50 states

89,000 localities

American diversity is reflected just as much in our governments as in our citizens. The key to understanding the similarities and differences across these governments lies in the comparative approach of *Governing States and Localities: The Essentials*.

A fresh, contemporary perspective on state and local politics, this new condensed edition covers the impact of the Great Recession, but with an eye toward the future. The economy is recovering, but budgets remain tight, the federal stimulus is ending, and the political climate is as polarized as ever. So what's next?

Find out in the pages of *Governing States and Localities: The Essentials*.

A blend of scholarship and news-style writing

- **Chapter-opening vignettes** pique student interest with headline-grabbing style through compelling stories that link to the broader themes of the chapter.

Louisiana governor Bobby Jindal used his executive power to order major spending cuts in the summer of 2012 to deal with the state's large budget shortfall. Although Louisiana's part-time legislators had gone home for the year, many objected to being cut out of the process, but they were wary of crossing the governor, who has the power to appoint top legislative leaders.

The Executive Branch and Bureaucracy

HOW GOVERNMENTS OPERATE AND WHO'S IN CHARGE

- How did governors get to be such powerful players, when for much of American history their offices were weak?
- Why do some states still give their governors more pomp than power?
- Why do we have so much bureaucracy?

ch. 8

Chapter 8 The Executive Branch and Bureaucracy   209

- **The Latest Research** boxes spotlight cutting-edge scholarship related to each chapter's discussion so students benefit from a deeper understanding of the social scientific study of states and localities.

- **A marginal glossary** defines key concepts as they are introduced.

Powers Granted to Government. Perhaps the most important and surprising difference between the U.S. Constitution and state constitutions is the scope of the documents. The U.S. Constitution's original purpose was to organize a federal government with sharply limited powers. In contrast, state governments have what is called **plenary power**,

Natural Law, or Higher Law
A set of moral and political rules based on divine law and binding on all people.

Constitutional Amendments
Proposals to change a constitution, typically enacted by a supermajority of the legislature or through a statewide referendum.

Plenary Power
Power that is not limited or constrained.

- **How It Works** boxes take one state and one government process and dive into how, exactly, it works.

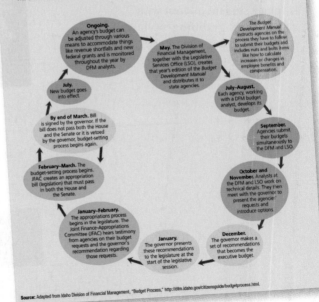

The Latest Research

The roles and responsibilities of federal and state governments are constantly evolving based on political and economic context, policy demands and innovation, Supreme Court rulings, and the political philosophies, ideological preferences, and partisan fortunes of lawmakers at both levels of government. Current scholars of federalism find themselves in a particularly interesting period in the development of intergovernmental relations. The worst of the recession is over, yet fiscal stresses remain. Federal, state, and local governments are trying to reset their relationships with each other to deal most effectively with what comes next—but no one is sure what comes next.

Below are summaries of some of the most recent research on federalism. Two constant themes emerge from this stream of scholarship: first, intergovernmental relations have undergone and are currently undergoing dramatic changes; and second, those changes have enormous implications not just for politics and policy but also for the day-to-day lives of citizens.

• **Gamkhar, Shama, and J. Mitchell Pickerill.** 2012. "The State of American Federalism 2011–2012: A Fend for Yourself and Activist Form of Bottom-Up Federalism." *Publius: The Journal of Federalism* 42: 357–386.

This study suggests that we may be witnessing the emergence of what the authors call "bottom-up" federalism. They argue that political, economic, and judicial trends are pushing states and localities to become more independent—to figure out how to solve the financial and social challenges they face without being propped up by the federal government. Multiple causes are driving these trends. For example, as divided government and gridlock slow government action at the federal level on a wide array of policy issues, state and local governments are being forced to step up and take action on their own. As federal stimulus dollars disappear, states and localities increasingly have to figure out how to make the books balance on their own. The decreased reliance on federal dollars seems to be encouraging more assertive declarations of state sovereignty. For example, states have begun reasserting their independence by opting out of federal programs (e.g., health insurance

exchanges, high-speed rail initiatives) that provide financial aid.

• **Rivlin, Alice.** 2012. "Rethinking Federalism for More Effective Governance." *Publius: The Journal of Federalism* 42: 387–400.

In this article, a companion piece to the Gamkhar and Pickerill study described above, Rivlin argues that the realities of postrecession governance create a pressing need for a reconsideration of the relationship between state and federal governments. In particular, Rivlin pushes for two key reforms. First, she argues that state and federal governments should rethink their job responsibilities. Rather than taking on increasingly shared responsibilities in areas such as education, she suggests, one level of government should take primary responsibility. Who gets the job should depend on who is best positioned to do that job and who has traditionally had the legal authority to do it (in the case of education, this would be the states). This is essentially an argument that a good dose of dual federalism is not necessarily a bad thing. The second big reform that Rivlin endorses is a fundamental rethinking of how government funds itself. She argues that the existing federal tax system is poorly suited for the twenty-first century and suggests the implementation of a kind of national sales tax, collected by the federal government but distributed to the states. This would allow states to recapture sales taxes lost to Internet sales as well as provide a more uniform and reliable revenue source for more distinct and defined policy responsibilities.

• **Robertson, David Brian.** 2012. *Federalism and the Making of America.* New York: Routledge.

The two articles described above are analyses of changes in intergovernmental relations more or less as they occur in real time. Robertson's book makes a good companion to these, placing such time-focused studies into perspective by offering a sweeping story of the historical development of federalism in America, from its birth at the founding of the Republic to the red-state–blue-state conflicts of the twenty-first century. The book is notable for its focus on federalism as the stage upon which most of the great policy battles in American history have been fought: racial relations, economic regulation, social welfare and regulation. All of these issues and more

---

FIGURE 4-1

HOW IT WORKS

A Year in the Life of a State Budget: Idaho's Budgetary Process

Most folks first hear about state budget priorities through their governor's state of the state address, the forum in which most state budgetary news is presented. In reality, budget planning begins well in advance of this address and involves all three branches of government to some degree. In Idaho, each year in May (after the last of the potatoes have been planted), that state's Division of Financial Management (DFM) starts sowing its own seeds: overseeing the development of that state's budget for the coming fiscal year. This is the beginning of what is really an eighteen-month process: the planning for fiscal year 2014, for instance, will actually get under way about mid-year in 2012.

This chart shows how the process works in Idaho:

Ongoing. An agency's budget can be adjusted through various means to accommodate things like revenue shortfalls and new federal grants and is monitored throughout the year by DFM analysts.

May. The Division of Financial Management, together with the Legislative Services Office (LSO), creates that year's edition of the Budget Development Manual and distributes it to state agencies.

The *Budget Development Manual* instructs agencies on the process they have to follow to submit their budgets and includes nuts and bolts items like how to calculate increases or changes in employee benefits and compensation.

July–August. Each agency, working with a DFM budget analyst, develops its budget.

September. Agencies submit their budgets simultaneously to the DFM and LSO.

October and November. Analysts at the DFM and LSO work on technical details. They then meet with the governor to present the agencies' requests and introduce options.

December. The governor makes a set of recommendations that becomes the executive budget.

January. The governor presents these recommendations to the legislature at the start of the legislative session.

January–February. The appropriations process begins in the legislature. The Joint Finance-Appropriations Committee (JFAC) hears testimony from agencies on their budget requests and the governor's recommendation regarding those requests.

February–March. The budget-setting process begins. JFAC creates an appropriation bill (legislation) that must pass in both the House and the Senate.

By end of March. Bill is signed by the governor. If the bill does not pass both the House and the Senate or it is vetoed by the governor, budget-setting process begins again.

July. New budget goes into effect.

Source: Adapted from Idaho Division of Financial Management, "Budget Process," http://dfm.idaho.gov/citizensguide/budgetprocess.html.

- **Marginal state facts** present quick, complementary info on a U.S. state.

populations are likely to promote different attitudes about and policies on welfare, affirmative action, bilingual education programs, even the role and responsibilities of government in general.

And it gets better. All these population characteristics are dynamic. That is [...]

for instance—cartograms use other variables to determine how size is represented. This cartogram depicts the size of each state's population, another useful way to compare states. Notice that some states that [are] geographically actually pretty [...] as New Mexico [...] square miles, are very [...] map because they [...] populations. Other [...] are geographically [...] ite small, such as [...] (with only 5,000 [...]), look much bigger [...] map because they [...] populations. Some [...] as Virginia, don't [...] rent in size at all [...] earance on a tra-

Texas is the country's fastest-growing state, with a 2.1 percent population increase in 2011. It narrowly beat out the previous population-growth champ, Utah, which came in second with an annual growth rate of 1.93 percent.

[...] age groups face a [...] education policy pressures than those with higher concentrations in younger groups. States with large aging populations are likely to face less demand for higher education spending and more demand for public programs that address the needs of the elderly, such as access to healthcare. Why do some states provide more support to higher [...]

[...] nd History

[...] ities have distinct "personalities" [...] t in everything from the "bloody [...] lder patch worn by the [...] tional Guard to the drawl that [...] e speech of West Texas natives. [...] ave been part of the Union for [...] re than two hundred years and still project an Old World connection to Europe. Hawaii and Alaska became states within living memory and are more associated with the exoticism of the Pacific and the Old West. New York City prides itself on being a cosmopolitan center of Western civilization. The visitor's bureau of Lincoln, Nebraska, touts the city's small-town ambience and Middle American values. These [...]

Key features encourage comparison

- **Chapter-opening, comparative questions** encourage students to look systematically for answers using the comparative method.

- What are the advantages and disadvantages of federalism?
- What is the comparative method, and why is it a useful way to talk about state and local governments?
- What role do state and local politics play in determining how much certain services—such as a college education—cost?

- **A Difference That Makes a Difference** boxes provide clear examples of how variation among states and localities can be used to explain a wide range of political and policy phenomena.

A Difference That Makes A Difference

State Constitutions and the Right to Marry

"By the power vested in me, by the state of . . ." These words are repeated by wedding officials every day, in every state. States control who can marry and when. In Nebraska, teens younger than nineteen need their parents' permission to marry, while over the state line in Kansas, people can walk down the aisle at eighteen. A number of states prohibited interracial couples from marrying until 1967, when the U.S. Supreme Court declared Virginia's law unconstitutional in *Loving v. Virginia*. Today, debate rages around gay marriage. Just six states—Connecticut, Iowa, Massachusetts, New Hampshire, New York, and Vermont—have legalized the unions, while thirty states have amended their constitutions to prohibit them. Several additional states recognize domestic partnerships or civil unions, which grant couples some of the same state-level benefits as marriage. Washington, DC, which is technically a federal city and not a state, allows gay marriage.

Legalization of gay marriage has been achieved through judicial review (in Connecticut, Iowa, and Massachusetts) and through legislation (New Hampshire, New York, and Vermont). Gay marriage has had a less fortunate time at the polls, where voters have rejected it time and time again—most recently in North Carolina in 2012. The most high-profile fight so far was waged in California in 2008 over Proposition 8, a ballot measure that sought to amend the state's constitution to define

marriage as a union between one man and one woman—and to put a stop to the same-sex marriages that had begun there in June 2008, after the state supreme court ruled that the state's ban was unconstitutional. After both sides spent more than $55 million on their campaigns, voters narrowly approved Prop. 8. Approval of new same-sex marriages was halted, but the state continues to consider the more than eighteen thousand couples who wed legally as married.

The victory of Proposition 8 prompted further debate among proponents of gay marriage, some of whom wonder whether, given their continued defeats at the polls, they should wait to wage new legalization campaigns across the states. But the fight over Prop. 8 isn't finished—and it's not even limited to within the state's borders anymore. In April 2009, Theodore Olson, the former U.S. solicitor general, filed a brief in federal court challenging the amendment. In 2010, a federal district court ruled that Proposition 8 unconstitutionally violated the due process and equal protection clauses of the Fourteenth Amendment, a decision that was upheld in 2012 by a federal appeals court. As of this writing, the case has been appealed to the U.S. Supreme Court. If the Court accepts the case, the justices could make a ruling that will clarify whether or not same-sex couples have the same right to marry as heterosexual couples.

Sources: Christine Vestal, "Gay Marriage Legal in Six States," *Stateline*, June 4, 2009, www.stateline.org/live/details/story?contentId=347390; Ballotwatch, Initiative and Referendum Institute, "Same-Sex Marriage: Breaking the Firewall in California?," October 2008; Jo Becker, "A Conservative's Road to Same-Sex Marriage Advocacy," *New York Times*, August 18, 2009, www.nytimes.com/2009/08/19/us/19olson.html.

- **Local Focus** boxes spotlight how localities function independently of states and show how they are both constrained and empowered by intergovernmental ties.

Local Focus
Bonds and Broken Budgets

The story of how Jefferson County, Alabama, waded into budget and bond muck stretches back to 1993, when the Cahaba River Society, a group dedicated to preserving the river that flows through Birmingham, complained that the county's sewer system was discharging raw sewage into waterways. Federal officials sent a consent decree in which Jefferson County promised to upgrade the system.

The county paid for the upgrade by issuing $3 billion in bonds. As sewer service rates rose to meet those costs and Jefferson County struggled under its debt, county officials looked for a way to lessen the loan payments. In 2002 and 2003, they refinanced their bonds with variable-rate and auction-rate securities. (Auction-rate securities are bonds for which the interest rate is reset at auction every few weeks.)

Auction-rate securities were supposed to be safe, but the auction-rate market collapsed in February 2008. Then the bond insurance companies that were backing the county's debt suffered their own fiscal problems and their credit was downgraded. The result: Jefferson County's interest rates skyrocketed, much like the rates of homeowners whose subprime mortgages had just reset. The county's revenue from sewer

fees could not cover the borrowing costs. On April Fool's Day 2008, Jefferson County failed to make its payment on its debt. Instead, it reached an agreement with its creditors to pay the interest and get an extension on the principal—an agreement that left the county of 660,000 teetering on the edge of bankruptcy.

County commissioners and other Alabama political players developed a variety of ideas to solve the sewer mess—to no avail. Without a solution in sight, the county made massive cutbacks: reducing department budgets by one-third, canceling road maintenance contracts, closing courthouses, and laying off hundreds of county workers. "We're having to downsize this government to the point that it may not be able to operate," County Commissioner Bettye Fine Collins said in 2009.

Collins's comments were prophetic. In December 2011, Jefferson County filed for bankruptcy; by that time its debt had ballooned to more than $4 billion, a crushing burden the county simply could not manage.

As discussed in the opening section of this chapter, variations on the Jefferson County story have played out across the country as the recession has significantly weakened local governments' financial footing.

Sources: Karen Pierog, "Default, Bankruptcy Fears Overhang U.S. Muni Market," Reuters, February 16, 2010; adapted from Josh Goodman, "Drained," Governing, August 2009.

Policy in Practice
Outwit, Outlast, Outplay: Who Really Got the Best Deal with Term Limits?

The biggest change to hit state legislatures over the past quarter century has been the advent of term limits. In the fifteen states with term limit laws—which were almost all approved through ballot initiatives by voters sick of career politicians—legislators are limited to serving no more than six, eight, or twelve years in either the house or the senate. Although that may sound like a long time, it turns out not to be enough for most legislators to master all the complexities of understanding and formulating a wide range of policy.

Term limits have failed the public's goal of bringing in more "citizen legislators." Instead, legislators are constantly seeking their next political jobs rather than carving out decades-long careers in one chamber. Term limits also have failed to bring the anticipated and hoped-for substantial numbers of women and minorities into the legislative ranks. The total number of women legislators is up nationwide, but their ranks have actually been slower to grow in states that impose term limits.[*]

But if they haven't fulfilled all their promises, term limits have not been quite the disaster the opponents predicted either. One of the most common predictions—that with new power so briefly, lobbyists hoarding institutional and policy knowledge would accrue all the power—appears to have missed the mark. Term limits pretty much have been a mixed bag for lobbyists, who must introduce themselves to a new, skeptical set of legislators every couple of years rather than relying on cozy relations with a few key committee chairs. "I don't know one lobbyist who thinks it's a good thing," said Rick Farmer, who wrote about term limits as an academic before going to work for the Oklahoma House. "If term limits are such a good thing for lobbyists, why do so many lobbyists hate them?"[*]

It does seem clear, however, that legislators in term-limited states have lost power to the executive branch—the governors and their staff who actually know how to operate the machinery of government. "Agency heads can outwit and outlast anyone and everyone on the playing field and they have consolidated their power," said one southern legislator-turned-lobbyist.

Academic studies in term limit states, including California, Colorado, and Maine, have found that legislators make far fewer changes to governors' budgets than they used to, representing many billions of dollars in legislative discretion that is no longer exercised. "The crumbling of legislative power is clear across states," said Thad Kousser, a political scientist at the University of California, San Diego, and author of a book about term limits. "There's no more clear finding in the research than a shift in power where the legislature is becoming a less than equal branch of government."

For all that, it's become common to hear governors and other executive branch officials complain about term limits because the laws mean they lack negotiating partners whose knowledge and expertise they can count on. It seems that no one who works in a state capitol—or in the law and lobbying shops that surround any capitol—likes term limits.

But there is one group that still finds them attractive—the voting public. Polls suggest that as much as 75 percent of the public favors them. "With new people in office, you have people with real world experience," says Stacie Rumenap, president of U.S. Term Limits, a group that advocates limits. "Under term limits, you might have a schoolteacher sitting on the education committee."[*]

That sort of suggestion is often made about term limits—you get rid of the professional politicians and get people who know what the real problems are because they themselves are real. And while Idaho and Utah have repealed their limits, efforts to extend terms or weaken term limits have been rejected several times since 2002 by voters in Arkansas, Maine, California, Florida, Montana, and South Dakota. California voters did relax the state's term limits slightly in 2012.

The main argument against term limits, after all, is procedural. It's difficult to make a convincing case that term limits have made any one particular policy worse, let alone imperiled the quality of life in any state that observes them, the underlying complaint of term limits opponents, that they make legislators less powerful, is one reason many people supported them to begin with.

Source: Adapted from Alan Greenblatt, "The Truth about Term Limits," Governing, January 2006, 24.
[*]Peter Slevin, "After Adopting Term Limits, States Lose Female Legislators," Washington Post, April 22, 2007, A4.
[*]Interview with Stacie Rumenap, October 4, 2002.

- **Policy in Practice** boxes demonstrate how different states and localities interpret and implement legislation.

States Under Stress
This Court Will Not Come to Order

In Birmingham, Alabama, domestic relations judge Suzanne Childers keeps a .38-caliber Smith & Wesson revolver under her bench. That, and a can of pepper spray, have served as protection for her courtroom since budget cuts eliminated two deputies' positions. Childers's story is extreme, but hers is not the only courtroom that has been left less safe as a result of the state and local fiscal crisis. In Massachusetts, open court officer positions were not filled between the end of 2008 and early 2010, and in Maine, metal detectors in courthouses go unstaffed. "It's a question of do you want to close courthouses and run [fewer] courthouses with full security? Or do you want to keep all your courthouses open and compromise on security?" said Mary Ann Lynch, a spokeswoman for Maine's court system.[*]

In many states, courts are opening later in the day, closing earlier, and shutting their doors entirely for several days per month. Kansas and Oregon have begun closing courts on Fridays, and one court in Georgia has stopped hearing civil matters altogether to focus time on critical criminal matters. In some parts of North Carolina and Ohio, cases have ground to a halt because the courts could not afford to buy more paper. With states facing severe budget shortfalls, almost every state court system is trying to get by with less. A survey conducted by the National Center for State Courts (NCSC) in 2011 estimated that at least forty-two state court systems were facing cutbacks in their 2012 budgets, leading most courts to shrink staff and reduce hours.[*] Iowa, for instance, now has fewer employees in the judicial branch than it had twenty-four years ago, even though case filings in the state increased by 54 percent in the same period.[*]

NCSC reported that the cuts would lead to increased backlogs in civil, criminal, and family court cases. Such backlogs lead inevitably to delays: in San Francisco, if you challenge a parking or traffic ticket, it "can now 'take up to a year from the time you first get a [traffic] ticket until you get a trial date,'" says Ann Donlan, communications director for San Francisco Superior Court.[*]

Making matters worse, states expected that the very programs they had implemented to help alleviate backlogs—alternative dispute resolution and problem-solving courts—would themselves end up on the chopping block.

When budget cuts eliminated courtroom security guards, Jefferson County, Alabama, domestic court judge Suzanne Childers resorted to keeping a .38-caliber pistol under her desk during session for protection.

[*]Quoted in Denise Lavoie, "Budget Cuts Force Tough Choices on Court Security," Seattle Times, January 10, 2010, http://seattletimes.nwsource.com/html/localnews/technology/2010758141_abacourtroomsecuritycuts.html
[*]National Center for State Courts, "State Budget Cuts Threaten Public's Access to Courts," November 29, 2011, www.ncsc.org/Newsroom/Backgrounder/2011/Court-Budget-Cuts.aspx.
[*]Alan Greenblatt, "See Me? Not a Chance This Year," NPR.org, April 12, 2012.
[*]Quoted in ibid.

- **States under Stress** boxes underscore how budgetary constraints are reshaping how state and local governments operate.

- **More than 80 tables, figures, and maps** provide an intuitively easy way for students to grasp the differences among states and localities, with up-to-date comparative data.

TABLE 2-3

Key U.S. Supreme Court Rulings Regarding Federalism, 1995–2012

Case	Decision
United States v. Lopez (1995)	Court strikes down a federal law prohibiting possession of firearms near public schools. State claim upheld.
Seminole Tribe of Florida v. Florida (1996)	Court rules Congress cannot allow citizens to sue states in a federal court except for civil rights violations. State claim upheld.
Printz v. United States (1997)	Court strikes down a federal law requiring mandatory background checks for firearms purchases. State claim upheld.
Alden v. Maine (1999)	Court rules that Congress does not have the power to authorize citizens to sue in state court on the basis of federal claims. State claim upheld.
United States v. Morrison (2000)	Court strikes down the federal Violence Against Women Act. State claim upheld.
Reno v. Condon (2000)	Court upholds a federal law preventing states from selling driver's license information. State claim overturned.
Bush v. Gore (2000)	Court overrules a Florida Supreme Court action allowing hand recounts of contested election ballots. State claim overturned.
Alabama v. Garrett (2001)	Court rules that state employees cannot sue their employers in federal court to recover monetary damages under the provisions of the Americans with Disabilities Act. State claim upheld.
Lorillard Tobacco Co. v. Reilly (2001)	Court strikes down Massachusetts laws regulating the advertising of tobacco products. State claim overturned.
Kelo v. City of New London (2005)	Court rules that government can seize private property for public purposes, including economic development. State claim upheld.
Gonzales v. Oregon (2006)	Court rules that the U.S. attorney general overstepped his authority by threatening to eliminate prescription-writing privileges for doctors who follow state law allowing physician-assisted suicide. State claim upheld.
Arizona v. United States (2012)	Court rules that states do not have the authority to enact and enforce immigration laws; however, it allows states to implement "show me your papers" regulations that require law enforcement officers to determine the immigration status of anyone they stop or detain.

FIGURE 6-2

State Party Fund-Raising over Time

2004 · $211m $190m
2006 · $344m $272m
2008 · $250m $261m
2010 · $283m $330m
2012 · $119m $125m

Republican ■ Democrat

Source: Data compiled from the National Institute for Money in State Politics, "Industry Influence 2000–2012," http://followthemoney.org/database/IndustryTotals.phtml?f=P&s=0.

Population by State

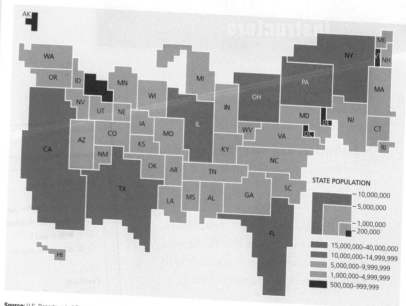

STATE POPULATION

— 10,000,000
— 5,000,000
— 1,000,000
— 200,000

15,000,000–40,000,000
10,000,000–14,999,999
5,000,000–9,999,999
1,000,000–4,999,999
500,000–999,999

Source: U.S. Department of Commerce, *Statistical Abstract of the United States, 2012* (Washington, DC: U.S. Census Bureau, 2012), "Table 16, Resident Population by Age and State: 2010," 21, www.census.gov/prod/2011pubs/12statab/pop.pdf.

STATE STATS

A new data product from CQ Press, State Stats allows students to investigate reliable, easy-to-use data from more than 80 different sources, covering such areas as health care, crime, and education. Intuitive mapping and graphing tools allow students to compare states through data visualization.

Free with purchase of a new book, students use State Stats icons throughout the book, linking to exercises in each chapter that challenge students to apply the comparative method, exploring what they find interesting about a particular state.

Local Government Total Expenditures
Category: Expenditures Topic: Government Finances: State and Local
National Total: $1,666,568,007,000 (2010)

State Stats on Local Government

Explore and compare data on the states! Go to **www.college.cqpress .com/sites/essentials-govstateandlocal** to do these exercises.

1. How has local government spending across the states changed between 2000 and 2010? Where has it changed the most and the least? What might account for some of the changes?

2. In which state does the local government have the highest level of direct general expenditures? Which has the least? How does state population affect these expenditures? Why?

3. How has the number of public high schools in Nebraska changed between 2001 and 2011? Why has this change occurred?

4. New York, northern New Jersey, and portions of Pennsylvania make up the largest metropolitan statistical area in the United States. What is the average household income in these states? What might this tell us about the relationship between these states? Do we have enough information here to make this analysis?

5. One of the drawbacks of metropolitan growth is the dependence on cars that it creates. Which states have the most cars per driver? Which have the least? Why is there such a large difference?

Support for instructors

college.cqpress
.com/sites/essentials-
govstateandlocal

Instructors can save time and effort by using these high-quality instructor resources:

- **Test Bank**—over 300 true/false, multiple-choice, fill-in-the-blank, and short essay questions are available with Respondus test generation software.

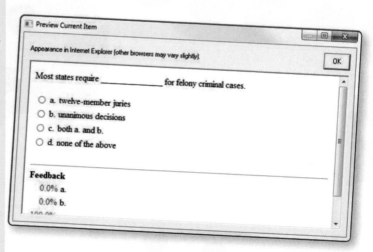

Preview Current Item

Appearance in Internet Explorer (other browsers may vary slightly).   OK

Most states require _____ for felony criminal cases.

○ a. twelve-member juries
○ b. unanimous decisions
○ c. both a. and b.
○ d. none of the above

Feedback
0.0% a.
0.0% b.

- **PowerPoint Lecture Presentations**—the presentation for each chapter includes all of the key concepts and important images from the text.
- **Instructor's manual**—includes chapter summaries, lecture outlines, and talking points for discussions and lectures.
- **Graphics for lectures and testing**—every table, figure, and map is provided as both a PDF file and a PowerPoint slide.
- **Course cartridge**—integrates with your course management system and includes the test bank, the PowerPoint presentations, the graphics from the book, useful Instructor's Manual content, quiz questions, and State Stats exercises from the student study site.

Support for students

college.cqpress.com/
sites/essentials-
govstateandlocal

Students can increase understanding and get a better grade using the **open access student study site** which includes:

- **Study**—chapter summaries with learning objectives.

Chapter 4. Finance: Filling the Till and Paying the Bills

Study

Chapter Summary

Dealing with finances is a highly politicized process for states and localities. Expenditures and the budgetary process in general provide clues to the political and policy priorities of a state's government and its local governments. State and local governments have six primary sources of revenue, including sales taxes, income taxes, excise taxes, and property taxes. Variation in state resources, geography, culture, history, and demographics has resulted in widespread variation in the use of such taxes among the states. For instance, states that forego income taxes rely heavily on property and sales taxes and are likely to have different tax rates to adjust to a different tax base. This variation among taxing mechanisms is reflected in variation in public policies.

The budget process among states and localities is defined primarily by the relationship between entitlement spending and discretionary spending. As entitlement spending (for example, Medicaid and welfare) increases, the ability of states to experiment with new policies and programs decreases. Meeting public expectations with regard to spending on education, healthcare services, highway infrastructure, and correctional institutions further limits the discretionary budgetary authority of states. Those states that adopted the referendum and initiative process also have had to deal with a strong "antitax" sentiment among their citizens, furthering limiting their ability to raise revenue. Such constraints have forced states and localities to be innovative. The resulting variation highlights the need for a comparative approach to studying finances in states and local governments.

Objectives

After reading this chapter, you should understand...

- the primary sources of revenue for states and localities
- the different types of taxes utilized by states and localities
- why tax capacity and tax effort vary among the states
- who controls the budget process
- how the state budget process differs from the federal budget process
- what the largest areas of expenditures are for state governments
- the difference between discretionary spending and entitlement spending

Study Questions

1. What are the primary sources of revenue for states and localities?
2. What is the difference between tax effort and tax capacity?
3. What are some reasons for tax variation among the states?
4. What are some options available to states for raising revenue?
5. Who initiates the budget process in the states, and what restricts the power of the governor in advancing his or her agenda in the budget?
6. What factors limit the use of discretionary spending in a state's budget?

- **Quiz**—mobile-friendly multiple-choice questions with automatic feedback.

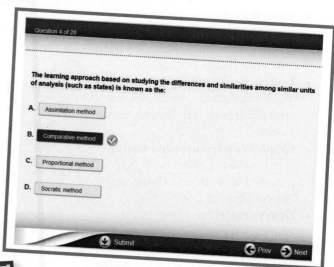

The learning approach based on studying the differences and similarities among similar units of analysis (such as states) is known as the:

A. Assimilation method

B. Comparative method ✓

C. Proportional method

D. Socratic method

⬇ Submit   ← Prev → Next

← Previous   🔄 Flip   → Next

Term
Definition
Remove ✕
Shuffle ✖
Reset ↻
Auto Play ◎
Total cards : 1

FISCAL FEDERALISM

Term 1 of 1

- **Flashcards**—mobile-friendly, viewable by definition or term, with marking and reshuffling.

▶ Study   ▶ Quiz   ▶ Flashcards   ▶ State Stats Exercises   ▶ Explore

Chapter 9. Courts: Turning Law into Politics

Explore

- www.abanet.org. — Web site of the American Bar Association, the largest voluntary professional association in the world, with a membership of more than 400,000.

- www.ajs.org. — Web site of the American Judicature Society, a nonpartisan organization with a national membership that works to maintain the independence and integrity of the courts and increase public understanding of the justice system.

- www.brennancenter.org. — Web site of the Brennan Center for Justice, a nonpartisan center at New York University that conducts research and advocates on a range of judicial topics, including state court reform and campaign financing.

- www.justiceatstake.org. — Web site of the Justice at Stake Campaign, a nonpartisan effort working to keep courts fair and impartial.

- www.ncsconline.org. Web site of the National Center for State Courts, an independent nonprofit organization that assists court officials to better serve the public.

- www.ojp.usdoj.gov/bjs. — Web site for the Bureau of Justice Statistics, which provides statistics and other information on a variety of justice system-related areas, including courts, sentencing, crimes, and victims.

- **Explore**—annotated web resources.

Governing STATES and LOCALITIES

The ESSENTIALS

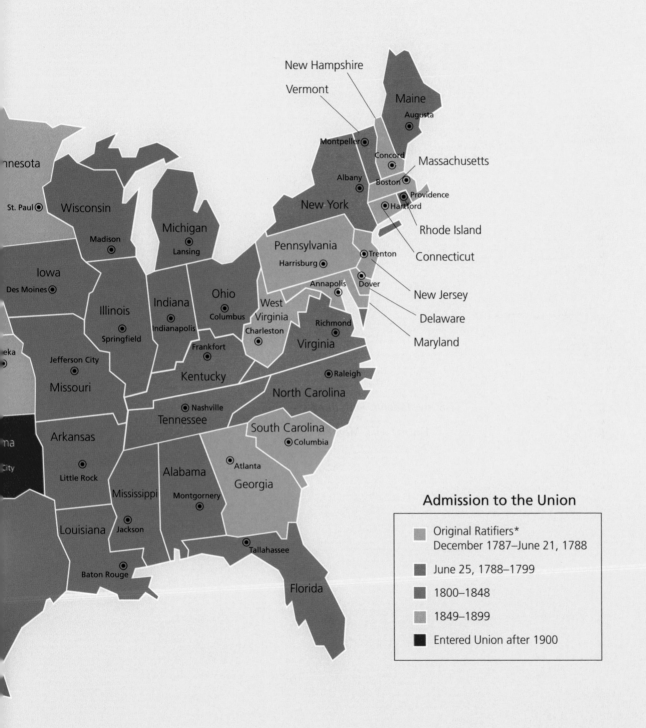

New Hampshire
Vermont

Maine
Augusta

Montpeller

Concord

Massachusetts

Albany

Boston

Providence

New York

Hartford

Rhode Island

Pennsylvania

Connecticut

Harrisburg

Trenton

New Jersey

Annapolis

Dover

Delaware

Maryland

Minnesota

Wisconsin

St. Paul

Michigan

Madison

Lansing

Iowa

Des Moines

Illinois

Indiana

Ohio

Springfield

Indianapolis

Columbus

West
Virginia

Charleston

Richmond

Virginia

Frankfort

eka

Jefferson City

Kentucky

Raleigh

Missouri

North Carolina

Nashville

Tennessee

South Carolina

ma

Arkansas

Columbia

City

Little Rock

Alabama

Atlanta

Mississippi

Montgornery

Georgia

Louisiana

Jackson

Baton Rouge

Tallahassee

Florida

Admission to the Union

Original Ratifiers*
December 1787–June 21, 1788

June 25, 1788–1799

1800–1848

1849–1899

Entered Union after 1900

For my students, with thanks — KBS

For my wife, Megan — AG

Governing STATES and LOCALITIES

The ESSENTIALS

KEVIN B. SMITH

University of Nebraska – Lincoln

ALAN GREENBLATT

NPR

Los Angeles | London | New Delhi
Singapore | Washington DC

Los Angeles | London | New Delhi
Singapore | Washington DC

FOR INFORMATION:

CQ Press
An Imprint of SAGE Publications, Inc.
2455 Teller Road
Thousand Oaks, California 91320
E-mail: order@sagepub.com

SAGE Publications Ltd.
1 Oliver's Yard
55 City Road
London EC1Y 1SP
United Kingdom

SAGE Publications India Pvt. Ltd.
B 1/I 1 Mohan Cooperative Industrial Area
Mathura Road, New Delhi 110 044
India

SAGE Publications Asia-Pacific Pte. Ltd.
3 Church Street
#10-04 Samsung Hub
Singapore 049483

Printed in the United States of America

A catalog record of this book is available from the Library of Congress.

ISBN 978-1-4833-0811-1

Publisher: Charisse Kiino
Development Editor: Nancy Matuszak
Editorial Assistant: Davia Grant
Digital Content Editor: Allison Hughes
Production Editor: Laura Barrett
Copy Editor: Rachel Keith
Typesetter: C&M Digitals (P) Ltd.
Proofreader: Eleni Georgiou
Indexer: Wendy Allex
Cover Designer: Scott Van Atta
Marketing Manager: Amy Whitaker

This book is printed on acid-free paper.

SUSTAINABLE FORESTRY INITIATIVE
Certified Chain of Custody
Promoting Sustainable Forestry
www.sfiprogram.org
SFI-01268
SFI label applies to text stock

14 15 16 17 10 9 8 7 6 5 4 3 2 1

Brief Contents

Detailed Contents

Chapter 4   81

Finance: Filling the Till and
Paying the Bills

Chapter 5   107

Political Attitudes and Participation:
Venting and Voting

Chapter 6   139

Parties and Interest Groups:
Elephants, Donkeys, and Cash Cows

Chapter 7   175

Legislatures: The Art of Herding Cats

Chapter 8   209

The Executive Branch and Bureaucracy:
How Governments Operate and
Who's in Charge

Tables, Figures, and Maps

Tables

Figures

Maps

Preface

This textbook is an abridged version of the fourth edition of *Governing States and Localities*. The difference between the two is encapsulated in this edition's subtitle: *The Essentials*. The new *Essentials* edition has exactly the same goals, aims, and authors as the full edition—it is designed to provide a comprehensive introduction to state and local governments, and it is a product of a unique collaboration between academic and professional writers that rests on a foundation of academic scholarship, more than two decades of experience in teaching undergraduates about state and local governments, and the insight and experience of a journalist who covers state and local politics.

The Essentials seeks to achieve the core pedagogical goals of the full edition of *Governing States and Localities* in a more compact package. We relied on extensive user feedback from the full edition to determine which elements instructors might consider optional in planning a basic survey course on state and local politics. *The Essentials* eliminates policy-specific chapters from the full edition (education, crime, health and welfare, and the environment), condenses treatments of elected executives and the bureaucracy into a single chapter, and includes one rather than two chapters on local government. The result is ten chapters, each further distilled to capture an essential survey of state and local government.

The book provides a fresh and contemporary perspective on state and local politics in terms of coverage and content as well as in its look and feel. The text deliberately follows a news magazine's crisp news-writing style, and the book employs magazine-quality, full-color layout and design. Our intent is to deliver a compact, focused text that meets the highest academic and pedagogical standards while remaining engaging and easily accessible to undergraduates.

The Essentials includes all of the significant updates and revisions of the latest full edition and reflects significant events that have occurred since that edition's publication. Streamlined graphics intuitively highlight key points in the text, which contains an overall theme of "What's next?" The Great Recession is technically over, but budgets remain tight and federal stimulus dollars are drying up. States and localities have cut budgets, reduced public sector employment, consolidated agencies, and pushed back against federal policy priorities that are accompanied by mandates but not money. The stage is set for a resetting of intergovernmental relations, and although the specifics of this ongoing reshuffling of power and responsibilities are not always clear, we attempt to lay out the possible directions of this latest evolution of the federal system and its impact on all branches of state and local politics.

The Essentials uses the pedagogical philosophy of the comparative method. This approach compares similar units of analysis to explain *why* differences exist. As scholars know well, state and local governments make excellent units of analysis for comparison because they operate within a single political system. The similarities and differences that mark their institutional structures, laws and regulations, political cultures, histories, demographics, economies, and geographies mean that they make exciting laboratories for asking and answering important questions about politics and government. Put simply, their differences make a difference.

The appeal of exploring state and local government through comparison is not just that it makes for good political science. It is also a great way to engage students because it gives undergraduates an accessible, practical, and systematic way to understand politics and policy in the real world. Students learn that even such seemingly personal concerns as why their tuition is so darned high are not just relevant to their particular situation and educational institution but also are fundamental to the interaction of that institution with its state's political culture, economy, history, and tax structure and even to the school's geographical and demographical position within the state and region. Using the comparative method, this book gives students the resources they need to ask and answer such questions themselves.

Key Features

This book includes a number of elements designed to showcase and promote its main themes. A set of chapter-opening questions engages student interest and prompts students to look systematically for answers using the comparative method. The idea is not simply to spoon-feed the answers to students, but rather to demonstrate how the comparative method can be used to explore and explain questions about politics and policy.

Following the comparative questions, each chapter moves on to an opening vignette modeled after a lead in a news magazine article—a compelling story that segues naturally into the broader themes of the chapter. Many of these vignettes (as well as many of the feature boxes) represent original reporting.

The feature boxes in each chapter also emphasize and reinforce the comparative theme:

- "A Difference That Makes a Difference" boxes provide clear examples of how variation among states and localities can be used to explain a wide range of political and policy phenomena. These pieces detail the ways in which the institutions, regulations, political culture, demographics, and other factors of a particular state shape its constitution, the way its political parties function, how its citizens tend to vote, how it allocates its financial resources, and why its courts are structured the way they are, to name a few.

- "Local Focus" boxes spotlight the ways localities function independently of the states and show how they are both constrained and empowered by intergovernmental ties.

- "Policy in Practice" boxes demonstrate how different states and localities have interpreted and implemented the legislation handed down from higher levels of government and the consequences of these decisions.

- "States Under Stress" boxes demonstrate how the Great Recession is reshaping how state and local governments operate.

- "The Latest Research" boxes feature an annotated list of important new scholarship, placed into the context of what students have just learned.

To help students assimilate content and review for tests, each chapter includes a set of highlighted key concepts. These terms are defined in the margins near the place where they are introduced and are compiled into a list at the end of each chapter with corresponding page numbers. Each chapter concludes with comparative exercises that encourage students to get more hands-on experience with data through the CQ Press database State Stats, accessible through the student companion site. State Stats features data from more than eighty government and nongovernment sources, and serves as a tool for students to research key information and trends on the states. Students can investigate reliable, easy-to-use data on areas such as state spending and federal grants, while intuitive mapping and graphing tools encourage them to compare data through visualization. A comprehensive glossary of key terms precedes the book's index.

Organization of the Book

Governing States and Localities: The Essentials is organized so that each chapter logically builds on previous chapters. The first chapter (subtitled "They Tax Dogs in West Virginia, Don't They?") is essentially a persuasive essay that lays the conceptual groundwork for the book. Its aim is to convince students that state and local politics are important in their day-to-day lives and critical to their futures as professionals and as citizens. That is, it makes the case for why students should care about state and local politics. Along the way, it introduces the advantages of the comparative method as a systematic way to explore this subject. In introducing the book's approach, the chapter provides the basic context for studying state and local governments, especially the differences in economics, culture, demographics, and geography that drive policy and politics at the regional level.

The next two chapters cover federalism and state constitutions. These chapters provide a basic understanding of what state and local governments are and what powers, responsibilities, and roles they have within the political system of the United States, as well as a sense of how they legally can make different political and policy choices.

Chapter 4 examines the finances of state and local governments. The key revenue streams for states and localities—income, sales, and property taxes—fell dramatically during the Great Recession and nearly six years later have yet to fully recover. Yet while revenue growth is stagnant, the demand for state and local services continues to increase. This ongoing imbalance between revenues and expenditures continues to be a dominant driver of politics and policy at the state and local level. This chapter gives students a fundamental sense of the revenues and expenditures of state and local governments and their central importance to virtually everything government does.

Chapter 5 examines political participation with an eye to helping students understand how citizens connect to the core policymaking institutions of government. Chapters 6 through 10 are separate treatments of those core institutions: parties and interest groups, legislatures, governors and the executive branch, courts, and local government.

Ancillaries

We are pleased to offer a suite of high-quality, classroom-ready instructor and student ancillaries to accompany the book. Written by Jayme L. Nieman of the University of Nebraska–Lincoln, the ancillaries are specifically tailored to the first edition of *Governing States and Localities: The Essentials*. A set of downloadable instructor's resources is available free to adopters, including a comprehensive test bank of more than three hundred true/false, multiple-choice, fill-in-the-blank, and short-answer questions. Available in a number of formats, this test bank can also be used with Respondus, a flexible and easy-to-use test-generation software program that allows professors to build, customize, and even integrate exams into course management platforms. In addition, instructors will find nearly two hundred PowerPoint lecture slides tailored to the text. These slides carefully detail the core concepts of each chapter, underscoring the book's comparative principles.

An instructor's manual with clear chapter summaries, downloadable lecture outlines, and points for discussion is included as well. Instructors have access to a full suite of .jpg and .ppt format files of all of the tables, figures, and maps in the book. These can be used to create additional PowerPoint slides or transparency masters when covering comparative data in the classroom or in discussion groups. In addition, these visuals can be imported into exams. Access them at **http://college.cqpress .com/sites/instructors-essentials-govstateand local.**

A host of updated student resources can be found on the book's website at **http://college .cqpress.com/sites/essentials-govstateandlocal**, including chapter summaries with clear chapter objectives and a set of self-testing study questions, nearly three hundred self-grading comprehensive quiz questions, a set of flashcards for review of key concepts, and a set of annotated links to important state and local websites. In addition, students and instructors alike will find *Governing* magazine's website especially useful for further research and in-class discussion. To help instructors bring the latest word from the states and localities into their classrooms, adopters may receive a free semester-long subscription to *Governing* magazine.

Acknowledgments

A lot of effort and dedication go into the making of a textbook like this, only a fraction of which is contributed by those whose names end up on the cover. Jayme L. Nieman, a Ph.D. student at the University of Nebraska–Lincoln, deserves special recognition for her important contributions as a research assistant, as does Laura Wiedlocher, a newly minted political scientist trained at the University of Missouri–St. Louis.

To Nancy Matuszak, Charisse Kiino, Laura Barrett, and Rachel Keith, the editorial team at CQ Press and SAGE responsible for much of what happened from game plan to actualization, a single word: Thanks! The word is miserly compensation for their work, effort, and dedication, and in no way makes up for all the trouble we caused. Nonetheless, our thanks are most sincerely meant (again). We heartily thank our many reviewers, past and present, for their careful and detailed assistance with reading and commenting on the manuscript:

Sharon Alter, William Rainey Harper Community College

Jeff Ashley, Eastern Illinois University

Margaret E. Banyan, Florida Gulf Coast University

Jenna Bednar, University of Michigan

Neil Berch, West Virginia University

Matthew Bergbower, Indiana State University

Nathaniel Birkhead, Kansas State University

John Bohte, University of Wisconsin–Milwaukee

Shannon Bow O'Brien, University of Texas–Austin

William Cassie, Appalachian State University

Douglas Clouatre, Mid Plains Community College

Gary Crawley, Ball State University

Warren Dixon, Texas A&M University

Nelson Dometrius, Texas Tech University

Jaime Dominguez, DePaul University

Deborah Dougherty, Illinois Central College

Georgia Duerst-Lahti, Beloit College

Nicholas Easton, Clark University

Craig Emmert, University of Texas–Permian Basin

David H. Folz, University of Tennessee

Patricia Freeland, University of Tennessee

Herbert Gooch, California Lutheran University

Michael E. Greenberg, Shippensburg University

Donald Haider-Markel, University of Kansas

George Hale, Kutztown University

William Hall, Bradley University

Susan Hansen, University of Pittsburgh

Dana Michael Harsell, University of North Dakota

June Lang, Suffolk County Community College

Lisa Langenbach, Middle Tennessee State University

William Lester, Jacksonville State University

Madhavi McCall, San Diego State University

William B. McLennan, William Peace University

Bryan McQuide, University of Idaho

Gary Moncrief, Boise State University

Scott Moore, Colorado State University

Lawrence Overlan, Bentley College

David Peterson, Iowa State University

Lori Riverstone-Newe, Illinois State University

Brett S. Sharp, University of Central Oklahoma

James Sheffield, University of Oklahoma–Norman

Kelly Sills, Washington State University–Vancouver

Lee Silvi, Lakeland Community College

Zachary Smith, Northern Arizona University

Kendra Stewart, Eastern Kentucky University

Charles Turner, California State University–Chico

James A. White, Concord University

John Woodcock, Central Connecticut State University

We hope and expect that each of them will be able to find traces of their numerous helpful suggestions throughout this final product.

Finally, in general, we express our appreciation to those political scientists and journalists who pay attention not only to Washington, DC, but also to what is happening throughout the rest of the country.

About the Authors

Kevin B. Smith is professor of political science at the University of Nebraska–Lincoln. He is coauthor of *The Public Policy Theory Primer* and numerous scholarly articles on state politics and policy, and longtime editor of CQ Press's annual *State and Local Government* reader. He is also a former associate editor of *State Politics & Policy Quarterly.* Prior to becoming an academic, he covered state and local politics as a newspaper reporter.

Alan Greenblatt, a reporter at NPR, has been writing about politics and government in Washington, DC, and the states for nearly two decades. As a reporter for *Congressional Quarterly*, he won the National Press Club's Sandy Hume award for political journalism. While on staff at *Governing* magazine, he covered many issues of concern to state and local governments, such as budgets, taxes, and higher education. Along the way, he has written about politics and culture for numerous other outlets, including the *New York Times* and the *Washington Post.*

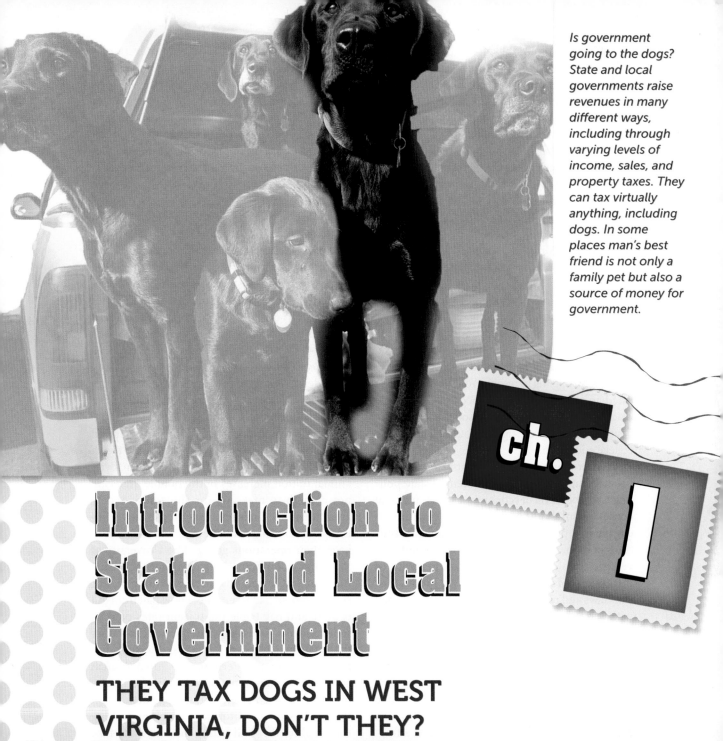

Is government going to the dogs? State and local governments raise revenues in many different ways, including through varying levels of income, sales, and property taxes. They can tax virtually anything, including dogs. In some places man's best friend is not only a family pet but also a source of money for government.

ch. 1

Introduction to State and Local Government

THEY TAX DOGS IN WEST VIRGINIA, DON'T THEY?

- What are the advantages and disadvantages of federalism?
- What is the comparative method, and why is it a useful way to talk about state and local governments?
- What role do state and local politics play in determining how much certain services—such as a college education—cost?

You could call Holden Thorp a pretty intelligent guy. He graduated from the University of North Carolina (UNC) with honors, got a Ph.D. from the California Institute of Technology, and then went on to Yale to do postgraduate work. He went back to UNC in 1993 and started rocketing through the ranks of one of the nation's premier research universities: from faculty member to department chair, from there to college dean, and not too long after that, at age forty-three, he became university chancellor. Along the way he cofounded a company that develops cancer-fighting drugs and wrote a widely respected book on entrepreneurship and innovation in universities. So you could call Holden Thorp pretty intelligent, but you'd be wrong. Holden Thorp is scary smart. That's a good thing for UNC, because it doesn't take a genius to figure out that his institution has a problem—a big problem that even the most engaged, active, and creative high-IQ types are struggling to resolve. You should be interested in this problem too, because if you are reading this book there's a reasonable chance it's your problem as well: figuring out how to fund a college education.

That problem is rooted not just in your bank balance but in a particular element of state politics, a combination of economic distress and fiscal conservatism that is pushing state legislatures to engage in a process of defunding public institutions of higher education. State colleges and universities, which is to say the vast majority of institutions of higher education, are products of state laws and regulations and are partially funded with state money. When states have less money, and most of them have less money these days, so does the entire nation's system of higher education. Good administrators such as Thorp are proactive—at UNC a stem-to-stern review designed to cut fat and make the institution more efficient is expected to cut $50 million in expenses. That will help, but it represents a fraction of the $230 million cut in state aid to the university in the past five years. This kind of thing is happening not just at UNC, but at pretty much all public colleges and universities. Adjusted for inflation, states are spending about 20 percent less on higher education than they were a decade ago. Twenty years ago, state appropriations covered about half of public university revenues; today that figure is about 30 percent and falling rapidly. Some of these cuts have been truly brutal—the California legislature cut all appropriations for higher education by $1.5 billion in a single year, the University of Wisconsin faced a similar quarter-billion haircut, and Florida slashed higher education spending by a quarter in four years.[1]

A number of public universities have been effectively privatized—for example, the University of Colorado Boulder and the University of Michigan at Ann Arbor now get only 6 or 7 percent of their revenues from their states. Yet, at the same time state revenues have fallen off a cliff, demand for a college education has skyrocketed. Something has to give in such a situation, and it has. At UNC class sizes have expanded, 556 class sections have been whacked, salaries have been frozen for years, admissions to some programs have been reduced, and the university is finding it harder to compete for top faculty with more well-heeled (especially private) universities. Oh, yes, and tuition has also increased. If you are enrolled at a public college or university, you can probably relate to this sort of thing—if anything, UNC is in better shape than most. But even annual tuition increases in the double digits are not enough to make up for shortfalls in state appropriations. Colleges are getting creative, figuring out how to tap into new revenue streams to keep their operations going. The University of Washington, for example, is admitting increasing numbers of foreign students who pay full sticker—about half its enrollees now hail from out of state and pay triple the tuition rates paid by state residents. Essentially, foreign students rather than state taxpayers are being asked to subsidize a state university. Perhaps the most radical approach to solving higher education's revenue problem has been given serious consideration at the University of California, Riverside: ditching tuition altogether and letting the university take a 5-percent share of students' salaries after they graduate.[2] Over the long term students will likely end up paying a lot more, but in the short term the idea of no tuition bills looks pretty attractive.

The bottom line is that if you are a student at a public institution of higher education, Holden Thorp's problem—figuring out how to pay for college with less state support—is your problem too. Actually, even if you are not a student at a public college, it's your problem. School revenues from states and localities come from taxes. If you get a paycheck, rent or own property, or buy anything, your state and local governments take a cut and pass some on to good old State U whether you go there or not. How do you feel about having your taxes jacked northward to help college students take a course in, say, state and local politics? For many people struggling in a tough economy, the answer to that question is emphatically negative and not printable in a PG-rated textbook.

It's not even just about money. Some argue that publicly supported higher education is a mediocre deal for taxpayers even in good economic times and that its underlying business model needs to be rethought. This is especially the case for well-known conservatives such as Pat Buchanan, who argue that administrator salaries are too high, college professors don't work hard enough, and universities teach too much that is economically and socially pointless. The hard economy may have forced the hand of state legislatures, but some argue that the time for higher education to be largely privatized and forced to yield to the discipline of the market is overdue.

So whose problem is the current challenge of funding higher education? Well, administrators, staff, faculty, and students at the affected institutions must deal with the problem, of course, but so must anyone who pays taxes or has an opinion on the appropriate role of higher education in shaping economic and social opportunity. Holden Thorp's problem turns out to be *everybody's* problem. The takeaway point here is that this massive problem that involves everyone is a problem of state politics. It is just one example of the importance of state and local governments and how the politics surrounding those governments shape the lives of all citizens of the United States.

One of the few positives of the Great Recession's impact on higher education is that it makes it a lot easier to convince college students that state and local politics is important and worthy of their attention. Holden Thorp's problem makes that point

pretty stark and pretty clear. It is worth emphasizing this point, though, because it represents the first and fundamental message of this book: everyone—not just college students—has a vested interest in knowing more about state and local government.

The Impact of State and Local Politics on Daily Life

Regardless of who you are and what you do, if you reside in the United States, state and local governments play a large role in your life. Regardless of what you are interested in—graduating, a career, relationships—state and local governments shape how, whether, and to what extent you are able to pursue these interests. To follow up on the example in the previous section, let's consider your college education. The vast majority of college students in the United States—about 70 percent—attend public institutions of higher education.[3] Public colleges and universities are created and supported by state governments. For many readers of this book, the opportunity to get a college education is possible only because each state government has created a system of higher education. For example, California has three major higher education systems: the University of California, the California State University, and the California Community College System. State governments require that taxpayers subsidize the operation of these education systems; in other words, the systems were designed not just to provide educational opportunities but also to make those opportunities broadly accessible, with tuition covering only a portion of the actual costs of a student's education. Much of the rest comes from the taxpayers' pockets via the state government. When that state subsidy falls, people like Holden Thorp get headaches and college students get higher tuition bills. Yet even with state governments putting less into higher education, they are still by far the single biggest revenue source for these

Many colleges and universities have raised tuition to offset declining appropriations from state legislatures, a move that critics argue is making higher education unaffordable for many. In February 2012, tuition hikes of 9 percent approved by the University of North Carolina Board of Governors prompted a student protest.

institutions. Tuition and fees cover about 20 percent of public college revenues, compared to 30 percent from state appropriations (the rest comes from investments, foundations, local governments, the federal government, and other miscellaneous sources).[4]

Even if you attend a private college, the state government may still play a significant role in covering the costs of your education. A quarter of the students at private, nonprofit schools receive grants or other forms of financial aid directly funded by state governments. In fact, undergraduates at private colleges receive on average more than $2,500 in state grants or other financial aid from the state or local government. Not including tuition, that amount of financial aid is several hundred dollars more than the average undergraduate at a public college receives from the state.[5]

State governments do not just determine what opportunities for higher education are available and what they cost. Some states have curriculum mandates. You may be taking a course on state and local politics—and reading this book—because your state government decided that it was a worthy investment of your time and money. In Texas, for example, a state politics course is not just a good idea—it's the law. According to Section 51.301 of the Texas Education Code, a student must successfully complete a course on state politics to receive a bachelor's degree from any publicly funded college in the state.

Think that's a lot of regulation? The government's role in shaping your college education is actually pretty small. Compared to the heavy involvement of state and local governments in shaping K–12 education, colleges have free rein. Roughly 90 percent of students in grades 9 through 12 attend public high schools.[6] Local units of government operate most of these schools. Private grade schools are also subject to a wide variety of state and local government regulations, ranging from teacher certification and minimum curriculum requirements to basic health and safety standards. Whether you attended public or private school—or were home-schooled—at the end of the day you had no choice in the decision to get a basic grade school education. Although the minimum requirements vary, every state in the union requires that children receive at least a grade school education.

State and local governments do not exist simply to regulate large areas of your life, even if it sometimes seems that way. Their primary purpose is to provide services to their respective populations. In providing these services, state and local governments shape the social and economic lives of their citizens. Education is a good example of a public service that extends deep into the daily lives of Americans, but it is far from the only one. The roads you use to get to school are there because state and local authorities built them and maintain them. The electricity that runs your computer comes from a utility grid regulated by your state government, local government, or both. State and local governments are responsible for the sewer and water systems that make the bathroom down the hall possible. They make sure that the water you drink is safe and that the burger, sushi, or salad you bought in your student union does not make you sick.[7] State governments determine the violations and punishments that constitute the criminal law. Local governments are responsible primarily for law enforcement and fire protection. The services that state and local governments supply are such a part of our lives that in many cases we notice only their absence—when the water does not run, when the road is closed, or when the educational subsidy either declines or disappears.

The Comparative Method in Practice: Yes, They Really Do Tax Dogs in West Virginia

Recognizing the impacts of state and local government may be a reasonable way to spark an interest in the topic, but interest alone does not convey knowledge. A systematic approach to learning about state and local government is necessary to gain a coherent understanding of the many activities, responsibilities, and levels involved. In this book, that systematic approach is the **comparative method**, which uses similarities and differences as the basis for systematic explanation. Any two states or localities that you can think of will differ in a number of ways. For example, they really do tax dogs in West Virginia. The state authorizes each county government to assess a fee for every dog within that county's jurisdiction. This is not the case in, say, Nebraska, where dogs have to be licensed but are not taxed.[8] Another example: Texas has executed hundreds of criminals since the moratorium, or ban, on the death penalty was lifted in the 1970s; other states have executed none.

Or consider the electoral differences between states. In recent elections, Kansans and Nebraskans sent only Republicans to the U.S. House of Representatives (in 2012, all seven House members from these two states were Republicans). The people of Massachusetts sent just Democrats (all ten seats were held by Democrats in 2012). Differences

between states and localities do not just involve such oddities as the tax status of the family pet or such big political questions as the balance of power in the House of Representatives. Those of you who do something as ordinary as buying a soda after class may pay more than your peers in other states or cities. Some readers of this book are certainly paying more in tuition and fees than those in other colleges. Why?

The comparative method answers such questions by systematically looking for **variance**, or differences, between comparable units of analysis. For our purposes, states are one comparable unit of analysis. Local governments—governments below the state level, such as county boards of commissioners and city councils—are another. Governments at each of these levels, state or local, have basic similarities that make meaningful comparisons possible. One way to think of this is that the comparative method is based on the idea that you can learn more about apples by comparing them to other apples than you can by comparing them to oranges or bananas.

For example, governmentally speaking, all fifty states have a lot in common. Their governmental structures are roughly the same. All have a basic division of powers among the executive, legislative,

> Governments at each of these levels, state or local, have basic similarities that make meaningful comparisons possible. One way to think of this is that the comparative method is based on the idea that you can learn more about apples by comparing them to other apples than you can by comparing them to oranges or bananas.

Comparative Method
A learning approach based on studying the differences and similarities among similar units of analysis (such as states).

Variance
The difference between units of analysis on a particular measure.

and judicial branches of government. All have to operate within the broad confines of the single set of rules that is the U.S. Constitution. There's a bit more variety below the state level, with many different kinds and levels of local government (counties, municipalities, townships, and so forth), but broadly speaking all these governments share a basic set of responsibilities and all have to operate within the rules set down within their respective state constitutions. These similarities among states and among local governments make meaningful comparisons possible. Paradoxically, what makes such comparisons meaningful are not the similarities but the differences. This is because even though states share similar political structures and follow the same overall set of rules, they make very different choices. These differences have consequences. Take, for example, college tuition and fees. As noted earlier, there is a direct relationship between the size of a state government's contribution to higher education and a student's average tuition bill.

Underlying this relationship is a set of differences that explains why your tuition bill is high (or low) compared to tuition charged by colleges in other states. Simply put, your tuition bill is comparatively higher (or lower) depending on the size of a state government's subsidy to higher education; this is a lesson hundreds of thousands of students have become all too painfully aware of in recent years. These sorts of meaningful differences extend far beyond how much you're paying for your college education. A similar difference explains why some of you will pay more for a soda after class than others. The sales tax on a can of soda ranges from 0 to 8 percent, depending on the city and state, hence the different prices in different locales.[9] These examples demonstrate the essence of the comparative method—from your tuition bills to the price of soda, differences between political jurisdictions make a difference in the daily lives of citizens.

Such differences can lend themselves to very sophisticated and very useful statistical analyses. For example, exactly how much is a tuition bill influenced by state support of public higher education? A professional policy analyst can use data on state higher education funding and tuition rates at state universities and colleges to provide a precise estimate of the relationship between the contributions from state government and your tuition bill. On average, for every appropriation of $1,000 per student by the state government, tuition and fees at public four-year universities fall by a little more than $200.[10] Of course, the reverse is also true: for every reduction of $1,000 per student in state aid, tuition goes up by an average of $200.

This basic approach of looking for "differences that make a difference" can be used to answer a broad range of "why" questions. For example, we know that how much a state gives to higher education helps determine how much you pay in tuition. So why do some states provide more support to higher education than others? This is a question about one difference (variation in how much state governments spend on higher education) that can be answered by looking at other differences. What might these differences be? Well, they could range from partisan politics in a state's legislature to a state's traditions and history to a state's relative wealth. As a starting point for using the comparative approach to analyze such questions, consider the following basic differences among states and among localities.

Sociodemographics

The populations of states and localities vary enormously in size, age, and ethnicity. The particular mix of these characteristics, or **sociodemographics**, in a specific state or community has a profound impact on the state or community's politics. California is the most populous state in the nation, with more than 37 million residents. It is a racially and ethnically diverse population, only 39.7 percent of which is non-Hispanic whites, and it includes many first- and second-generation immigrants. Roughly 13.7 percent of Californians live in poverty. Compare this with New Hampshire, which has about 1.3 million residents, 92.2 percent of whom

Sociodemographics
The characteristics of a population, including size, age, and ethnicity.

are non-Hispanic whites and only about 7.8 percent of whom live below the poverty line.[11] These population characteristics present different challenges to the governments in these two states. Differences in populations are likely to promote different attitudes about and policies on welfare, affirmative action, bilingual education programs, and even the role and responsibilities of government in general.

And it gets better. All these population characteristics are dynamic. That is, they change. From 2000 to 2010, the population of McKinney, Texas, grew by more than 200 percent.[12] During roughly the same period, the population of Parkersburg, West Virginia, shrank by more than 21 percent. Such population expansions and contractions create very different problems and policy priorities for local governments—the struggle to accommodate new growth in a fast-developing area versus the challenge of maintaining even basic services in a rural county in which there are ever fewer taxpayers to tax. Or consider the population of the entire state of Florida, which was still growing in 2010, but at the slowest annual rate seen in three decades. That gearing down of population growth is expected to influence everything from housing starts to job creation to state and local tax collections.[13]

How might sociodemographics be related to, say, your tuition bill? Consider the age distribution of a state's population, from young to old. There is less demand for college education among those older than sixty-five than there is among those in the traditional undergraduate demographic of eighteen to twenty-four. Given this, states with higher percentages of their populations in older age groups face a different set of education policy pressures than those with higher concentrations in younger groups. States with large aging populations are likely to face less demand for higher education spending and more demand for public programs that address the needs of the elderly, such as access to healthcare. Why do some states provide more support to higher education than others? At least a partial answer to this question is that different sociodemographics create different demands for higher education.

Study Map 1-1 for a moment. Believe it or not, you are actually looking at the United States. The reason the states look so strange is that this is a special kind of map called a cartogram. Instead of using actual geographical space to determine the size of a particular area represented in the map—the number of square miles in each state, for instance—cartograms use other variables to determine how size is represented. This cartogram depicts the size of each state's population, another useful way to compare states. Notice that some states that are geographically actually pretty big, such as New Mexico at 122,000 square miles, are very small on this map because they have small populations. Other states that are geographically actually quite small, such as Connecticut (with only 5,000 square miles), look much bigger on this map because they have large populations. Some states, such as Virginia, don't look all that different in size from their appearance on a traditional map.

Texas is the country's fastest-growing state, with a 2.1-percent population increase in 2011. It narrowly beat out the previous population-growth champ, Utah, which came in second with an annual growth rate of 1.93 percent.

Culture and History

States and localities have distinct "personalities" that are apparent in everything from the "bloody bucket" shoulder patch worn by the Pennsylvania National Guard to the drawl that distinguishes the speech of West Texas natives. Some states have been part of the Union for more than two hundred years and still project an Old World connection to Europe. Hawaii and Alaska became states within living memory and are more associated with the exoticism of the Pacific and the Old West. New York City prides itself on being a cosmopolitan center of Western civilization. The visitor's bureau of Lincoln, Nebraska, touts the city's small-town ambience and Middle American values. These differences are more than interesting variations in accent and local points of pride. They are visible symbols that represent distinct values and attitudes. Political scientists generally accept that these differences extend to government and that each state has a distinct **political culture**—identifiable

---

Political Culture
The attitudes and beliefs broadly shared by a polity about the role and responsibilities of government.

MAP 1-1

Population by State

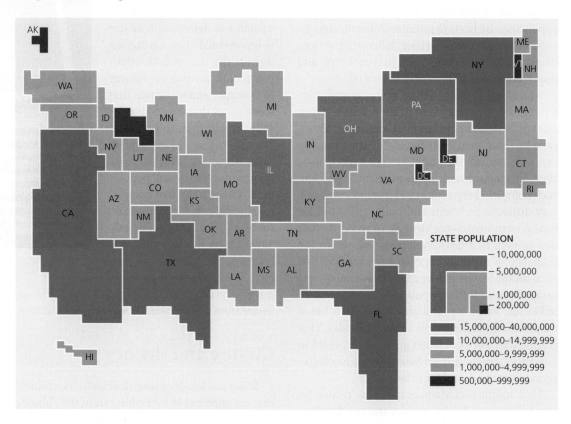

STATE POPULATION

- 10,000,000
- 5,000,000
- 1,000,000
- 200,000

	15,000,000–40,000,000
	10,000,000–14,999,999
	5,000,000–9,999,999
	1,000,000–4,999,999
	500,000–999,999

Source: U.S. Department of Commerce, *Statistical Abstract of the United States, 2012* (Washington, DC: U.S. Census Bureau, 2012), "Table 16, Resident Population by Age and State: 2010," 21, www.census.gov/prod/2011pubs/12statab/pop.pdf.

general attitudes and beliefs about the role and responsibilities of government.

Daniel Elazar's *American Federalism: A View from the States* is the classic study of political culture. In this book, first published more than forty years ago, Elazar not only describes different state cultures and creates a classification of state cultures still in use today but also explains why states have distinctly different political cultures. Elazar argues that political culture is a product of how the United States was settled. He says that people's religious and ethnic backgrounds played the dominant role in establishing political cultures. On this basis, there were three distinct types of settlers who fanned out across the United States in more or less straight lines from the East Coast to the West Coast. These distinct migration patterns created three different types of state political cultures: moralistic, individualistic, and traditionalistic.[14]

States with **moralistic cultures** are those in which politics is the means used to achieve a good and just society. Such states tend to be clustered in the northern parts of the country (New England, the Upper Midwest, and the Pacific Northwest). Elazar argues that the Puritans who originally settled the Northeast came to the New World seeking religious freedom. Their political culture reflected a desire to use politics to construct the best possible society. This notion—that government and politics represent the means to the greater good—creates a society that values involvement in politics and views government as a positive force for addressing social problems.

Moralistic Culture
A political culture that views politics and government as the means of achieving the collective good.

Demographics and culture give each state and locality a unique "personality." Here teenagers celebrate the Chinese New Year by blowing confetti into the air in New York City's Chinatown.

This general orientation toward government and politics spread along the northern and middle parts of the country in successive waves of migration. Wisconsin, for example, is a classic moralistic state. First settled by Yankees and later by Scandinavians, Germans, and Eastern Europeans, the state has long had a reputation for high levels of participation in politics (for example, high levels of voter turnout), policy innovation, and scandal-free government.

States with **individualistic cultures** have a different view of government and politics. In individualistic cultures, people view government as an extension of the marketplace, something in which people participate for individual reasons and to achieve individual goals. Government should provide the services that people want, but it is not a vehicle for creating a "good society" or intervening in private activities. Politics in individualistic states is viewed like any other business. Officeholders expect to be paid like professionals, and political parties are, in essence, corporations that compete to provide goods and services to people. Unlike folks in moralistic states, people in individualistic states tend to tolerate more corruption in government—as long as the roads are paved and the trains run on time.

Why? In individualistic states, "both politicians and citizens look upon political activity as a specialized one," Elazar writes, "and no place for amateurs to play an active role."[15] The roots of this view of government, according to Elazar, come from the English, Scottish, Irish, and

Germans who initially settled in states such as Maryland, New Jersey, and Pennsylvania. They came to the United States in search of individual opportunity, not to construct some idealized vision of the good society. This "every man for himself" attitude was reflected in politics, and the individualistic culture was carried by subsequent waves of migration into places such as Illinois and Missouri.

New Jersey is a good example of an individualistic state. This state, as political scientist Maureen Moakley puts it, "has always been more of a polyglot than a melting pot."[16] Originally settled by waves of poor and uneducated immigrants in pursuit of the American Dream, it has in more recent times become home to more than a million foreign-born residents and large racial and ethnic minority populations. The result is a fragmented political culture in which many residents feel more connected to their local communities than to the state. Not surprisingly, given all this, New Jersey has a long tradition of strong, independent local government, with laws that give the state's nearly six hundred general-purpose local governments more power than localities in other states.

Individualistic Culture
A political culture that views politics and government as just another way to achieve individual goals.

A Difference That Makes a Difference

Is It Better to Be a Woman in Vermont or a Gal in Mississippi?

According to the Institute for Women's Policy Research (IWPR), it is better to be a woman in Vermont than a gal in Mississippi.

Why? Well, in an analysis of the status of women in the states, the IWPR found several reasons for ranking Vermont as the best state for women and Mississippi as the worst. For example, in Vermont women had greater economic autonomy and enjoyed greater reproductive rights than women in Mississippi. This is only a partial answer to the question, however. To learn the rest of it, we must ask: *Why* would women have greater economic autonomy and more reproductive rights in Vermont than in Mississippi?

The comparative approach to answering this question involves looking for other differences between Vermont and Mississippi—differences that might explain the variance in the status of women. Some candidates for those explanatory differences are presented in Table 1-1. This table shows the top five and the bottom five states in the IWPR rankings, the dominant political culture in each state, and the percentage of state legislators in each state who were women in 2012. Notice any patterns?

You may have caught that all of the top five states have either moralistic or individualistic cultures. All of the bottom five states have traditionalistic cultures. Therefore, political culture might explain some of the difference in women's status. States in which the dominant political values stress the importance of everyone getting involved might offer more opportunities for women. So might states in which such values emphasize hard work as the predominant basis for getting ahead in life. States in which the dominant political values stress leaving the important decisions to established elites might offer fewer opportunities for women because, traditionally, elites have been male.

Also, take a look at the proportions of women in the state legislatures. On average, about one-third of state legislators in the top five states are women. In the bottom five states, that average is halved—only about 16 percent of state legislators are women. This is a difference that can have considerable impact. A number of studies show that women legislators tend to support more progressive policies, are more likely to pay attention to women's issues, and are more likely to push these issues into law.*

Thus states that have more women in their legislatures are more likely to respond to issues such as reproductive rights, violence against women, child-support policies, and family-leave benefits. All these contribute to the IWPR's calculations. Why is Vermont a better state for women than Mississippi? A comparative answer to that question is that Vermont has a political culture that is more likely to encourage and support political participation by women and it also has a greater female presence in its state legislature.

TABLE 1-1

Politics and the Status of Women in the States: Some Variables

Five Best States for Women	Dominant Political Culture	Percentage of State Legislators Who Are Women
1. Vermont	Moralistic	38.9
2. Connecticut	Individualistic	29.9
3. Minnesota	Moralistic	32.8
4. Washington	Moralistic	32
5. Oregon	Moralistic	28.9
Five Worst States for Women	**Dominant Political Culture**	**Percentage of State Legislators Who Are Women**
46. Oklahoma	Traditionalistic	12.8
47. Arkansas	Traditionalistic	22.2
48. Kentucky	Traditionalistic	18.8
49. South Carolina	Traditionalistic	9.4
50. Mississippi	Traditionalistic	16.7

Sources: National Conference of State Legislatures, "Women in State Legislatures: 2012 Legislative Session," www.ncsl.org/legislatures-elections/wln/women-in-state-legislatures-2012.aspx; Institute for Women's Policy Research, *The Status of Women in the States*, 2004, www.iwpr.org/States2004/SWS2004/index.htm; Daniel J. Elazar, *American Federalism: A View from the States* (New York: Crowell, 1966).

*Michele Swers, "Understanding the Policy Impact of Electing Women: Evidence from Research on Congress and State Legislatures," *PS: Political Science & Politics* 34, no. 2 (2001): 217–220.

In **traditionalistic cultures**, politics is the province of elites, something that average citizens should not concern themselves with. Traditionalistic states are, as their name suggests, fundamentally conservative, in the sense that they are concerned with preserving a well-established society. Like moralistic states, traditionalistic states believe that government serves a positive role. But there is one big difference—traditionalistic states believe the larger purpose of government is to maintain the existing social order. Those at the top of the social structure are expected to play a dominant role in politics, and power is concentrated in the hands of these elites. Traditionalistic states tend to be rural states (at least historically) in which agriculture, rather than a broader mix of competing commercial activities, is the main economic driver.

Traditionalistic cultures tend to be concentrated in the Deep South, in states such as Georgia, Mississippi, and South Carolina. In these states, politics is significantly shaped by tradition and history. Like the settlers of individualistic states, those who settled the South sought personal opportunity. The preindustrial, agrarian economy of the South, however, led to a culture that was little more than a variation of the feudal order of the European Middle Ages. As far back as the 1830s, French aristocrat and writer Alexis de Tocqueville, writing about the United States, noted that "as one goes farther south . . . the population does not exercise such a direct influence on affairs. . . . The power of the elected officials is comparatively greater and that of the voter less."[17]

Few states today can be considered "pure" examples of any of these cultures. In other words, most states have elements of two of the cultures or of all three. For example, a number of traditionalistic states, such as Florida and Georgia, have seen huge influxes of people from northern states, people who often are not from traditionalistic cultures. The Deep South is also considerably more urban than it used to be. Such changes tend to add elements of the moralistic and individualistic cultures into the traditionalistic mix.

Even with such changes, however, for most states one of Elazar's three political cultures is likely to be dominant, as Map 1-2 shows. Numerous studies have found that the dominant political culture shapes politics and policy in important ways. Policy change and innovation, for example, are more likely in moralistic states. Individualistic states are more likely to offer businesses tax breaks. Traditionalistic states tend to commit less public money to areas such as education.[18] Faced with similar problems, therefore, the Texas and Wisconsin state legislatures may propose radically different policy responses. These differences are at least partially products of the political cultures that still distinguish each state. In other words, culture and history matter.

These cultural differences certainly are apparent when it comes to supporting higher education. Moralistic states commit considerably more resources to higher education than do individualistic and traditionalistic states. They spend about 13 percent more per capita on colleges and universities than states with the other two cultures. Because moralistic states are those in which attitudes support higher levels of commitment to the public sector, these spending differences make sense in cultural terms. Why do some states provide more support to higher education than others? Apparently, another part of the answer is that some political cultures see higher education more in communal than in individual terms.

Economy

The relative size and health of a state's economy has a huge impact on its capacity to govern and provide public services. The per capita gross domestic product (GDP)—the state equivalent of the gross national product—varies from about $28,000 in Mississippi to $63,000 in Delaware.[19] This means that the government in Delaware has the ability to tap a greater amount of resources than the government in Mississippi. In effect, this difference in wealth means that if Delaware and

Traditionalistic Culture
A political culture that views politics and government as the means of maintaining the existing social order.

MAP 1-2

Dominant Political Culture by State

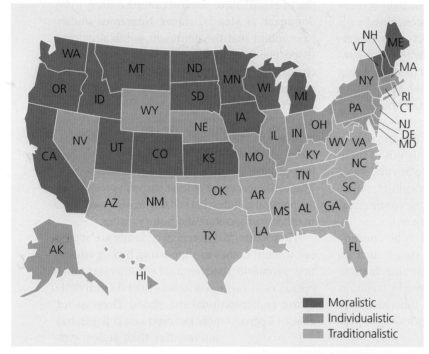

Moralistic
Individualistic
Traditionalistic

Source: Virginia Gray, "The Socioeconomic and Political Contexts of States," in *Politics in the American States: A Comparative Analysis*, 10th ed., ed. Virginia Gray and Russell Hanson (Washington, DC: CQ Press, 2013), 22.

places such as Kansas and Nevada, although agriculture in the former and gambling in the latter create just as many policy challenges and demands for government action.

Regardless of the basis of a state's economy, greater wealth does not always translate into more support for public programs. States with above-average incomes actually tend to spend *less* per capita on higher education. Why would less wealthy states concentrate more of their resources on higher education? There are a number of possible explanations. Education is a critical component of a postindustrial economy, so states that are less well off may direct more of their resources into education in hopes of building a better economic future. Citizens in wealthy states may simply be better able to afford higher tuition costs. Whatever the explanation, this example suggests another advantage of employing the comparative method—it shows that the obvious assumptions are not always the correct ones.

Mississippi were to implement identical and equivalent public services, Mississippi would have a considerably higher tax rate. This is because Mississippi would have to use a greater proportion of its smaller amount of resources for these services than Delaware would. These sorts of differences are also visible at the local level. Wealthy suburbs can enjoy lower tax rates and still spend more on public services than economically struggling urban or rural communities.

Regional economic differences do not just determine tax burdens and the level of public services. They also determine the relative priorities of particular policy and regulatory issues. Fishing, for example, is a sizable industry in coastal states in the Northeast and Northwest. States such as Maine and Washington have numerous laws, regulations, and enforcement responsibilities tied to the catching, processing, and transporting of fish. Regulating the economic exploitation of marine life occupies very little government attention and resources in

Geography and Topography

There is wide variation in the physical environments in which state and local governments operate. Hawaii is a lush tropical island chain in the middle of the Pacific Ocean, Nevada encompasses a large desert, Michigan is mostly heavily forested, and Colorado is split by the Rocky Mountains. Such geographical and topographical variation presents different challenges to governments. State and local authorities in California devote considerable time and resources to preparing for earthquakes. Their counterparts in Texas spend less time thinking about earthquakes, but they do concern themselves with tornadoes, grass fires, and hurricanes.

Combine geography with population characteristics and the challenges become even more

TABLE 1-2

Political Cultures at a Glance

	Elazar Classification		
	Moralistic	**Individualistic**	**Traditionalistic**
Role of Government	Government should act to promote the public interest and policy innovation.	Government should be utilitarian, a service provider.	Government should help preserve the status quo.
Attitude of Public Representatives	Politicians can effect change; public service is worthwhile and an honor.	Businesslike. Politics is a career like any other, and individual politicians are oriented toward personal power. High levels of corruption are more common.	Politicians can effect change, but politics is the province of the elites.
Role of Citizens	Citizens actively participate in voting and other political activities; individuals seek public office.	The state exists to advance the economic and personal self-interest of citizens; citizens leave politics to the professionals.	Ordinary citizens are not expected to be politically involved.
Degree of Party Competition	Highly competitive	Moderate	Weak
Government Spending on Services	High	Moderate; money goes to basic services but not to perceived "extras."	Low
Political Culture	Strong	Fragmented	Strong
Most Common in . . .	Northeast, northern Midwest, Northwest	Middle parts of the country, such as the Mid-Atlantic; parts of the Midwest, such as Missouri and Illinois; parts of the West, such as Nevada	Southern states, rural areas

Source: Adapted from Daniel J. Elazar, *American Federalism: A View from the States*, 2nd ed. (New York: Crowell, 1972).

complex. Montana is a large rural state in which transportation logistics—simply getting students to school—can present something of a conundrum. Is it better to bus students long distances to large, centrally located schools, or should there be many smaller schools within easy commuting distance for relatively few students? The first option is cheaper. Larger schools can offer academic and extracurricular activities that smaller schools cannot afford. But the busing exacts a considerable cost on students and families. The second alternative eases transportation burdens, but it requires building more schools and hiring more teachers, which means more taxes. Geographical and population differences often not only shape the answers to such difficult policy issues but also pose the questions.

Consider the variety of seasonal weather patterns that occur within the enormous geographical confines of the United States. In Wisconsin, snow removal is a key service provided by local governments. Road-clearing crews are often at work around the clock during bad weather. The plows, the crews, and the road salt all cost money. Considerable investment in administration and coordination is required to do the job effectively. In Florida, snow removal is low on local governments' lists of priorities, for good reason—it rarely snows in the Sunshine State. On the other hand, state and local authorities in Florida do need to prepare for the occasional hurricane. Hurricanes are less predictable and less common than snow in Wisconsin, but it only takes one to create serious demands on the resources of local authorities.

And, yes, even basic geography affects your tuition bill, especially when combined with some of the other characteristics discussed here. Many large public colleges and universities are located in urban centers because central geographical locations serve more people more efficiently. Delivering higher education in rural areas is a more expensive proposition simply because there are fewer people in the service area. States with below-average population densities tend to be larger and more sparsely populated. They also tend to spend more on higher education. Larger government subsidies are necessary to make tuition affordable.

Recognizing the Stakes

The variation across states and localities offers more than a way to help make sense of your tuition bill or to explain why some public school systems are better funded or to understand why taxes are lower in some states. These differences also serve to underline the central role of states and localities in the American political system. Compared to the federal government, state and local governments employ more people and buy more goods and services from the private sector. They have the primary responsibility for addressing many of the issues that people care about most, including education, crime prevention, transportation, healthcare, and the environment. Public opinion polls often show that citizens place more trust in their state and local governments than in the federal government. These polls frequently express citizens' preference for having the former relieve the latter of a greater range of policy responsibilities.[20] With these responsibilities and expectations, it should be obvious that state and local politics are played for high stakes.

High stakes, yes, but it is somewhat ironic that state and local governments tend to get less attention in the media, in private conversation, and in curricula and classrooms than does their federal counterpart.[21] Ask most people to think about American government, and chances are they will think first about the president, Congress, Social Security, or some other feature of the national government. Yet most American governments are state or local. Only 535 elected legislators serve in the U.S. Congress.

> Compared to the federal government, state and local governments employ more people and buy more goods and services from the private sector. They have the primary responsibility for addressing many of the issues that people care about most, including education, crime prevention, transportation, healthcare, and the environment.

Thousands of legislators are elected at the state level, and tens of thousands more serve in the legislative branches of local government.

In terms of people, state and local governments dwarf the federal government. The combined civilian workforce of the federal government (about 3 million) is less than half the number of people working for a single category of local government—more than 6 million people work for public elementary and secondary schools alone.[22] Roughly 5 million state employees and more than 14 million local government employees punch the time clock every day. In terms of dollars, state and local governments combined represent about the same spending force as the federal government. In 2009, state and local government expenditures totaled approximately $3 trillion.[23]

The size of state and local government operations is commensurate with these governments' twenty-first-century role in the political system. After spending much of the twentieth century being drawn closer into the orbit and influence of the federal government, states and localities spent the century's last two decades, and much of the first decade of the twenty-first, aggressively asserting their independence. This maturing of nonfederal, or subnational, government made its leaders and its policies—not to mention its differences—among the most important characteristics of our political system. The Great Recession of 2008–2009 made that importance all too clear. As the economy went south and the budget gaps went north, state and local governments were forced into a painful process of cutting budgets. As pretty much any college student at a publicly supported college or university can attest, when state and local governments start hurting, the pain is felt by, well, everyone. What is at stake in state and local politics turns out to be not just what *you* are interested in, but just about anything that anyone is interested in. This is one of the reasons the federal government passed a massive economic stimulus package that sent billions of dollars pouring into state and local treasuries in 2010 and 2011. If you want a quick and direct way to reach the nation's economic, social, and political heart, then state and local governments are the obvious routes.

The context of the federal system of government, and the role of state and local governments within that system, is given more in-depth coverage in chapter 2. For now, it is important to recognize that governance in the United States is more of a network than a hierarchy. The policies and politics of any single level of government are connected and intertwined with the policies and politics of the other levels of government in a complex web of interdependent relationships. The role of states and localities in these governance partnerships has changed considerably in the past few decades.

What states and localities do, and how they go about doing it, turns out to shape national life overall as well as the lives of individual citizens. Given what is at stake at the state and local levels, no citizen can fully comprehend the role and importance of government without understanding subnational politics.

Laboratories of Democracy: Devolution and the Limits of Government

U.S. Supreme Court Justice Louis Brandeis famously described the states as **laboratories of democracy**. This metaphor refers to the ability of states—and, to a lesser extent, localities—to experiment with policy. Successful experiments can be replicated by other states or adopted by the national government. For much of the past thirty years, state-federal relations have been characterized by **devolution**, or the process of taking power and responsibility away from the federal government and giving it to state and local governments. As a result, the states for a time aggressively promoted new ways to solve old problems in such high-profile policy areas as welfare, gun control, and education. That trend of increasing state policy autonomy came to a screeching halt with the severe economic contraction of 2008–2009; in the next few years states became critically dependent on federal money to stay solvent, and that meant they had to pay attention to federal policy priorities. Currently the federal government is in the process of drawing down its massive intergovernmental grants to state and local governments. Whether this will herald a reduction in federal influence and a resurgence of state policy independence remains to be seen—as we shall see in chapter 4, state budgetary conditions are far from rosy, and only the federal government has the power to print money.

We'll take a closer look at the details of intergovernmental relations in the next chapter, but it is important here to recognize that how state and local governments exercise their independent decision-making authority is dependent on a number of factors. Some of these factors are external. The U.S. Constitution, federal laws and regulations, nationwide recessions, and the like constrain what states and localities can and cannot do. Internal factors, such as the characteristics of a particular state, also play a critical role in setting limits on what the state decides to do.

The big three of these internal factors are wealth, the characteristics of the state's political system, and

Laboratories Of Democracy
A metaphor that emphasizes the states' ability to engage in different policy experiments without interference from the federal government.

Devolution
The process of taking power and responsibility away from the federal government and giving it to state and local governments.

the relative presence of organized interest groups, those individuals who organize to support policy issues that concern them. Public programs cost money. Wealth sets the limits of possible government action. Simply speaking, wealthier states can afford to do more than poorer states. For most states, lack of funds is currently the biggest factor limiting independent policy action at the state and local levels. That is, many subnational governments do not have the money to launch expensive new policy initiatives. Indeed, in recent years many of these governments have not had the money to keep funding their existing programs and services (higher education, for example) at previous levels. While money is important, however, it is not the only factor that influences policy directions at the subnational level. Political system characteristics are the elements of the political environment that are specific to a state. States in which public opinion is relatively conservative are likely to pursue different policy avenues than states in which public opinion is more liberal. States in which Republicans dominate the government are likely to opt for different policy choices than states in which Democrats dominate. States with professional full-time legislatures are more likely to formulate and pursue sustained policy agendas than are states in which legislators

are part-timers who meet only periodically. States in which the government perceives an electoral mandate to reform government are more likely to be innovative than are states in which the government perceives an electoral mandate to retain the status quo.[24] Organized interest group activity also helps determine what sort of policy demands government responds to. Governments in states with powerful teachers' unions, for example, experience different education policy pressures than do governments in states in which teachers' unions are politically weak. These three factors constitute the basic ingredients for policymaking in the states. Specifics vary enormously from state to state, and the potential combinations in this democratic laboratory are virtually infinite.

Localities face more policymaking constraints than states do because they typically are not sovereign governments. This means that, unlike states, local governments get their power from the level of government above them rather than directly from citizens. The states have much greater control over local governments than the federal government has over the states. Yet, even though local governments are much more subordinate to state government than state government is to the federal government, they do not simply take orders from the state capital. Many have independent taxing authority and broad discretion to act within their designated policy jurisdictions.

These policy jurisdictions, nevertheless, are frequently subject to formal limits. The authority of school districts, for example, extends only to funding and operating public

It has a local government much like any other major municipality and electoral votes like a state, but it is ultimately ruled by Congress even though it has no representatives with full voting rights in the national legislature. Technically, Washington, DC, is a federal city, the only political jurisdiction of its kind in the United States.

Local Focus

The Federal City

Riddle me this. It is a city. It is sort of a state. It is ruled by Congress. What is it? It is the District of Columbia, otherwise known as Washington, DC. It is also the nation's capital, and it is surely the most unusual local government in the country.

Technically, Washington, DC, is a federal city. Article I, Section 8, Paragraph 17, of the U.S. Constitution gives Congress the power to rule over an area not to exceed ten square miles that constitutes the seat of national government. Yet it has never been quite clear what that means in terms of governance. Should Congress rule the city directly? Should the citizens of the city be given the right to elect a representative government? If they do this, should the government be subordinate to Congress, or should it be counted as equivalent to a state and thus free to make any laws that do not violate the U.S. Constitution?

Throughout the city's history, these questions have been answered very differently. In the early 1800s, the district was a strange collection of cities and counties, each governed by different means. Washington City and Georgetown were municipalities run by a chief executive (a mayor) and a legislature (a council). Depending on the time period, however, the mayors were sometimes appointed by the federal government and sometimes elected. In addition to the two cities there were also two counties. Maryland laws governed Washington County; Virginia laws governed Alexandria County.

In the 1870s, Washington City, Georgetown, and Washington County were combined into a single governmental unit, a federal territory with a governor appointed by the president and a legislature elected by the territorial residents. This eventually became the District of Columbia, or Washington, DC. For most of its history, commissioners appointed by the federal government governed the district. It was not until 1974 that the residents of Washington, DC, gained home rule and the right to elect their own mayor and council.

This mayor-council arrangement, however, is unlike any other municipal government in the United States. The laws passed by the council have to be reviewed and approved by Congress. The laws that govern federal-state relationships treat the district as a state, even though it is not a state and cannot operate like one. The mayor is not considered the head of a federal agency, but he or she is expected to act like one when seeking appropriations from Congress.

This odd hybrid of local, state, and federal governments is reflected in the unique electoral status of Washington, DC, voters. Voters in the district have a local vote but only half of a federal vote. They can vote for the president but not for a member of Congress. They can vote for a mayor and council, but they have no voting representative in Congress. Yet Congress has the power to overturn laws passed by the council. The district now has three electoral votes. Prior to 1963, it had none and DC voters could not cast a ballot for president.

All of this makes Washington, DC, the nation's most unusual local government. It is the only municipality that is a creature of the United States rather than of a state constitution, and, as such, it is the only really national city in the country.

Source: Selected material from Council of the District of Columbia, "History of Self-Government in the District of Columbia," 1997, www.dccouncil.washington.dc.us.

schools. State government may place limits on districts' tax rates and set everything from minimal employment qualifications to maximum teacher-to-pupil ratios. Even within this range of tighter restrictions, however, local governments retain considerable leeway to act independently. School districts often decide to contract out cafeteria and janitorial services, cities and counties actively seek to foster economic development with tax abatements and loan guarantees, and police commissions experiment with community-based law enforcement. During the past two decades, many of the reforms enthusiastically pursued at all levels of government—reforms ranging from innovative management practices to the outright privatization of public services—have had their origins in local government.[25]

> States and localities are not just safe places to engage in limited experimentation; they are the primary mechanisms connecting citizens to the actions of government.

What all this activity shows is that states and localities are not only the laboratories of democracy but also the engines of the American republic. States and localities are not just safe places to engage in limited experimentation; they are the primary mechanisms connecting citizens to the actions of government. It is for exactly this reason that one of the central federal government responses to the economic crisis of 2008–2009 was to shore up local and state governments financially.

Conclusion

There are good reasons for developing a curiosity about state and local governments. State politics determines everything from how much you pay for college to whether your course in state and local governments is required or elective. Above and beyond understanding the impact of state and local governments on your own life and interests, studying such governments is important because of their critical role in the governance and life of the nation.

Subnational, or nonfederal, governments employ more people than the federal government and spend as much money. Their responsibilities include everything from repairing potholes to regulating pot. It is difficult, if not impossible, to understand government in the United States and the rights, obligations, and benefits of citizenship without first understanding state and local governments.

This book fosters such an understanding through the comparative method. This approach involves looking for patterns in the differences among states and localities. Rather than advocating a particular perspective on state and local politics, the comparative method is predicated, or based, on a systematic way of asking and answering questions. Why is my tuition bill so high? Why does Massachusetts send mostly Democrats to the U.S. House of Representatives? Why are those convicted of capital crimes in Texas more likely to be executed than those convicted of comparable crimes in Connecticut? Why are sales taxes high in Alabama? Why is there no state income tax in South Dakota? We can answer each of these questions by comparing states and looking for systematic patterns in their differences. The essence of the comparative method is to use one difference to explain another.

This book's examination of state and local politics is organized so that each chapter logically builds on previous chapters. The next two chapters, on federalism and state constitutions, are designed to explain the basic structure, organization, responsibilities, and powers of state and local political systems. Chapter 4 examines how an era of austerity and constraint is reshaping federalism and creating long-term challenges for state and local governments in meeting their constitutional obligations and policy responsibilities. Chapters 5 and 6 examine political participation and the mechanisms—elections, parties, and interest groups—that connect citizens to state and local governments. Chapters 7, 8, and 9 are separate treatments of core government institutions: legislatures, the executive branch, and the courts. Finally, Chapter 10 examines local governments and their unique role within state political systems.

The Latest Research

As discussed extensively in this chapter, the comparative method is an important tool used by scholars to understand how state-level differences translate into meaningful political and policy differences. A lot of these differences that make a difference are not static—indeed, some may be changing even as you read this textbook. Recently some of the most foundational state differences have been the subject of a series of studies that may change our understanding of those differences and their implications.

The "granddaddy" of all differences is political culture, a concept originated by Daniel Elazar that continues to be widely respected for its explanatory power. Yet, however powerful its explanatory capacities, Elazar's classification of state political cultures is not based on intensive statistical analysis; it is much more impressionistic. It is also static—in other words, the basic state classifications of moralistic, traditionalistic, and individualistic have not changed since Elazar defined them nearly half a century ago. Since then, large shifts in demographics have taken place as the result of new waves of immigration, population and other relevant data have become more widely available, and sophisticated statistical analysis techniques have been developed and broadly employed. All of this gives state scholars the opportunity to undertake much more fine-grained analyses of regional value systems, how they translate into culture, how that culture might change, and what those changes might mean for state politics and policy.

Related to the renewed interest in studying and tracking cultural changes is a spate of new scholarship that focuses on measuring state-level political orientations and ideology, in effect capturing the political nuances of what makes a "red" state or a "blue" state or even a "happy" state. Several teams of scholars have been developing new measures of state-level policy attitudes and orientations, and these improved measures of political differences are proving themselves useful for predicting important policy differences.

Below we summarize some of the cutting-edge research on the differences that make a difference.

• •

- **Lieske, Joel.** 2010. "The Changing Regional Subcultures of the American States and the Utility of a New Cultural Measure." *Political Research Quarterly* 63: 538–552.

Joel Lieske, a political scientist at Cleveland State University, is the scholar most associated with the continuing study of state political culture. Lieske's scholarship tackles one of the toughest questions in this area: How can we measure culture? Elazar's classifications are very useful but impressionistic, and efforts to quantify those classifications into "yardsticks" to measure degrees of cultural difference often amount to nothing more than putting numbers on Elazar's classifications. Lieske has long argued that immigration settlement patterns and degrees of self-governance have nurtured the development of regional subcultures that may be more expansive than Elazar's threefold classification. Here he uses county-level data on racial origin, ethnic ancestry, religious affiliation, and various indicators of social structure to create a composite statistical measure of political culture. This is a much more sophisticated analysis than that employed by Elazar, and it results in not three primary subcultures but eleven. In Lieske's analysis, for example, moralistic cultures are actually made up of three related but distinct political subcultures—Nordic, Mormon, and Anglo-French, the labels representing the cultural elements of particular ethnic groups (especially Germans and Scandinavians) and different sects of dissenting Protestantism.

- **Lieske, Joel.** 2012. "American State Cultures: Testing a New Measure and Theory." *Publius: The Journal of Federalism* 42: 108–133.

In this article Lieske puts his new measure of state culture to the test. In a statistical contest, he pits his new measure against Elazar's typology and the most often used quantitative index of that typology (an index created in 1969 by political scientist Ira Sharkansky) to see which measure can better predict various indicators of state performance. Lieske's new measure of state cultural differences does the better job, suggesting that the new measure—which, unlike Elazar's, can at least theoretically be updated with new census data—better captures cultural differences.

- **Berry, William D., Richard C. Fording, Evan J. Ringquist, Russell L. Hanson, and Carl E.**

Klarner. 2010. "Measuring Citizen and Government Ideology in the U.S. States: A Re-appraisal." *State Politics & Policy Quarterly* 10: 117–135.

One of the most important differences among states lies in the general political attitudes or orientations of the states' citizens. Scholars consider it critical to tap into those state-level attitudes for many reasons. For example, if we do not know the political orientations and attitudes of citizens, we have no means of assessing whether state lawmakers actually reflect and represent the wishes of their constituents. State-level measures of ideology are incredibly hard to construct. The central problem is that no comparable state-level scientific polls are done in all fifty states at the same time. One way to get around this problem is to infer state preferences by looking at the ideologies and policy preferences of the candidates who win congressional elections. This study employs these kinds of data to create a measure of state ideology that has been found to do a good job of explaining differences in policies ranging from social welfare to incarceration rates.

- **Carsey, Thomas M., and Jeffrey J. Harden.** 2010. "New Measures of Partisanship, Ideology, and Policy Mood in the American States." *State Politics & Policy Quarterly* 10: 136–156.

This article takes an alternate approach to tackling the same measurement problem that Berry et al. address in the study cited above. Rather than inferring from lawmaker characteristics, however, Carsey and Harden put together measures of state partisan identification, ideology, and policy mood using data from a series of polls taken in congressional election years from 2000 through 2006. The resulting measures are found to be good estimates of state-level differences on these dimensions.

- **Álvarez-Diaz, Ángel, Lucas González, and Benjamin Radcliff.** 2010. "The Politics of Happiness: On the Political Determinants of Quality of Life in the American States." *Journal of Politics* 72: 894–905.

This is a study of the differences that influence perhaps the most important difference: the quality of life of citizens. The authors examine the ideology and partisanship of state governments and the policies these governments pursue, seeking to correlate these with measures of citizen satisfaction. Some may find the results surprising. States with more generous social welfare policies and more economic regulation—in other words, states that more closely resemble the social democratic countries of northern Europe—tend to have happier citizens who are more satisfied with their quality of life.

Chapter Review

Key Concepts

- comparative method (p. 5)
- devolution (p. 15)
- individualistic culture (p. 9)
- laboratories of democracy (p. 15)
- moralistic culture (p. 8)
- political culture (p. 7)
- sociodemographics (p. 6)
- traditionalistic culture (p. 11)
- variance (p. 5)

Suggested Websites

- **http://academic.udayton.edu/sppq-TPR/index.htm.** Data archive website of *State Politics & Policy Quarterly*, an academic research journal devoted to the study of state-level questions.

- **http://library.cqpress.com/statestats.** A comprehensive and searchable database of state-level information (requires subscription).

- **http://quickfacts.census.gov/qfd.** U.S. Bureau of the Census website that lists state rankings on population, per capita income, employment, poverty, and other social and economic indexes.

- **www.csg.org/csg/default.** Website of the Council of State Governments (CSG), an organization that represents elected and appointed officials in all three branches of state government. Publishes on a wide variety of topics and issues relevant to state politics and policy.

State Stats on State and Local Government

Explore and compare data on the states! Go to **college.cqpress .com/sites/essentials-govstateandlocal** to do these exercises.

1. How many state and local government employees are there in your state? Which state has the most? The least? How have these numbers changed in the past ten years? Why do you think these changes have occurred?

2. States with which political culture (individualistic, traditionalistic, or moralistic) spend the most, per capita, on higher education? Why might that be?

3. In your state, did the percentage of households headed by single mothers increase, decrease, or stay the same between 2006 and 2010? How might any changes in this percentage influence your state's budgeting decisions? How does this compare to states that neighbor yours?

4. What is the per capita state and local sales tax revenue in Delaware? What about in the states immediately surrounding Delaware? How are those states able to collect sales taxes? Why wouldn't neighboring citizens just drive to Delaware to do all of their shopping?

5. What is the per capita gross domestic product in your state? Is it above or below the national figure? Did your state's per capita GDP increase, decrease, or stay the same between 2010 and 2011? What differences between your state and others might explain why your state is above/below the national average?

States and the federal government, like it or not, need each other. President Barack Obama and New Jersey governor Chris Christie may have different party loyalties and different policy preferences, but they set aside their differences to work together effectively to help New Jersey recover from the aftermath of a hurricane that devastated the state's coastal regions in fall 2012.

ch. 2

Federalism

THE POWER PLAN

- Why does the federal government seem to be gaining power while the states are losing it?
- What are the advantages and disadvantages of federalism?
- Why would some businesses prefer to be regulated by the federal government rather than by state governments?

In 1883, the poet Emma Lazarus was asked to pen a few words that might be donated to a charitable auction. The auction's purpose was to sell works of art and literature to raise money for a pedestal designed to hold a very big sculpture. You might have heard of the sculpture—the Statue of Liberty, which has raised high the torch of freedom over New York Harbor for more than a century and is one of the most iconic symbols of the United States. You might also know at least a few lines of "The New Colossus," the sonnet Lazarus composed for the cause—especially the bit that says, "Give me your tired, your poor, your huddled masses yearning to breathe free." These words express the idea of the United States as a nation of immigrants, founded not on race or religion but on a universal idea of individual liberty. *E pluribus unum* and all that. That sentiment of international roots and values, proudly engraved on a bronze plaque below Lady Liberty's tootsies, has been in pretty short supply in many states over the past couple of years. Indeed, state attitudes toward immigration have been less about welcoming the tired, poor, huddled masses than about telling them to get lost.

To be fair, the standoffish attitude of many states toward immigration these days is targeted specifically at illegal (or undocumented) immigration rather than at immigration in general. Immigration is an issue that sparks furious controversy. It is also an issue that highlights the often contentious and fractious relationship between state and federal governments. Historically and constitutionally, regulating immigration falls under the jurisdiction of the federal government. During the first decade of the twenty-first century, though, many states thought the federal government had punted on its responsibilities. (By some estimates nearly 12 million people, many of them from South American countries, have come to live in the United States in violation of federal residence laws, seeking to emulate Europeans of an earlier century by immigrating in search of social and economic freedom and opportunity.) For many state and local officials the rising rate of illegal immigration created a massive headache; it increased demand on public services and resulted in a sort of shadow society that posed challenges for everything from law enforcement to tax collections to accurate population estimates. States wanted the feds to do something—it was their job, after all. The feds did nothing. The states decided to take on the job themselves.

One of the most restrictive, and certainly the most famous, of the new state-level immigration laws is Arizona's Support Our Law Enforcement and Safe Neighborhoods Act (SB 1070), signed into law by Governor Jan Brewer in 2010. In a nutshell, SB 1070 made it a *state* crime to be in the United States illegally. Under its provisions immigrants had to carry paperwork proving their legal residence status and law enforcement officers were required to ask for that proof if they suspected someone of being in the state illegally. The law also made it illegal to hire, shelter, or transport those without proper documentation.

The bill, to put it mildly, was enormously controversial. Proponents saw it as an appropriate response to a problem Washington was ignoring. Critics saw it as barely veiled racism. Regardless, it put the state government into direct confrontation with the federal government. When that happens—and it has happened a lot—the United States Supreme Court gets to serve as referee. In 2012, the Supreme Court struck down most, but not all, of SB 1070. The Court essentially ruled that federal immigration laws preempt state law, that under the Constitution's supremacy clause what the federal government wants takes precedence, and that if the federal government wants to do nothing about illegal immigration, well, tough. Critically, though, the Court left intact SB 1070's requirement that immigrants carry documents proving they are legal residents of the United States, the "show me your papers" provision. As many other states had followed Arizona's lead and adopted immigration regulations, many immigrants will now likely have to deal with some form of a "show me your papers" law, whether they live in Arizona or not. This puts immigrants without those documents in a sensitive spot—any contact with law enforcement, even something as trivial as a speeding ticket, means they could be reported to federal authorities and, at least in theory, targeted for deportation. The feds might have supremacy in this area, but that does not mean the states will not play an important and high-profile role.

While it is too soon to assess the long-term impact of such state-level regulations, the whole immigration controversy is a good example of how subnational governments are, by design, assigned a central domestic policymaking role. In short, states and localities enjoy a high degree of independence from the central government. This importance and independence are products of **federalism**, a political system in which national and regional governments share powers and are considered independent equals. An understanding of this system of shared powers is critical to an understanding of the politics of states and localities and the central role they play in the U.S. political system. One of the most important questions in the American political system is: Who—the federal government or the state governments—has the power to do what? In the words of University of Chicago law professor Cass Sunstein, the debate over the distribution of powers between the state and federal levels holds "the ultimate fate of measures safeguarding the environment, protecting consumers, upholding civil rights, protecting violence against women, protecting endangered species, and defining criminal conduct in general and banning hate crimes in particular."[1]

> One of the most important questions in the American political system is: Who—the federal government or the state governments—has the power to do what?

Who gets the power to do what will affect the lives of virtually all citizens in the United States. This chapter provides a basic understanding of federalism, its history and evolution in the United States, and its implications for politics and governance in states and localities.

Federalism
Political system in which national and regional governments share powers and are considered independent equals.

Systems of Power

We typically think of a nation as being ruled by a single sovereign government, that is, a government that depends on no other government for its political authority or power. This does not mean, however, that every nation has one government. Power and policy responsibility are distributed throughout any given political system in one of three ways, and all typically involve multiple levels of government. (See Figure 2-1.) The first option is to concentrate power in a single central government. Nations in which legal authority is held exclusively by a central government are known as **unitary systems**. Unitary systems typically do have regional and/or local governments, but these can exercise only the powers and responsibilities granted them by the central government. In other words, these governments are not sovereign; how much or how little power they are allowed to wield is up to the central government, not the citizens of the particular localities. The United Kingdom is a good example of a unitary system. Although the United Kingdom has a strong tradition of local government and has set up regional legislatures in Scotland and Wales and (intermittently) in Northern Ireland, power is concentrated in the nation's parliament. If it so chooses, Parliament can expand or contract the powers and responsibilities of these lower governments or even shut them down entirely (this has actually happened in Northern Ireland).

In contrast to unitary systems, confederal systems concentrate power in regional governments. A **confederacy** is defined as a voluntary association of independent, sovereign states or governments. This association stands the power hierarchy of a unitary system on its head. In a confederacy, it is the central government that depends on the regional governments for its legal authority. The United States has experimented with confederal systems twice during its history. The Articles of Confederation was the first constitution of the United States. It organized the U.S. political system

---

Unitary Systems
Political systems in which power is concentrated in a central government.

Confederacy
Political system in which power is concentrated in regional governments.

FIGURE 2-1

HOW IT WORKS

Systems of Government

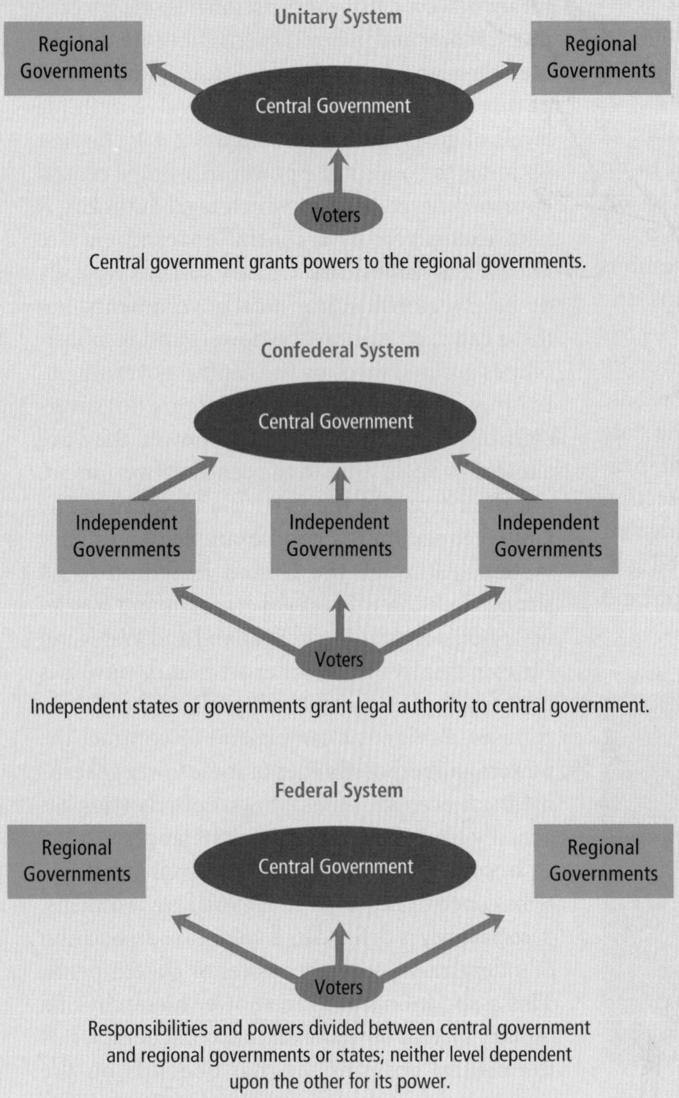

Unitary System

Regional Governments

Central Government

Regional Governments

Voters

Central government grants powers to the regional governments.

Confederal System

Central Government

Independent Governments

Independent Governments

Independent Governments

Voters

Independent states or governments grant legal authority to central government.

Federal System

Regional Governments

Central Government

Regional Governments

Voters

Responsibilities and powers divided between central government and regional governments or states; neither level dependent upon the other for its power.

as an agreement of union among sovereign states. The national government consisted of a legislature in which all states had equal representation. There was no national executive branch, such as the presidency, and no national judiciary, such as the Supreme Court.

This confederal system was adopted during the Revolutionary War and remained in effect for

more than a decade. Many of the nation's founders saw its many flaws, however, and wrote its replacement at the Constitutional Convention of 1787 in Philadelphia. The product of that gathering—the U.S. Constitution—was ratified in 1788 and replaced the Articles of Confederation as the basis of the U.S. political system.[2] The second experiment with confederacy began in 1861 at the onset of the Civil War. Southern states seeking to secede from the Union organized their political system as a confederacy. All of this ended with the South's surrender in 1865 and the return of the seceded states to the Union.

Federal systems operate in a middle range between unitary systems and confederacies. Responsibilities in a federal system are divided between the two levels of government, and each is given the appropriate power and legal authority to fulfill those responsibilities. The system's defining feature is that neither level of government is dependent on the other for its power. Within its defined areas of responsibility, each is considered independent and autonomous. In the United States, the two levels of government considered sovereign are the federal government and state governments. States are legally equal partners with the national government and occupy a central role in the political system. Although required to operate within the rules laid down by the U.S. Constitution, states are considered sovereign because their power and legal authority are drawn not just from the U.S. Constitution but from their own citizens as codified in their own state constitutions. Local governments are treated very differently from states. Within their own borders, states are very much like unitary systems;

substate governments such as cities and counties get their power from the state, and they exercise only the policymaking authority the state is willing to grant. The specifics of local governments' powers and policy responsibilities are discussed in more depth in chapter 10.

Why Federalism? The Origins of the Federal System in the United States

There are a number of reasons the United States is a federal system. Largely because of their experiences with the Articles of Confederation, the framers of the Constitution rejected the possibility of a confederacy. The national government was so weak under the Articles that prominent figures such as James Madison and George Washington feared it doomed the newly independent republic to failure.

These fears were not unfounded. Following the successful conclusion of the Revolutionary War in 1783, the new United States found itself in the grip of an economic recession, and the central government had little power to address the crisis. Indeed, it actually contributed to the problem by constantly threatening to default on its debts. Independence had brought political freedom, but it also meant American-made products now were in head-to-head competition with cheap, high-quality goods from Great Britain. This made consumers happy but threatened to cripple American businesses. The economic difficulties pitted state against state, farmer against manufacturer, and debtor against banker. The weak central government really did not have the power to attempt a coordinated, nationwide response to the problem. It could do little but stand by and hope for the best.

As internal tensions mounted within the United States, European powers still active in the Americas threatened the nation's survival. Spain

shut down shipping on the Mississippi River. The British refused to withdraw from some military posts until the U.S. government paid off its debts to British creditors. George Washington believed the United States, having won the war, was in real danger of losing the peace. He said that something had to change in order "to avert the humiliating and contemptible figure we are about to make on the annals of mankind."[3]

For a loose coalition of the professional classes who called themselves Federalists, that "something" was obviously the central government. This group of lawyers, businessmen, and other individuals, drawn mostly from the upper social strata, sought to create a stronger and more powerful national government. Americans, however, were not particularly enthusiastic about handing more power to the central government, an attitude not so different from today. Most recognized that the Articles had numerous flaws, but few were ready to copy the example of the British and adopt a unitary system.

Two events in fall 1786 allowed the Federalists to overcome this resistance and achieve their goal of creating a more powerful national government. The first was the Annapolis Convention. This meeting in Maryland's capital convened to try to hammer out an interstate trade agreement. Few states sent delegates. Those who did show up had strong Federalist sympathies. They took advantage of the meeting and petitioned Congress to call for a commission to rewrite the Articles of Confederation.

The second event was Shays's Rebellion, named for its leader, Daniel Shays, a hero of the recently won Revolutionary War. The rebellion was an uprising of Massachusetts farmers who took up arms in protest of state efforts to take their property to pay off taxes and other debts. It was quickly crushed, but with further civil unrest threatening to boil over into civil war and with mounting pressure from powerful elites within the Federalist ranks, the Continental Congress was pushed to call for states to send delegates to Philadelphia in summer 1787. The purpose of the meeting, which came to be known as the Constitutional Convention, was the rewriting of the Articles of Confederation.

Once convened, the group quickly abandoned its mandate to modify the Articles and decided to write an entirely new constitution. In doing so, the Federalists who dominated the convention rejected confederacy as an adequate basis for the American political system. Their experience under the Articles had taught them that a central government subordinate to the states was not much of a government at all. What they wanted was a government capable of dealing effectively with national problems, and this meant a strong central government whose power was independent of the states. Yet while the Federalists wanted to get rid of the confederal system, neither popular sentiment nor political reality favored replacing it with a unitary system. To have any legal force the new constitution would have to be ratified by the states, and it was highly unlikely the states would voluntarily agree to give up all of their powers to a national government. Federalism was thus the only practical option.

A federal system represented more than just the political price paid to achieve a stronger national government. The founders were attempting to construct a new form of **representative government**, one where citizens exercise power indirectly. Convention delegates wanted a more powerful national government, but at the same time they did not want to concentrate power for fear that would lead to tyranny. Their solution to this problem was to create a system of separated powers and checks and balances. They divided their new and stronger national government into three branches—legislative, executive, and judicial—and made each branch partially reliant on the others to carry out its own responsibilities. This made it difficult for any single group to gain the upper hand in all three divisions of government and gave each branch the power to check the excesses of the other branches.

The delegates achieved a similar set of goals by making state and national governments coequal partners. By letting states remain independent decision makers in a wide range of policy arenas, they divided power between the national and subnational levels of government. The national government was made more powerful by the new

Representative Government
A form of government in which citizens exercise power indirectly by choosing representatives to legislate on their behalf.

constitution, but the independence of the states helped set clear limits on this power.

The Advantages and Disadvantages of Federalism

Federalism solved a political conundrum for the founders and helped achieve their philosophical aims of dispersing and separating power. Yet federalism is not necessarily better than a confederal or a unitary system, just different. In the United States, the pros and cons of federalism have benefited and bedeviled the American political system for more than two centuries.

There are four key advantages to the federal system. (See Table 2-1.) First, it keeps government closer to the people. Rather than the federal government's imposing a "one size fits all" policy, states have the freedom and authority to match government decisions to local preferences. This freedom also results in the local variance in laws, institutions, and traditions that characterizes the U.S. political system and provides the comparative method with its explanatory strength.

Second, federalism allows local differences to be reflected in state and local government policy and thereby reduces conflict. Massachusetts, for example,

TABLE 2-1

Advantages and Disadvantages of Federalism

Advantages	Disadvantages
Allows for flexibility among state laws and institutions.	Increases complexity and confusion.
Reduces conflict because states can accommodate citizens' interests.	Sometimes increases conflict when jurisdictional lines are unclear.
Allows for experimentation at the state level.	Duplicates efforts and reduces accountability.
Enables the achievement of national goals.	Makes coordination difficult.
	Creates inequality in services and policy.

tends to be more liberal than, say, Alabama. California has a much more ethnically and culturally diverse population than Nebraska. Rather than having the various interests and preferences that spring from state-to-state differences engage in a winner-take-all policy struggle at the federal level, they can be accommodated at the state level. This reduces the friction among interests and lessens conflict.

Third, independent subnational governments allow for flexibility and experimentation. The states, as Supreme Court justice Louis Brandeis famously put it, are "the laboratories of democracy." Successful policy innovations in one state can be adopted by other states and copied by the federal government (see the box "Policy in Practice: Squeezing Lemons").

Fourth, the achievement of at least some national goals is made easier by the participation of independent subnational governments. For example, the federal government's 2010 Patient Protection and Affordable Care Act (popularly known as Obamacare) is the most sweeping reform of healthcare regulation in half a century. The primary goal of Obamacare is to reduce the number of people without health insurance, and one of the law's key provisions is the establishment of health insurance exchanges, basically centralized places where people can buy federally subsidized health insurance packages. As state governments constitute ready-made centralized regulatory bodies geographically distributed across the nation, it makes sense to have them set

Policy in Practice

Squeezing Lemons

Dan Brochu claimed that his new Oldsmobile Omega traveled well only when it was going up and down a repair lift. Maybe he wasn't exaggerating—inside a year the car went through four transmissions and a complete electrical system failure, and to add insult to injury, the paint started to peel. Thomas Ziemba could relate. His new Chevy Caprice had a skipping engine, a defroster that spewed steam, and a radio that seemed possessed—it would work only if he blew the horn first. Brochu and Ziemba had lemons, they knew it, and in 1982 they wanted the Connecticut state government to know it.

The state government not only got the message but also did something about the problem. The legislature passed Connecticut General Statute 743b, colloquially known as the "lemon law." When it was passed in the 1980s, it was a new and innovative policy. The lemon law basically said that if a car was defective and its defects could not be repaired by reasonable effort (defined as four attempts or thirty days in the shop), it was legally a lemon and the consumer could sue the car's

manufacturer. The upshot was that if someone could prove he or she had a lemon, the manufacturer had to cough up a refund or replace the car.

These days, this sort of law does not seem so innovative or unusual. There's a reason for that. After Connecticut passed its lemon law and it generally seemed to be effective in making manufacturers stand behind their products and warranty claims, other states, in so many words, said, "That's a good idea; let's get us a lemon law, too." And they did. Today all fifty states have some version of a lemon law.

The spread of lemon laws is a good example of one of the key advantages of federalism. By allowing states to experiment, federalism enables them to formulate effective policy innovations, which may then be adopted by other states. Effective policies will spread, while not-so-effective policies will not. While federalism clearly has some downsides, the laboratories of democracy, at least in this instance, were pretty good at whipping up some lemon-aid.

Sources: "Lemon Laws: Mixed Signals," *Newsweek,* May 31, 1982, 50; Better Business Bureau, "Standards of the Connecticut Lemon Law," www.bbb.org/us/Storage/16/Documents/BBBAutoLine/CT-LLsummary.pdf.

Emergency management provides a classic example of how federalism shapes policy. The Federal Emergency Management Agency (FEMA) is a critical component of any government response to disaster, but its effectiveness is tied to its coordination with state and local agencies.

of the Federal Bureau of Investigation and the U.S. Drug Enforcement Agency. The responsibilities and jurisdictions of these organizations overlap, which means taxpayers end up paying twice for some law enforcement activities. Also, when these agencies are unsuccessful or ineffective, it can be very difficult to figure out which is responsible and what needs to change.

up and run these exchanges rather than have the federal government do it from scratch.

A federal system also has some clear disadvantages. First, while allowing local differences does keep government closer to the people, it also creates complexity and confusion. For example, if you own a nationwide business, you have to deal with state *and* federal regulations—fifty-one sets of regulations in all. That means, among other things, fifty-one tax codes and fifty-one sets of licensing requirements. And many communities have their own restrictions and requirements that businesses must meet as well.

Second, federalism can increase conflict as easily as reduce it. The Constitution is very vague on the exact division of powers between state and federal governments. This results in a constant struggle—and a lot of litigation—to resolve which level of government has the responsibility and legal authority to take the lead role in a given policy area. Third, although federalism promotes flexibility and experimentation, it also promotes duplication and reduces accountability. For example, local, state, and national governments have all taken on law enforcement responsibilities. This means in one area there may be municipal police departments, a county sheriff's department, and the state patrol, plus local offices

Fourth, the federal system can make it hard to coordinate policy efforts nationwide. For example, police and fire departments on opposite sides of a state border, or even within adjacent jurisdictions in the same state, may have different communication systems. It is hard to coordinate a response to a large-scale emergency if the relevant organizations cannot talk to each other, but the federal government cannot force state and local governments to standardize their radio equipment.

Finally, a federal system creates inequality in services and policies. The quality of public schools and welfare services, for example, depends heavily on the choices state and local governments make. This inevitably means that some states offer better educational opportunities and do more for the needy than others.

The Constitutional Basis of Federalism

The relationship between national and state governments is like a sibling rivalry. It is hard to imagine either level of government getting along without the other, yet because each is independent and focused on its own interests, conflict is common. The ink was barely dry on the newly ratified Constitution before the federal government and the states were squabbling over who had the power and authority in this or that policy area. In writing the Constitution, the founders recognized that the differences between states and the federal government were likely to be a central and lasting feature of the political system. Accordingly, they attempted to head off the worst of the disputes—or at least to provide a basis for resolving them—by making a basic division of powers between the national and state governments.

The Constitution grants the federal government both enumerated and implied powers. **Enumerated powers** are grants of authority explicitly given by the Constitution. Among the most important of these is the **national supremacy clause** contained in Article VI. This states that the Constitution "shall be the supreme law of the land; and the judges in every state shall be bound thereby." In other words, federal law takes precedence over all other laws. This allows the federal government to preempt, or override, areas regulated by state law. In recent decades, the federal government has aggressively used this power to extend its authority over states in a wide range of policy issues, so much so that **preemption** has been called "the gorilla that swallows state laws."[4]

Other enumerated powers are laid out in Article I, Section 8. This part of the Constitution details a set of **exclusive powers**—grants of authority that belong solely to the national government. These include the powers to regulate commerce, to declare war, and to raise and maintain an army and navy. Article I, Section 8, also confers a set of **concurrent powers** on the national government. Concurrent powers are those granted to the national government but not denied to the states. Both levels of government are free to exercise these prerogatives. Concurrent powers include the powers to tax, borrow, and spend.

Finally, this same section of the Constitution gives the national government **implied powers**. The basic idea behind implied powers is that the authors of the Constitution realized they could not possibly list every specific power that the national government would require to meet the needs of a developing nation. Accordingly, they gave Congress the flexibility to meet unforeseen challenges by granting the federal government a set of broad and largely undefined powers. These include the **general welfare clause**, which gives the federal government the authority to provide for "the general welfare of the United States," and the **necessary and proper clause**, which authorizes Congress "to make all laws which shall be necessary and proper" to carry out its responsibilities as defined by the Constitution. (See Table 2-2 for explanations of these and other provisions.)

The Constitution says a good deal about the powers of the federal government but very little about the powers of the states. The original, unamended Constitution spent much more time specifying the obligations of the states than it did defining their power and authority. The obligations list includes Article IV, Section 2, better

Enumerated Powers
Grants of authority explicitly given by the Constitution.

National Supremacy Clause
Constitutional clause that states that federal law takes precedence over all other laws.

Preemption
The process by which the federal government overrides areas regulated by state law.

Exclusive Powers
Powers given by the Constitution solely to the federal government.

Concurrent Powers
Powers that both federal and state governments can exercise. These include the powers to tax, borrow, and spend.

Implied Powers
Broad but undefined powers given to the federal government by the Constitution.

General Welfare Clause
Constitutional clause that gives Congress an implied power through the authority to provide for the "general welfare."

Necessary and Proper Clause
Constitutional clause that gives Congress an implied power through the right to pass all laws considered "necessary and proper" to carry out the federal government's responsibilities as defined by the Constitution.

TABLE 2-2

The U.S. Constitution's Provisions for Federalism

What It Is . . .	What It Says . . .	What It Means . . .
Article I, Section 8 (commerce clause)	The Congress shall have Power . . . To regulate Commerce with foreign Nations, and among the several States, and with the Indian Tribes.	Gives Congress the right to regulate interstate commerce. This clause has been broadly interpreted to give Congress a number of implied powers.
Article I, Section 8 (necessary and proper clause)	The Congress shall have Power . . . To make all Laws which shall be necessary and proper for carrying into Execution the foregoing Powers, and all other Powers vested by this Constitution in the Government of the United States, or in any Department or Officer thereof.	An implied power giving Congress the right to pass all laws considered "necessary and proper" to carry out the federal government's responsibilities as defined by the Constitution.
Article IV, Section 3 (admission of new states)	New States may be admitted by the Congress into this Union; but no new State shall be formed or erected within the Jurisdiction of any other State; nor any State be formed by the Junction of two or more States, or Parts of States, without the Consent of the Legislatures of the States concerned as well as of the Congress.	Allows the U.S. Congress to admit new states to the union and guarantees each state sovereignty and jurisdiction over its territory.
Article IV, Section 4 (enforcement of republican form of government)	The United States shall guarantee to every State in this Union a Republican Form of Government, and shall protect each of them against Invasion; and on Application of the Legislature, or of the Executive (when the Legislature cannot be convened) against domestic Violence.	Ensures that a democratic government exists in each state and protects states against foreign invasion or insurrection.
Article VI (supremacy clause)	This Constitution, and the Laws of the United States which shall be made in Pursuance thereof; and all Treaties made, or which shall be made, under the Authority of the United States, shall be the supreme Law of the Land; and the Judges in every State shall be bound thereby, any Thing in the Constitution or Laws of any State to the Contrary notwithstanding.	States that federal law takes precedence over all other laws.
Tenth Amendment	The powers not delegated to the United States by the Constitution, nor prohibited by it to the States, are reserved to the States respectively, or to the people.	Guarantees that a broad but undefined set of powers is reserved for the states and the people as opposed to the federal government.
Fourteenth Amendment	All persons born or naturalized in the United States, and subject to the jurisdiction thereof, are citizens of the United States and of the state wherein they reside. No state shall make or enforce any law which shall abridge the privileges or immunities of citizens of the United States; nor shall any state deprive any person of life, liberty, or property, without due process of law; nor deny to any person within its jurisdiction the equal protection of the laws.	Prohibits any state from depriving individuals of the rights and privileges of citizenship and requires states to provide due process and equal protection guarantees to all citizens.
Sixteenth Amendment	The Congress shall have the power to lay and collect taxes on incomes, from whatever source derived, without apportionment among the several States, and without regard to any census or enumeration.	Enables the federal government to levy a national income tax. This amendment helped further national policies and programs in the years following its passage.
Seventeenth Amendment	The Senate of the United States shall be composed of two Senators from each State, elected by the people thereof, for six years; and each Senator shall have one vote. . . . When vacancies happen in the representation of any State in the Senate, the executive authority of each State shall issue writs of election to fill such vacancies: Provided that the legislature of any State may empower the executive thereof to make temporary appointments until the people fill the vacancies by election as the legislature may direct.	Provides for direct election of U.S. senators, rather than election by each state's legislature.

known as the **full faith and credit clause**. This clause requires all states to grant "full faith and credit" to each other's public acts and records. This means that wills, contracts, and marriages that are valid under one state's laws are valid under all. Under the **privileges and immunities clause**, states are prohibited from discriminating against citizens from other states. The idea here was to prevent people traveling across state boundaries or temporarily residing in a state because of business or personal reasons from becoming the targets of discriminatory regulation or taxation.

The Constitution also sets out an often criticized system for electing the nation's president and vice president. The presidency goes not to the candidate who wins the most votes but rather to the one who wins the most states. Article II, Section 1, charges the states with appointing electors—one for each of a state's U.S. senators and representatives—who actually choose the president based on the winner of the state's popular vote. (If the Republican candidate gets the most votes in a state, the state's delegation to the electoral college is made up of Republican Party loyalists who vote for the Republican nominee.) A presidential candidate needs a majority in the electoral college, which requires the votes of at least 270 of the 538 state electors, to be named the winner.

Other than outlining these responsibilities and explicitly granting the states the right to enter into compacts, or binding agreements, with each other on matters of regional concern, the Constitution is virtually silent on the powers of the states. This lopsided attention to the powers of the federal government was a contentious issue in the battle to ratify the Constitution. Opponents of the document, collectively known as Anti-Federalists, feared that states would become little more than puppets of the new central government. Supporters of the Constitution sought to calm these fears by

arguing that states would remain sovereign and independent and that the powers not specifically granted to the federal government would be reserved for the states. As James Madison put it, in writing the Constitution the Federalists were seeking "a middle ground which may at once support due supremacy of the national authority" and also preserve a strong independent role for the states.[5]

Madison and his fellow Federalists offered to put these assurances in writing. In effect, they promised that if the Constitution were ratified, the first order of business for the new Congress would be to draft a set of amendments that would spell out the limits of central government power and specify the independence of the states. Although Anti-Federalist skepticism remained, the Federalists kept their promise. The First Congress formulated a series of changes that eventually became the first ten amendments to the Constitution and are collectively known as the **Bill of Rights**.

Most of these amendments set specific limits on government power. The aim was to guarantee certain individual rights and freedoms, and, at least initially, they were directed at the federal government rather than at state governments. The **Tenth Amendment**, however, finally addressed the power of the states. In full, the Tenth Amendment states: "The powers not delegated to the United States by the Constitution, nor prohibited by it to the states, are reserved to the states respectively, or to the people." This provided no enumerated, or specific, powers to the states, but those implied by the language of the amendment are considerable. The so-called reserved powers encompass all of the concurrent powers that allow the states to tax, borrow, and spend; to make laws and enforce them; to regulate trade within their borders; and to practice eminent domain, which is the power to take private property

---

Full Faith and Credit Clause
Constitutional clause that requires states to recognize each other's public records and acts as valid.

Privileges and Immunities Clause
Constitutional clause that prohibits states from discriminating against citizens of other states.

Bill of Rights
The first ten amendments to the Constitution, which set limits on the power of the federal government and set out the rights of individuals and the states.

Tenth Amendment
Constitutional amendment guaranteeing that a broad but undefined set of powers is reserved for the states and the people.

for public use. The reserved powers also have been traditionally understood to mean that states have the primary power to make laws that involve the health, safety, and morals of their citizens. Yet the powers reserved for the states are more implied than explicit, and they all rest in an uneasy tension with the national supremacy clause of Article VI.

After the Tenth Amendment, the **Fourteenth Amendment** is the most important in terms of specifying state powers. Ratified in 1868, the Fourteenth Amendment is one of the so-called Civil War Amendments that came in the immediate wake of the bloody conflict between the North, or the Union, and the South, or the Confederacy. The Fourteenth Amendment prohibits any state from depriving individuals of the rights and privileges of citizenship and requires states to provide due process and equal protection guarantees to all citizens. The Supreme Court has used these guarantees to apply the Bill of Rights to state governments as well as to the federal government and to assert national power over state power in issues ranging from the desegregation of public education to the reapportioning of state legislatures.

The implied powers of the federal government, the limitations set on states by the Fourteenth Amendment, and the undefined "leftovers" given to the states by the Tenth Amendment mean that the scope and the authority of both levels of government are, in many cases, dependent on how the Constitution is interpreted. The Constitution, in other words, provides a basic framework for solving the sibling-rivalry squabbles between the states and the federal government. (See Figure 2-2.) It does not provide, however, an unambiguous guide to which level of government has the primary power, responsibility, and authority on a broad range of policy issues. This, as we will see, means that the U.S. Supreme Court is repeatedly thrust into the role of refereeing power disputes between national and state governments.

Fourteenth Amendment

Constitutional amendment that prohibits states from depriving individuals of the rights and privileges of citizenship and requires states to provide due process and equal protection guarantees.

The Development of Federalism

Although clearly establishing a federal political system, the U.S. Constitution leaves considerable room for disagreement about which level of government—federal or state—has the power to do what. Disagreements about the scope and authority of the national government happened almost immediately when the First Congress convened in 1789. The issue of a national bank was one of the most controversial of these early conflicts and the one with the most lasting implications. Alexander Hamilton, secretary of the treasury under President George Washington, believed a central bank was critical to stabilizing the national economy, but there was nothing in the Constitution that specifically granted the federal government the authority to create and regulate such an institution.

Lacking a clear enumerated power, Hamilton justified his proposal for a national bank by using an implied power. He argued that the necessary and proper clause implied the federal government's power to create a national bank because the bank would help the government manage its finances as it went about its expressly conferred authority to tax and spend. Essentially, Hamilton was interpreting *necessary* as "convenient" or "appropriate." Secretary of State Thomas Jefferson objected, arguing that if the Constitution was going to establish a government of truly limited powers, the federal government needed to stick to its enumerated powers and interpret its implied powers very narrowly. He thus argued that the *necessary* in the necessary and proper clause should properly be interpreted as "essential" or "indispensable." This argument was not fully resolved until 1819, when the Supreme Court decided the case of *McCulloch v. Maryland* and, in essence, backed Hamilton's interpretation of the Constitution over Jefferson's. This was important above and beyond the issue of a national bank. It suggested that the Constitution gave the national government a broad set of powers relative to the states. Key to this early affirmation of the federal government's power was U.S. Chief Justice John Marshall, whose backing

FIGURE 2-2

Powers of National and State Governments

National Government Powers

Coin money

Regulate interstate and foreign commerce

Tax imports and exports

Make treaties

Make all laws "necessary and proper" to fulfill responsibilities

Make war

Regulate postal system

Powers Denied

Tax state exports

Change state boundaries

Impose religious tests

Pass laws in conflict with the Bill of Rights

Concurrent Powers

Tax

Borrow money

Charter banks and corporations

Take property (eminent domain)

Make and enforce laws and administer a judiciary

State Government Powers

Run elections

Regulate intrastate commerce

Establish republican forms of state and local government

Protect public health, safety, and morals

All powers not delegated to the national government or denied to the states by the Constitution

Powers Denied

Tax imports and exports

Coin money

Enter into treaties

Impair obligation of contracts

Enter compacts with other states without congressional consent

Source: Adapted from Samuel Kernell, Gary C. Jacobson, and Thad Kousser, *The Logic of American Politics*, 6th ed. (Washington, DC: CQ Press, 2013), Figure 3-2.

of a broad interpretation of implied powers laid the foundation for later expansions in the scope and authority of the federal government.

The full impact of *McCulloch v. Maryland*, however, would not be felt for some time. For the most part, the federal government began to feel its way into the gray areas of its constitutional powers pretty cautiously. Federalism went on to develop in four distinct stages—dual federalism, cooperative federalism, centralized federalism, and New Federalism—and the first of these stages leaned toward the more limited role of the federal government favored by Jefferson.

Dual Federalism (1789–1933)

Dual federalism is the idea that state and federal governments have separate jurisdictions and responsibilities. Within these separate spheres of authority, each level of government is sovereign and free to operate without interference from the

other. Dual federalism represents something of a middle ground in the initial interpretations of how the Constitution divided power. On one side of the debate were Federalists such as Hamilton, who championed a nation-centered view of federalism. They wanted to interpret the Constitution as broadly as possible to give the national government supremacy over the states.

On the other side were fierce **states' rights** advocates such as John Calhoun of South Carolina, who served as vice president in the administrations of John Quincy Adams and Andrew Jackson. Supporters of states' rights wanted the federal government's power limited to the greatest possible extent and saw any expansion of that power as an encroachment on the sovereignty of the states. In the 1820s and 1830s, Calhoun formulated what became known as the **compact theory** of

Dual Federalism

The idea that state and federal governments have separate and distinct jurisdictions and responsibilities.

States' Rights

The belief that states should be free to make their own decisions with little interference from the federal government.

Compact Theory

The idea that the Constitution represents an agreement among sovereign states to form a common government.

Chapter 2   Federalism   35

The Sixteenth Amendment gave the federal government the power to levy an income tax. Some of the money collected by the federal government in income taxes is returned to the states in the form of grants to support a wide range of domestic policies and programs.

○ ⊙•○ ⊙•◐•○ ⊙•◐ ○•◐ ○•◐ ○•◐•○ ⊙•◐ ○•◐ ○•◐•○ ⊙•◐ ○ ⊙•○

federalism. The idea was that the Constitution represented an agreement among sovereign states to form a common government. Calhoun interpreted the Constitution as essentially an extension of the Articles of Confederation, thus viewing the U.S. political system as more confederal than federal.

The compact theory argued that if sovereignty ultimately rested with the states, then the states rather than the Supreme Court had the final say in how the Constitution should be interpreted. The states also had the right to reject federal laws and make them invalid within their own borders. This process was known as **nullification**, and the compact theory took it to an extreme. Calhoun argued that states could reject the entire Constitution and choose to withdraw, or secede, from the Union. In the 1820s, national policies—especially a trade tariff—triggered an economic downturn in the southern states, which created wide support for nullification and **secession** arguments. These extreme states' rights views were not completely resolved until the Union victory in the Civil War ended them for good.

Dual federalism walked a line between the extremes of **nation-centered federalism** and **state-centered federalism**. Basically, dual federalism looks at the U.S. political system as a layered cake. The state and federal governments represent distinct and separate layers of this cake. To keep them separate, advocates of dual federalism sought to limit the federal government to exercising only a narrow interpretation of its enumerated powers. If the Constitution was to be interpreted broadly, that interpretation should favor the states rather than Congress. This became the central operating philosophy of the U.S. Supreme Court for much of the nineteenth century and is most closely associated with the tenure of Chief Justice Roger B. Taney, who served from 1836 to 1864. Compared with his immediate predecessor, John Marshall, Taney was much less sympathetic to arguments that interpreted the federal government's powers broadly.

The dual federalism doctrine gave rise to some infamous Supreme Court decisions on the powers and limitations of the federal government. Perhaps the best known is *Scott v. Sandford* (1857). This case dealt with Dred Scott, a slave taken by his master from Missouri, a slave state, to Illinois, a free state, and on into what was then called the Wisconsin Territory, where slavery had been outlawed by the Missouri Compromise of 1820. This federal law stipulated which new states and territories could and could not make slavery legal. After his master's death, Scott sued for his freedom, arguing that his residence in a free territory had legally ended his bondage. Scott's case was tied to the Missouri Compromise, which the

Nullification
The process of a state's rejecting a federal law and making it invalid within state borders.

Secession
A government's or political jurisdiction's withdrawal from a political system or alliance.

Nation-Centered Federalism
The belief that the nation is the basis of the federal system and that the federal government should take precedence over the states.

State-Centered Federalism
The belief that states are the basis of the federal system and that state governments should take precedence over the federal government.

Supreme Court subsequently ruled unconstitutional. The justices' justification was that Congress did not have the enumerated, or the implied, power to prohibit slavery in the territories. Thus Scott remained a slave, although his owners voluntarily gave him his freedom shortly after the Supreme Court decision. He died of tuberculosis in 1858, having spent only one of his nearly sixty years as a free man.

Cooperative Federalism (1933–1964)

In theory, dual federalism defines and maintains a clear division between state and national governments and sets a clear standard for doing so. If the federal government has the enumerated power to take the disputed action or make the disputed law, it has supremacy over the states in that particular case; if it does not have the enumerated power, then the Tenth Amendment reserves that power for the states, and state preferences take precedence.

The problem was that theoretical clarity rarely matched the complex realities of governance. State and national governments share interests in a wide range of issues, from education to transportation. To divide these cleanly into separate spheres of influence was not only difficult, but impractical and undesirable. Even at the height of the dual federalism era, state and federal governments were collaborating as much as they were fighting. The federal government, for example, owned vast tracts of land in the Midwest and West, and it made extensive grants of these lands to the states to help develop transportation and education systems. Many of the nation's best-known state universities got their start this way, as land-grant colleges.

In the nineteenth century, the federal government also gave out cash grants to support Civil War veterans housed in state institutions, gave money to the states to support agricultural research, and lent federal manpower—primarily U.S. Army engineers—to help state and local development projects.[6] Rather than a layered cake, a more appropriate metaphor for federalism is a marble cake, with the different levels of government so thoroughly mixed with each other that they are impossible to separate. (See Figure 2-3.)

Certainly as the nation became increasingly industrialized and more urban, state and federal interests became increasingly intertwined. As the nineteenth century drew to a close and the twentieth century began, the federal government undertook a significant expansion of its policy responsibilities. In 1887, it began to regulate the

FIGURE 2-3

The Varieties of Federalism

Dual or "Layer Cake" Federalism

Cooperative or "Marble Cake" Federalism

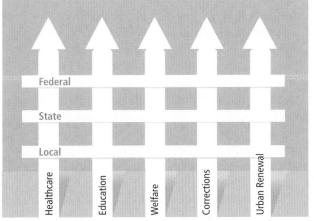

Centralized or "Picket Fence" Federalism

> **Even at the height of the dual federalism era, state and federal governments were collaborating as much as they were fighting.**

railroads, a policy area with enormous significance for the economic development of states and localities. In economic and social terms, this was roughly equivalent to the federal government of today announcing its comprehensive regulation of the Internet and software manufacturers. By fits and starts, dual federalism gradually fell out of favor with the Supreme Court.

Several events accelerated this trend. In 1913, the Sixteenth Amendment was ratified, giving the federal government the ability to levy a nationwide income tax. The new taxing and spending authority helped further national policies designed during the next decades.[7] World War I (1914–1918) resulted in a significant centralization of power in the federal government. During World War II (1939–1945) that power was centralized even further. The need to fight global conflicts pushed the federal government to assert the lead role on a wide range of economic and social issues. Even more important to the long-term relationship between state and national governments was the Great Depression of the 1930s, a social and economic catastrophe that swept aside any remaining vestiges of dual federalism.

The central catalyst for a fundamental change in the nature of state-federal relations was the election of Franklin Delano Roosevelt to the presidency in 1932. In an effort to combat economic and social malaise, Roosevelt aggressively pushed the federal government into taking a lead role in areas traditionally left to the states, and in the 1930s the federal government became deeply involved in regulating the labor market, creating and managing welfare programs, and providing significant amounts of direct aid to cities. The general approach of Roosevelt's so-called New Deal agenda defined the central characteristics of

cooperative federalism—using the federal government to identify a problem, set up the basic outline of a program to address the problem, and make money available to fund that program and then turning over much of the responsibility for implementing and running the program to the states and localities. This arrangement dominated state and federal relations for the next three decades.

Centralized Federalism (1964–1980)

Cooperative federalism signaled a significant shift in power away from the states and toward the federal government. The key to this power shift was money, specifically federal **grants-in-aid**, which are cash appropriations given by the federal government to the states. An ever-increasing proportion of state and local budgets came from federal coffers. At the beginning of the nineteenth century, federal grants constituted less than 1 percent of state and local government revenues. By the middle of the 1930s, federal grants accounted for close to 20 percent of state and local revenues.[8]

For the next thirty years, the federal government continued to rely on grants to administer programs, including the 1950s construction of the federal highway system that Americans drive on today. The 1960s marked a shift, however. **Centralized federalism**, ushered in with Lyndon Baines Johnson's presidency, further increased the federal government's involvement in policy areas previously left to state and local governments. It is commonly associated with Johnson's Great

---

Cooperative Federalism
The notion that it is impossible for state and national governments to have separate and distinct jurisdictions and that both levels of government must work together.

Grants-In-Aid
Cash appropriations given by the federal government to the states.

Centralized Federalism
The notion that the federal government should take the leading role in setting national policy, with state and local governments helping to implement the policies.

FIGURE 2-4

Key Dates in the History of American Federalism

Revolutionary War starts	1775	1776	Declaration of Independence adopted
Articles of Confederation ratified	1781	1783	Revolutionary War ends
Annapolis Convention	1786	1786	Shays's Rebellion
Constitutional Convention drafts new constitution	1787	1788	U.S. Constitution ratified
First Congress adopts Bill of Rights	1791		
McCulloch v. Maryland establishes that the federal government has a broad set of powers over the states	1819		
Roger Taney sworn in as chief justice; adopts dual federalism as model for federal-state relations	1836	1832	South Carolina attempts to nullify federal law
		1857	*Scott v. Sanford* demonstrates the limits of the federal government
Southern states experiment with confederacy as Civil War starts	1861	1860	South Carolina secedes from the Union in December; hostilities between North and South begin a month later
		1865	Civil War ends with Union victory; Thirteenth Amendment abolishes slavery
Fourteenth Amendment passes	1868		
		1887	Federal government regulates the railroads
Sixteenth Amendment passes	1913		
Great Depression	1930	1933	Franklin Delano Roosevelt takes office; era of cooperative federalism begins
Era of centralized federalism begins	1964		
Election of Ronald Reagan and emergence of New Federalism	1980	1972	Richard Nixon begins revenue sharing
Supreme Court decides *Bush v. Gore;* George W. Bush receives Florida's contested electoral votes and becomes president	2000	1986	William Rehnquist becomes chief justice; Supreme Court begins to look more favorably on states' rights arguments
		2008 –2009	Great Recession

Society program, which used state and local governments to help implement such national initiatives as the Civil Rights Act and the War on Poverty. Sometimes it is referred to as "picket-fence federalism" because of its many crosscutting regulations.

Those initiatives meant more money—and more regulations—for states and localities. The federal government aggressively began attaching strings to this money through **categorical grants**. Federal-state relations evolved into a rough embodiment of the Golden Rule of politics—he who has the gold gets to make the rules.

Richard Nixon's presidential administration took a slightly different tack. It cut some strings but continued to increase the number of grants doled out by the federal government.[9] In the late 1960s, the administration pioneered the idea of **general revenue sharing grants**, federal funds turned over to the states and localities with essentially no strings attached. Although popular with states and localities—from their perspective it was "free" money—this type of grant-in-aid had a short life span; it was killed by the Ronald Reagan administration in the early 1980s.

A central feature of cooperative federalism was the often fierce state competition to control and access federal grant revenues. The politics became complex. One form of conflict arose between the states and the federal government over what types of grants should be used for particular policies or programs. States and localities favored federal grants with fewer strings. Congress and the president often favored putting tight guidelines on federal money because this allowed them to take a greater share of the credit for the benefits of federal spending.

Perhaps the most important dimension of the politics of grants-in-aid, however, was the federal government's increasing desire to use its purse strings to pressure states and localities into adopting particular policies and laws. Beginning in the 1960s and 1970s, cooperative federalism began a new, more coercive era with the rise of ever more stringent grant conditions. These included **crosscutting requirements**, or strings that applied to all federal grants. For example, one requirement a state or locality must meet to receive virtually any federal government grant is an assessment of the environmental impact of the proposed program or policy. Accordingly, most state and local governments began writing—and defending—environmental impact statements for any construction project that involved federal funds.

The federal government also began applying **crossover sanctions**. Crossover sanctions are strings that require grant recipients to pass and enforce certain laws or policies as a condition of receiving funds. One example is the drinking age. The federal government requires states to set twenty-one as the minimum legal age for drinking alcohol as a condition of receiving federal highway funds.

Increasingly, the strings came even if there were no grants. State and local governments were essentially commanded to adopt certain laws or rules, such as clean water standards and minimum wage laws.[10] These **unfunded mandates** became a particular irritant to state and local governments. Even when there was broad agreement on the substance of a mandate, subnational governments resented the federal government's taking all the credit while leaving the dirty work of finding funds and actually running the programs to the states and localities.

Congress eventually passed a law banning unfunded mandates in the mid-1990s, but it is full of loopholes. For example, the law does not apply to appropriations bills—the laws that actually authorize the government to spend money. The National Conference of State Legislatures has estimated that in a recent five-year period the federal government shifted $131 billion in costs

Crosscutting Requirements
Constraints that apply to all federal grants.

Crossover Sanctions
Federal requirements mandating that grant recipients pass and enforce certain laws or regulations as a condition of receiving funds.

Unfunded Mandates
Federal laws that direct state action but provide no financial support for that action.

Categorical Grants
Federal grants-in-aid given for specific programs that leave states and localities with little discretion over how to spend the money.

General Revenue Sharing Grants
Federal grants-in-aid given with few constraints, leaving states and localities with almost complete discretion over how to spend the money.

to the states in unfunded mandates.[11] Congress, in other words, continues to pass laws that subnational governments must obey and to pass on the costs of implementing these laws to the states.

New Federalism (1980–2002)

Centralized federalism's shift of power toward the national government always faced opposition from states' rights advocates, who viewed the growing influence of the national government with alarm. By the end of the 1970s, centralized federalism also was starting to face a practical crisis—the federal government's revenues could not keep up with the demand for grants. With the election of Ronald Reagan in 1980, the practical and ideological combined to create pressure for a fundamental shift in state and federal relations.

Reagan was not the first president to raise concerns about the centralization of power in the national government. A primary reason for Nixon's support of general revenue sharing, for example, was the attraction of giving states more flexibility by cutting the strings attached to federal grants. It was not until Reagan, however, that a sustained attempt was made to reverse the course of centralized federalism. Reagan believed the federal government had overreached its boundaries, and he wanted to return power and flexibility to the states. At the core of his vision of state-centered **New Federalism** was the desire to reduce federal grants-in-aid. In return, states would be given more policymaking leeway with the money they did get through **block grants**.

Reagan's drive to make this vision a reality had mixed success. The massive budget deficits of the 1980s made cutting grants-in-aid a practical necessity. We can see this in Figure 2-5, which shows federal government grants to state and local governments in billions of constant dollars from 1940 through 2011. There was a clear upward trend beginning in the 1960s that peaked in about 1978. After that, federal grants to states stayed relatively constant for about a decade—while the federal government was not really drastically cutting grants in the 1980s, in real terms it did not increase them either. At least for a while, the federal government managed to rein in the grant dollars flowing to states and localities. Reducing the federal government's influence over states and localities turned out to be another matter.

Reagan, like many conservatives, was a modern heir to a states' rights perspective dating to the Anti-Federalist movement. He believed that government should be as close to the voters as possible—in the city hall or the state capitol—rather than far away in Washington, DC. Yet believing that government should be closer to the people in the abstract is far different from putting that belief into practice. Taking power from the federal government did advance a core philosophical belief of the Reagan administration, but it also created problems for Reagan supporters, who were not shy about voicing their displeasure.

Such core conservative constituencies as business and industry quickly realized that dealing with one government was much less of a headache than dealing with fifty governments. They almost immediately began to put counterpressure on the movement toward expanded state policymaking authority. The result was something of a push-and-pull, with the Reagan administration trying to shove power onto the states with one set of legislative priorities and yank it back to the federal government with another. Ultimately, Reagan did succeed in cutting grants-in-aid. He consolidated fifty-seven categorical grants into nine new block grants. General revenue sharing and another sixty categorical grants were eliminated entirely. This reduced the amount of money sent to the states while increasing the states' ability to act independently.[12] Yet Reagan also engaged in a number of fairly aggressive preemption movements and backed a number of unfunded

---

New Federalism
The belief that states should receive more power and authority and less money from the federal government.

Block Grants
Federal grants-in-aid given for general policy areas that leave states and localities with wide discretion over how to spend the money within the designated policy area.

FIGURE 2-5

Federal Grants to States, 1940–2011 (in billions)

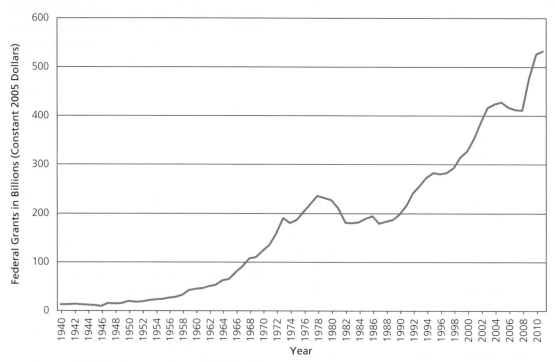

Source: U.S. Office of Management and Budget, *Budget of the United States*, Historical Tables, Table 431, "Federal Grants-in-Aid to State and Local Governments: 1990 to 2011," data released September 30, 2011.

mandates. This reduced the independence of states and forced them to fund programs they did not necessarily support.

The seeds of New Federalism had a hard time taking root at the national level, but its roots sank fast and deep at the state and local levels. States were caught between the proverbial rock of a cash-strapped federal government and the hard place of the demand for the programs traditionally supported by federal funds. They slowly and often painfully worked themselves out of this dilemma by becoming less reliant on the federal government. States began aggressively pursuing innovative policy approaches to a wide range of social and economic problems. By the 1990s, as one author puts it, there was "a developing agreement among state and national political elites that states should have greater authority and flexibility in operating public programs."[13]

The effort to take power away from the federal government and give it to the states was broadly supported by public opinion, as polls consistently showed that Americans placed more trust in state and local governments than they did in the federal government.[14] In the 1990s, the Clinton administration championed the idea of devolution, an extension of New Federalism that sought a systematic transition of power from the federal to the state level in certain policy areas.

Probably the best-known example of devolution is the Personal Responsibility and Work Opportunity Reconciliation Act of 1996, popularly known as the law that "ended welfare as we know it." The law, which Clinton signed under Republican pressure during the 1996 presidential campaign after vetoing it twice, ended Aid to Families with Dependent Children (AFDC) and replaced it with a block grant. In essence, the law embodied the deal between state and federal governments that constituted devolution—the federal government would provide less money, and the states would get more policymaking authority.

Like its parent, New Federalism, the devolution revolution faced strong resistance, often from an old enemy. Conservatives, at least rhetorically, still were the strongest states' rights advocates. Yet when states' rights conflicted with key portions of the conservative political agenda, conservative groups still fought tenaciously for federal supremacy over the states, just as they had during the 1980s. An example of this contradictory behavior is the 1996 Defense of Marriage Act. This federal law was proposed in the wake of movements in Hawaii and Vermont to legalize same-sex civil unions. The full faith and credit clause requires a contract made under the laws of one state to be legally recognized and binding in all states. So, if one state made same-sex unions legal, it raised the possibility that the other forty-nine would have to recognize such civil unions as the legal equivalent of marriages. There was a strong push from many traditional states' rights advocates for the federal government to, in essence, grant states exceptions from their full faith and credit obligations. The Defense of Marriage Act did this. It also put the federal government into the business of defining what constitutes a marriage, an area traditionally left to the states.[15]

Ad Hoc Federalism . . . and a Return to Centralized Federalism? (2002–present)

The mixed commitment to New Federalism is perhaps best exemplified by the presidency of George W. Bush. Bush came to the White House from the Texas governor's mansion and, at least on the surface, was a strong supporter of the principles of New Federalism. The policy record of the Bush administration, though, was considerably at odds with New Federalism sentiments. For example, Bush's signature domestic policy was the No Child Left Behind Act, which asserted federal control over important aspects of public education, a policy area traditionally under the jurisdiction of state and local governments. Peter Harkness, editor of *Governing* magazine, summed up the Bush administration's record on federalism thus: "The administration has mandated more, preempted more and run roughshod over state initiatives that didn't conform to its own ideology."[16]

Part of Bush's departure from the New Federalism philosophy was driven by recession and war. Throughout the history of the United States, during times of crisis, power has become centralized in the national government—it simply is better equipped than the individual states to deal with national economic challenges or international conflict. The Bush administration found itself struggling with a soft economy at the beginning of its term and a disastrous slide into economic recession at the end of its term. In between, much of its focus was devoted to a global war on terrorism in response to the devastating attacks of September 11, 2001.

During the eight years of the Bush administration, the commitment to New Federalism dissolved more or less entirely. This did not necessarily mean that federal-state relations in the Bush era shifted from a commitment to devolution to a commitment to centralizing power in Washington, DC. What it meant was that a principled guiding philosophy of state-federal relations like dual federalism, cooperative federalism, or New Federalism was abandoned. Instead a new, more partisan or ideologically based approach to state-federal relations came to the fore, an approach described as **ad hoc federalism**.[17] Ad hoc federalism is the process of choosing a state-centered or nation-centered view of federalism on the basis of political or partisan convenience. In other words, the issue at hand, not a core philosophical commitment to a particular vision of federalism, determines a policymaker's commitment to state or federal supremacy.

This is not necessarily a bad thing for states or localities. For example, when the federal government failed to ratify the Kyoto Protocol, a treaty addressing climate change—an international agreement considered the province of the federal

Michigan was the first state to plow its roads and to use the yellow dividing line on its highways.

Ad Hoc Federalism
The process of choosing a state-centered or nation-centered view of federalism on the basis of political or partisan convenience.

government—more than seven hundred generally liberal-leaning U.S. cities decided independently to adopt the treaty's provisions. In other words, based on the issue at hand, more liberal cities decided that treaties concerning global warming were within their jurisdiction. Similarly, as we have already seen, when the federal government would not pass an immigration law, more conservative states decided based on the issue at hand that this was within their jurisdiction. States such as Alabama, Arizona, Georgia, Indiana, South Carolina, and Utah, accordingly, passed immigration laws.[18] The big concern of ad hoc federalism is that it treats the key institutional feature of the American political system not as a consistent and stable basis for organizing policy and constitutional responsibilities, but as a more incoherent structure that is viewed differently depending on ideological convenience. Thus conservatives champion states' rights while arguing against the federal government's constitutional authority to mandate the purchase of a health insurance policy, but ignore states' rights when arguing for the federal government's authority to pass laws outlawing gay marriage. Similarly, while liberals traditionally are more inclined to downplay states' rights arguments in favor of centralizing federal government power over a wide range of issues, they discover a commitment to states' rights when it suits them (on gay marriage, for example). Ad hoc federalism makes everyone an equal-opportunity hypocrite.

The shift toward ad hoc federalism was at least temporarily slowed by the Great Recession of 2008–2009, which shook up state-federal relations and shifted power decisively toward the federal government. This was prompted in part by the nature of economic shock. For example, the financial industry was widely seen as helping to precipitate the economic downturn by making irresponsible loans and underestimating risk. To prop up the financial system, the federal government spent billions, in the process becoming a major stockholder in many banks (not to mention part owner of the world's largest insurance company and two major domestic car manufacturers). Historically, banks and insurance companies have been regulated by state and federal governments, but with the federal government the only entity with deep enough pockets to prevent an implosion on Wall Street, few doubt that the regulatory authority over these sectors of the economy will take a significant shift toward Washington, DC, and away from the states.

Those same deep pockets also paid for what amounted to a resurrection of centralized federalism, with the federal government setting policy priorities, deciding what to spend on those priorities, and delegating to the states the administration of the approved programs. This was not so much a premeditated attempt by the federal government to usurp the power of the states as it was a recognition that the empty coffers of states and localities needed to be filled, that only the federal government had the capacity to provide that much cash, and that the federal government was not going to give away that money without getting its policy priorities attended to. Accordingly, out of budgetary necessity states and localities found themselves orbiting the policy preferences of the federal government. As the economy returned to modest growth and the tide of federal grants-in-aid began to recede in the past few years, however, states and localities seemed increasingly eager to break the gravitational pull of the federal government. It is too soon to tell whether this heralds the resurrection of New Federalism or just the resumption of ad hoc federalism (see the box "States under Stress: What Brand of Federalism Is Next?").

The Supreme Court: The Umpire of Federalism

Article VI of the Constitution contains the national supremacy clause, which declares that the Constitution, laws passed by Congress, and national treaties are the "supreme law of the land." This does not mean that the states are always subordinate to the national government. Don't

States Under Stress

What Brand of Federalism Is Next?

A quarter century ago, John Herbers, a former national correspondent for the *New York Times*, wrote a cover story for *Governing* magazine heralding the advent of a largely unplanned, unpredicted new sort of federalism. More responsibility and authority would be devolved down to the states and their localities as the Reagan administration reduced the federal imprint on American governance, and at the time states and localities seemed to be ready to accept a greater, more independent role.

State and local management capacity had improved substantially, mostly because during the era of cooperative and centralized federalism Washington had relied on state and local bureaucracies to manage federal money rather than expand its own. Also, states and localities were becoming more financially independent; they had raised as much in new taxes as the Reagan administration had cut. Most surprising from a contemporary perspective is not Herbers's assessment of subnational governments' mature management or revenue capacities but his description of the broad, bipartisan agreement on the direction federalism would take and what that would imply—devolution was the name of the game, and this would lead to less friction between states and the federal government.

In terms of the states being well positioned to handle the management and financial side of things, Herbers was spot-on. Indeed, in the four years following the recession of 1980–1982, states grew their revenues by one-third, to $228 billion. And that didn't include mushrooming cash inflows from nontax sources such as lotteries, which had expanded into a majority of the states. Because the national economy was humming along quite nicely and the tax base had significantly expanded, state and local governments experienced what would be an almost three-decade run of solid increases in tax revenue—interrupted slightly by two mild recessions.

The political side of it, though, didn't go quite as Herbers had imagined. State-federal relations were sometimes rocky in the 1980s and 1990s, although there was agreement on a general direction of greater state independence. That general agreement disappeared and intergovernmental relations tipped into acrimony in the following decade. Somewhat surprisingly, this happened during the administration of George W. Bush. Though a conservative and an ex-governor, Bush showed little interest in following a traditional conservative, states' rights script as president and made a series of moves that yanked power back from the states and toward the federal government: the No Child Left Behind education law, the Real ID Act, and a wave of preemptions of state regulations and thinly disguised unfunded mandates (which supposedly had been banned). At the same time, Washington lobbyists pushed for more centralization, with the idea that their industries could cut a better deal at the federal level and avoid a patchwork of statutes and regulations. It was a time of what Don Borut, executive director of the National League of Cities, called "coercive federalism" or, when he was being more blunt, "shift-and-shaft federalism."

As relationships between the states and the federal government were souring, the Great Recession hit, weakening the financial and management capacities of the states. The Obama administration further centralized power, using a series of financial carrots and regulatory sticks to get states and localities to pay attention to federal policy priorities. Above all, intergovernmental relationships were influenced by a rising tide of partisanship and ideological rigidity that swamped both Washington and many of the states. That mixture has been pretty toxic for intergovernmental relations and has made it hard to replicate Herbers's crystal-ball gazing for the next twenty-five days, let alone the next twenty-five years.

So what brand of federalism will we see next? Will it be the kind John Herbers foresaw? Will federal and state governments share a broad understanding of the direction of intergovernmental relations and be willing to work across partisan and ideological lines to make it happen? Or will a mixture of crippling recession, massive cutbacks in discretionary federal spending, and continued political dysfunction at the national and state levels exacerbate the disadvantages of federalism and minimize its advantages? It is too early to tell.

Source: Adapted from Peter Harkness, "Potomac Chronicle: What Brand of Federalism Is Next?," *Governing*, January 2012.

forget—the Tenth Amendment also counts as part of that supreme law. However, it does mean that federal courts often have to referee national-state conflicts. Because it has the final say in interpreting the Constitution, the Supreme Court is, in effect, the umpire of federalism. Its rulings ultimately decide the powers and limitations of the different levels of government.

The Rise of Nation-Centered Federalism on the Court

Throughout U.S. history, the Supreme Court has cycled through trends of state-centered and nation-centered philosophies of federalism. As we have already seen, the early Supreme Court under Chief Justice John Marshall pursued a fairly broad interpretation of the federal government's powers in such cases as *McCulloch v. Maryland*. Marshall's successor, Roger Taney, took the Court in a more state-centered direction by establishing dual federalism as the Court's central operating philosophy. The shift from dual federalism to cooperative federalism required a return to a more nation-centered judicial philosophy. Although the Court initially took a more nation-centered direction in its rulings following the Civil War, it was not until the Great Depression and Roosevelt's New Deal that a decisive tilt in the Court's rulings cleared the way for the rise of cooperative federalism and the centralization of power in the national government.

The shift toward a liberal interpretation of the federal government's powers dominated the Supreme Court's operating philosophy for much of the next sixty years and is exemplified by its decision in *United States v. Darby Lumber Co.* (1941). The substantive issue at stake in this case was whether the federal government had the power to regulate wages. The Supreme Court said yes, but the decision is of more lasting interest because of the majority opinion's dismissive comment on the Tenth Amendment. Once considered the constitutional lockbox of state power, the amendment, according to the Court's ruling, now did little more than state "a truism that all is retained which has not been surrendered." In other words, the Tenth Amendment was simply a basket for "leftover" powers the federal government did not seek or want.

During and after the New Deal era, the Supreme Court also accelerated a trend of broadly interpreting Congress's powers to regulate interstate commerce. It did this through its interpretation of the **interstate commerce clause**. In *Wickard v. Filburn* (1942), the Court ruled that the clause gave Congress the power to regulate what a farmer can feed his chickens. In *Heart of Atlanta Motel v. United States* (1964) and *Katzenbach v. McClung* (1964), the justices ruled that it gave Congress the power to regulate private acts of racial discrimination.

A series of such decisions over the course of more than fifty years led some judicial scholars to conclude that the Supreme Court had essentially turned the concept of enumerated and reserved powers on its head. In effect, the assumption now seemed to be that the federal government had the power to do anything the Constitution did not specifically prohibit.[19] The states and localities were drawn ever closer into subordinate satellite roles in orbit around the federal government. This situation continued until just before the end of the twentieth century. At that point, the Court once again began siding with the states over the federal government.

A Tenth Amendment Renaissance or Ad Hoc Federalism?

By the mid-1990s, the Supreme Court was dominated by justices appointed by New Federalists. Reagan, who had campaigned on his intention to nominate federal judges who shared his conservative philosophy, appointed four. He also elevated a fifth, William Rehnquist—originally appointed as an associate justice by Nixon—to the position of chief justice. Reagan's vice president and presidential successor, George H. W. Bush, appointed two more justices. The

Interstate Commerce Clause
Constitutional clause that gives Congress the right to regulate interstate commerce. This clause has been broadly interpreted to give Congress a number of implied powers.

end result was a mid-1990s Supreme Court chosen largely by conservative Republican presidents who wanted limits set on the federal government's powers and responsibilities. The justices obliged.

In a series of narrow—mostly 5–4—decisions in the 1990s, the Court began to back away from the nation-centered interpretation of the Constitution that had dominated its rulings during the era of cooperative federalism (see Table 2-3). *United States v. Lopez* (1995) was a significant victory for states' rights and a clear break from a half century of precedent. This case involved the Drug Free School Zone Act of 1990, which made it a federal crime to possess a firearm within one thousand feet of a school. Following a good deal of precedent, Congress justified its authority to regulate local law enforcement by using a very liberal interpretation of the interstate commerce clause. The Supreme Court disagreed and argued that the commerce clause granted no such authority.

Similar reasoning was used by the justices in *United States v. Morrison* (2000) to strike down the Violence Against Women Act (VAWA). Congress had passed this law in 1994 out of concern that the states, although having primary responsibility for criminal law, were not adequately dealing with the problem of violence against women. The key provision of the VAWA gave assault victims the right to

TABLE 2-3

Key U.S. Supreme Court Rulings Regarding Federalism, 1995–2012

Case	Decision
United States v. Lopez (1995)	Court strikes down a federal law prohibiting possession of firearms near public schools. State claim upheld.
Seminole Tribe of Florida v. Florida (1996)	Court rules Congress cannot allow citizens to sue states in a federal court except for civil rights violations. State claim upheld.
Printz v. United States (1997)	Court strikes down a federal law requiring mandatory background checks for firearms purchases. State claim upheld.
Alden v. Maine (1999)	Court rules that Congress does not have the power to authorize citizens to sue in state court on the basis of federal claims. State claim upheld.
United States v. Morrison (2000)	Court strikes down the federal Violence Against Women Act. State claim upheld.
Reno v. Condon (2000)	Court upholds a federal law preventing states from selling driver's license information. State claim overturned.
Bush v. Gore (2000)	Court overrules a Florida Supreme Court action allowing hand recounts of contested election ballots. State claim overturned.
Alabama v. Garrett (2001)	Court rules that state employees cannot sue their employers in federal court to recover monetary damages under the provisions of the Americans with Disabilities Act. State claim upheld.
Lorillard Tobacco Co. v. Reilly (2001)	Court strikes down Massachusetts laws regulating the advertising of tobacco products. State claim overturned.
Kelo v. City of New London (2005)	Court rules that government can seize private property for public purposes, including economic development. State claim upheld.
Gonzales v. Oregon (2006)	Court rules that the U.S. attorney general overstepped his authority by threatening to eliminate prescription-writing privileges for doctors who follow state law allowing physician-assisted suicide. State claim upheld.
Arizona v. United States (2012)	Court rules that states do not have the authority to enact and enforce immigration laws; however, it allows states to implement "show me your papers" regulations that require law enforcement officers to determine the immigration status of anyone they stop or detain.

sue their assailants in federal court. Congress argued that it was authorized to pass such a law because fear of violence prevented women from using public transportation or going out unescorted at night. Such fears, the reasoning went, placed limits on economic opportunities for women. This argument made the connection to commerce and Congress's constitutional authority. The Supreme Court again rejected this broad interpretation of the commerce clause.

After 1990, at the same time that it was narrowly interpreting the Constitution to limit federal power, the Supreme Court began to interpret the Constitution broadly to expand state power. Notably, the Court made a series of rulings that broadly interpreted the Eleventh Amendment's guarantee of **sovereign immunity** to the states. Sovereign immunity is essentially "the right of a government to be free from suits brought without its consent."[20] In cases such as *Seminole Tribe of Florida v. Florida* (1996) and *Alden v. Maine* (1999), the Supreme Court adopted an interpretation of the Eleventh Amendment that limited the right of citizens to sue states for violations of federal law. These rulings not only lessened the power of the federal government over the states but also arguably gave the states more power over their own citizens.

Although these and other rulings resurrected the Tenth Amendment and underlined the independent power of the states, there has been an element of inconsistency to Supreme Court decisions since 1990. In *Bush v. Gore* (2000), the Court abandoned its commitment to states' rights by overruling the Florida Supreme Court and ordering a halt to the contested recount of presidential ballots. In effect, the U.S. Supreme Court overturned the state court's interpretation of state law—which allowed recounts—and decided the presidency in favor of George W. Bush. Another decision that favored federal power over state power came in *Lorillard Tobacco Co. v. Reilly* (2001). Here, the Court overturned a Massachusetts law that regulated the advertising of

tobacco products. The Court argued that federal law—specifically, the Federal Cigarette Labeling and Advertising Act—legitimately preempts state law on this issue.

The Court also trumped ten states that have legalized the use of marijuana for medical purposes. In *Gonzales v. Raich* (2005), the Court, led by its more liberal justices, ruled that federal law enforcement officers, prosecutors, and judges can prosecute and punish anyone possessing marijuana. The ruling weakened the states' laws; however, it did not overturn them because state and local officials need not participate in any federal efforts to seize medical marijuana.[21] Just six months later, however, the Court upheld a state law related to serious illnesses when it ruled in *Gonzales v. Oregon* (2006) against the federal government's challenge of Oregon's law that allows physician-assisted suicide. In recent years, the Court has reviewed a number of preemptions of state law on everything from banking regulation to labor arbitration, and, for the most part, it has sided with federal authority.[22]

This was certainly the case in the Court's 2012 landmark ruling in *National Federal of Independent Business v. Sebelius*, which bitterly disappointed many conservatives. This case decided the federal government's power to enact the Patient Protection and Affordable Care Act ("Obamacare"), in particular the federal government's authority to require individuals to purchase health insurance. Chief Justice John Roberts, appointed by President George W. Bush and typically seen as a member of the Court's conservative bloc, surprised many by voting with the more liberal justices to affirm that power. Yet in another landmark case decided the same year, the Court put caveats on federal supremacy. In *Arizona v. United States* (2012), the case that decided Arizona's immigration law discussed in the opening section of this chapter, the Supreme Court ruled that only the federal government has the power to set immigration policy but that states can check the immigration status of people within their borders. In other words, the Court sort of split the difference between state and federal claims to power.

Sovereign Immunity
The right of a government to not be sued without its consent.

So over the past quarter century or so, the Supreme Court has sometimes zigged and sometimes zagged on state-federal relations. In the 1990s its rulings seemed to herald a resurrection of states' rights by conservative justices, but this commitment was never consistent, and something of that inconsistency is seen in the big landmark cases affecting state-federal relations of the past few years. Some scholars argue that these sorts of inconsistencies have always been characteristic of the Supreme Court's federalism rulings. Ideology—not a firm commitment to a particular vision of state-national relations—is what ultimately decides how a justice rules in a particular case.[23] Therefore, a Court dominated by conservative appointees will occasionally depart from the state-centered notion of federalism if a nation-centered view is more ideologically pleasing, whereas a Court dominated by liberal appointees will do the opposite. The Supreme Court, like the president, finds it hard to resist the temptations of ad hoc federalism.

> Ideology—not a firm commitment to a particular vision of state-national relations—is what ultimately decides how a justice rules in a particular case.

Conclusion

The Constitution organizes the United States into a federal political system. This means that the states are powerful independent political actors that dominate important policy areas. Many of these policy areas are those with the most obvious and far-reaching roles in the day-to-day lives of citizens. Education, law enforcement, utility regulation, and road construction are but a handful of examples. The independence they are granted under the federal system allows states broad leeway to go their own way in these and many other policy areas.

The resulting variation has a number of advantages, such as making it easier to match local preferences with government action and allowing states and localities to experiment with innovative programs and policies. There are also a number of disadvantages. These include the complexity of and difficulty in coordinating policy at the national level. The interests of state and national governments overlap in many areas. Because of this and because the Constitution does not clearly resolve the question of who has the power to do what in these arenas of shared interest, conflict is inevitable.

What is the future of federalism? In the past decade, the federal government's commitment to New Federalism all but collapsed and was replaced by a much more ad hoc approach to state-federal relations. Under the George W. Bush administration, the federal government veered away from the devolutionary trends of the 1990s and made numerous efforts to shift power to the national government. The economic shocks of 2008–2009 caused a significant retrenchment among subnational governments, which suddenly found themselves heavily reliant on the federal government as a major revenue source. As state budgets and an overextended federal government have slowed grants-in-aid, there are signs that states are looking to assert more independence. It is not at all clear, though, that New Federalism is back. If states' rights are championed only when they coincide with ideological or partisan preferences on given issues, what we are more likely to see is the resumption of ad hoc federalism. Regardless of what the future brings, there is no doubt that the federal system has evolved into a complex web of intergovernmental relationships that recognizes the practical necessity of cooperation among all levels of government. This creates a situation ripe for continued conflicts between state and federal governments, conflicts that in many cases will have to be resolved by the Supreme Court. Regardless of how these conflicts are ultimately resolved, the future undoubtedly will find states and localities continuing to play a central role in the U.S. political system, both as independent policymakers and as cooperative partners with the federal government.

The Latest Research

The roles and responsibilities of federal and state governments are constantly evolving based on political and economic context, policy demands and innovation, Supreme Court rulings, and the political philosophies, ideological preferences, and partisan fortunes of lawmakers at both levels of government. Current scholars of federalism find themselves in a particularly interesting period in the development of intergovernmental relations. The worst of the recession is over, yet fiscal stresses remain. Federal, state, and local governments are trying to reset their relationships with each other to deal most effectively with what comes next—but no one is sure what comes next.

Below are summaries of some of the most recent research on federalism. Two constant themes emerge from this stream of scholarship: first, intergovernmental relations have undergone and are currently undergoing dramatic changes; and second, those changes have enormous implications not just for politics and policy but also for the day-to-day lives of citizens.

* * * * * * * * * * * * * * * * * * * *

• **Gamkhar, Shama, and J. Mitchell Pickerill.** 2012. "The State of American Federalism 2011–2012: A Fend for Yourself and Activist Form of Bottom-Up Federalism." *Publius: The Journal of Federalism* 42: 357–386.

This study suggests that we may be witnessing the emergence of what the authors call "bottom-up" federalism. They argue that political, economic, and judicial trends are pushing states and localities to become more independent—to figure out how to solve the financial and social challenges they face without being propped up by the federal government. Multiple causes are driving these trends. For example, as divided government and gridlock slow government action at the federal level on a wide array of policy issues, state and local governments are being forced to step up and take action on their own. As federal stimulus dollars disappear, states and localities increasingly have to figure out how to make the books balance on their own. The decreased reliance on federal dollars seems to be encouraging more assertive declarations of state sovereignty. For example, states have begun reasserting their independence by opting out of federal programs (e.g., health insurance exchanges, high-speed rail initiatives) that provide financial aid.

• **Rivlin, Alice**. 2012. "Rethinking Federalism for More Effective Governance." *Publius: The Journal of Federalism* 42: 387–400.

In this article, a companion piece to the Gamkhar and Pickerill study described above, Rivlin argues that the realities of postrecession governance create a pressing need for a reconsideration of the relationship between state and federal governments. In particular, Rivlin pushes for two key reforms. First, she argues that state and federal governments should rethink their job responsibilities. Rather than taking on increasingly shared responsibilities in areas such as education, she suggests, one level of government should take primary responsibility. Who gets the job should depend on who is best positioned to do that job and who has traditionally had the legal authority to do it (in the case of education, this would be the states). This is essentially an argument that a good dose of dual federalism is not necessarily a bad thing. The second big reform that Rivlin endorses is a fundamental rethinking of how government funds itself. She argues that the existing federal tax system is poorly suited for the twenty-first century and suggests the implementation of a kind of national sales tax, collected by the federal government but distributed to the states. This would allow states to recapture sales taxes lost to Internet sales as well as provide a more uniform and reliable revenue source for more distinct and defined policy responsibilities.

• **Robertson, David Brian**. 2012. *Federalism and the Making of America.* New York: Routledge.

The two articles described above are analyses of changes in intergovernmental relations more or less as they occur in real time. Robertson's book makes a good companion to these, placing such time-focused studies into perspective by offering a sweeping story of the historical development of federalism in America, from its birth at the founding of the Republic to the red-state–blue-state conflicts of the twenty-first century. The book is notable for its focus on federalism as the stage upon which most of the great policy battles in American history have been fought: racial relations, economic regulation, social welfare and regulation. All of these issues and more have been critically shaped by America's system of intergovernmental relations.

- **Weissert, Carol S**. 2011. "Beyond Marble Cakes and Picket Fences: What U.S. Federalism Scholars Can Learn from Comparative Work." *Journal of Politics* 73: 965–979.

This article is Weissert's presidential address to the Southern Political Science Association, one of the more prestigious professional associations in the discipline. In it Weissert examines an issue critical to readers of this textbook: the comparative method. She argues that while there is no doubt that state scholars put the comparative method to good use, they have a blind spot—they fail to learn from scholars of other federal systems that employ the same method. If we want to learn what differences really make a difference—not just in the United States, but anywhere at any time—we need to pay attention to differences that make a difference in other federal systems, not just federalism in the United States.

Chapter Review

Key Concepts

- ad hoc federalism (p. 43)
- Bill of Rights (p. 33)
- block grants (p. 41)
- categorical grants (p. 40)
- centralized federalism (p. 38)
- compact theory (p. 35)
- concurrent powers (p. 31)
- confederacy (p. 25)
- cooperative federalism (p. 38)
- crosscutting requirements (p. 40)
- crossover sanctions (p. 40)
- dual federalism (p. 35)
- enumerated powers (p. 31)
- exclusive powers (p. 31)
- federalism (p. 25)
- Fourteenth Amendment (p. 34)
- full faith and credit clause (p. 33)
- general revenue sharing grants (p. 40)
- general welfare clause (p. 31)

Suggested Websites

- **www.ncsl.org/statefed/statefed.htm.** Website sponsored by the National Conference of State Legislatures and dedicated to state-federal issues.

- **www.nga.org.** Website of the National Governors Association, which includes a section devoted to state-federal relations.

- **www.publius.oxfordjournals.org.** Website of *Publius*, a scholarly journal dedicated to the study of federalism.

- **www.supremecourtus.gov.** Website of the U.S. Supreme Court; includes text of the Court's opinions.

State Stats on Federalism

Explore and compare data on the states! Go to **college.cqpress .com/sites/essentials-govstateandlocal** to do these exercises.

1. On average, the federal government contributes around 10 percent, the state government around 47 percent, and local governments around 44 percent of the funding for public K–12 schools. How much money, per pupil, does your state spend on elementary and secondary education? Is this an example of compact federalism, dual federalism, or cooperative federalism? Why?

2. What percentage of your state's population is enrolled in Medicaid? How does your state compare to the states around it? How might the Affordable Care Act change this number moving forward?

3. How many immigrants were admitted to New Mexico in 1997? How many were admitted to Arizona in the same year? How might this difference affect variations in policies regarding immigration?

4. What was the incarceration rate per one hundred thousand people in Utah in 2010? What was the rate in neighboring Idaho? Why might this difference be concerning?

5. What was the per capita net income that your state received from corporate taxes in 2011? What was the amount in a neighboring state? How might these differences affect a business that would like to have offices in both locations?

A CONSTITUTION

or

FRAME of GOVERNMENT,

Agreed upon by the DELEGATES of the People of the State of
MASSACHUSETTS-BAY,

IN

CONVENTION,

Begun and held at CAMBRIDGE on the First of *September*, 1779,

AND

Continued by Adjournments to the Second of *March*, 1780.

[Revised and Corrected.]

B O S T O N:
STATE OF MASSACHUSETTS-BAY,
Printed by BENJAMIN EDES & SONS, in State-Street,
M,DCC,LXXX.

State constitutions differ from the U.S. Constitution in many ways. Some are older—the Massachusetts Constitution, shown here, was written about a decade before the U.S. Constitution was adopted. Most state constitutions are longer, more detailed, and much easier to change than their federal counterpart.

ch.

3

Constitutions

OPERATING INSTRUCTIONS

- What impact do state constitutions have on our lives?
- Why do state constitutions differ?
- How do constitutions determine what state and local governments can and cannot do?

You do not need a Ph.D. to help change the state constitution in Colorado. You just need to be a registered voter. Want to understand what you are being asked to change? Well, keep studying. For that, you really might need a Ph.D.

Like many states, Colorado has a process of **direct democracy**, in other words a system that allows citizens to make laws themselves rather than outsourcing the job to elected representatives. This includes the ability to vote on proposed amendments to the state constitution. Voting on amendments is one thing, though; understanding them is quite another. For example, consider the following proposed amendment (fair warning—prepare to go cross-eyed):

> Concerning reform of the state civil service system, and in connection therewith, modifying the merit principle, exempting certain positions from the system, modifying the number of eligible applicants from which an appointment is to be made, modifying the residency requirement, expanding the duration of temporary employment, specifying the rulemaking authority of the state personnel board and the state personnel director, allowing the general assembly to reallocate the rulemaking authority of the state personnel board and state personnel director, authorizing a modification to the veterans' preference, and making conforming amendments.[1]

Eh? Don't get it? Us neither—and one of us actually has a Ph.D. According to one study, the language of policy proposals put to voters in direct democratic processes is written at a seventeenth-grade level. That means these proposals are, on average, written for people who have at least a college degree. In Colorado, such proposals are written at a twenty-sixth-grade level—they are literally written so you need a Ph.D. to understand them (or not—having a Ph.D. sure didn't help us make sense of the mouthful in the previous paragraph).[2]

This is important because, as we shall see, state constitutions have an enormous impact on state governments and policymaking—and on us. They affect the education we receive, the employment opportunities we enjoy, the political cultures of the states in which we live, and the rights we do (or don't) have. State constitutions and the rights and powers they provide also vary widely. Thus it would be nice if we could at least get a plain-English general gist of what these all-important sets of rules and laws mean and what they imply. Ballot initiatives written in dense legalese probably won't get you there, but hopefully we can help you understand the importance of state constitutions—no Ph.D. required.

This chapter explores how the role that state constitutions allow citizens to play significantly affects governing. For example, Colorado, as we have already seen, embraces the idea of direct democracy. In that state the constitution allows the **electorate**, or those individuals who can vote, to take policy matters into their own hands (even if the voters are not quite sure what they are holding). Ballot initiatives and referendums allow Colorado voters to amend the constitution or override the decisions of the state's elected officials—or even remove the officials entirely—with ease. In contrast, New York's constitution does not allow these things. New York politicians are famously insulated from voters' demands, and state-level decisions are made by a handful of senior elected officials.

So here's one difference that can make a big difference—some state constitutions allow direct democratic processes such as ballot initiatives and referendums and other states do not. That's far from the only difference, though. State constitutions include everything from rules about who can hold elective office (some states have term limits, others do not) to parking regulations for major municipalities. What explains the tremendous variation among state constitutions? A state constitution reflects particular historical experiences and notions of what makes for good government. Alabama's constitution, for instance, was drafted in 1901 by a small group of

---

Direct Democracy
A system in which citizens make laws themselves rather than relying on elected representatives.

Electorate
The population of individuals who can vote.

wealthy planters and reflects their fears that rapid industrial development would threaten the "best" form of government—that is, planter government. The state's generally traditional political culture made this idea of "best" government broadly acceptable.[3] Alabama has remained a traditional state at least in part because its constitution, despite more than eight hundred amendments, has thwarted industrialization and modernization.

State constitutions have taken on increasing importance in the last decade or two because of judicial activity at the state and federal levels. In the 1990s, the U.S. Supreme Court's insistence on determining the boundaries of federalism and evaluating state laws and regulations—a form of activism sometimes referred to as **judicial federalism**—gained former Chief Justice William Rehnquist the nickname "Governor Rehnquist."[4] State supreme courts have also become more assertive by interpreting state constitutions as guaranteeing rights that, at least currently, have no such guarantee in the U.S. Constitution. This activity can be traced in part to a famous 1977 *Harvard Law Review* article penned by Supreme Court justice William Brennan, a former justice of the New Jersey Supreme Court. Brennan argued that state constitutions afforded their citizens a layer of rights above and beyond those protected in the U.S. Constitution and urged state courts to be forceful about paying attention to these rights. They have. In the past decade, for example, state supreme courts in Connecticut, Iowa, Massachusetts, New Hampshire, New York, and Vermont have ruled that their constitutions guarantee equal marriage rights to same-sex couples. (See the box "A Difference That Makes a Difference: State Constitutions and the Right to Marry.") Ever more assertive courts, in other words, have found new rights in state constitutions. This means that the documents that reflect and determine what state and local governments can and cannot do have become even more important to an understanding of politics in the United States.

Judicial Federalism
The idea that the courts determine the boundaries of state-federal relations.

What State Constitutions Do: It's Probably Different from What You Think

Residents of the United States live under a system of **dual constitutionalism**, which means federal and state governments are both sovereign powers run in accordance with the rules laid out in their respective constitutions. Most citizens have at least some rudimentary knowledge of the U.S. Constitution; these same citizens generally know very little about state constitutions.

All state constitutions as well as the U.S. Constitution have common purposes and functions. They all describe the roles and responsibilities of government as well as its organizational structure. All create three primary branches of government (legislative, executive, and judicial) and all contain something like a bill of rights that spells out the rights of citizens and places specific limits on governmental powers. Most state constitutions place these rights firmly in the context of **natural law**, also known as **higher law**, a tradition that holds that these rights are not political creations but divine endowments. The constitutions and any subsequent **constitutional amendments**, or changes, are meant to ensure these rights for citizens.

While they share important features with the U.S. Constitution, state constitutions differ from their federal counterpart in important ways. These differences include:

Powers Granted to Government. The most important difference between the U.S. Constitution and state constitutions is the scope of the documents. The U.S. Constitution's original purpose was

Dual Constitutionalism
A system of government in which people live under two sovereign powers. In the United States, these are the government of their state of residence and the federal government.

Natural Law, or Higher Law
A set of moral and political rules based on divine law and binding on all people.

Constitutional Amendments
Proposals to change a constitution, typically enacted by a supermajority of the legislature or through a statewide referendum.

FIGURE 3-1

HOW IT WORKS

Alabama's State Constitution: The More Things Change, the More They Stay the Same

Since 1819, Alabama has adopted six different constitutions. The most recent was ratified in 1901 and consists of more than 360,000 words (that's about forty-five times longer than the U.S. Constitution). The bulk of this comes from the 835 (and counting) amendments that make it the world's longest operating constitution. It was the product of a constitutional delegation comprising 155 white males who, like convention president John Knox, were mostly large planters. They wished to hold back the industrialization that had left Alabama in great debt. Knox, however, described the constitution's primary purpose as "secur[ing] white supremacy." African American voters were stripped of voting rights, and interracial marriage was forbidden (as recently as 2012 the state's legislature was still working to strip racist language from the constitution). Civil rights advocate Booker T. Washington, among others, condemned the document.

Many of its original provisions are now defunct or have been retracted, but that doesn't mean there are not still big problems with the constitution. Some provisions allow the continuing disfranchisement of many citizens, delay of economic development, and denial of governing powers to localities. Critics have accused the constitution of encouraging unproductive government action; the state legislature spends more than half of its time debating issues that have only local relevance, and two-thirds of the constitutional amendments address issues specific to one town or county.

There have been numerous efforts to alter Alabama's constitution—six different governors have tried to change the existing 1901 document. In each case, they were met with resistance from the legislature, the state supreme court, or powerful planters and industrialists. The latest attempt at reform involves a constitutional revision commission created in 2011 by the legislature. The job of this sixteen-member commission is to comb through the constitution and recommend changes. These are recommendations, though, not mandates. Recommendations by the commission can be rejected by the legislature and must be approved by voters before taking effect. So while Alabama's constitution is likely not set in stone forever, the prospects of a start-from-scratch do-over still seem slim.

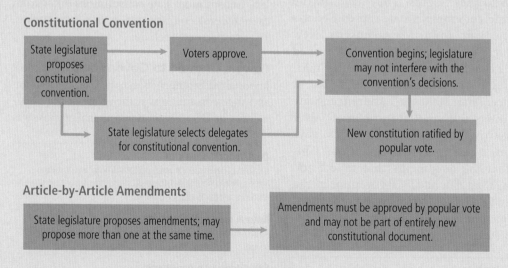

Source: Alabama Citizens for Constitutional Reform, www.constitutionalreform.org.

to organize a federal government with sharply limited powers. In contrast, state governments have what is called **plenary power**, which means their powers are not limited to those laid down in the U.S. Constitution or their own state constitutions. As the Tenth Amendment of the U.S. Constitution makes clear, *all* powers not expressly delegated or forbidden to the federal government are reserved for the states. In other words, this is not a limited grant of power in the sense of laying out the specifics of what states have the authority to do or not to do. It basically says that states can do whatever they want—they have complete or plenary power—as long as they do not contravene the U.S. Constitution.

This plenary power is vested in state legislatures and means that these legislatures do not need the express permission of the constitution to act. As long as their actions are not constitutionally prohibited (and state constitutions often place strict restrictions on government action), they are good to go. Think of it like this: When passing a law, Congress must address the key question, "Is this allowed?" (by the U.S. Constitution). For state legislatures the key question is, "Is this prohibited?" (by the state constitution). That's the difference between limited and plenary powers in the federal system. The bottom line is that state constitutions do not establish limited governments in the same way the U.S. Constitution establishes a limited federal government.[5]

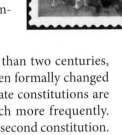

Permanence. Over more than two centuries, the U.S. Constitution has been formally changed only twenty-seven times. State constitutions are replaced and amended much more frequently. California is currently on its second constitution. New York is on its fourth. Louisiana is on its eleventh. By one estimate, the average state constitution lasts for only about seventy years.[6]

Length. At about 7,400 words, the U.S. Constitutions is about half as long as this chapter. In contrast, state constitutions tend to be much longer—the average is about 26,000 words or roughly twice the length of this chapter. Some are much longer. New York's constitution and California's ruling document are each roughly 50,000 words long. The longest state constitution, Alabama's, is more than forty-five times the length of the U.S. Constitution.[7]

Specificity. Why are state constitutions so much longer than the federal constitution and so much more likely to change? Part of the answer has to do with details. The U.S. Constitution is primarily concerned with setting up the general structures and procedures of government. State constitutions do these things too, but they often get into policy specifics. Oklahoma's constitution mandates that home economics be taught in school; Maryland's regulates off-street parking in Baltimore. Political scientist Christopher Hammonds has estimated that 39 percent of the total provisions in state constitutions are devoted to specific policy matters of this sort. In contrast, only 6 percent of the U.S. Constitution deals with such specific issues.[8]

Embrace of Democracy. The U.S. Constitution creates a system of representative democracy; it purposefully rejects direct democracy as a basis for governance. The founders went to great pains to check "the whimsies of the majority" by designing a system of checks and balances that deliberately keeps policymaking at arm's length from the shifting winds of popular opinion. During the Progressive Era in the early 1900s, many states revamped their constitutions to do just the opposite. This was particularly true of the newer western and midwestern states, in which old-school politics was less entrenched and political cultures tended toward the moralistic or individualistic.

Progressive reformers believed old constitutional arrangements were outmoded and that citizens should have the opportunity to participate directly in making laws. Moreover, they worried that state legislatures had been captured by wealthy special interests. In other words, they thought that representative democracy was working for the

---

Plenary Power
Power that is not limited or constrained.

State constitutions contain provisions on everything from free speech to parking fees, from how to organize government to how to build a pipe. Oklahoma's constitution, for example, requires schools to offer courses in the "domestic sciences." Unsurprisingly, state constitutions tend to be considerably longer than the U.S. Constitution.

benefit of a few rather than for the benefit of all. Their solution was to give the people the ability to amend their constitutions and pass laws directly through the use of referendums and ballot initiatives. Thus, in about half the states, state constitutions champion direct democracy in a way that the U.S. Constitution purposefully does not.

Finances. Congress and the White House can run up as much national debt as they can persuade bond buyers to swallow. In contrast, thirty-two state constitutions require the legislative and executive branches to balance their budgets. Another seventeen states have statutes that mandate balanced budgets. Only Vermont can choose to run up debt like the feds. Even state constitutions that do not require a balanced budget take a much more proscriptive, or restrictive, view of budget matters than does the U.S. Constitution. California's constitution, for instance, mandates that almost 40 percent of the state budget go toward education, a requirement that has constrained legislators' options when the state has been faced with budget shortfalls.

Other state constitutions mandate a specific style and format for laws that allow the transfer of money to the executive branch. These are known as **appropriations bills**. During the 1990s, some states, including Arizona, Colorado, Nevada, Oklahoma, and South Dakota, amended their constitutions to

require supermajorities—two-thirds or three-fifths of the electorate—instead of simple majorities of the legislature to increase revenues or taxes.[9] Sometimes constitutions get more specific still, prohibiting legislators from attaching "riders" to appropriations bills and requiring a single subject for each bill. (Riders are amendments or additions unrelated to the main bill.) Not surprisingly, state legislators sometimes try to evade these strict requirements. As a result, state judges tend to be much more involved in monitoring the government's budget process than their federal counterparts.

The Evolution of State Constitutions

The first state constitutions were not technically constitutions but **colonial charters** awarded by the king of England. These typically were brief documents giving individuals or corporations the right to establish "plantations" over certain areas and govern the inhabitants therein. King James I of England granted the first charter in 1606. It created the Virginia Company of London, which in 1607 established the first English settlement in North America at Jamestown in what is now the state of Virginia.

As the colonies expanded, many of these charters were amended to give the colonists "the rights of Englishmen." Just what those rights were, however,

Appropriations Bills
Laws passed by legislatures authorizing the transfer of money to the executive branch.

Colonial Charters
Legal documents drawn up by the British Crown that spelled out how the colonies were to be governed.

was not entirely clear. Britain's constitution was not (and is not) a written document, but a tradition based on the Magna Carta of 1215 and on a shared understanding of what government should and should not do. Some colonies took an expansive view of their rights and privileges as Englishmen. The Massachusetts Bay Colony, like other English settlements in North America, was organized as a corporation and was controlled by a small group of stockholders. But whereas the charters of the other companies remained in England within easy reach of the British courts, Puritan leader John Winthrop took his colony's charter with him when he sailed for the New World in 1630. This made it difficult for the English government to seize and revoke the charter if the company misbehaved or operated illegally, which it soon did. The Puritans excluded non-churchgoers from local governments, punished people who violated their sense of morals, and generally behaved like an independent polity. This misbehavior eventually incurred the displeasure of King Charles II, who revoked the charter in 1691. Massachusetts then received a new royal charter that provided for a royal governor and a general assembly—a form of governance that lasted until the Revolutionary War, nearly a century later.[10]

When the colonies won their independence, it was clear that the colonial charters had to be replaced or at least modified. It was less clear what should replace them. Some believed that the Continental Congress should draft a model constitution for every state to adopt. Richard Henry Lee, a Virginia politician, explained this idea in a letter to John Adams in May 1776: "Would not a uniform plan of government, prepared for America by the Congress, and approved by the colonies, be a surer foundation of unceasing harmony to the whole?"[11]

Adams thought not. He liked the idea of uniform state constitutions in principle but worried about what would happen in practice. The colonists' experience in dealing with royal governors had created an aversion to executive power, yet Adams thought a strong executive was necessary for effective government. He feared that the Continental Congress would create governments with weak executives dominated by powerful **unicameral legislatures** or perhaps even do away with executives (i.e., governors) altogether. This would violate what he saw as the wise precautionary principle of the **separation of powers**. Ultimately,

instead of suggesting a model constitution, the Continental Congress passed a resolution urging the thirteen colonies to reorganize their authority solely "on the basis of the authority of the people."[12] This set the stage for the states to create their own varied blueprints for government.

After independence was declared and secured, the states convened special assemblies to draft new constitutions. Most adopted lightly modified versions of their old colonial charters. References to the king of England were deleted and bills of rights added. In most of the new states, power was concentrated in the legislative branch to diminish the possibility of tyrannical governors appearing in the political arena.

The First Generation of State Constitutions

This first generation of state constitutions created powerful **bicameral legislatures**—with a few exceptions. Georgia, Pennsylvania, and Vermont opted for unicameral legislatures. In most cases governors and state judiciaries were made subordinate to the legislature, with legislatures often assuming the power to appoint both the governor and judges. No one envisioned a state supreme court with the power to overrule the acts of a legislature on the grounds that its laws were unconstitutional. Indeed, the states that did provide for a constitutional review entrusted that function to a special "council of revision" or to "councils of censor."

Nor did the early state constitutions embrace the now commonplace idea of "one person, one vote." Every early state constitution except Vermont's restricted voting access to white males who met certain minimum property requirements. Vermont gave the vote to every adult male. Supporters of a

---

Unicameral Legislature
A legislature having only one chamber. Nebraska is currently the only U.S. state with a unicameral legislature.

Separation of Powers
The principle that government should be divided into separate legislative, executive, and judicial branches, each with its own powers and responsibilities.

Bicameral Legislature
A legislature made up of two chambers, typically a house of representatives, or assembly, and a senate.

limited **franchise** defended these limitations as essential to the new republic. Without property qualifications, John Adams warned,

> there will be no end to it. New claims will arise; women will demand a vote; lads from 12 to 21 will think their rights are not enough attended to; and every man who has not a farthing will demand an equal voice with any other, in all acts of the state. It tends to confound and destroy all distinctions, and prostrate all ranks to one common level.[13]

Indeed, Adams wanted to restrict the franchise even further by setting still higher property requirements.

In practice, the requirements necessary to achieve the right to vote varied widely. Some states, such as New Hampshire, let all white male taxpayers vote. This reflected the fact that New Hampshire was a state of small landowners with a fairly egalitarian political culture. However, even this fair state specified a higher threshold of property ownership that must be met should a man wish to hold office. In Virginia, a state with a more hierarchical political culture dominated by a small group of wealthy landowners and planters, the property qualifications were stiff. Only white males who owned at least twenty-five acres and a twelve-foot-by-twelve-foot house, or fifty acres unsettled, or a town lot with a twelve-foot-by-twelve-foot house, could vote. Needless to say, women and nonwhites could not vote.

Over the course of the nineteenth century, the franchise was expanded gradually, although in a very uneven and often unjust fashion. A number of southern states, for example, rewrote their constitutions to allow minorities to vote only when such changes were forced on them as part of the price for their readmission to the Union after the Civil War. African American rights were enshrined in the Fourteenth Amendment of the U.S. Constitution. Yet, despite these protections, gains for African Americans proved short-lived. In the last decade of the 1800s, African Americans' ability to vote and to participate in all aspects of society were harshly limited by the passage of **Jim Crow laws**. These laws provided for the systematic separation of races, sharply restricted access to the franchise, and permitted the outright intimidation of African Americans.

Women fared slightly better. Wyoming began to allow women the vote in 1869. By 1912, only thirteen states had followed suit. It took the Nineteenth Amendment, ratified in 1920, to secure the right to vote, or suffrage, for all women nationwide. The limitations on the franchise imposed by many early state constitutions did little to promote good governance. State legislatures quickly developed an impressive record of corruption and fiscal extravagance because some of the men who had the legal right to vote also had money to influence politicians, an easy task in many states. But the era of unlimited legislative power did not last very long. New territories entering the Union, such as Indiana and Mississippi, opted for elected governors, as did older states that began to revise or replace their constitutions in the 1820s. The intention was to create more balance among the branches of government and allow all voters (not just the rich ones) more of a voice in deciding who would run a state. By 1860, South Carolina was the only state with a governor selected by the legislature.[14]

Formal Constitutional Changes

Every state constitution provides a method for making changes. Fourteen states actually require citizens to vote periodically on whether or not they want to convene a **constitutional convention**. Voters can decide if they want to amend or replace their state's constitution.[15]

Franchise
The right to vote.

Jim Crow Laws
Legislative measures passed in the last decade of the nineteenth century that sought to systematically separate blacks and whites.

Constitutional Convention
An assembly convened for the express purpose of amending or replacing a constitution.

In the early nineteenth century, suggesting such change could be an exciting—and dangerous—business. In 1841, a patrician attorney and renegade lawmaker by the name of Thomas Wilson Dorr convened an illegal constitutional convention. Its task was to replace Rhode Island's colonial charter with a more modern and progressive constitution. The aged document still limited the franchise to voters owning land valued at $134 or more at a time when other states had long since abandoned such requirements. Dorr's supporters elected him "governor" the following year on a platform that proposed allowing all white males—even Catholic immigrants, a group viewed with great suspicion—to vote, which caused the sitting governor to order Dorr arrested and tried for treason. Thus began the Dorr War, or Dorr's Rebellion. Dorr's supporters attempted to seize the arsenal in Providence but were repelled when their cannons failed to discharge. A month later, Dorr and his followers tried again. This time a force of militiamen and free blacks from Providence repelled them.[16] Still, Rhode Island's establishment got the hint. A new, more liberal constitution was quickly enacted.

The amendment process has since become a bit more routinized in most states. Amending or replacing a state constitution is typically a two-step process. First, a constitutional amendment or a new constitution must be proposed and meet a certain threshold of support. Then it must be ratified.

More than 2,300 initiatives have been included on state ballots since 1904. Oregon leads the nation, with 355 initiatives presented by December 2010.

MAP 3-1

Number of Constitutions per State

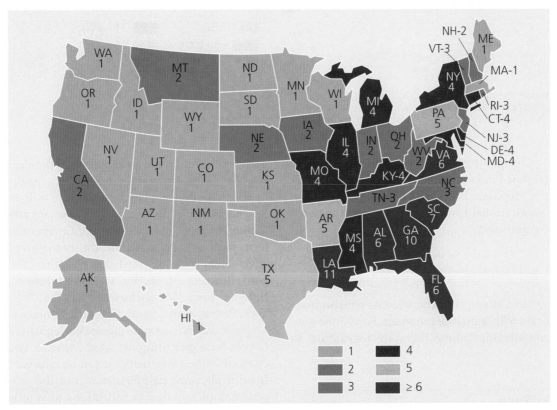

WA 1 · OR 1 · MT 2 · ND 1 · MN 1 · WI 1 · MI 4 · NH-2 · VT-3 · ME 1 · MA-1 · NY 4 · RI-3 · CT-4 · NJ-3 · DE-4 · MD-4 · ID 1 · WY 1 · SD 1 · IA 2 · IL 4 · IN 2 · OH 2 · PA 5 · WV 2 · VA 6 · NV 1 · UT 1 · CO 1 · NE 2 · KS 1 · MO 4 · KY-4 · NC 3 · CA 2 · AZ 1 · NM 1 · OK 1 · AR 5 · TN-3 · SC 7 · MS 4 · AL 6 · GA 10 · TX 5 · LA 11 · FL 6 · AK 1 · HI 1

Legend: 1 · 2 · 3 · 4 · 5 · ≥ 6

Source: Data from *The Book of the States 2012* (Lexington, KY: Council of State Governments, 2012), Table 1.1, http://knowledgecenter.csg.org/drupal/content/book-states-2012-chapter-1-state-constitutions.

MAP 3-2

Number of Amendments Adopted per State

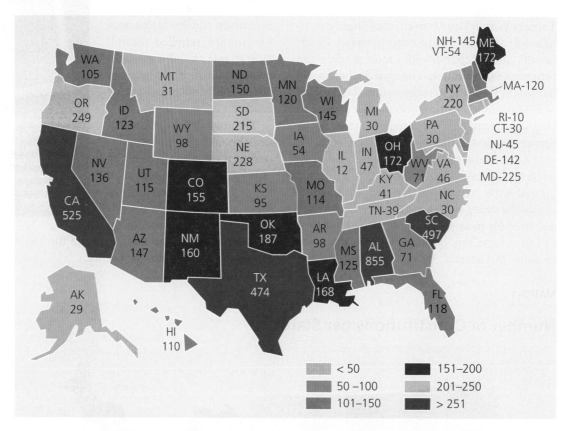

< 50	151–200
50–100	201–250
101–150	> 251

Source: Data from *The Book of the States 2009* (Lexington, KY: Council of State Governments, 2009), 12; and *The Book of the States 2012* (Lexington, KY: Council of State Governments, 2012), Table 1.1, http://knowledgecenter.csg.org/drupal/content/book-states-2012-chapter-1-state-constitutions.

Changes to state constitutions are generally proposed in four primary ways: through legislative proposals, ballot initiatives or referendums, constitutional conventions, and constitutional commissions.

Legislative Proposals

Most attempts to change state constitutions begin with legislative proposals. Forty-nine state constitutions allow the state legislature to propose constitutional amendments to the electorate as a whole.[17] In seventeen states, a majority vote in both houses of the legislature suffices to send a constitutional amendment on for **ratification**. However, most states require a supermajority for a constitutional amendment to go into effect. Some states set the bar even higher. The constitutions of eleven states—Delaware, Indiana, Iowa, Massachusetts, Nevada, New York, Pennsylvania, South Carolina, Tennessee, Virginia, and Wisconsin—require the legislature to vote for a constitutional amendment in two consecutive sessions before it can be ratified.[18] In principle, some state legislatures can also propose completely new constitutions to voters, although this has not been done since Georgia did so in 1982.

Ratification
A vote of the entire electorate to approve a constitutional change, referendum, or ballot initiative.

Ballot Initiatives and Referendums

Twenty-four states give voters another way to propose constitutional amendments—through **ballot initiatives** or popular **referendums**. These ballot measures offer citizens a way to amend the constitution or to enact new legislation without working through the legislature. South Dakota was the first state to provide voters with the option of ballot initiatives, in 1898, but it was only after Oregon embraced them in 1902 that the push for direct democracy really got under way. In the sixteen years that followed, nearly two dozen states followed Oregon's lead. The last state to approve ballot initiatives was Mississippi in 1992, some seventy years after its state supreme court tossed out its first ruling allowing initiatives.[19]

How ballot measures work in practice varies widely from state to state, although there are some common elements to the process. In most states, citizens must first provide the text of their proposal to an oversight body, usually the secretary of state's office or a legislative review committee. Then they need to gather enough signatures to place the proposal on the ballot. This threshold varies widely. Wyoming sets the bar high, requiring a number of signatures equal to 15 percent of the votes cast for governor in the most recent election. The bar is lower in Colorado, where proponents need only gather signatures equal to 5 percent of the votes tallied for secretary of state in the previous election. The signatures are then verified, again by the secretary of state or the attorney general. Proposals that pass each test make it onto the ballot at the next election.

Ballot measures typically combine the proposal and ratification stages of the amendment process. Once a proposed amendment is on the ballot, it usually requires a simple majority to pass and become part of the constitution, although some state constitutions do require a supermajority. The practical result is laws without lawmakers; the initiative is commonly employed to seek policy changes that, for whatever reason, are not being considered or undertaken by the legislature.

Constitutional Conventions

The most freewheeling approach to changing or replacing a state constitution is to convene a constitutional convention. Massachusetts, whose constitution was drafted in 1780 and is the nation's oldest, was the first state to adopt a constitution via a convention. Most other states quickly followed. Currently, the only states that make no provisions for changing their constitutions through the use of constitutional conventions are Arkansas, Indiana, Mississippi, New Jersey, Pennsylvania, and Texas.

A constitutional convention typically begins when a state legislature passes a resolution that calls for a statewide referendum on whether a convention should be held. If voters approve the proposal, the next step is to hold elections for convention delegates. In most states, a law is passed providing for convention members to be elected from local districts. Of course, there are exceptions. The legislatures of Georgia, Louisiana, Maine, South Dakota, and Virginia can call a constitutional convention without the approval of the electorate. Iowa holds an automatic constitutional assembly every ten years, and Alaska's lieutenant governor can propose a constitutional convention through a ballot question if one has not occurred within the last decade.

Once delegates are selected, a constitutional convention can convene, and once it is convened the delegates are free to amend, revise, or even replace their state's constitution. They can change the existing document in any way they see fit or write an entirely new constitution. Ultimately, the convention's handiwork goes before the electorate as a whole to be voted in or cast out. Or a constitutional convention can do nothing at all. In 1974, Texas convened a convention to rewrite its creaky

---

Ballot Initiative
A process through which voters directly convey instructions to the legislature, approve a law, or amend the constitution.

Referendum
A procedure that allows the electorate to either accept or reject a law passed by the legislature.

> State legislators tend to be wary of constitutional conventions and rarely convene them. The reason for this caution is that, once convened, a constitutional convention theoretically can examine any and all aspects of state and local government.

1876 constitution. After months of drafting a new constitution, a majority of the delegates unexpectedly voted against it. The state legislature voted to put the newly drafted constitution to a statewide referendum anyway. The voters turned it down.[20]

State legislators tend to be wary of constitutional conventions and rarely convene them. The reason for this caution is that, once convened, a constitutional convention theoretically can examine any and all aspects of state and local government. Lawmakers thus might end up initiating a process that leads to more far-reaching changes than expected. Increasingly, voters seem to share this skepticism. Voters in Alaska, Montana, and New Hampshire, among others, have rejected referendums that would have provided for constitutional conventions. The last U.S. state constitutional convention was held in 1986 in Rhode Island.[21] The most serious recent calls for a convention have been made in California, where the constitution is broadly acknowledged to be overly complex and contradictory (for example, some provisions of the California constitution mandate spending while others restrict taxation).

Constitutional Revision Commissions

If constitutional conventions are for the bold and trusting, then **constitutional revision commissions**

Constitutional Revision Commission
An expert committee formed to assess a constitution and suggest changes.

are the cautious technocrat's preferred route to constitutional change. A revision commission typically consists of a panel of citizens appointed by the governor, by the state legislature, or by both. The commission suggests—but cannot mandate—changes to the state constitution. Between 1990 and 2000, seven states—Alaska, Arkansas, California, Florida, New York, Oklahoma, and Utah—convened constitutional revision commissions. Alabama's legislature created a constitutional revision commission in 2011 and charged it with a multiyear effort to recommend piecemeal changes to that state's bloated constitution (see Figure 3-1).

Two states go even further in their enthusiasm for constitutional commissions. Florida's constitution requires that a constitutional revision commission convene every twenty years. It also gives this commission a unique power—the right to present proposed changes directly to voters for their approval or rejection. Florida's last constitutional revision commission met in 1998. It recommended thirteen changes to the state constitution, including a provision that would allow local governments to expand their requirements for background checks and waiting periods for firearms purchases. That led the head of Florida's chapter of the National Rifle Association (NRA) to decry the proposal as a power grab and to issue a warning that gun owners might vote down all of the proposed constitutional changes, even changes with universal support, should the firearms provision be included.[22] The commission refused to back down. Six months later, more than 70 percent of voters supported the measure.

The other state with an unusual constitutional revision commission is Utah, the only state whose commission is permanent. Members of the Utah Constitutional Revision Commission are appointed by the governor, by the leaders of both houses of the legislature, and by sitting commission members. Unlike Florida's commission, Utah's commission can issue its recommendations only in the form of a public report to the governor. Although it is a permanent body, the Utah commission has not met much lately—it got into hot water for not supporting (or opposing) amendments favored by partisan interests in the state legislature. In response, the legislature passed a law mandating that the commission can meet only if it is specifically requested to do so by the governor or legislature, and neither has proven particularly eager to make such a request.

Ratification

Once an amendment has been proposed and found acceptable, it must be ratified before it can go into effect. In most states, this is a straightforward process: the proposed constitutional amendment or new constitution is put before the voting public in the next statewide election for an up or down vote. Two states add a twist. In South Carolina, a majority of both houses of the state legislature must approve a constitutional amendment after a successful popular referendum before the amendment can go into effect. In Delaware, approval by a two-thirds vote in two successive general assemblies gets a constitutional amendment ratified. As already discussed, a ballot initiative essentially combines the proposal and ratification stages. Once a proposed amendment is qualified for the ballot, it usually requires only a simple majority to become part of the constitution.

Informal Methods for Changing Constitutions

Many state constitutions change dramatically without a formal amendment process. The most common route of informal constitutional change is via the state supreme courts—for example, when a court interprets an existing constitution in a way that creates a new right, such as the right to an adequate or equitable education.

Sometimes constitutional changes also come about from **judicial review**. In December 1999, the Vermont Supreme Court directed the state legislature to pass a law that would provide for civil unions. Its rationale? The court found that because the state constitution was "instituted for the common benefit, protection and security of the people," the state government could not refuse to provide

the benefit of marriage to gay people. To those who objected that the state constitution, which was enacted in 1793 and at the time was a model of brevity at 8,200 words, said nothing about gay marriage, the court explained that its job was "to distill the essence, the motivating idea of the framers," not to be bound by eighteenth-century notions of jurisprudence.[23] In November 2003, the Massachusetts Supreme Court went further when it declared the state's ban on same-sex marriage unconstitutional, which prompted efforts to amend not just state constitutions but the U.S. Constitution as well to define marriage explicitly as a union between a man and a woman. While the attempt to amend the U.S. Constitution mostly fizzled, as of 2012 thirty states had amended their constitutions specifically to ban same-sex marriage.

State constitutions can also change when other branches of government successfully lay claim to broader powers. For example, Rhode Island's legislature has used its strong constitutional position—a clause in the state constitution says that the General Assembly "can exercise any power" unless the constitution explicitly forbids it—to take control of functions that most states delegate to governors. This means that in Rhode Island legislators not only sit on the boards and commissions that oversee a range of state agencies, but also dominate the board that sets the salaries for high-ranking executive branch officials. Not surprisingly, this has given the legislature a great deal of power over executive branch decisions. In short, Rhode Island has just the type of government that John Adams feared.

Southern states such as Florida, Mississippi, and Texas also tend to have constitutions that provide for weak governors. In these cases, this arrangement is a legacy of the post–Civil War **Reconstruction** period. During Reconstruction, the victorious Union Army forced most of the former Confederate states to replace their constitutions. Reconstruction ended in 1876, and the Union troops withdrew. With the exception of Arkansas, North Carolina, and Tennessee, the southern states soon abandoned their revised constitutions in favor of new ones that greatly weakened gubernatorial powers.[24] Part of the reasoning for this was that weak governors could be

---

Judicial Review
The power of courts to assess whether a law is in compliance with the constitution.

Reconstruction
The period following the Civil War when the southern states were governed under the direction of the Union army.

Procedures for Constitutional Amendment by Legislature

MAP 3-3

Legislative Vote Required for Proposal

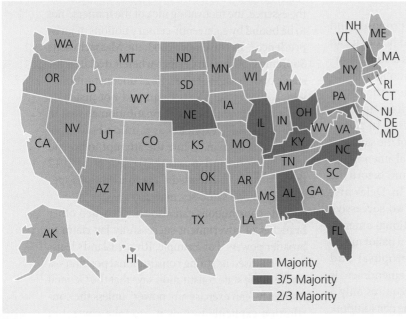

Majority

3/5 Majority

2/3 Majority

Source: Data from *The Book of the States 2012* (Lexington, KY: Council of State Governments, 2012), Table 1.1, http://knowledgecenter.csg.org/drupal/content/book-states-2012-chapter-1-state-constitutions.

MAP 3-4

Vote Required for Ratification

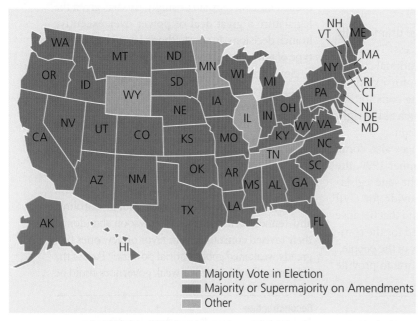

Majority Vote in Election

Majority or Supermajority on Amendments

Other

Source: Data from *The Book of the States 2012* (Lexington, KY: Council of State Governments, 2012), Table 1.1, http://knowledgecenter.csg.org/drupal/content/book-states-2012-chapter-1-state-constitutions.

kept from enacting policies that the federal government encouraged but that were contrary to the norms of these traditionalistic states. This had happened during Reconstruction, when the governors of the states that had seceded from the Union were replaced by individuals sympathetic to the federal government in Washington or were forced to cooperate with federal policy in regard to such issues as African American rights. For example, in 1885, Florida passed a constitution that took away the governor's right to appoint his own cabinet; members were elected instead. Although it has been amended many times since, that constitution is still in effect today. As a result, Florida has one of the weakest governorships in the country.[25]

Of course, state legislatures do not always gain the upper hand. In states whose constitutions give governors the edge, some chief executives have been very aggressive in expanding their powers. Although their techniques do not involve written amendments to the state constitutions themselves, they do affect the distribution of powers within state government—a function that is a primary concern of state constitutions.

State constitutions may also be changed in another way—through simple neglect. Sometimes state governments just stop enforcing obscure or repugnant sections of their state constitutions, effectively changing the constitutions in the process. No politician today would dare to argue for denying the vote to individuals simply because they are poor or do not own land or belong to a minority group. Yet

A Difference
That Makes *a Difference*

State Constitutions and the Right to Marry

"By the power vested in me, by the state of . . ." These words are repeated by wedding officials every day, in every state. States control who can marry and when. In Nebraska, teens younger than nineteen need their parents' permission to marry, while over the state line in Kansas, people can walk down the aisle at eighteen. A number of states prohibited interracial couples from marrying until 1967, when the U.S. Supreme Court declared Virginia's law unconstitutional in *Loving v. Virginia.* Today, debate rages around gay marriage. Just six states—Connecticut, Iowa, Massachusetts, New Hampshire, New York, and Vermont—have legalized the unions, while thirty states have amended their constitutions to prohibit them. Several additional states recognize domestic partnerships or civil unions, which grant couples some of the same state-level benefits as marriage. Washington, DC, which is technically a federal city and not a state, allows gay marriage.

Legalization of gay marriage has been achieved through judicial review (in Connecticut, Iowa, and Massachusetts) and through legislation (New Hampshire, New York, and Vermont). Gay marriage has had a less fortunate time at the polls, where voters have rejected it time and time again—most recently in North Carolina in 2012. The most high-profile fight so far was waged in California in 2008 over Proposition 8, a ballot measure that sought to amend the state's constitution to define marriage as a union between one man and one woman—and to put a stop to the same-sex marriages that had begun there in June 2008, after the state supreme court ruled that the state's ban was unconstitutional. After both sides spent more than $55 million on their campaigns, voters narrowly approved Prop. 8. Approval of new same-sex marriages was halted, but the state continues to consider the more than eighteen thousand couples who wed legally as married.

The victory of Proposition 8 prompted further debate among proponents of gay marriage, some of whom wonder whether, given their continued defeats at the polls, they should wait to wage new legalization campaigns across the states. But the fight over Prop. 8 isn't finished—and it's not even limited to within the state's borders anymore. In April 2009, Theodore Olson, the former U.S. solicitor general, filed a brief in federal court challenging the amendment. In 2010, a federal district court ruled that Proposition 8 unconstitutionally violated the due process and equal protection clauses of the Fourteenth Amendment, a decision that was upheld in 2012 by a federal appeals court. As of this writing, the case has been appealed to the U.S. Supreme Court. If the Court accepts the case, the justices could make a ruling that will clarify whether or not same-sex couples have the same right to marry as heterosexual couples.

Sources: Christine Vestal, "Gay Marriage Legal in Six States," *Stateline*, June 4, 2009, www.stateline.org/live/details/story?contentId=347390; Ballotwatch, Initiative and Referendum Institute, "Same-Sex Marriage: Breaking the Firewall in California?," October 2008; Jo Becker, "A Conservative's Road to Same-Sex Marriage Advocacy," *New York Times*, August 18, 2009, www.nytimes.com/2009/08/19/us/19olson.html.

until 1999, Texas's constitution contained a provision limiting the right to vote to citizens who owned land and paid a poll tax. The state government had stopped enforcing these objectionable requirements long before but had neglected to actually repeal them. Likewise, Alabama's constitution outlawed interracial marriages until an amendment overturned the ban in 2000; the state had informally dropped enforcement of the provision years earlier.

Why State Constitutions Vary

Without a doubt, state constitutions vary widely from state to state. What explains these differences? Four factors seem particularly important: historical circumstances, political culture, geography, and changing notions of good government.

To understand how historical circumstances and culture can create a constitution—and then be shaped by that constitution—consider the case of Texas. The Lone Star State's current constitution was written in 1876, soon after federal troops had withdrawn and Reconstruction had ended. During Reconstruction, a strong Unionist governor backed by federal troops had governed the state, centralized police and education functions in state hands in Austin, and generally defied the white Democrats who had been in power before the Civil War. So Texas followed in the footsteps of other southern states and drew up a constitution designed to ensure that the state would never again have an activist state government. Toward that end, the new constitution allowed the legislature to meet only infrequently, limited the governor's power over the executive branch, and provided for an elected judiciary. The document's sole progressive feature was a provision that for the first time allowed women to continue to own their own property after they were married.[26]

White Democrats' antipathy toward Reconstruction explains much of the content of Texas's 1876 constitution. The state's political culture explains why its constitution has endured to the present. Political scientist Daniel Elazar classifies Texas as a traditionalistic/individualistic state that, in his words, "places a premium on limiting community intervention" and "accepts a natural hierarchical society as part of the ordered nature of things."[27] Although Elazar's categories have blurred in recent years, state constitutions continue to bear them out. In short, Texas's constitution is well suited to the state's political culture—a culture that views strong activist government with suspicion.

In contrast, a constitution that allowed the legislature to meet only every other year would suit a moralistic state poorly. Not surprisingly, moralistic states such as Michigan, Minnesota, and Wisconsin allow their legislatures to meet far more frequently than does Texas. Because they envision fairly robust styles of governance, the constitutions in these states allow the legislatures to meet throughout the year, creating what are, for all intents and purposes, full-time professional legislatures.

New England's propensity for short, framework-oriented constitutions is a variation based noticeably on geography. One political scientist has hypothesized that such a variation may reflect the fact that New England states are small and relatively homogeneous and that their citizens are thus less inclined to fight to include policies they support in their states' constitutions.[28]

Of course, history, political culture, and geography aren't the only factors that determine the kind of constitution a state will have. Another important factor is the changing sense of what works best. In the early nineteenth century, many states concluded that a system in which the legislature operates with unbridled power simply did not work well, so they changed their constitutions in ways that strengthened the chief executive. Eighty years ago, groups such as the National Municipal League argued that state constitutions should be more like the federal constitution; that is, they should be much shorter documents that provide a framework for governance rather than long documents that get into the details of policies. That argument gave rise to the **model constitution**, a kind of ideal that states interested in "improving" could adopt. During the 1960s and 1970s, many states did revise their constitutions in ways designed to make their governments more effective, although the last edition of the model constitution was written in 1968.

Since the mid–twentieth century, however, some political scientists have questioned the assumptions behind the model constitution movement. To these revisionists, the fact that most state constitutions outside New England are long and policy rich is actually a good thing—a healthy sign of an engaged electorate. Revisionists

> Of course, history, political culture, and geography aren't the only factors that determine the kind of constitution a state will have. Another important factor is the changing sense of what works best.

Model Constitution
An expert-approved generic or "ideal" constitution that states sometimes use as a yardstick against which they can measure their existing constitutions.

argue that citizens have defended their right to participate by shaping their state constitutions.[29]

How State Constitutions Differ

The most obvious ways in which state constitutions differ involve their length and ease of amendment. These differences are not simply cosmetic; they almost always reflect the different functions that state constitutions serve. Vermont has the shortest state constitution. Like the U.S. Constitution, its goal is primarily to establish a framework for effective government, not to regulate the details of specific policy matters. This is true to a lesser extent of the constitutions of other states in New England as well.

In contrast, constitutions in other regions tend to be longer and more specific in their policy prescriptions. In most states, voters and interest groups that want to accomplish such goals as increased state spending on education will lobby the governor or the legislature. In California, a state with a long, policy-specific constitution that provides for a high degree of direct democracy, people often try to amend the constitution instead. Although the majority of political scientists wring their hands about this tendency, it is undeniable that Californians play a role in shaping their constitution that voters in New England cannot. Also note that these two differences—length and ease of amendment—not only reflect differences in goals and purposes but also directly influence each other. If a constitution is easier to amend, it makes sense that it is more likely to get amended—and that usually means it gets longer. Again, a difference makes a difference.

Operating Rules and Selection for Office

State constitutions create varying organizational structures and operating rules for the constituent elements of the state government. They establish different methods and requirements for serving in state politics. Some of these differences reflect the historical differences among states as well as variations in political culture and geography.

Other differences reflect differing notions of what makes good government. Sometimes these notions can be quite quirky. For example, to serve as the governor of Oklahoma, a state of 3.7 million people, you must be at least thirty-one years old, but to be the chief executive of California—population 37 million—you need only be eighteen. You might be eligible to lead one of the nation's largest states, but don't plan on buying beer or wine, even at your own fund-raisers!

In addition, state constitutions differ widely in how many statewide elected positions they create and how those positions are filled. One of the most important of these differences has to do with the judiciary. At the federal level, judges are selected by the president and approved by the U.S. Senate. Things work very differently in the states. Some states elect their judges, some states appoint their judges, many states use a combination of appointment and election, and some states use different selection methods for different types of courts. The details of these various systems and their particular pros and cons are discussed in depth in chapter 9. What's important for our purposes here is that there are big differences from state to state in how judges end up on the bench, and those differences are products of different constitutional approaches to structuring and staffing the judicial branch of government.

Virginia's executive mansion is the oldest continuously occupied governor's residence in the United States. It has been the home of Virginia's governors since 1813

Even seemingly small institutional differences created by different constitutional approaches can have big impacts on how state governments work. For example, if a state's constitution gives the executive strong veto powers, the governor may have an easier time getting a recalcitrant legislature to consider his or her point of view on a particular piece of legislation than would a governor with weak veto powers. Similarly, some studies show that elected judges are more likely than those more insulated from the ballot box to uphold the death penalty in cases involving capital crimes.[30] In short, the different operating rules embedded in state constitutions lead to very different types of governance.

Distribution of Power

State constitutions make widely differing decisions about where power should reside. Although all state constitutions make at least a bow toward the principle of the separation of powers, in actuality many give one branch of government a preponderance of power. Under some state constitutions, the reins of government are clearly in the hands of the legislature or general assembly. Other states have amended their constitutions to give executives the upper hand.

Traditionally, state constitutions tended to create stronger legislatures and weaker executives. In recent decades, however, even though strong state legislatures are still the norm, constitutional changes in many states have bolstered governors' powers. More than forty state constitutions now give governors the important power of the **line-item veto**, the ability to veto certain portions of appropriations bills while approving the rest. Exactly what counts as an item, and thus what is fair game for a governor's veto pen, is often unclear. As a result, line-item veto court cases have become a common part of the legal landscape.

Some states go even further. In Wisconsin, for example, the state constitution allows the governor the power to strike out an appropriation entirely and write in a lower figure.[31] During his term in office, Wisconsin governor Tommy Thompson pushed the power of the partial veto to strike passages and even individual words from bills that came to his desk. In some cases, Thompson would strike individual letters from bills to create entirely new words, changing the entire meaning of the legislation. Critics came to call Thompson's creative writing "the Vanna White veto." In one case, Thompson used the Vanna White veto and his Scrabble skills to transform a piece of legislation from a bill that set the maximum detention period for juvenile offenders at forty-eight hours into one that allowed for a ten-day detention period, a move that enraged the Democratic legislature.[32] Voters later amended the constitution to prohibit that particular veto maneuver. Yet, despite the controversies that surrounded such actions, during his record fourteen-year reign, none of Thompson's more than 1,900 budget vetoes was ever overturned by the legislature.[33]

The power structures set up by the constitutional systems of some states resist easy classification. Take Texas, for example. The fact that the legislature meets for only five or six months every other year might lead you to think that power in Texas resides primarily with the governor. Not so. In fact, the Texas constitution arguably makes the office of lieutenant governor the most powerful in the state. In Texas, the lieutenant governor presides over the Senate, appoints Senate committees and assigns bills, and chairs the powerful Texas Legislative Council, which is responsible for researching and drafting bills. Indeed, many observers attribute George W. Bush's two successful

Line-Item Veto
The power to reject a portion of a bill while leaving the rest intact.

terms as governor to his close relationship with his lieutenant governor, Bob Bullock, a Democrat.

Rights Granted

State constitutions differ not only in the mechanisms of governance they create and the sets of constraints and powers they give to government but also in the rights they confer on citizens. For example, the U.S. Constitution does not explicitly mention a right to privacy, although the U.S. Supreme Court did define a limited right to privacy in *Griswold v. Connecticut* (1965). In contrast, Montana's constitution states that "the right to individual privacy is essential to the well-being of a free society and shall not be infringed without the showing of a compelling state interest."[34] As a result, courts in Montana—and in Kentucky and Tennessee—have interpreted the state constitution to protect adults' freedom to engage in consensual oral or anal sex, which until quite recently was illegal in many other states.[35]

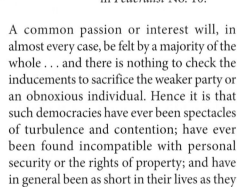

Even rights that are directly addressed by the U.S. Constitution are often expanded, clarified, or given more specifics in state constitutions. For example, the Second Amendment says, "A well regulated Militia, being necessary to the security of a free State, the right of the people to keep and bear Arms, shall not be infringed." Legal scholars have been arguing over the meaning of this vaguely worded amendment for a long time—is the right purely an individual right? If so, the government has a narrow basis for regulating private ownership of firearms. Or is the right attached to the necessity of a "well regulated Militia"? If that's the case, it suggests a more expansive basis for government regulation of firearms. No such confusion is raised by Nebraska's state constitution, which says that "the right to keep and bear arms for security or defense of self, family, home, and others, and for lawful common defense, hunting, recreational use, and all other lawful purposes, and such rights shall not be denied or infringed."

Representative Government versus Direct Democracy

One of the most striking differences among state constitutions is the degree to which they have (or have not) embraced direct democracy. Most Americans celebrate the United States as a democracy, but the founders believed that they were establishing something different—a representative democracy. This is a form of government in which qualified representatives of the public make the decisions. Most of the founders viewed direct, or pure, democracy with suspicion. A "pure democracy, by which I mean a society consisting of a small number of citizens, who assemble and administer the government in person, can admit of no cure for the mischiefs of faction," warned James Madison, one of the primary authors of the U.S. Constitution, in his famous argument for the document in *Federalist* No. 10:

A common passion or interest will, in almost every case, be felt by a majority of the whole . . . and there is nothing to check the inducements to sacrifice the weaker party or an obnoxious individual. Hence it is that such democracies have ever been spectacles of turbulence and contention; have ever been found incompatible with personal security or the rights of property; and have in general been as short in their lives as they have been violent in their deaths.[36]

In other words, Madison believed that entrusting a simple majority with the power to carry out its will would lead to fickle and tyrannical behavior and to a government that would teeter between anarchy and autocracy.

The U.S. Constitution's solution to the problem of pure democracy was to create a representative government, or, as Madison saw it, government by a small group of elected officials "whose wisdom may best discern the true interest of their country."[37] In accordance with this belief, the U.S. Constitution created an upper chamber—the

Senate—whose members would be selected by state legislatures from among their eminent men. The document also created an electoral college to elect the president. Both of these decisions were made to insulate the federal government from the whims of the majority. The Constitution makes no provision for direct democratic processes. There is not a single federal officeholder *directly* elected by the entire nation. Whereas the creators of the federal government took great care to ensure it was insulated from direct democratic processes, many states decided to do just the opposite during the Progressive Era. By giving their citizens the chance to make laws and change their constitutions directly, the Progressives sought to circumvent legislatures and executives they viewed as being beholden to wealthy special interests. As Robert M. La Follette, a leader of the Progressive Party in Wisconsin and later a governor and senator from the state, put it,

the forces of the special privileges are deeply entrenched. Their resources are inexhaustible. Their efforts are never lax. Their political methods are insidious. It is impossible for the people to maintain perfect organization in mass. They are often taken unaware and are liable to lose at one stroke the achievements of years of effort. In such a crisis, nothing but the united power of the people expressed directly through the ballot can overthrow the enemy.[38]

For politicians like La Follette, direct democratic mechanisms, such as the ballot initiative and the referendum, represented the general populace's best hope for breaking the power of political bosses and moneyed interests. From 1902 through 1918, direct democracy enjoyed a great vogue in the states. Sixteen states adopted the ballot initiative in that period. After World War I, ballot initiatives lost some of their luster as popular enthusiasm for Progressive ideas waned. Only five states—Alaska (1959), Florida (1968), Wyoming (1968), Illinois (1970), and Mississippi (1992)—have amended their constitutions to allow for ballot initiatives since the end of the Progressive Era.[39] What's more,

note where these states are located. The majority of the states that allow direct democracy lie west of the Mississippi River, where the practice fits with much of the West's populist history.[40]

For decades, initiatives and referendums were used sparingly. Then came Proposition 13 in California. In the 1970s, taxpayer activist Howard Jarvis and retired real estate salesman Paul Gann launched what at first seemed a foolishly impractical campaign to roll back California property taxes and cap the rate at which they could grow. Their campaign struck a chord with many Californians. The state's booming economy had sent property values skyrocketing. Higher property assessments led to higher real estate taxes, which created a huge revenue boom for the state and local governments. Indeed, at the time the state government had a $5 billion annual surplus. Yet despite the public outcry for relief from rising property costs, Governor Jerry Brown and the rest of the politicians in Sacramento could not agree on a tax reduction plan.

In 1978, California voters passed Proposition 13 and took the decision out of their hands. It directed the state to roll back real estate taxes to 1975 levels and decreed that property assessments could not increase by more than 2 percent a year, regardless of inflation. Most localities previously had reassessed real estate taxes every two years. Proposition 13 decreed that property could be reassessed only when it was sold. The legislation also cut property tax receipts in half and marked the beginning of a nationwide "taxpayer revolt."

California's political establishment viewed the passage of Proposition 13 with great trepidation. Politicians worried that it would cripple their ability to pay for the schools and infrastructure that had contributed so much to California's post–World War II successes. These fears proved well founded. In the wake of Proposition 13, California went from having one of the nation's best-funded public school systems (in the top third in terms of per-pupil spending) to having one of the worst (in the bottom third). The proposition put such draconian limits on the ability of local governments to raise revenues that municipalities and counties became increasingly dependent on the state for their funding—so much so that ten years later, in 1988, California teachers' unions pushed through Proposition 98, which mandated that upward of 40 percent of California's general revenue go to education.[41]

In addition to complicating government finances and drastically reducing the flexibility of lawmakers in California, the success of Proposition 13 revived interest in ballot initiatives in the twenty-four other states in which they were permitted. In the three decades from 1940 through 1970, an average of nineteen initiatives appeared on ballots per two-year election cycle in the United States. In the 1980s, that number shot up to fifty initiatives in the average election cycle. In the 1990s, it hit seventy-six per election cycle.[42] Many of these initiatives were proposed constitutional amendments, and their sheer numbers suggest that states allowing ballot initiatives are now engaged in an almost continuous cycle of changing their constitutions. These changes are increasingly less about broad questions of good governance and more about pushing narrow agendas.

In the past two decades, the initiative process has been used to push through legislation on some of the most controversial political issues in the entire country. Oregon voters used a ballot initiative to narrowly (51–49 percent) approve physician-assisted suicide in 1994. In California, voters have used initiatives to impose some of the nation's strictest term limits on elected officials (Proposition 140), to end affirmative action (Propositions 209 and 96), to deny education and health benefits to families of illegal immigrants (Proposition 87), to spend $3 billion on stem-cell research (Proposition 71),

and to recall a sitting governor and replace him with an action movie star.

The initiative process has become big business. In 2004, more than $200 million was spent in the battles waged over California's ballot measures alone.[43] Several companies are devoted to gathering the signatures needed to get issues placed on ballots for anyone who can afford their services. Signature gathering can be a pretty lucrative business—in 2010 and 2012, it cost, on average, more than a million dollars to collect enough signatures to get a proposal certified and on a state ballot.[44] Those who have used ballot initiatives successfully see them as tools for circumventing hostile legislatures and acting on the will of the majority. Most political scientists and close observers of state politics have a different viewpoint. They argue that the record of ballot initiatives confirms that the founders were wise to keep direct democratic processes out of the U.S. Constitution because at the state level these processes have been hijacked by individuals who use initiatives to further their own self-interests.

Veteran *Washington Post* political reporter David Broder describes ballot initiatives in scathing terms:

> At the start of a new century—and millennium—a new form of government is

Qwest Field, home of the Seattle Seahawks, was made possible by a ballot initiative that provided $300 million in public financing for construction of the stadium. The team's owner, billionaire and Microsoft cofounder Paul Allen, financed the successful ballot initiative.

spreading in the United States. It is alien to the spirit of the Constitution and its careful system of checks and balances. Though derived from a reform favored by Populists and Progressives as a cure for special-interest influence, this method of lawmaking has become the favored tool of millionaires and interest groups that use their wealth to achieve their own policy goals—a lucrative business for a new set of political entrepreneurs.[45]

Exploiting the public's disdain for politics and distrust of politicians, interest groups with deep pockets now have a mechanism through which they can literally rewrite state constitutions to advance their own agendas. For example, in 1997, Microsoft cofounder and Seattle Seahawks owner Paul Allen made an end run around a balky state legislature and spent $6 million on a ballot initiative that required the state of Washington to foot much of the cost for a new stadium for his team. It proved to be a good investment; the initiative passed with 51 percent of the vote. Although this was welcome news for many football fans, most political scientists probably see it as an illustration of the very problem that Madison identified in *Federalist* No. 10. In some ways, the initiative has created a very odd form of governance in which citizens vote for and live under laws that are often opposed by their elected governments.

Constitutions for Local Government?

For the most part, substate governments, such as school districts, counties, and municipalities, are considered subordinate arms of the state. They draw their legal authority from state law and the discretion of state governments, not from their own citizens in the form of their own constitutions.

There are some exceptions to this rule. The **municipal charter** is a key example. In a rough sense, municipal charters are similar to the charters that served as the governing documents for the original colonies. Legally, most municipalities are corporations, and their charters describe the purposes of the municipality and the processes for achieving these objectives. A charter is not a constitution;

rather, it is a grant of authority derived from a constitution or from state law. Some states have **home rule**, which allows municipalities the right to draft and amend their own charters and to regulate local matters within their jurisdictions without interference from the state. Some states have municipal home rule provisions in their constitutions; others grant home rule to municipalities through legislation. Municipal home rule means that some local governments are operated by charters that "can take on many characteristics of a constitution."[46] Even in the most liberal home rule states, however, state constitutions and state law generally take precedence over municipal charters.

Conclusion

Even though you rarely read about them in the newspaper—much less hear about them on the evening news—state constitutions play *the* critical role in defining the possibilities of politics in most states. All state constitutions set the basic structure of government, apportion power and responsibilities to particular institutions and political actors, and determine the rights and privileges of citizenship. State constitutions reflect states' distinctive political cultures and, over time, reinforce or alter those traditions.

Beyond this common core of shared functions, however, state constitutions vary greatly. Some protect and extend the rights of the individual beyond the guarantees of the U.S. Constitution; others do not. Perhaps the single biggest difference among state constitutions is the degree to which they serve as a venue for policymaking. In western states, whose constitutions provide for a high degree of direct democracy, advocates and interest groups often attempt to enshrine their policy positions in the state constitutions. As a result, these states have long, detailed constitutions. In contrast, the constitutions of the eastern states, particularly in New England, more closely resemble the U.S. Constitution.

Municipal Charter
A document that establishes operating procedures for a local government.

Home Rule
A form of self-governance granted to towns and cities by the state.

State constitutions tend to have a bad reputation with political scientists, for understandable reasons. Although many function well, in more than a few instances they play an outright disruptive role. In states such as Alabama and Texas, antiquated state constitutions have made it difficult for state governments to promote economic development—a function that most people believe the state government should serve. In California and other states, interest groups have used state constitutions to ensure that the states' general revenues flow toward the programs they support. In the process, they have reduced—in some areas drastically—the flexibility of legislatures to make independent decisions, a set of constraints that amounts to putting limits on representative democracy.

But, as political scientist Christopher Hammonds has argued from another perspective, the fact that constitutions continue to be a contentious venue for politics in many states is not necessarily all bad. Although it is still theoretically possible to change the U.S. Constitution, for all practical purposes we as a society have given that right over to the U.S. Supreme Court. It takes an extraordinarily contentious issue, such as reproductive rights, to provoke talk about changing the federal constitution. In contrast, citizens continue to exercise their right to tamper with and tweak their state constitutions. Is that all bad?

The Latest Research

State constitutions are one of the most important and understudied aspects of subnational government. While it is not hard to find constitutional scholars in political science, the vast majority of these study the U.S. Constitution, not its state counterparts. There is more attention paid to state constitutions in the field of law, but even here scholars focusing on state constitutions regularly lament the relative lack of research available on these centrally important legal documents.

This lack of attention is surprising because, as the studies listed below demonstrate, state constitutions reflect different philosophical notions of what a government is, what it should do, and what rights citizens should or should not have. These are not just abstract theoretical arguments; your marriage rights, to take one prominent example, are almost wholly determined by the constitution and the laws it authorizes in the state in which you reside.

Below we summarize some of the more recent and prominent research on state constitutions. All of these studies reflect a constant theme: not just the central importance of state constitutions to the American political system but also how those constitutions are constantly changing and creating differences in state-level legal structure that have big, real-world impacts on the lives of state residents.

• •

- **Williams, Robert F.** 2009. *The Law of American State Constitutions*. New York: Oxford University Press.

   Robert Williams is a one of the most widely recognized scholars of state constitutional law, and this book is one of the most comprehensive and up-to-date scholarly analyses available of the nature and purpose of state constitutions. This work is notable not just for its overview of the historical development of state constitutions, their structure, and their legal implications, but also for staking out a strong "positivist" position on these documents. Essentially, Williams argues that state constitutions should not be viewed as mini-versions of the U.S. Constitution. Instead, each should be viewed as a unique text and interpreted—by scholars and judges—within that framework. This argument amounts to a strong rejection of the so-called common principles approach, which views and interprets state constitutions basically as a branch of common law—that is, a set of cases or precedents.

- **Dinan, John J.** 2006. *The American State Constitutional Tradition.* Lawrence: University Press of Kansas.

   Many scholars have studied the U.S. Constitutional Convention of 1787 and debated the debates and negotiations among the delegates on the purposes of government, its appropriate structure and process, its proper limitations, and the rights it should or should not grant to citizens. Much less attention has been paid to the debates of state constitutional conventions, perhaps because there have been so many of them (more than one hundred, and for many of them we have much more detailed records than we have for the federal Constitutional Convention). Dinan sets out to rectify this, providing a sweeping study of the development of state constitutions. He finds that the delegates to state constitutional conventions have often taken different paths than those taken by their federal counterparts. For example, federal constitutional delegates mostly had a negative concept of individual liberty; they worried about protecting citizens from the intrusions of government. State constitutional delegates have been much more willing to adopt a positive concept of liberty, seeing the government as a tool to enforce and maintain individual rights. These differences make a big difference in the substance and structure of state constitutions compared to the federal constitution.

- **Krislov, Marvin, and Daniel Katz**. 2008. "Taking State Constitutions Seriously." *Cornell Journal of Law and Public Policy* 71: 295–342.

This is a study of how state constitutions change. In comparison with the federal constitution, state constitutions generally have much less restrictive amendment processes, and even within individual states there may be multiple avenues to constitutional change. While noting the huge variation across states in these amendment processes, Krislov and Katz pay particular attention to direct democratic processes. Their analysis shows that such processes, in particular constitutional initiatives, have become a primary method of amending state constitutions. Yet even among states that allow ballot initiatives there is substantial variation in the rules and procedures for passage of a constitutional initiative. This study suggests that those differences create different sets of incentives for groups to pursue constitutional change and that the rapid shifts in state constitutional content create particular challenges for the process of state-level judicial review.

- **Lupia, Arthur, Yanna Krupnikov, Adam Seth Levine, Spencer Piston, and Alexander Von Hagen-Jamar**. 2010. "Why State Constitutions Differ in Their Treatment of Same-Sex Marriage." *Journal of Politics* 72: 1222–1235.

This is an interesting companion study to the Krislov and Katz article. This team of researchers examines state-level variation in attitudes toward same-sex marriage and constitutional outcomes. One of the surprising findings of their study is that attitudes correlate fairly poorly with constitutional amendments on same-sex marriage. Public opinion regarding same-sex marriage does not differ greatly between states with constitutional amendments banning the practice and those without such amendments. The authors find that the differences that do exist are explained, at least in part, by the relative complexity of the rules and regulations associated with constitutional amendment. In other words, the fact that U.S. state constitutions differ in the legal status of same-sex marriage has less to do with attitudes on that topic in the states and much more to do with the institutional arrangements established by those constitutions to translate the will of the people into state law.

Chapter Review

Key Concepts

- appropriations bills (p. 60)
- ballot initiative (p. 64)
- bicameral legislature (p. 61)
- colonial charters (p. 60)
- constitutional amendments (p. 57)

- constitutional convention (p. 62)
- constitutional revision commission (p. 66)
- direct democracy (p. 56)
- dual constitutionalism (p. 57)
- electorate (p. 56)
- franchise (p. 62)
- home rule (p. 76)
- Jim Crow laws (p. 62)
- judicial federalism (p. 57)
- judicial review (p. 67)
- line-item veto (p. 72)
- model constitution (p. 70)
- municipal charter (p. 76)
- natural law, or higher law (p. 57)
- plenary power (p. 59)
- ratification (p. 64)
- Reconstruction (p. 67)
- referendum (p. 64)
- separation of powers (p. 61)
- unicameral legislature (p. 61)

Suggested Websites

- **http://camlaw.rutgers.edu/statecon/statecon_1.html.** Website for Rutgers University's Center for State Constitutional Studies.

- **www.iandrinstitute.org.** Website for the Initiative and Referendum Institute at the University of Southern California, a clearinghouse for information about the initiative and referendum processes of the states.

State Stats on Constitutions

Explore and compare data on the states! Go to **college.cqpress .com/sites/essentials-govstateandlocal** to do these exercises.

1. Some scholars say that unicameral government works best when its citizens are a relatively small, homogenous group. Explore the demographic information for Nebraska. What about Nebraska's population makes it suited for unicameral government? Are there any states that are more homogeneous than Nebraska? Why don't they have unicameral governments?

2. Vermont is the only state that does not have a balanced budget requirement. How does its outstanding government debt load

compare to its neighboring states' debt load? Is this surprising? Why or why not?

3. Recall this chapter's example of a Colorado ballot initiative written at the postgraduate reading level. What percentage of the population in Colorado is college graduates? Why might the ballot initiative, as written, be a problem for voters? Are there any states with lower college graduation rates? What are the implications of these numbers?

4. What percentage of the population in California is foreign born? What about Montana? How might differences in the makeup of the electorate in these states impact their laws?

5. What was the percentage change in Nevada's population of eighteen to twenty-four year olds from 1990 to 2000? How might this type of change influence (or not) the kinds of policies that the citizens want? What does this kind of change generally do to voter turnout? Did this happen in Nevada?

State governments aren't the only ones that have had to deal with lingering revenue shortfalls as a result of recession. In the past few years, some local governments have been so financially stressed they've been forced into bankruptcy. In 2012, Stockton, California, became the largest municipality ever to go bust.

Finance

FILLING THE TILL
AND PAYING THE BILLS

- What are the differences between progressive and regressive tax systems?
- Why are property taxes so important to communities?
- How does the federal government support state and local budgets?
- Are states' revenue and spending programs sustainable?

A combination of poor economic conditions and bad fiscal decisions had been pushing Detroit, Michigan, toward a financial cliff for years. On July 18, 2013, the city fell off the edge—right into the arms of Chapter 9 bankruptcy and the record books. It now has the dubious honor of being the largest city in U.S. history to go bust.

Detroit is far from being the only local government in the United States to find itself in financial straits. While the economy may have stabilized since the Great Recession, it has not fully recovered, and the coffers of some governments have simply not been able to support the wait for better economic times. Harrisburg, the capital of Pennsylvania, went into receivership in 2011. Montgomery County, the largest county in Alabama, filed for bankruptcy the same year. Central Falls, Rhode Island, became insolvent in 2010. Stockton, California, went bust in 2012.

Step up a level of government and the picture is just a little less alarming. No state has declared bankruptcy—at least not yet—and the budget situation in many states is actually improving compared to a few years ago. No one is popping champagne corks though. Finances at the state level have managed to advance only from the catastrophic to the merely very bad. For fiscal year 2013, states faced a combined shortfall of $55 billion.[1] That's a whopping combined budgetary shortfall, but it is still a big improvement over a few years ago when a single state—California— was struggling to close a $50 billion hole in its budget. In other words, states are a long way from the let-the-good-times-roll numbers that policymakers would prefer to see on their balance sheets. Revenues still struggle to keep pace with obligations, and many states still face uncomfortable choices between cutting spending and raising taxes—or doing both.

Deficits are a bigger problem for state and local governments than they are for their national counterpart. For the federal government, a budget shortfall is an embarrassment, not a crisis. Virtually all the states (Vermont is the only exception) are required by law to balance their operating budgets every year, and most local governments are in the same boat. When the bills add up to more than what's coming in at the federal level, Congress is free to borrow to cover the gap. In other words, the federal government can run **budget deficits** as much as it likes. Not so for state and local governments. They can delay the inevitable by jiggering the books with fancy accounting tricks and hoping for the best, but the sharpest of bean counters cannot shield them from the hard fact that the law requires their ledgers to be balanced. When income minus expenditure results in a negative number, they cannot just borrow or print money and hope the future will somehow provide an easy way out; they have to figure out how to get more revenue and/or cut spending.

The Great Recession of 2008–2009 pushed many states toward a financial implosion because they simply could not manage that balancing act. The **revenues** that keep states functioning—especially income, sales, and property taxes—dropped precipitously, and unemployment rates rose above 10 percent. In a single year's span, between June 2008 and June 2009, state income tax receipts plunged by more than a quarter.[2] At the same time, consumer demand dried up, taking with it state sales tax revenues, and the housing crisis sent property values— and their resulting taxes—tumbling. That all happened just as demand for state services jumped; the demand for Medicaid, unemployment insurance, public colleges, and even libraries increases during a downturn.

States were rescued from this crisis by the **American Recovery and Reinvestment Act (ARRA)**, a $787 billion package passed by Congress that was designed to stimulate the economy with targeted tax cuts, job creation, and government investments. Almost $300 billion of the stimulus was earmarked to help prop up state and local government programs, including $87 billion for state Medicaid programs and a $53.6 billion state fiscal stabilization fund, which most states used in 2009 and 2010 to stave off deep cuts to education and emergency services.[3] This massive financial injection made the federal government the single largest

---

American Recovery and Reinvestment Act (ARRA)
A $787 billion federal government package intended to stimulate economic growth during the recession of 2008–2009.

Budget Deficit, or Shortfall
Cash shortage that results when the amount of money coming in to the government falls below the amount being spent.

Revenues
The money governments bring in, mainly from taxes.

source of revenue for state and local governments for a year or two, but by 2012 the federal government was turning off the tap. This kept states and localities in a tough financial bind; their income sources were slowly starting to rise, but they were still struggling to approach prerecession levels, and the federal government was no longing shoveling cash their way. So state and local governments went right on looking for new revenue sources and spending cuts and resigned themselves to being less hopeful of finding a billion or two of extra federal aid between the couch cushions. The upshot is that these days there is less danger of a massive, widespread fiscal tsunami swamping all states and localities than there is of the odd government being unable to keep treading financial water and slipping under a sea of red ink.

In 2009, residents of the United States paid approximately $4,160 in state and local taxes per person.[4] Along with **user fees**, those collections raised about $2.2 trillion.[5] State and local governments use these funds along with federal grant dollars to do everything from financing local schools and state universities to providing health insurance for low-income families and people with disabilities to building highways. The money also helps maintain correctional facilities that house more than 2 million people per year and provides police and fire protection to the remaining approximately 310 million of the population. In short, state and local taxes pay for the programs that Americans care most about and that most directly affect their daily lives.

There is a tendency to think of taxes and budgets as a bit of a yawn—isn't this topic dry, technical, and, boring? We'll be the first to admit that *The Fiscal Survey of States* is not exactly most people's idea of a rollicking good read, but this topic is actually among the most important and consequential in this book. Budgets are the subject of some of the most intense political struggles in state and local politics, and not just because people care about money. Budgets are extremely important because they are fundamentally about policy. Indeed, in many ways they are *the* central policy

documents of government. They determine and reflect the policy orientations of elected leaders. If you want to know what your state or local government's priorities are, its budget will tell you.

> Budgets are extremely important because they are fundamentally about policy. Indeed, in many ways they are *the* central policy documents of government. They determine and reflect the policy orientations of elected leaders. If you want to know what your state or local government's priorities are, its budget will tell you.

This chapter discusses how state and local governments raise money, how they decide to spend it via the budget process, and what they spend it on. It examines why state and local governments make such different taxing and spending choices, and it explores the consequences of these varying choices. The chapter concludes with a discussion of how budgetary constraints and challenges are forcing many state and local governments to rethink how they pay for public services.

Show Me the Money: Where State Revenues Come From

More than half of the revenues of state and local governments in 2008 (the latest year for which comprehensive figures are available), or about $1.9 trillion, came from six primary taxes.[6] These were sales taxes, including **excise taxes**, often referred to as **sin taxes**, on tobacco and alcohol; property taxes;

User Fees
Charges levied by governments in exchange for services. Such fees constitute a type of hidden tax.

Excise, or Sin, Taxes
Taxes on alcohol, tobacco, and similar products that are designed to raise revenues and reduce use.

income taxes; motor vehicle taxes; **estate taxes**, also called death taxes; and **gift taxes**. As states struggled to balance their budgets in the last years of the decade, they increasingly turned to all of these taxes for help; they raised almost $24 billion in tax and fee increases in their 2010 budgets alone.[7]

Sales Taxes

Sales taxes account for roughly a third of total state and local government tax revenues. The lion's share—about 81 percent—of these funds are generated by state sales taxes, but roughly 7,500 local governments also levy a sales tax. Some states, such as California, also return a small percentage of sales taxes to the localities where the purchases were made. Overall, sales tax revenues account for nearly 16 percent of local government tax revenues nationwide.[8]

State governments also take in significant sums from gasoline taxes and sin taxes on tobacco and alcohol. Different states interpret these types of taxes very differently. Other factors often influence what gets taxed and for how much. North Carolina has a large tobacco-growing industry and imposes a tax of only $0.45 on each pack of cigarettes. New York has no large-scale tobacco industry and levies a tax of $4.35 per pack of cigarettes sold.[9]

Politicians like sales taxes because they tend to be less visible to their constituents than an income tax. As such, they are less likely to cause voters to retaliate against them at the polls. Economists like sales taxes because they are **focused consumption taxes** that do not distort consumer behavior. That is, sales taxes, even relatively high ones, often do not cause consumers to buy less.

Many liberals and advocates for low-income people, however, are critics of sales taxes. They complain that these are **regressive taxes**. If Bill Gates buys a grande latte at Seattle Starbucks, he pays about $0.28 in sales tax; a freshman at the University of Washington pays exactly the same. Although the amount of tax is the same, there is a big difference. The student is paying a much higher percentage of his or her income to the government than Mr. Gates. If Bill Gates's income were a mere $5 million a year and a typical student's income $2,500 a year, Mr. Gates would have to pay $566.20 in sales taxes on that latte to face the same **tax burden** as a typical student. To address concerns about low-income tax burden, states often exempt necessities such as food, clothing, and electric and gas utilities from taxation. In general, however, states relying heavily on sales taxes as primary funding sources unavoidably have more regressive tax systems.

Take, for example, Tennessee, a state that relies heavily on sales taxes rather than assessing personal income taxes. Rich and poor alike paid a 7-percent sales tax at the cash register in 2012. However, Memphis residents earning $25,000 a year or less paid an average of 12 percent of their incomes in state and local taxes—that is, about $2,993 for a family of three. In contrast, those residents earning $150,000 or more a year paid only 6.5 percent, or $9,718, of their incomes in taxes.[10] In other words, the better-off family paid more in absolute terms, but the less well-off family paid nearly twice as much in terms of proportion of income. That makes Tennessee's tax system highly regressive.

Besides being regressive, sales taxes have another problem—they simply are not bringing in as much revenue as they used to. In the words of James Hine,

---

Estate Taxes
Taxes levied on a person's estate or total holdings after that person's death.

Gift Taxes
Taxes imposed on money transfers made during an individual's lifetime.

Sales Taxes
Taxes levied by state and local governments on purchases.

Focused Consumption Taxes
Taxes that do not alter spending habits or behavior patterns and therefore do not distort the distribution of resources.

Regressive Taxes
Taxes levied on all taxpayers, regardless of income or ability to pay; they tend to place proportionately more of a burden on those with lower incomes.

Tax Burden
A measurement of taxes paid as a proportion of income.

a finance expert at Clemson University, relying on the sales tax "is like riding a horse that is rapidly dying." Two developments account for this. First, services have become a much more important part of the economy. In 1960, 41 percent of U.S. consumer dollars was spent on services. By 2000, that percentage had risen to 58 percent. Yet most sales taxes are still skewed toward the purchase of products rather than the purchase of services. Buy a robotic massage chair at the Mall of America in Bloomington, Minnesota, and you'll pay $58.20 in sales tax on that $800 item.[11] Hire an acupuncturist for an hour from a holistic medical center in Bloomington, and you'll pay no sales tax at all. Hawaii, New Mexico, South Dakota, and Wyoming have changed their tax codes so that sales taxes now apply to most professional and personal services.[12] However, most other states have been reluctant to follow suit because taxing services could put them at a competitive disadvantage. For instance, if Illinois were to place a sales tax on accounting services, there would probably be a sudden boom in business for CPAs in nearby Indiana.[13]

The second factor behind faltering sales tax revenues is the rise of the Internet and online shopping. In 1992, the U.S. Supreme Court ruled that states could not force companies to collect sales taxes for them in places where the companies had no physical presence. As a result, most online purchases are tax free. A study by William F. Fox and Donald Bruce of the University of Tennessee, Knoxville, found that the overall losses of sales tax revenue from Internet sales were $8.6 billion in 2010, and the researchers predicted losses as high as $11.4 billion per year by 2012.[14] For states such as Texas and Tennessee that don't have income taxes and that rely heavily on sales tax revenue, this trend is a big problem. To make up for the kind of revenue loss that Fox and Bruce have predicted, Texas would have to raise its current statewide sales tax rate from 6.25 percent to 7.86 percent.[15]

Absent federal intervention, states have banded together to collect taxes on online sales. Dozens of states have joined the Streamlined Sales Tax Project, agreeing to simplify their tax codes in exchange for the chance to convince retailers to collect the taxes voluntarily. The project went live in October 2005, with 150 retailers signing on in eighteen states.[16] By June 2011, more than 1,400 companies were participating in twenty-four states.[17] Several states, led by New York, jumped ahead of the project by passing laws mandating that Amazon.com and similar companies collect sales tax on purchases residents make from affiliates located in state. Amazon challenged the law, but the New York Superior Court upheld the state's law in 2009.[18] After years of controversy and legal battles, in 2012 California also managed to introduce a law requiring Amazon to collect local and state sales taxes. This was a big deal for the cash-strapped state government, which needed the revenue, but not such a good deal for California consumers—it added 7 to 10 percent to the cost of an Amazon purchase.[19]

Property Taxes

The second-largest source of tax revenue for state and local governments is property taxes. In 2009, property taxes raised approximately 33 percent, or $424 billion, of total state and local government tax revenues.[20] Most sales

Will that be cash or charge? Either way, these shoppers at the Mall of America in Bloomington, Minnesota, got a break from sales tax on their clothing purchases. Minnesota is one of numerous states that consider clothing an essential item and, therefore, waive any sales taxes. Other states, such as New Hampshire, have no sales tax at all, which makes their malls and shopping outlets very popular with shoppers from neighboring states.

tax revenues go to state governments, but almost all property taxes go to local governments. As a result, property taxes are by far the most important source of revenue for local governments. Approximately 72 percent of local government tax revenues, but only a tiny fraction (2 percent) of state tax revenues, comes from property taxes.[21]

Just about every local government relies on property tax revenues, but property tax rates vary widely from community to community. Most Americans who own homes or condominiums face an effective tax rate of about 1.39 percent.[22] The word *effective* simply acknowledges that some places have exemptions and adjustments that make the effective tax rate lower than the nominal tax rate. You can figure out the nominal tax rate by dividing the amount of tax paid by the amount of taxable income. You find the effective tax rate by dividing the amount of tax paid by the amount of total economic income.

In other words, if you own a condo worth $100,000, you probably pay about $1,390 a year in property taxes. In Manchester, New Hampshire, however, you'd pay $2,840 in property taxes on that same condo. That's because New Hampshire has an effective tax rate of 2.84 percent, which is one of the highest among cities across the country. Why are New Hampshire's property tax rates so high? Largely because the state has no income tax and no sales tax. That limits the state government's ability to raise funds. It also means that the state does not offer its towns the level of financial support that most state governments do. As a result, whereas most local governments receive 25 percent of their total revenues from property taxes, local governments in New Hampshire are forced to rely on property taxes for 53 percent of their total revenues.[23]

The Education Connection. Property taxes are important for another reason: they pretty much finance public schools. On average, school districts receive about 44 percent of their funding from local governments.[24] In most states, where you live determines how many education dollars your children receive. Wealthy communities with high housing values raise the most money from property taxes. School districts in these areas tend to have the most

educational resources. Conversely, school districts in the poorest areas have the fewest resources. In recent years state and federal governments have stepped in to try to ease these funding gaps by providing more resources to poor schools that cannot compete resource-wise with schools that have strong property tax bases, but the gaps are persistent. For example, the federal government's main effort to reduce resource inequality comes through Title I of the Elementary and Secondary Education Act, which sends billions of dollars to schools that serve socioeconomically distressed students. One analysis of education spending in New York City found that schools in poorer communities make do with less per-pupil revenue even with the help of Title I funds. Some schools serving the poorest communities do so with about 85 percent of the average per-pupil expenditure in New York.

The bottom line is that when schools are heavily dependent on property taxes, it is all but impossible to equalize resources. If states do nothing, schools in areas with high property values will have bigger budgets; if they try to equalize resources, they have to find the money (read: raise taxes), which is never popular and is especially resented if it is viewed as a tactic to divert money from local schools to nonlocal schools.

The Pros and Cons of Property Taxes. Property owners generally pay their property taxes twice a year in large lump sums. As such, these taxes tend to be highly visible and extremely unpopular with the public. However, local officials like them because property tax receipts are historically less volatile and more predictable than other types of tax revenues. Local revenue departments assess the values of houses and businesses and then send the owners their tax bills, so the local government knows exactly how much revenue a property tax will yield.

In most instances, taxes seem worse when the economy is bad. Property taxes are the exception. They tend to rise most sharply when a town or city is experiencing an economic boom and housing prices are soaring. In these circumstances, an upsurge in property values can lead to a backlash.

The most famous of such backlashes occurred in California in 1978. In response to years of rising property values and related taxes, Californians passed Proposition 13. This piece of legislation capped the property tax rate at 1 percent of a property's purchase price and froze property assessments at their 1978 levels until the property was resold. Newcomers to a neighborhood have to pay property taxes based on the actual value of their houses.

To this day, Proposition 13 is hotly debated. Conservatives have long praised the movement that gave rise to it. They say it was the harbinger of the conservative politics that former California governor Ronald Reagan brought to Washington three years later. Most experts, however, believe that its effects have been devastating to education. Prior to Proposition 13, California was one of the most generous funders of public education among the U.S. states; in the years since, it has become one of the least generous.

Even the most liberal electorates can be goaded into atypical action by rising property tax rates. In 1980, Massachusetts voters passed Proposition 2½, which capped property tax increases at, you guessed it, 2.5 percent. As a result, towns that want to increase spending by more than that, for such needs as increased funding for education, have to hold special override sessions. Towns have also come to rely on user fees.

Many state and local governments have attempted to ease the burden of property taxes on senior citizens and, in some cases, on other low-income individuals. In about fifty Massachusetts towns, senior citizens can reduce their property taxes by performing volunteer work. Cook County, Illinois, limits property tax rate increases by tying them to the national rate of inflation.[25] Despite these efforts, tensions between retirees living on fixed incomes and parents eager to spend more on local schools are commonplace. These pressures can be particularly acute in areas with large numbers of retirees.

Income Taxes

Personal **income taxes** account for 21 percent of state and local tax revenues,[26] although in some ways this figure conceals more than it reveals. Almost all nonfederal income tax revenues go to

state governments.[27] In many states, personal income taxes are assessed on a graduated scale, so higher-wage earners pay a greater percentage of their income in taxes. This structure tends to make state tax systems that rely more heavily on the income tax than on the sales tax more **progressive**.

As with property taxes, states have different approaches to income taxes, with some using such taxes as a primary revenue source and others shunning them altogether. Alaska, Florida, Nevada, South Dakota, Texas, Washington, and Wyoming impose no income taxes at all, and New Hampshire and Tennessee impose taxes only on certain types of income. Your state's reliance (or lack of reliance) on income taxes influences not just how much you take home in your paycheck but also how much stuff costs. This is because states that do not collect income taxes usually rely heavily on sales tax revenues. States that have no sales tax tend to make up the loss by taking a bigger bite out of income. Oregon, for example, has no sales tax and is thus heavily reliant on income taxes (individual and corporate) as a primary revenue source. In 2009, Oregon's income tax provided 75 percent of the state's total tax revenues—the most of any state.[28] Voters in Oregon endorsed, and even increased, the state's reliance on its income tax in January 2010 by approving an increase in the tax rate on the highest-wage earners—the first time they have approved such an increase since 1930.

Two states, Alaska and New Hampshire, have neither income taxes nor sales taxes. How do they manage to function without two of the primary sources of revenue for most state governments? For Alaska, geology is the difference that makes a difference: the Prudhoe Bay oil fields bring in so much money that the state has little need for other revenue streams. The difference that makes a difference for New Hampshire is mostly the residents' hardheaded resistance to taxation. Unlike Alaska, New Hampshire has no big alternate revenue source—it just makes do. According to Donald Boyd of the

Income Taxes
Taxes on wages and interest earned.

Progressive Tax System
A system of taxation in which the rate paid reflects ability to pay.

Rockefeller Institute, New Hampshire's state government simply does less than most state governments. The state relies almost exclusively on local governments to finance elementary and secondary education rather than raising state revenue for this purpose. Unlike many other states, it has also managed to avoid court orders to spend dramatically more on secondary school education. It is able to do all this, in part, because the average New Hampshire resident has one of the highest levels of income in the country. The people of New Hampshire are able to pay for a lot of goods and services for themselves.

These states are the exceptions. On average, Americans pay about $767 a year in state income taxes.[29] However, residents of states with high tax rates, such as Maryland, Massachusetts, New York, and Oregon, pay significantly more in income taxes. (See Table 4-1.)

TABLE 4-1

State Individual Income Tax Collections per Capita, Fiscal Year 2010

State	Individual Income Tax Collections per Capita ($)	Rank	State	Individual Income Tax Collections per Capita ($)	Rank
Alabama	543	35	Nebraska	832	18
Alaska[a]	0	44	Nevada[a]	0	44
Arizona	379	41	New Hampshire[b]	63	42
Arkansas	719	29	New Jersey	1,176	7
California	1,229	5	New Mexico	466	38
Colorado	816	19	New York	1,796	1
Connecticut	1,616	2	North Carolina	961	13
Delaware	952	14	North Dakota	454	40
Florida[a]	0	44	Ohio	684	30
Georgia	726	26	Oklahoma	595	33
Hawaii	1,127	8	Oregon	1,293	4
Idaho	684	31	Pennsylvania	737	23
Illinois	736	24	Rhode Island	864	17
Indiana	597	32	South Carolina	473	37
Iowa	871	16	South Dakota[a]	0	44
Kansas	944	15	Tennessee[b]	27	43
Kentucky	728	25	Texas[a]	0	44
Louisiana	506	36	Utah	765	22
Maine	981	12	Vermont	782	20
Maryland	1,077	10	Virginia	1,086	9
Massachusetts	1,549	3	Washington[a]	0	44
Michigan	555	34	West Virginia	782	21
Minnesota	1,219	6	Wisconsin	1,020	11
Mississippi	456	39	Wyoming[a]	0	44
Missouri	724	28	United States (average)	767	–
Montana	724	27			

Source: Tax Foundation, "State Individual Income Tax Collections, 2010," http://taxfoundation.org/article/facts-figures-handbook-how-does-your-state-compare-0.

a. State does not tax wage income.

b. State does not tax wage income but does tax interest and dividend income.

Other Tax Revenue Sources: Cars, Oil, and Death

Car registrations, deaths, and oil and other natural resources are also major sources of state revenues. In 2008, car registration fees brought in almost $20 billion to state and local governments. Estate taxes, sometimes called death taxes, and gift taxes brought in another $5.3 billion.[30]

Thirty-two states levy **severance taxes** on natural resources that are removed, or severed, from the state. Some states are quite creative about devising severance taxes. Washington, for example, taxes oysters and salmon and other game fish caught in state. But despite some creative taxing, the only states that raise real money from severance taxes are states with significant coal, oil, and natural gas reserves, such as Wyoming and Alaska.

Other Sources of Income: Fees, Charges, and Uncle Sam

The total tax revenues discussed so far add up to a lot of money (nearly $2 trillion), but that only covers about two-thirds of the roughly $3 trillion in annual spending that state and local governments racked up in 2012. The rest of the money came from user fees and other charges, insurance trust money, and intergovernmental transfers.

These sources of revenue can be significant. In 2008, state and local governments raised $613 billion from "charges and miscellaneous fees." This is $165 billion more than they raised from sales taxes.[31] Government levies in the form of things such as university tuitions, public hospital charges, airport use fees, school lunch sales, and park permits obviously can make a big difference to the bottom line. Recently, states have increased fees to help close budget deficits and avoid more prominent tax increases. The pattern accelerated as tax revenues fell off in recent years; in 2010, state budgets included $5.3 billion in fee increases.[32] In 2013, state budgets tacked on another $500 million in new fee increases. State and local governments earned another $144 million from utility fees and, yes, from liquor sales and licenses.[33]

Insurance Trust Funds

The amount of money shown on a pay stub before any deductions are taken out can be pretty impressive. The actual amount of the paycheck can be a bit disappointing. What many wage earners may not realize is that they are not the only ones paying the taxes and fees they see deducted from their paychecks. Their employers often have to match these payroll taxes and deductions. These **insurance trust funds** go to their state governments and to the federal government. Ultimately, the contributions are invested to support Social Security and retirement programs, workers' compensation and disability programs, and other related insurance programs that benefit employees.

Intergovernmental Transfers

The final portion of state and local government revenues comes from **intergovernmental transfers**. In the case of state governments, that means transfers from the federal government. In the case of local governments, it means transfers from state governments. In 2011, the federal government provided some $575 billion to state and local governments, making it the single largest source of revenues for these governments.[34] That situation is most likely to be temporary, however—a good portion of that money from the federal government came from the stimulus funds appropriated by the ARRA, as discussed in the introductory section of this chapter. Much of that money was disbursed to states and spent by 2012–2013.

Thanks to unprecedented revenues from oil production, North Dakota is expected to have a $2 billion budget reserve at the end of fiscal year 2013. North Dakota recently surpassed Alaska to become the nation's second-biggest oil producer, following only Texas.

Severance Taxes
Taxes on natural resources removed from a state.

Insurance Trust Funds
Money collected from contributions, assessments, insurance premiums, and payroll taxes.

Intergovernmental Transfers
Funds provided by the federal government to state governments and by state governments to local governments.

A Difference That Makes a Difference

The Blessing and Curse of a Booming Economy

While the economic doldrums have left many states awash in red ink, North Dakota has found itself awash in cash. While most states struggle to deal with the lingering budgetary effects of a recession, North Dakota struggles to deal with the impact of a massive economic boom. While the cupboards are bare for many states, North Dakota's treasury is amply stocked.

How has North Dakota managed all this? Mostly by being the location of certain events predating the Great Recession—and we mean *way* predating the Great Recession. Like 417 million years ago. Somewhere around the time a large oil deposit formed under what is now the border between North Dakota and Canada. The first well sunk to try to tap that oil was drilled on land owned by a farmer named Henry Bakken; what is now known as the Bakken formation is believed to hold a massive 4.3 billion barrels of oil.

While the Bakken formation's potential has been known for a long time, it wasn't until relatively recently that the technology existed to allow anyone to tap that oil cost-effectively. Coincidentally, that technology came online and opened up the taps on the Bakken formation pretty much at the same time the United States was hit by the worst financial crisis in five generations. Geology was thus a difference that made a big difference to this state. The happy coincidence that the sea of fossil fuel on which it sat was newly open to extraction meant that North Dakota pretty much missed the financial hard times of the Great Recession.

Taxes on oil and gas production netted the state $839 million in fiscal year 2011 and are expected to generate $1 billion a year to the state's bottom line for the foreseeable future. That's a big number for a small-population state like North Dakota. While other states have been cutting budgets, North Dakota has increased its biennial budget by 12 percent.

In these tough economic times, the oil boom makes North Dakota seem like some sort of alternate universe. While unemployment hovers around 8 percent nationally and is much higher in some pockets, North Dakota has more jobs than people. In Williams County there are nine jobs for every person looking for work. The average oil and gas worker there earns $90,000 per year. Average household income in municipalities such as Stanley (population 1,458) has jumped 130 percent in a decade.

While the oil boom means that North Dakota does not have to worry much about budget deficits, the effects are not all positive. The state is undergoing a population boom that is straining public services and creating housing shortages. The impact of the oil and gas industry on the environment and on the largely rural, agricultural way of life that has defined generations of North Dakotans has raised worry and criticism in some quarters. And local governments do not benefit directly from taxes on oil and gas—these revenues flow mostly to the state.

Still, some states that are cutting services, raising taxes, and generally struggling to make ends meet might be forgiven if they look at North Dakota's problems with envy. At least North Dakota has extra money to deal with its problems, which is more than many states can say.

Source: Ryan Holeywell, "North Dakota's Oil Boom Is a Blessing and a Curse," *Governing*, August 2011, www.governing.com/topics/energy-env/north-dakotas-oil-boom-blessing-curse.html.

Approximately 90 percent of federal funds go to specific state programs. Medicaid, the joint state-federal health insurance program for low-income people and people with disabilities, is by far the largest recipient. It receives about 64.6 percent of all federal funds that go to state

MAP 4-1

American Recovery and Reinvestment Act Funds Awarded by State, 2012

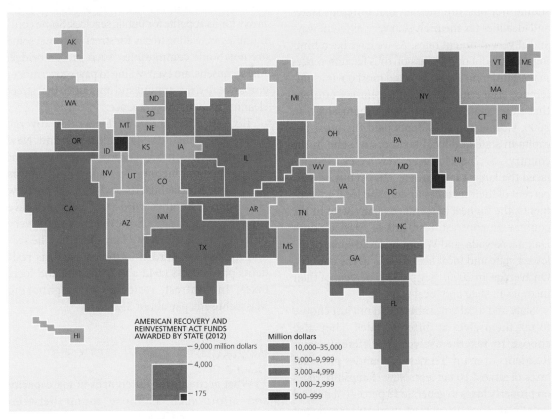

Source: "State/Territory Totals as Reported by Recipients," Recovery.gov, reporting period February 7, 2009–March 31, 2012, www.recovery.gov/pages/textview.aspx?data=recipientHomeMap.

governments.[35] Education (both K–12 and post-secondary school), transportation projects, and public welfare also receive significant federal funding. Most of these funds cannot be used on just anything—states must spend them on certain programs and often in a certain fashion.

During the 1960s, local governments and some neighborhood organizations also received substantial federal funding. Many of these programs have since ended or been scaled back drastically. Aside from the stimulus bill, local governments get only about 4 percent of their total revenues from the federal government. Adding to the problem for localities is that states have also reduced their support for local governments to help balance their own budgets. Still, intergovernmental revenue

transfers—mostly from state governments—account for about a third of local government spending.[36]

Localities generally have welcomed the money, but relationships between state governments and county and city governments have not always been easy. Over the course of the past decade, many city and county governments have found themselves stuck with unfunded mandates. These requirements have been imposed on them by federal or state legislation that forces them to perform certain tasks but fails to provide them with the money to carry out those tasks. Transfers of money and responsibilities, however, continue to be commonplace during economic downturns.[37]

Taxing Variations Among State and Local Governments

Generalizations about state and local finances should not obscure the fact that different states and localities tax themselves in very different ways and at very different rates. As we have been hinting throughout our discussion thus far, differences make a difference. The first and most obvious difference concerns the very different tax burdens that states choose to impose on themselves. In 2009, Connecticut residents paid the most per capita in state and local taxes of any state in the country—$7,256. However, New Jersey residents faced the largest tax burden. They returned 12.2 percent of their incomes to state and local governments, the highest percentage of any state in the country. In contrast, residents of Alaska, South Dakota, Nevada, and Wyoming faced some of the lowest state and local tax burdens in the country. On average, in 2009, they paid 9.5 percent of their incomes in state and local taxes.[38]

State and local governments do not just choose to tax themselves at different rates. They also choose to tax themselves in different ways. Residents of many Tennessee counties pay sales taxes of almost 10 percent. New Hampshire relies on property taxes to generate 18 percent of its total state tax revenue. In contrast, property taxes do not contribute anything to state coffers in fourteen states, although localities rely heavily on them.[39]

In thinking about a state's tax burden, it is helpful to distinguish between its **tax capacity** and its **tax effort**. In Newport Beach, California, for example, many homes are worth more than $1 million—a far cry from the price tags of a few years ago—but on that much value, even low property tax rates are going to bring in serious money. Conversely, Odessa, Texas, with a median home price of $66,700, is not going to generate a lot of property tax revenue no matter how high its rates are. Newport Beach's tax capacity is high; Odessa's tax capacity is low.

Rather than tax capacity, many political scientists prefer to look at a different measurement—tax effort, which is the aggregate-level equivalent of individual-level tax burden. Basically, measurements of tax effort seek to determine the proportion of a given community's income that it chooses to pay out in taxes. A community's tax effort is also a good proxy for its appetite for public services. Some communities are willing to pay for street cleaning; some are not. Some communities, such as Cambridge, Massachusetts, are even willing to pay a government employee to drive around and announce that street cleaning is about to commence.

Tax capacities and tax efforts often diverge markedly. Consider Massachusetts and New Hampshire. Both are comparatively affluent states. Personal income per capita in 2007 was $49,142 in Massachusetts and $41,144 in New Hampshire.[40] In other words, the two states have similar tax capacities. However, they make very different tax efforts. New Hampshire has the second-lightest tax burden in the country. Its residents pay about $3,642 a year in state and local taxes. In contrast, residents of neighboring Massachusetts pay about $5,377.[41]

Explaining Tax Variations

What accounts for differences in tax capacity and effort such as those found between Massachusetts and New Hampshire? Political culture is one difference that helps explain the difference. New Hampshire prides itself on its rugged individualism. Its motto is "Live Free or Die." Residents tend to want the government to stay out of their way. In contrast, Massachusetts was founded as a commonwealth. The founding document of the Massachusetts Bay Colony describes a single "Body Politic" dedicated to the "general good" of the colony.[42] In this tradition, state and local governments are seen as effective ways of advancing that general good so higher taxes and larger governments are more acceptable.

Political culture, however, is not the only important variable that explains the very different tax efforts among states. Factors such as geography, geology, demographics, and history also influence the choices that state and local governments make.

Geography. One obvious, but easily overlooked, factor that influences state tax policies is geography.

Tax Capacity
A measure of the ability to pay taxes.

Tax Effort
A measure of taxes paid relative to the ability to pay taxes.

Some states use sales tax policy as a competitive edge. Delaware proudly recruits shoppers from nearby Mid-Atlantic states to its outlet malls with "no sales tax" advertisements. In contrast, Hawaii charges a 4.5-percent tax on nearly everything sold, including many services. How can it get away with this practice? Well, unless residents are willing to fly to the mainland for their sundries, they don't have much choice but to pay up.

Geology. As we have already seen, geology plays an important role in some state economies. This is most notably true in oil-rich and natural-gas-rich states such as Alaska, Wyoming, and North Dakota (see the box "A Difference That Makes a Difference: The Blessing and Curse of a Booming Economy"). Thanks in large part to Prudhoe Bay, state and local governments in Alaska are able to maintain high levels of spending with very low tax burdens. Alaska has used its mineral riches to help establish the Alaska Permanent Fund, which is a sovereign wealth fund—basically a state-owned investment corporation. The fund's profits are partially redistributed to state citizens, so rather than the state taxing residents, the fund pays Alaskans for being Alaskans. The fund sends each eligible citizen a yearly **dividend** check; in 2012, the amount per person was about $878.

Demographics. Demographics also play an important role in determining the attitudes of state and local governments toward taxes. This is particularly true at the local level. Consider a city with a strong local economy and rising house prices. Such a city attracts a large number of young workers with children. These are people who might very well want to spend more money on local schools and are willing to deal with rising property tax revenues. However, as mentioned previously, for seniors living on fixed incomes, rising house prices and rising property taxes might spell disaster. During economic booms, conflicts between

Dividend
A payment made to stockholders (or, in Alaska's case, residents) from the interest generated by an investment.

parents of school-age children and retirees are a common feature of local politics.

The Economic Cycle. Even when states make similar tax efforts and have similar cultures, their state and local finances can still vary widely because states (and even cities) can have very different economies. The national economic numbers that most people are familiar with—unemployment, productivity gains, income, and the like—are not necessarily accurate reflections of state economic conditions. Depending on the makeup of their economies, states can find themselves at very different points on an economic cycle at the same point in time. For example, industrial states such as Michigan and Indiana tend to experience economic downturns first. Texas historically has had a countercyclical economy. When rising oil prices threaten to push industrial states into recession, Texas tends to do well. The same is true of Wyoming, Alaska, and, most recently, North Dakota.

Demographics, geography, history, political culture, and the swings of the economic cycle are all important, but these variables do not explain all the financial choices that state and local governments make. Take Mississippi, for example. One of the most religious and politically conservative states in the country, Mississippi is the buckle of the Bible Belt. In 1990, however, Mississippi passed riverboat gambling legislation. This legislation allowed casino operators to build full-size casinos on barges moored permanently to the shoreline on the Mississippi River and the Gulf Coast. The goal was to turn the northwestern town of Tunica, which had gained a measure of renown after the television newsmagazine *60 Minutes* profiled it as the poorest city in America, into Las Vegas East.

What's important to keep in mind here is that Nevada and Mississippi have completely different political cultures. Political scientist Daniel Elazar describes Mississippi as a traditionalistic state and Nevada as an individualistic state. In short, Nevada has the kind of political culture that we might expect to produce, well, Las Vegas. Mississippi does not. Today, however, the hamlet of Tunica has more casino square footage than the East Coast gambling hot spot Atlantic City, in the individualistic state of New Jersey. Clearly, political culture isn't everything.

Debt

The final source of money for state and local governments is debt, generally issued in the form of **bonds**. These are financial instruments with which state and local governments promise to pay back borrowed money at a fixed rate of interest on a specified date. The interest rates paid by a government depend largely on the government's bond rating. Bond ratings are issued by three private companies—Moody's, Standard & Poor's, and Fitch—and are based on the governments' fiscal health; many states' bond ratings have fallen during the current recession. A rating of AAA is the best, and anything lower than BBB is considered "junk bond status" and would send a government's interest rates skyrocketing. No state has ever fallen below BBB rating.[43]

State and local governments, as well as quasi-governmental entities such as utility and water authorities, use bonds to finance **capital investments**, typically infrastructure upgrades such as new roads, new schools, and new airports. There are two types of bonds: **general obligation bonds**, which are secured by the taxing power of the jurisdiction that issues them, and **revenue bonds**, which are secured by the revenue from a given project, such as a new toll road. For state governments, capital investments are projects such as highway construction, power plant construction and pollution control, and even land conservation. Because the issuance of general obligation bonds must be approved by voters, state and local governments turn to revenue bonds more often.

Bonds
Certificates that are evidence of debts on which the issuer promises to pay the holders a specified amount of interest for a specified length of time and to repay the loans on their maturity.

Capital Investments
Investments in infrastructure, such as roads.

General Obligation Bonds
Investments secured by the taxing power of the jurisdiction that issues them.

Revenue Bonds
Investments secured by the revenue generated by a state or municipal project.

Local governments use bonds to finance projects such as construction or improvement of schools, sewage and water lines, airports, and affordable housing. Investors like them too, in part because the earnings from most state bonds are exempt from state income taxes.

In 2012, state and local governments issued about $295 billion in bonds.[44] **Municipal bonds**, called munis, are generally safe and attractive investments, particularly for the rich. Municipal bondholders usually are exempted from paying federal or state taxes on income they receive from bonds. Sometimes, however, municipal finances go disastrously awry. In 2009, Jefferson County, Alabama, the largest county in the state, announced it would file for bankruptcy after defaulting on $3 billion in bonds to finance improvements to its sewer system.

The Budget Process

Once state and local governments have raised money from taxes, user fees, and bonds and have received money from intergovernmental transfers, they must decide how to spend it. These decisions are made during the **budget process**.

Most state and local governments budget for one **fiscal year**. Unfortunately for fans of simplicity in government, the fiscal year is not the same as the calendar year. The federal government's fiscal year runs from October 1 to September 30. Most state and local governments begin their fiscal year on July 1; Alabama, Michigan, New York, and Texas are exceptions. Thus, when legislatures debate the budget, they are almost always debating the budget for the coming fiscal year.[45] Nineteen states pass two-year budgets.[46]

Municipal Bonds
Bonds issued by states, counties, cities, and towns to fund large projects as well as operating budgets. Income from such bonds is exempt from federal taxes and from state and local taxes for the investors who live in the state where they are issued.

Budget Process
The procedure by which state and local governments assess revenues and set budgets.

Fiscal Year
The annual accounting period used by a government.

Local Focus

Bonds and Broken Budgets

The story of how Jefferson County, Alabama, waded into budget and bond muck stretches back to 1993, when the Cahaba River Society, a group dedicated to preserving the river that flows through Birmingham, complained that the county's sewer system was discharging raw sewage into waterways. Federal officials issued a consent decree in which Jefferson County promised to upgrade the system.

The county paid for the upgrade by issuing $3 billion in bonds. As sewer service rates rose to meet those costs and Jefferson County struggled under its debt, county officials looked for a way to lessen the loan payments. In 2002 and 2003, they refinanced their bonds with variable-rate and auction-rate securities. (Auction-rate securities are bonds for which the interest rate is reset at auction every few weeks.)

Auction-rate securities were supposed to be safe, but the auction-rate market collapsed in February 2008. Then the bond insurance companies that were backing the county's debt suffered their own fiscal problems and their credit was downgraded. The result: Jefferson County's interest rates skyrocketed, much like the rates of homeowners whose subprime mortgages had just reset. The county's revenue from sewer fees could not cover the borrowing costs. On April Fool's Day 2008, Jefferson County failed to make its payment on its debt. Instead, it reached an agreement with its creditors to pay the interest and get an extension on the principal—an agreement that left the county of 660,000 teetering on the edge of bankruptcy.

County commissioners and other Alabama political players developed a variety of ideas to solve the sewer mess—to no avail. Without a solution in sight, the county made massive cutbacks: reducing department budgets by one-third, canceling road maintenance contracts, closing courthouses, and laying off hundreds of county workers. "We're having to downsize this government to the point that it may not be able to operate," County Commissioner Bettye Fine Collins said in 2009.

Collins's comments were prophetic. In December 2011, Jefferson Country filed for bankruptcy; by that time its debt had ballooned to more than $4 billion, a crushing burden the county simply could not manage.

As discussed in the opening section of this chapter, variations on the Jefferson County story have played out across the country as the recession has significantly weakened local governments' financial footing.

Sources: Karen Pierog, "Default, Bankruptcy Fears Overhang U.S. Muni Market," Reuters, February 16, 2010; adapted from Josh Goodman, "Drained," *Governing*, August 2009.

Budget time lines do vary from state to state, but the budget process itself is quite similar across states. It begins with instructions from the governor's budget office. The executive branch agencies are told to draw up funding requests for the upcoming year. During the fall (assuming the typical fiscal year beginning on July 1), the budget office reviews the spending requests and helps the chief executive develop a unified budget for the executive branch.

Most chief executives unveil their budgets in State of the State addresses in January. In forty-five states, governors and mayors are required by law to submit a **balanced budget** to the legislature or city council. The legislative body reviews the budget, authorizes spending on certain programs, appropriates the necessary money, and presents its budget to the chief executive to sign into law.

As a guard against fiscal excess and abuse, forty-nine states have statutory or constitutional requirements that the state legislature must enact a balanced budget. Only Vermont

Balanced Budget
A budget in which current expenditures are equal to or less than income.

MAP 4-2

Municipal Bankruptcies as of April 2013

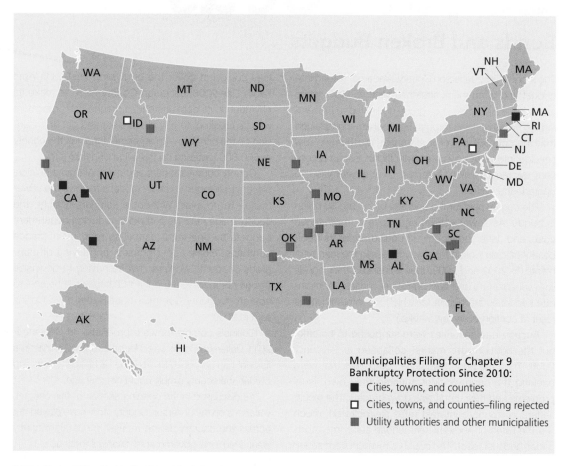

Source: "Bankrupt Cities, Municipalities List and Map," *Governing*, www.governing.com/gov-data/other/municipal-cities-counties-bankruptcies-and-defaults.html.

Note: Only about half of the U.S. states allow municipalities to file for Chapter 9 bankruptcy; laws in other states prohibit such filings. Not all bankruptcy filings were approved.

is free to run up debt as it pleases.[47] All but five states also have laws that require lawmakers to save a certain portion of state revenues in so-called rainy day, or budget stabilization, funds. States can draw on these funds during times of recession, when revenues fall. Although rainy day funds rarely offset the revenue drops that occur during a recession, they do provide some cushion for the lawmakers who have to balance state budgets. In 2009 and 2010, for example, rainy day funds helped close more than $35 billion of states' budget gaps—funds that would have otherwise had to come from more severe program cuts or greater tax increases.[48] Many local governments face similar requirements because of state laws or their own municipal codes.

There are, of course, exceptions. In states such as Arkansas, Mississippi, and South Carolina, legislatures take the lead role in formulating the initial budget plan. Legislative bodies also take the lead in county and city governments with weak chief executives, such as Los Angeles, California. In many western states, citizens and special interests have become players in the budgeting process via ballot initiatives.

Despite some groups' moral objections to gambling, states have turned to casinos like this one floating on the Mississippi River in Dubuque, Iowa, to help raise much-needed revenues.

Expenditures, or Where the Money Goes

State and local governments spend a lot of money. In fiscal year 2010, state governments alone spent nearly $2 trillion. (See Table 4-2.) In 2012, state and local governments combined spent approximately $9,762.50 for every man, woman, and child in the country.[49] So, where did the money go?

Wages. Salaries are the single largest source of **expenditures** for state and local governments—roughly $800 billion in 2008. State and local governments are the biggest employers in the United States. In 2008, state governments employed 5.1 million people nationwide. Local governments employed another 14.6 million people.[50]

Education. Education has long been the single largest functional spending category for state and local governments. In 2010, state governments alone spent $571 billion on education, the majority of it (about $316 billion) in the forms of transfers to schools and school districts.[51]

Despite the big financial commitment by states—they provide about half the funding— primary and secondary education traditionally has been the preserve of local governments. In most states, elected local school boards hire superintendents and principals, select curricula that align with state standards, and develop school budgets. Local governments typically devote about 38 percent of their budgets to education.[52]

State governments also devote a portion of their expenditures to higher education; in 2012, this amounted to a total of about $72.4 billion. That number has been steadily declining, however—in

2007, states spent more than $75 billion.[53] Funding for higher education has been cut largely because it comes out of general revenue funds; that is, it is part of what is known as **discretionary spending.** In tight economic times, discretionary spending is one of the first parts of a government budget to come under stress—when revenues shrink, legislatures have to reduce annual appropriations, and that means cutting discretionary spending. As publicly supported colleges and universities have ways to deal with spending cuts from state government (read: jack up your tuition and increase your class size), higher education funds have been particularly hard-hit by budget retrenchment.

Healthcare. Since the late 1990s, healthcare spending has surged dramatically. For state governments, spending on healthcare is now greater than spending for any other single item. Medicaid is the largest and most expensive state-run health program. When it was established in 1965, it was

---

Expenditures
Money spent by government.

Discretionary Spending
Spending controlled in annual appropriations acts.

TABLE 4-2

State Revenue, Expenditures, and Debt, 2010 (in millions of dollars)

Item	Total revenue	Total expenditure	Debt at end of fiscal year
UNITED STATES	2,035,700	1,942,822	1,113,355
ALABAMA	26,824	27,700	8,785
ALASKA	12,375	11,000	6,381
ARIZONA	32,842	33,016	13,956
ARKANSAS	19,595	17,354	4,261
CALIFORNIA	278,495	257,249	148,929
COLORADO	27,991	27,661	16,710
CONNECTICUT	26,840	27	30
DELAWARE	8	7,827	5,515
FLORIDA	91,653	81,629	40,403
GEORGIA	44,878	44,482	13,789
HAWAII	11,566	11,178	7,701
IDAHO	8,859	8,514	3,873
ILLINOIS	73,275	75,270	61,412
INDIANA	35,575	35,474	23,635
IOWA	21,265	19,109	5,140
KANSAS	16,546	16,584	6,478
KENTUCKY	26,993	29,098	14,393
LOUISIANA	32,188	33,616	17,443
MAINE	9,539	9,024	6,034
MARYLAND	37,394	37,488	24,475
MASSACHUSETTS	50,472	51,731	73,940
MICHIGAN	65,972	63,918	32,146
MINNESOTA	39,887	37,942	11,683
MISSISSIPPI	20,979	20,023	6,468
MISSOURI	33,916	30,772	20,421
MONTANA	7,141	7,052	4,374
NEBRASKA	10,063	9,585	2,330
NEVADA	14,053	12,935	4,436
NEW HAMPSHIRE	7,828	7,708	8,347
NEW JERSEY	66,740	67,971	60,958
NEW MEXICO	17,567	17,996	8,740
NEW YORK	195,460	174,308	129,530
NORTH CAROLINA	57,467	52,190	18,853
NORTH DAKOTA	6,119	5,134	2,198
OHIO	89,664	76,737	31,177
OKLAHOMA	23,692	22,640	9,963
OREGON	28,703	26,978	13,510
PENNSYLVANIA	83,287	87,285	44,738
RHODE ISLAND	8,809	8,211	9,498
SOUTH CAROLINA	28,869	28,927	15,771

Item	Total revenue	Total expenditure	Debt at end of fiscal year
SOUTH DAKOTA	4,493	4,429	3,483
TENNESSEE	29,720	29,675	5,835
TEXAS	120,390	119,605	42,034
UTAH	16,022	16,263	6,478
VERMONT	6,001	5,726	3,493
VIRGINIA	46,357	43,457	24,967
WASHINGTON	44,299	46,238	27,478
WEST VIRGINIA	13,564	12,343	7,144
WISCONSIN	48,088	38,590	22,319
WYOMING	7,411	5,757	1,514

Source: *State and Local Sourcebook*, online supplement to *Governing*, 2010, http://sourcebook.governing.com.

viewed as a limited safety net for the very poor and disabled. However, the numbers of low-income, uninsured Americans have grown, and medical care has become more expensive. The program has grown at an enormous rate as a result. In 1970, state governments spent $2 billion on Medicaid, and the federal government kicked in another $3 billion. By 2008, the states and the federal government had spent $311 billion on the program, up from $298 billion just a year earlier.[54] State Medicaid programs provide health insurance to more than 60 million people and account for 20.7 percent of total state spending.[55]

These numbers may be about to go up. In 2010 the federal government enacted the Patient Protection and Affordable Care Act—commonly known as Obamacare—which has the explicit aim of extending health insurance coverage to millions of uninsured people. The law is of central interest to the states because Medicaid is a program cooperatively run—and paid for—by both state and federal governments. As such, it is an example of **fiscal federalism**, a system of delivering public services that involves the federal government picking up most of the costs while states take responsibility for administering the services.

Fiscal Federalism
The system by which federal grants are used to fund programs and services provided by state and local governments.

Obamacare was a contentious and controversial law opposed by some state officials, who viewed it as federal encroachment on state sovereignty. In 2012, however, the Supreme Court ruled its major provisions constitutional, so like it or not states have to learn to live with it. While a number of objections were raised against Obamacare, its potential budgetary impact was one of the biggest sources of concern for state officials. By some estimates Obamacare could add an extra 17 million people to the numbers covered by Medicaid, which is an **entitlement** program. This means states and the federal government are obligated by law to provide health insurance to low-income individuals who qualify for the program, regardless of the cost. If states have an unexpected surge of applicants and they have not set aside enough money for Medicaid, tough. The federal government has committed to covering many of the increased costs associated with Obamacare (which also has the overall goal of reining in the spiraling costs of healthcare), but at this point it is not certain how the program will affect the states' bottom lines.

What is not in doubt is that Medicaid and other healthcare programs are expensive for both the states and the federal government. In 2010 total Medicaid costs were about $389 billion; states contributed about $126 billion, with the rest coming from the federal government.[56] The State Children's Health Insurance Program (SCHIP) is another joint state-federal program that helps provide health insurance for children in poor families. In 2009, SCHIP was a $10 billion program, with about $7 billion funded by the federal government and the rest provided by the states.

States do have some leeway in determining how generous they want to be with programs such as Medicaid and SCHIP. Eligibility for these sorts of programs is typically determined by family or wage earner income relative to federally established poverty levels. While the federal government sets basic guidelines on those eligibility requirements, states can use more generous guidelines if they choose.

For example, in Mississippi children under the age of five are eligible for Medicaid benefits in families earning up to 133 percent of the federal poverty level. In Wisconsin they are eligible if their families earn up to 300 percent of the federal poverty level.[57] In other words, whether someone is eligible for Medicaid benefits is dependent not just on how much his or her family earns but also on what state the family lives in.

Welfare. Welfare has been one of the most contentious issues in U.S. politics for a long time. Like Medicaid, welfare is an entitlement program; states have some leeway to determine eligibility, but they cannot deny or restrict benefits to qualified individuals. From 1965 to 1996, women with young children were eligible to receive monetary assistance through a welfare program known as Aid to Families with Dependent Children (AFDC).

In 1996, Republicans in Congress and President Bill Clinton joined forces to pass the Personal Responsibility and Work Reconciliation Act, which abolished AFDC and replaced it with the Temporary Assistance for Needy Families (TANF) program. TANF disbursed federal money to states in block grants and gave them considerable freedom in determining how they wanted to spend those funds. Many liberals predicted that such welfare "reform" would result in disaster. Instead, the number of people on welfare rolls declined dramatically. From 1994 to 1999, the welfare caseload declined by nearly 50 percent, from approximately 4 million people to 2 million people.[58]

Welfare continues to be a politically contentious issue even though, from a financial viewpoint, it is actually a pretty minor program. In 2011 states spent about $15 billion on TANF, with the federal government kicking in another $15 billion—that's no more than a percentage point or two of total state spending.[59]

Firefighting, Police, and Prisons. In 2008 state and local governments spent $129 billion on fire and police protection. They spent an additional $73 billion on prisons and correctional facilities.[60] State and local government spending on police

---

Entitlement
A service that government must provide, regardless of the cost.

FIGURE 4-1

HOW IT WORKS

A Year in the Life of a State Budget: Idaho's Budgetary Process

Most folks first hear about state budget priorities through their governor's State of the State address, the forum in which most state budgetary news is presented. In reality, budget planning begins well in advance of this address and involves all three branches of government to some degree. In Idaho, each year in May (after the last of the potatoes have been planted), the Division of Financial Management (DFM) starts sowing its own seeds: overseeing the development of the state's budget for the coming fiscal year. This is the beginning of what is really an eighteen-month process; the planning for fiscal year 2014, for instance, actually got under way about midyear in 2012.

This chart shows how the process works in Idaho:

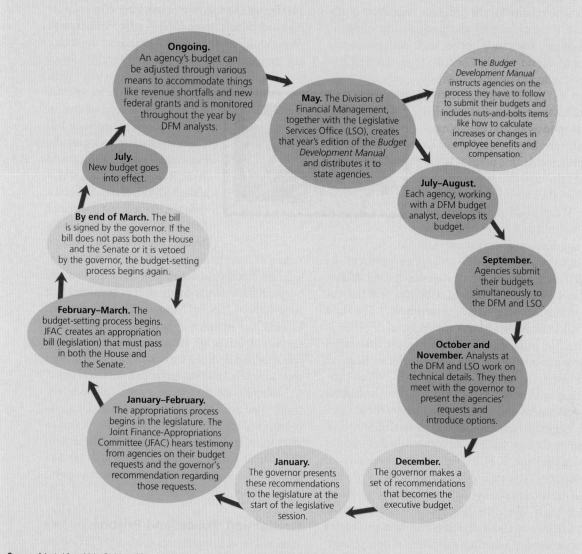

Ongoing. An agency's budget can be adjusted through various means to accommodate things like revenue shortfalls and new federal grants and is monitored throughout the year by DFM analysts.

May. The Division of Financial Management, together with the Legislative Services Office (LSO), creates that year's edition of the *Budget Development Manual* and distributes it to state agencies.

The *Budget Development Manual* instructs agencies on the process they have to follow to submit their budgets and includes nuts-and-bolts items like how to calculate increases or changes in employee benefits and compensation.

July–August. Each agency, working with a DFM budget analyst, develops its budget.

September. Agencies submit their budgets simultaneously to the DFM and LSO.

October and November. Analysts at the DFM and LSO work on technical details. They then meet with the governor to present the agencies' requests and introduce options.

December. The governor makes a set of recommendations that becomes the executive budget.

January. The governor presents these recommendations to the legislature at the start of the legislative session.

January–February. The appropriations process begins in the legislature. The Joint Finance-Appropriations Committee (JFAC) hears testimony from agencies on their budget requests and the governor's recommendation regarding those requests.

February–March. The budget-setting process begins. JFAC creates an appropriation bill (legislation) that must pass in both the House and the Senate.

By end of March. The bill is signed by the governor. If the bill does not pass both the House and the Senate or it is vetoed by the governor, the budget-setting process begins again.

July. New budget goes into effect.

Source: Adapted from Idaho Division of Financial Management, "Budget Process," http://dfm.idaho.gov/citizensguide/budgetprocess.html.

protection and prisons varies widely. New York City, with a population of 8 million, employs a police force of thirty-seven thousand. That works out to one police officer for every 216 people. In contrast, Los Angeles, a city of 3.8 million, employees only ten thousand police officers. That equals only one police officer for every 380 people.

States also have very different levels of enthusiasm for funding prisons. In fiscal year 2008 Florida devoted 4.8 percent of its state spending to prisons. This level of spending is more than 1 percentage point higher than the national average and reflects Florida's incarceration rate, which is among the ten highest in the country. In contrast, West Virginia's state government spent only 1.1 percent of its state budget on corrections.[61]

Highways. In 2009 state and local governments spent about $120 billion on transportation, much of it devoted to highways and roads.[62] Most of this money came from dedicated revenue sources, such as the gasoline tax, but the federal government accounted for nearly a third of these funds.[63] The federal contribution to state transportation spending has been unusually high for several years because of the ARRA, which channeled billions in federal stimulus money to the states in the form of highway funds.

Not surprisingly, states with wide-open spaces spend more money on highway construction and transportation. In 2008 Utah devoted 22.1 percent of total state expenditures to transportation. This was the highest percentage for any state in the country, followed by Montana at 13.4 percent and South Dakota at 12.7 percent. Nationwide, state governments spent 7.9 percent of total revenues on transportation in 2008.[64]

Restraints on State and Local Budgeteers

Politicians and journalists usually talk about "the budget" in the singular, as if elected officials meet every year or two to divvy up a single pot of money. That's misleading. State and local officials cannot actually lay their hands on all the revenues

flowing into state and local coffers. Most of the money that comes from the federal government is earmarked for specific programs, such as Medicaid. Revenue streams from many state sources, such as the car registration tax, are likewise dedicated to specific purposes, such as highway construction. State and local officials develop their budgets under several additional restraints as well.

The Governmental Accounting Standards Board. States conduct their accounting and financial reporting according to standards set by the Governmental Accounting Standards Board (GASB). In 2004, the organization issued GASB 45, a rule that mandated that states tally and disclose the cost of healthcare benefits pledged to current and retired state employees. As if that were not daunting enough, the states also had to find a way to begin saving enough to cover their pension liabilities, or they risked damaging their credit ratings. GASB 45 helped expose a massive gap between what states promised public-sector retirees and what they could actually pay for, a gap that was pushed wider by the revenue crunch of the Great Recession. The basic problem is that while state pension schemes have the funds to pay for promised retiree pensions and healthcare benefits in the short term, they do not have the money set aside to pay for the expected long-term increases in those costs. As of 2010 the gap between the assets of state pension funds and their financial obligation to cover promised pension and healthcare benefits was $1.4 trillion (yes, that's trillion with a *t*).[65] States have taken some steps to try to close the gap by reducing benefits and increasing employee contributions to those benefits, but even with those reductions it is not clear that states will be able to cover their promises without resorting to getting more from taxpayers.

Unfunded Mandates. For years, state officials complained bitterly about the federal government's habit of mandating that states achieve a goal, such as an environmental cleanup, but then failing to provide any money to pay for it. State officials viewed such unfunded mandates as an affront to the notion of federalism itself. In 1995, Congress passed legislation designed to curtail unfunded mandates imposed on states, but this did not end the problem. Ironically, in the late 1990s, state governments increasingly imposed unfunded mandates on county and city governments. Evidently, many state governments were no more able to resist the temptation to set goals and make someone else pay for them than the federal government had long been.

As detailed in chapter 2, under federalism the state governments and the federal government are coequals, at least in theory. If the federal government encroaches too much on state prerogatives, the U.S. Supreme Court can step in and strike federal actions down. But states are not federations; indeed, within their own borders they are more accurately described as unitary systems. Local governments are not equal partners with state governments. In most cases, state governments are free to intervene in local arrangements as they please. Beginning in the late nineteenth century, many states did extend the sovereign powers of government to local governments by passing legislation that provided for home rule. Communities could enact charters and ordinances, change their names, and annex their neighbors without the permission of the legislature. They also controlled their own budgets and property taxes.

At the time, California was one of the strongest home rule states. In recent years, however, that has changed. California cities now control less than half of their discretionary spending. The state tells them what they must do with the rest. The situation is even worse for California's counties. They have the final say over less than one-third of the money they spend.[66]

Ballot Initiatives and the Budget Process.

California's experience illustrates one of the most significant trends in state finances—the growing use of ballot initiatives to shape and restrain state tax systems. According to Bill Piper of the Initiative and Referendum Institute, voters put 130 tax initiatives on ballots nationwide from 1978 through 1999. Roughly two-thirds were antitax initiatives that cut, limited, or eliminated taxes in some way. Of these, 41 passed. In fact, a whopping 67 percent of all antitax initiatives that came up for a vote from 1996 through 1999 passed.[67] The net effect of all those initiatives was to create a massive headache for California's budget makers in the twenty-first century—in simple terms, they got to control less

and less of the state's financial affairs, which were increasingly constrained or just put on automatic pilot.

The big problem with using direct democracy to make far-reaching budgetary decisions is that while citizens generally prefer low taxes, they also tend to favor fairly high levels of spending on a wide range of government programs and services. The end result is that state and local governments are required to do a lot of expensive things even as they are being legally required to limit their revenues. These same constraints also made it hard for some states to respond effectively to the fast-moving economic hits brought on by the Great Recession. California is just one of a number of ballot initiative states that are choking on tax and spending policies put in place by voters.

At their worst, antitax budget initiatives can paralyze state legislatures and local governments. At least fifteen states have passed initiatives or referendums that require tax decisions to gain supermajorities in a legislature in order to be approved. Assembling those supermajorities—typically two-thirds or three-quarters of the legislature—is an enormous challenge. In Montana, for example, the required supermajority is three-quarters of the legislature. State Senator Roy Brown once commented on the slim chances of changing tax policy with that obstacle in place: "We can't even get a three-fourths majority vote to go to the bathroom."[68]

Conclusion

State and local governments rely on six major types of taxes to fund the operations of government: property taxes; income taxes; sales taxes; sin, or excise, taxes; user fees; and gift taxes. Each of these taxes has distinct pros and cons. Local governments like property taxes because they set the rates and thus control exactly how much revenue is raised. However, when property taxes rise, seniors and people on fixed incomes often suffer. Income taxes tend to be more progressive; sales taxes are more regressive. The exact configuration of taxes in any given state reflects that state's history and political culture. Tax revenues, in turn, support the budget process by which state and local governments set their spending priorities. Increasingly, governments are relying on user fees—collected in relatively small amounts, but frequently—to supply key revenues.

State and local government finances can be difficult to unravel. However, this is an area that citizens are well advised to watch. Not only do the budget decisions of state and local governments determine the services that individuals enjoy and how much they pay in taxes, but this is also often the arena in which the priorities of public life are sorted out. Is it fair or unfair to ask wealthy citizens to pay a higher percentage of their income in taxes? States such as Texas and Florida, which have no income taxes, have in a sense decided that it is unfair. States such as California, which has an income tax, have reached a different conclusion. Should everyone pay more in taxes to extend healthcare to low-income citizens? Massachusetts's tax policies suggest that its answer is yes. Many states in the Deep South would seem to feel otherwise. In short, the consequences of budget decisions are very real.

There is another reason to pay close attention to state and local finances. Over the past few years, the recovery from the most severe recession since World War II has been sluggish, and states' revenue systems are not set up to make the most of today's evolving economy. To get consistently back in the black, state financial structures almost certainly will need to change. States such as Tennessee that rely heavily on sales tax revenues face particularly serious long-term challenges. As Internet sales and dollars spent on untaxed services continue to grow, sales tax revenues in particular will most likely continue to falter. This will create a need for new revenue-raising measures. Yet states with ballot initiatives may well find new approaches to be blocked by antitax sentiments at the voting booth.

The Latest Research

The running theme of this chapter is that state and local budgets are all-important. The process of how subnational governments get their money, spend their money, and keep revenue and expenditures in a legally mandated balance is ground zero for the most important current policy debates in state and local politics.

Academic research typically lags behind current events by several years, so most of the latest research on taxing and spending is not based on data from the past fiscal year or two. Nevertheless, the latest research has plenty of lessons for states and localities facing tough fiscal decisions and for voters who want to hold policymakers accountable for those decisions. The research discussed below reflects two central themes: (1) the real-life impact of state-level economic conditions and who does or does not get held responsible for those conditions, and (2) the efforts of states to deal with the effects of taxing and spending limitations.

• • • • • • • • • • • • • • • • • • • •

- **Brown, Adam R.** 2010. "Are Governors Responsible for the State Economy? Partisanship, Blame, and Divided Federalism." *Journal of Politics* 72: 605–615.

One of the long-standing debates in state politics scholarship is who gets held accountable for economic performance: the president, governors, or a combination of both. This is a particularly interesting time to revisit this question, as governors are pursuing different approaches to addressing state-level fiscal problems and President Barack Obama was recently reelected to a second term despite sluggish economic growth and unemployment rates flirting with double digits. Brown's study is noteworthy because it shows that voters assign blame or credit for economic fortunes not based on state or national economic conditions or the policies of policymakers, but on the partisanship of whoever holds high executive office. Essentially, if the economy is doing poorly, voters who share their governor's partisanship will give the governor a pass—and they will blame the president if he is from the opposite party. If the economy is doing well, voters who identify with the governor's party will give that official the credit. This has the interesting implication that objective economic conditions are not as important to voters' judgment of the performance of a chief executive's taxing and spending policies as one might think.

- **Bifuloco, Robert, Beverly Bunch, William Duncombe, Mark Robbins, and William Simonsen.** 2012. "Debt and Deception: How States Avoid Making Hard Fiscal Decisions." *Public Administration Review* 72: 659–667.

The vast majority of state governments, as noted in this chapter, are legally required to have balanced budgets. This seems simple enough; doesn't it just mean that revenue has to equal expenditure? Well, sort of. Over the past few years, states have tried all sorts of accounting gimmicks to satisfy the letter if not the spirit of balanced budget mandates. Some of those gimmicks can obscure the real health of state government balance sheets. Bifuloco and his colleagues examine how several states borrow to finance current operating expenditures—something that seems mighty close to the deficit spending that state governments are supposedly prevented from doing. To make their financial statements look balanced, states underfund long-term obligations, defer payments, restructure debt, and borrow money from designated funds to cover general fund deficits. These moves are largely designed to get state governments cash in the short term while piling up debt obligations in the long term. This study reveals the extent to which this sort of deficit financing in all but name goes on and raises questions about the transparency of state financial statements.

- **Bae, Suho, Seong-gin Moon, and Changhoon Jung.** 2012. "Economic Effects of State-Level Tax and Expenditure Limitations." *Public Administration Review* 72: 649–658.

More than thirty states have tax and expenditure limitations, or TELs. TELs are designed to place limits on how much state governments can tax and, at least according to their advocates, to help boost economic growth by keeping government smaller. This study, however, uses the comparative method to show that the theory does not work in practice. It looks at state economic data over a twenty-year period, comparing economic performance between states and the particular types of TEL mechanisms the states do or do not employ. The authors conclude that TELs have no impact on per capita income in states and have a negative effect on employment. Rather than boosting private-sector economic activity, TELs are more likely to simply reduce the production of public goods and services. The results of this study impart a cautionary—and controversial—lesson for states that are balancing budgets by cutting spending and avoiding tax hikes.

- **Kelly, Nathan, and Christopher Witko.** 2012. "Federalism and American Inequality." *Journal of Politics* 74: 414–426.

One of the most contentious issues in current American politics is income inequality. Do the haves get too much and the have-nots too little? If so, should government do anything to balance things out? In an era of tight budgets and bruising arguments over who, if anyone, should be taxed more and how that money should or should not be spent, answers to these questions are contested and controversial. This debate has played out primarily on a national stage, but this study uses the comparative method to show that state-level factors contribute greatly to income inequality. Kelly and Witko look at more than three decades' worth of state-level data and find that things such as a state's demographics, the degree of unionization in its labor pool, and the partisan makeup of its government are differences that make a difference to income inequality.

Chapter Review

Key Concepts

- American Recovery and Reinvestment Act (ARRA) (p. 82)
- balanced budget (p. 95)
- bonds (p. 94)
- budget deficit, or shortfall (p. 82)

- budget process (p. 94)

- capital investments (p. 94)

- discretionary spending (p. 97)

- dividend (p. 93)

- entitlement (p. 99)

- estate taxes (p. 84)

- excise, or sin, taxes (p. 83)

- expenditures (p. 97)

- fiscal federalism (p. 98)

- fiscal year (p. 94)

- focused consumption taxes (p. 84)

- general obligation bonds (p. 94)

- gift taxes (p. 84)

- income taxes (p. 87)

- insurance trust funds (p. 89)

- intergovernmental transfers (p. 89)

- municipal bonds (p. 94)

- progressive tax system (p. 87)

- regressive taxes (p. 84)

- revenue bonds (p. 94)

- revenues (p. 82)

- sales taxes (p. 84)

- severance taxes (p. 89)

- tax burden (p. 84)

- tax capacity (p. 92)

- tax effort (p. 92)

- user fees (p. 83)

Suggested Websites

- **www.cbpp.org.** Website of the Center on Budget and Policy Priorities. Founded in 1981, the center studies fiscal policy and public programs at the federal and state levels that affect low-income and moderate-income families and individuals. An excellent source of information on state budget issues.

- **www.census.gov/compendia/statab.** The U.S. Census Bureau provides an online version of the *Statistical Abstract of the United States.* Section 8, "State and Local Government Finances and Employment," provides a wealth of information on state and local government revenue and spending. The Census Bureau has announced that it is ceasing publication of the *Abstract* after 2012 as a budget-cutting measure. The 2013 version is to be published by a private company, ProQuest.

- **www.gao.gov.** Home page of the Government Accountability Office, which is tracking the use of ARRA stimulus funds in sixteen of the largest states.

- **www.nasbo.org.** Website of the National Association of State Budget Officers.

- **www.ncsl.org.** Website of the National Conference of State Legislatures. NCSL's fiscal program produces periodic state budget and tax updates and tracks state actions to close budget gaps.

- **www.recovery.gov.** The federal government's web page dedicated to tracking ARRA.

State Stats on Finance

Explore and compare data on the states! Go to **college.cqpress .com/sites/essentials-govstateandlocal** to do these exercises.

1. In 2011, the national per capita federal economic stimulus fund amount was $855. How does your state compare to this average? What might account for some of the variation? Is this the same trend as usual when it comes to your state receiving money from the federal government?

2. Does your state collect income tax? Sales tax? Which source of revenue does your state most heavily rely on? Do you think that this is a good thing? How do your state's methods of obtaining revenue compare with those of neighboring states?

3. Mississippi collects a relatively high amount of sales tax revenue per capita. Considering its population, why might some people have a problem with this taxation system? Explain why you agree or disagree. Now, look next door at Alabama. Why might these two neighboring states be so different in terms of sales tax revenue?

4. How much outstanding debt does your state have? If your state mandates a balanced budget, where did this debt come from? How does your state's debt load compare to that of the states around it?

5. Which state has the most local government direct general expenditures? Which state has the least? Why do you think that there is so much variation? Do these expenditures translate into jobs and services in these states?

Long lines were the order of the day for many voters on election day 2012, even though turnout was not at record levels. Many states have passed controversial laws in recent years that require individuals to present identification before they can vote.

ch.

5

Political Attitudes and Participation

VENTING AND VOTING

- What causes some states or localities to change party preferences?
- How do state regulations affect voting?
- How do politicians tune in to what citizens are thinking?

Political power in the U.S. is no longer held strictly by white males. In fact, there seem to be fewer white, Anglo-Saxon Protestants (or WASPs) running things than there have ever been. Barack Obama, of course, is the nation's first African American president. Joe Biden, his vice president, is Catholic—as are John Boehner, speaker of the House, and Nancy Pelosi, House minority leader. Every member of the U.S. Supreme Court is either Jewish or Catholic, and Harry Reid, the Senate Democratic leader, is Mormon. Only Mitch McConnell, the Republican leader in the Senate, is a WASP. "The top male WASP in government is the Senate minority leader—who's married to an Asian American," tweeted John J. Pitney Jr., a professor of government at Claremont McKenna College.[1]

While there are still a lot of white males in that bunch, the complete political dominance of WASPs with a Y chromosome is increasingly a thing of the past. Women and racial, ethnic, and religious minorities are becoming a greater presence at the peak of government power, and not just federal government power. Across the fifty states in 2012, there were six women governors, two Hispanic governors, one African American governor, and two governors of Indian descent. This all reflects demographic changes taking place in the country at large. William H. Frey, a demographer at the Brookings Institution, has suggested that the electorate that propelled Obama to power in 2008 offers a possible glimpse into the future of American politics. It is both "post-ethnic" (meaning candidates can appeal to upper-income whites as well as racial minorities) and "post-boomer" (meaning candidates can appeal across age groups). Frey cautioned that the political future hasn't yet fully arrived, but the long-term trends point in that direction.[2] Consider that during the 1950s, whites made up more than 90 percent of the electorate (95 percent in 1952).[3] In 2012, whites made up 72 percent, African Americans made up 13 percent, and Hispanics constituted 10 percent. Generally speaking, voting participation has increased among ethnic minorities since 2004, while among eligible whites voting has declined. In 2012, African Americans voted in higher proportions than whites for the first time in U.S. history.

Although these trends reflect a shift toward demographics traditionally associated with Democratic voters, Republicans have won plenty of elections. In 2012, they retained a majority in the House of Representatives and at the state level consolidated some of the huge electoral gains the GOP made in the 2010 elections. Demographics are clearly not political destiny. Although many groups show a propensity for voting for one party or the other—for example, African Americans for Democrats, regular churchgoers for the GOP— no group votes entirely as a bloc. And even groups that give overwhelming support to one party's candidates at a particular time do not do so forever.

Some states have tended to vote one way for president but the opposite for governor or other important offices, although that is becoming increasingly less true. Localities such as counties do tend to vote for one party over the other— that's one reason there are so few competitive U.S. House or state legislative seats. Still, even in the bluest of blue or reddest of red communities there are always exceptions. This is why political pros are increasingly borrowing technology and demographic breakdowns from consumer marketers. Political data mining has evolved far beyond the old idea that you can guess a voter's partisan leanings by looking at the types of magazines he or she subscribes to. Now, campaigns access all manner of consumer databases, gleaning such near-complete portraits of individuals' habits and inclinations as to threaten the sanctity of the secret ballot, according to Chris Evans, managing editor of the *Minnesota Journal of Law, Science & Technology*. Campaigns use "big data" to test messages online and get the right, tailored messages to voters as individuals rather than mass groups within the population. "The goal of these 'digital dossiers' is to profile likely voters and identify traits that predict voting habits," Evans wrote in 2012. "Political data-mining has proven to be a winning election tactic, but the resulting erosion of voter privacy has gone unabated."[4]

But politicians still struggle to figure out what the voters back home are thinking, since sometimes it seems that the only people they hear from at the capitol or city hall are part of some organized group. How can they pay attention to the needs and desires of the majority of constituents who do not send them e-mails, belong to interest groups, or even read the local newspaper?

This chapter answers those questions, and also looks at how voters maintain or change the political cultures and preferences of their states and districts over time. Some of the mechanisms for change discussed include elections and the avenues for direct democracy, such as ballot initiatives and referendums. Public opinion—and how and whether politicians respond to it—is another factor that influences political outcomes.

Elections

Unquestionably, we have created an odd paradox as a nation. We like elections—we hold more of them than any other country on earth—yet we consistently score one of the lowest voter turnout rates of any democracy in the world.

State political cultures are reflected and sustained through elections, when a majority or **plurality** of voters elects officials who more or less reflect the political beliefs of the majority or plurality. Elections represent the fundamental process of representative democracies; they are the primary mechanism used to connect the will of the people to the actions of government. Election laws are set and controlled by the states, and each state must determine what constitutes a valid vote. There has long been a great deal of variation among states regarding how easy or how hard it is for citizens to vote. Some of the differences have been smoothed away in recent years by federal laws and court decisions, but many remain, and they largely reflect the types of political cultures that Elazar describes (and that are outlined in the preceding chapters).

These differences, in turn, affect national politics. The way that people vote in their own states—the type of access they have to the ballot—helps determine the success or failure of presidential candidates and the makeup of Congress. With numerous states in recent years enacting voter identification requirements and other restrictions

---

Plurality
The highest number of votes garnered by any of the candidates for a particular office but short of an outright majority.

that make it harder for people to register and vote, voting rights have reemerged as one of the most salient issues in American politics.

But differences in election laws are not the only reason one state may tend to vote differently than its neighbors. For about one hundred years after the Civil War, for example, Republicans were not a true national party. They had next to no presence in the South, which still resented Republican intrusions during the Civil War and Reconstruction in support of abolition, suffrage, and greater opportunity for African Americans. That is one reason Democrats held the region for decades. In fact, the Republican Party of the nineteenth century bore a closer resemblance in some ways to the Democratic Party of today than to its own twenty-first-century GOP descendant. Times and political parties change, however. These days, the South is one of the pillars of Republican strength. The region's continuing conservatism now fits well within the GOP.

Southern states and the less populous, heavily rural states of the Mountain West, such as Idaho, Wyoming, and Montana, tilt toward Republican interests and form a bloc that has helped elect presidents through its disproportionate share of the electoral college. Each state's electoral college votes are equal to the size of its congressional delegation. Because each state is guaranteed at least two U.S. senators and one U.S. representative, the electoral college gives a minimum of three votes to each state, regardless of population. This means that the voting power of smaller states in the electoral college is disproportionately larger than the states' population, whereas the voting power of bigger states is disproportionately lower.

For example, in 2012, California had fifty-five electoral votes to represent a population of nearly 37.7 million. In that presidential election, then, each of California's electoral college votes represented about 685,000 people. Contrast that with Wyoming, which had the minimum of three electoral college votes but a population of only about 568,000. Each of Wyoming's electoral college votes represented not quite 190,000 people. Political analyst Steven Hill, director of the political reform program at the New America Foundation, calls this "affirmative action for low-population states."[5] This is one reason George W. Bush won the presidency in 2000 despite losing the popular vote. Imbalance in the representation of electoral college votes leads to periodic efforts by groups that want to make sure no one ends up in the White House with fewer popular votes than the opponent—an incredibly tough reform to pull off without amending the Constitution. In recent years, for example, states such as Maryland, Massachusetts, and California have enacted laws that will require them to award their electoral votes according to national popular vote percentages, but those measures won't take effect until a preponderance of states are on board with the idea. In states where the GOP controls the legislature but voters have tended to prefer Democratic presidential candidates, such as Pennsylvania and Virginia, legislators have talked about awarding electoral votes by congressional district rather than sticking with the traditional winner-take-all system. But those efforts have yet to meet with success.

The Mountain West, meanwhile, may also be shifting in terms of partisan leanings. No state within the region supported a Democrat for president between 1968 and 1998, but in 2008 Barack Obama carried Colorado, Nevada, and New Mexico. He won all three states again in 2012, and Democrats have their eye on Arizona for the future. The region retains its traditional libertarian response to government in that it wants to be left alone by a federal government that owns the vast majority of the land in many western states. But the region's demographics have changed, and this shift has changed its politics to some extent. There have been dramatic increases in the minority share of the population as well as large influxes of other new citizens from outside the region, with the bulk of folks now living in metropolitan areas.[6]

Similar resistance in the suburbs to conservative stances on social issues has helped Democrats in recent elections. In Missouri, as the Democratic core vote continued to extend outward from the central city of St. Louis, Republicans were left with less room with which to work. They dominate Missouri's legislature and congressional delegation, but in statewide races they need to turn out voters en masse in dozens of sparsely populated rural and exurban counties to offset not just the big cities but also their recent losses in the suburbs. In 2012, Republicans gained a supermajority in both legislative chambers, but Democrats won every statewide race but one. "Running statewide for a Republican is a harder challenge," said Mike Gibbons, a former GOP state senator from St. Louis County who lost in his 2008 bid for state attorney general. "You have to gain a substantial margin in the smaller counties. That means you have to travel all over the state, and you also have to compete in suburban areas to hold them close."[7]

A similar dynamic has played out in suburban parts of California, Virginia, New York, and numerous other states in recent years, as suburbs have become more dense and diverse, with more immigrants settling outside the central cities that were long most attractive to newcomers. "The so-called inner-ring suburbs are now almost as dense and almost as politically Democratic as the central cities," says Lawrence Levy, director of the Center for Suburban Studies at Long Island's Hofstra University.[8]

A Voice for the Public

Elections may be how citizens can speak out for their beliefs, and they may give states a voice in national politics, but you wouldn't know it from the interest they generate among the general public. Voter turnout levels are perpetually disappointing. Less than half the voting-age population cast ballots in presidential elections. In elections in which congressional or statewide offices are at the top of the ticket, the percentage drops to less than 40 percent. For municipal elections, turnout rates are generally less than 20 percent. Voting does tend to pick up for competitive races, when voters feel they have a genuine choice and might make a real difference. Turnout may also tick upward if voters perceive that core issues are at stake.

The idea that voters are motivated by appeals to a few core issues underlies the growing use of ballot initiatives as a means of promoting turnout. For instance, the numbers of conservative Ohio voters who turned out to cast their ballots in favor of a

> The idea that voters are motivated by appeals to a few core issues underlies the growing use of ballot initiatives as a means of promoting turnout. For instance, the numbers of conservative Ohio voters who turned out to cast their ballots in favor of a constitutional ban on gay marriage in 2004 may have helped Bush carry that year's most contested state.

constitutional ban on gay marriage in 2004 may have helped Bush carry that year's most contested state. Two years later, liberals, looking for weapons of their own, ran initiatives for minimum wage increases on half a dozen state ballots. Some political scientists have found evidence that controversial ballot initiatives do increase turnout, particularly in nonpresidential election years.[9]

But the idea that most voters are motivated by a single issue or handful of issues oversimplifies matters. It is true that the majority of voters remain loyal to one party over the other throughout most of their voting lives. They can be convinced to cast their votes—or even to change their votes—by any number of factors. The state of the economy, the health of a state's budget, corruption scandals, or the course of a military conflict may change minds and voting habits. "Each election forces one to revisit such topics as to what's effective in voter mobilization or who you aim at," says independent political analyst Rhodes Cook.[10]

After 2008, the story seemed to be young voters. Turnout rates are traditionally abysmal for young people. Young voters turned out in record numbers for Obama in 2008 but returned to their usual habits of apathy in the congressional and state elections of 2010. However, people under 30 defied widespread media predictions that they would stay home in 2012. They once again gave heavy support to Obama and made up a slightly larger share of the electorate than they had four years earlier.

State Supervision of Elections

The U.S. Constitution gives states the authority to determine "the times, places and manner of holding elections." In nearly every state, the secretary of state has the practical duty of running elections: setting dates, qualifying candidates, and printing and counting the ballots. In a few states, the lieutenant governor or a state election board oversees these chores. The states, in turn, rely on the counties or, in some cases, cities to run the polls themselves. The localities draw precinct boundaries and set up and supervise polling places. In many cases, they have the main responsibility for registering voters. Following an election, county officials count up the ballots and report the results to the appropriate individual, such as the secretary of state, who then tabulates and certifies the totals.

The styles of the ballots used vary from state to state. California currently uses a random alphabet system to decide the order in which candidate names appear, rotating the starting letter of that alphabet in each state assembly district. The **office group ballot**, also known as the **Massachusetts ballot**, lists candidates' names, followed by their party designations, under the title of the office they are seeking (governor, state representative, and so on). The other major type of ballot is the **party column ballot**, or the **Indiana ballot**, which "arranges the candidates for each office in columns according to their party designation."[11] Fifteen states make it even easier for citizens to vote for party nominees—voters can cast a **straight ticket** vote for all of one party's candidates with one computer click or pull of the lever. This is a practice in decline, however; several states have abolished it, most recently Wisconsin in 2011.[12]

Office Group (Massachusetts) Ballot
A ballot in which candidates are listed by name under the title of the office they are seeking.

Party Column (Indiana) Ballot
A ballot in which the names of candidates are divided into columns arranged according to political party.

Straight Ticket
Originally, a type of ballot that allowed voters to pick all of one party's candidates at once; today, voting a straight ticket refers to voting for all of one party's candidates for various offices—for instance, voting for all Democrats or all Republicans.

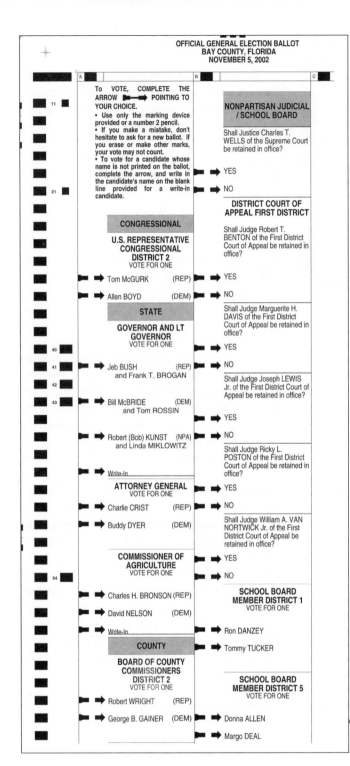

The two main types of ballots are the office group ballot and the party column ballot. These sample ballots from elections in Florida and West Virginia show the differences between the two basic approaches to ballot design. The West Virginia ballot exemplifies the party column ballot, which lists the candidates in columns that indicate their party designations. The Florida ballot, on the other hand, emphasizes office rather than party. This is the key feature of the office group ballot, which lists candidates by name and party under the title of the office they are running for.

Each state's election code determines the specific details about ballots and what exact form the ballot takes. By the early 1990s, about 80 percent of the states had replaced traditional paper ballots with punch cards, machines in which voters pull a lever next to the names of the candidates of their choice, or optical-scan voting machines.[13] Voters in most states now use electronic systems resembling automated teller machines (ATMs), but many states require a paper trail to allow for verification of the electronic results. All but a handful of states tabulate votes for write-in candidates, although victories or even significant showings by such candidates are few and far between.

A few cities, including Minneapolis and San Francisco, use instant-runoff voting (IRV) for municipal elections. Rather than picking one candidate, voters rank all the choices. If one candidate receives more than 50 percent of the first-choice vote, he or she wins. If no one receives a majority of first-choice votes, the candidate with the lowest number of votes is disqualified and his or her supporters' second-place choices are redistributed among the remaining candidates. This process continues until someone emerges with a majority. Supporters argue that such a system means a candidate who is acceptable to a majority of voters will win, as opposed to the outcome in a winner-take-all election in which a candidate with only, say, 30 to 40 percent of the vote comes out on top of a large split field. Both the Heisman Trophy winner and the winner of the Academy Award for Best Picture are now determined by an IRV or preferential voting system. But instant-runoff voting has its critics, who say it can result in victories for candidates who are the first choice of few. Jean Quan, for instance, was elected mayor of Oakland, California, in 2010 after being picked as the first choice of just 24 percent of voters. Burlington, Vermont, and Aspen, Colorado, have abandoned the IRV method following complaints that it left voters confused.[14]

Regulating the Parties

A state's authority to print ballots or purchase voting software gives it enormous control over which parties and candidates are presented to the voters. Until the late nineteenth century, parties themselves printed the ballots, a system that obviously encouraged voters to select a straight ticket of their chosen party's nominees. The advent of the **secret ballot**, also known as the **Australian ballot**, led the states to print their own ballots and, therefore, to determine which parties should appear on ballots. "From there," writes Kay Lawson, a retired San Francisco State University political scientist,

"it seemed but a short step to requiring that parties show a minimum level of support to qualify."[15]

The Republican and Democratic parties are themselves regulated at the state level by a bewildering array of varying state laws. Some states provide detailed regulations for party organization, activities, and nominating procedures. Others are silent on many specific matters. According to political scientist V. O. Key, the traditional Democratic one-party control of the South, although now a thing of the past, led to the introduction of the political primary. Voters had no real choice in the general election, so primaries gave them a say in who ultimately would hold an office.[16] These days, nearly all states hold primary elections to pick party nominees for state offices, although some states, such as Virginia, still nominate candidates at party conventions. (A fuller discussion of political parties is found in chapter 6.)

The two major parties may not like all the state ballot regulations they have to comply with, but rules in many states favor the major parties over new or minor parties and independent candidates. Prior to the 1968 Supreme Court decision in *Williams v. Rhodes*, it was possible for states to have no mechanism at all to qualify new parties for their ballots. Even today, according to Richard Winger, editor of the newsletter *Ballot Access News*, in eleven states new parties cannot qualify for the ballot before they have picked their candidates, who must be listed on their ballot access petition, the collection of voters' signatures.[17]

The Court's decision meant that a state no longer could require that a certain percentage of signatures be collected in each county. But that did not mean states could not erect new roadblocks to keep out aspiring parties or candidates. Nine states changed their laws to require that signatures be collected in each congressional district. This kept ballot access elusive for candidates or parties that had most of their support in particular cities or regions. Fifteen states also placed time constraints on when signatures could be collected.

Secret (Australian) Ballot
A ballot printed by a state that allows voters to pick and choose among different candidates and party preferences in private.

Policy in Practice

Vote Counts More Accurate—but Still Not Perfect

Perhaps nothing demonstrates more clearly how much better states and counties have gotten at counting votes than a look at how other entities do it.

Republican presidential caucuses in 2012 were plagued with problems. Several states were embarrassed by snafus following their caucuses, which are run by political parties rather than by public officials.

In Iowa, an eight-vote election-night win for Mitt Romney was later converted into a thirty-four-vote victory for Rick Santorum, with party officials admitting that they didn't, in fact, know the actual number. (The state party chair resigned.) Counting of caucus votes was slow enough in Nevada to raise doubts during the delay, while in Maine, the GOP decided to declare Romney the statewide winner even before some counties had held their caucuses. "It's been stunning to watch," said Cathy Cox, a former Georgia secretary of state. "Caucus voting looks like the Wild West of voting."

Election experts agree that vote counting has generally gotten quicker and more accurate since presidential election results in Florida were disputed all the way up to the U.S. Supreme Court in 2000. After that controversy, the federal government devoted billions of dollars to help states modernize their voting machinery, leading to widespread adoption of electronic, touch-screen voting.

But voting in the United States is a highly decentralized process. Every state has its own rules, which are then generally implemented separately by individual counties. State and county election officials continue to suffer embarrassing moments, as when New York City found nearly two hundred thousand uncounted votes a month after the general election in 2010, an oversight Mayor Michael Bloomberg called "a royal screw-up."

Despite concerns raised from the start about electronic voting, such screw-ups are generally caused by human error. Most New York State jurisdictions download the votes cast on voting machines onto flash drives, which are taken to a central computer for counting. The problems in New York City were the result of a system of counting votes by hand, in which district poll workers write results out on tally sheets that get delivered (one hopes) by hand to a central counting house.

Those kinds of problems might recur in other places. With federal dollars from the Help America Vote Act (HAVA) of 2002 pretty much having run dry, many jurisdictions are strapped when it comes time to buy new machines. And some don't want to. After being pressed by activists nervous about the lack of paper trails from electronic machines and the risks of vote tampering through hacking, the Virginia General Assembly in 2007 banned local governments from buying new touch-screen voting machines when the current electronic models wear out. Voters instead will be using a scanning system that requires them to mark paper ballots and then scan them into a machine.

Problems caused by the improper reading of paper ballots are what have spurred innovations in voting machines over the past decade. And concerns about electronic voting machines remain. In at least some polling places in sixteen states, machines don't produce any paper trail that can be used as a backup in case of a recount or dispute. And about half the states have systems that are vulnerable to hacking, especially when it comes to military personnel voting overseas, according to a 2012 study by researchers at Rutgers Law School. This means that the job of counting votes remains more complicated than it looks—as GOP caucus organizers have found. "If you can't produce pretty instantaneous results, people are going to lose confidence in the results and you're going to open up the floodgates to opportunities for fraud," says Cox, the former Georgia official.

Source: Adapted from Alan Greenblatt, "Caucus System Cracks Revealed during 2012 GOP Primary Season," *Governing*, May 2012.

Some of the most restrictive ballot access laws have been repealed by various state and federal courts. For example, Ohio and California used to require new parties to qualify even before the election year began, but these laws were struck down in 2006 and 2012, respectively. Virginia formerly blocked petitioners from gathering signatures outside their home congressional districts, but that law was also struck down in 2012. In West Virginia the law used to require petition circulators who were trying to collect signatures to tell everyone they approached, "If you sign my petition, you can't vote in the primary." That happened to not be true—but it was the law, until a court struck it down in 2004. Why make a law requiring circulators to lie to voters? Well, such a fib benefits the major parties by keeping out the competition, and the major parties write the laws.

These sorts of laws benefiting political parties, if not the democratic process, remain on the books in various places. In Texas, voters who participate in major-party primaries are not allowed to sign petitions to get new parties on the ballot; the state also requires citizens to know their voter registration numbers and to affix those numbers next to their signatures on petitions. Quick—what's your voter registration number? In its 1971 decision in *Jenness v. Fortson*, the Supreme Court upheld a Georgia law that requires minor parties or independent candidates to collect signatures that represent 5 percent of registered voters. In 1986, the Georgia legislature lowered that threshold to 1 percent, but that still means more than fifty thousand signatures, a bar no one has been able to meet since 2000. "This is a very, very major organizational undertaking," Larry Jacobs, a political scientist at the University of Minnesota, said about minor-party ballot access. "It's like building an army from scratch."[18]

For third-party and independent candidates, then, it can be a real challenge to gain access to the ballot. Of course, how hard or easy it is for these political outsiders to get on the ballot varies from state to state. As with everything else, there are differences that make a difference. Given what we know about Elazar's theory regarding southern, or traditionalistic, states and their hierarchical attitude toward politics, it should not surprise us that states such as Alabama, North Carolina, and Oklahoma have the most restrictive ballot access laws. That does not mean that hundreds of minor-party and independent candidates have not overcome all these hurdles and more to win spots on statewide ballots. A few of them have even won election as governor—for instance, in Minnesota in 1998, Maine in 1994 and 1998, and Rhode Island in 2010. (Note that all three of these examples involve moralistic or individualistic states.) Lincoln Chafee, who was elected Rhode Island governor as an independent in 2010, decided it would be easier to run for reelection as a Democrat and announced he was joining that party in 2013.

Even winning a place on a ballot one year is no guarantee that members of minor parties will qualify the next time around. Alabama requires that a minor party poll at least 20 percent of the vote for governor to win an automatic qualification for the next ballot. New Jersey, Oklahoma, and Virginia require at least 10 percent, and Pennsylvania requires 15 percent, or more than 1 million votes. Given all the restrictions, Lawson concludes, "The laws have been effective in keeping minor parties off the ballot in election after election."[19]

Minor-party candidates are concerned about ballot access in more progressive states as well. Since 2008, Washington State has used a top-two or **blanket primary** system, in which the top two finishers proceed to the general election, regardless of party. California voters adopted the same system in 2010. The blanket primary presents a big obstacle to minor parties and independent candidates; primary elections tend to be low-turnout affairs dominated by voters who are major-party partisans. As a result, independents and minor-party candidates rarely have the chance to appear on general election ballots. "It's the biggest threat to

---

Blanket Primary
An initial round of voting in which candidates from all parties appear on the same ballot, with the top two vote-getters proceeding on to the general election.

independent and third parties in the last 50 years," complained Christina Tobin, a Libertarian Party candidate for California secretary of state in 2010.[20]

Why all the restrictions? Keeping minor parties off the ballot naturally helps the two major parties. Those who are in power control the rules that keep them in power. "VA's D legislature thought the rules up, knowing they would benefit themselves & friends," tweeted Larry Sabato, director of the University of Virginia's Center for Politics, in 2011. "Then Rs, once in power, liked restrictions too."[21]

Restricting Voters

States do not just regulate the access of parties to the ballot; they also regulate the interaction of citizens with that ballot. They determine who can register to vote and how they can register. Changes in federal law over the years have removed many of the barriers that states once imposed to restrict voting rights, those based on property ownership, literacy, race, sex, and age. But there are still differences among states in how easy or difficult it is for citizens to register to vote—a necessary step toward having the chance to vote in every state except North Dakota, which does not require voter registration. A majority of states now register voters automatically in various ways, for instance when they get driver's licenses. But the differences between states when it comes to ballot access have become more pronounced in recent years, with 17 states passing new laws to tighten registration or voter identification requirements in 2011 and 2012 alone.

In the early years of the nation, most eastern states required citizens to own property in order to be eligible to vote. Such requirements diminished over time, in large part because the western frontier states lacked the type of class structure that reinforced them. The eastern states, however, soon came up with the idea of imposing literacy tests. Before they could vote, new immigrants had to demonstrate knowledge of the state constitution or other complex issues to the satisfaction of the local election official.[22] Native whites who were illiterate often were exempted

from this requirement. Southern states took up literacy testing as a means of keeping African Americans from voting, as African Americans generally received an inadequate education in schools segregated by race. Literacy tests remained a part of the southern legal landscape until the federal Voting Rights Act of 1965 barred them. Southern states also sometimes imposed poll taxes as a means of disenfranchising African Americans and some poor whites until the Supreme Court found them unconstitutional in 1966. (See the box "A Difference That Makes a Difference: How Some States Discourage Voters.")

Several amendments to the U.S. Constitution expanded voting rights to include minorities and women. The Fifteenth Amendment, passed following the Civil War, was meant to end discrimination against black men seeking to vote. Until the civil rights movement of the 1960s, however, southern states effectively bypassed the provisions of the amendment for a century through literacy tests, intimidation, and other means. The Voting Rights Act of 1965 gave the federal government the authority to review state requirements for registration and voting. In 1964, the Twenty-Fourth Amendment banned the use of poll taxes meant to keep African Americans and other poor people from voting. Women received the right to vote with the ratification of the Nineteenth Amendment in 1920. The voting age was lowered to eighteen by the Twenty-Sixth Amendment in 1971. In 1993, Congress passed what became known as the "motor voter" law, which requires states to allow citizens to register to vote when they take tests to receive their driver's licenses.

Why all the effort to get people registered to vote? The purpose of registering voters is to prevent fraud. Registration is intended to stop people from voting more than once or outside their home jurisdictions. This makes sense, but throughout the nation's history, many states have used registration laws as a means of making voting inaccessible to some.

Voter fraud has become a contentious topic in recent years, with opinion largely split along partisan lines. Republicans say such measures as requiring each voter to show a form of photo identification are necessary to guard against fraud, while Democrats argue that the GOP is simply trying to block access by poor people and members of minority groups, who are least likely to have such identification—and most likely to vote Democratic. In 2008, the Supreme Court upheld a 2005 Indiana law requiring that anyone seeking to vote produce a government-issued photo ID at the polls, such as a passport or driver's license. "This notion that somehow voter fraud is a dirty word, I don't understand it, because you're talking about people stealing votes, canceling out legitimate votes," Attorney General Alberto Gonzales testified in 2007.[23]

Political scientist Andrew Hacker wrote after the decision that the justices failed to take into account the hardships that requiring a "license to vote" would impose on the 15 percent of Indiana's voting-age population who have no driver's license or other photo identification. Hacker noted that in Milwaukee County, Wisconsin, 53 percent of African Americans lacked a driver's license, compared with 15 percent of the adult white population statewide. "Requiring a driver's license to vote has a disparate racial impact, a finding that once commanded judicial notice," Hacker wrote.[24]

Voter Turnout

Even as some states are tightening requirements for voter registration, with some now requiring individuals to provide proof of citizenship, others are seeking to make the mechanics of registering easier. As of July 2013, 17 states allow citizens to register to vote online.[25] In 2012, Washington State unveiled an app that allows citizens to register using personal data through Facebook. "In this age of social media and more people going online for services, this is a natural way to introduce people to online registration and leverage the power of friends on Facebook to get more people registered," said Shane Hamlin, Washington's co-director of elections.[26]

But efforts to ease registration do not always lead to higher voter turnout. The motor voter law produced an initial spike in registration, but it had little or no effect on the number of people voting. According to Curtis Gans of the Committee for the Study of the American Electorate at American University, **voter turnout** rates have declined by about 25 percent over the past forty years.[27] Turnout did spike for the hotly contested 2004 presidential race, but it dropped again in 2006. A record 131 million Americans cast votes in 2008, but that number dropped by about 5 million four years later. There are countless reasons voter turnout has decreased, including a general disaffection with politics and government, a measurable decline in civic education and newspaper reading, a weakening of such civic-minded institutions as student government and unions, and the changing role of political parties away from engaging and educating voters and toward raising money and providing services to candidates.

Turnout rates are in decline, but they are not declining uniformly across the states. There are many reasons some states have turnout rates 20 percentage points higher than others, most of which are related to political culture, demographics, and party competition.

In general, the closer you live to Canada, the more likely you are to vote. The states with turnout rates of more than 65 percent for the 2012 presidential election, including New Hampshire, Iowa, and Wisconsin, were mostly in the northern tier of the country. The states with lower turnout rates, including Arkansas, Hawaii, Tennessee, and Utah, are in the South or Far West. (See Table 5-1.) What explains the difference? Culture, for one thing. Elazar's theory about moralistic states appears to hold up, at least as far as voter turnout goes. "You're talking about states with fairly vigorous political parties, communications media that do cover politics and an educational system more geared toward citizen engagement than other parts of the country," says Gans. A big state such as California has a mix of cultures—individualistic and moralistic—according to Elazar.

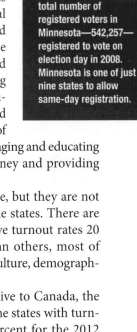

About 18 percent of the total number of registered voters in Minnesota—542,257—registered to vote on election day in 2008. Minnesota is one of just nine states to allow same-day registration.

Voter Turnout
The percentage of voting-eligible citizens who register to vote and do vote.

TABLE 5-1

Percentage of the Voting-Age Population Casting Ballots in the 2012 Presidential Election

Rank	State	Percentage of Total Voting-Age Population	Elazar Classification	Rank	State	Percentage of Total Voting-Age Population	Elazar Classification
1	Minnesota	71.3	Moralistic	27	District of Columbia	56.8	
2	Wisconsin	69.4	Moralistic	28	Connecticut	55.6	Individualistic
3	New Hampshire	67.8	Moralistic	29	Idaho	55.5	Moralistic
4	Iowa	67.1	Moralistic	30	Florida	55.2	Traditionalistic
5	Maine	66.9	Moralistic	31	Alaska	55.1	Individualistic
6	Colorado	68.1	Moralistic	32	South Carolina	53.8	Traditionalistic
7	Ohio	65.2	Individualistic	33	Kansas	53.5	Moralistic
8	Michigan	62.0	Moralistic	34	Rhode Island	53.4	Individualistic
9	Montana	61.6	Moralistic	35	Illinois	53.3	Individualistic
10	Virginia	60.8	Traditionalistic	36	New Jersey	53.3	Individualistic
11	Massachusetts	60.4	Individualistic	37	Kentucky	53.2	Traditionalistic
12	North Carolina	60.2	Traditionalistic	38	Indiana	56.0	Individualistic
13	Maryland	59.6	Individualistic	39	Georgia	52.2	Traditionalistic
14	Missouri	59.5	Individualistic	40	Utah	51.4	Moralistic
15	North Dakota	59.4	Moralistic	41	New Mexico	49.5	Traditionalistic
16	Vermont	59.3	Moralistic	42	Tennessee	49.4	Traditionalistic
17	Oregon	58.6	Moralistic	43	Nevada	48.7	Individualistic
18	Washington	58.3	Moralistic	44	Arkansas	47.5	Traditionalistic
19	Delaware	58.0	Individualistic	45	Arizona	46.5	Traditionalistic
20	South Dakota	57.7	Moralistic	46	New York	46.2	Individualistic
21	Mississippi	57.3	Traditionalistic	47	Oklahoma	46.2	Traditionalistic
22	Louisiana	57.1	Traditionalistic	48	West Virginia	45.5	Traditionalistic
23	Pennsylvania	57.1	Individualistic	49	California	45.1	Moralistic
24	Nebraska	56.8	Individualistic	50	Texas	41.7	Traditionalistic
25	Wyoming	56.8	Individualistic	51	Hawaii	40.0	Individualistic
26	Alabama	56.0	Traditionalistic				

Source: United States Election Project, "2012 General Election Turnout Rates," http://elections.gmu.edu/Turnout_2012G.html.

It is not just political culture that makes a difference. Demographics also matter, and moralistic states tend to be more likely to have demographic profiles favorable to turnout. People are more likely to vote if they are better educated, if they are elderly, and if they are white. "In states with a high percentage of minorities, you're going to have low turnout," says Steven Hill of the New America Foundation. "States with higher voter turnout, such as Minnesota and Maine, tend to be fairly white states."[28] Such moralistic states historically have also bred strong two-party competition. This tends to increase turnout. Citizens in states or districts dominated by one party tend not to vote as eagerly. Their candidate of choice is certain to win—or to lose if they are "orphaned" voters whose party is weak in their home state or district. What we see here are differences that interact with other differences to produce variation in turnout.

Voter turnout rates actually have increased in the South, where many of the historical impediments to registration and voting have declined and the major parties have become more competitive than was the case for more than one hundred years. But the region has merely stabilized at a turnout rate that is slightly lower than that in the rest of the country. Its high proportion of African Americans and its historical legacy of suppressing their votes and the votes of some whites

> Hispanics have long been considered the "sleeping giant" of American politics because of their failure to vote in numbers commensurate with their share of the population—and they're now waking up. They cast just 6 percent of the ballots in the United States in 2004, barely half as many as African Americans even though they constitute a larger portion of the national population.

keep the South's turnout rates sluggish even though African Americans do tend to vote in greater numbers than do other minorities, such as Hispanics.

Hispanics have long been considered the "sleeping giant" of American politics because of their failure to vote in numbers commensurate with their share of the population—and they're now waking up. They cast just 6 percent of the ballots in the United States in 2004, barely half as many as African Americans even though they constitute a larger portion of the national population. Their numbers ticked upward in 2008 but still trailed well behind those of African Americans, who turned out in high numbers in support of Obama. A record number of Hispanics voted in 2010, with their share of the electorate ticking up to nearly 7 percent; still, less than a third of eligible Hispanics cast ballots that year.[29] Hispanics made up 10 percent of voters in 2012,

though, and their share of the electorate—and their influence—is considered certain to grow.

But growth in the Latino electorate is still lagging well behind the rate of growth of the Hispanic population as a whole. The standard explanation is that Hispanics simply lack the well-established political organizations needed to encourage registration and turnout. But other factors are involved as well. More than 20 percent of voting-age Hispanics are noncitizens, and thus not eligible to vote. Then there's age. The median age of Hispanics in the United States is just twenty-seven, compared with forty-two for non-Hispanic whites. A much higher percentage of Hispanics do not vote because they are simply too young. That will change. About fifty thousand Hispanics will turn eighteen every month for the next fifteen years. This could mean that Hispanic voting rolls will swell enormously—or it could mean that young Hispanics, just like young Americans of every race, will fail to exercise their right to vote in great numbers. Hispanics, in short, already behave pretty much like everybody else.

As previously mentioned, many other factors also determine rates of voter turnout. Elderly people tend to vote in high numbers—which is one reason Social Security and Medicare are always important political issues. Young people, by contrast, vote in lower numbers, in percentage terms. People who are wealthy tend to vote more than the poor, and people with higher levels of education vote much more regularly than do people with limited education. These are some of the reasons a high-income state with an educated population, such as Connecticut, has much higher turnout rates than a low-income state where the population is poorly educated on the whole, such as Hawaii.

A competitive election will draw a crowd even in a state that normally has low voter turnout. When people feel they have a real choice, they are more likely to make the effort to vote. A close three-way race for governor, such as the one that took place in Minnesota in 1998, will produce record turnout, whereas a yawner between a popular incumbent and a no-name opponent will make people sit on their hands. Some states tend to have consistently competitive elections because the two major parties are matched fairly evenly, each getting a roughly equal share of support from the electorate. Other states are one-party states, with Republicans or Democrats dominant. One-party states rarely have competitive elections—but when they do, voter turnout is certain to go up.

In his best-selling 2000 book *Bowling Alone,* Robert Putnam notes that moralistic states such as Minnesota and the Dakotas have much higher rates of volunteering, attendance at public meetings, and "social trust," as measured by polls, than do traditionalistic states.[30] In other words, voter turnout is just one indication of the overall sense of civic engagement in a place. States with strong "socializing institutions"—anything from membership organizations to news media that still cover politics—are more likely to be places where people are engaged enough to vote.

What Elections Are Used For

Forty-nine states elect a governor and two sets of state legislators: state senators and members of a state house of representatives, delegates, or assemblymen. Nebraska, the only exception, elects a governor and a one-chamber legislature. Beyond that, there is quite a bit of variation among the states in what they allow people to vote for. Some states allow voters to pick a number of statewide officeholders, such as attorney general and secretary of state, whereas in a few places these are appointed positions. Judges are elected at the voting booth in most places, although not in about a dozen states. Roughly half the states allow voters to make policy decisions directly through ballot initiatives and referendums.

A look at state elections shows that states have quite different rules about who gets to vote for whom. That, in turn, can affect how a state makes policy. A governor who can appoint his or her entire cabinet is likely to have better success at pushing through policies than is a governor who has to contend with a group of elected officials, each with his or her own agenda.

All this is putting aside local elections, which also vary considerably. Most large cities, such as Chicago and San Francisco, allow voters to elect a mayor directly. Many smaller cities have what is called a council-mayor format, in which the city council picks one of its own members to serve as mayor, while the city is administered by a city manager, who is not elected. The same holds true for counties. In some places a county commission picks its own leader, whereas in others voters pick a county executive on their own. Local elections are, for the most part, **nonpartisan**—that is, candidates do not run under a party label. But, again, there are exceptions, such as the highly partisan elections for mayor of New York City.

Electing the Executive Branch

Until recently, New Jersey voters elected only their governor out of all statewide officeholders. This system helped to create one of the most powerful governorships in the country. It wasn't always so. For centuries, New Jersey governors were much weaker players than the state's legislatures. They were limited to a single term and had weak veto and appointment powers. County officials in the state also were quite powerful, at the expense of state officials. That all changed, however, beginning with the new state constitution of 1947. The constitution was pushed through by reformers of the moralistic strain that had always been present, although usually not dominant, in New Jersey politics. The reformers got new powers for the state's governors, including the ability to succeed themselves, authority to appoint not just cabinet officials but also about five hundred board and commission members, and broad authority to reject legislation. New Jersey's governors now can veto all or part of many bills and can issue conditional vetoes, meaning a governor can reject portions of a bill while suggesting new language for it.[31] (New Jersey for many years did not even bother with the office of lieutenant governor, but following a string of gubernatorial vacancies, voters

---

Nonpartisan Election

An election in which the candidates do not have to declare party affiliation or receive a party's nomination; local offices and elections are often nonpartisan.

A Difference
That Makes *a Difference*

How Some States Discourage Voters

The notion of equal access to the ballot for all—one person, one vote—is a cornerstone of American democracy. But how do you determine whether the person seeking to vote has the right to vote?

That question is at the center of one of the major debates in U.S. politics in recent years. Numerous states have put in place greater safeguards to protect against voter fraud, demanding evidence of identification such as driver's licenses at polling places and sometimes requiring that those wishing to register to vote produce documents such as birth certificates.

These laws were given the green light by the U.S. Supreme Court in 2008, when it upheld a 2005 Indiana law requiring that voters produce government-issued photo ID at the polls. Kris Kobach, the Republican secretary of state in Kansas and sponsor of his state's 2011 voter ID law, says that requiring voters to show a photo ID is no burden at a time when they have to do the same to board an airplane, enter a federal building, or even "buy the kind of Sudafed that works."

Such arguments have been persuasive, at least with the general public. Polling in 2012 showed that about three-quarters of Americans supported voter ID laws.

Still, critics of the laws—mostly Democrats—complain that they amount to attempts at voter suppression. The people least likely to be able to produce government-issued IDs are minorities and the young and the old, all groups expected to favor Democratic candidates in general. "He's doing a better job as secretary of state than he did when he was the Republican state chair," Kansas state representative Ann Mah, a Democrat, said of Kobach.

Voter ID laws are a solution in search of a problem, the argument goes. The 41 incidents of improper voting or registration activity for 2010 that Kobach's office cited are mostly accounted for by honest mistakes, Mah argued, such as snowbirds accidentally seeking to vote in two states or felons being allowed to vote although they were ineligible. There was no evidence that Kansas was seeing large numbers of illegal aliens voting, or that there was a conspiracy on the part of any party or group to affect the outcomes of elections, said Chris Biggs, Kobach's Democratic predecessor as secretary of state.

Those findings track those of national studies. An analysis of 2,068 reported fraud cases dating back to 2000 by a Carnegie-Knight investigative reporting project in 2012 found that there had been just ten cases of alleged in-person voter impersonation since 2000. "With 146 million registered voters in the United States, those represent about one for every 15 million prospective voters," reported the *Washington Post*.[a]

During the 2012 election year, media reports appeared frequently about senior citizens who had voted for decades but had been turned away from the polls when they were unable to produce long-lost documents that were suddenly the key to the franchise. Matt Barreto, a

Voter identification laws became controversial in 2012. Democrats argued that Republicans were seeking to suppress Democratic supporters, their fears fueled by remarks from Pennsylvania House GOP leader Mike Turzai that a new voter ID law would "allow" Republican presidential nominee Mitt Romney to win the state.

Herman Fredrick, a resident of Norristown, Pennsylvania, had to show photo identification to vote in a primary election in April 2012. Pennsylvania was among a number of states that had controversial voter ID requirements in place for that year's presidential election.

University of Washington political scientist, conducted a survey in 2012 that found that, while most Pennsylvanians believed they had proper ID, 13 percent of registered voters lacked the kind of identification required by the state's new law.[b]

Eric Holder, President Obama's attorney general, likened voter ID requirements to "poll taxes," a long-discredited and abandoned tool meant to disenfranchise African American voters. Despite the Supreme Court ruling, the U.S. Justice Department and other entities challenged numerous voter ID laws in court.

Pennsylvania lawmakers were chagrined when their own attorneys had to concede in court that the state had no awareness "of in-person voter fraud in Pennsylvania and [did] not have direct personal knowledge of in-person voter fraud elsewhere." They were even more embarrassed when Mike Turzai, the Pennsylvania House Republican leader, seemed to verify critics' complaints that the state had passed the law for partisan purposes when he said at a June 2012 rally, "Voter ID . . . is going to allow Governor [Mitt] Romney to win the state of Pennsylvania."

Much of the debate ultimately swirled around competing visions of election regulation—whether the goal should be to ensure that access to the ballot is strictly enforced to protect against abuse, or whether chances for fraud are too slim to justify denying eligible voters their right to vote simply because they lack certain forms of documentation. Both political debate and court cases turned not only on voter ID requirements but also on efforts to purge voter rolls and limit the numbers of hours polling places would be open.

Most people—and certainly most Republican lawmakers—seemed to feel that protecting the ballot box and insisting that citizens make the extra effort to obtain proper identification was the way to go. During debate over Florida's voter ID law in 2011, Republican senator Mike Bennett said, "I don't have a problem making [voting] harder. I want people in Florida to want to vote as bad as that person in Africa who walks 200 miles across the desert. This should be something you do with a passion."

Still, plenty of people believed this view of the matter was too harsh and that too many Americans had to endure long lines on election day or, worse, were at risk of being unfairly turned away for lack of knowledge about the new laws and difficulty in acquiring the right kinds of ID.

In May 2012, a federal judge threw out a portion of a Florida law that made it more difficult for independent groups such as the League of Women Voters to register voters. With such groups shying away from the state, voter registration by that point was down significantly from 2008 levels. "If the goal is to discourage voter registration drives and thus also to make it harder for new voters to register, this may work," Judge Robert L. Hinkle wrote. "Otherwise, there is little reason for such a requirement."

But a month later, Hinkle blocked a Justice Department request to stop the state from purging its voter rolls of noncitizens and other people ineligible to vote, saying that leaving such persons on the rolls could do "irreparable harm" to legitimate voters.[c]

---

[a]Katasha Khan and Corbin Carson, "Election Day Impersonation, an Impetus for Voter ID Laws, a Rarity, Data Show," *Washington Post*, August 11, 2012, www.washingtonpost.com/politics/election-day-impersonation-an-impetus-for-voter-id-laws-a-rarity-data-show/2012/08/11/7002911e-df20-11e1-a19c-fcfa365396c8_story.html.

[b]Angela Couloumbis, "Numbers Behind Pa. Voter-ID Law Debated in Court," *Philadelphia Inquirer*, July 27, 2012, http://articles.philly.com/2012-07-27/news/32870331_1_voter-law-form-of-photo-identification-thousands-of-inactive-voters.

[c]Lizette Alvarez, "Judge Sides with Florida on Purging Voter Rolls," *New York Times*, June 28, 2012, A14.

created the position in 2005; the change took effect following the 2009 elections.)

Compare all that influence with the limited powers of the governor of Texas. In Texas, the governor is only one of twenty-five elected statewide officials—and he or she is not even generally considered the most powerful one among them. That distinction belongs to the lieutenant governor. In most states, the lieutenant governor holds a purely symbolic office, with little to do but wait around for something crippling to befall the governor. In Texas, the lieutenant governor is president of the Senate and therefore wields tremendous influence over the course of legislation.

In contrast, the governor of Texas can recommend a budget, but he or she has no authority to make the legislature grapple with it seriously. Compare that to Maryland, where legislators can only accept or defeat the governor's spending proposals; they can make no fresh additions of their own. The Texas governor appoints the secretary of state and members of many boards and commissions, but many of the latter serve staggered terms. This means that the governor might have to work with people who were appointed by his or her predecessor.

Bills have been put forward to provide the governor of Texas with more power. Generally, they have gone nowhere. The state's **plural executive system** illustrates the desires of the framers of the 1876 state constitution to keep any one person or institution from having too much power. They believed in a separation of powers not just between branches of government but also within the executive branch.[32] The weakened powers of the governor are a reflection of the distrust that Texans had for strong government, in keeping with their constitution's many restrictions on raising taxes.

A couple of other southern and traditionalistic states, such as Alabama and Georgia, also divide power within the executive branch. In 1999, Democrats in the Alabama Senate sought to strip control of their chamber along with other powers from Lieutenant Governor Steve Windom, a Republican. And they could have done it if only he had left the Senate floor, but Windom refused. To stay present in and to keep control of the chamber for that day, and thus for the rest of his term, he did what was necessary, even urinating into a plastic jug in the chamber.[33]

Other states chart more of a middle-of-the-road course, electing a handful of statewide officials. In most states, in addition to a governor, voters elect a lieutenant governor, treasurer, secretary of state, and attorney general. A few states elect other officers as well, such as an insurance commissioner. Some observers believe that appointed officials are removed from political concerns and can make decisions without regard to partisan interests. Others believe that having to answer directly to the public makes individual officeholders more responsive to the public's needs and desires. Regardless of which side is correct, the fact that many statewide officeholders run for office independent of the governor gives them a power base of their own.

Attorneys general, treasurers, and other statewide officials often have aspirations of becoming governor themselves one day. This often leads to conflict with the sitting governor. Some of these fights occur along partisan lines. New Mexico attorney general Gary King, a Democrat, complained in 2012 that Republican legislators were trying to examine his office e-mails in retaliation for his office's investigation of the state Department of Public Education to determine whether resources were being used for political gain. "This is not the first time that the Republican Party has done such a thing where there are allegations made at Governor [Susana] Martinez for some sort of wrongdoing and just days after, the Republican Party filed a complaint or something that appeared to be designed to at a minimum take up the time of the attorney general's office," King said.[34]

Legal Offices

Voters pay comparatively little attention to candidates running for some state executive branch offices. Races for, say, state treasurer or

Plural Executive System

A state government system in which the governor is not the dominant figure in the executive branch but, instead, is more of a first among equals, serving alongside numerous other officials who are elected to their offices rather than appointed by the governor.

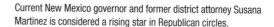

secretary of state are, for the most part, just not seen as all that exciting. Most often, the party that wins the governorship takes the lion's share of the secondary executive branch offices anyway, as there is not much ticket splitting. These are offices often pursued by legislators or other politicians looking to move up the political ladder. They hope these second-tier positions will firm up their résumés for their future bids for prominent offices such as governor.

One office for which the majority-party-takes-all dynamic no longer holds is that of attorney general, the chief law enforcement officer in the state. For many years, Democrats completely dominated the office in most states, but that began to change in the late 1990s. For one thing, the job came to be seen as a more important stepping-stone to the governorship than in the past; in 2012, eight former state attorneys general were serving as governors. Attorneys general in ten other states, including Michigan, Pennsylvania, and California, ran for governor in 2010. Republicans, understandably, became increasingly unwilling to concede this important gateway to the chief executive's office.

Moreover, state attorneys general, who traditionally had concentrated on law enforcement and consumer protection disputes within their states, had joined in a series of multistate settlements that represented important challenges to

corporate interests. They forced a series of settlements in 1998, for instance, that pushed the major tobacco companies to change their marketing strategies and to pay states an estimated $246 billion over twenty-five years. Some Republicans believed that these activist attorneys general were engaging in "government lawsuit abuse"—not targeting criminal behavior but, instead, going after companies to achieve changes in policy and regulation that could not be accomplished in the legislative arena. They founded the Republican Attorneys General Association (RAGA) as a campaign wing to elect members of their party to the office and funneled contributions from businesses and conservative interest groups that were threatened by the new activism to their candidates. "Historically . . . attorney general races were off most business people's radar screens," according to Bob LaBrant of the Michigan Chamber of Commerce. In the new environment, he says, "there's greater incentive to get involved in an attorney general race because of the increased involvement of attorneys general across the country in litigation against the business community."[35]

Interest group money and influence make a difference. In 2002, the Law Enforcement Alliance of America, an arm of the gun lobby, ran an estimated $1.5 million late-season ad campaign that helped keep the Texas attorney general's office in Republican hands. This was an expanded version of the U.S. Chamber of Commerce's effort in Indiana in 2000, when a $200,000 ad campaign was widely viewed as a leading factor in driving an incumbent Democrat attorney general out of office.[36] Such numbers, once eye-popping, have become routine. All told, Republicans improved their numbers after RAGA's founding from just twelve attorneys general in 1999 to twenty in 2003 and twenty-six by 2012. Both parties now believe that campaigns for attorney general will remain more expensive and competitive than they were historically.

A related phenomenon is affecting judicial elections, which traditionally were sleepy affairs. All but eleven states hold some type of elections for judicial posts. These are either direct elections by voters or retention elections used by voters to grant additional terms to justices appointed by the governor or the state legislature. Until the mid-1990s, judicial campaigns were cheap and fairly ho-hum. What campaign contributions candidates did receive came mainly from trial lawyers, along with contributions from unions and other constituencies allied with the Democratic Party. All of that began to change, however, when Republicans and their business allies grew weary of seeing their legislative victories in areas such as tort law and workers' compensation overturned by the high courts. In 2000, candidates in supreme court races in twenty states raised a total of $45.5 million, a 61-percent increase over the previous record. The average cost of winning a judicial election jumped 45 percent between 2002 and 2004, while individual races also kept breaking records, with one Illinois contest nearing the $10 million mark in 2004.[37] Elections for individual lower-level judgeships have broken through the million-dollar

barrier also. In 2007 and 2008, judicial candidates raised $62 million, with more than $18 million of that coming from lawyers, lobbyists, and their firms, according to the National Institute on Money in State Politics.

Direct Democracy

In addition to electing officials to state and local offices, voters can participate in certain forms of direct democracy. As discussed in chapter 3, in about half the states, voters can pass legislation on their own through ballot initiatives or referendums, which are also available in hundreds of municipalities across the country. In twenty-four states, citizens can petition to place a piece of legislation or a constitutional amendment on the ballot for approval or rejection by voters. Also in twenty-four states—mostly the same states—citizens can petition to review a law passed by the legislature and the governor, which they then can accept or reject. (See Table 5-2.)

TABLE 5-2

Avenues for Direct Democracy

State	Popular Referendum	Ballot Initiative	Constitutional Amendment by Initiative	Recall of State Officials
Alabama	No	No	No	No
Alaska	Yes	Yes	No	Yes
Arizona	Yes	Yes	Yes	Yes
Arkansas	Yes	Yes	Yes	No
California	Yes	Yes	Yes	Yes
Colorado	Yes	Yes	Yes	Yes
Connecticut	No	No	No	No
Delaware	No	No	No	No
Florida	No	Yes	Yes	No
Georgia	No	No	No	Yes
Hawaii	No	No	No	No
Idaho	Yes	Yes	Yes	Yes
Illinois	Yes	Yes	No	No
Indiana	No	No	No	No
Iowa	No	No	No	No
Kansas	No	No	No	Yes
Kentucky	Yes	No	No	No
Louisiana	No	No	No	Yes

(Continued)

TABLE 5-2 (Continued)

State	Popular Referendum	Ballot Initiative	Constitutional Amendment by Initiative	Recall of State Officials
Maine	Yes	Yes	No	No
Maryland	Yes	No	No	No
Massachusetts	Yes	Yes	Yes	No
Michigan	Yes	Yes	Yes	Yes
Minnesota	No	No	No	Yes
Mississippi	No	Yes	Yes	No
Missouri	Yes	Yes	Yes	No
Montana	Yes	Yes	Yes	Yes
Nebraska	Yes	Yes	Yes	No
Nevada	Yes	Yes	Yes	Yes
New Hampshire	No	No	No	No
New Jersey	No	No	No	Yes
New Mexico	Yes	No	No	No
New York	No	No	No	No
North Carolina	No	No	No	No
North Dakota	Yes	Yes	Yes	Yes
Ohio	Yes	Yes	Yes	No
Oklahoma	Yes	Yes	Yes	No
Oregon	Yes	Yes	Yes	Yes
Pennsylvania	No	No	No	No
Rhode Island	No	No	No	Yes
South Carolina	No	No	No	No
South Dakota	Yes	Yes	Yes	No
Tennessee	No	No	No	No
Texas	No	No	No	No
Utah	Yes	Yes	No	No
Vermont	No	No	No	No
Virginia	No	No	No	No
Washington	Yes	Yes	No	Yes
West Virginia	No	No	No	No
Wisconsin	No	No	No	Yes
Wyoming	Yes	Yes	No	No
Total number of states with	25	24	18	18

Sources: Data compiled from the Initiative and Referendum Institute at the University of Southern California, www.iandrinstitute.org/statewide_i&r.htm; and the National Conference of State Legislatures, www.ncsl.org/LegislaturesElections/ElectionsCampaigns/RecallofStateOfficials/tabid/16581/Default.aspx.

When citizens or groups other than elected officials put a measure on the ballot to become a law, this is called a popular initiative. When citizens put a measure on the ballot to affirm or reject an action of the legislature or other political actor, this is called a popular referendum. When the legislature places a measure on the ballot to win voter approval (such as a constitutional amendment or bond issue), it is called a legislative referendum. Some referendums are nonbinding—expressing the will of the people but not becoming law—but most are binding and do have the force of law once passed.

In all fifty states, the legislature or other government agencies have the power of legislative referendum. In the decades following independence, citizens in several northeastern states ratified new constitutions; Congress subsequently made legislative referendums for constitutional amendments mandatory for all new states entering the union after 1857.[38]

States Under Stress

Protest Movements Achieve Different Levels of Success

Two large-scale populist movements emerged during the first term of Barack Obama's presidency: the Tea Party movement and the Occupy movement. Participants in both were angry about the influence and power of large institutional forces in society. The two movements' platforms were diametrically opposed, however, and the approaches they took to trying to influence American politics were completely different.

The fast-growing Tea Party movement began in 2009, shortly after Obama became president. It was made up of individuals angry about the size of government—a backlash against the president's $800 billion stimulus program, a bank bailout plan that Congress had passed under President George W. Bush to the tune of $700 billion, and a deficit that in 2009 topped $1.4 trillion. "The Republicans for the last two decades have been a party whose litmus tests have been cultural issues, especially abortion," explained conservative columnist Michael Barone in 2010. "The tea partiers have helped to change their focus to issues of government overreach and spending."[a]

Members of the movement also derided Obama's healthcare legislation, which they saw as obtrusive and a threat to individual liberty, since it mandated that most people buy health insurance. Not surprisingly, they aligned themselves largely with the Republican Party—even if many participants in the Tea Party movement insisted that they were independent.

The Tea Party movement, which derived its name from colonial-era protests against British taxation, quickly claimed more than one thousand different affiliate groups around the country.[b] (Perhaps ironically, the Tea Party gained renewed prominence in 2013 with news that a field branch of the IRS had singled out the applications for tax-exempt status from Tea Party branches and other conservative groups for additional scrutiny.) Tea Party–endorsed candidates prevailed in numerous GOP primaries in both 2010 and 2012. Republican strategists largely welcomed the burst of energy that Tea Partiers brought to their cause, which had been discouraged by widespread electoral losses in 2006 and 2008.

Some criticized the Tea Party for being too unyielding. Some of the candidates backed by Tea Party groups in primaries were unable to prevail in contests Republicans might have won had they nominated more "establishment" or mainstream candidates. And those Tea Party favorites who did win elections drew criticism once in office for refusing to compromise at all on budget matters, nearly forcing the country into default in 2011.

But while the Tea Party was influencing Republican politicians in Congress and the statehouses, those politicians were trying to co-opt the Tea Party, to harness its energy and enthusiasm without letting its agenda dominate the party's direction. "That's the secret to politics," GOP consultant Scott Reed said in 2011. "Trying to control a segment of people without those people recognizing that you're trying to control them."[c]

Being co-opted in this way seemed to be the main thing the Occupy movement wanted to avoid. The movement began with a protest beginning in September 2011 in a park near Wall Street in Lower Manhattan; the demonstrators complained that too much wealth was concentrated in the hands of too few individuals.

The slogan "We are the 99 percent" went global, as did the idea of protesting by camping in place for twenty-four hours a day, which quickly spread to hundreds of cities. The issue of income inequality and the question of whether the wealthiest 1 percent held too much power soon became central concerns of the movement.

But Occupy was not able to translate its complaints into a policy agenda. It wasn't clear what the members of the movement wanted to have happen. The mere act of their camping out itself became problematic as winter set in and issues of sanitation and crowd control grew worse; in many cities, authorities ordered police to remove the protesters from public spaces.

As Rosemary Feurer, a historian at Northern Illinois University, has noted, protest movements typically don't start out with set lists of goals that they want politicians to achieve. The populist movements of the nineteenth century and early labor union activity began in ways similar to the beginnings of the Occupy movement: an encampment of people came together, found they shared a sense of dissatisfaction with the status quo, and worked to change it. As Feurer has observed, "What starts these movements is a list of grievances. You don't start with a list of goals, but with a sense of what's wrong."[d]

Occupy gatherings sought to run by consensus, with those gathered expressing approval or disapproval of simple items, such as the order of speakers, through hand gestures. The movement, by its nature, was suspicious of leaders. "Don't lose sight of the bigger message of this movement being driven from the bottom up by consensus and not affiliation or deference to any group that's out there," said Ed Needham, a media spokesman for Occupy Wall Street.[e]

As such, Occupy had a hard time finding allegiance even with politicians who might have been sympathetic. This was exemplified when John Lewis, a Democratic congressman from Georgia and hero of the civil rights movement, showed up at the Occupy Atlanta site. Protesters there praised Lewis but refused to let him speak right away, as that would have disrupted the scheduled agenda.

Lewis, who had other obligations, decided to leave, although he said he took no offense. Recalling his own days as head of the Student Nonviolent Coordinating Committee during the 1960s, he said civil rights groups sometimes reached consensus slowly and refused to be deferential to more established leaders. "It is growing, it is maturing, it will work out," Lewis told reporters, speaking about the Occupy movement at the Atlanta site. "It will come of age."

Just a few months after the protests began, however, it didn't appear that Occupy would have continuing relevance. What were highly visible encampments had already given way to sporadic, sparsely attended marches. "Occupy does not have a traditional leadership structure, making it difficult for the movement to engage in conventional political organizing in support of state legislators and members of Congress, like the Tea Party has," the *New York Times* reported in April 2012. "And some activists, angry at politicians across the board, do not see electoral politics as the best avenue for the movement, complicating efforts to chart its direction."[f]

Source: Original piece written for this book by Alan Greenblatt.

[a]Michael Barone, "Tea Party Brings Energy, Change and Tumult to GOP," *Washington Examiner*, March 14, 2010, http://townhall.com/columnists/michaelbarone/2010/03/15/tea_party_brings_energy,_change_and_tumult_to_gop/page/full.

[b]Peter Katel, "Tea Party Movement," *CQ Researcher*, May 19, 2010, p. 243.

[c]Quoted in Matt Bai, "'You're Nuts!,'" *New York Times Magazine*, October 16, 2001, 44.

[d]Quoted in Alan Greenblatt, "For Wall Street Protests, What Constitutes Success?," NPR.org, October 14, 2011, www.npr.org/2011/10/14/141347126/for-wall-street-protests-what-constitutes-success.

[e]Phone interview with Ed Needham, October 12, 2011.

[f]Michael S. Schmidt, "For Occupy Movement, a Challenge to Recapture Momentum," *New York Times*, April 1, 2012, A21.

As discussed in chapter 3, the notion of popular referendums and initiatives really took root because of the efforts of reformers from the Populist and Progressive movements. These individuals sought to give citizens more influence over state political systems that they saw as dominated by moneyed interests such as banks, railroads, and mining companies. A majority of the states that have adopted the popular initiative process (under which citizens can collect a certain number of signatures to place issues directly on the ballot) did so in the late 1800s and early 1900s. Most of these states are in the West and the Upper Midwest, which had political cultures that welcomed the idea of populist control. Much of the opposition in the southern and eastern states grew out of racist concerns that giving people direct authority to make laws would give too much power to African Americans or to new immigrants such as the Irish.

Recent ballot initiatives and referendums have covered a wide range of topics, from banning or allowing gay marriage and legalizing marijuana to making sure that pregnant pigs are housed in large-enough pens (an amendment to the Florida constitution approved by voters in 2002). Many initiatives have to do with tax and spending issues. Sometimes voters send contradictory signals. For instance, in Washington State, voters in recent years have approved limitations on property and other taxes while at the same time approving such expensive programs as teacher pay increases and school class size limitations.

Those who favor the initiative process say that it gives voters a chance to control government directly. Voters know that they are voting for an environmental safety program or a campaign finance law, as opposed to voting for candidates who say that they favor these things but who may act differently once in office. Initiative states do tend to have lower state spending per capita, but that gap is generally bridged by local spending, which tends to run higher in initiative states.[39]

Critics of the initiative process say that it creates more problems than it solves. Because voters are presented with a straight yes-or-no choice about spending more on, say, elementary and secondary education, they do not take into account other competing state priorities, such as transportation or colleges, the way legislators must. Voters can say, as those in Washington have, that they want both lower taxes and more services but leave legislators and governors few tools for balancing the budget or responding to economic recessions. In many states—particularly California—initiatives have become big business. They are not necessarily the expressions of grassroots ideals anymore; instead, they are proposed and paid for by wealthy individuals or interest groups, such as teachers' unions or the owners of gambling casinos.

Far and away the most famous and influential modern ballot initiative was Proposition 13, approved by California voters in 1978, which limited property tax rates and made other changes to the state's tax and spending laws (see chapter 3). The initiative was copied successfully in Michigan and Massachusetts, and most states soon placed limitations on their own property tax rates. The success of Proposition 13 fueled the modern initiative movement. Only eighty-seven statewide initiatives were proposed during the entire decade of the 1960s. Since 1978, however, about three hundred initiatives have been proposed per decade. Ninety-three statewide initiatives were placed on ballots in 1996 alone. That appears to have been the peak year, with supporters of the initiative process complaining since then that state legislatures have placed new restrictions on ballot access and signature collection. But following a long decline, the numbers of initiatives started going up again in 2012 and are likely to continue to climb, according to Jennie Bowser, a senior fellow with the National Conference of State Legislatures, because there is "an industry" that relies on an active initiative process.[40]

The power of initiatives can be seen in the establishment of legislative term limits, which exist in nearly every state that allows ballot initiatives but in only a couple of states that do not. Term limits have been imposed in nearly every case by voters through ballot measures, not by legislators themselves. State legislators are subject to term limits in fifteen states, but the defeat of a term limits initiative in Oregon in 2006 seems to have signaled the end of the movement.

Perhaps the most prominent measures to appear on ballots in recent years have been those addressing gay marriage. Many states already had defined marriage as the union of a man and a woman, but following a Massachusetts court decision that found gays had a right to marry, thirty states have changed their constitutions to ban same-sex marriage. In May 2012, North Carolina voters approved such a ban, but the next day, President Obama announced that he was in favor of legalizing same-sex marriage (while stressing it was a policy best handled by the states). Supporters of gay marriage enjoyed their first successes at the ballot box in November 2012. Minnesota voters rejected a ban on same-sex marriage, while voters in Maine and Washington granted marriage rights to same-sex couples and Maryland voters approved the legislature's decision to allow gay marriage.

As noted earlier, some political scientists have suggested that high-profile initiatives do lead more people to vote. Given the attention a proposed gay marriage ban received in Ohio in 2004, when that state's electoral votes ultimately decided the presidency, there was much coverage in the media that looked at the question of whether the initiative helped President Bush by encouraging social conservatives to vote. "I'd be naïve if I didn't say it helped," Robert T. Bennett, chair of the Ohio Republican Party, told the *New York Times*. "And it helped most in what we refer to as the Bible Belt area of southeastern and southwestern Ohio, where we had the largest percentage increase in support for the president."[41]

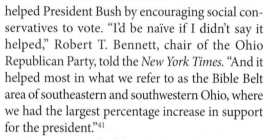

Not surprisingly, liberals decided to jump on this particular bandwagon, finding causes, such as minimum wage increases and stem-cell research support, to place on ballots in hopes that more progressive voters would turn out as well. But there is a school of thought that argues that they need not have bothered. Simon Jackman, a statistician at Stanford University, has shown that same-sex marriage initiatives boosted turnout by about 3 percent in the eleven states that had them on the ballot in 2004. On examining data from all of Ohio's counties, however, he concluded that that state's initiative did not boost support for Bush.[42]

Beyond initiatives and referendums is perhaps the ultimate expression of popular dissatisfaction—the **recall**. Recalls of local officials are allowed in thirty-six states and 61 percent of U.S. municipalities—more local governments than allow initiatives or referendums. Like ballot initiatives, recall laws are mainly by-products of the intention of early twentieth-century reformers to make state governments more responsive to average citizens. Recalls of state officials are allowed in eighteen states. No governor had faced a recall since the 1920s when, in 2003, California Democrat Gray Davis was

recalled and replaced by Republican Arnold Schwarzenegger. In 2012, Wisconsin governor Scott Walker, a Republican, survived a recall attempt in what became one of the most expensive elections in U.S. history. These high-profile recalls helped promote growth in recalls at the local level, with everyone from county commissioners to school board members being shown the door. In 2011, at least fifty-seven mayors faced recall attempts—up from twenty-three in 2009. Not all of these recall attempts succeeded, but in recent years, serious recall attempts have been launched against mayors in cities such as Omaha, Kansas City, and Portland, Oregon. The overwhelming recall election loss of Carlos Alvarez, mayor of Miami-Dade County, Florida, in 2011 makes him perhaps the most prominent victim of the recall trend at the local level.[43]

Still, over the past one hundred years, fewer than two dozen recall elections have involved state officials, including legislators (although Wisconsin Democrats, who failed to recall Walker, did manage in the same election to recall several members of the Republican state Senate and temporarily regain control of that chamber).[44] The only governor to be recalled before Davis in California was Lynn Frazier of North Dakota in 1921. Frazier, the state attorney general, and the agricultural commissioner all lost their offices after a grassroots movement swelled against scandals in Frazier's government. The only other governor who has ever faced a scheduled recall election was Evan Mecham of Arizona; the legislature saved voters the trouble by removing him from office in 1987.

California makes the recall process relatively easy, requiring the gathering of proportionately fewer signatures than are necessary in other states to place the recall before the voters. California requires a number of signatures equal to only 12 percent of the number of people who voted in the last election for the office, whereas most states require 25 percent and Kansas requires 40 percent. Gray Davis was unpopular, having won reelection

---

Recall

A way for voters to oust an incumbent politician prior to the next regularly scheduled election; they collect signatures to qualify the recall proposal for the ballot and then vote on the ouster of the politician.

the year before by a small plurality. He also had come to be blamed for the state's $38 billion deficit and electricity crisis.

Public Opinion

Randall Gnant, a former president of the Arizona Senate, says that there is quite a contrast between the politics of today and those of the 1800s. Back then, he says, "it seemed that everybody took part in the political process—there were torchlight parades, party-run newspapers for and against candidates." Today, "we're into sort of a reverse kind of period. Now, almost nobody participates in the electoral process—voter turnout rates are abysmally low." But that does not mean that citizens are not paying any attention to the political process. Given the importance of websites, Twitter, and other social media that quickly spread public opinion—or at least a share of it—the old idea that voters agree to a sort of contract with politicians whom they elect to two- or four-year terms is rapidly becoming dated. Voters are more than willing to express their displeasure about a given policy well before the next scheduled election day. "Try to get somebody interested in electing a candidate and they just don't want to get involved," Gnant points out. "But they are perfectly willing to get involved if somebody does something they don't want them to do."[45]

Citizen opinion usually does not register loudly enough to result in a recall or other formal protest. On most issues that come before policymakers at the state level, citizen opinion hardly seems to exist or be formulated at all. After all, how many citizens are going to take the time to follow—let alone express an opinion about—an obscure regulatory issue concerning overnight transactions between banks and insurance companies?

This lack of interest, or, at the very least, this lack of time, raises an important question. If citizens do not or cannot make their feelings known on every issue addressed in the hundreds of bills that wend through the average state legislature each year, how can legislators know that their votes will reflect the will of their constituents? After all, as V. O. Key writes, "unless mass views have some place in the shaping of policy, all the talk about democracy is nonsense."[46]

Responding to Opinion

Doug Duncan served for a dozen years as county executive of Montgomery County, Maryland, before giving up the job in 2006. Like many veteran officeholders, he found that one of the biggest changes in his job came in the area of communications. "Doing it is half the job," he says, "and the other half is telling people about it so they know how you're spending their money."[47] The old outlets for government officials making announcements or responding to criticism—local daily newspapers and evening TV news broadcasts—have had declines in their audiences or even gone away completely in some cases. Nevertheless, with the growth of the Internet, more information sources are available now than ever before. "The information's there," Duncan says. "It's just a question of how you make it available."

E-mail, Twitter, and websites devoted to neighborhood concerns or services such as libraries have made it easier for public officials to know what their constituents are thinking—at least, those constituents who are motivated enough to make their opinions known on a given issue. And elected officials have become fairly quick to adopt new platforms, such as Facebook and Twitter. But let's be realistic—state officials, in particular, cannot know what the majority opinions are in their districts on every issue they confront. Mike Haridopolos, a former GOP president of the Florida Senate, cautions officials against reading too much into what they hear through social media. "I tell my members, just because you get a tweet or an e-mail doesn't mean your whole district is concerned about something," he says.[48] And even multiple e-mails might be the work of just one or two individuals using multiple aliases.

On most issues, legislators do not hear from any constituents at all. A few high-profile concerns, such as tax increases or the legalization of casino gambling, may lead a newspaper or an interested party to conduct a statewide poll, but even on the rare occasions when polls are conducted on state issues, the resulting data are not broken down by legislative district. Given their lack of specific information about how constituents view particular areas, public officials have to rely on a series of clues.

Some political scientists have taken data from various nationwide polls, broken them down by state, and analyzed how well elected officials have reflected the general ideologies and desires of the public in their states.[49] What they have found is that average state opinion does seem to be reflected in the policy decisions made in individual states. What does *average state opinion* mean? It encompasses the types of things we discussed earlier in regard to Daniel Elazar's classifications of the states. Some states tend to be more liberal overall, whereas others are more conservative. The average citizen's desires—whether in a conservative state such as Texas or a more progressive one such as Vermont—tend to be pretty well reflected by state laws on issues that range from restrictions on abortion services to welfare spending, the death penalty, environmental protections, and gay rights.[50]

> For one thing, elected officials devote an enormous amount of time to trying to gauge how opinion is running in their districts. They may not hear from constituents on every issue, but they pay close attention to those concerns that are registered through letters and phone calls.

How does this happen? For one thing, elected officials devote an enormous amount of time to trying to gauge how opinion is running in their districts. They may not hear from constituents on every issue, but they pay close attention to those concerns that are registered through letters and phone calls. They go out and seek opinions by attending religious services and civic events where they can hear the concerns of constituents directly. They use surrogates—such as newspaper articles and interest groups—as ways of determining what is on their constituents' minds. Susan Herbst, executive vice chancellor and chief academic officer for the University System of Georgia, spent some time earlier in her career hanging out with legislators in Springfield, Illinois. She found that the media were important in shaping public opinion by giving a voice to average people in their stories. The media also shaped the terms of debate. Herbst noted that people in the capital thought that lobbyists often provided good indicators of how people felt about an issue: "Staffers seem to think that the nuances and intensity of public opinion are best captured in the communications of interest groups."[51] More recently, political scientists at the University of Minnesota have found that media coverage of debates among political elites—those most directly engaged in actual legislative debates, such as trade associations—does help to shape mass public opinion on issues.[52]

This is not to say that using interest groups as surrogates can't be misleading sometimes. The National Rifle Association, for example, may call on its state members to send letters to legislators in numbers that dwarf those mustered by gun control advocates—even in places where a majority favors gun control. "Intense minorities can come off potentially sounding like majorities when in fact they're not," says Illinois Wesleyan University political scientist Greg Shaw.[53] Legislators like to think that they have a pretty good sense of whether a mail-writing campaign has sprung up spontaneously or shows signs of having been organized—multiple participants signing their names to the same form letter, for example—but sometimes this is easier said than done.

Formal interest groups do not represent every constituent. Some people may favor environmental protection but not give money to the Sierra Club or the World Wildlife Fund. Some older people resist invitations to join AARP. Still, legislators do gain some sense of how active such groups are in their states and whether they seem to have favorable support at home. A lot of this is inexact, but legislators learn from talking to people whether their constituents are most upset about crime or transportation problems. They are convinced that if they vote for things that voters broadly support, such as mandatory sentencing guidelines for drug

Elected officials do not just have to address the issues they campaigned on, respond to views expressed at the ballot box, deal with the demands of special interest groups, and be attentive to the expectations of political parties. They also have to be prepared to deal with the unexpected. On May 20, 2013, a major tornado struck Moore, Oklahoma, killing 23 people, injuring hundreds, and devastating the town. Here Moore mayor Glenn Lewis (left), Oklahoma governor Mary Fallin (right), Rep. Tom Cole, R-Okla., and President Obama (center) survey the damage left in the tornado's wake. State and local emergency agencies were first responders to this disaster, while federal agencies helped deal with the aftermath.

offenders or limits on welfare benefits, they will be rewarded politically.

Conversely, a legislator's major fear is of being punished politically. Failure to get reelected can be the death knell of a political career. It is important to note, however, that if legislators or governors did not broadly reflect the wishes of the populace that elected them, they would never have won their positions in the first place. In this age of computer-assisted **redistricting**, legislative districts in particular are shaped according to the local political culture, which tends to lean in one ideological direction. Ninety-five times out of a hundred, a liberal is not going to get elected to a conservative district.

Once elected, legislators who want to get reelected are careful not to stray too far from the public opinion in their districts, as best as they can perceive it. They cannot know what public opinion is on the specifics of every bill, but the fact that not every individual is paying close attention to state politics does not mean that legislators can do whatever they want. Political officials recognize that lobbyists and other interested parties are watching their voting records carefully and can use such information against them if necessary. "Legislators aren't worried about what their constituents know—they are worried about what an opponent might do with their record in the next election," says Paul Brace, a Rice University political scientist. They act, therefore, as if there is someone or some group out there who has a

chance of using a potentially unpopular record against them. "Legislation is written in minutiae, but you know if you vote for it, you'll get an opponent who can dumb it down and use it against you in the next election, and you won't do it."[54]

Some states offer less opportunity for using a politician's record against him or her. In a moralistic state such as Minnesota, there are more daily newspapers paying close attention to state policy matters than in, say, individualistic Wyoming. There are more public interest groups and state-level think tanks closely monitoring St. Paul than there are monitoring Cheyenne. Citizens in states with higher levels of civic engagement are more likely to keep their politicians "honest"—reflecting voters' overall policy desires—than are citizens in less engaged states.

In a state such as Idaho or Maryland, one party so completely dominates state politics that only rarely are politicians voted out of office because their records do not reflect public opinion. But even Idaho Republicans or Maryland Democrats can lose—if only in the party primary—if voters sour on their records. Every state capital has engendered enough of an echo chamber that examines and discusses the work of legislators and other elected officials that an overall sense of their records—conservative or liberal, sellout or crusading—is known to people who care enough about politics to vote. If those records do not reflect local opinion, the jobs will go to other candidates in the next election.

Redistricting
The drawing of new boundaries for congressional and state legislative districts, usually following a decennial census.

Conclusion

This is a highly partisan era, with little civility or cooperation, it seems, between Republicans and Democrats. But the war between the red and the blue will never be as heated as the war between the blue and the gray—the North and the South during the Civil War. Although voters today are divided, they are not as deeply divided as they have been at other moments in the country's past, such as during the Civil War or at the time of the Watergate scandal in the 1970s.

This fact is reflected in the recent series of contentious but ultimately narrowly won presidential contests, and on down through other levels of government. As with Congress and the electoral college, state legislatures have been closely divided, with the two main parties switching leads in total number of seats nationwide throughout the early twenty-first century. The lead among governorships has switched around, too, with Republicans currently up.

The outcomes of recent elections reflect the divided public mood. State and local officials have less ability to control who participates in the political process because of the many changes in voting laws passed at the federal level. They do still maintain a lot of control over whom citizens can vote for through their regulation of political parties and their ability to decide who deserves to get their names on the ballot.

Which state officials citizens get to vote for differs depending on where the citizens live. In most states, citizens vote for several statewide officials such as governor, attorney general, and secretary of state. In others, they may vote only for the governor. Similarly, in some localities citizens elect the mayor directly, whereas in others the mayor is chosen by the city council from among its own membership. Some states allow people to vote directly for judges, while in other states judges are appointed to office. Some localities allow residents to vote for school board members; in others, these positions are appointed.

In general, citizens vote for enough officeholders with the authority to control policies that the majority's will becomes law. However, because polling is done far more often at the national level than it is at the local or even the state level, officeholders sometimes have only an anecdotal sense of what their constituents are thinking. They do pay close attention to the clues they are given and monitor opinion as closely as they can. They are well aware that if they do not create the types of policies that most people want, they are not going to stay in office for long.

The Latest Research

This chapter has explained in some depth the role of state and local governments in structuring elections. As discussed above, what citizens need to do in order to register to vote, where they vote, when they vote, and the mechanics of how they vote are largely decisions made by state and local governments. States have differences on all these matters, and it should come as no surprise after reading this chapter that these are differences that make a difference. Tougher registration requirements, for example, tend to result in lower voter turnout.

The studies discussed below represent some of the latest research on how the basic mechanics of elections—for example, deciding what type of ballot to use or where to set up polling stations—can have big impacts on electoral participation. The common theme here is that how states decide to regulate elections is one of the most important, and often overlooked, influences on political participation in local, state, and federal elections.

• •

- **Herrnson, Paul, Michael Hanmer, and Richard Niemi.** 2012. "The Impact of Ballot Type on Voter Errors." *American Journal of Political Science* 56: 716–730.

This study examines how ballot format and type of voting system (paper or electronic) influence voter error. Specifically, the researchers examined two types of error: (1) wrong-candidate error, which happens when a voter mistakenly casts a ballot for the wrong candidate; and (2) unintentional undervoting, which happens when a voter plans to cast a ballot for a particular elective office but does not. They found that there was not much difference in these sorts of errors across voting systems (paper ballots had a slightly higher error rate); however, there was a big difference between standard office group (Massachusetts) ballots and ballots that offered the option of voting a straight ticket. The straight ticket option led to significantly more errors. For example, voters in elections using ballots with this option were more likely not to vote in nonpartisan races they had intended to vote in (such races would not be included in a straight ticket option), and, more disturbingly, they were more likely to vote unintentionally for the wrong candidate. The error rate was small, generally less than 5 percent, but it was still enough to make a difference in an election.

- **Brady, Henry, and John McNulty.** 2011. "Turning Out to Vote: The Costs of Finding and Getting to the Polling Place." *American Political Science Review* 105: 115–134.

One of the most important aspects of voting controlled by state and local governments is the determination of where voters can cast their ballots. This study shows that locations of polling places can make a big difference in turnout. Los Angeles County consolidated its voting districts during the 2003 gubernatorial recall election, thus changing the polling places of large numbers of voters. Did these changes in polling stations make a difference? This study suggests that they did: the consolidation was associated with a reduction in polling place turnout by a bit more than three percentage points. One of the implications of this finding is that changing polling places can make a big enough difference in turnout to theoretically make a difference in a close election.

- **Hood, M. V., III, and Charles Bullock III.** 2012. "Much Ado about Nothing? An Empirical Assessment of the Georgia Voter Identification Statute." *State Politics & Policy Quarterly* 12: 393–414.

As discussed above, among the more controversial reforms of voting regulations in recent years has been the decision by some states to require voters to provide proof of identification before casting ballots. Opponents of these laws worry that they will suppress turnout, especially among certain disadvantaged (especially racial minority) groups who are less likely to have typical government-approved IDs such as driver's licenses. This study examines the impact of Georgia's decision to implement a voter ID law beginning in 2007. The researchers did not find that the new law suppressed turnout in any particular racial demographic. However, they did find that the law reduced voter turnout, although not by much. The new regulation was associated with a decrease in turnout of less than one-half of a percentage point.

- **Davidson, Chandler.** 2009. "The Historical Context of Voter Photo-ID Laws." *PS: Political Science & Politics* 42: 93–96.

This essay argues that regardless of the empirical impact of voter ID laws, their adoption raises some disturbing questions about their intent given the history in numerous states of attempts to suppress minority voting. The author notes that proponents in Indiana argued that a voter ID law was needed to reduce the possibility of one particular type of voter fraud: somebody impersonating someone else in order to vote at a polling place. They could produce little evidence, however, that this sort of fraud was ever a problem in that state. While the historical record reveals almost no significant amount of voter impersonation, the author points out, attempts to suppress minority voting have a deep and extensive history. Thus it seems less likely that these laws are designed to prevent a type of fraud that is not happening than it is that they are intended to suppress turnout among targeted groups. What this essay highlights is that empirical findings such as those reported in the Hood and Bullock study discussed above are not likely to end the voter ID controversy. The debate is fueled not just by the impact of the laws but by the underlying intent motivating them.

Chapter Review

Key Concepts

- blanket primary (p. 115)
- nonpartisan election (p. 120)
- office group (Massachusetts) ballot (p. 111)
- party column (Indiana) ballot (p. 111)
- plural executive system (p. 123)
- plurality (p. 109)
- recall (p. 130)
- redistricting (p. 133)
- secret (Australian) ballot (p. 113)
- straight ticket (p. 111)
- voter turnout (p. 117)

Suggested Websites

- **http://fairvote.org.** Website of the Center for Voting and Democracy, which promotes voting and advocates instant-runoff voting and the abolition of the electoral college.

- **http://pewresearch.org.** Website of the Pew Research Center for the People & the Press, which conducts surveys and publishes studies that look at the demographic trends affecting politics.

- **www.lwv.org.** Website of the League of Women Voters. Provides a wealth of voter education information.

- **www.nass.org.** Website of the National Association of Secretaries of State. Secretaries of state typically serve as chief election officials, and their offices have primary responsibility for recording official election outcomes.

State Stats on Political Attitudes and Participation

Explore and compare data on the states! Go to **college.cqpress .com/sites/essentials-govstateandlocal** to do these exercises.

1. Considering the historical support of African Americans for one political party over the other, if you were running for president as a Democrat, would you be more likely to win in Michigan or West Virginia? Why?

2. If voters in lower income brackets are less likely to vote than their richer counterparts, would you expect to see higher voter turnout in Texas or Utah? Why?

3. What is Nebraska's per capita expenditure on welfare programs? What is Maine's? What political variables might account for such a big difference between the two states?

4. This chapter notes that government leadership is not nearly as white and Protestant as it used to be. How has the percentage of the population in your state that is white changed between 2000 and 2010? What (if anything) does this mean for politics?

5. Which states have the largest percentage of the population who are marijuana users? How does this correlate with the results of the recent election that legalized marijuana for recreational use in two states? If this trend continues, which states might we expect to see legalize marijuana next? Why?

Once seen as a fringe cause, legalization of marijuana use won voter approval in two states in 2012. But demonstrators such as Joe Tremolada in Oakland, California, are still protesting federal enforcement of drug laws.

Parties and Interest Groups

ELEPHANTS, DONKEYS, AND CASH COWS

- Why are political parties weaker than they used to be?
- Why are political parties stronger in some states than in others?
- How do interest groups influence policymakers?

How did Thomas Massie get elected as a Republican congressman from Kentucky? Many people think it had a lot to do with a twenty-one-year-old college student from Texas.

Massie was considered an underdog in a western Kentucky congressional district, but he won the support of several outside interest groups—as well as James Ramsey, a college student who had inherited a fortune from his grandfather. Ramsey started his own campaign committee, known as a **super PAC**, which devoted some $500,000 to the race—roughly double what either Massie or his opponent, Rep. Alecia Webb-Edgington, was able to raise in support of their campaigns. Just before the primary election in 2012, Massie said he had never met Ramsey, but admitted he was likely to send him a Christmas card. Because the district votes so reliably Republican, Massie's primary win was tantamount to his election to Congress. "It shows the role you can play in congressional districts, where you don't have to have that much money," said Trey Grayson, director of the Harvard University Institute of Politics. "Essentially one person, a college kid who inherited a lot of money, created a super PAC that swung the race dramatically in Massie's direction."[1]

Massie's victory showcases a number of important trends. One of these is the increasing **polarization** of U.S. politics. Voters increasingly live in districts, like Massie's, that tend to favor one party or the other. There is little ideological overlap between the parties and less bipartisan cooperation in Congress or statehouses than there used to be. As a result, the key electoral contests in many cases have become the **primary elections** in which party nominees are decided.

Massie's ability to prevail over a candidate who had the backing of top elected officials from her party also illustrates the shifting dynamics in U.S. politics. So-called **establishment** candidates, who typically would have been expected to garner most nominations in the past, now often struggle against opponents who may have lighter political résumés but can win over voters by portraying themselves as insurgents who will challenge the status quo. In large part, that's because such insurgents have new organizing and fund-raising tools at hand. Thanks to recent court decisions, money is able to flow more freely into campaigns than has been the case for the past hundred years. Sometimes insurgent candidates are able to raise funds themselves, but often, as in Massie's case, dollars finds their way into their races through independent **political action committees (PACs)**, including super PACs.

Super PACs are not allowed to coordinate their messages directly with candidates, but sometimes these organizations are run by close allies of candidates, such as former aides. Other times, they have no connection to candidates at all—which leads some observers to worry that such groups could end up dominating the political conversation. With the rise of super PACs, "candidates, those on the ballots, will be much more of an afterthought than they ever were before," said Wisconsin state senator Jon Erpenbach, a Democrat. "In some cases, candidates don't even matter."[2]

In any event, the changing financial landscape is having one certain effect: the line between **political parties** and **interest groups**—individuals, corporations, or associations that seek to influence the actions of elected and appointed public officials on behalf of specific companies or causes—is becoming more blurred. Historically, political parties have helped select, groom, and promote candidates who largely

---

Super PAC
A political action committee that can spend unlimited funds on behalf of a political candidate but cannot directly coordinate its plans with that candidate.

Polarization
A split among elected officials or an electorate along strictly partisan lines.

Primary Election
An election that determines a party's nominees for offices in a general election against other parties' nominees.

Establishment
The nexus of people holding power over an extended period of time, including top elected officials, lobbyists, and party strategists

Political Action Committee
A group formed for the purpose of raising money to elect or defeat political candidates. PACs traditionally represent business, union, or ideological interests.

Political Parties
Organizations that nominate and support candidates for elected offices.

Interest Groups
Individuals, corporations, or associations that seek to influence the actions of elected and appointed public officials on behalf of specific companies or causes.

align with their parties' platforms. Today, candidates at both the state and federal level may end up relying more heavily on outside interest groups. Such a group may have a broad political agenda that closely mirrors that of a party—helping to support and elect more Republicans, for instance—or it may be more concerned with a single issue, such as protecting the environment or keeping taxes low.

Parties still have an important role to play—arguably a more important one than was the case a generation ago. This chapter explores the roles political parties play and how they vary by state, as well as the influence that interest groups have, not only on elections but also on governance.

A Primer on Political Parties

Political parties are not as dominant in American life as they once were. From roughly the 1820s until the 1940s, political parties constituted a leading organizing force in this country. They not only provided citizens with political identities but also were major sources of social activity and entertainment—and, in many cases, jobs. Today, parties are not as effective as they used to be at getting people out to vote or even at organizing them around an issue. However, they do remain important to candidates, giving them a kind of "brand" identification and acting as fund-raisers.

Although there are two major national parties, the party organizations play larger roles at the state level than they do as national forces. Their respective strength varies widely from state to state and is affected by such factors as the different ways states regulate parties, the differences in the historical roles that parties have played within each state, and the amount of competition between the major parties within a given state. In general, the more closely balanced the two main parties are in a state, the more likely it is that they will have well-funded and well-organized state-level party organizations.

Political parties recruit candidates for offices and provide them with support for their campaigns. They give candidates money or

help them to raise it and offer logistical and strategic assistance. Just as important, they help coordinate the candidates' messages with those of candidates running for other offices under the party's banner.

Since the 1850s, the vast majority of candidates for political office in the United States have run as members of either the Democratic or the Republican Party. The Democratic Party as we know it today evolved from **factional splits** in the earliest days of the American republic. The country started without a two-party system, but factions soon developed. The Federalists, led by Alexander Hamilton, favored a strong central government with power rooted in the industrial North. The Democratic-Republicans, led by Thomas Jefferson, emerged as the party opposing the Federalists. They argued for states' rights against a "monarchical" rule by the aristocracy and declared that farmers, craftspeople, and shopkeepers should control their own interests without interference from the capitol.

Jefferson's party, which eventually morphed into the Democratic Party, dominated politics throughout the first half of the nineteenth century. That same period saw the creation of numerous parties: Whigs, Know-Nothings, Barnburners, Softshells, Hunkers, and Free Soilers. They all had some success, but the Democratic Party of Jefferson and Andrew Jackson dominated so completely that, as the main source of political power, the party split into factions, with northern and southern Democrats arguing over the expansion of slavery. That argument created an opening for a new major party.

The Republican Party was formed in 1854 in opposition to slavery. It soon replaced the Whig Party, which had been formed in 1834 to protest the spoils-system politics of Andrew Jackson. The Republican Party, also known as the Grand Old Party (GOP), quickly enjoyed congressional success. Following the election of Abraham Lincoln in 1860, Republicans dominated the presidency for decades to come. Their antislavery stance,

---

Factional Splits, Or Factions
Groups that struggle to control the message within a party; for example, a party may be split into competing regional factions.

however, guaranteed that the party remained practically nonexistent in the South until the civil rights era of the 1950s and 1960s. Democrats reemerged as the nation's dominant party in the 1930s, when Republicans were blamed for the Great Depression. The Democrats' New Deal coalition of southerners, union workers, African Americans, the poor, and the elderly drove American politics well into the 1960s but fragmented after that, resulting in a loss of political control.

Long-standing Democratic majorities at the congressional and state levels eroded. Republicans dominated presidential elections from 1968 through 1988, winning five out of the six contests. Since then, however, Democrats have met with more success, carrying the popular vote five of six times. In 2012, Democrat Barack Obama won reelection with 51 percent of the vote—down from 53 percent in 2008, making him just the third president in U.S. history to be reelected with a smaller share of the vote than he received during his initial election. (The other two were Franklin D. Roosevelt, whose winning percentage ticked down in both 1940 and 1944, and Andrew Jackson, who took less of the popular vote in 1832. These are also the only three Democrats to win twice by majority votes.)

Although most Americans are familiar with the Republican and Democratic parties, many may not realize that political parties technically take many different shapes. When people refer to Democrats or Republicans, they are actually referring to officials belonging to two umbrella groups that cover a wide variety of parties. Each of the national parties is really consortium of state parties. Party chairs and other representatives from the state parties dominate the national party committees. State parties, in turn, are consortia of local parties. In some states local parties are defined by counties, whereas in others they are defined by congressional districts. Although both the Democratic and Republican parties are active in every state, some state and local parties are more active than others. Parties in densely populated states such as Florida and California are well-funded, professionally run organizations. In less populated states such as Montana and Idaho, the parties have very small full-time staffs and take on

more personnel just during the few months leading up to an election.

A given state may have a particularly dominant political party, but overall, the political parties in most of the world's other Western-style democracies are much stronger than those in the United States. For example, in the United States, party leaders are not able to nominate candidates of their own choosing. Most candidates are now chosen directly by the voting public through primaries. In fact, even a party's top nominee—its presidential candidate—may not have been the first choice of party leaders. This is much different from the way party politics operates in, say, Great Britain. There, political parties are much more centralized. Leadership within a party translates more cleanly into leadership in government. The parties, not voters, select the parties' nominees for the office of prime minister.

After Ronald Reagan and other Republicans chipped into Democratic support among certain groups in the New Deal coalition, the Democrats became a famously argumentative group, with various factions within the party finding it hard to find common cause with one another. As recently as 2006, a Democratic strategist wrote about "the Democratic Party's well-deserved reputation for being a fractious coalition of infighting special interests."[3] But following their poor showing in that year's elections, Republicans began to argue more

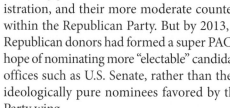

loudly among themselves about which ideas should prevail within the party—a fractious debate that continued through and after the party's losing presidential campaigns in 2008 and 2012. Conservative, populist Tea Party groups began holding large rallies in 2009 to decry big government, President Obama's administration, and their more moderate counterparts within the Republican Party. But by 2013, major Republican donors had formed a super PAC in the hope of nominating more "electable" candidates for offices such as U.S. Senate, rather than the more ideologically pure nominees favored by the Tea Party wing.

Swing Voters
Individuals who are not consistently loyal to candidates of any one party. They are true independents whose allegiance is fought for in every election.

Other groups are made up of so-called **swing voters**—that is, voters who might support candidates of either major party. Swing voters include farmers, suburbanites, and the elderly. Neither party can take their votes for granted, so they are highly sought after. Young people have tended not to vote much at all, or at least not in proportion to their share of the population, which is why their concerns have often been ignored, but they have emerged more recently as a key source of Democratic support. Pulling together as wide an assortment of interests as they can, political parties help voters and groups connect with the government while furthering their own ideals.

Political parties, however, remain different from other groups that participate in the political process, including interest groups. As already noted, a political candidate runs under a single party label, such as Republican, Democratic, or Green. The candidate campaigns for office and is nominated as a member of that party. In contrast to political parties, an interest group may support a candidate, but that person's candidacy is not based on affiliation with the group. The interest group did not recruit the candidate to run in its name. The interest group, in fact, might be supporting candidates from several parties. Increasingly, however, politically engaged interest groups tend to be associated with one party or another.

Candidates still may rely on parties to serve as conduits to interest groups and voters, but the importance of parties to individual candidates has not been as great recently as in the past. Academics have noted a shift to **candidate-centered politics** over the past thirty years or so. What this means is that parties play less of a role in determining who is going to run for which office. Instead, candidates, in effect, select themselves. Ambitious people interested in politics and government run for the offices of their choice rather than working their way up the party ranks in roles their parties might have chosen for them. Arnold Schwarzenegger

decided in 2003 to suspend his acting career to run for governor of California and won the support of the state's Republican Party. In the old days, a party's gubernatorial candidate first would have had to put in years in lower offices. He or she would have had to earn the support of party leaders throughout the state before running for the state's highest office. Another example is the case of Thomas Massie, the congressman from Kentucky, who did not need the blessing of his party's elders to make his successful run for office in 2012. The parties' own fund-raising role is now sometimes overshadowed by outside groups such as super PACs.

However important interest group spending is during an election, parties remain the primary mechanisms for the organization of government. Except for Nebraska, which is nonpartisan, all state legislatures are organized by party. If Democrats have a majority of the seats in the Maine House of Representatives, for example, the speaker of the House and other top leaders will be Democrats and the party will control each committee as well. Not everyone supports this system. George Norris, a U.S. senator from Nebraska who promoted many changes to his home state's political system during the 1930s, argued that state politicians should be nonpartisan. That way, he claimed, they would be judged on their record of dealing with issues at home rather than on the question of whether they adhered to positions taken by national parties.

Some things have changed, however. Once the dominant force in U.S. politics, deciding who ran for which office and with how much support, political parties have become such loose conglomerations of differing interests that they might be best described as marketing organizations. They are brand names that individual candidates choose to apply as a shortcut to identification in the marketplace. For example, to say that you are a Democratic candidate provides voters with a fairly reliable indication that you are for abortion rights legislation. Republicans—those who run for office, if not all rank-and-file party

Candidate-Centered Politics
Politics in which candidates promote themselves and their own campaigns rather than relying on party organizations.

FIGURE 6-1

HOW IT WORKS

Democratic and Republican Party Organization in Ohio and Cuyahoga County

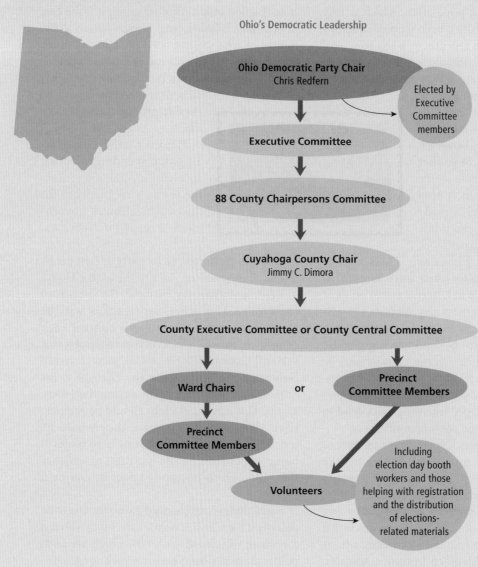

Ohio's Democratic Leadership

Ohio Democratic Party Chair
Chris Redfern

Elected by Executive Committee members

Executive Committee

88 County Chairpersons Committee

Cuyahoga County Chair
Jimmy C. Dimora

County Executive Committee or County Central Committee

Ward Chairs   or   Precinct Committee Members

Precinct Committee Members

Volunteers

Including election day booth workers and those helping with registration and the distribution of elections-related materials

members—nearly always feel the opposite. These days, there is little overlap between the parties on a whole host of issues, including tax policy, gun ownership rights, and environmental protections. As a theoretical ideal, or baseline, political scientists use the **responsible party model** as a way to measure and assess political parties. The responsible party model holds that political parties should present clear policy options to voters, that voters will cast ballots based on the options they favor

Responsible Party Model
The theory that political parties offer clear policy choices to voters, try to deliver on those policies when they take office, and are held accountable by voters for the success or failure of those policies.

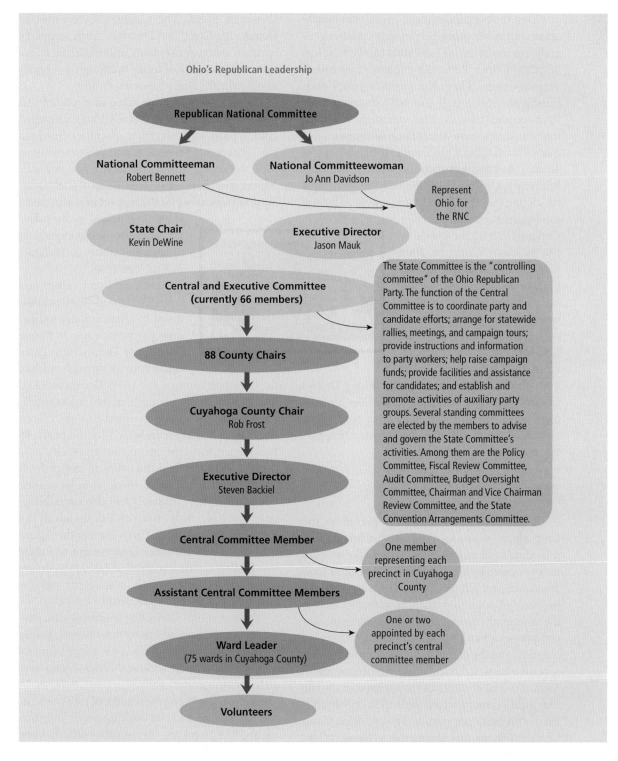

Ohio's Republican Leadership

Republican National Committee

National Committeeman
Robert Bennett

National Committeewoman
Jo Ann Davidson

Represent Ohio for the RNC

State Chair
Kevin DeWine

Executive Director
Jason Mauk

Central and Executive Committee
(currently 66 members)

The State Committee is the "controlling committee" of the Ohio Republican Party. The function of the Central Committee is to coordinate party and candidate efforts; arrange for statewide rallies, meetings, and campaign tours; provide instructions and information to party workers; help raise campaign funds; provide facilities and assistance for candidates; and establish and promote activities of auxiliary party groups. Several standing committees are elected by the members to advise and govern the State Committee's activities. Among them are the Policy Committee, Fiscal Review Committee, Audit Committee, Budget Oversight Committee, Chairman and Vice Chairman Review Committee, and the State Convention Arrangements Committee.

88 County Chairs

Cuyahoga County Chair
Rob Frost

Executive Director
Steven Backiel

Central Committee Member

One member representing each precinct in Cuyahoga County

Assistant Central Committee Members

One or two appointed by each precinct's central committee member

Ward Leader
(75 wards in Cuyahoga County)

Volunteers

the most, that while in office parties try to create and implement the programs they promise, and that in the next election the parties will be judged by their performance in delivering these programs. In short, this model views political parties as connecting the wishes of citizens to government programs and policies, organizing the government to deliver on those wishes, and acting as the agents used to hold government accountable for delivering on what it promises.

Given the overall decline of strong **voter identification** with either major party, today's politics generally centers more on individual candidates than on party politics. Parties have found a new role as support organs. They offer consulting and fundraising services to self-selected aspirants. They have become "basically what you might call holding companies," says Walter Dean Burnham, a former political science professor at the University of Texas. "They organize cash and spread it around."[4] But now parties are being forced to adapt to legal restrictions on those functions as well. A federal campaign finance law passed by Congress in 2002 and upheld by the Supreme Court in 2003 makes it more complicated for parties to spend money on activities designed to register voters or encourage them to vote. (The Supreme Court reaffirmed the law's constitutionality in 2007 and, as pertains to party fund-raising limits, again in 2010.) Thanks to subsequent court decisions, such roles are now often played by super PACs and other groups that are at least technically separated from political parties and their candidates.

What Parties Were Like

In their early years, political parties in the United States were a lot more than just brand identifiers and fund-raisers. Many of the social services now provided by local governments, such as food assistance and job placement services, were the province of political parties throughout much of the nineteenth century. For all of the contemporary complaints about the "liberal media," one-sided bloggers, and the domination of talk radio by conservative hosts, today's nonpartisan "mainstream" media are a far cry from the newspapers of the late nineteenth century, which were often openly affiliated with particular parties. The pro-Republican *Chicago Tribune*, on learning that a Democrat had won the 1876 presidential election, ran a headline that read, "Lost. The Country Given over to Democratic Greed and Plunder."[5] Such an openly partisan statement remains unimaginable in the mainstream media of today (although not nearly as unlikely in a blog post or on Twitter).

People's party loyalties were so strong in this period because many of their livelihoods revolved around party interests. Party machines doled out jobs, government contracts, and other benefits to their workers and supporters. The idea was that "offices exist not as a necessary means of administering government but for the support of party leaders at public expense," as one political scientist wrote regarding nineteenth-century party cliques in New York State.[6]

Politics in many cities and some states was totally dominated by these usually indigenous party machines. In Rhode Island, the Democratic Party was dominant through much of the twentieth century, and party leaders brooked little dissent. Only a handful of free-agent candidates were able to pry nominations away from those who had been endorsed by the party. In Providence, the state capital and largest city, only three individuals held the office of mayor from 1941 until 1974. Two of those men were state Democratic Party leaders. Over the same thirty-year period, only two chairs headed the Providence Democratic Party. Both of them doubled as head of the city's Department of Public Works. Party leaders controlled 2,800 jobs, doling them out roughly equally among the various wards, or political districts, within the city.[7]

The close links connecting control of jobs, government spending, and party activity were hardly unique to Rhode Island. Chicago, Nassau County on Long Island, New York, and Pennsylvania were all home to legendary **political**, or party, **machines**. In Oklahoma, the state gave control of most government jobs—the decision-making power over hiring and firing workers—to individual officeholders. These individuals were not afraid to exploit such

---

Voter Identification
When a voter identifies strongly with one of the major parties, he or she is considered a Democrat or a Republican; many voters, however, are considered weakly aligned with either major party.

Political Machines
Political organizations controlled by small numbers of people and run for partisan ends. In the nineteenth and twentieth centuries, these organizations controlled party nominations for public office and rewarded supporters with government jobs and contracts.

control for their own benefit. "I have 85 employees—garage men, road workers, janitors, elevator operators—and they work for me when I need them," said a county commissioner. "These people care if I stay in office."[8]

> "I have 85 employees—garage men, road workers, janitors, elevator operators—and they work for me when I need them," said a county commissioner. "These people care if I stay in office."

The machine system was self-perpetuating, with control of jobs and power and offices feeding off one another. "Each succeeding election was viewed not as a separate contest involving new issues or new personalities," wrote political scientist Joel Sibley, "but as yet another opportunity to vote for, and reaffirm, an individual's support for his or her party and what it represented."[9] Party machines and rival factions ran "slates," or specific lists, of endorsed candidates for offices and lent their backing to the favored candidates. Sometimes this support came at a price.

Given party contacts and contracts with private-sector entities, party control of jobs often extended well beyond the borders of government. Sometimes—as was the case in Jersey City, New Jersey—the machines would charge an automatic kickback, demanding, say, 3 percent of public employee salaries. Such trimmings were not always enough to satisfy machine leaders. The exposure of clear cases of corruption, such as evidence that a party was extorting union funds, running gambling operations, and taking kickbacks on government contracts, often led to the election of reform candidates for mayor and other city and state offices.

In many states, such as Alabama, Florida, and Michigan, elected officials and party leaders had little opportunity to practice **patronage**—that is, to hand out jobs to their friends and supporters rather than hiring people based on qualifications. Therefore, there was little motivation to build

up a machine. In some places, such as Texas, nineteenth-century political parties were weak. They helped administer the election code and tried to remain acceptable to all candidates. In other places, disgust over corruption in politics led to antimachine statutes, such as the imposition of civil service requirements for many government jobs and tougher anticorruption laws. The widespread use of **nonpartisan ballots** for municipal offices was the direct result of reforms imposed in reaction to political machines. These ballots, which do not list candidates by political party, are designed to separate city government from party voting.

California may be the best example of a state that had such a progressive reaction against the machines. The state was hostile toward parties, lacked any type of patronage system, and held nonpartisan elections. Precinct and ward organizations were weak, whereas individual candidates were assertive.[10] Party organizations were once banned from endorsing candidates in primary contests. The law also limited state party chairs to two-year terms and required the rotation of chairs on a geographical basis every two years. In 1989, the U.S. Supreme Court threw out the statute and declared it unconstitutional.[11]

But California was the exception to the rule. Throughout the 1800s, most states essentially treated parties as private associations and chose not to regulate them. This remains the position of many other countries today. But, during the twentieth century, that all changed in the United States. States began to regulate parties as though they were public utilities. Such state regulation of political parties is examined later in this chapter.

Parties in the Twentieth Century

At the dawn of the twentieth century, political machines were generally locally based, and local parties were much more important political

---

Patronage
The practice of elected officials or party leaders handing out jobs to their friends and supporters rather than hiring people based on merit.

Nonpartisan Ballot
A ballot that does not list candidates by political party; this type of ballot is still often used in local elections.

CIVIL SERVICE REFORM.

Office-Seeker. "St. Jackson, can't you save us? Can't *you* give us something?"

supporters. At conventions, party leaders closely controlled most votes and thus had enormous influence over who would or would not become the party's official nominee in the general election. This influence is lost in a primary election; in a primary, members of the general public have the chance to cast secret ballots. This gives party officials less direct control over the nominating process. Some states, such as Virginia, still allow for the option of nominating candidates by party conventions, but every state now has a system in place to nominate candidates through primaries. Every party holds statewide conventions, and many hold conventions at the local or district level as well. Nowadays, practically anyone who cares to attend a state or local party convention can do so, but it still takes some effort or connections to attend a national party convention, especially as a voting delegate.

Direct primaries allow rank-and-file voters to choose nominees for public office through means of a direct ballot. This contrasts with the convention system, in which the role of voters is indirect—voters choose delegates to a convention, and the delegates choose the nominee. At the state level, there are three basic types of direct primaries. In a **closed primary**, only registered members of the party holding the primary are allowed to vote, meaning that an individual must be a registered Democrat to vote for the Democratic nominee for office or a registered

actors than state parties in states where there were powerful big-city machines. Elsewhere, state parties often were funded and controlled by corporate interests—in many cases by just one interest, such as the DuPont Corporation in Delaware or the Anaconda Copper Company in Montana. Following the Progressive Era reforms in states such as California, state parties became little more than empty shells. As late as the 1970s, many state parties lacked permanent headquarters and were run out of their chairs' homes.[12]

State parties lost much of their influence because of the rise of primary elections. In primary elections, voters select the candidates who will represent the parties in **general elections**, the contests between party nominees that decide which candidates will actually win political office. Before primary elections became common, parties picked their nominees through **party conventions**, meetings of a few hundred party officials or

General Election
A decisive election in which all registered voters cast ballots for their preferred candidates for a political office.

Party Convention
A meeting of party delegates called to nominate candidates for office and establish party agendas.

Closed Primary
A nominating election in which only voters belonging to that party may participate. Only registered Democrats can vote in a closed Democratic primary, for example.

Republican to vote for the Republican nominee. This type of primary prevents **crossover voting**, in which a member of one party votes in another party's primary (a Democrat voting in a Republican primary, for instance). This practice is not allowed in all states. In an **open primary**, independents—and in some cases members of both parties—can vote in the primary of any party they choose. In a blanket primary—a type of primary invalidated in 2000 in the U.S. Supreme Court case *California Democratic Party v. Jones*—all candidates from all parties are listed on a single ballot and voters are allowed, in effect, to mix and match the primaries they participate in. That is, a voter could vote in one party's primary for a particular office, then switch to another party's primary for another office. Louisiana holds what is essentially a nonpartisan blanket primary—sometimes called a jungle primary—in which all candidates run in the same primary regardless of party. If no candidate wins an outright majority in the primary, the two top vote-getters—regardless of party—go on to a general election face-off. A **runoff primary** sometimes occurs in some states if no candidate receives a majority of the vote in an initial primary. In that case, the top two candidates face off. Washington State and California voters in recent years have established similar "top-two" primary systems, in which candidates from all parties appear together on a single primary ballot, and the top two finishers, regardless of party, proceed to the general election. Map 6-1 shows a state-by-state breakdown of the main types of primaries.

As late as 1968, party officials selected about 600 of the 2,600 delegates to the Democratic Party's national convention—almost 25 percent—two to four years ahead of the convention. Senator

Eugene McCarthy, D-Minn., had made such a surprisingly strong showing in the New Hampshire primary that he drove President Lyndon Johnson from the race. But Johnson's backing was still significant enough to help his vice president, Hubert H. Humphrey, win the support of delegates controlled by party officials. McCarthy believed he had been cheated by the party rules, so he proposed that all delegates to the nominating convention be chosen through "procedures open to public participation" in the same year in which the convention was to take place.[13]

Humphrey recognized that McCarthy and Senator Robert F. Kennedy, D-N.Y., both of whom had campaigned on anti-Vietnam platforms, had taken 69 percent of the primary vote. Respectful of what that number meant, he wanted to reward their followers with a consolation prize. So Humphrey coupled McCarthy's changes with one proposed by Senator George McGovern, D-S.D. McGovern wanted to see delegations demographically match—or at least reflect—the compositions of the states they represented. More and more states threw up their figurative hands as they tried to meet each of these new requirements. Taking the path of least resistance, they decided that the easiest thing to do would be to hold popular-vote primaries. Democratic primaries were held in only fifteen states in 1968, but by 1980 the number had risen to thirty-five. Conventions were reduced to little more than coronation ceremonies.[14]

How State Parties Recovered: Campaign Reform in the Late Twentieth Century

By the time the conventions are held, candidates have already been selected by voters through primary elections. Yet the conventions are still important networking occasions for officeholders and activists; they also provide occasions for parties to change their internal rules. The action for candidates now is in the primary and general election seasons. This is when they have the chance to woo voters directly, if not personally. Candidates no longer need hierarchical machines

---

Crossover Voting
Members of one party voting in another party's primary. This practice is not allowed in all states.

Open Primary
A nominating election that is open to all registered voters regardless of their party affiliations.

Runoff Primary
An election held if no candidate receives a majority of the vote during the regular primary. The two top finishers face off again in a runoff to determine the nominee for the general election. Such elections are held only in some states, primarily in the South.

MAP 6-1

Party Affiliation Requirements for Voting in Direct Primaries

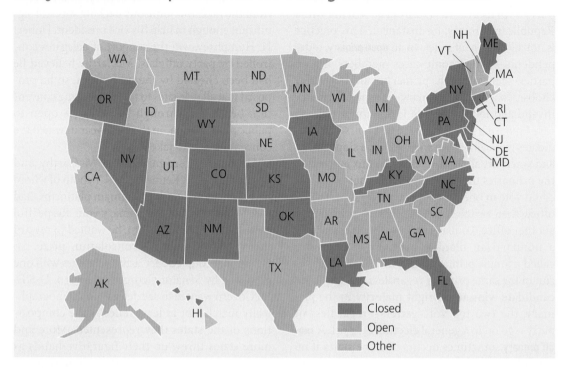

Closed
Open
Other

Source: Center for Voting and Democracy, "Primaries: Open and Closed," www.fairvote.org/congressional-and-presidential-primaries-open-closed-semi-closed-and-top-two#.UNt5xXfNmSq.

Notes:

Alaska: Closed caucuses for both parties, but voters may change party affiliation at polls or caucus.

California: In 2010, California approved a system in which all candidates compete on the same primary ballot, with the two top finishers, regardless of party, proceeding to the general election.

Idaho: Democrats have an open caucus, while the Republicans have an open primary.

Illinois: Voters may vote only in the primary of the same party as the last primary they participated in. Loosely enforced. Voters may change party affiliation at polls or caucus.

Iowa: Closed caucuses, but voters may change registration at polls.

Kansas: In the Democratic caucus, independent voters can register as Democrats on caucus day. For Republicans it is a closed caucus.

Louisiana: Primaries are closed for presidential elections. For congressional elections, they are effectively open, because Louisiana currently uses a top-two runoff system. The state switched to a closed primary for congressional races after 2006.

Maryland: Parties can choose to open primaries, but both Democrats and Republicans have chosen not to. If a voter does not choose a party, he or she will be recorded as "unaffiliated" and is permitted to vote in any nonpartisan primary in his or her local jurisdiction.

Massachusetts: Registered Democrats and Republicans can vote only for their own party in the primary, but independent voters may decide which party they would like to vote for.

Montana: Republicans have a closed caucus, while Democrats have an open primary.

New Hampshire: Registered Democrats and Republicans can vote only for their own party in the primary, but independent voters may decide which party they would like to vote for. Unregistered voters can register on election day.

New Jersey: Registered Democrats and Republicans can vote only for their own party in the primary. Any New Jersey voter who has never before voted in a New Jersey primary election may declare a party affiliation at the polling place. Independents may also decide which party to vote for.

North Carolina: A person registered with a party must vote in that party's primary. Unaffiliated voters may choose a party on the day of the primary election.

North Dakota: North Dakota has no voter registration. Voters must only prove that they have been a resident for at least thirty days.

Ohio: A voter must vote in the primary of the same party he or she participated in at the last primary election.

Rhode Island: If voters are registered as "unaffiliated," they may vote in the primary of any party they choose. Once they vote in a primary, however, they are considered a member of that party until and unless they "disaffiliate."

Utah: Currently only Republicans close their primary. Democrats and independents can vote in the Democratic primary. Conventions are held by the political parties prior to the primary.

Virginia: Parties may choose to nominate by convention rather than by primary election.

Washington: The state in 2004 moved to an open, "top-two" primary system, which the Supreme Court upheld in 2008.

West Virginia: Republicans have a closed convention, while Democrats hold a primary in which unaffiliated voters and independents may participate.

to reach voters. The decline of party machines was followed in time by the advent of televised campaign commercials as the dominant mode for trying to persuade citizens to vote.

The increasing reliance on campaign ads, ironically, led to restored strength for state and national political parties and spelled the decline of local party strength in federal elections. The move from greeting potential voters in person at party dinners and county fairs to airing TV ads meant that politicians had to run more professional campaigns. They now hire pollsters to figure out which issues will resonate best in their ads. Consultants help shape their message on these issues, and media gurus produce the ads and place them during favorable time slots. Once more changing with the times, state parties became important clearinghouses, connecting candidates with consultants. Eventually, they evolved into important consulting organizations themselves.

Every Democratic and Republican state party now has a full-time chair or executive director. Most have other professional staffers as well, who handle fund-raising, communications, field operations, and campaigns.[15] In general, Republican state parties tend to be better funded and, therefore, better run than their Democratic counterparts. Democratic state parties, however, often gain support from their allied groups, such as labor unions.

With their massive computer databases, maintained and updated from year to year, political parties help candidates target and reach voters who are sympathetic to their messages. It's common now for candidates to carry iPads and smartphones loaded with the latest voter registration data instead of the old-fashioned clipboards full of paper printouts on which they could scribble notes. Parties also play an important role in helping interested groups and potential contributors determine which of their candidates have a realistic shot at winning. The major parties are not the voter organizers they were in the machine days, when individuals were encouraged to vote "early and often," but they do still contact up to 25 percent of the electorate in any election cycle. While the national parties typically

play a greater role in polling and developing issues, "local and state parties [are] particularly important for registering voters and conducting get out the vote campaigns."[16]

One state chair in the 1950s exemplified the move that parties made toward professionalized consulting services. Ray Bliss took over the Ohio Republican Party after it suffered an electoral drubbing in 1948. He immediately began to identify and recruit better candidates. He also looked at ways to encourage citizens to vote, noting that, in 1948, 140,000 rural Republicans did not vote and 150,000 potential Republican voters in urban areas were not even registered. Following Bliss's registration and get-out-the-vote drives, Ohio Republicans in 1950 reelected a U.S. senator, won three statewide offices, and regained control of the state legislature.[17]

Minority-party members enviously keep close tabs on the governing party, and they alert the public and the press to every perceived misstep and abuse. It is also important for minority parties to avoid being demoralized and to continue to offer voters alternatives, so that candidates from their parties will be in place once the public is ready for a change. For instance, conservative Republicans dominated the Arizona Senate during the late 1990s. It seemed certain that Arizona speaker of the House Jeff Groscost would join their ranks in 2000 because he was running in a Senate district that heavily favored the GOP. Late in the campaign season, however, Groscost was implicated in a scandal surrounding a massive tax break that aided sports utility vehicle (SUV) owners—including a friend of Groscost's who sold the vehicles—and cost the state hundreds of millions of dollars. Groscost was defeated by his previously unknown Democratic challenger, and the Senate ended up operating under divided control between the parties.

Today, the two parties remain so closely competitive nationally that political scientists refer to a period of **dealignment**, meaning that neither party is dominant. In earlier periods of American history,

Dealignment
The lack of nationwide dominance by any one political party.

one party or another generally dominated politics, holding most of the important offices. The two major examples are Republican dominance from the time of the Civil War into the 1920s and the Democratic New Deal coalition, which held power from the presidential election of 1932 into the 1960s. The 1932 election of Franklin D. Roosevelt is the best example of a **realignment**, the switching of popular support from one party to another. Neither party has pulled off a similarly lasting realignment since then, in that voters seem about equally supportive of both major parties. Indeed, Republican hopes of creating a "permanent majority" following George W. Bush's 2004 win were dashed quickly when Democrats took control of the U.S. Congress in the 2006 midterm elections, followed by Barack Obama's win in the 2008 presidential election. Conversely, Democrats took a shellacking in 2010. They were able to recover to some extent by 2012 with Obama's reelection, but still lack control of the House.

State Party Regulation and Finance

State Party Regulation

Remember that states did not regulate political parties until the beginning of the twentieth century, when the progressive backlash against machine abuse led states to intervene. Political scientists now refer to parties as equivalent to public utilities, such as water and electricity, in which the public has a sufficient interest to justify state regulation.[18] Political parties, after all, are the main conduits through which elections are contested and government is organized. The legal justifications that states have used to regulate parties revolve around registration requirements—twenty-nine states and Washington, DC, register voters by party[19]—because party names are printed alongside the names of candidates on ballots.

Thirty-eight states regulate aspects of the structure of their state and local parties, often in explicit detail, to prevent antidemocratic,

machine-boss control.[20] Some states determine, for instance, how the members of state parties' central committees should be selected and how often those committees will meet. A state might specify which party organization can name a substitute candidate if a nominee dies or withdraws prior to an election. Such regulation is practiced whether in regard to a state party in Minnesota or a local party in Pennsylvania.

A relatively limited number of state parties have challenged the laws regulating parties in the wake of the 1989 Supreme Court decision, mentioned previously, in which the Court ruled that the state of California did not have the authority to dictate how political parties are organized. The major parties in New Jersey did adopt a number of changes in party structure, but for the most part the parties seem satisfied with the way things are being run under the systems imposed on them by the states.

The decision in 1989 was neither the first time nor the last time the U.S. Supreme Court weighed in on concerns related to political parties. The nation's highest court has issued a number of other decisions in recent years to clarify the legal rights of parties. In a series of cases emanating from Illinois during the 1970s and 1980s, the Court made it clear that "party affiliations and support" are unconstitutional bases for the granting of a majority of government or public jobs, except at the highest levels.[21] In 1986, it ruled that the state of Connecticut could not prevent independents from voting in Republican Party primaries if the GOP welcomed them.[22] This precedent, which allowed the parties rather than the state to determine who could participate in the parties' primaries, was later followed in several other states. The parties have not always gotten their way, however. In 1999, the Court determined that states have the constitutional right to regulate elections and prevent manipulation. The ruling blocked a new party in Minnesota from "fusing" with the state's Democratic Party by nominating candidates for election that the Democrats already had nominated.[23]

Campaign Finance

In 1996, the U.S. Supreme Court lifted federal limits on how much parties could spend. Under the new rules, a party could spend as much as it liked to

---

Realignment
The switching of popular support from one party to another.

support a candidate, as long as the candidate did not approve the party's strategy or ads or have any say over what the party was doing. The Court decided that no one had the right to restrict **independent expenditures**—that is, funds spent on activities or advertising without the candidate's knowledge or approval. "We do not see how a Constitution that grants to individuals, candidates, and ordinary political committees the right to make unlimited independent expenditures could deny the same right to political parties," wrote Justice Stephen G. Breyer.[24] A decade later, the Court tossed out a Vermont law that sought to limit fund-raising and the amounts that candidates could spend on state campaigns.

In addition to this legal windfall, state parties already had been exempted from a number of federal campaign finance limits. In 1974 and 1976, Congress had enacted laws that limited the amount of money candidates could collect from individuals and political action committees. Congress revised the law in 1979 following complaints from party leaders that the new laws almost completely eliminated state and local party organizations from participation in presidential campaigns. The old law, party leaders contended, put too many restrictions on how parties could spend money during a presidential election year. The revised law lifted all limits on what state and local parties could raise or spend for "party-building" activities. These included purchasing campaign materials, such as buttons, bumper stickers, and yard signs, and conducting voter registration and get-out-the-vote drives.[25]

It quickly became clear that the laxer restrictions were broad enough to allow for the purchase of TV ads and the funding of other campaign-related activities with so-called **soft money** donations, which were nominally meant to support party building.

Meanwhile, the state parties proved themselves no slouches at raising money, as Figure 6-2 shows. Democrats and Republicans at the state level raised more than $500 million during the 2008 election cycle—a slight dip because of the loss of federal party transfers under McCain-Feingold.[26] But no matter what limitations are placed on campaign finance, money finds its way into the system because the U.S. Supreme Court has held that political expenditures are equivalent to free speech. In January 2010, in *Citizens United v. Federal Election Commission*, the Court ruled that political spending by corporations in candidate elections cannot be restricted. That finding was at odds with long precedent and the campaign finance laws of at least two dozen states, but in a 2012 ruling, the Court made clear that states cannot ban direct political spending by corporations. Says University of Virginia government professor Larry J. Sabato,

> There is no way to stop the flow of interested money and there will always be constitutional ways around the restrictions enacted into law. What is so fundamental is that politics and government determine the allocation of goods and values in society. Those goods and values are critical to the success or failure of hundreds of interest groups and millions of individuals. Those groups and individuals are going to spend the money to defend their interests, period.[27]

A total of $8,713,918 was contributed to Hawaii's Democratic and Republican candidates and committees in 2012, with $7,414,853 of that going to Democrats.

FIGURE 6-2

State Party Fund-Raising Over Time

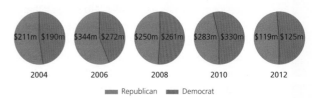

2004	2006	2008	2010	2012
$211m $190m	$344m $272m	$250m $261m	$283m $330m	$119m $125m

■ Republican ■ Democrat

Source: Data compiled from the National Institute for Money in State Politics, "Industry Influence 2000–2012," http://followthemoney.org/database/IndustryTotals.phtml?f=P&s=0.

Independent Expenditures
Funds spent on ad campaigns or other political activities that are run by a party or an outside group without the direct knowledge or approval of a particular candidate for office.

Soft Money
Money not subject to federal regulation that can be raised and spent by state political parties. A 2002 law banned the use of soft money in federal elections.

Policy in Practice

Does It Make Sense to Limit Campaign Finance?

Politicians seem to have no trouble raising money these days. Presidential contests have become billion-dollar affairs, the cost of gubernatorial contests in some states has approached or even exceeded $100 million, and million-dollar state legislative races are not uncommon.

Nevertheless, many candidates are being outgunned by super PACs and other outside groups with nearly unlimited funds at their disposal. With billionaires dashing off multimillion-dollar checks to super PACs, political scientists and some politicians themselves are worried that candidates have become mere bystanders in their own campaigns.

This situation has triggered a debate about whether it makes sense to have a system in which campaign finance limits apply mainly to political parties and candidates. Opinion on how best to fix the problem remains split roughly along party lines.

An increasing number of Republicans want to close what they consider the opposite of a loophole, saying it makes no sense to handcuff candidates when money is otherwise flowing so freely. "The problem is the limits," Tennessee GOP senator Lamar Alexander said at a committee hearing in 2012. "These new super PACs exist because of the contribution limits we've placed upon parties and candidates. Get rid of the limits on contributions, and super PACs will go away."

Abolishing those limits, however, would only open the door to outright influence peddling, according to Democrats and others who advocate keeping the rules in place for candidates and parties. "To suggest that the solution to the problem is for candidates to raise the money themselves would just double down the possibilities for corruption," says Josh Orton, political director of Progressives United, a Wisconsin-based group that favors campaign finance limits. "Can you imagine the kind of conversations that could happen if we lifted the restrictions on corporations giving to candidates themselves?"

Individuals are limited to donations of $2,500 per federal candidate per election, which means they can contribute that amount for both primary and general election campaigns. Limits on gifts to parties are higher; for instance, an individual may give a national party $30,800 per year and a state party $10,000. About half the states had banned corporations from spending money directly on campaigns, but such strictures were struck down by the Supreme Court in 2012.

Other limits on what outside groups can spend on campaigns have largely been eroded since the Supreme Court's *Citizens United* ruling in 2010. That decision has been hailed—and derided—for ushering in a new era of campaign finance law. But it was an earlier Supreme Court decision, in *Buckley v. Valeo*, that made it hard to make campaign finance restrictions stick. That case found that money in politics is protected as equivalent to free speech. Ever since the 1976 *Buckley* decision, money has been like water, finding its way into the political system through new means, regardless of what restrictions have been enacted. "Right now, you have the worst of all worlds—unlimited contributions to third-party entities, with some, but certainly not instant, disclosure," says Trey Grayson, a former Republican secretary of state from Kentucky who now directs the Harvard University Institute of Politics.

Grayson says he'd rather see money put in the hands of candidates and parties, who are more accountable to voters than campaign committees that may disappear after the election. Currently, messages from candidates themselves in a contested race are likely to make up only a "small sliver" of total campaign advertising, says Ed Goeas, a Republican consultant who favors lifting limits while requiring disclosure of donors. "Money is now at the end that's furthest away from the candidates and furthest away from the parties," Goeas says. "The money is with these other groups that are having more impact on the campaign than the campaign itself."

Super PACs are not supposed to coordinate their messages or strategies with candidates, but many political observers agree that the line often gets blurry, with former aides to candidates sometimes running super PACs that support their campaigns. Still, erasing the line entirely would do great damage to the political system, argue the proponents of maintaining campaign finance limits. Having politicians directly receive large or unlimited funds from entities they might regulate would be a surefire recipe for corruption. "We're in pretty bad shape right now, but there are still some lines," says Meredith McGehee, policy director for the Campaign Legal Center. "By funneling large amounts of money to politicians, what you would actually have is just more candidates elected who are beholden to a small elite."

Supporters of such limits point to possible models to stem the tide of money. Public financing systems in Maine and Arizona, for example, give politicians incentive to raise small amounts of money from constituents.

But even those who would seek to level the playing field by allowing candidates and parties to raise more money directly believe that the genie may already be out of the bottle. Many rich donors have come to like super PACs, which allow them to control their own messages through advertising, without relying on politicians to have to deliver them.

Source: Original piece written for this book by Alan Greenblatt.

Party Competition: Why Some States Are More Competitive Than Others

In 2002, Republicans took their first majority in the number of state legislative seats controlled nationwide since the early 1950s. But four years later, the Democratic Party made impressive gains at the state level as well. Following the 2006 elections, Democrats held twenty-eight of the fifty state governorships—their first majority in a dozen years. In addition, Democrats emerged with a 660-seat advantage in state legislative seats. By 2008, Democrats controlled both legislative chambers in twenty-seven states, compared to the Republicans' fourteen. That year, the party didn't win legislative races in only the states where Democrats traditionally dominate; it ran up its margins in states where Republicans only recently had controlled at least one house, such as Minnesota and Oregon.[28]

These gains were wiped out, however, in the strong Republican year of 2010. The GOP made a net gain of sixty-three seats in the U.S. House—enough to win back control of that chamber—and six seats in the U.S. Senate. Republicans made a net gain of six governorships and nearly seven hundred seats in state legislatures—giving them their best showing at that level since 1928. Once again, however, the tide soon shifted back, if only slightly. Democrats in 2012 took control of about two hundred additional state legislative seats while picking up a net gain of eight seats in the U.S. House and two in the U.S. Senate.

Historically, most state political cultures have heavily favored one party or the other, as shown in Map 6-2. A well-known example of this is the old Democratic "Solid South." For more than a century, most southern voters were "yellow-dog Democrats," meaning they would sooner vote for a yellow dog than for a Republican. From 1880 to 1944, all eleven states of the old Confederacy voted for Democrats in every presidential election—with a couple of exceptions in 1920 and 1928. These states elected only Democrats and a few independents governor, and they elected only Democrats to the U.S. Senate after popular voting for senators began in 1916.[29] The Democratic hegemony in the South began to break up with the civil rights era that began, roughly, with the elections of 1948.

A decade ago, both parties started out with a fair chance of winning statewide elections in just about every state. That was actually a big change. Republicans are now dominant politically in the South, but they have lost their edge in the Northeast, which has become one of the more Democratic sections of the country. Republicans hold the advantage in many states of the Mountain West, but Democrats are stronger along the Pacific Coast.

In the 2002 gubernatorial elections, old party strangleholds finally broke. Georgia elected a

MAP 6-2

Interparty Competition, 2007–2011

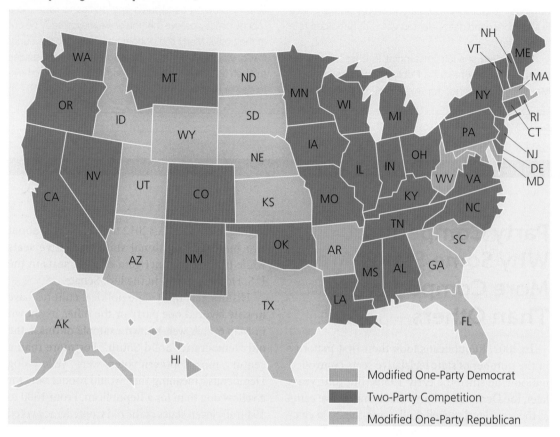

Modified One-Party Democrat

Two-Party Competition

Modified One-Party Republican

Source: Data compiled from Thomas Holbrook and Raymond La Raja, "Parties and Elections," in *Politics in the American States: A Comparative Analysis*, 10th ed., ed. Virginia Gray and Russell L. Hanson (Washington, DC: CQ Press, 2013), 88.

Republican governor for the first time since 1868, ending the longest drought for either party in any state before or since. The GOP also took the governor's mansion in other states that had traditionally gone Democratic. These states included Maryland, which elected a Republican for the first time since 1966, and Hawaii, which chose the GOP for the first time since 1959. Democrats, meanwhile, won in Illinois, Maine, Michigan, and Wisconsin for the first time in well over a decade, and they seated governors in Arizona, Kansas, Oklahoma, and Wyoming—states that had been supporting mostly Republicans in recent years.[30] Of the twenty-four new governors elected in 2002, twenty wrested control from a governor of another party.

Since then, however, many states have shown their true colors, ending up either Democratic blue or Republican red. Following the 2012 elections,

only three states had divided legislatures (Iowa, Kentucky, and New Hampshire). One party holds both the governorship and legislative control in most states—often by supermajorities. Once a party loses power, it is at a disadvantage in recovering power. Its traditional allies also have a harder time pushing their agendas. Republicans currently control every statewide office in Texas and have enjoyed control of that state's legislature since the 2002 elections. That means that Democrats have less power in Texas now than they have had for more than a century. This, in turn, means that interest groups are more likely to support Republican candidates because they believe that members of that party will have more say in the function of state government.

Interest groups recognize the fluid nature of political power. Trial lawyers make up one of the most important Democratic constituencies, for example, because of their ability to contribute large amounts of campaign cash. In Florida, a state that has become more Republican in recent years, trial lawyers are splitting their donations and support. They are lining up more and more often behind Republicans because they want to get a hearing from the currently dominant party. Some groups, however, are forever on the outs in certain states and communities. Environmentalists have a harder time pushing their legislation in Michigan, because of its historic dependence on the automotive industry, than they do in California. Labor unions have a harder time organizing in traditional right-to-work states in the South than they do in the Northeast or Midwest, but even there, unions—particularly those representing public-sector workers—have come under attack in recent years.

Also important to remember is that even though many state legislative chambers are politically competitive and have switched hands several times in recent years, most of the seats within them are dominated by one party or the other. Legislative districts are redrawn following each decennial census. Given computerization and other tools, political leaders are able to predict the likely voting patterns of people on a block-by-block or sometimes house-by-house basis. Following the 2010 census, nearly every district in the country was redrawn in such a way that it became reasonably safe for a candidate of one party over the other. In other words, there are now many safe Democratic districts and safe Republican districts, and there are not a lot of districts that are competitive. This means that most of the competition for any given seat will take place in the primary race of the dominant party.

Party Factions and Activists

Parties are no longer generally able to reward their followers directly with jobs or other payoffs. Decisions handed down by the U.S. Supreme Court have made it clear that party affiliation is not a constitutional basis on which to decide government hires. Kentucky governor Ernie Fletcher learned that the hard way in 2006 when he and several other top state officials were indicted for hiring supporters. Fletcher had been the first Republican elected to run the state in more than thirty years, and members of his administration were apparently too eager to hire party loyalists for government positions, disregarding the state's merit-hiring law in some instances.

With party leaders prevented from dispensing prizes such as jobs, party activism and various party tasks are now largely carried out by volunteers. And because people seldom work for free unless they believe in something very strongly, political volunteers have become more ideological. People work for candidates and parties because they believe in specific causes, such as handgun control legislation or protections for small business owners.

Just because jobs are no longer the parties' golden eggs does not mean that politicians and parties do not seek to pluck favors from their constituents through policies or promises. Both major parties court the elderly with assurances of healthcare benefits, such as Medicare, because senior citizens vote and thus are worth courting. Young people, by contrast, have historically tended not to vote. Only 24 percent of Americans thirty years of age and younger voted in 2006, which was the best midterm showing for the young in twenty years.[31] The young voter turnout increased in the 2004 and 2008 presidential elections—51 percent of the population between the ages of eighteen and twenty-nine cast ballots in 2008—but the group's participation continued to trail that of older voters by almost 15 percentage points.[32] In 2012, the number of voters between the ages of eighteen and twenty-nine stayed about the same as in 2008—about 23 million—but because of a decline in voter participation overall, their share of the total electorate ticked up by one percentage point to 19 percent.

Each party has its main constituent groups, but that does not preclude both parties from trying to poach supporters from the other side. Remember, however, that each party is a kaleidoscope of interest groups and can only appeal so much to any one group before it risks alienating support among other groups. Given the growth of Hispanics as a share of the electorate and the nation's overall population, some Republicans have supported changes to immigration law that would reduce penalties against those in the country illegally, but many others in the party still favor restrictive policies and more secure borders.

Politicians must perform the neat trick of motivating the true believers within party ranks to support their candidacies during primary elections without pinning themselves down so much that they do not appeal to members of the other party and independents during the general election. Often, the more contentious the issue, the more a party will try to blur its differences with the other party. Candidates do not want to promise so much to their core supporters—known as the base—that they cannot then reach other voters. By promising a lot of money for public transportation, for instance, a candidate might gain support in the city but lose it in the suburbs.

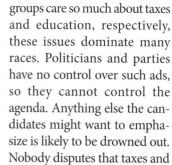

Both major parties try to appeal to as much of the populace as possible, but their supporters sometimes care more about promoting particular issues than they do about winning elections. Interest groups now raise their own funds and use them freely to promote their issues in campaigns. A 2009 special election for a vacant congressional seat based in Watertown, New York, demonstrates the difficulty the parties have in maintaining discipline in message and candidate selection. The state GOP nominated Dede Scozzafava, a pro-choice, pro–gay marriage state assemblywoman. Notable figures within the national Republican Party, including former vice presidential nominee Sarah Palin and Minnesota governor Tim Pawlenty, were opposed to Scozzafava's candidacy and publicly backed the Conservative Party candidate instead. Scozzafava dropped out of the race three days before the election and threw her support to Bill Owens, the Democratic candidate and eventual winner.[33]

Numerous interests took an active role in that particular general election campaign that fall, including pro–term limits groups, antiabortion and pro-choice advocates, labor unions, environmental organizations, and antitax groups. In fact, the amount of money the candidates spent on their own campaigns was dwarfed by the amount spent by these and other outside groups. Such situations have become more the rule and less the exception in recent years. In Wisconsin, political races were dominated for years by issue ads run by Wisconsin Manufacturers & Commerce and the Wisconsin Education Association Council. Because these two groups care so much about taxes and education, respectively, these issues dominate many races. Politicians and parties have no control over such ads, so they cannot control the agenda. Anything else the candidates might want to emphasize is likely to be drowned out. Nobody disputes that taxes and schools are important, but making them the only subjects in an election detracts from other issues.[34]

Now those well-established groups sometimes find themselves outgunned as well, with numerous organizations from inside and outside the state making their opinions known. This dynamic was heightened with the recall elections that dominated the state's politics in 2009 and 2010. Jennifer Shilling, a Democratic state representative, decided to challenge Republican senator Dan Kapanke in one of several recall contests that took place in 2009 after GOP leaders slashed budgets and eliminated collective bargaining rights for most public-sector employees. Shilling raised $400,000 for the race, against Kapanke's $1.6 million. But both candidates' treasuries were dwarfed by the millions spent by outside groups that ran independent expenditure campaigns. Shilling won, but, she said, "It was just numbing to look at my financial report, knowing what we needed to be competitive and get our messages out."[35]

During the 1980s, it appeared that candidates were fairly free agents. Today's campaigns, however, have become such big business that the candidates' funds and self-motivation often are not enough. Plus, candidates need votes, and to get these votes, they must join ranks with party officials and interests. Candidates can sometimes become mere pawns in campaigns that have been overtaken by deep-pocketed interest groups. They stand on the sidelines and watch as the parties or other groups run the greater volume of ads, redefining their campaigns for them.

Pragmatism Versus Idealism

Interest groups, just like parties, are most likely to play a prominent role in races that are closely contested or that can tip the partisan balance in a legislature. Redistricting at both the federal and state legislative levels, however, has grown so sophisticated—with so much emphasis placed on making districts safe for incumbents—that relatively few of these races are closely contested. Much of the action takes place in primary contests. But in true swing districts, where either party has a shot at winning, both major parties and all their allies will spend as much money as they can muster to win.

In these cases, party leaders grow frustrated when interest groups trumpet issues that do not appeal to a wider public. The main goal of parties is to win elections, so they are much more interested in fielding candidates who fit the profile of the office in contention than they are in promoting a specific ideology. The Republican National Committee, for example, defeated an attempt in 1998 to pass a party resolution that would have blocked the party from giving any money to candidates opposed to a ban on late-term abortions. Social conservatives were angry that the national committee had spent $760,000 supporting the reelection effort of New Jersey governor Christine Todd Whitman, who had vetoed a state ban on the procedure. "I'm about as pro-life as anybody," said Bob Hiler, Indiana's member of the national committee, "but I just cannot accept a situation in the Republican Party where there is a litmus test if you want to join or be a candidate. I respect the decisions of our national party leaders to place money where it needs to go to ensure that we win that seat."[36]

With just two broad-based national parties, neither can afford to preach an unyielding gospel on any single issue. The people most interested in politics may be motivated by their investment in particular issues, but if they hang around long enough, they come to realize that the best way to promote their cause is to win and hold political power. Still, perversely, the parties that are best able to keep their troops in line and satisfied with less-than-perfect ideological purity are the parties currently out of power. In other words, the desire to get back into the White House or to hold majority control of a legislature is often strong enough to convince all the quarreling factions to back someone who looks like a winner— even if that candidate is not "perfect" on all of the issues.

But the fact that both parties spend a good deal of time blurring their positions on the most important issues of the day to try to appeal to the most people while alienating the fewest number has made a lot of voters sour on them. Many Americans believe that politicians do not stand for anything and are more interested in preserving their power than in doing the right thing. That is a major reason increasing numbers of voters have declared themselves independent in recent decades and have refused to give lifelong allegiance to one party over the other in the same way that their grandparents did.

Third Parties and Independents

If millions of people are disenchanted with the Republican and Democratic parties for a variety of reasons, why isn't there more of a movement toward establishing a viable third, or minor, party as an alternative? Every election cycle seems to find more people dissatisfied with the major parties and more willing to identify themselves as independent. In 2008, a greater share of the electorate— 39 percent—identified itself as independent rather than as either Democratic (34 percent) or Republican (26 percent); that was the fifth straight election year in which independents were a plurality.[37] In 2012, slightly more people identified themselves as Democrats than as independents.

Still, in 2012 there was nothing resembling a strong third-party movement in the presidential race. If anything, the opposite was true. An organization known as Americans Elect sought to create a place for a strong third-party candidacy, spending $35 million on marketing, social media and other technology tools, and ballot access, securing a spot on the ballots of twenty-eight states by May 2012. But it shut down its crusade that month, having been unable to persuade a viable candidate to run under its banner.[38]

In most other democracies, numerous parties exist, each with strong support. In countries such as Israel and Italy, the leading party typically does not have enough seats in parliament to construct a government on its own and has to enter into a coalition with other parties.

That has never been the case in the United States, for a number of reasons. Democrats and Republicans, as we have been exploring, have established wide networks of contacts and supporters—individuals and groups that have long loyalties to one party or the other. They have office-holders at all levels who can help with strategy and fund-raising.

The major parties also have many other institutional advantages. For one thing, the United States favors a winner-take-all system in which the person receiving the most votes in a district wins. In some countries, seats in the legislature are distributed on a percentage basis, so that if a party gets 5 percent of the vote it receives about 5 percent of the total seats available. But if a party took only 5 percent of the vote across the United States, it probably would not win a seat anywhere. In 1992, Texas computer billionaire Ross Perot, the most successful third-party presidential candidate in decades, took 19 percent of the vote but did not carry a single state and therefore won no electoral college votes.

For the 1996 presidential race, Perot established the Reform Party, which he called his gift to the American people. Perot used that gift himself, running for a second time but not doing nearly so well. He had a hard time getting on the ballot in some states—rules regarding ballot access differ across states and are often complicated. In the state of New York, for instance, a candidate must collect a certain number of signatures from each of the congressional districts to get on the ballot. Many candidates with more modest financial means than Perot have had difficulty gaining access to ballots. Perot himself was excluded from the presidential debates. The commission running the debates—composed of officials from the Democratic and Republican parties—decided he was not showing enough strength in the polls to warrant being included.

Excluded though he was, Perot nevertheless took 8 percent of the vote in 1996. This was enough to guarantee the Reform nominee in 2000 a spot on all fifty state ballots, as well as $12 million in federal campaign funds. With Perot out of the running, however, the Reform nomination dissolved into chaos. Two separate conventions nominated two different candidates. The states were left having to decide which candidate deserved the spot on the ballot. "There are no statutes to guide us," said Mike Cooney, Montana's former secretary of state, in 2000. "The Reform Party needed to resolve this issue before it got to this point. It's an internal party problem that has been foisted upon the states and put us all in a bad situation."[39] The eventual Reform nominee proved not to be as much of a factor in the race as did Green Party nominee Ralph Nader. The Reform Party seemed to have self-destructed. Several of the old minor parties that had taken up its banner, such as Minnesota's Independence Party, soon returned to their original names.

Difficulties of Building Support

Many Democrats blamed Nader for the defeat of their candidate in 2000, Al Gore. Gore won more popular votes than Republican George W. Bush but was defeated in the electoral college. Some people believe that a third-party candidate will never be anything more than a "spoiler" who deprives major-party candidates of needed votes. Others believe that third parties help present a real and needed alternative to the Democrats and Republicans. Unless the major parties are challenged, the thinking goes, they will never change.

Minor-party candidates have enjoyed more success running for lower offices, but not much. Within a state or a legislative district, there is a better chance that an individual will enjoy enough personal popularity to equalize the playing field against Democrats and Republicans, who typically are better funded and connected. Still, only a half dozen governors elected during the past fifty years have been neither Democrats nor Republicans.

Three of those six—Walter Hickel of Alaska, Lowell Weicker of Connecticut, and Lincoln Chafee of Rhode Island—had earlier won statewide office as Republicans. Another two were elected in Maine, a state noted for the independent-mindedness of its electorate. The fifth, Jesse Ventura of Minnesota, served only one term, and the would-be successor from his Independence Party finished a distant third in 2002. Further demonstrating the difficulty of going it alone, Chafee became a Democrat in 2013, believing that running under a party banner would boost his chances of winning reelection.

At the legislative level, things are just as grim for third-party candidates. Following the 2012 elections, there were only twenty-nine third-party or independent state legislators in the United States (not counting nonpartisan Nebraska) out of a total of 7,400. Each of these candidates had dedicated followers. But from a pragmatic perspective—say, that of a voter interested in seeing his or her agenda become law—it may make better sense to support a Democrat or Republican who has a chance of serving in the majority party than it does to pull for a person who will hold just one vote.

Ultimately, it is the states that publish the ballots and have the authority to decide which parties' nominees are going to be listed on them. It is the states that grant ballot access to parties based on their having won a minimum percentage of the vote in a previous statewide general election. The threshold varies from 1 percent in Wisconsin to as much as 20 percent in Georgia. Such high institutional barriers make minor parties' complaints about two-party dominance of American politics about as fruitless as trying to hold back the tide.

Major-Party Support

One other reason minor parties have trouble gaining traction is that people are not, in the main, terribly unhappy with the major parties. The major parties, after all, do devote themselves to appealing to as broad a range of citizens as possible. That said, voter identification with the parties has declined. Some states once allowed voters to vote a straight ticket, meaning they could pull one lever to vote for all the Democratic or Republican candidates on the ballot. Such procedures are now considered quaint. Voters are more and more willing to divide their ballots, a practice called **ticket splitting**. One voter joked, "I vote for the man for president, and give him a Congress he can't work with."

In 1960, the Gallup Organization found that 47 percent of respondents identified themselves as Democrats, 30 percent as Republicans, and just 23 percent as independents or members of other parties. By the 1990s, those numbers had converged. Polling by the Pew Research Center for the People & the Press over a fifty-four-month period in the mid-1990s found that an average of 33 percent of the respondents called themselves Democrats, 29 percent identified as Republicans, and 33 percent said they were independents, with a handful naming other specific parties.[40] A poll released by the Pew Research Center in 2009 found that as the proportion of Republicans continued to shrink, Democrats picked up strength, but self-described independents had become the largest of the three groups, with 39 percent of respondents choosing the label—the highest such proportion in seventy years.[41]

As subsequent polling by Pew and other groups has found, however, most self-identified independents are not true independents. Their preferences generally do lean toward one of the major parties. "Partisan loyalties in the American populace have rebounded significantly since the mid-1970s, especially among those who actually turn out to vote," concluded political scientist Larry M. Bartels in 2000.[42] The proportion of pure independents, those who do not lean toward either party, peaked at 16 percent in 1976. Twenty years later, true independents were just 9 percent of the populace.[43]

Many people may not choose to identify themselves with either major party, but they mostly tend to vote one way or the other, a team of political

---

Ticket Splitting

Voters' or districts' voting for different parties' nominees for different offices—for instance, supporting a Republican for president while supporting a Democrat for Congress.

scientists concluded in the 1992 book *The Myth of the Independent Voter*.[44] "Independents have a great pride factor—'I vote for the person, not the party,'" said Jane Jech, a Republican candidate for the Iowa Senate in 2012. "But in truth, they lean one way or the other."[45]

The Republicans and Democrats have dominated American politics for 150 years. They have met every challenge—both ideological and structural—and found a way to preserve their near-total control. As political scientist Jeff Fishel puts it,

> if there's any lesson of history about the two major parties in American politics, it is that they're incredible adaptive survivors. They lost the monopoly they had, particularly on candidate recruitment and finance. That certainly does not mean that they're going out of business, just that they have to compete with other groups.[46]

Interest Groups and Lobbies

If many citizens are cynical about political parties, they're even more put off by interest groups. It's true that lobbyists representing big companies, unions, and other organizations often push for legislation to promote or protect their own narrow interests. But lobbying is how citizens and private companies make their views known to policymakers between election seasons. Sometimes people even lobby for altruistic reasons rather than self-interest.

College students of this generation will be familiar with Invisible Children, a group that sought to influence U.S. policy in Africa. The group called for people—primarily teenagers and young people—to pressure politicians, celebrities, and adults of their acquaintance to bring Central African warlord Joseph Kony to justice for murder, child abduction, and rape. Invisible Children, which had shown films about Kony to countless school groups, released a video on the web known as *Kony 2012* that became one of the greatest Internet sensations in history. As the word spread through Twitter and other social media, the video drew more than 100 million views on YouTube and Vimeo within days of being posted in March 2012. Invisible Children had already enjoyed some success in influencing policymakers, helping to convince Congress to pass a law that led to the United States sending one hundred military advisers to Uganda. *Kony 2012* called on young people to "cover the night" on April 20, putting up posters wherever they lived, to sear Kony into the nation's consciousness. But almost as soon as the video reached mass attention, a backlash set in. Invisible Children was criticized for simplifying the issues involved and for how it spent its funds. By the time April 20 rolled around, it appeared that most students had moved on. "Just a few weeks ago, students were ready to participate in fund-raising efforts or the Cover the Night event," said Alison Decker, a nineteen-year-old sophomore at Northwestern University. "Unfortunately, most of the fervor has seemed to change to apathy or eye rolls about the legitimacy of Invisible Children."[47]

It's not just that some of the group's claims and strategies drew criticism. Ten days after the release of *Kony 2012*, Jason Russell, a cofounder of Invisible Children and leading character in the video, was hospitalized by police in San Diego after he stood naked and screaming on a street corner. He was the apparent victim of exhaustion and dehydration, but a video of his breakdown—which was itself widely disseminated and viewed—undermined his group's credibility. Part of the power of *Kony 2012* was the way Russell was able to personalize the cause, showing how he and his young son had come to understand the menace and impact of Kony and his group, the Lord's Resistance Army. But Russell's having made himself central to the film's message created a public relations crisis when he was caught acting out on tape, said Marcus Messner, a communications professor at Virginia Commonwealth University. The incident was parodied in an episode of *South Park* that showed a character named Stan stripping his clothes off in San Diego after an antibullying video he directed had become a huge success and was then roundly reviled. "What was really a turnoff, particularly for young people, was the amateur video showing the [Invisible Children] organizer dancing naked on a street corner," Messner said. "While most people did not personally hear the criticism of the [*Kony 2012*] video, they did see the video of the breakdown." The VCU chapter of Invisible Children broke its ties with the group, changed its name, and decided to donate funds directly to children's programs in Uganda.[48]

Other student-led campaigns in recent years—such as attempts to pressure universities to divest from companies that supply arms to the government in Sudan—have been more successful. But such cause campaigns are different in kind than the average work done by interest groups, which tend to have long-standing interests in issues or regulations that affect the groups or their members directly. As should be apparent by now, interest groups have always been important resources for candidates, providing volunteers and other services as well as money. They have taken on even greater importance in the current era of high-stakes fund-raising and super PACs. They are the organizations that take a direct interest in political activity—both in terms of supporting candidates during an election season and in terms of lobbying elected and appointed government officials regarding policy and spending matters. Still, they differ from parties in that politics and elections are not their whole reason for being. As political scientist Frank J. Sorauf notes, "the American Medical Association devotes only part of its energies to protecting its interests through political action. Not so the political party. It arises and exists solely as a response to the problems of organizing the political process."[49] In other words, the American Medical Association (AMA) may spend millions of dollars annually trying to affect elections and legislation, but it devotes more of its energy and resources to educating its members, promoting good healthcare techniques, and other private activities. This difference in focus illustrates a fundamental and obvious trait that separates political parties from special interest groups—political parties run candidates for office under their own labels, whereas special interest groups do not.

Interest groups basically come in five flavors. One is the membership group, such as the AMA or the Sierra Club, made up of individual members with a common interest. A second type is the trade association, which represents individuals or organizations in a particular industry or field, such as the National Restaurant Association or the Alliance of Automobile Manufacturers. The third type of interest group is an individual institution; many large organizations, such as Microsoft and General Motors, have lobbyists on staff or devote a significant portion of their executives' time to lobbying. The fourth type consists of government lobbyists (sometimes called legislative liaisons), those who represent the interests of one branch of government to another. Executive branch officials have aides designated to lobby Congress or a legislature on their behalf, and cities, counties, and states hire lobbyists to make their cases in Washington. The fifth, and smallest, category comprises interest groups made up of private individuals who lobby on their own behalf for a pet project or against a policy that they find reprehensible.[50]

People and organizations have a constitutional right to petition the government for redress of grievances. That means that they have the right to complain to lawmakers and regulators about their disagreements with laws and how they are enforced. That is what lobbying is. It is worth noting that the government runs some of the most active lobbies. The White House maintains a lobbying shop to try to persuade Congress of the wisdom of its policies. Municipal governments hire lobbyists and associations to protect their interests in their state capitals. Currently about forty thousand lobbyists are working in state capitals, and the number of associations and related groups has quintupled over the last fifty years. Lobbying in the states is now a billion-dollar business every year.[51]

The Internet has made it easy to track which interest groups are active in which states. Open up a search engine and type in the name of a state and "lobbying registration," and you'll quickly find the website of an ethics commission or other state board with which all lobbyists must register. The National Institute on Money in State Politics (www.followthemoney.org) and the Center for Public Integrity (www.publicintegrity.org) also offer detailed information about campaign finance and lobbying activity in the states, as well as studies about overall trends.

The raw numbers—who is spending what where—tell only part of the story, however. It is often difficult to find out which group has influenced the outcome of a specific piece of legislation. Some interest groups, such as Invisible

Children, play a very public game, but others are more secretive, playing an insider game in which influence is a matter of quiet access to legislators.

That is why many interest groups hire **contract lobbyists**, usually lawyers or former government staffers or elected officials who are valued for possessing insider knowledge and contacts within particular state capitals. Contract lobbyists generally have a number of clients, as lawyers do. About 20 percent of lobbyists registered to ply their trade in a given capital are contract.[52] They use their relationships and contacts to convince legislators that they should or should not pass particular bills. And although lobbyists ignore the executive branch at their peril, given that spending decisions and regulatory action are carried out there, more lobbying activity happens in the legislative arena. "You don't change their minds," said a California lobbyist. "You find ways of making them think they agreed with you all along."[53]

Legislators often rely on lobbyists to provide them with information, whether simply data about an industry's economic outlook or their opinions about whether a bill would cost jobs in the legislators' districts. Legislators are always grappling with many issues at once: the state budget, education, the environment, and so on. It is up to lobbyists to keep legislators and their staffs apprised of who favors a particular bill and who would benefit from or be hurt by it. Lobbyists build up relationships with legislators over time, and legislators come to trust some of them for reliable information, even if they hold differing positions on particular issues. Often, members of trade associations and other groups will seek to inform legislators about their views without necessarily knowing whether the politicians they're meeting with agree with them or not; this is "lobbying as primarily engaged in providing information about constituency views, with groups pressing lawmakers to enact particular policies based on how constituents will respond," as one academic wrote after spending time working on Capitol Hill.[54]

Standing in contrast to contract lobbyists are **cause lobbyists** who promote a single-issue agenda, such as medical marijuana or campaign finance reform. A cause lobbyist often plays an outsider's game, using the media to sway public opinion and pressure public officials. Groups that do not have an economic interest in legislative outcomes are able to get away with this tactic because their ideological position is clear for all to see. Major industries also occasionally play outside games as they seek to pressure politicians by stirring up interest through issue advertising.[55] Contract lobbyists, by contrast, engage in **direct lobbying**, dealing personally with legislators and their staff in hopes of persuading them. The students trying to get public officials to divest from Sudan were taking part in **indirect lobbying**, building support for their cause through the media, through rallies, and through other ways of influencing public opinion, hoping that legislators would be swayed by the resulting buzz.

Using the media effectively can be trickier for private corporations and other entities directly affected by legislation. The media nearly always portray this third type of lobbyist in a negative light. If a politician sponsors a bill favoring a particular industry and individuals in that industry have made substantial donations to his or her campaign treasury, news stories are bound to be written about that money trail. Numerous states, including Kentucky, Massachusetts, and Minnesota, have passed ethics laws in recent years that preclude lobbyists, who used to wine and dine legislators, from giving legislators anything of value, even a cup of coffee.[56]

Cause Lobbyist
A person who works for an organization that tracks and promotes an issue, for example, environmental issues for the Sierra Club or gun ownership rights for the National Rifle Association.

Direct Lobbying
A form of lobbying in which lobbyists deal directly with legislators to gain their support.

Indirect Lobbying
A form of lobbying in which lobbyists build support for their cause through the media, rallies, and other ways of influencing public opinion, with the ultimate goal of swaying legislators to support their cause.

Contract Lobbyist
A lobbyist who works for different causes for different clients in the same way that a lawyer represents more than one client.

Policy in Practice

Why Companies Avoid Overt Partisanship

Michael Jordan, the basketball legend, refused to engage publicly in partisan politics. The reason was simple, he explained: Republicans buy shoes, too, he said, and Jordan didn't want to antagonize any potential customers for Nike, whose products he endorsed. Major corporations tend to employ the same logic. They don't want to risk angering potential consumers who disagree with their politics.

Target, the big retailer, found itself the target of boycott campaigns in 2010 after it donated $150,000 to a super PAC that supported a gubernatorial candidate who opposed gay marriage. Perhaps more striking, however, was the defection of many major corporations from a previously obscure legislative group that had become the center of controversy in 2012.

The American Legislative Exchange Council, known as ALEC, had long championed conservative legislation. The group brought together state legislators and corporations to craft policy that was turned into model bills introduced in many states. Much of it had to do with fiscal matters, such as tax policy, or policies that had some direct benefit to the group's corporate members—including prison sentencing laws that helped bring business to ALEC's active private prison affiliates. Roughly a thousand bills based on ALEC language are introduced in an average year, with about 20 percent enacted into law.

With the GOP sweep in the 2010 elections, ALEC was poised to be more influential than ever. Legislation promoted by the group dominated discussion in many capitols around such issues as climate change, voter ID requirements, illegal immigration, and limits on public-sector pensions. Versions of ALEC's Freedom of Choice in Health Care Act, which was a direct challenge to the federal law championed by President Barack Obama, were introduced in more than forty states. "It's really no secret," said state senator Jane Cunningham, the lead sponsor of Missouri's version. "I learned about the idea from ALEC and brought it back to Missouri."

For years, liberal advocacy groups decried ALEC's influence, but they were unable to alarm very many members of the public, since the group remained little known. That began to shift, however, in 2011, when 850 model bills generated by ALEC, along with other documents, were published on a website run by the liberal Center for Media and Democracy. That made it easier for journalists and the group's ideological opponents in individual states to compare proposed legislation with language crafted by ALEC. In addition, Common Cause, a group that supports campaign finance restrictions, called on the Internal Revenue Service to audit ALEC's books, claiming that the organization acted more like a full-fledged lobbying shop than a tax-exempt nonprofit.

ALEC was facing some public relations headaches, but its problems really began with the high-profile shooting of Trayvon Martin, an unarmed African American youth, in Florida in February 2012. The man who shot Martin, George Zimmerman, maintained that he was innocent of murder charges thanks to the state's "stand your ground" law, which allows people to use force when they feel they may be at risk.

That type of law had been promoted by ALEC. The group soon backed away from the issue, announcing two months after the shooting that it was disbanding the task force that dealt with public safety and elections issues. From now on, ALEC leaders said, they would stick purely to economic matters.

By then, it was too late for many of ALEC's corporate members. Several major companies, including Coca-Cola, Pepsi, McDonald's, and Kraft, had cut their ties with the group. Nearly three dozen corporations and foundations would ultimately make the decision that being associated with ALEC, however effective the group had been in the past, had become bad for business.

That's why most of the major donors to super PACs during the 2012 election cycle were not big corporations. Rather, they were wealthy individuals or owners of privately held companies who didn't have to worry about what their shareholders would think about their politics.

Source: Adapted from Alan Greenblatt, "ALEC Enjoys a New Wave of Influence and Criticism," *Governing,* December 2011.

TED CRUZ
NO PRINCIPLES

PAID FOR BY TEXAS CONSERVATIVES FUND WHICH IS RESPONSIBLE FOR THIS MESSAGE. NOT AUTHORIZED BY ANY CANDIDATE OR CANDIDATE'S COMMITTEE. WWW.TEXASCONSERVATIVESFUND.COM

This super PAC–sponsored ad targeted Texas solicitor general Ted Cruz with an allegation of corruption. Cruz ran for—and won—an open seat in the Texas Senate, but like many candidates for office in the 2012 election, he faced an increase in opposition ads from interest groups, which are now allowed to organize into super PACs and dig into deeper spending pockets.

Today, many interest groups try to combine the direct and indirect approaches, hitting up legislators for favors in private meetings while also running public relations campaigns through the media. Groups are also likely to join together in coalitions, hoping that a united front will not only present a more coherent and persuasive message but also prevent any individual group from looking as if it is pleading from narrow self-interest. Interest groups often look for surprising allies who will plead their case. For instance, groups wanting to increase funding for after-school programs will enlist law enforcement agencies to argue that the programs help cut crime by giving young people something constructive to do.

As mentioned earlier, some interest groups, particularly those with ideological agendas, tend to be loyal to one party over the other. Interest groups as a whole, however, do not give most of their support to candidates of a particular party. Rather, they give most of their support to the *incumbents* of either party. One reason for this is that incumbents are reelected the vast majority of the time, so betting on their victory is pretty safe. It makes more sense, pragmatically speaking, to curry favor with someone who possesses power than with someone who does not. Even if the incumbent does not subscribe to an interest group's entire program, the group may

find it is able to work with the individual on an issue or two.

Interest groups also favor incumbents because the campaign contributions such groups make are based more on rewarding public officials for positions they have already taken than on trying to persuade them to take new positions altogether. In other words, if a legislator already has demonstrated support for gun owners' rights, the NRA will be inclined to support him or her. The group does not give donations to gun control advocates in the hope of changing their minds. The money follows the vote, in most cases, rather than the other way around. "Someone isn't going to vote one way or the other on gun control based on whether or not they received a contribution from the NRA," says John Weingart, associate director of the Eagleton Institute of Politics at Rutgers University. "But the example we always use here is that if there's a fight between ophthalmologists and opticians about what the regulations should be, a campaign contribution might make a difference because most people don't care."[57]

About 1,100 different occupations are regulated by states today, and, as Weingart suggests, fighting among those industries is never ending. Orthopedic surgeons and podiatrists face off over who gets to treat ankle injuries and force legislators to debate whether the ankle is part of the foot. (The Colorado legislature decided it was, opening up the field to podiatrists.) Dog groomers fight veterinarians for the right to brush canine teeth.[58]

Although states got into the professional licensing business in a big way to protect public health and safety, they are also pushed to enforce regulations by groups that want to set a bar high enough

MAP 6-3

State Corruption Report Card

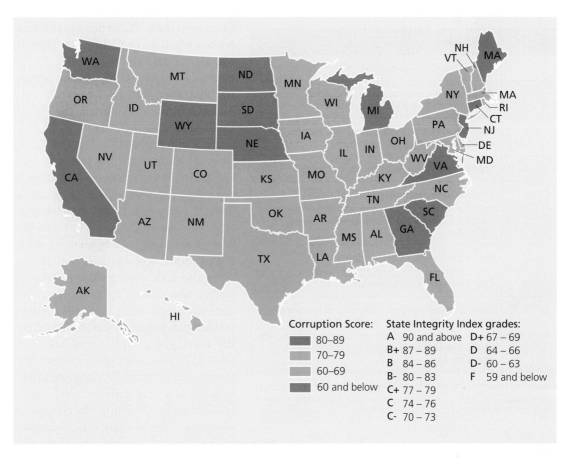

Corruption Score:
- 80–89
- 70–79
- 60–69
- 60 and below

State Integrity Index grades:

A	90 and above	D+	67 – 69
B+	87 – 89	D	64 – 66
B	84 – 86	D-	60 – 63
B-	80 – 83	F	59 and below
C+	77 – 79		
C	74 – 76		
C-	70 – 73		

Source: State Integrity Investigation, The Center for Public Integrity, www.stateintegrity.org/your_state.

to discourage competition. Consider the case of Jestina Clayton, who moved at age twenty-two from a village in the West African nation of Sierra Leone to a town called Centerville in Utah. She started a business offering traditional African hair braiding, but soon enough she was warned that in order to practice her trade she needed a cosmetology license, which would require two years of schooling costing approximately $16,000 in tuition. She appealed to the state governing body—the Barber, Cosmetology/Barber, Esthetics, Electrology and Nail Technology Licensing Board—for an exemption. The board, made up mainly of licensed barbers and cosmetologists, shot her down. Clayton then enlisted the help of a sympathetic state representative, but his bill to exempt hair

braiding from the licensing law was blocked by full-force lobbying by the Professional Beauty Association, which favored regulation that would keep hair care the exclusive province of its professionals. Such scenarios are not uncommon, said Morris Kleiner, a University of Minnesota economist who coauthored a proposal at the federal level to abolish state licensing rules that do more harm than good. Approving such a proposal is good policy but "political suicide," Kleiner said. "When you talk about reductions in licensing, you have every occupation from the plumbers to the CPA's to the electricians lining up to argue why regulation should not be reduced."[59]

Beer is regulated at the state level, which is why Anheuser-Busch InBev, the maker of

TABLE 6-1

Top Ten Most Influential Interests in the States, 2007

Ranking	Organization
1	General business organizations
2	Schoolteacher organizations (National Education Association and American Federation of Teachers)
3	Utility companies and associations (electric, gas, water, telephone/telecommunications)
4	Manufacturers (companies and associations)
5	Hospital/nursing home associations
6	Insurance: general and medical (companies and associations)
7	Physicians/state medical associations
8	Contractors, builders, developers
9	General local government organizations (municipal leagues, county associations, elected officials)
10	Lawyers (predominantly trial lawyers, state bar associations)

Source: Data compiled from Anthony J. Nownes, Clive S. Thomas, and Ronald J. Hrebenar, "Interest Groups in the States," in *Politics in the American States: A Comparative Analysis*, 9th ed., eds. Virginia Gray and Russell L. Hanson (Washington, DC: CQ Press, 2008), 117.

organizations in its home state, such as the New Jersey Chamber of Commerce, the state's Business and Industry Association, and the New Jersey Health Products Company Group. It also belongs to industry associations in California, Illinois, Massachusetts, and elsewhere. At the national level, Johnson & Johnson belongs to Pharmaceutical Research and Manufacturers of America, the Health Care Industry Manufacturers' Association, and still other groups.[60]

When an industry has relatively little credibility, it often will turn to allies to represent the public face of its cause. Tobacco companies favor hiring lobbyists who have earned the respect of state legislators as former colleagues or by working for other, less controversial clients. They also seek other groups to take the lead on a lot of their fights. When a state considers legislation that will regulate smoking in public places, for example, the most public opponents are more likely to be restaurant groups rather than the tobacco industry. "We're going to participate in a very upfront way," said a spokesman for the Philip Morris tobacco company. "But like any other industry, we're going to look to people who share that point of view on any given issue" to take a role as well.[61]

Budweiser, hires lobbyists in all fifty states. Insurance is also regulated at the state level. Many more industries, in fact, are turning their attention to the states because that is where the federal government and the courts have sent increasing amounts of power. The states have assumed authority over issues such as securities regulation and have taken the lead on issues that have not progressed in Congress, such as energy policies meant to address climate change. The active role of the states in regulating economic and social activities has induced some business interests, such as the pharmaceutical industry, to maintain lobbies that are just as powerful in the states as they are in Washington. National companies that are not based in particular states are likely to hire local contract lobbyists to work in those states to lend clout to their causes. The consumer products company Johnson & Johnson has its own lobbyists but also maintains memberships in

> When an industry has relatively little credibility, it often will turn to allies to represent the public face of its cause. Tobacco companies favor hiring lobbyists who have earned the respect of state legislators as former colleagues or by working for other, less controversial clients. They also seek other groups to take the lead on a lot of their fights.

As in the case of tobacco companies fighting smoking bans, lobbyists spend the majority of their time playing defense, trying to kill bills they believe would harm their companies or clients. Still, interest groups and their desires stir up much of the activity in state capitals. "Frankly, the legislature in New Jersey exists for the lobbyist," said one lobbyist there.[62] What he was suggesting is that the governor may want five or six bills passed during a session, while individual legislators may want one or two of their own passed as well. The remaining 95 percent of the thousands of bills introduced in a given year are a wish list of the wants and needs of the lobbyists and the interests they represent.

That is why interest groups are an important part of the political landscape in every state. Certain groups play a disproportionate role in particular states—for example, gambling in Nevada or the poultry industry in Arkansas[63]—but the full range of interest groups has crucial influence over the workings of every state. Clive S. Thomas and Ronald J. Hrebenar, two political scientists who have been studying interest group activity in the states for decades, rank the states according to which have policies that are most influenced by interest groups. In no state are interest groups subordinate to—that is, consistently outgunned by—other policy players, such as governors or political parties.

Those players are stronger in some states than in others. The relative weakness of political parties led Thomas and Hrebenar to argue that interest groups are most powerful in a few states in the South and West, such as Alabama, Nevada, and West Virginia.[64] Certain interest groups may hold greater sway at specific times. The importance of environmental issues, in particular, seems to ebb and flow. But Thomas and Hrebenar note that in the majority of states, the influence of interest groups as a whole remains fairly constant—and fairly strong.

The influence of interest groups is difficult to measure, but it is nonetheless quite apparent, part of the very air that policymakers breathe. Some groups may score a victory here and there: dentists looking for a regulatory change or animal rights activists looking to ban cockfighting. Other groups have become a permanent part of the landscape, such as business lobbies concerned with taxes, transportation, and education.

There are some interest groups that are powerful everywhere because their members are everywhere. Groups such as teachers' unions and associations of car dealers, restaurant owners, and real estate agents hold particular sway because they have members in every legislative district, and legislators are more likely to be persuaded by individuals or employers from their home districts. Most lobbying by the National Association of Realtors, for example, is handled by volunteer members and state association staff rather than by hired contract lobbyists, because realtors tend to be well connected in their communities. They also make it a point to have particular members of their professional community get to know individual legislators from their districts and keep them up to date about their issues of concern. Realtors, like members of other professions affected at the state policy level, also seek office themselves in part-time legislatures. During the 2005–2006 session, no fewer than twenty-two people who made their livings in real estate also served as members of the Utah legislature—including the president of the National Association of Realtors.[65]

Taken together, interest groups are the means through which individual citizens and private companies, as well as governmental bodies, influence the policy decisions that affect their lives or ways of doing business. "I don't believe there are some states where interest groups are stronger and others where they're weaker," said Alan Rosenthal, who was an expert on state politics at Rutgers University. "In every state, interest groups are important. That's the way interests are represented, through groups."[66]

Conclusion

The essential job of political parties is to nominate candidates for public office. The parties no longer control many government jobs, but despite changes in campaign finance laws, they have maintained their positions as crucial fundraising organizations. They also perform many

Politicians in the past have worked hard to gain the support of unions, many of which are strong, outspoken, and well organized. While union support may still be sought in many states, in others the tide has turned. Wisconsin union supporters staged mammoth protests in 2011 when Governor Scott Walker proposed ending collective bargaining rights for public employees.

other functions in American democracy. They aggregate and articulate political interests and create and maintain majorities within the electorate and within government. They are not the dominant organizing forces they once were, in part because voters and candidates—and non-party fund-raising organizations such as super PACs—have become more independent than they were decades ago. Parties, however, do still play important roles in recruiting political candidates, supporting them financially and logistically and helping them market themselves to like-minded voters.

For the past 150 years, two major parties—the Democrats and the Republicans—have dominated politics in the United States. Few candidates not belonging to either of these parties have won office at any level of government, and in most cases, the victories of those few have been based on personal appeal rather than support for the third party they represented. The Republican and Democratic parties have been able to adapt to changing times and tastes in ways that have kept them in power, if not always in perfect favor.

With states regulating increasing numbers of industries, interest groups have proliferated so that there are now far more lobbyists than elected officials. Interest groups help push agendas subscribed to by individuals or corporations. Other interest groups push back. Their primary mission is to win as many political offices as possible, so the parties, with varying success, collate and mute the ideological agendas of their interest group allies. Parties cannot afford to have any one group's ideas play such a prominent role that other groups or voters are alienated. It is a difficult balancing act to try to appeal to the majority of voters at any given time while also standing for principles that are clear enough that most people are willing to support them.

The Latest Research

This chapter makes clear that political parties have critically important roles to play in democratic governance. How they go about fulfilling those roles has an enormous impact on politics and policy, in effect setting the boundaries of what will or can be done by the government. One aspect of how parties are executing those responsibilities has evolved into one of the dominant issues in contemporary American politics: the increasing polarization of the two major parties. Scholars of state politics are intensely interested in the development and direction of political parties and their associated interest groups, and by employing the comparative method they have uncovered some fascinating insights about the polarized stances of political parties.

Indeed, the research discussed below suggests that if we want to know why political parties and interest groups are the way they are, polarized or not, we need a deeper understanding of what is happening outside government, especially at the local level. It is increasingly what happens there—especially in terms of interest group activity—that ultimately determines not just levels of partisanship but the very definition of what a political party is.

• •

- **Masket, Seth.** 2011. *No Middle Ground: How Informal Party Organizations Control Nominations and Polarize Legislatures.* Ann Arbor: University of Michigan Press.

In this provocative book, Seth Masket, a political scientist at the University of Denver, takes a sustained look at what political parties are and what has caused the increasing partisanship in American politics. Traditionally, political scientists have viewed political parties as products of politicians. The basic argument is that political elites create formal organizations (that is, political parties) to help them gain office, run government, and pursue particular sets of policies. Masket turns conventional wisdom on its head. Rather than centralized and hierarchical organizations, he argues, political parties, at least in the contemporary world, are characterized by what he terms informal party organizations (IPOs). These organizations, loose affiliations of individuals and interest groups, have enormous influence over primary elections. If elected officials—be they state legislators or members of Congress—want to keep their jobs, they need the support of these IPOs. This is because IPOs have the resources to mobilize enough voters to decide who wins in low-turnout primaries. This ends up distorting democratic representation. IPOs often have more extremely partisan viewpoints than do members of the general electorate, but an elected official who moderates his or her views once in office runs the risk of not making it through the next primary. Thus politicians end up being creatures of (informal) political parties, rather than the other way around.

- **Bawn, Kathleen, Martin Cohen, David Karol, Seth Masket, Hans Noel, and John Zaller**. 2012. "A Theory of Political Parties: Groups, Policy Demands, and Nominations in American Politics." *Perspectives on Politics* 10: 571–597.

This article picks up on and develops a number of the ideas expressed in Masket's *No Middle Ground.* The central argument is that interest groups and activists are now the key actors in shaping political parties. Rather than political parties being tools of elected officials to help them win and keep office, parties are now dominated by interest groups and activists—essentially the IPOs described in Masket's book—who are less interested in the preferences of voters than in their own narrow agendas. These groups focus their efforts on controlling the nomination process—that is, primary elections. This control provides them the whip they need to keep elected officials focused on narrow rather than general interests.

- **Koger, Gregory, Seth Masket, and Hans Noel**. 2010. "Cooperative Party Factions in American Politics." *American Politics Research* 38: 33–53.

This study takes a closer look at the interest groups and factions that are driving party politics. The authors examine how parties, candidates, and interest groups share information and money-raising resources and find that lying underneath the two political parties are two distinct networks. They find separate "teams" of interest groups and media outlets working with one political party but not the other. Furthermore, these teams appear to be fairly cohesive, at least internally. The various members of the two big partisan networks cooperate with each other, but not with players on the other team. Again, we see evidence of political parties being influenced by powerful nongovernmental actors.

- **Shor, Boris, and Nolan McCarty.** 2011. "The Ideological Mapping of American Legislatures." *American Political Science Review* 105: 502–551.

Political scientists have extensively mapped the growing partisan divide in Congress. While scholars have done similar studies at the state level, data collection challenges have prevented large-scale studies employing the comparative method. This study goes a long way to filling that gap. Boris and McCarty combine roll-call data from all states since the mid-1990s with surveys of state legislatures to examine how partisanship compares across state legislatures, as well as between state legislatures and Congress. This reveals some clear differences across states and equally clear differences between state and federal legislatures. Notably, in Congress it is well established that the most liberal Republicans are still to the right of the most conservative Democrats, and vice versa. This ideological gap is seen as one of the primary reasons that the bipartisan compromise crucial to action on pressing issues has proven so elusive for recent Congresses. At the state level, however, there are still some legislatures in which the most liberal Republicans are to the left of the most conservative Democrats, and vice versa. This makes finding that all-important bipartisan compromise more likely.

Chapter Review

Key Concepts

- candidate-centered politics (p. 143)
- cause lobbyist (p. 164)
- closed primary (p. 148)
- contract lobbyist (p. 164)
- crossover voting (p. 149)
- dealignment (p. 151)
- direct lobbying (p. 164)
- establishment (p. 140)
- factional splits, or factions (p. 141)
- general election (p. 148)
- independent expenditures (p. 153)
- indirect lobbying (p. 164)
- interest groups (p. 140)
- nonpartisan ballot (p. 147)
- open primary (p. 149)
- party convention (p. 148)
- patronage (p. 147)
- polarization (p. 140)

- political action committee (p. 140)
- political machines (p. 146)
- political parties (p. 140)
- primary election (p. 140)
- realignment (p. 151)
- responsible party model (p. 143)
- runoff primary (p. 149)
- soft money (p. 153)
- super PAC (p. 140)
- swing voters (p. 142)
- ticket splitting (p. 161)
- voter identification (p. 146)

Suggested Websites

- **http://ballotpedia.org.** A wiki providing information on candidates and ballot measures in all the states.
- **www.fivethirtyeight.com.** Nate Silver's blog, now hosted by ESPN, covering electoral polling and politics at the national and state levels.
- **http://influenceexplorer.com.** This website, run by the Sunlight Foundation, provides data on campaign finance and lobbying expenditures.
- **http://moneyline.cq.com.** CQ-Roll Call's Political MoneyLine website, which provides information on campaign finance, lobbying and lobbyists, and parties and candidates.
- **www.dnc.org.** Website of the Democratic National Committee.
- **www.followthemoney.org.** Website of the National Institute on Money in State Politics, which tracks political donations and lobbying in all fifty states.
- **www.gop.com.** Website of the Republican National Committee.
- **www.irs.gov/Charities-&-Non-Profits/Political-Organizations/Political-Organization-Filing-and-Disclosure.** The Internal Revenue Service's Political Organization Filing and Disclosure website.
- **www.ncsl.org.** Website of the National Conference of State Legislatures.
- **www.opensecrets.org.** Website of the Center for Responsive Politics, a nonpartisan organization tracking money in politics.
- **www.publicintegrity.org.** Website of the Center for Public Integrity, which produces, among other investigative journalism reports, pieces on campaign finance and lobbying activity in the states and Washington, DC.

State Stats on
Parties and Interest Groups

Explore and compare data on the states! Go to **college.cqpress
.com/sites/essentials-govstateandlocal** to do these exercises.

1. If you were a lobbyist for the oil industry, would you devote your
   time to working in North Dakota or in Louisiana? Why? Would your
   answer have been different ten years ago? Why?

2. What is the percentage of the population in Mississippi enrolled
   in Medicaid? Based on this information alone, would you expect
   Mississippi to favor Democratic or Republican candidates for
   office? Is your expectation correct? Why or why not? Now, what
   percentage of the population in Wisconsin is enrolled in Medicaid?
   Why might Mississippi and Wisconsin have different political
   leanings considering this information?

3. How does the per capita state government tax revenue in New
   Hampshire compare to neighboring Vermont's? What factors in the
   states' history and politics led to this disparity? What are some of
   the possible implications?

4. How has the percentage of Hispanic residents in Colorado changed
   since 1995? What do you expect that this has done for Colorado's
   political leanings and why?

5. In the 1950s, Ray Bliss identified pockets of rural Americans
   who were not mobilizing to vote. Which states have the highest
   percentages of rural residents now? Which have the least? How do
   those states tend to lean politically? Why?

Every state capitol attracts school groups, protesters, lobbyists, and people only casually interested in getting a glimpse of their government in action.

Legislatures

THE ART OF HERDING CATS

- Why do so many citizens think that legislatures accomplish so little—or accomplish the wrong things altogether?
- What constraints do legislatures face in making effective laws?
- Why are some legislators more powerful than others?

State legislatures operate in complex ways, especially when it comes to how members negotiate with their colleagues as they attempt to make laws. The basic dynamics, though, are fairly similar to ordering pizza.

Let's say you're really hungry for pizza. You're broke, so to get pizza, you need friends. If friends go in on the order, however, you're pretty sure that you won't get your ideal pizza—hamburger with onions and red peppers—because your friends think that's a disgusting combination. You need to make a deal, and that involves compromise. You go around your dorm and pretty quickly find four others willing to go in on a delivery. Of the five people ordering, two want some kind of meat, but three are vegetarians. If all votes are counted as equal, you're going meatless. This is called **majority rule**.

But legislation—and pizza orders—aren't always decided by predictable partisan majorities. Let's say it's just you (a young man), your roommate (also a man), and your girlfriend. Your roommate doesn't want hamburger or sausage or pepperoni—and your girlfriend, instead of siding with you, agrees with him! Something similar can happen in legislatures, when some members abandon their fellow Democrats or Republicans to vote with the opposing party. For instance, most Democrats might want to pass stricter gun control laws, but some of their rural, more conservative Democratic colleagues might block them by joining with the GOP. This is called **coalition building**.

Although your girlfriend initially voted with your roommate, she actually finds the idea of splurging on pepperoni pretty enticing. She also figures it is not smart relationship-wise to favor your roommate's taste over yours. Maybe she can get you to watch that romantic comedy you've been avoiding if she supports your order. In much the same way, legislators often vote for bills that they do not particularly like in order to win support for other priorities. They might want to curry favor with their party leaders, or they might simply want to earn a colleague's help in the future by voting for the colleague's pet bill now. This is called trading votes, or **logrolling**.

Or maybe you have learned that you cannot count on your girlfriend to stick up for you when it's time to call the pizza parlor. So you go around to all your pals in the dorm and plant the idea that what would really be fun tonight would be getting a pizza. You ask only people you are pretty sure will be good with pepperoni. Legislators—and other people concerned with what legislators are up to—do this all the time. They try to solicit support from people who are going to vote long before a vote actually takes place so that the result will come out the way they want. This is called lobbying and is similar to the kind of lobbying that interest groups do, as we have seen in chapters 5 and 6.

But let's say that while you are busy polling your friends, one of them unexpectedly says that he hates pepperoni worse than poison and that he refuses even to think about sausage. This sort of thing often happens in legislatures. If there is a bill to increase state spending for abortion clinics, for instance, you can bet that one or more legislators will do everything in their power to block that spending.

An adamant opponent can stop a hated piece of legislation's progress through a chamber in many ways, including by mounting a **filibuster**, a kind of endless debate sometimes used in the U.S. Senate. Another way is to attach unwanted amendments, or **riders**, to a bill. The road to a bill's passage into law is twisty and sometimes full of unexpected hurdles. John Dingell, D-Mich., the longest-serving member of the Congress, perhaps best described the strange relationship between the actual substance of a bill and how it moves

Majority Rule
The process in which the decision of a numerical majority is made binding on a group.

Coalition Building
The assembling of an alliance of groups to pursue a common goal or interest.

Logrolling
The practice in which a legislator gives a colleague a vote on a particular bill in return for that colleague's vote on another bill to be considered later.

Filibuster
A debate that under U.S. Senate rules can drag on, blocking final action on the bill under consideration and preventing other bills from being debated.

Rider
An amendment to a bill that is not central to the bill's intent.

through the House when he said in 1984, "If you let me write procedure and I let you write substance, I'll screw you every time."[1]

All these complicated dynamics are why legislative leadership has sometimes been compared to the job of herding cats. "You come into the Senate every day with a wheelbarrow of 33 cats," writes William Bulger, a former president of the Massachusetts Senate. "Your job is to get the wheelbarrow with 17 of those cats to the other side of the chamber."[2]

In fairness, legislatures are not designed to be simple. The congressional system was designed to prevent bad laws—defined as laws that were not properly thought through and did not enjoy at least acquiescence from a broad majority—rather than promote good laws. "The injury which may possibly be done by defeating a few good laws will be amply compensated by the advantage of preventing a number of bad ones," wrote Alexander Hamilton in *Federalist* No. 73.[3] Most state legislatures have the same basic structure as the U.S. Congress, with a house and a senate, each of which must approve a bill before it can go to the governor to be signed into law. That means that even if a bill makes its way through all the circuitous steps of getting passed by the house, including **committee** fights and winning a majority in the chamber, it can easily die if the senate refuses to sign off on an identical version. "If we passed the Lord's Prayer, we'd send it to the Senate and they'd amend it and send it back," said Bob Bergren, speaker of the Montana House.[4]

The consequence of this complexity is a misperception by the general public about how well legislatures work and how competent individual legislators are. Even when they don't seem to accomplish much, legislators work hard. They address thousands of bills and constituent complaints every year, but the institutional structures of the legislatures make it difficult for them to respond quickly to the issues of the day.

Studies show that the average person knows little about his or her state legislature but is firmly convinced it is unnecessarily contentious, and that legislators are guilty of talking when they

> Even when they don't seem to accomplish much, legislators work hard. They address thousands of bills and constituent complaints every year, but the institutional structures of the legislatures make it difficult for them to respond quickly to the issues of the day.

should be acting. Many people believe that legislators are too cozy with interest groups. Voters wonder why their representatives do not simply vote the "right" way and go home.

The problem is that there is no one "right" way. Some legislators represent liberal **districts**; others represent conservative areas. Some represent cities; others represent farmlands grappling with entirely different, nonurban issues. Legislators acting in good faith will come to different conclusions about what is the right approach to take on any number of issues, from education and transportation to job creation and taxes. All sides get to present their most convincing arguments, but only rarely can a majority of members of a legislature come to an agreement that pleases them all. In their disagreement, they reflect the different opinions of their **constituents**, the citizens back home.

Let's say that you and your friends are still arguing over pepperoni and the vegetarian combo, only this time each choice has the same number of fans. In the end, you decide that you will just go with cheese. Nobody is thrilled about this—none of you gets the toppings you were hoping for—but everyone can live with the choice. This is called **compromise**, and it's exactly the kind

Committee
A group of legislators who have the formal task of considering and writing bills in a particular issue area.

District
The geographical area represented by a member of a legislature.

Constituents
Residents of a district.

Compromise
The result when there is no consensus on a policy change or spending amount but legislators find a central point on which a majority can agree.

of unsatisfying choice legislators often arrive at. The purpose of this chapter is to give you a sense of how state legislators come to their decisions, who they are, what they do, and how they organize themselves in their institutions.

The Job of Legislatures

On June 24, 2011, the New York State legislature voted to make the state the sixth to legalize gay marriage. The decision came as a significant surprise. Just two years earlier, when Democrats had the majority in the New York Senate, a bill to legalize gay marriage had failed on a lopsided vote. In the 2010 elections, Republicans won the edge in the New York Senate. In New York, as in most places, Democrats are more likely than Republicans to favor gay marriage, yet even with Republicans in charge, the legislation passed in the Senate because four Republicans joined with all but one of the chamber's Democrats in voting in favor.

The four Republicans had several reasons to break with their party. Polling showed that a strong majority of New Yorkers thought same-sex nuptials should be legal, so senators risked voter anger if they said no. Legalizing gay marriage was a top priority of the state's popular Democratic governor, Andrew Cuomo, and senators needed to stay in the governor's good graces to enact their own priorities. Still, the senators said that they had merely done what they thought was right. "I apologize for those who feel offended," said Mark Grisanti, one of the four Republicans. "I cannot deny a person, a human being, a taxpayer, a worker, the people of my district and across this state, the State of New York, and those people who make this the great state that it is the same rights that I have with my wife."[5]

Not surprisingly, some were offended. Social conservatives who oppose gay marriage play a key role in the Republican Party's coalition. "Marriage has always been, is now and always will be the union of one man and one woman in lifelong, life-giving union," the New York State Catholic Conference said in a statement. "Government does not have the authority to change this most basic of truths."[6] In 2012, the next time they were up for reelection, all four of the Republicans who had voted yes faced serious primary opposition

from fellow Republicans, with foes spending hundreds of thousands of dollars to oust them. But gay marriage supporters also kicked in large amounts of campaign cash in their defense. One decided to retire rather than run again. Another lost in the Republican primary. A third lost to a Democratic opponent in the November election. As a result, when the legislature reconvened in 2013, Grisanti was the only one of the four left in the Senate.

This story demonstrates several key points about how legislatures operate. Everyone understands that it is the job of the legislature to set policy for the state, in consultation with the governor—or sometimes despite the governor's wishes, if there are sufficient votes to override his or her veto. Nevertheless, the decisions that legislators make are, by their nature, political. It's difficult to please everybody, and often legislators have to balance competing interests. In this case, they had to choose between the desires of their party on one hand and the majority view of the state on the other. They had to choose which of two opposing interest groups they would offend, knowing that either choice would likely put their political careers at risk. And they had to consult their consciences too.

Many state legislatures are not as polarized as Congress, where the members of the two political parties barely speak to one another and the two sides seem to treat each other as treacherous enemies as much as potential collaborators. State legislatures, though, seem increasingly headed in this direction. The case of the New York gay marriage vote, in which just a few legislators broke with their party—and paid a high price for doing so--is typical. In Virginia in 2012, the legislature was weeks late completing its most basic job, writing a new state budget, because the Virginia Senate was evenly split between Democrats and Republicans—twenty members on each side—and not a single member was willing to cross over and vote with the rival party.

What Legislatures Do

All state legislatures share four basic interrelated and often overlapping functions:

- *A lawmaking function:* They pass laws and create policy for their states.

- *A representative function:* They provide a means for various groups and individuals to have their interests represented in state policymaking.

- *A constituent service function:* They offer personalized constituent service to help residents sort out their problems with the state government.

- *An oversight function:* They oversee the activities of the governor and the executive branch and some private businesses through public hearings, budget reviews, and formal investigations.

Although state legislatures all address similar issues, including taxes, budgets, and a broad range of other matters (such as regulating office safety and requiring sex offenders to register their places of residence with police), differences in timing, state history, and political culture may cause one state's laws on a topic to differ widely from those of other states. Occasionally, legislatures are pressured to pass uniform laws, as when the federal government, through the National Minimum Drinking Age Act of 1984, insisted that the states raise their legal drinking ages to twenty-one or lose highway funding. These days, states seem more often to be pulling in opposite directions, with Democratic legislatures in places like Colorado and California taking entirely different approaches to tax policy and gun regulation than Republican lawmakers in states such as Kansas and North Carolina.

Regardless, the media and the public tend to register the failures of a legislature while not giving it credit for successes in balancing competing interests within the state. Ethics scandals generally receive greater coverage than do substantial debates, yet legislators debate and pass laws that cover everything from levels of Medicaid health insurance funding to clean water protections to aid for local governments to workers' compensation payments. In most legislatures, 90 percent of the bills receive almost no media attention and are of interest only to those they directly affect. The news media—and the voting public—pay attention only when issues that affect the broadest range of people are considered, such as increases (or cuts) in property tax rates. Legislators do not have the luxury of tuning out when complex and boring but important issues crop up.

The biggest legislative fights tend to be over budgets. Dealing with how much money the state devotes to each of its programs is a way of revisiting all the problems that never go away. How much is enough to spend on education? How much of that education tab should the state pick up? How much money should be spent on healthcare? How long should prison terms be for all manner of crimes, and what should be done to reintegrate offenders into society once they've served their time? How big an investment should the state make in roads or public transportation? State legislatures annually address hundreds of such issues, large and small.

Denver Democratic representative Mark Ferrandino is the first openly gay lawmaker in Colorado to hold the title of House speaker. He became speaker in January 2013.

Lawmaking

The Texas state legislature grappled with more than ten thousand bills in 2011, and even much mellower Montana took up more than a thousand that year.[7] Despite this amount of activity—or perhaps because of it—legislators generally do not go looking for issues to address. The typical bill is introduced for one of several reasons: it is a bill that has to be considered, such as the annual state budget; it is a bill dealing with a common problem modeled on another state's legislation; or it is something that an individual or a group outside the legislature—such as constituents, the governor, or lobbyists—wants considered.

Finally, lobbyists representing a client such as a beer company or auto manufacturer will often promote draft legislation in the hope that a member of the legislature or general assembly—as the legislatures are known in Colorado, Georgia, Pennsylvania, and several other states—will sponsor it as a bill. True.com, an online dating service, convinced legislators in several states in 2006 to introduce legislation requiring such websites to conduct background checks of all their users. "I was shocked when I found out that dating services, which market themselves as finding someone's true soulmate, don't provide any kind of even cursory background checks," said Illinois state representative John Bradley, whose bill passed the state House that year. But, even though True.com's founder said he was motivated by an online meeting that ended in murder, his competitors were able to convince legislators that the bill was only a "PR stunt" designed to make True.com's services, which included background checks, look more enticing. They said there was no way of checking on customers, whom everyone knew to be fibbers. "There's sort of a joke in the industry that the average person lies by 10 pounds and 10 years," said Eric Straus of Cupid.com.[8]

Although lobbyists promote bills, they also devote an enormous amount of energy to trying to kill bills. Part of the job of the legislative process is to act as a sort of referee among a lot of competing interests. Any proposed change in state law that someone views as a positive step is likely to adversely affect—or at least frighten—someone else. In 2011, the Kentucky Medical Association and the Kentucky Academy of Eye Physicians fought to kill a bill that would allow optometrists to perform laser eye surgeries. The groups argued that optometrists lack the right training to perform the surgery, but they were also defending their turf—they represent ophthalmologists, not optometrists. Their adversary, the Kentucky Optometric Association, proved to be too strong. The optometrists hired eighteen lobbyists and contributed campaign cash to all but one of the legislature's 138 members.[9] The bill passed. Disputes like this are common: doctors battle with nurse practitioners or dentists disagree with dental hygienists. When a bill comes up for a vote, state legislators are forced to pick a side.

Legislators react most strongly to bills in which they have a personal stake or that they know will affect their constituents directly. The bulk of the work they do involves formulating the law and trying to keep an eye on the executive branch, but legislators' primary responsibility is to provide **representation** for their constituents. Basically, they ensure that the interests of those for whom they speak are properly considered as part of decision making at the state level. Let's say that environmentalists are concerned about a river's water quality and want to require new water filters at a paper mill. The mill's owners, concerned that the cost of the filters will be exorbitant, warn that they will have to lay off three hundred employees if the bill goes through. A legislator from that area will have to worry about whether creating a healthier environment is worth being accused of costing people their jobs. Legislators who live clear across the state from the river and its mill, however, will hold the deciding votes. The people directly affected—the company, the workers, and the downstream residents worried about pollution—will all try to portray themselves as standing for the greater good. If no side is clearly right and favoring one side over the other might

---

Representation
Individual legislators acting as the voices of their constituencies within the house of representatives or senate.

Local Focus

Taking on the Law in the Land of the Free . . . and the Home of the Silly

Rich Smith, a British journalism student, spent one Christmas Day playing board games. He came across a reference to an obscure law in Florida that made it illegal for divorced women to go parachuting on Sundays. Enchanted by this and a treasure trove of other dumb American laws, he decided to spend the summer after graduation driving all across the United States and breaking every outdated or just plain absurd law he could find. "Tying giraffes to lampposts seemed a funnier way in which to become a felon" than arson or murder, Smith writes in his book about the spree, *You Can Get Arrested for That.*[a]

Smith and a friend attempted to break two dozen laws in all, succeeding in most cases. Many of the laws concerned personal behavior. Traveling east from San Francisco, Smith carried out his first successful crime by peeling an orange in a hotel room, an action illegal throughout California.

He then drove to Globe, Arizona, where it is illegal to play cards on the street against an American Indian, and did just that. He made sure to order plenty of garlic bread along with his pizza in Indianapolis because in that city it is illegal to enter a theater within three hours of eating garlic. He also broke the law by eating watermelon in a cemetery in Spartanburg, South Carolina, and by sleeping on top of a refrigerator in Pennsylvania.

The fashion police have made it illegal to wear a goatee in Massachusetts, so Smith grew one in plenty of time for his visit to that state. He also broke several laws concerning fishing, including his attempt to hunt down marine mammals in a lake in Utah and, of course, his blatant disregard for Chicago's ban on fishing while wearing pajamas. But he lacked sufficient skill to violate Tennessee's stricture against catching a fish with a lasso.

Although Smith managed to break numerous laws, several others defeated him. He failed to find a bathtub to carry illegally across the village green in Longmeadow, Massachusetts, and he couldn't persuade a woman in Iowa to kiss him for longer than five minutes (or at all).

Several of his crimes were witnessed by police or private security guards, but perhaps it's in the nature of "dumb" laws that they aren't rigorously enforced. The only time Smith and his buddy got into serious trouble was when they drove at ninety-seven miles per hour in a seventy-five-mile-per-hour zone in Wyoming. That time, they got nailed.

[a]Published by Three Rivers Press, New York, 2006.

---

do political damage, the bill may easily die. Legislators can then be accused of doing nothing when in reality they are merely reflecting the lack of statewide consensus about how to solve the problem.[10]

Legislatures often finish their work on an issue not because of outside pressure but because of internal changes. New leaders in the Arizona Senate in 2001 brought with them solutions to long-standing issues, including understaffing in the state's highway patrol, underfunding of the state's mental health system, and provisioning for water through new contracts. Legislators even managed to repeal antiquated sex laws that made it a crime for unmarried couples to live together.[11] More recently, in 2008, Republicans won control of both legislative chambers in Tennessee for the first time since the Civil War. They quickly began pushing long-sought legislation in areas such as the regulation of guns, charter schools, and abortion. "I think every bad bill I've seen in my 10 years got resurrected this year and had a chance of passing," complained Mike Turner, chair of the House Democratic caucus.[12] Two years later, the Republicans won even bigger legislative majorities and one of their own, Bill Haslam, was elected governor. They quickly enacted an ambitious agenda that included many party priorities, phasing out the inheritance tax, weakening teacher tenure, enacting tort reform, and overhauling civil service rules.

Not surprisingly, states with stagnant leadership or long-term control by one party have a harder time making breakthroughs. Changes in partisan control bring in new leaders and, with them, new agendas

FIGURE 7-1

HOW IT WORKS

A One-Eyed Frog's View of the Legislative Process, or How a Bill Really Became a Law in Minnesota

The mechanisms by which a bill becomes a law at the state level are similar to the mechanisms at work at the federal level. And we've all seen the flowcharts that outline the ins and outs: a bill goes in one side, gets debated, marked up, and reported out, and then comes out the other side as a real-life law to be implemented, or it gets returned to the legislature for an override, or it gets "killed." You'd be forgiven for thinking that beneath that abstraction lies a more complex and interesting process.

You'd be right. Below is a different flowchart, this one fleshing out what actually happened when a group of Minnesota teens brought to light the fact that the frog population in their area was turning up with extra limbs and missing eyes. About eight months and $151,000 later, the frogs were in much better shape.

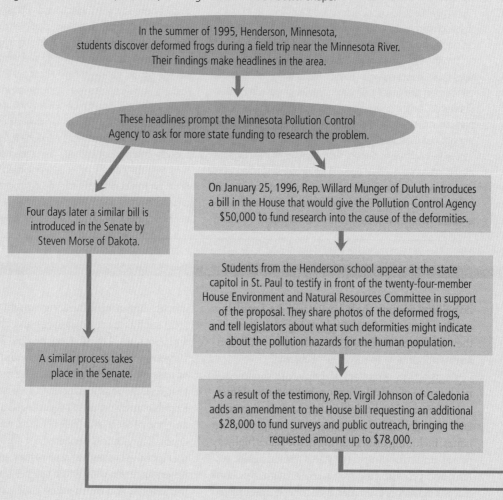

In the summer of 1995, Henderson, Minnesota, students discover deformed frogs during a field trip near the Minnesota River. Their findings make headlines in the area.

These headlines prompt the Minnesota Pollution Control Agency to ask for more state funding to research the problem.

On January 25, 1996, Rep. Willard Munger of Duluth introduces a bill in the House that would give the Pollution Control Agency $50,000 to fund research into the cause of the deformities.

Four days later a similar bill is introduced in the Senate by Steven Morse of Dakota.

Students from the Henderson school appear at the state capitol in St. Paul to testify in front of the twenty-four-member House Environment and Natural Resources Committee in support of the proposal. They share photos of the deformed frogs, and tell legislators about what such deformities might indicate about the pollution hazards for the human population.

A similar process takes place in the Senate.

As a result of the testimony, Rep. Virgil Johnson of Caledonia adds an amendment to the House bill requesting an additional $28,000 to fund surveys and public outreach, bringing the requested amount up to $78,000.

Source: Minnesota House of Representatives Public Information Office, "Capitol Steps: How Six Bills Became Law," www.house.leg.state.mn.us/hinfo/How6bil.pdf.

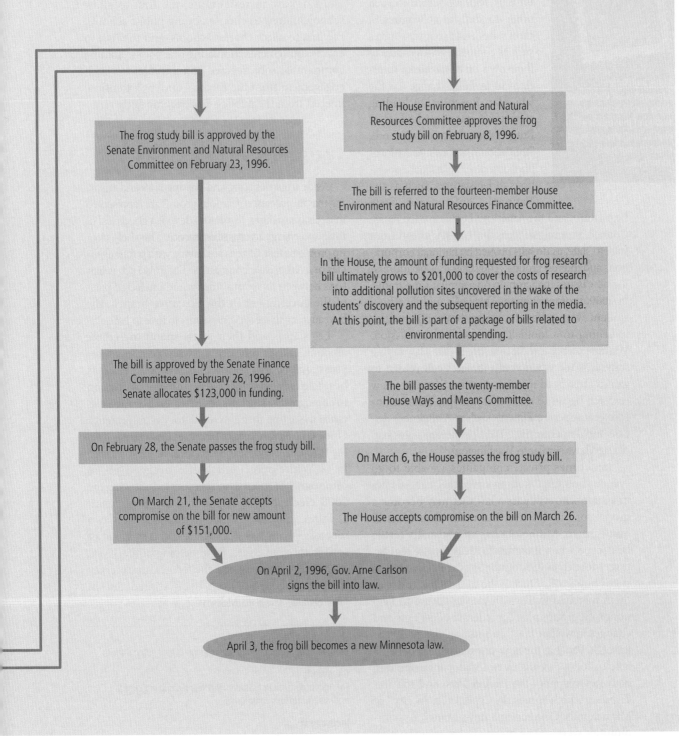

The House Environment and Natural Resources Committee approves the frog study bill on February 8, 1996.

The frog study bill is approved by the Senate Environment and Natural Resources Committee on February 23, 1996.

The bill is referred to the fourteen-member House Environment and Natural Resources Finance Committee.

In the House, the amount of funding requested for frog research bill ultimately grows to $201,000 to cover the costs of research into additional pollution sites uncovered in the wake of the students' discovery and the subsequent reporting in the media. At this point, the bill is part of a package of bills related to environmental spending.

The bill is approved by the Senate Finance Committee on February 26, 1996. Senate allocates $123,000 in funding.

The bill passes the twenty-member House Ways and Means Committee.

On February 28, the Senate passes the frog study bill.

On March 6, the House passes the frog study bill.

On March 21, the Senate accepts compromise on the bill for new amount of $151,000.

The House accepts compromise on the bill on March 26.

On April 2, 1996, Gov. Arne Carlson signs the bill into law.

April 3, the frog bill becomes a new Minnesota law.

Texas legislators approved a bill that would allow for random drug testing of thousands of high school athletes in an effort to stamp out steroid use.

that reflect new priorities and different constituencies. After all, before a bill can even get far enough to be debated, the idea for it must be developed. To get ideas for bills, legislators turn to each other, to staff, to colleagues in other states, and to outside sources such as companies with causes of their own or think tanks interested in pushing change. As the late Alan Rosenthal, a leading expert on state legislatures at Rutgers University, pointed out, "legislation is becoming a national phenomenon."[13] National associations of legislatures, such as the National Conference of State Legislatures and the American Legislative Exchange Council, promulgate ideas that quickly spread from state to state, as do bills pushed by national corporations and interest groups. And states may be addressing new issues that crop up on a similar time frame. In 2009, prompted by the story of a middle school student who suffered a severe brain injury after returning to a football game with a concussion, Washington became the first state to pass a law setting standards for when youth athletes can return to games after head injuries. Around that time, new research began to show that multiple concussions could cause severe ailments such as Alzheimer's disease and dementia. By 2012, thirty-eight states had enacted laws similar to Washington's.[14]

Sometimes private companies are able to go "venue shopping," finding sympathetic legislators in a state who will pass a law that may become a model for other states. But most ideas are still homegrown. Minnesota has an unusually fertile landscape when it comes to ideas for the legislature. More than 750 foundations are active in the state's public life. During the mid-1990s, thirty of them matched funds with the legislature to help nonprofit groups plan for federal budget cuts and changes in welfare law.[15] In addition, the state capital of St. Paul has the now-unusual benefit of being able to follow trends in two major metropolitan daily newspapers—the *Pioneer Press* and the *Star Tribune*, which serves the capital's "twin city" of Minneapolis. Once upon a time, numerous communities were served by two or more competing

newspapers. Today, consolidations and closures have forced most areas to make do with one, if that. Fortunately for Minnesota's legislators, both of the Twin Cities' papers actively cover public policy. Perhaps partly as a result, the state was the first to ban smoking in restaurants, the first to allow schoolchildren to choose among public schools, the first to allow charter schools, and the first to enact requirements stipulating that people holding comparable jobs receive comparable pay. Such engagement from the media—and, by extension, interest from the public—has become fairly rare.

Constituent Service

Aside from debating and passing laws and ensuring that the interests of various groups are represented in decision making, legislators devote a good deal of time and energy to **constituent service**. They help clear up problems that citizens are having with public agencies or even private companies. They also act as liaisons between their constituents and unelected parts of the government in the executive branch, the bureaucracy that everyone seems to love to hate.

Legislators and their staffs spend incredible amounts of their time dealing with constituent service requests, also known as **casework**.[16] Residents of a state may experience all manner of frustration in coping with state laws or may merely want assistance in sorting through regulatory requirements. One of the advantages of being an **incumbent** is having the ability to dole out this kind of personalized help. While a recount battle dragged on in Minnesota for more than six months following the 2008 election, U.S. senator Amy Klobuchar, D-Minn., and her staff had to do the work of two senators—handling double the usual caseload of sorting through issues, from helping military veterans in the state navigate the federal bureaucracy "to adoptions that have been stalled out in Guatemala," she told MSNBC.[17]

Constituent Service
The work done by legislators to help residents in their voting districts.

Casework
The work undertaken by legislators and their staffs in response to requests for help from constituents.

Incumbent
A person holding office.

Being mayor means constantly meeting with constituents, as Tom Barrett (in tie and gray hair) does here outside a Milwaukee post office.

At the state level, some legislators have staff members devoted solely to helping constituents. This is particularly true in their district offices—offices located in the area back home that they represent, as opposed to their capitol offices. Typical issues include tracking down deadbeat dads for child support, figuring out how constituents can receive proper health coverage under Medicaid programs, and determining which federal agency to contact with questions about military matters.

In one humorous case, Jim Townsend received a call from a constituent complaining that the grass in the median strip of a state road near his house had become overgrown. Townsend was not only a legislator but also the majority leader of the Oklahoma House. When he called the highway department, he expected action. He was promised prompt service, but the same constituent called him back two weeks later to report that nothing had been done. Townsend took matters into his own hands, putting his own riding mower in the back of his pickup truck and doing the mowing himself.[18] The problem with constituent service is that attempts to help individuals sometimes morph into policy decisions. That is, a legislator might not only write a letter to help a particular person but also write a bill that changes the way the state approaches a program, such as health insurance. Helping an individual may be all well and good, but changing the system based on the personal story of one constituent is not necessarily the best way to change policies that will affect thousands.

Undoubtedly, it is important for legislators to hear about the real-world experiences of their constituents. Because they cannot meet with everybody, however, they need to rely on reports and studies to get a complete picture. They otherwise might be swayed too greatly by anecdotes and personal interactions. The danger of politicians' having to raise significant campaign finance treasuries is not so much that their votes can be bought but that they are much more likely to meet with the people or interest groups that give them the campaign contributions. Campaign donors often give money simply so that they can have access to a legislator when they hand over the check. That means that people who do not or cannot give money may not get heard.

Oversight

Under the U.S. system of checks and balances, legislatures are charged with **oversight**, the task of making sure that the governor and the executive branch agencies are functioning properly. Legislators are only doing their job when they call governors and executive branch agencies to account through hearings, investigations, and audits for how they are carrying out those laws. Unfortunately, the most ubiquitous form of oversight is a legislator's intervening with administrative agencies on behalf of constituents or constituent groups in ways that are "episodic and punitive."[19]

For example, several years ago, the Arkansas Livestock and Poultry Commission filed suit against a livestock sales barn for failure to meet state regulations concerning an infectious livestock disease called brucellosis. The state senator from that

Oversight
The legislature's role in making sure that the governor and executive branch agencies are properly implementing the laws.

district placed language to weaken those regulations in the bill to fund the commission, which prompted the commissioner to resign.[20] The commissioner had taken the funding cut as a signal that his authority was being undermined, so he quit. That kind of scattershot approach—helping a particular constituent at the expense of the public good—is by its nature inequitable. The point of bureaucratic norms is to make sure that regulations and laws are applied fairly and evenly across the board.

Legislators may attack agencies for pursuing policies that hurt their constituents, but it's unfortunately pretty rare for the legislative branch—despite its duty to keep an eye on executive branch functions—to be consistent about taking a hard look at whether ongoing programs are functioning as they should. Aside from unearthing an occasional scandal involving misspent funds, legislators reap little political reward for poking around in the business of the state. And for each program there are not only agency officials but also program beneficiaries and lobbyists who will question the motives of legislators or staffers who seek to audit the program's work. For example, in 2007, the North Carolina legislature created the Program Evaluation Division, which was charged with compiling a scorecard to show how state agencies were performing, in much the same way information about the performance of private companies might be compiled for investors. The first report looked at agricultural research stations. North Carolina had the most of any state in the country—twenty-one, compared with only eleven in the much larger state of California—and evaluators concluded that there was no economic or strategic justification for the state to support so many. "That report was like setting off a nuclear weapon in the area of Raleigh," said John Turcotte, the division's founding director. "Any time you question the necessity of an institution or a major component of a program, you will create massive opposition."[21]

Organization and Operation of Legislatures

While every state legislature is unique, the vast majority share similarities in how they divide and manage labor and in the institutional rules that help determine who governs and how.

Bicameralism

Legislatures are not, of course, random groups of people hanging around a dorm and picking pizza toppings. Every state has a constitution that describes a body that can pass state laws. In every state but Nebraska, which has a unicameral (or one-house) legislature, the legislature is bicameral (or divided into two houses), pretty much like the U.S. Congress. As mentioned earlier in this chapter, one chamber is normally called either the house of representatives or the assembly and the other is called the senate. The Tenth Amendment of the U.S. Constitution reserves to the states all powers not given to the federal government, and state legislatures can write any state law that does not interfere with federal laws.

The house always has more members, known as state representatives, than the senate. There are 163 representatives in the Missouri General Assembly, for example, but only 34 senators. There are some exceptions, but generally senators serve four-year terms, whereas house members have to be reelected every two years. The two chambers operate independently, with separate leaders, committees, and agendas, although both chambers have to pass the same version of a bill before it can be sent to the governor to be signed into law or vetoed.

Legislative Leadership

Most state legislatures have essentially the same leadership structure, at least for their top positions. At the beginning of a session, each house votes in its speaker. This is generally someone picked beforehand by a **caucus**, or meeting, of members of the majority party. The majority leader and the minority leader rank just below the speaker of the house. *Majority* and *minority* here refer to the respective strengths of the major parties. Either the Democratic or the Republican Party may hold the

---

Caucus
All the members of a party—Republican or Democrat—within a legislative chamber. Also refers to meetings of members of a political party in a chamber.

majority of seats in a chamber. (In 2012, fewer than ten legislators—out of more than seven thousand nationwide—were independents or members of third parties.) In the senate, the top leader is known as the president, president pro tempore, president pro tem, or majority leader.

Certain aspects of the leadership positions remain constant across all the states. For example, a speaker will typically preside over daily sessions of the house or assembly, refer bills to the appropriate committees, and sign legislation as it makes its way over to the senate or the governor's desk. Leaders appoint committee chairs (in some states, all the members of committees), set or change committee jurisdictions, and offer staff or legislative help to rank-and-file members. They also often help with campaigns, including providing financial support.

The amount of power invested in the office of speaker or senate president varies by state. In the Texas Senate, leadership powers are invested in the office of lieutenant governor. But regardless of how the formal duties are divided up, usually there is one individual who emerges as holding the most power and speaking for the chamber in negotiating with the other chamber and the governor.

With the exception of Nebraska, where parties are actually banned from the nonpartisan unicameral legislature, legislatures are divided along party lines (and even in Nebraska, the Democratic and Republican parties endorse candidates for the legislature, so it's well known which lawmakers affiliate with which party). Not only does the majority party get to pick the top leader, but it gets to fill virtually all of the important committee chairs as well. A party majority is worth much more than the comfort of knowing that your fellow Democrats or Republicans will help you outvote the opposition on most bills. Holding the leadership and chair positions means that the majority party gets to set the agenda—deciding which bills will be heard for a vote. At the end of World War II, all but seven of the forty-eight states had united governments, meaning one party controlled the governorship and both legislative chambers. By 1986, only twenty-one of fifty states had united governments.[22] Since then the tide has turned.

Following the 2012 elections, only three states had divided legislatures, with one chamber controlled by each party. One party or the other controlled both the legislature and the governorship in thirty-seven states, there being veto-proof majorities in almost half the legislative chambers nationwide.

Climbing the leadership ladder can take no time at all in states with term limits, such as California and Florida, where House members can serve only six and eight years, respectively, and speakers are sometimes chosen as freshmen. In contrast, Joe Hackney, who became speaker of the North Carolina House in 2007, had to serve more than a quarter century before attaining that post. "When I came to the legislature, I more or less regarded it as a long-term thing," he says. "It wasn't my plan to be there two or four or six years and quit. It was my plan to make a contribution, and I saw that those who make a contribution built up seniority and experience."[23] Hackney held the position of speaker for four years, before Republican victories in 2010 forced him from power.

Voters unhappy with the status quo often will unseat top leaders in symbolic decapitations. That happened in 2006 to Bob Garton, who had led the Indiana Senate for twenty-six years but lost his seat when voters grew unhappy about a health insurance perk for senators. That same year, Robert Jubelirer, a twenty-five-year leader in the Pennsylvania Senate, was one of seventeen incumbents ousted in primaries by voters angry about a legislative pay raise.

Committees

Legislatures are divided into committees—usually about fifteen or twenty per chamber—that grapple with particular issues, such as education, transportation, and taxes. Thousands of bills are introduced annually in each legislature. Most of these bills never reach the floor where the full house or senate meets. Basically, they never make it past the committee stage to be debated or voted on by the house or senate as a whole. Instead, they are sent to the appropriate committee, where they may be debated and amended but

TABLE 7-1

Total Number of State Legislators (House and Senate), 2012

State	Senate Members	House Members	Total Members
Alabama	35	105	140
Alaska	20	40	60
Arizona	30	60	90
Arkansas	35	100	135
California	40	80	120
Colorado	35	65	100
Connecticut	36	151	187
Delaware	21	41	62
Florida	40	120	160
Georgia	56	180	236
Hawaii	25	51	76
Idaho	35	70	105
Illinois	59	118	177
Indiana	50	100	150
Iowa	50	100	150
Kansas	40	125	165
Kentucky	38	100	138
Louisiana	39	105	144
Maine	35	151	186
Maryland	47	141	188
Massachusetts	40	160	200
Michigan	38	110	148
Minnesota	67	134	201
Mississippi	52	122	174
Missouri	34	163	197
Montana	50	100	150

State	Senate Members	House Members	Total Members
Nebraska	49	n/a	49
Nevada	21	42	63
New Hampshire	24	400	424
New Jersey	40	80	120
New Mexico	42	70	112
New York	62[a]	150	212
North Carolina	50	120	170
North Dakota	47	94	141
Ohio	33	99	132
Oklahoma	48	101	149
Oregon	30	60	90
Pennsylvania	50	203	253
Rhode Island	38	75	113
South Carolina	46	124	170
South Dakota	35	70	105
Tennessee	33	99	132
Texas	31	150	181
Utah	29	75	104
Vermont	30	150	180
Virginia	40	100	140
Washington	49	98	147
West Virginia	34	100	134
Wisconsin	33	99	132
Wyoming	30	60	90
Total	**1,971**	**5,411**	**7,382**

Source: National Conference of State Legislatures, "2012 State and Legislative Partisan Composition," www.ncsl.org/documents/statevote/2012_Legis_and_State.pdf.

a. New York added a Senate district with the 2012 election, which increased the number of senators to 63.

MAP 7-1

Partisan Control of State Government, 1954

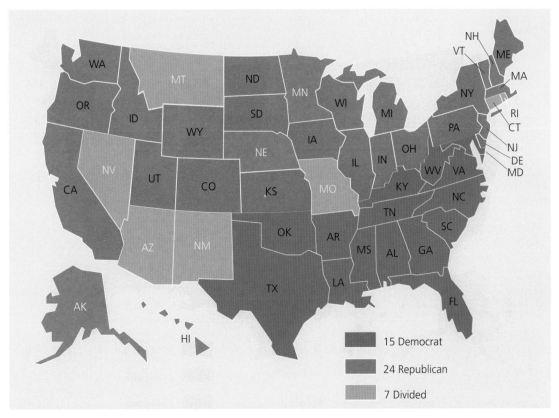

15 Democrat

24 Republican

7 Divided

Source: All data from Klarner Data Set, *State Politics & Policy Quarterly* Data Resource, www.unl.edu/SPPQ/journal_datasets/klarner.html.

Note: Alaska and Hawaii were still territories in 1954 and had not yet received full statehood. The data for Minnesota are incomplete. Although the governor was Republican, there are no data demonstrating whether Democrats or Republicans controlled the legislature. Nebraska's unicameral legislature is not included because candidates run in nonpartisan elections.

usually die without a hearing. Just as the senate president, house speaker, or other leader sets the agenda for floor action on bills, the committee chair decides which bills are going to be heard and receive priority treatment at the committee level.

Legislators try to serve on the committees where they will have the most influence. The most prestigious committees are the budget committees, which set tax and spending levels. Other committees debate policies, but unless funding is provided to pay for those policies, they do not matter as much. Seats on a finance or appropriations committee are highly sought after, but members will also "request appointment to committees which will give them the most visibility and interest in their districts."[24] Thus a senator from a rural district may want to serve on an agriculture committee. A representative who previously served on a city council may want a seat on the local government committee.

While any member can introduce legislation on any topic, members of the education committee, for example, are more likely to introduce and influence bills that affect schools. When an education bill is being debated in the full house or senate, other members, who have other specialties, will turn to members of the education committee for guidance about what the bill would do and how they should vote. The same holds true for other issues, such as transportation and healthcare.

Rank-and-File Members

The majority of legislators—those who provide leaders with their votes—are known as **rank-and-file members** of the legislature. And no legislator—leader

Rank-And-File Members
Legislators who do not hold leadership positions or senior committee posts.

MAP 7-2

Partisan Control of State Government, 2012

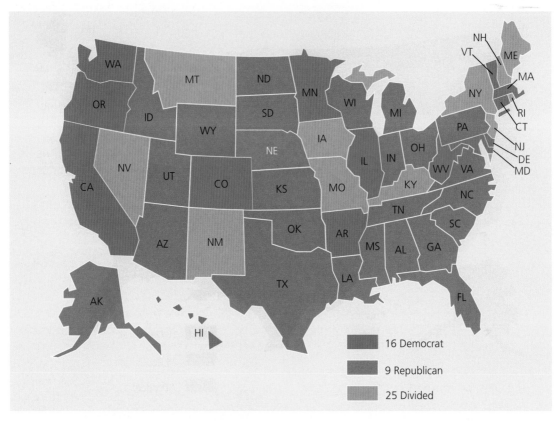

16 Democrat

9 Republican

25 Divided

Source: Data compiled from National Conference of State Legislatures, "2012 Live Election Night Coverage of State Legislative Races," www.ncsl.org/legislatures-elections/elections/statevote-2012-election-night-results-map.aspx; and National Conference of State Legislatures, "Live 2012 Election Night Results: Governors," www.ncsl.org/legislatures-elections/elections/statevote-election-night-governor-map.aspx.

or rank-and-file member—can be fully versed on the details of all of the dozens of bills that confront him or her every day during a session. Legislators turn to many sources for information on how to vote. There is a classic notion, posited by political philosopher and statesman Edmund Burke, that divides legislators into **delegates**, who vote according to the wishes of their districts, and **trustees**, who vote according to their own consciences.[25] Given the proliferation of legislation, however, members never hear from a single constituent on probably 90 percent of the bills that they must consider. Instead, they rely for guidance on staffers, other legislators, interest groups and lobbyists, executive branch officials, foundations, think tanks, and other sources.

The fact that legislators cannot rely solely on their own judgment to vote is the source of many people's sense that legislators' votes can be bought—or at least rented. This is ironic, considering that political scientists consistently find that most legislators are extremely attentive to their districts and vote according to their sense of their constituents' desires. Their primary goal, after all, is to win reelection. In addition, most states have made it tougher for lobbyists to get lawmakers' attention. It is difficult under the new ethics rules for a lobbyist to spring for a legislator's cup of coffee, much less treat him or her to lunch. In

Delegates
Legislators who primarily see their role as voting according to their constituents' beliefs as they understand them.

Trustees
Legislators who believe they were elected to exercise their own judgment and to approach issues accordingly.

Kentucky, for example, there are fewer of the nightly receptions that once kept Frankfort well fed, and lobbyists are prohibited from making any personal contributions to candidates for the legislature. "A lot of the principal lobbyists are still here, so folks have had to learn to adapt," says Bobby Sherman, head of the Kentucky legislature's nonpartisan research staff. "It's more work for them. They have to build relationships in a different way, and information delivery is much more important."[26]

All of this is necessary because, as with most things, times have changed. It used to be that rank-and-file members voted pretty much the way they were instructed by their party leaders. In Connecticut, the legislature of the early 1960s was an assemblage of party hacks—members beholden to the party chair for patronage. This meant that most of the legislature's important decisions were made in small meetings to which the public—or even most rank-and-file members—were not invited.

The wishes of leaders often carry much less weight with members than they did even a generation ago. Leaders these days are no stronger than members want them to be; they often lead by listening. They have to pay attention to customer service, and their main customers are rank-and-file legislators. Leaders help other legislators intervene with the governor or the rest of the executive branch and help green-light bills in order to build up political chits. "As long as it wasn't against the law, didn't require that I go to confession, or wouldn't break up my marriage, I did it," recalled Ralph Wright, onetime speaker of the Vermont House.[27]

Leaders cannot bully their way through as they did a generation ago, for two reasons. First, leadership offices control direct fund-raising efforts designed to build or maintain majorities, but the leadership's efforts are mainly directed at the relatively few contests that will make or break a majority. Dick Saslaw, the Democratic Senate president in Virginia, for example, spent about $1.5 million in campaign cash in 2011 trying to defend his party's narrow majority, funneling money to incumbents and challengers in the most competitive races.[28] Most rank-and-file members today raise their own money and have greater access to expert advice for hire and

separate sources of money, whether from political action committees run by industries or labor unions or elsewhere. The politician who spent the most on Virginia's 2011 legislative elections wasn't a member of the legislature at all. It was Bob McDonnell, the state's Republican governor, who contributed $3.7 million to candidates through a PAC he controls.[29]

We have already touched on the other factor—members do not have to rely on leaders as much as they once did for information about bills or for help in writing legislation. The proliferation of lobbyists and the **professionalization** of legislatures have meant that members have their own resources to draw on.[30]

Apportionment

One more issue that profoundly affects all legislators is **apportionment**. Following the nationwide census that occurs every ten years, each state draws new lines for its legislative districts. In states with more than one member of Congress, congressional districts are redrawn as well. The redistricting process is the most naked exercise of political power in the states. Within the legal limits that exist—Supreme Court rulings in the 1960s set the requirement that districts be roughly even in population—the incumbent party will do everything it can to preserve its hold or, preferably, increase its numbers. Each party will seek to draw the maximum number of districts possible that are likely to elect members of its own party. The two major parties will fight each other as best they can to make certain that the other side does not gain the upper hand. "Just like there are no atheists in foxholes, there are no nonpartisans in redistricting," says Paul Green, director of the School of Policy Studies at Roosevelt University in Chicago.[31]

Professionalization
The process of providing legislators with the resources they need to make politics their main career, such as making their positions full time or providing them with full-time staff.

Apportionment
The allotting of districts according to population shifts. The number of congressional districts that a state has may be reapportioned every ten years, following the national census.

Political district boundaries that link disparate communities or have odd shapes that resemble earmuffs or moose antlers are known as **gerrymanders,** a term derived from the name of Elbridge Gerry, an early nineteenth-century governor of Massachusetts. **Malapportionment** occurs when districts violate the principle of equal representation. In the past, some state legislative districts could have many times the numbers of constituents in other districts. Votes in the smaller districts, in effect, counted for more.

Travis County, Texas, where Austin is located, is one of the most Democratic jurisdictions in the state. President Obama won almost 64 percent of the vote in Travis County in 2008. In 2011, the Republican-controlled Texas legislature sliced and diced Travis County so that four of the five congressional districts that include parts of the county lean toward Republicans. They did that by packing Democrats into a single district that includes both parts of Austin and parts of San Antonio, three counties away—with the two halves connected only by a narrow strip of land. The district outline looks so strange on a map that the *Washington Post* held a contest to describe it: the winning entry was "Upside-down elephant (spraying water)."[32] Travis County's government, among other groups, challenged the redistricting in court, but judges allowed the five-way split to go into effect for the 2012 elections.[33]

Legislatures define district boundaries in most states, but there are exceptions. Since the 1980s, Iowa's political maps have been created by the nonpartisan Legislative Services Agency. The agency uses computer software to draw one hundred House districts and fifty Senate districts according to rules that keep population as equal as possible from district to district, avoid splitting counties, and keep the districts compact. In contrast to legislature-drawn maps, those drawn by the agency do not take into account party registration, voting patterns, or the political territory of incumbents. Largely as a result, partisan control of the Iowa legislature has flipped often since the agency was created.

Gerrymanders

Districts clearly drawn with the intent of pressing partisan advantage at the expense of other considerations.

Malapportionment

A situation in which the principle of equal representation is violated.

MAP 7-3

The Upside-Down Elephant District

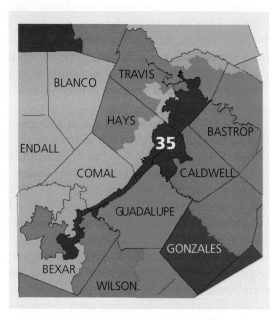

Texas's Thirty-Fifth Congressional District drew attention for its odd shape, the result of what many viewed as a partisan effort to redraw the district's lines.

Source: Texas Legislative Council.

While Iowa's system is unique, reformers elsewhere regularly try to find ways to prevent redistricting from flagrantly favoring one party over the other. Lately, the reformers have won some important victories. In Florida in 2010, voters approved a constitutional amendment that mandated rules for redistricting, including forbidding the drawing of lines for the purpose of favoring incumbent officeholders or political parties. Meanwhile, California approved a pair of citizen initiatives in 2008 and 2010 that took redistricting out of the hands of state legislators and entrusted it to an independent commission.

Partisanship is the primary concern of redistricting, but it is not the only one. Issues of representation also play a big part. African Americans are overwhelmingly Democratic, but some joined with Republicans following the 1980 and 1990 censuses to create black-majority districts, especially in the South. It wasn't that they joined the Republican Party; they simply allied themselves

with the GOP to draw **majority-minority districts**, which guaranteed the election of more African Americans but also made the neighboring "bleached" districts more likely to elect Republicans.

Redistricting also changes representation in ways that go beyond black and white. With each new round of redistricting, power shifts to places that are growing quickly and away from ones that are not. One of the major themes of the 2010 round of redistricting was a shift in power away from rural areas and to suburbs and exurbs that had experienced far stronger population growth in the previous ten years.[34] Alaska legislators were so concerned about having fewer lawmakers representing rural areas—and about the remaining rural districts becoming even more massive—that they submitted a constitutional amendment to voters in 2010 to add more seats to the legislature. One of the lawmakers supporting this change was state senator Albert Kookesh, who represented the largest state legislative district in the country. From its southeastern corner, Kookesh's district extended 1,185 miles west, about the same distance as that from Jacksonville, Florida, to Minneapolis, Minnesota, and about 1,000 miles north, about the same distance as that from Phoenix, Arizona, to Portland, Oregon.[35] Getting around an area of that size cannot be done efficiently in a car; it's hard enough to do it by plane. "In order for me to get to one of my villages, Lime Village, I would have to go from Angoon to Juneau, Juneau to Anchorage, Anchorage to Fairbanks, Fairbanks to Aniak, and Aniak to Lime Village," Kookesh said.[36] Alaska voters rejected the plan to add legislative seats.

Majority-Minority District
A district in which members of a minority group, such as African Americans or Hispanics, make up a majority of the population or electorate.

State Legislators

If you were to make a composite drawing of the average state legislator, he—and it would be a he—would be white and in his fifties. He would have had at least some college education, have an income topping $50,000, describe himself as moderate or conservative, and have lived in the community he was representing for at least ten years.[37] There are many, many exceptions to all the aspects of this composite. The type of person who runs for state legislative office has changed a good deal over the past thirty years—for example, there are far more women and African Americans in office and fewer lawyers—but nonetheless, the type of middle- to upper-middle-class American male described here still predominates.

The nation's 7,383 state legislators come from all backgrounds, particularly in the states where the house and senate meet for only part of the year. In states with full-time legislatures, such as California and Pennsylvania, the legislators tend, not surprisingly, to be career politicians who have served in local or other elected offices or perhaps as members of legislative staffs. In states with part-time legislatures, such as Arkansas and Indiana, members come from many different walks of life, devoting perhaps one-third of their working hours to politics while earning their livings through some other means.

Professional Background

Some employers encourage the political hopes of their employees because they know legislative service can be good for business. This holds true especially for professions most directly affected by state lawmaking. In 2006, Al Mansell stepped down from his leadership role as president of the Utah Senate to become president of the National Association of Realtors. He stayed in the Senate, however, sponsoring legislation that helped members of his profession. He was one of twenty-two people who worked in real estate who were serving in the Utah legislature at that time. "I've got people who are on county commissions, mayors, state senators," said Chris Kyler, CEO of the Utah Association of Realtors. "Our lieutenant governor was president of our state association about 20 years ago. Our people are involved in the parties, too. We've got precinct chairs and vice chairs and county delegates throughout the state."[38]

Consider public education. Teachers' unions are usually among the most active lobbying groups in any state, but schools do not necessarily have to rely on outsiders to influence the legislature. Teachers themselves are often members of legislatures, and employees of other institutions of higher learning also serve. In Maine, state law requires that teachers be granted leave from their jobs if they want to run for office. Maine's legislature meets for only six months every other year. About 15 percent of legislators are lawyers—a big decline from past decades. In New York, 60 percent of the Assembly and 70 percent of the Senate used to be made up of lawyers.[39] Nowadays, the dominant group in legislatures nationwide comprises people with business backgrounds. They make up about 30 percent of today's legislators. The remaining half or so come from education, healthcare, real estate, insurance, and agriculture.

Demographic Diversity

The number of women legislators has risen dramatically since the "second wave" feminist era of the late 1960s and early 1970s, but they still do not reflect the female share of the overall population. In 1970, women held just 4 percent of all state legislative seats.[40] Their numbers doubled quickly, to 8 percent of all legislators by 1975, and they climbed to 18 percent by 1991. The ranks of women legislators held steady at just over 20 percent for about a dozen years before spiking to 23.5 percent after the 2006 elections. The figure ticked up to just above 24 percent following the 2008 campaigns. Only six states—Arizona, Colorado, Maryland, Minnesota, New Hampshire, and Vermont—could brag in 2007 that one-third or more of their legislators were women.[41] In 2009, the New Hampshire Senate became the first legislative chamber in the nation to have a majority of women members. Women served as its president and majority leader, and another woman served as speaker of the New Hampshire House.[42] Republican victories in the 2010 elections dropped the national number back below 24 percent—about 60 percent of the women in state legislatures are Democrats.[43] Following the 2012 elections, the number ticked back above 24 percent.

The numbers of women entering state legislatures may not be growing exponentially, but the types of women holding house and senate seats have changed. In the old days of the 1970s—many years before most readers of this book were born—most women running for office came to politics later in life than did their male counterparts. They had not been tapped to run by party professionals or other "queenmakers." Instead, they jump-started their own careers, drawn into the policy realm out of concerns about their children's schools or their local communities. Men may know from the time they are in school that they want to run for office, said Barbara Lee, who runs a foundation dedicated to helping women run for office, but women often find out later in life that it is important to enter the game because of their specific concerns and experiences.[44] This dynamic has changed to some extent. Women now enter politics at ages comparable to men. Many still tend to care about particular issues (education, healthcare, and the environment) that are noticeably different from the top priorities of men (taxes and budgets), but sometimes they focus on such issues because they still find it harder than men to gain seats on the more powerful finance committees in representative numbers. But over the past few

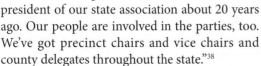

decades, their backgrounds became more varied, and they also became more conservative, although they still were more liberal than men—and significantly more likely than their male colleagues to initiate legislation.[45] Women also became more likely than men to get their priority bills through the legislative process successfully.[46]

Still, gender composition of a state legislature is a difference that makes a difference: women legislators do tend to bring up issues and concerns that would not be raised by an all-male legislature. This tendency is even truer of issues of concern to minorities. African Americans have made gains similar to those of women in legislatures over the past forty years, growing from a microscopic minority to a larger minority, albeit one that still does not reflect their overall share of the population. The numbers of African American legislators have nearly quadrupled, to about 625—less than 10 percent of all the legislators nationwide.

Although it can be both dangerous and wrong to generalize about any group, it has been observed that the interests of African Americans as a whole have long been fairly stable and predictable. "On questions of public policy, ideology, and candidate choice," writes Kerry L. Haynie in his 2001 book on black state legislators, "African Americans have been the most cohesive and consistent policy subgroup in United States politics."[47] In short, the racial composition of state legislatures is also a difference that makes a difference. This is especially the case given that state influence over issues important to African American legislators increased just as their numbers were increasing. Since the 1970s, decisions about many issues of importance to African Americans, including Medicaid, student aid, school lunch programs, community development, welfare, and environmental protection, have devolved from the federal level to the states.[48] In his study of how representatives in Arkansas, Illinois, Mississippi, New Jersey, and North Carolina acted in three different sessions, Haynie found that 55 to 82 percent of African American legislators introduced bills that addressed issues of particular interest to blacks. White legislators, by contrast, almost never introduced such legislation. In only one of the three years that Haynie studied (1969, 1979, and 1989) did more than one-quarter of nonblack legislators introduce even one bill of interest to African Americans.[49] It may sound obvious, but so-called black issues are much more likely to be addressed when African Americans are serving in state legislatures.

Black legislators, of course, do not focus solely or even mostly on issues that are specific to their racial group. One reflection of this is that in recent years African American legislators have been voted into leadership roles by their colleagues in states with relatively few black voters. At the start of the 2009 legislative sessions, in the same month President Obama first took the oath of office, Colorado became the first state with a black Senate president and a black House speaker simultaneously. Malcolm Smith was elected New York's first African American Senate president, and Steve Horsford became Nevada's first African American Senate majority leader that same year.

Professional Versus Citizen Legislators

As discussed above, legislatures, strictly white male playgrounds in the past, have become more inclusive of women and minorities and more attentive to their concerns. But even bigger changes in legislatures over the past thirty-five years have come in the very ways that they do business. Whereas once legislatures were sleepy backwaters where not much got done—and even less got done ethically—now many chambers are highly professional operations. Most legislatures used to meet for short periods every other year. These days all but a handful meet every year and, in a few cases, nearly year-round. "No single factor has a greater effect on the legislative environment than the constitutional restriction on length of session," two leading legislative scholars wrote long ago.[50]

The most pronounced differences among the states are between "professional" legislatures that meet full time, pay members high salaries, and employ large staffs; and "amateur," or "citizen," legislatures that meet part time, have members who usually hold other jobs, and have smaller staffs. To some extent, all legislatures have become more professional.

A Difference
That Makes a Difference

Life in the Minority: Stall Tactics and "Sacred Sperm"

After Republicans won historic victories in the 2010 elections, they quickly used their new power to pursue an ambitious conservative agenda across a broad range of cultural, economic, and fiscal issues. Every Republican cause, from tax cuts to private school vouchers to gun rights expansions, suddenly had a better chance of passing in many states. Democrats were left reeling—and searching for any tactic to slow the Republicans down. For example, many legislative chambers have rules that a certain number of legislators, a "quorum," must be present for bills to advance. When Republicans in Wisconsin and Indiana began to move bills to weaken labor unions, a key Democratic Party constituency, Democrats in those states fled the legislative chambers—and the states entirely—as a way to prevent the Republicans from reaching the quorum they needed to act. Dozens of Indiana Democrats, for example, holed up at the Comfort Inn and Suites in Urbana, Illinois, in February 2011. These tactics succeeded in bringing national attention to the disagreements, but they didn't ultimately stop the legislation from passing.

When Republicans pushed forward new restrictions on women's access to abortion and birth control—eighty such bills were enacted in 2011 alone—Democratic women legislators found a different way to fight back. They introduced bills using language meant to sound equally intrusive when it came to men and their bodies. Their legislation was also intended to make male legislators squirm. An Ohio bill would have required Viagra-seeking men to undergo psychological counseling and to produce a notarized affidavit from a sex partner attesting to recent erectile dysfunction before being allowed to purchase the drug. A Georgia bill would have banned vasectomies except when needed to avoid death or "impairment of a major bodily function." And in Oklahoma, an "every sperm is sacred" amendment to a "personhood" bill would have defined life as beginning at ejaculation and made it clear that depositing semen anywhere but in a woman's vagina is a crime against the unborn. "It wasn't until I got graphic that people finally heard what I was saying," says Oklahoma senator Constance Johnson, sponsor of the ejaculation bill.

These graphic bills indeed received a lot of media attention. Not surprisingly, pro-life legislators and advocacy groups were ticked off by the tactic. "On acts that are meant to mock or parody something that is seen as a very serious issue by the caucus, the life or pro-life issues, it's about gravitas," said David Atkins, the spokesman for Oklahoma Senate leader Brian Bingman. "At the end of the day you would hope that elected officials would recognize that and they would treat the issue seriously."

The women legislators argued that their amendments were no less serious—or at least no less demeaning—than the abortion and birth control legislation coasting through so many capitols. Democratic women in many red states know that they are fighting at best a rearguard action. Putting in legislation that holds up an unflattering mirror to the majority party's agenda may be the best minority legislators can do.

And, at least in a few instances, their efforts have done more than that. In response to a bill in Virginia that originally would have required a woman seeking an abortion to undergo a transvaginal ultrasound exam with what *Doonesbury* called a "10-inch shaming wand," Democratic senator Janet Howell put forward an amendment that would have required men to undergo rectal exams and counseling before they could receive Viagra or other erectile dysfunction drugs. The amendment fueled national media exposure, including bits on both *The Daily Show* and *Saturday Night Live.* That bright spotlight forced the bill's sponsors to back down some before the bill was signed into law. Women seeking abortions in Virginia now do have to undergo ultrasounds, but not transvaginal ones.

Source: Original piece written for this book by Alan Greenblatt.

Even "amateur" legislators devote a third of their time to legislative work. In the early 1940s, the legislatures of only four states—New Jersey, New York, Rhode Island, and South Carolina—met in annual sessions, but the number meeting yearly has climbed continuously.[51] Today, only four states do not meet in regular annual sessions. Expenditures per legislator have increased above the rate of inflation in nearly every state, and today, the most professional legislatures have resources that rival those of the U.S. Congress.[52] Lately, however, that trend has slowed. The number of legislative staffers nationwide dropped from 1996 to 2009 after decades of increases.[53]

With the exception of Texas, the more populous states have highly professional legislatures. Such legislatures are able to provide more resources to their chambers, which allows these chambers to keep up with the wider variety of issues that arise in densely populated states in comparison with most of their less populous neighbors. Legislatures in some states, such as Pennsylvania and California, meet essentially year-round; in contrast, Montana's part-time legislature meets for only ninety days and only in odd-numbered years.

More populous states have the money to invest in the full-time legislatures that are necessary for their governments to keep on top of issues facing these states' more complicated and developed economies and diverse populations. The reason that Texas, with a population second only to California's, has a part-time legislature lies in the state's distrust of government in general. Texas is one of only nine states that do not impose an income tax, and a legislature that meets only part time every other year is in keeping with this general low-tax, low-service point of view. Other states have traditions of embracing more expansive government. States with strong progressive traditions, such as Michigan and Wisconsin, have long used full-time, professional legislators with substantial staffs at their command.

As distrust of government has spread to more state capitols, there have been some moves to reverse the trend toward better-staffed, more expensive, more professionalized legislatures. It was a sure sign of unhappiness with the Michigan legislature amid its struggles to pass budgets in a difficult economic time that serious, although ultimately unsuccessful, petition drives were

launched in 2008, including one by a local area chamber of commerce, to turn it into a part-time body. In Pennsylvania, efforts to scale back the legislature's spending on itself grew out of a double-digit pay increase legislators approved for themselves at 2:00 A.M. on July 7, 2005. Since then, one perennial idea promoted by some in the state has been to save money by having fewer legislators. No one could accuse Pennsylvania's House members of serving their own career interests when they voted in 2012 for a constitutional amendment that would have cut the House from 203 to 153 members.[54] The Senate, which the amendment would have shrunk from 50 members to 38, did not act on the proposal.

Some states impose severe restrictions on the meeting times of their legislatures. In Colorado, the state constitution limits the House and the Senate to no more than 120 days per year. Sometimes such limits are honored mostly in the breach. The governor may insist that the legislature meet in special session to address a budget crisis or other issue that cannot wait until the next regular session. Or the legislature may simply carve out a little more time for itself, as happened in 2002 in North Carolina. House rules require that the chamber be shut down by 9:00 P.M., so members stopped the clock one night at 8:50, essentially "freezing time," so they could continue debate until 3:35 A.M. and finish a session that had run for months longer than expected.

Just like most of us, legislators feel intensely the pressure to get their work done on time. The fact that they have deadlines—for passing budgets or for adjournment—usually keeps them focused in much the same way that a final exam will make college students finally hit the books or do their serious Googling at term's end. Newspapers, however, routinely report on legislatures missing their budget deadlines and often publish commentary critical of the practice. The reality is that a legislature is pretty cheap to operate—in no state does it cost much more than 0.5 percent of the state budget—but elected officials know that their overtime does not play well with voters.[55]

Mississippi's largest paper, the *Clarion Ledger,* for instance, ran a typical editorial condemning legislators for wasting money in a special session in 2008, even though the extra time cost the state

TABLE 7-2

State House Demographic Diversity: Total Numbers and Percentages of Legislators Who Are Women, African American, and Hispanic

State	Total Number of Legislative Seats	Women State Legislators		African American State Legislators		Hispanic State Legislators	
		Total	Percentage of Total Seats	Total	Percentage of Total Seats	Total	Percentage of Total Seats
Alabama	140	18	12.9	34	24	0	0
Alaska	60	17	28.3	1	2	0	0
Arizona	90	32	35.6	2	2	17	19
Arkansas	135	23	17	15	11	0	0
California	120	31	25.8	9	8	28	23
Colorado	100	42	42	3	3	5	5
Connecticut	187	55	29.4	19	10	6	3
Delaware	62	16	26	5	8	1	2
Florida	160	40	25	25	16	17	11
Georgia	236	54	23	56	24	3	1
Hawaii	76	24	32	0	0	1	1
Idaho	105	27	26	0	0	1	1
Illinois	177	57	32	29	16	11	6
Indiana	150	3	21	13	9	1	1
Iowa	150	35	23	3	2	0	0
Kansas	165	39	24	6	4	4	2
Kentucky	138	25	18	7	5	0	0
Louisiana	144	16	11	29	20	0	0
Maine	186	54	29	0	0	0	0
Maryland	188	57	30	42	22	4	2
Massachusetts	200	51	26	8	4	5	3
Michigan	148	28	19	19	13	3	2
Minnesota	201	67	33	1	>1	3	1
Mississippi	174	28	16	42	24	0	0
Missouri	197	43	22	12	6	1	1
Montana	150	42	28	0	0	1	1
Nebraska	49	10	20	1	2	1	2
Nevada	63	18	29	7	11	3	5
New Hampshire	424	139	33	1	>1	2	<1
New Jersey	120	35	29	10	8	5	4
New Mexico	112	31	28	2	2	44	39
New York	213	47	22	43	20	17	8
North Carolina	170	39	23	26	15	2	1

State	Total Number of Legislative Seats	Women State Legislators		African American State Legislators		Hispanic State Legislators	
		Total	Percentage of Total Seats	Total	Percentage of Total Seats	Total	Percentage of Total Seats
North Dakota	141	24	17	0	0	0	0
Ohio	132	31	24	16	12	0	0
Oklahoma	149	20	13	6	4	0	0
Oregon	90	26	29	3	3	1	1
Pennsylvania	253	45	18	21	8	1	< 1
Rhode Island	113	31	27	1	1	3	3
South Carolina	170	22	13	28	17	1	1
South Dakota	105	24	23	0	0	0	0
Tennessee	132	23	17	12	9	1	1
Texas	181	37	20	14	8	36	20
Utah	104	17	16	0	0	2	2
Vermont	180	73	41	1	1	0	0
Virginia	140	25	18	17	12	1	1
Washington	147	45	31	3	2	3	2
West Virginia	134	22	16	0	0	0	0
Wisconsin	132	33	25	8	6	1	1
Wyoming	90	15	17	0	0	2	2
Total	7,383	1,784	24	600	6	238	4

Source: National Conference of State Legislatures, "Women in State Legislatures: 2013 Legislative Session," http://www.ncsl.org/legislatures-elections/wln/women-in-state-legislatures-for-2013.aspx; National Conference of State Legislatures, "Number of African American Legislators 2009," www.ncsl.org/default.aspx?tabid=14781; National Conference of State Legislatures, "2009 Latino Legislators," www.ncsl.org/Default.aspx?TabId=14766.

Note: Percentages are rounded to the nearest whole number. Numbers are the latest available; those for women legislators are from 2013, and those for African American and Hispanic legislators are from 2009.

only $59,895 for the first day and $39,420 a day for each one after that. At that rate, the session would have had to drag on for weeks to add just 1 percent to the $90 million budget deficit the state faced the next year.[79] Such media coverage is one reason legislatures, even as they get more professional and better at their jobs, remain unpopular with the public. Map 7-4 shows the breakdown of full-time, hybrid, and part-time legislatures among the states.

The Citizens' Whipping Boy: Legislators and Public Opinion

Thirty or forty years ago, legislatures were, to put it bluntly, sexist, racist, secretive, boss ruled, malapportioned, and uninformed. Alabama's legislature was an extreme but representative case. In 1971, it ranked fiftieth out of the fifty state legislatures in independence, fiftieth in accountability, and forty-eighth in overall performance in a Ford Foundation study. Yet, just three years earlier, 65 percent of the respondents in a statewide poll had judged the institution favorably. By 1990, the legislature had freed itself of its institutional racism, secrecy, and malapportionment and was fully equipped to gather information and operate in a new state-of-the-art legislative facility. That year it received an approval rating of 24 percent.[56] Remarkably, some legislatures have fallen even further than that in recent years. During a leadership crisis in 2009, just 11 percent of New Yorkers said the state Senate was doing an excellent or good job.[57] The California legislature's approval

MAP 7-4

Full-Time, Hybrid, and Part-Time Legislatures

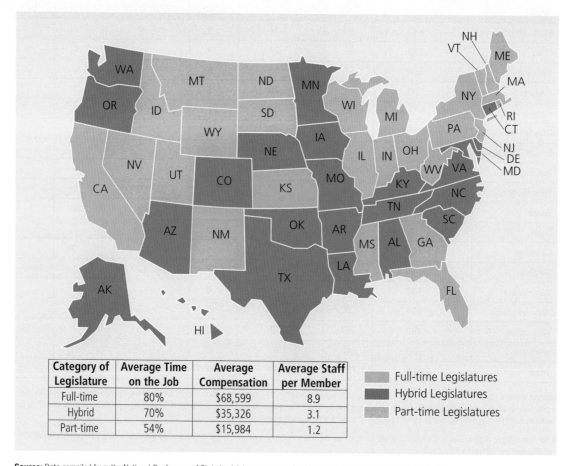

Category of Legislature	Average Time on the Job	Average Compensation	Average Staff per Member
Full-time	80%	$68,599	8.9
Hybrid	70%	$35,326	3.1
Part-time	54%	$15,984	1.2

Full-time Legislatures
Hybrid Legislatures
Part-time Legislatures

Source: Data compiled from the National Conference of State Legislatures, www.ncsl.org/programs/legman/about/partfulllegis.htm.

rating fell to 10 percent in fall 2010 and never exceeded 23 percent from September 2008 to February 2012.[58]

Performance and approval ratings and other information about legislators and what they are up to are out there in the open for all to see. Legislatures are much more transparent institutions than the other branches of government and certainly are more open about what they are doing than are private-sector businesses or unions. This is not to say that many legislative decisions are not still made behind closed doors, but they are acted on out in the open. Interested citizens can find out how their legislators have represented them by paging through their voting records on the web, by reading the newsletters that their representatives and senators

mail to them, and by watching their legislatures in action on video. As of 2012, every state but Rhode Island made their legislatures' proceedings available for audio or video streaming online.[59]

All this transparency and openness—yet legislatures still manage to get a bad rap. It is a curious reality of U.S. political life. State legislatures have, by and large, gotten much better at their jobs. The diversity of their membership has moved steadily toward reflecting the population as a whole. Legislatures have reformed themselves and have become more honest, ethical, and competent in the process. Yet the average person still views them as out-of-control institutions that would do less harm by meeting as little as possible.

> Performance and approval ratings and other information about legislators and what they are up to are out there in the open for all to see. Legislatures are much more transparent institutions than the other branches of government and certainly are more open about what they are doing than are private-sector businesses or unions.

"The legislature is an ideal whipping boy (or girl)," wrote Alan Rosenthal in his book *Engines of Democracy*. It is an institution, after all. Although it is made up of individuals, a legislature as a whole is not a flesh-and-blood person, like a governor. Everyone can easily complain about something the legislature has done recently—including legislators, many of whom campaign by promising to be the ones who will bring sanity and righteousness back to the capitol. Average citizens are disturbed by the influence that interest groups wield, but members of interest groups themselves are often unhappy because things don't always break their way. Finally, as Rosenthal wrote, "people generalize from the worst cases, not the best cases." They do not assume that most legislators are like their own representative or senator, whom they tend to like; rather, they think most are like "the relative few who are convicted or indicted in a court of law, reprimanded by a state ethics commission, or are accused . . . in the media."[60]

By now, however, it should be evident that legislatures, just like books, cannot be judged by the average person's perception of their covers. State legislatures may have become more efficient and effective units of government over the past thirty years, but legislators may have actually become more unpopular than they were a generation ago. The increases in staff, in salaries, and in other professional tools that legislators have acquired in recent decades probably have made them better at their jobs. But as they have become more professional, legislatures also have become larger

targets of disdain for a public that believes it has little or no use for professional or career politicians. Amateur legislatures hold a stronger appeal to deeply rooted American desires for limited government and limited governmental power.

To a large extent, the general public does not view large staffs and good salaries as ways of ensuring that legislators do their jobs in a professional manner. Instead, these increases in legislative resources are seen as yet more proof that politicians want to exploit their offices for personal gain. Rather than reacting strongly to policy issues, the public is quick to anger over such ethical questions as legislative pay raises and other perks for elected officials. "The public does not want the same thing out of a legislature that you think they might want," says John Hibbing, a University of Nebraska political scientist who has written about the unpopularity of legislatures. "The public wants a legislature whose members are not in a position to feather their own nests."[61]

Legislators have done a poor job of selling the idea that what they do is important and necessary in a democracy. "It's our fault" that the legislature is viewed as "dysfunctional," "sheep," and "not independent," says Richard Brodsky, a member of the New York Assembly. "We have never gotten the message out in a coherent way of what we do well and right."[62]

For their part, the media are more concerned with dramatizing conflicts than with explaining what are sometimes awfully dry policy matters; therefore, they have not helped legislators to make their case. A primary job of the media in a democracy is to report on what the government is up to, but less and less media attention is devoted to legislatures. Books about such media failings are even more tiresome, if you can believe it, than books about state and local government—but a few points are worth making here.

First, ever since Watergate, the scandal that forced President Richard Nixon to resign in 1974, the press has taken an adversarial position toward the government. People in government, including legislators, are not very good in the first place at getting out the good news about what they are doing or publicizing their successes. And reporters, who are by their nature skeptics, are good at covering scandals and mistakes. "Skepticism is not just a personality quirk of journalists," says one reporter. "It's a core value, the wellspring of all our best work."[63] The media have made boo-boo coverage practically the mainstay of government reporting. This is not true in 100 percent of cases, of course, but the press's general attitude toward government was summed up well a few years ago by a reporter in Pennsylvania who told a public official, "Your job is to manage the public business and mine is to report when you do it wrong."[64] To be fair, legislators do it wrong a fair amount of the time. Two former speakers of the Pennsylvania House began sharing a jail cell in 2012 after they were convicted in separate corruption scandals. A year doesn't go by without several legislators being charged with crimes. In covering these scandals, though, what the press sometimes loses sight of is that the vast majority of legislators are law-abiding lawmakers who mostly try to do their best.

Reporters may be too cynical about what legislators are up to, but a bigger problem might be that there are so few reporters watching them. An *American Journalism Review* survey in 2009 found that there were only 355 full-time newspaper reporters covering the state capitols—a drop of 32 percent since 2003 and only about one-thirteenth the number of journalists who covered the Super Bowl that year. (Although, given the parlous state of journalism, even the number reporting on that event has come down in recent years.)[65] That is an average of seven reporters per state, but Georgia, for instance, had only five full-time statehouse reporters. The number of capitol reporters in some other states, such as Michigan, had dropped by nearly half in the previous decade or so. Several states had seen formerly competing papers, such as the *St. Petersburg Times* and the *Miami Herald*, combine forces and share reporters and coverage. The numbers are even weaker for television coverage.[66]

Fewer reporters translates into fewer stories about what legislators are doing to earn their taxpayer-financed livings. The more populous states, such as New York and California, still boast relatively sizable, if diminished, capitol press corps, but even in these states the legislatures lose out because their stories get lost in the clutter of other news. The South Dakota legislature, when it is in session, is a major source of news in that underpopulated state, whereas the Illinois General Assembly loses out to coverage of other activities in Chicago and the surrounding area.[67] As a result of diminished coverage, says Gary Moncrief, a political scientist at Boise State University, "I'm not sure the American public is very attuned to the inner workings of legislatures and the fact that they probably do work better today than thirty or forty years ago."[68]

Some of the slack has been taken up by online-only publications, from blogs written by solitary activists or political junkies to nonprofit outlets with something closer to traditional newsrooms and staffs. Many of the nonprofits, such as *MinnPost* and the *Texas Tribune*, have gone quickly from start-ups to leading sources of news for state government officials, lobbyists, and fellow reporters. They've broken big stories, such as California Watch's investigation of the earthquake risk of state schools. As newspapers can attest, however, good statehouse reporting does not guarantee a viable business model. These publications are counting on continued donations, ad revenue,

Many state legislators attempt to keep their constituents informed about their doings through social media. On his blog, Alabama Republican Sen. Bill Holtzclaw runs through his day, describing meetings and including links to legislation occupying his time.

Policy in Practice

Outwit, Outlast, Outplay: Who Really Got the Best Deal with Term Limits?

The biggest change to hit state legislatures over the past quarter century has been the advent of term limits. In the fifteen states with term limit laws—which were almost all approved through ballot initiatives by voters sick of career politicians—legislators are limited to serving no more than six, eight, or twelve years in either the house or the senate. Although that may sound like a long time, it turns out not to be enough for most legislators to master all the complexities of understanding and formulating a wide range of policy.

Term limits have failed the public's goal of bringing in more "citizen legislators." Instead, legislators are constantly seeking their next political jobs rather than carving out decades-long careers in one chamber. Term limits also have failed to bring the anticipated and hoped-for substantial numbers of women and minorities into the legislative ranks. The total number of women legislators is up nationwide, but their ranks have actually been slower to grow in states that impose term limits.[a]

But if they haven't fulfilled all their promises, term limits have not been quite the disaster their opponents predicted either. One of the most common predictions—that with members serving so briefly, lobbyists hoarding institutional and policy knowledge would accrue all the power—appears to have missed the mark. Term limits pretty much have been a mixed bag for lobbyists, who must introduce themselves to a new, skeptical set of legislators every couple of years rather than relying on cozy relations with a few key committee chairs. "I don't know one lobbyist who thinks it's a good thing," said Rick Farmer, who wrote about term limits as an academic before going to work for the Oklahoma House. "If term limits are such a good thing for lobbyists, why do so many lobbyists hate them?"

It does seem clear, however, that legislators in term-limited states have lost power to the executive branch—the governors and their staff who actually know how to operate the machinery of government. "Agency heads can outwit and outlast anyone and everyone on the playing field and they have consolidated their power," said one southern legislator-turned-lobbyist.

Academic studies in term limit states, including California, Colorado, and Maine, have found that legislators make far fewer changes to governors' budgets than they used to, representing many billions of dollars in legislative discretion that is no longer exercised. "The crumbling of legislative power is clear across states," said Thad Kousser, a political scientist at the University of California, San Diego, and author of a book about term limits. "There's no more clear finding in the research than a shift in power where the legislature is becoming a less than equal branch of government."

For all that, it's become common to hear governors and other executive branch officials complain about term limits because the laws mean they lack negotiating partners whose knowledge and expertise they can count on. It seems that no one who works in a state capitol—or in the law and lobbying shops that surround any capitol—likes term limits.

But there is one group that still finds them attractive—the voting public. Polls suggest that as much as 75 percent of the public favors them. "With new people in office, you have people with real world experience," says Stacie Rumenap, president of U.S. Term Limits, a group that advocates limits. "Under term limits, you might have a schoolteacher sitting on the education committee."[b]

That sort of suggestion is often made about term limits—you get rid of the professional politicians and get people who know what the real problems are because they themselves are real. And while Idaho and Utah have repealed their limits, efforts to extend terms or weaken term limits have been rejected several times since 2002 by voters in Arkansas, Maine, California, Florida, Montana, and South Dakota. California voters did relax the state's term limits slightly in 2012.

The main effects of term limits, after all, are procedural. It's difficult to make a convincing case that term limits have made any one particular policy worse, let alone imperiled the quality of life in any state that observes them. The underlying complaint of term limits opponents, that they make legislators less powerful, is one reason many people supported them to begin with.

Source: Adapted from Alan Greenblatt, "The Truth about Term Limits," *Governing,* January 2006, 24.

[a]Peter Slevin, "After Adopting Term Limits, States Lose Female Legislators," *Washington Post,* April 22, 2007, A4.

[b]Interview with Stacie Rumenap, October 4, 2002.

and other more unconventional sources of funding to survive. "There's no question in my mind that with the right team of journalists and leadership, you can do consistent and high-quality journalism," says Robert Rosenthal, a former *New York Times* reporter and *Philadelphia Inquirer* editor who is now executive director of California's Center for Investigative Reporting. "How you keep that going financially, though, is still a huge question mark."[69]

While fewer reporters are covering statehouses, legislators have found ways to cut out the middleman. Through social media sites such as Facebook, YouTube, and Twitter, legislators are able to communicate directly with their constituents and the wider world more easily than ever before. In a typical example, New Jersey senator Jim Whelan held a town hall meeting in July 2012 during which he answered questions from a radio host on the Senate Democrats' Ustream channel while simultaneously accepting tweeted questions from the public via his own Twitter feed. Afterward, the chat was posted on the Democrats' Ustream channel, their YouTube page, and Whelan's own YouTube page.[70]

Twitter has had a particularly profound effect on state capitols, allowing breaking news, policy arguments, and snarky comments to spread instantaneously. The direct interactions with the public that Twitter makes possible, however, have been a mixed blessing for legislators. Feuds that once would have been private—or wouldn't have had a venue in which to happen at all—are now public. For example, after New York Senate majority leader Dean Skelos criticized actor Alec Baldwin for supporting an income tax increase on the wealthy, the *30 Rock* star fired back on Twitter. "His partisanship doesn't bother me," Baldwin tweeted, using hashtags such as #noonelieslikedeanskelos. "It's that he's so dumb." Skelos didn't back down from the fight, tweeting back, "Hypocritical @AlecBaldwin rages against corporate greed yet is a paid spokesperson for corporate giant (Capital One Bank)."[71]

Many political figures have learned the hard way that some inside knowledge and some thoughts are best left untweeted. In 2009, when Democrats held an edge of only two seats in the Virginia Senate (twenty-one to the Republicans' nineteen), Republicans nearly persuaded one Democratic senator, Ralph Northam, to leave his party's caucus. If Northam had switched sides, the Democrats' majority would have been gone. But before the move was a done deal, Jeff Frederick, the chairman of the Virginia Republican Party, tweeted, "Big news coming out of Senate: apparently one dem is either switching or leaving the dem caucus. Negotiations for power sharing underway." Democrats sprang into action, calling in Governor Tim Kaine to help persuade Northam to stick with the party. Ultimately, Northam agreed to stay with the Democrats. Some observers believed it was Frederick's premature tweet that alerted the Democrats and prevented them from closing the deal.[72] A couple of months later, Frederick was removed as party chairman.

The decline of general coverage and the rise of often partisan commentary and news sites on the web are among the reasons that amateur legislatures are much more popular with their constituents than are more professional chambers. The urge to return legislatures to their more humble but lovable position as citizen institutions has been the main driver behind the term limits movement. Limits on the number of terms an individual may serve in the house or senate have been approved in most of the states that allow ballot initiatives. As of 2009, there were fifteen states with term limits. The limits range from a low of six years of service per legislative chamber in states such as Arkansas and Michigan to twelve years of service in Nevada, Oklahoma, and Louisiana.

Term limits are especially strict in states where the public thinks there has not been enough turnover in the legislature. "The lower the existing turnover rate in the legislature," a pair of political scientists concluded in 1996, "the harsher the term limits they tend to adopt."[73] In California, for example, Assemblyman Willie Brown became the poster child for a term limits initiative because of his fourteen years as Assembly speaker. In 1990, California voters sent a strong message. When they limited terms, they also cut the legislature's budget and staffing levels by 40 percent—the third cut in six years. The same year, Colorado voters imposed eight-year term limits on legislators and limited sessions to no more than 120 days a year.

In keeping with the public disdain for professional or full-time legislatures, policy competence in legislators is often viewed as a negative. The idea is that if they are too distracted by details and special interest wishes, they will never shut up and actually do something to serve the common good.[74] Political nominees are eager to appeal to this public sentiment. "I just want to get things done," one candidate said in 2002 in a typical statement. "Hewing to the party line—any party's line—does not interest me."[75]

The American electorate clearly remains divided, and even in states in which one party is clearly dominant there still can be plenty of disagreement. To cite one example, although the GOP controlled both of Kansas's legislative chambers in 2012, relations deteriorated so far between the conservative House and the more moderate Senate—the sides disagreed on tax cuts and a host of social issues—that one House Republican tried to secretly record a conversation with a Senate colleague about contentious healthcare changes.[76] The Senate moderates were routed by conservatives in Republican primaries that year, and many of the challengers were House members.

If there is no agreement in your dorm room about whether to get pepperoni on the pizza or leave it off, why should anyone in a society as diverse as ours expect easy agreement among legislators about tax rates, budgets, healthcare, guns, or the environment? Legislators simply reflect the messiness of public opinion. No matter which way they decide an issue—even if it is only to decide to maintain the law as it stands—they are bound to make some people angry. People prefer decisions to be neat and simple and harmonious. Maybe that is why no one likes legislatures.

Conclusion

Legislatures have one of the toughest jobs in the political system. It's hard enough trying to get a group of friends to agree on pizza toppings. Imagine trying to get a hundred or more people—many of whom flat-out oppose your preferred choice—to sign off on something as controversial as, say, a welfare bill. Now imagine trying to do that over and over again—researching; negotiating; meeting; balancing partisan interests, special interests, and constituent interests; and, finally, hammering out an agreement that no one is fully satisfied with and everyone is willing to criticize. That gives you some idea of the reality of a legislator's job.

Historically speaking, legislators today do their jobs more effectively and more fairly than at any previous time. For this achievement, they are mistrusted and disliked. Why? Ultimately, this is perhaps because a legislature can never give all the people everything they want. Democracy is simply not set up to do this because people want very different things. Legislatures do not really create conflict; they simply reflect the disagreements that exist in the electorate. Or at least they do if the legislators are reasonably effective at representing the preferences of their constituencies. What democracy promises, and what state legislatures largely deliver, is not what everyone wants—on most issues no such option exists—but reasonable compromises that most people can live with. Like a group with differing tastes in pizza, legislatures are successful when they can agree on second best.

The Latest Research

This chapter has noted at various points the impact of term limits, which constitute arguably the biggest institutional reform of state legislatures in the past quarter century. As discussed in some detail above, roughly one-third of all states limit in some fashion how long state legislators can serve. Although term limits are popular with the public, academic analyses give them a much more mixed review.

The impacts of term limits are still not fully understood. Only a limited number of election cycles have occurred in which term limits have forced big turnovers in legislative membership, and the impact of filling statehouses with rookies can take some time to assess. Still, term limits provide a golden opportunity for researchers to put the comparative method into action. We now have states that have term limits and states that do not. Is this a difference that makes a difference, and, if so, a difference in what? Below we summarize some of the latest research seeking answers to this question. As you will see, those answers are not what term limit advocates or opponents expected.

• •

- **Cummins, Jeff.** 2012. "The Effects of Legislative Term Limits on State Fiscal Conditions." *American Politics Research* 20: 1–26.

One of the themes running throughout this entire book, not just this chapter, is how battered state finances continue to be a major influence on policy and politics. This study analyzes state budgets between 1983 and 2008 and finds that as legislative turnover increases, budgets are more likely to head toward the red. This happens for several reasons. More experienced legislators may be better equipped to handle fiscal crises, in the same fashion that a veteran pilot is better prepared for in-air emergencies. Legislators who have short time horizons are less likely to take into account the long-term implications of policy. The findings of this study have particular resonance given that term limits were increasing legislative turnover during and after the Great Recession.

- **Susan Miller, Jill Nicholson-Crotty, and Sean Nicholson-Crotty.** 2011. "Reexamining the Institutional Effects of Term Limits in U.S. State Legislatures." *Legislative Studies Quarterly* 36: 71–97.

By now a number of studies have documented that term limits tend to pull power away from legislatures and toward other political actors, such as governors and interest groups. Based on an extensive series of statistical analyses, this study provides a more nuanced picture of these shifts in power. It turns out that a governor or interest groups do not automatically gain more influence once a legislature is term limited. The legislature's decrease in power is contingent on a number of factors. Upper chambers (state senates), for example, tend not

to lose much at all. As legislatures and legislative leaders tend to have different levels of influence in different states, term limits might leave a legislature less powerful than it was—but still more powerful than its counterparts in other states.

- **Masket, Seth, and Jeffrey Lewis.** 2007. "A Return to Normalcy? Revisiting the Effects of Term Limits on Competitiveness and Spending in California Assembly Elections." *State Politics & Policy Quarterly* 7: 20–38.

Some of the positive impacts uncovered by some early studies of term limits were that they led to more electoral competition and drove down campaign spending. This study reassesses these findings to see if they hold up over time. The research focuses on differences in elections for the California Assembly between the periods 1976–1990 (before term limits) and 1992–2004 (after term limits). The findings suggest that the impact of term limits over time is fairly insignificant. In the term limits era, incumbents were more likely to be involved in close races but were slightly less likely to lose them. In other words, term limits have not done much to reduce the electoral advantage of incumbents. Campaign spending is as high in the term limits era as it was in the pre–term limits era. In short, the positive effects of term limits found by earlier studies, at least in California, are found to be fairly short lived.

- **Wright, Gerald.** 2007. "Do Term Limits Affect Legislative Roll Call Voting? Representation, Polarization, and Participation." *State Politics & Policy Quarterly* 7: 256–280.

One of the more startling findings of early research on the impact of term limits was that term-limited legislators became less representative of their constituents. This raised worries that term limits might cut the electoral connection—in other words, result in a reduction in legislator concern about constituent interests. After all, why worry about representing the interests of your district if you are going to be booted from office regardless of how good a job you do? Wright's findings suggest that some of those concerns were exaggerated. This comparative study of roll-call voting in state legislatures finds that term-limited legislators are just as representative as legislators who are not term limited.

7

Chapter Review

Key Concepts

- apportionment (p. 191)
- casework (p. 184)
- caucus (p. 186)
- coalition building (p. 176)
- committee (p. 177)
- compromise (p. 177)
- constituent service (p. 184)
- constituents (p. 177)
- delegates (p. 190)
- district (p. 177)
- filibuster (p. 176)
- gerrymanders (p. 192)
- incumbent (p. 184)
- logrolling (p. 176)
- majority-minority district (p. 193)
- majority rule (p. 176)
- malapportionment (p. 192)
- oversight (p. 185)
- professionalization (p. 191)
- rank-and-file members (p. 189)
- representation (p. 180)
- rider (p. 176)
- trustees (p. 190)

Suggested Websites

- **http://ncsl.typepad.com/the_thicket.** The National Conference of State Legislatures website offers coverage of state issues in its blog The Thicket.
- **http://stateline.org.** A foundation-sponsored news service that provides daily news about state government.
- **www.alec.org.** Website for the American Legislative Exchange Council, an influential conservative organization that drafts model legislation. Both legislators and private-sector interests are members.

- **www.csg.org.** Website for the Council of State Governments, which provides training and information to state government officials.

- **www.ncsl.org.** Website of the National Conference of State Legislatures; provides a wealth of information about legislative structures and procedures as well as the major issues faced by legislators.

State Stats on Legislatures

Explore and compare data on the states! Go to **college.cqpress.com/sites/essentials-govstateandlocal** to do these exercises.

1. According to the ballots, in 2010, 54.3 percent of the eligible population turned out to vote in Washington state. What percentage of the eligible population *reported* voting? Why might there be a discrepancy here?

2. In 2012, the Virginia legislature was late in passing its state budget. What was its budget in 2010? Was this higher or lower than the national average? What is the problem with comparing the total budget amounts between states?

3. Utah has a very Republican state legislature, while Vermont has a very Democratic one. What is the difference in the state and local tax burden of these states? How might the partisan makeup of the state legislatures influence this?

4. State legislatures determine most of the budgetary allocations in their states, including spending on health programs like Medicaid. Which state spends the largest percentage of its budget on healthcare? Which spends the least? What might account for the differences?

5. How has the crime rate in your state changed since 2000? Is this what you expected? Why or why not?

Louisiana governor Bobby Jindal used his executive power to order major spending cuts in the summer of 2012 to deal with the state's large budget shortfall. Although Louisiana's part-time legislators had gone home for the year, many objected to being cut out of the process, but they were wary of crossing the governor, who has the power to appoint top legislative leaders.

ch.

8

The Executive Branch and Bureaucracy

HOW GOVERNMENTS OPERATE AND WHO'S IN CHARGE

- How did governors get to be such powerful players, when for much of American history their offices were weak?

- Why do some states still give their governors more pomp than power?

- Why do we have so much bureaucracy?

Bobby Jindal, the Republican governor of Louisiana, faced a big budget shortfall in the summer of 2012. The state's part-time legislature had gone home for the year, so Jindal decided to take care of the problem himself. He ordered nearly $1 billion in spending cuts, slashing some programs by 34.5 percent (reductions of 35 percent or more would have required legislative approval). He shut down major state-run facilities, including a prison and a mental hospital, in some cases giving local legislators less than an hour's notice before publicly announcing the shutdowns.

Needless to say, many legislators were unhappy. Some called for a special session to address the cuts. "I think legislators ought to be involved," said Dee Richard, a state representative. "Most of the cuts might be right, but we have no input."[1] Richard gained no traction with his call to bring the legislature back into session, however. Not only is Louisiana's legislature dominated by Republicans largely sympathetic to Jindal's desires, but the governor in that state gets to appoint top legislative leaders, including the House speaker and committee chairs. Legislators in Louisiana think carefully before crossing the governor. Even in states where the governors hold fewer cards than Jindal, legislators hesitate to go up against them. "If you're a legislator and you look at the governor, he's calling the shots, whoever he is," Rutgers University political scientist Alan Rosenthal said—at the annual meeting of the National Conference of State Legislatures, no less.[2]

Governors are the prime political actors in virtually all states. The governor sets the agenda, largely determining which policy issues will be pursued and how the state budget will look. Governors are unique among state-level politicians in terms of the media attention they can attract. This helps them promote their causes, but they must rely on other institutional players if they are going to accomplish more than making speeches.

Recently, governors have also become a lot better equipped to control the rest of the executive branch, and they are running states in fact as well as in theory. Throughout the last decades of the twentieth century, governors were given more and more formal control over the machinery of government at the same time that the federal government was shifting greater control of many programs,

> Governors are like mini-presidents in their states. Like the president, the governor commands the lion's share of political attention in a state, is generally seen as setting the agenda for the legislative branch, and is basically the lead political actor—the figure most likely to appear on television on a regular basis. Also like the president, the governor tends to receive the blame or enjoy the credit for the performance of the economy.

including welfare, to the states. Governors are now, with few exceptions, not just the most famous politicians in their states but also the most powerful. "The weakest governor has a built-in advantage over the strongest legislature," said Rosenthal, the late author of a recent book on governors titled *The Best Job in Politics.*[3]

Governors are like mini-presidents in their states. Like the president, the governor commands the lion's share of political attention in a state, is generally seen as setting the agenda for the legislative branch, and is basically the lead political actor—the figure most likely to appear on television on a regular basis. Also like the president, the governor tends to receive the blame or enjoy the credit for the performance of the economy.

And, again like the president, the governor shares responsibility for running the government—implementing laws, issuing regulations, and building the roads, maintaining the parks, and performing other public functions—with the help of a cabinet. Presidents appoint their cabinet officials to run the Departments of Defense and Agriculture and the like. Governors have help in running state-level departments of agriculture, finance, environmental protection, and so on. In most cases, the governor appoints officials to head these departments, but some other statewide officials, such as attorneys general, are often elected on their own and may even represent another party. We explore the roles of these other executive branch officials later in this chapter. We will also examine the agencies and departments, known as the bureaucracy, that carry out the work of governments.

The Job of Governor

Following the American Revolution, governors had very little power for one simple reason—distrust. Colonial governors, appointed by the British, had imposed unpopular taxes and exploited their positions to make themselves rich. Americans did not want to invest too much power in individuals who might turn into mini-dictators. There was no national president, after all, under the original Articles of Confederation. In the states, most of the power was disbursed among many individuals holding office in legislatures and on state boards and commissions. Governors in all but three of the original states were limited to one-year terms. While in office, they were not given control over state departments and agencies. Separately elected individuals, boards, or commissions ran these instead. After the North Carolina constitutional convention, one delegate said that the governor had been given just enough power "to sign the receipt for his salary."[4]

The number of agencies grew as government became more complex, and lack of central control over these agencies meant that states had difficulty functioning coherently. Governors were at the top of the political pyramid but lacked the authority to control and lead the executive branch in ways that the public expected of them, a problem that persisted well into the twentieth century. In recent decades, governors have been granted greater powers, including much more power over appointments than they once had. This means that they are able to put their own teams in place to carry out their policies.

Terry Sanford, a former governor of North Carolina, sums up the job of the contemporary governor well:

The governor by his very office embodies his state. He must . . . energize his administration, search out the experts, formulate the programs, mobilize the support, and carry new ideas into action. . . . Few major undertakings ever get off the ground without his support and leadership. The governor sets the agenda for public debate; frames the issues; decides on the timing; and can blanket the state with good ideas by using his access to the mass media. . . . The governor is the most potent political power in the state.[5]

Chief Legislator

Just as the president does not serve in Congress, governors do not sit as members of state legislatures. Like the president, however, they have enormous influence over the work legislatures do. Governors outline their broad proposals in inaugural and annual State of the State addresses. They and their staffs then work with individual legislators and committees to translate these proposals into bills.

Governors never get everything they want from state legislatures, but they do have a great deal of impact on which bills become laws. Legislators can get around a **veto**, or gubernatorial rejection of a bill, but that often means that they have to pass the bill again by a **supermajority vote**. Supermajority votes are usually votes of two-thirds or more. That means a governor needs the support of only one-third plus one vote in either chamber to sustain a veto. If you can only rarely pass a law without the governor's approval, it stands to reason that you will want to work with him or her to create a version of the bill that will win such approval.

Another factor that makes governors enormously influential in the legislative process is their command of state budgets. In nearly every state, the

Veto
The power to reject a proposed law.

Supermajority Vote
A legislative vote of much more than a simple majority, for instance, a vote by two-thirds of a legislative chamber to override a governor's veto.

main responsibility for creating a state budget rests in the office of the governor. The governor proposes a budget that details the amounts of money that will go to every state agency, welfare program, highway department, and school district. There are often restrictions on how a state must spend much of its money from year to year, whether because of old laws or federal requirements. But the governor gets first crack at deciding how most of the state's money is going to be spent. "As far as legislators are concerned," one political scientist writes, "the ability to create the budget is so powerful that it becomes *the* major tool for a governor in achieving his legislative programs."[6]

While the legislature might set the overall dollar amount that goes to the transportation department, the governor might get to decide, for instance, whether bridges are going to be built in particular districts. To get those bridges—or any other goodies they might want—legislators often have to give the governor what he or she wants in terms of passing major initiatives. "Any legislator who says he needs nothing from the governor's office is either lying or stupid," according to one observer of the Alabama political scene.[7]

Head of State Agencies

Governors at one time had very little control over who ran their states' departments. This meant that people with other agendas could set policy on taxes or healthcare or other issues. Only about half of the governors chose their own cabinet officials in 1969, but nearly all of them do today.[8] The power to appoint people to run state departments offers obvious benefits for governors. They can pick their own people, who they know will pursue their policy preferences. If those people fail, they can be fired.

Chief Spokesperson for the State

Mississippi governor Haley Barbour was the first to credit the countless government workers who helped southern Mississippi cope with Hurricane Katrina, which devastated the Gulf Coast in 2005. But a major crisis such as Katrina also demands a strong leader who can communicate calm to the public and provide "a central decision-making point for when things get balled up or go sideways, which they do," as Barbour says.

A governor acts as the chief spokesperson and the public face of state government in good times as well as bad. Governors regularly send out press releases about their role in helping to land new jobs and companies through tax incentives, the creation of cooperative business ventures, and other economic development activities. The day after his election in 2002, New Mexico governor Bill Richardson got on a plane to talk to executives in California's Silicon Valley in the hope of persuading them to set up operations in New Mexico. Once in office, Richardson proudly boasted that he calls CEOs on a daily basis and "sucks up to them big time."[9]

Governors are also important lobbyists in Washington, seeking more federal money for their states. They are just about the only people who lobby in the nation's capital who can be sure that members of Congress and cabinet officials will meet with them directly rather than having them meet with staff.

Party Chief

Governors are also the leading figures in their parties within their states. U.S. senators arguably might be more influential figures, but governors are more important politically at home. Governors command more foot soldiers. A governor may be able to call on thousands of state workers, whereas a senator's staff numbers in the dozens at most. Not all of a governor's workers are loyal members of the same party—in fact, governors appoint far fewer state employees than they did some decades ago. Governors, however, have more people whose jobs depend on them than do any other elected officials.

Governors often pick state party chairs of their liking. They help to recruit and raise money for candidates for other statewide offices and the legislature. They use the media attention they attract to campaign for those they support. They are still the titular heads of their parties in their states, and no modern politician (who isn't already rich) can avoid the duties of raising campaign contributions.

Commander in Chief of the National Guard

Even in this country's earliest days, when governors had few powers, each governor's military position was strong, "with all states designating him as commander-in-chief."[10] The National Guard in each state is a state agency—governors can and do call out these units to respond to natural disasters or civil unrest—but the president has the power to federalize it, calling up units to perform federal service. That happened in the civil rights era, when the Guard was ordered to work for the feds against southern governors who were resisting integration. Those serving in today's National Guard are more likely to fight alongside federal soldiers in such places as Iraq.

The Powers of Governors

Anyone who follows sports understands that natural ability does not necessarily translate into success. Some players look great on paper—they're strong, fast, and possess the skills that should help them dominate their sport. But, for whatever reason, these players sometimes are shown up by less talented athletes who have a greater understanding of the game, work harder, or simply find a way to win. It is the same with governors. Some look incredibly strong on paper and their states' constitutions give them powers that their neighbors can only envy. Yet sometimes they simply cannot translate those assets into political success. Conversely, states in which the governor's **formal powers** are weak may sometimes

have individuals in that office who completely dominate their states' politics. They are able to exploit the **informal powers** of their office—that is, they manage to create personal powers as opposed to relying on relatively weak institutional powers.

Formal Powers

Most governors have a wide variety of formal powers granted to them by state constitutions or other laws. Among the most important of these are the power to appoint officials to run state agencies, the power to veto legislation, the power to craft budgets, the power to grant pardons, and the power to call legislatures into session.

The Power to Appoint. The first governors lacked **appointment powers**. They could not pick their own people to run state agencies, which made those agencies more independent. Nowadays, governors can pick their own teams, giving them greater authority to set policy. When John Engler served as governor of Michigan during the 1990s, for example, he put in place a series of appointees with a strong ideological commitment to limited government. These appointees helped him carry out his desire to shrink the state's government. Engler's contemporary, Ann Richards of Texas, set out to change the face of state government by changing the faces of the people within it, appointing women, African Americans, and Hispanics to replace the white men who had always run things in Austin.

Governors get to appoint dozens and sometimes thousands of people to full-time government jobs and to commissions and boards. For instance, if you are attending a public college,

More than 2,100 National Guard troops were called on to support relief efforts in New Jersey after Superstorm Sandy ravaged the state's coastline in 2012.

Informal Powers
The things a governor is able to do, such as command media attention and persuade party members, based on personality or position, not on formal authority.

Appointment Powers
A governor's ability to pick individuals to run the state government, such as cabinet secretaries.

Formal Powers
The powers explicitly granted to a governor according to state law, such as being able to veto legislation and to appoint heads of state agencies.

Texas governor Rick Perry (left) is introduced by Texas lieutenant governor David Dewhurst. Although technically the second-ranking executive in the Texas state government, Dewhurst actually may wield more power than the governor, who has very few formal powers. The lieutenant governor presides over the state Senate, sets the agenda, and appoints senators to the committees. This makes Dewhurst the executive with the most direct influence over the Texas legislature.

The Power to Veto.

Every governor has the power to veto legislation (North Carolina's governor was the last to win this power, in 1997). Legislators can override vetoes, but that rarely happens because of supermajority vote requirements. Members of the governor's own party are usually reluctant to vote to override a veto. This means that if the governor's party holds just one-third of the seats in a legislative chamber, plus one, a veto is likely to be sustained—meaning the governor wins.

Still, legislatures sometimes pass a bill just to get it vetoed, to make the governor's opposition official and public. That happened often when Gary Johnson was governor of New Mexico during the 1990s. "During his eight years as New Mexico's governor, Gary Johnson competed in the Ironman Triathlon World Championship, won the America's Challenge Gas Balloon Race, played guitar with Van Halen's Sammy Hagar, and helped save a house when massive wildfires struck Los Alamos," political scientists Thad Kousser and Justin H. Phillips write in their 2012 book *The Power of American Governors*.[11] Yet, they note, he never succeeded in persuading legislators to enact items on his legislative agenda.

All but six governors—those in Indiana, Nevada, New Hampshire, North Carolina, Rhode Island, and Vermont—have a power known as the line-item veto; that is, they can reject just a portion of a bill. If there is a bill funding education, for example, the governor can accept all of it except for an increase in funding for a school in the district of a legislator who is a political enemy. The governor's ability to cut legislators' pet projects out of the budget forces most of them to support that governor's major initiatives. Congress tried to give the

chances are that the governor appointed the board of governors of your school or university system. These are considered plum jobs, and giving them out is a way for a governor not only to influence policy but also to reward campaign contributors and other political allies.

The Power to Prepare State Budgets.

The most powerful tool governors have may be their ability to shape their states' budgets. In most states, agencies and departments submit their budget proposals to a central budget office that works as part of the governor's team. The governor's ability to deny them funds or shift money among departments helps make sure that agencies remain focused, at least to some extent, on the governor's priorities.

A governor can use the budget process to override old agency decisions, for example, to make sure that the transportation department fully funds bike trails that previously have been ignored. Even when an agency has some independence about how it spends its money, a governor can persuade officials to fund other priorities—such as a new law school at a state university—by threatening to withhold some percentage of their agency's overall budget.

president line-item veto authority, but the U.S. Supreme Court ruled the practice unconstitutional in 1998.

Some governors can strike not only projects from bills, but individual words and letters as well. Wisconsin Republican Tommy Thompson became notorious for vetoing just enough letters in a bill's wording to alter the meaning of the bill when he was governor in the 1990s. The courts upheld his right to do so, but that power was soon curbed. Nevertheless, in 2005, Jim Doyle, the state's Democratic governor, was able to strike 752 words from a budget bill in order to cobble together a new twenty-word sentence that shifted $427 million from transportation to education.[12]

The Power to Grant Pardons. Governors, like the president, can forgive crimes or commute (change) sentences if they feel that particular persons have been convicted unfairly. They sometimes act on the recommendations of pardon boards, but the decision to pardon is theirs alone and not reversible.

A famous example of the use of pardon power happened in Illinois in 2003. During his last week in office, Governor George Ryan pardoned four prisoners condemned to death and commuted the sentences of the other 167 death-row prisoners to life in prison. Ryan had grown concerned that the number of capital cases that were being overturned because of new evidence, such as DNA lab work, indicated that the death penalty was being unfairly and inequitably applied. He appointed a commission to study the application of the death sentence and became convinced that the state could not impose the death penalty with such absolute certainty that innocent people would not be put to death. The move gained Ryan international celebrity among death penalty opponents but was criticized by prosecutors and others at home.

Not all governors use their pardon powers in such a high-minded way. In Tennessee in 1979, Lamar Alexander was sworn in as governor three days early to prevent outgoing governor Ray Blanton from commuting the sentences of any more prisoners. Blanton already had granted fifty-two last-minute pardons, and the Federal Bureau of Investigation (FBI) had arrested members of his staff for extorting money to sell pardons, paroles, and commutations. More recently,

outgoing governor Haley Barbour of Mississippi drew national condemnation by pardoning some two hundred people during his final days in office in 2012, including five who were still in prison and five others who had worked in the governor's mansion. Despite a challenge from Mississippi's attorney general, the state Supreme Court quickly ruled that Barbour's actions had been perfectly in keeping with his power. In part because they fear political backlash if pardoned criminals should reoffend, the practice of pardoning has become increasingly rare among governors since the 1960s, with some governors currently in office never having pardoned anyone at all.[13]

The Power to Call Special Sessions. Many legislatures meet only part time and have fixed session schedules. Every governor, however, has the power to call legislatures into special session. Nearly half the nation's governors have the ability to set the agenda of a special session. This means that in such a session legislators can deal only with those issues that the governor wants addressed.

Special sessions can be useful for governors who want to deal with particular issues right away. In recent years, many governors have called special sessions when their states' revenues have fallen short so that the legislatures can help them cut spending. Even though governors are able to call legislators into special session, they cannot necessarily make them do anything. In Iowa in 2002, Governor Tom Vilsack called the legislature back into session in the hope that it would increase funding for education and health, but the legislators adjourned after a single day without debating any bill. "We just came in and went home," said House majority leader Christopher Rants. Vilsack then signed a package of budget cuts he had accepted in meetings with legislators and went on to call a second special session later in the month.[14]

Informal Powers

The powers just outlined are spelled out in state constitutions and statutes. Governors either have line-item veto authority or they do not. Much of the outcome of a governor's program, however, depends on the governor's individual ability to wield informal powers—the ability to leverage the power and

TABLE 8-1

The Governors: Powers

State or Other Jurisdiction	Budget-Making Power		Item Veto Power			Item Veto—2/3 Legislators Present or 3/5 Elected to Override	Item Veto—Majority Legislators Elected to Override	Authorization for Reorganization through Executive Order
	Full Responsibility	Shares Responsibility	Governor Has Item Veto Power on All Bills	Governor Has Item Veto Power on Appropriations Only	Governor Has No Item Veto Power			
Alabama	*(a)	...	*	...	...	...	*	...
Alaska	*	...	...	*	...	*	...	*
Arizona	*(a)	...	...	*	...	*	(b)	...
Arkansas	...	*	...	*	...	...	*	*
California	*(a)	...	...	*	...	*	...	*(c)
Colorado	...	*	...	*	...	...	*	*
Connecticut	...	*	...	*	...	*	...	...
Delaware	*(a)	...	*	...	...	*	...	*
Florida	...	*	...	*	...	*	...	*
Georgia	*	...	...	*	...	(b)	...	*
Hawaii	...	*	*	...	...	*	...	*
Idaho	(d)	(d)	...	*	...	*	...	*
Illinois	...	*	*	...	...	*	...	*
Indiana	*	...	...	...	*	...	...	*
Iowa	...	*	...	*	...	*	...	*
Kansas	*	...	...	*	...	*	...	*
Kentucky	*(a)	...	...	*(e)	...	*	*	*
Louisiana	...	*	...	*	...	...	*(f)	*(g)
Maine	...	*	...	*	...	...	*	...
Maryland	*	...	*	...	...	*	...	*
Massachusetts	*	...	*	...	...	...	*(f)	*(c)
Michigan	*(h)	...	...	*(e)	...	...	*(f)	*
Minnesota	...	*	...	*	...	...	*(f)	*(i)
Mississippi	...	*(j)	*	...	...	*	...	*
Missouri	*(a)	...	...	*	...	*	...	*
Montana	*	...	...	*	...	*(k)	...	*(l)
Nebraska	...	*	...	*	...	*(m)	...	...
Nevada	*	...	...	...	*	...	...	...
New Hampshire	*(a)	...	...	...	*	...	...	...
New Jersey	*(a)	...	...	*	...	...	*(f)	*(n)
New Mexico	*	...	...	*	...	*	...	...
New York	...	*	*	...	...	*	...	...
North Carolina	...	*	...	...	*	...	...	*(o)
North Dakota	*	...	...	*	...	*	...	*
Ohio	*	...	...	*	...	*	...	...
Oklahoma	...	*	...	*	...	...	*(f)	...

State or Other Jurisdiction	Budget-Making Power		Item Veto Power					Authorization for Reorganization through Executive Order
	Full Responsibility	Shares Responsibility	Governor Has Item Veto Power on All Bills	Governor Has Item Veto Power on Appropriations Only	Governor Has No Item Veto Power	Item Veto—2/3 Legislators Present or 3/5 Elected to Override	Item Veto—Majority Legislators Elected to Override	
Oregon	...	*	...	*	...	*	...	*
Pennsylvania	*	...	...	*	...	*	...	...
Rhode Island	...	*	...	...	*	...	...	...
South Carolina	...	*	...	*	...	*	...	...
South Dakota	*	...	...	*	...	*(p)	...	*
Tennessee	...	*	...	*	...	...	*	*
Texas	...	*	...	*	...	*	...	...
Utah	...	*	...	*	...	*	...	*
Vermont	*	...	...	...	*	...	...	*
Virginia	*	...	...	*	...	*(p)	...	*
Washington	*	...	*(q)	...	...	*	...	...
West Virginia	*	...	...	*	...	*	...	...
Wisconsin	*(a)	...	...	*(r)	...	*	...	...
Wyoming	...	*	*	...	...	*	...	...
American Samoa	...	*	...	...	...	...	...	*
Guam	*	...	*	...	...	*	...	*
No. Mariana Islands	...	*	...	*	...	*	...	*
Puerto Rico	...	*	...	*	...	*	...	*(s)
U.S. Virgin Islands	*	...	...	*	...	*	...	*

Key:

*   Yes; provision for.

...   No; not applicable.

(a)   Full responsibility to propose; legislature adopts or revises and governor signs or vetoes.

(b)   Two-thirds of members to which each house is entitled required to override veto.

(c)   Authorization for reorganization provided for in state constitution.

(d)   Legislature has full responsibility with regard to setting the state's budget.

(e)   Governor may veto any distinct item or items appropriating money in any appropriations bill.

(f)   Two-thirds of elected legislators of each house required to override.

(g)   Only for agencies and offices within the governor's office.

(h)   Governor has sole authority to propose annual budget. No money may be paid out of state treasury except in pursuance of appropriations made by law.

(i)   Statute provides for reorganization by the commissioner of administration with the approval of the governor.

(j)   Governor has the responsibility of presenting a balanced budget. The budget is based on revenue estimated by the governor's office and the Legislative Budget Committee.

(k)   If the legislature is not in session when the governor vetoes a bill, the secretary of state must poll the legislature as to the question of an override, but only if the bill had passed by a vote of two-thirds of the members present.

(l)   The office of the governor shall continuously study and evaluate the organizational structure, management practices, and functions of the executive branch and each agency. The governor shall, by executive order or other means within his authority, take action to improve the manageability of the executive branch. The governor may not, however, create an agency of state government by administrative action, except that the governor may establish advisory councils and must approve the internal organizational structures of departments.

(m)   Three-fifths majority required to override line-item veto.

(n)   Executive reorganization plans can be disapproved by majority vote in both houses of the legislature.

(o)   Executive order must be approved by the legislature if changes affect existing law.

(p)   Two-thirds of legislators present required to override.

(q)   Governor has veto power of selections for nonappropriations and item veto in appropriations.

(r)   In Wisconsin, governor has "partial" veto over appropriation bills. The partial veto is broader than the item veto.

(s)   Only if it is not prohibited by law.

Source: The Council of State Governments' survey of governor's offices, December 2011. Reprinted with permission of The Knowledge Center, Council of State Governments.

FIGURE 8-1

HOW IT WORKS

Merging Formal and Informal Gubernatorial Powers: Florida's Governor Crist Takes on Category 5 Insurance Problems

As powerful as they are, there are some things governors may not be able to control. The weather is one. The insurance industry may be another. Florida's Republican governor Charlie Crist tackled both in his first term as he worked behind the scenes and in front of the cameras to pass legislation to stem rising insurance costs in the state.

THE PROBLEM. The disastrous 2004 and 2005 hurricane seasons left many of Florida's homeowners with more than just flattened roofs: it landed them with crushing insurance bills. The cost of insuring a home more than doubled in 2006, and many residents considered leaving the state altogether. Joining a chorus of voices advocating for a host of insurance reforms, Governor Crist urged Floridians to stay put and promised to work with lawmakers to help bring down insurance rates.

That's no small feat. Insuring property in a state that saw nearly $36 billion in storm damages in one year alone is an expensive business—and regulating that industry is the state's responsibility. Even the industry's harshest critics understand that the premiums homeowners pay on a regular basis to insure their homes must keep pace with the amounts that agencies anticipate will be paid out in future claims. That's basic math. But, critics say, insurers' profits have soared in recent years. Some agencies have adopted such misleading or unfair practices as creating differently named subsidiary companies that offer different rates than their parent agencies. Others offer restricted insurance plans to Floridians (for example, they offer auto but not homeowners insurance). Still others refused to offer policies in that state, leaving many without coverage.

In their wake stands Citizens Property Insurance, a state-run agency created in 2002 by the Florida legislature as an insurance "safety net." Under its original rules, homeowners were allowed to switch to Citizens only if they had been denied coverage by a national company or if their premiums were quoted at more than 25 percent higher than Citizens's rates. By 2006, however, Citizens was set to become the insurer for more than half of all of Florida's homeowners—about 1.3 million policyholders—making it the state's largest insurance company rather than the agency of last resort.

With so many homeowners forced to pay exorbitant rates or cut loose from national policies altogether and Citizens stepping in to fill the gap, Governor Crist and Florida's lawmakers were made to reconsider the role that Citizens should (or could) play in wholesale insurance reform.

THE PROCESS. In January 2007 Crist called a weeklong special legislative session to try to hammer out a plan. Crist himself brought several aggressive measures to the table, including recommendations to lower threshold requirements for homeowners to get coverage through Citizens, to cap the agency's ability to raise rates, and to crack down on subsidiaries. He also asked for the power to appoint the company's director. But the hallmark of his plan was to make Citizens more competitive with private insurers. After the special session, the legislature continued the reform debate during its regular session.

Early predictions of Crist's likelihood of success were not good. The insurance lobby came on strong, as did a handful of legislators from his own party, who warned the public that increasing the role of the state-sponsored Citizens was tantamount to socialism and potentially could bankrupt the state. But having once been a state legislator himself, Crist knew how to work the ropes. His main advantage was his stratospheric popularity: he had plenty of political capital, and he wasn't shy about spending it.

To promote his plan, Crist put in rare appearances before several House and Senate committees and stumped to persuade homeowners that the promised rate relief wasn't an illusion. He also traveled to Washington, D.C., to help Florida lawmakers appeal for a national disaster relief fund to help defray costs to that state's homeowners.

Crist and his staff continued to work behind the scenes, too, with the governor's staff "buttonholing" legislators. State senator J. D. Alexander reported that "there had been some political arm-twisting," adding, "You don't go against a governor with a 77-percent approval rating." [a]

Both the House and Senate took up bills that included a number of Crist's original proposals; by the end of their regular session, they'd reached resolutions.

THE OUTCOMES. Crist got a lot of what he wanted. Legislators agreed to freeze Citizens's rates at 2006 levels through 2009. Policyholders will be allowed to choose coverage through Citizens if they receive quotes from national insurers that are more than 15 percent higher than Citizens's annual premiums. Other provisions also are in place to allow the agency to be more competitive with private insurers.

"You put the nail in the coffin this afternoon on the industry that was hurting our people. That's right and just fair and important, and you did it, and God bless you for fighting for the people of Florida," Crist told legislators. "I hear some groans from insurance lobbyists? Tough. That's right. We work for the people, not them." [b]

But Crist didn't get everything he asked for. Legislators killed an amendment giving him the power to appoint Citizens's director. Also rejected was a proposal that would have allowed the agency to write policies for auto, theft, and fire insurance that would have made it better able to amass greater financial reserves and offer lower premiums.

[a] Paige St. John, "Crist Still Pushing for Property-insurance Legislation," *Tallahassee Democrat*. www.tallahassee.com/apps/pbcs.dll/article?AID=2007705030346.

[b] S. V. Date, "Sessions End More Like Recess Than Finale," Palm Beach Post.com. www.palmbeachpost.com/state/content/state/epaper/2007/05/05/m1a_XGR_session_0505.html.

prestige of the office into real influence in a way that may not be replicated by successors. Governors may be personally popular, have a special gift for working with legislators, or have some other skills that help them do their jobs well but that are not based on any authority granted by the state. They can "exert leadership," as onetime South Carolina governor Richard Riley put it, using informal powers "such as negotiations, public relations and strategizing."[15]

Popular Support. One thing that will always help a governor is popular support. A governor who wins with 51 percent of the vote has the same formal powers as a governor who wins with 73 percent, but the more popular governor is clearly going to have an edge. Legislators and other officials accept more readily the need to go along with a popular governor's program because they believe that program is what most voters in the state want. This is especially true if the governor had strong support for election in their districts. "I think if a governor has strong popularity ratings, he's got a bigger **bully pulpit,**" said former Ohio governor Bob Taft. "If a governor is strong and popular, whether or not he's going to use the electoral power that gives him, legislators still think that he might use that either for or against them in their reelection."[16]

Party Support in the Legislature. Having members of their own party dominate the legislature certainly helps governors get their agendas passed. Governors can be successful if the other party controls the legislature, but it is a lot tougher. The reasons are fairly obvious. Republican legislators want to see a Republican governor succeed and likely share many of the same values, while the same holds true, obviously, for Democratic legislators serving under Democratic governors. Governors are more likely to grant favors to legislators of their own party or raise money for them. This, in turn, makes those legislators more likely to support the governors' programs.

Ability to Communicate. We have already touched on the advantage governors have over legislators in regard to media exposure. There is

no law that says newspapers and TV stations have to pay more attention to pronouncements from the governor—but that is what happens. Whereas a governor speaks clearly with one voice, a legislature speaks with many—not just because it is made up of many individuals, but also because there are differing points of view between the chambers and between the majority and minority parties.[17] "In any squabble, the governor had a distinct edge over what amounted to a gang of unknowns in the legislature," writes former Vermont House speaker Ralph Wright.[18]

Governors, though, have to play both an inside game and an outside game. They have to appeal to capital insiders as well as to the public at large. A governor who makes every move based on the ability to turn it into a press release or who appeals to the public by bashing the "corruption" in the capital may score points with the media and the public but soon will have few friends in the legislature.

Still, governors often enjoy the upper hand in their relations with the legislature. Roy Barnes, who served one term as governor of Georgia from 1999 until 2003, had said during his days in the state legislature, "When you are called down to the governor's office, it is a very impressive office, you're talking to the governor, and you know that he controls things that could be good or ill for your district. He controls grants, he controls roads, and other things."[19] In other words, the formal powers of the governor (the ability to control projects) merge with informal powers (the mystique of the office) to influence legislators and other supplicants.

Becoming Governor and Staying Governor

Given the history of politics in this country, it should come as little surprise that middle-aged white males have dominated the job of being governor. Women are being elected to governorships with greater frequency—only three women were elected governor during the nation's first two centuries—but plenty of states have yet to elect a woman for the top job.[20] In 2007, nine women served as governor, the highest number ever to serve at one time. (Their ranks have since been slightly depleted by retirements and presidential appointments; just five women governors were in

---

Bully Pulpit
The platform from which a high-profile public official, such as a governor or president, commands considerable public and media attention by virtue of holding office.

office following the 2012 elections.) In 1873, P. B. S. Pinchback, the black lieutenant governor of Louisiana, was elevated to the post of acting governor for forty-three days, but only two African Americans have ever been elected as governor of any state:[21] Douglas Wilder of Virginia held the job during the first half of the 1990s, and Deval Patrick was first elected to the office in Massachusetts in 2006. David A. Paterson, who is African American and legally blind, became governor of New York following Eliot Spitzer's 2008 resignation due to a sex scandal. There have been a handful of Hispanic and Asian American governors, including Brian Sandoval of Nevada and Susana Martinez of New Mexico. In 2007, Bobby Jindal of Louisiana became the first Indian American to be elected governor; he was joined by Nikki Haley of South Carolina in 2010.

Many nonpoliticians have been elected governor, including film star Arnold Schwarzenegger of California, former wrestler Jesse Ventura of Minnesota, and business executives Mark Warner of Virginia and John Lynch of New Hampshire. Most governors, however, have had a good deal of previous government experience. They have served in the U.S. Congress or the state legislature or held other statewide positions, such as lieutenant governor, attorney general, or even state supreme court justice. Throughout the twentieth century, in fact, only about 10 percent of governors had no prior elective experience.[22] Only a handful of independent or third-party candidates have been elected governor in recent years, including Lincoln Chafee of Rhode Island, who had served in the U.S. Senate as a Republican, was elected in 2010 as an independent, and switched to the Democratic Party in 2013.

One qualification for modern governors is quite clear—they must have the ability to raise money. Gubernatorial campaigns are multimillion-dollar affairs, particularly in heavily populated states, where television ads are expensive to run because the media markets are competitive and costly. The total cost of the campaigns for the thirty-seven governors' races in 2010 was $1.1 billion—the first time gubernatorial campaign costs exceeded $1

billion. Contributing mightily to that total were two self-funding candidates, both Republicans: Meg Whitman, the former head of eBay, who lost the California governorship despite spending $140 million of her own money; and hospital executive Rick Scott, who became governor of Florida thanks in part to his ability to devote $78 million in personal funds to his own campaign.

Factors Driving Gubernatorial Elections

Like the Winter Olympics, gubernatorial elections in most states have been moved to the second year of the presidential term in what are called off-year elections. Thirty-four states now hold their gubernatorial elections in the off year. Another five states—Virginia, New Jersey, Kentucky, Mississippi, and Louisiana—hold their elections in odd-numbered years. Nine states—Delaware, Indiana, Missouri, Montana, New Hampshire, North Carolina, North Dakota, Utah, and Vermont—hold their elections at the same time as the presidential contest. In addition, New Hampshire and Vermont, the only states that have clung to the old tradition of two-year terms, hold elections for governor every even-numbered year.

Many states from the 1960s to the 1980s moved their gubernatorial elections to the presidential midterm because they hoped this would allow voters to concentrate on matters of importance to the states without having their attention diverted to federal issues brought up in presidential campaigns. This plan has not been 100 percent successful. In gubernatorial elections the office of governor is often the biggest thing on the ballot, so voters use these races as a way of expressing their opinions about who is *not* on the ballot. "There is simply no question that the primary motivation was to reduce presidential coattails on the election for governor and to increase the voters' attention on state rather than national issues," says Larry J. Sabato, director of the University of Virginia's Center for Politics. "What changed? Party polarization increased. It is easier to link the president and governor (and Congress and state legislatures)

TABLE 8-2

Who's Who Among U.S. Governors, 2013

State	Governor	Party	Education (highest degree obtained)	First Elected in[a]	Previous Political Life
Alabama	Robert Bentley	Republican	University of Alabama	2010	Member, Alabama House of Representatives
Alaska	Sean Parnell	Republican	Seattle University (JD)	—	Lieutenant governor
Arizona	Jan Brewer	Republican	Radiology technician	—	Elected Arizona secretary of state
Arkansas	Mike Beebe	Democrat	University of Arkansas (JD)	2006	State attorney general
California	Jerry Brown	Democrat	Yale University (JD)	1974	California attorney general
Colorado	John Hickenlooper	Democrat	Wesleyan University	2010	Mayor of Denver
Connecticut	Dan Malloy	Democrat	Boston College (JD)	2010	Mayor of Stamford
Delaware	Jack Markell	Democrat	University of Chicago (MBA)	2008	State treasurer
Florida	Rick Scott	Republican	Southern Methodist University (JD)	2010	Started at the top as governor; previously a businessman
Georgia	Nathan Deal	Republican	Walter F. George School of Law (JD)	2010	Member, U.S. House of Representatives
Hawaii	Neil Abercrombie	Democrat	University of Hawaii, Mamoa	2010	Member, U.S. House of Representatives
Idaho	C. L. "Butch" Otter	Republican	College of Idaho	2006	Member, U.S. House of Representatives
Illinois	Pat Quinn	Democrat	Northwestern University (JD)	—	Lieutenant governor
Indiana	Mike Pence	Republican	Indiana University (JD)	2012	Member, U.S. House of Representatives
Iowa	Terry Branstad	Republican	University of Iowa	1982	Member, Iowa House of Representatives
Kansas	Sam Brownback	Republican	Kansas State University	2010	Member, U.S. Senate
Kentucky	Steve Beshear	Democrat	University of Kentucky (JD)	2007	Lieutenant governor
Louisiana	Bobby Jindal	Republican	Brown University (also Rhodes scholar at Oxford University)	2007	Member, U.S. House of Representatives
Maine	Paul LePage	Republican	University of Maine	2010	Mayor of Waterville
Maryland	Martin O'Malley	Democrat	University of Maryland (JD)	2006	State field director for Barbara Mikulski's 1986 campaign

State	Governor	Party	Education (highest degree obtained)	First Elected in[a]	Previous Political Life
Massachusetts	Deval Patrick	Democrat	Harvard University (JD)	2006	Appointed assistant attorney general for civil rights by Bill Clinton
Michigan	Rick Snyder	Republican	University of Michigan (JD)	2010	Chair of the Michigan Economic Corporation
Minnesota	Mark Dayton	Democrat	Yale University	2010	Member, U.S. Senate
Mississippi	Phil Bryant	Republican	Mississippi College	2011	Lieutenant governor
Missouri	Jay Nixon	Democrat	University of Missouri (JD)	2008	Missouri attorney general
Montana	Steven Bullock	Democrat	Columbia University (JD)	2012	Montana attorney general
Nebraska	Dave Heineman	Republican	U.S. Military Academy	------	Lieutenant governor
Nevada	Brian Sandoval	Republican	Ohio State University	2010	District judge for the District of Nevada
New Hampshire	Maggie Hassan	Democrat	Northeastern University (JD)	2012	Member, New Hampshire Senate
New Jersey	Chris Christie	Republican	Seton Hall University (JD)	2009	U.S. attorney for New Jersey
New Mexico	Susana Martinez	Republican	University of Oklahoma (JD)	2010	Elected district attorney
New York	Andrew Cuomo	Democrat	Albany Law School (JD)	2010	New York attorney general
North Carolina	Pat McCrory	Republican	Catawba College	2012	Mayor of Charlotte
North Dakota	Jack Dalrymple	Republican	Yale University	—	Lieutenant governor
Ohio	John Kasich	Republican	Ohio State University	2010	Member, U.S. House of Representatives
Oklahoma	Mary Fallin	Republican	University of Oklahoma	2010	Member, U.S. House of Representatives
Oregon	John Kitzhaber	Democrat	University of Oregon Medical School	1994	President, Oregon State Senate
Pennsylvania	Tom Corbett	Republican	St. Mary's University School of Law (JD)	2010	Pennsylvania attorney general
Rhode Island	Lincoln Chafee	Democrat	Brown University	2010	Member, U.S. Senate
South Carolina	Nikki Haley	Republican	Clemson University	2010	Member, South Carolina House of Representatives
South Dakota	Dennis Daugaard	Republican	Northwestern University (JD)	2010	Lieutenant governor
Tennessee	Bill Haslam	Republican	Emory University	2010	Mayor of Knoxville

(Continued)

TABLE 8-2   (Continued)

State	Governor	Party	Education (highest degree obtained)	First Elected in[a]	Previous Political Life
Texas	Rick Perry	Republican	Texas A&M University	2000	Member, Texas House of Representatives
Utah	Gary Herbert	Republican	Brigham Young University (no degree)	—	Lieutenant governor
Vermont	Peter Shumlin	Democrat	Wesleyan University	2010	Member, Vermont House of Representatives
Virginia	Bob McDonnell	Republican	Regent University (JD)	2009	State attorney general
Washington	Jay Inslee	Democrat	Willamette University (JD)	2012	Member, U.S. House of Representatives
West Virginia	Earl Ray Tomblin	Democrat	University of Charleston	—	President, West Virginia Senate
Wisconsin	Scott Walker	Republican	Marquette University	2010	County executive of Milwaukee
Wyoming	Matthew Mead	Republican	University of Wyoming College of Law (JD)	2010	U.S. attorney for Wyoming

Source: National Governors Association, "Governors of the American States, Commonwealths and Territories, 2013," http://www.nga.org/files/live/sites/NGA/files/pdf/BIOBOOK.PDF.

a. Those individuals with no dates shown in this column (—) were not elected to the governorship when they first took that office; rather, each was elevated to the position after the elected governor left office for some reason.

because almost all Democrats now are liberal and almost all Republicans are conservative, at least on critical social, tax, and spending issues."[23]

Overall, however, gubernatorial races are still less prone to following national trends than, say, elections for the U.S. Senate. Voters more often use party as a guide in lower-profile contests, such as state legislative races, but are better informed about individual gubernatorial candidates. One reason is the greater news coverage of the races. Another important factor is the amount of money that candidates for governor spend to publicize themselves. Candidates create extensive organizations that promote their campaigns and use all the modern techniques of political consultants, polling, and media buys. Voters are far more likely, even in less populous states, to get to know the candidates through TV ads and brochures than through speeches or other personal appearances. As noted above, gubernatorial elections are now a billion-dollar business, with individual races sometimes costing in excess of $100 million. Candidates and outside groups spent more than $80 million in the unsuccessful recall election of Wisconsin Republican Scott Walker in 2012 (roughly $14 for every man, woman, and child in Wisconsin.), more than doubling the previous gubernatorial record in that state.[24]

Leaving Office

Governors are rarely booted out of office prematurely. In June 2004, Connecticut governor John Rowland resigned after being investigated by the legislature for accepting gifts from a contractor with business before the state. Faced with possible **impeachment** and a federal criminal investigation, Rowland, one of the nation's longest-serving governors at the time, chose to step down. Rod Blagojevich, the disgraced Illinois governor caught by the FBI on tape plotting to sell the appointment to President Obama's old Senate seat, continued to insist on his innocence even after he was impeached

Impeachment
A process by which the legislature can remove executive branch officials, such as the governor, or judges from office for corruption or other reasons.

in 2009, but he was convicted in 2011 and sentenced to fourteen years in prison. In 2003, Gray Davis of California was the first governor forced to leave office by a **recall election** since Lynn Frazier of North Dakota was booted out more than eighty years earlier on charges of corruption. Voters felt that Davis had dug the state into such a deep hole financially that it would take years to recover. Wisconsin's Scott Walker in 2012 became the first governor to survive a recall election.

Arizona governor Evan Mecham was impeached and convicted in 1987 for impeding an investigation and lending state money to a car dealership that he owned. The most recent previous conviction dates back to 1929, when Henry Johnston of Oklahoma was removed for general incompetence by a legislature with possible political motives. A few governors, including Fife Symington of Arizona (1997), Jim Guy Tucker of Arkansas (1996), and Guy Hunt of Alabama (1993), have resigned following criminal convictions. More recently, two governors have resigned amid sex scandals: Eliot Spitzer of New York (2008) and Jim McGreevey of New Jersey (2004).

A more common threat to gubernatorial staying power is term limits. Governors in thirty-six states are limited to either two terms or two consecutive terms in office. The governor of Utah can spend no more than three terms in office. The only two states that have two-year terms instead of four-year terms—Vermont and New Hampshire—place no limits on the number of terms a governor may serve. Howard Dean served five full terms as governor of Vermont before running for president in 2004.

What do governors do once they leave office? Several of them, like Dean, run for higher offices, such as the presidency or a Senate seat. Four of the five presidents prior to Barack Obama, in fact, were governors before winning the White House (see the box "A Difference That Makes a Difference: From State House to White House: Translating a Governorship into a Presidency"). Governors also regularly run for the U.S. Senate. A dozen senators and one representative serving in 2010 previously had been governors. Entering

> A more common threat to gubernatorial staying power is term limits. Governors in thirty-six states are limited to either two terms or two consecutive terms in office.

the Senate or serving as a cabinet official is generally considered a step up the professional ladder from being a governor.

Many former governors, though, complain that they never had it so good as back when they were running their states. "My worst day as governor was better than my best day as a United States senator," Thomas Carper, D-Del., said in 2009.[25] Wisconsin's Tommy Thompson openly lamented the second-guessing to which he was subjected as President George W. Bush's secretary of health and human services during a 2006 appearance before the National Governors Association, an organization he had once chaired. "When you're a Governor, you can wake up in the morning and you can have an idea and you can have somebody working on it by 11 o'clock in the morning," Thompson said. "When you go to Washington . . . I get up, get the same idea, go in. Then you have to vet it with 67,000 people who all believe sincerely they're smarter than you."[26]

Other Executive Offices

The governor is the only statewide official elected in every state. Most states, however, also have several other statewide officials elected in their own right. This is a holdover from earlier times when the governor was not invested with much power and authority was distributed among a number of officeholders. Texas still has two dozen officials who are elected statewide, whereas New Jersey for many years elected only the governor (that changed in 2009, when Garden State voters elected a lieutenant governor for the first time). Most states have handfuls of officials

---

Recall Election
A special election allowing voters to remove an elected official from office before the end of his or her term.

A Difference
That Makes *a Difference*

From State House to White House: Translating a Governorship Into a Presidency

How big of an advantage is it to run for the presidency as a sitting governor as opposed to holding some other position? For more than a quarter century prior to Barack Obama's election in 2008, it looked as if it was about as big as they come.

Four of the previous five presidents had been governors: Jimmy Carter, Ronald Reagan, Bill Clinton, and George W. Bush. The one exception was George W. Bush's father, George H. W. Bush, who came to the Oval Office after serving as Reagan's vice president. Seventeen presidents in all had served earlier as governors.

Lately, though, governors have had bad luck. Former Massachusetts governor Mitt Romney lost to Obama in 2012, after beating Texas governor Rick Perry and former Minnesota governor Tim Pawlenty, among other opponents, in the GOP primaries.

Obama's first race had been dominated by senators, including John McCain, Hillary Rodham Clinton, and Obama himself. (Obama had served four years in the U.S. Senate when he was first elected, after spending eight years in the Illinois Senate.) They outpolled a large number of gubernatorial contenders, including Romney, Bill Richardson of New Mexico, Mike Huckabee of Arkansas, and Mark Warner of Virginia. Sarah Palin was serving as governor of Alaska when McCain picked her as his running mate (she resigned her post in Juneau the following year).

But if their recent track record isn't so great, compare governors to holders of other offices. No sitting U.S. senator before Obama had been elected president since John F. Kennedy in 1960. No member of the U.S. House has been elected since James Garfield, all the way back in 1880.

What makes governors such attractive candidates for the nation's most powerful office? And what makes legislators usually so *un*attractive?

For one thing, governors are the only politicians aside from presidents who have run governments that are anywhere near as complicated as the federal government. True, governors do not formulate foreign policy, but they do have to become experts in running departments that cover everything from taxes and education to public health and public safety. Governors have to run things. Members of Congress just vote. "Because the presidency is no place to begin to develop executive talents, the executive careerist clearly is preferable to the legislator," writes political scientist Larry J. Sabato.[a]

Also, Congress is a major part of "official" Washington, and senators and representatives can hardly say they have no connection with what occurs there. Conversely, governors running for the White House can always claim they are Washington "outsiders" who are going to sweep in and clean up the town. Former governor-turned-president Bill Clinton reportedly advised then senator Joseph Biden, D-Del., that senators had to overcome big handicaps to run for president. Not only did they have their records to explain, but they also had forgotten how to speak the language of the average person. "When you get to Washington, the only people you talk to are the elites: elites in the press, elites among the lobbyists, elites that you hire on your own staff," Clinton told Biden. "You're not regularly talking to ordinary, everyday people."[b] Biden didn't listen to Clinton, launching his second bid for the presidency in 2008 and ultimately being elected at Obama's side as vice president. But, then, neither did Clinton's wife, who served as Obama's first secretary of state after losing to him in the 2008 primaries.

Still, the out-of-touch image of Congress and Washington in the public mind hampers members of Congress who seek national office. "It could probably be shown by facts and figures that there is no distinctly native American criminal class except Congress," Mark Twain wrote in his 1897 book *Following the Equator*. Governors running for national office invariably present themselves as fresh alternatives to the tired habits of Washington, promising to change the culture and tone of the nation's capital.

That they fail to do so is almost a given. That opens up the field for the next fresh face from the state of California or Arkansas or Texas. Within hours of Obama's reelection, attention turned to governors as potential candidates in 2016—among Republicans and Democrats alike.

[a]Larry J. Sabato, *Goodbye to Good-Time Charlie: The American Governorship Transformed*, 2nd ed. (Washington, DC: CQ Press, 1983), 33.

[b]Quoted in E. J. Dionne Jr., "Govs 4, Senators 0. Tough Odds," *Washington Post*, January 4, 2004, E4.

elected statewide; we outline the responsibilities of a few of them below.

Lieutenant Governor

The office of lieutenant governor traditionally has been seen as something of a joke. Lieutenant governors, it's been said, have nothing to do but wait for their governors to resign or die so that they can accrue some real power. That situation has changed in just the past few years. Some states, such as Georgia and Virginia, responded to budget shortfalls of recent years by slashing the budgets and limiting the powers of their lieutenant governors' offices. More states, however, have expanded the purview of the office, recognizing that the security demands created by the terrorist attacks of 2001 mean that there is plenty of work to go around and that the skills of the second in command should be used more fully. Today, "it's rare that the lieutenant governor doesn't have some specific duties," says Julia Hurst, director of the National Lieutenant Governors Association.[27]

In many states, the lieutenant governor's responsibilities are laid out by law. In Indiana, for example, the lieutenant governor's portfolio includes the departments of commerce and agriculture. In half the states, the lieutenant governor presides over the state senate, having varying degrees of authority in that chamber from state to state.

Twenty-five states elect their governors and lieutenant governors as part of the same ticket. In eighteen other states, the two are elected separately. The other seven states—Arizona, Maine, New Hampshire, Oregon, Tennessee, West Virginia, and Wyoming—don't elect lieutenant governors, although in Tennessee the speaker of the Senate is given the title and in West Virginia the honor falls to the Senate president.

Attorney General

Perhaps the statewide office that has undergone the greatest transformation in recent years is that of attorney general. Always referred to as the top law enforcement officer in the state, the attorney general sometimes has had duties that have been quite minimal because most criminal prosecutions are taken care of at the county level. But attorneys general have become major political players, finding new power by banding together in multistate consumer protection cases against Microsoft, financial firms, toy manufacturers, drug companies, and shoe manufacturers, among many other examples.

Beginning in 2007, New York State attorney general Andrew Cuomo won $13 million in settlements from lenders and universities that had violated state laws with their student loan policies. One of the first things Cuomo did after taking office as governor in 2011 was to use the money to set up a national student loan center that would offer "unbiased" financial advice to students and their parents.

Not surprisingly, there has been a backlash against these newly powerful officials. In part, this has been based on the fact that for many attorneys general the job has been a successful launching pad toward the governorship. In 2010, nine former attorneys general were serving as governors, with about as many seeking the office in elections that year. "It seems to be considered the second most prominent and important position to governor," says veteran Arkansas newspaper columnist John Brummett. "The other statewide offices are mostly clerical and pointless."[28]

Attorneys general have traditionally been Democrats, their campaigns funded by trial lawyers. In recent years, the U.S. Chamber of Commerce and many other business groups have spent millions trying to defeat "activist" attorney general candidates. "Historically . . . attorney general races were off most business people's radar screens," says Bob LaBrant of the Michigan Chamber of Commerce. Today, "there's greater incentive to get involved in an attorney general race because of the increased involvement of attorneys general across the country in litigation against the business community."[29] The Republican Attorneys General Association was founded in 1999 to elect candidates who believe that their colleagues have gone too far in pursuit of business regulations and the revenues

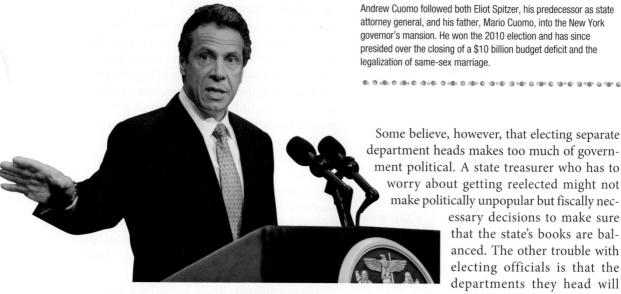

Andrew Cuomo followed both Eliot Spitzer, his predecessor as state attorney general, and his father, Mario Cuomo, into the New York governor's mansion. He won the 2010 election and has since presided over the closing of a $10 billion budget deficit and the legalization of same-sex marriage.

such cases can generate. Their strategy appears to have worked—the number of GOP attorneys general climbed from twelve in 1999 to twenty by 2003; as of 2012, the two major parties could each boast of twenty-five attorneys general.

Other Offices

Every state elects its governor, and most states elect a lieutenant governor and attorney general. In terms of which other offices are held by elected officials—as opposed to officials appointed by the governor or by boards and commissions—the states vary widely. The theory behind electing many officials directly is that it gives the public a greater voice in shaping a variety of state programs, instead of just selecting a governor and leaving it all up to him or her.

Only a few states, including Georgia, Montana, and Oregon, elect a state superintendent of education. In Nebraska, a state board of education is elected and the board in turn selects a superintendent. Several states, mostly in the South, directly elect a secretary of agriculture. An increasing number of states allow citizens to vote for an insurance commissioner. Most states elect a secretary of state who, in turn, regulates elections in those states. Overall, many states structure their executive branches similarly—if there isn't an elected agriculture secretary, there is certain to be an appointed one.

Some believe, however, that electing separate department heads makes too much of government political. A state treasurer who has to worry about getting reelected might not make politically unpopular but fiscally necessary decisions to make sure that the state's books are balanced. The other trouble with electing officials is that the departments they head will squabble over money and power instead of working together as part of a team to promote the greater good.

Election officials themselves have become controversial in some cases. Secretaries of state often oversee elections, and some have been accused of partisan bias in this role. Colorado secretary of state Scott Gessler came to his job after a career as one of the GOP's top campaign lawyers in the state. He was accused by Democrats of retaining a partisan bias in office, notably in participating in a fund-raiser to pay off a campaign fine levied by his office. He was sued no fewer than eight times during his first year in office.[30] Similarly, Democrats in other states complained that GOP secretaries of state favored their parties by making changes to early-voting rules and implementing voter identification laws that they claimed were meant to suppress voting by those likely to vote Democratic. Kris Kobach had served as chair of the Kansas Republican Party before becoming secretary of state and sponsoring that state's voter ID law. "He's doing a better job as Republican state chair as secretary of state than he did when he was the Republican state chair," complained Democratic state representative Ann Mah.[31]

What Is Bureaucracy?

Elected executives head the agencies and departments that implement and manage most public programs and services. In other words,

TABLE 8-3

The Powers of the Offices

In Many States, Lieutenant Governors . . .	Secretaries of State . . .	Attorneys General . . .
Preside over the senate	File and/or archive state records and regulations, other corporate documents	Institute civil suits
Appoint committees	Administer uniform commercial code provisions	Represent state agencies and defend and/or challenge the constitutionality of legislative or administrative actions
Break roll-call ties	Publish the state manual or directory, session laws, the state constitution, statutes, and/or administrative rules and regulations	Enforce open meetings and records laws
Assign bills	Open legislative sessions	Revoke corporate charters
May be assigned special duties by governors	Enroll and/or retain copies of bills	Enforce antitrust prohibitions against monopolistic enterprises
Serve as cabinet members or members of advisory bodies	Register lobbyists	Enforce air pollution, water pollution, and hazardous waste laws in a majority of states
Serve as acting governors when the governors are out of state		Handle criminal appeals and serious statewide criminal prosecutions • Intervene in public utility rate cases • Enforce the provisions of charitable trusts

Source: Compiled from the National Lieutenant Governors Association, www.nlga.us/Members.htm; *The Book of the States* 2003 (Lexington, KY: Council of State Governments, 2003), 215, 221, and 224; and the National Association of Attorneys General, www.naag.org/ag/duties.php.

they are in charge of the government's bureaucracy. For our purposes, **bureaucracy** consists of the public agencies and the public programs and services that these agencies implement and manage. Thus **bureaucrats** are simply the employees of the public agencies. The vast majority of these agencies—generically known as government bureaucracies—are located in the executive branches of state and local governments. Although these agencies vary greatly in terms of the programs and services they manage and deliver, the vast majority of them are organizationally very similar. There is a specific set of organizational characteristics associated with bureaucracy:

- *Division of labor.* Labor is divided according to task and function. Most large bureaucracies, for example, have separate

technical, personnel, and financial specialists.

- *Hierarchy.* There is a clear vertical chain of command. Authority is concentrated at the top and flows down from superiors to subordinates.

- *Formal rules.* Bureaucracies are impartial rather than impulsive. They operate on the basis of formulated guidelines and standardized operating procedures.

- *Maintenance of files and records.* Bureaucracies record their actions.

- *Professionalization.* Employees of bureaucratic agencies typically earn their jobs based on qualifications and merit.[32]

Virtually all large, complex organizations have these characteristics, not just government agencies. Wal-Mart and IBM have these traits and can thus be considered bureaucratic organizations, even though they are private companies. In the

Bureaucracy
Public agencies and the programs and services they implement and manage.

Bureaucrats
Employees of public agencies.

end, what separates public bureaucracies from private bureaucracies is not what they are, but what they do.

What Does Bureaucracy Do?

Public bureaucracies play two fundamental roles in state and local political systems. First, they are the key administrators in the democratic process. They are charged with carrying out the decisions and instructions of elected public officials. This is the central focus of the academic discipline of public administration. Their second role is more controversial. Bureaucracies not only carry out the decisions of the democratic process, but, as it turns out, they also have a fairly important say in what those decisions are.

Bureaucracy as Policy Implementer

The first job of bureaucracy is to carry out what the government wants or needs done.[33] The whole process is known as **policy implementation**. Agencies implement policy by issuing grants and contracts, by enforcing laws and regulations, and by undertaking and managing programs directly.

For example, when elected officials decide to build a new road, they do not adjourn the legislature to go survey land, drive bulldozers, and lay asphalt. It is a public agency that negotiates to buy and survey the land. It is the transportation department that either issues the contracts to build the road or takes on the job of construction using its own employees and equipment.

State and local bureaucracies manage not only state and local programs but federal programs as well. The federal government relies on state and local agencies

Inside Erie County, New York, there are three cities, twenty-five towns, fifteen villages, and almost one thousand special fire, sewer, and lighting districts.

> State and local bureaucracies manage not only state and local programs but federal programs as well. The federal government relies on state and local agencies to implement the vast majority of its welfare, education, and highway programs and much of its health policy.

to implement the vast majority of its welfare, education, and highway programs and much of its health policy as well.[34]

The single largest form of bureaucracy in the United States is a fundamental part of virtually every community: public schools. Employing more than 3 million teachers, public schools serve almost 50 million students and have a combined budget of $519 billion.[35]

Bureaucracy as Policymaker

The second fundamental role of bureaucracy is more controversial. Put bluntly, bureaucracies do not just implement policy; they also make it.[36] They do this in at least three ways.

The first way is through what has been called the power of the **street-level bureaucrat**. Street-level bureaucrats are the lower-level public employees who actually carry out the actions that represent government law or policy. In many cases, street-level bureaucrats have the discretion, or ability, to make choices about what actions they do or do not perform. In making these choices, they are essentially making policy. For example, the street-level bureaucrat associated with speed limits is the traffic cop. This public employee is actually on the highway with a radar gun making

Policy Implementation
The process of translating the express wishes of government into action.

Street-Level Bureaucrat
A lower-level public agency employee who actually carries out the actions that represent law or policy.

Cutting red tape? Most people do not associate barbers or beauticians with bureaucracy, yet most barbers and beauticians must be licensed and regulated by the state and/or local government.

certain that motorists abide by the speed limits specified by state or local law. The legislature may have passed a law setting a maximum highway speed of 65 miles per hour, but if the traffic cop decides to go after only those motorists doing 75 miles per hour or faster, what really is the speed limit that motorists must obey? And who has set that limit? Arguably, it is not the legislature but, rather, the cop.[37]

The second way in which bureaucracies make policy is through rulemaking. **Rulemaking** is the process by which laws or mandates approved by legislatures are turned into detailed written instructions on what public agencies will or will not do.[38] For example, the Nebraska state legislature created the Nebraska Games and Parks Commission to enforce a number of laws related to hunting, fishing, wildlife preservation, and boating. The details of enforcing those laws—such as setting permit fees, determining bag limits for particular types of fish, and designating

---

Rulemaking
The process of translating laws into written instructions on what public agencies will or will not do.

no-wake zones on lakes—are rules established by the commission rather than laws passed by the legislature. These sorts of details are often left to individual agencies.

Finally, bureaucracies also contribute to policymaking directly by pursuing political agendas. Street-level discretion and rulemaking are *passive* policymaking in the sense that they involve bureaucrats' responding or not responding to something such as a speeding car or a newly signed bill. Yet bureaucracies and bureaucrats also take *active* roles in politics. They do this in a number of ways. At the state and local levels, the heads of many public agencies are elected. Such positions include everything from county sheriff to state attorney general. As elected officials, these agency heads often make campaign promises, and, once in office, they try to get their agencies to deliver on those promises.

The implementation and political roles of bureaucracy make it a particular target for citizen concern and, at times, scorn. It is easy to see that we need some bureaucracy. Somebody has to manage all those programs and services we want from government. Yet government bureaucracy has a terrible reputation for inefficiency, incompetence, and mismanagement.[39] Why do we have so much bureaucracy? How good a job does it really do? Could we get by with less of it? Is there a better way to run public programs and services? These are reasonable questions that the comparative method can help answer.

What Is "Enough" Bureaucracy?

Most people believe that, whatever the virtues of bureaucracy, there is too much bureaucracy in government and in our lives. Undeniably, state and local governments have a lot of bureaucracy. How much? Look at Table 8-4, which lists the numbers of employees on state and local government payrolls by function. Combined, state and local governments have more than 19 million

TABLE 8-4

State and Local Government Employment by Function

Function	Total Individuals (in thousands)	State Government (in thousands)	Local Government (in thousands)
Elementary and secondary education	8,037	67	7,970
Higher education	3,093	2,487	606
Hospitals	1,090	446	644
Police protection	1,017	107	909
Corrections	763	489	274
Streets and highways	560	240	320
Public welfare	549	247	303
Other government administration	429	62	366
Electric power and gas supply	94	4	90
Judicial and legal	456	183	273
Financial administration	432	173	258
Fire protection	429	0	429
Natural resources	208	159	49
Social insurance	83	83	0
State liquor stores	10	10	0
Other	514	201	313
All functions	19,809	5,329	14,480

Source: U.S. Department of Commerce, *Statistical Abstract of the United States*, 2012 (Washington, DC: U.S. Census Bureau, 2012).

full-time and part-time employees. Most of these—approximately 14 million—are employees of local rather than state governments.[40]

But numbers alone give little insight into whether there is too much or too little bureaucracy. In reality, the size of the bureaucracy varies from state to state and from locality to locality for two main reasons. First, in each locality, citizens make different kinds of demands on each state and local government agency. Some localities need more of one particular resource, whereas others need less. In Eden Prairie, Minnesota, the public demands more cross-country ski trails, and in Yuma, Arizona, the citizens need more public swimming pools. As a result, the size and role of the public sector can vary significantly from place to place— more services equals more bureaucracy. There is no universally agreed on yardstick for measuring what constitutes a "reasonably" sized bureaucracy.

Measured on a per capita basis, the mostly large, urban, and populous states have the *smallest* bureaucracies. More rural, less populous states, conversely,

have the *largest* bureaucracies. How can this be? Why would North Dakota have more bureaucracy than California? The answer is actually pretty simple. Even the most rural state still needs an educational system, roads, and law enforcement. These are all labor-intensive propositions. Indeed, they may be even more labor-intensive in rural states. For example, to serve a widely dispersed population, an educational system either has to build lots of small schools or figure out a way to transport lots of students over considerable distances to a smaller number of large schools. The same tale is told when we use expenditures—in this case, the amount of money states spent for services—to measure the size of bureaucracy. (See Table 8-6.)

Expenditures and employees tell us something about the size of the bureaucracy, but they do not tell us much about its influence or power over the daily lives of citizens. If you have ever spent time in a university financial aid office, you probably already understand the point here—when people complain about bureaucracy being too big or

TABLE 8-5

States With the Most and the Least Bureaucracy by Number of Employees

State	State Employees (per 10,000 citizens)
Top Five	
Hawaii	602
North Dakota	374
Alaska	372
Delaware	362
New Mexico	314
Bottom Five	
Florida	119
Illinois	122
Pennsylvania	131
California	138
New York	139

Source: U.S. Bureau of Labor Statistics data for 2008, as reprinted in *State and Local Sourcebook*, online supplement to *Governing* magazine, 2009.

TABLE 8-6

States With the Most and the Least Bureaucracy by Expenditures

State	State and Local Expenditures (dollars per capita)
Top Five	
Alaska	15,924
New York	12,499
Wyoming	11,647
California	10,100
Massachusetts	9,622
Bottom Five	
Idaho	6,373
Arkansas	6,587
South Dakota	6,608
Oklahoma	6,699
Missouri	6,775

Source: U.S. Census Bureau data, as reprinted in *State and Local Sourcebook*, online supplement to *Governing* magazine, 2009.

intrusive, they often mean the red tape and rules that come with it, not its budget or payroll.

Measuring Bureaucratic Effectiveness: It Does a Better Job Than You Think

Different demands translate into public agencies of different sizes and with varying levels of involvement in our day-to-day lives. What the comparative method has not told us is how good (or bad) a job public agencies do. The widespread belief is that such agencies are, at best, mediocre managers of public programs and services.[41] Although many if not most people believe this, for the most part this notion is wrong. Public agencies, as it turns out, are very good at what they do.

The assumption is that the private sector is more efficient and more effective than the public sector, but numerous studies have found that this assumption is based more on stereotypes than on facts.[42] For example, **contracting out** is a term used to describe having private or nonprofit organizations rather than government agencies deliver public services. The basic idea is that private companies should be able to deliver services more efficiently. But the record of contracting out services in practice is much more mixed. While it certainly works well in some circumstances, it is far from a panacea.

For example, faced with rising healthcare costs and a reluctance to increase student fees on top of rising tuition bills, a number of colleges and universities have experimented with contracting out student healthcare services. The University of Northern Colorado outsourced its student health center in 2003, but the large healthcare provider that took over the operation asked to be released from its contract a few years later when it found it couldn't make a profit. At the University of Denver, an experiment with privatization was also largely a failure. The healthcare company that took over the university's student healthcare services seemed to focus too

Contracting Out
Government hiring of private or nonprofit organizations to deliver public goods or services.

much on its bottom line and too little on the outreach services central to the original health center's mission. The university brought its health center back in-house and funded it with student fees.[43]

Some of the problems associated with contracting out often include a loss of accountability and transparency, difficulty in specifying contracts to cover all possible contingencies (for example, who bears the costs if bad weather delays road construction), and a clash between public service and make-a-profit value systems. All this can create conflict between private contractors and governments, conflict that can be messy, litigious, and expensive. After experimenting with contracting out, some governments—like the University of Denver—end up deciding it causes more headaches than it's worth. This is a pretty common experience; local governments that contract out services frequently bring those services back in-house after a year or two.[44] A public bureaucracy might be old-fashioned, but it generally can be counted on not just to get the job done, but also to be responsive to its elected bosses rather than a profit-loss statement.

Compared to private-sector employees, public-sector employees tend to have higher levels of education, express a greater commitment to civic duty and public service, abide by more stringent codes of ethical behavior, and be more committed to helping other people.[45] Various studies have shown that over the past thirty years, state and local agencies have become more productive and more professional, and they have done so during an era when they have shouldered an increasing share of the burden for delivering programs and services from the federal government.[46]

Many of the faults attributed to public bureaucracies actually can be traced to legislatures, which give agencies conflicting and confusing missions and often do not provide them with adequate resources to fulfill these missions. The real surprise is not that some bureaucracies are ineffective or poorly run but that the vast majority of them, most of the time, manage to more or less serve the public interest. At least one professional student of bureaucracy has suggested that any objective view of the joint performance of bureaucracy and representative democracy would lead to the conclusion that what we need is more bureaucracy and less democracy![47]

Is There a Better Way to Run Public Programs and Services?

Is that a ridiculous idea (not to mention antidemocratic)? Do we really need less democracy and more bureaucracy? The short answer is no. As we have already discussed, public services and programs could be contracted out and delivered through a competitive bidding process by the private sector. Public agencies could be staffed and run by political party loyalists or special interest supporters. Things could be done differently. Before we abandon the traditional public bureaucracy, however, it is worth considering why public agencies are so, well, bureaucratic.

Remember the key characteristics of bureaucratic organizations listed earlier? These turn out to be important factors when it comes to running public programs and services. For one thing, bureaucracies tend to be impartial because they operate using formal rules, not partisan preference, bribes, or arbitrary judgment. If you need some form of license or permit, if your shop is subject to some form of environmental or business regulation, or if you are trying to receive benefits from a public program, it does not matter to the bureaucracy if you are rich or poor, liberal or conservative, an influential high-roller or an average citizen. What matters to the bureaucracy are the rules that define the application process, eligibility requirements, and delivery of the necessary service or program. Following bureaucratic rules can be maddening, but these rules do help ensure that public agencies are more or less impartial. In addition, setting rules, requiring records, and setting up a clear chain of authority help ensure that bureaucrats and bureaucracies do not exceed their authority or act unfairly.

Professionalization is another bureaucratic characteristic that is desirable in public agencies

---

Professionalization
The rewarding of jobs in a bureaucratic agency based on applicants' specific qualifications and merit.

because it promotes competence and expertise. Job qualifications help ensure that merit—rather than partisan loyalty, family connections, or political influence—is the basis for an individual's gaining public-sector employment.

The great irony of public bureaucracy is that the very characteristics that help ensure neutrality, fairness, and accountability also produce the things that people dislike about bureaucracy: red tape and inefficiency. Formal rules help guarantee equity and fairness, but—as anyone who has spent time filling out forms and waiting in line can attest—they can be a pain. Enforcing rules, or "going by the book," may mean bureaucracy is fair, but it is not particularly flexible.

Still, as maddening as current systems may be, they have largely been seen as preferable to the old patronage systems that handed out government jobs through much of the nineteenth and twentieth centuries based on partisan loyalty. In the old days, machine politics meant that getting a government job was based on whom you knew rather than on what you knew. Job security lasted only as long as you kept in your political patron's good graces or until the next election. Understandably, then, there was a tremendous incentive to make the most of a government position. Kickbacks and bribery inevitably made their way into many state and local agencies.

The founders of the modern conception of government bureaucracy were the progressive reformers of the late nineteenth and early twentieth centuries. They wanted a lasting solution to the gross dishonesty and inefficiency they saw in public administration, and their thinking centered on the idea that the administrative side of government needed to be more insulated from the political arena.[48] Reformers promoted **neutral competence**, the idea that public agencies should be the impartial implementers of democratic decisions, not partisan extensions of whoever happened to win the election.

To achieve these ends, progressive reformers began to push for public agencies to adopt the formal characteristics of bureaucratic organizations. This was accomplished in no small part through lobbying for the merit system as an alternative to the political spoils system. In a **merit system**, jobs and promotions are awarded on the basis of technical qualifications and demonstrated ability instead of given out as rewards for political loyalty. A merit system also makes it harder for public employees to be dismissed without due cause. But this does not mean a guaranteed job. The idea is to create a system within which public employees can be fired only for failing to do their jobs and not because they missed a payment to a political boss. The overall goal was to make government bureaucracies less political and more professional.

New York was the first state to adopt a merit system in 1883. In 1935, the federal Social Security Act made merit systems a requirement for related state agencies if they wished to receive federal grants. This generated another wave of merit-based reforms of state and local bureaucracies. By 1949, nearly half the states had created merit-based civil service systems. Fifty years later, virtually all states and many municipalities had adopted merit systems. All of this helped professionalize state and local bureaucracies and turned what had been sinkholes of patronage and corruption or marginally competent old-boy networks into effective instruments of democratic policymaking.

Politics and the Merit System

In some ways, merit-based bureaucracy is a victim of its own success. The whole idea of shifting to a merit system was to insulate public agencies and their employees from undue political influence. But merit systems did not eliminate the political role of the bureaucracy; they merely changed it. Under the spoils system, bureaucracy was an agent of a particular boss, party, or political agenda, and it favored the supporters of electoral winners. The merit system cut the connection

---

Neutral Competence
The idea that public agencies should be the impartial implementers of democratic decisions.

Merit System
A system used in public agencies in which employment and promotion are based on qualifications and demonstrated ability; such a system blends very well with the organizational characteristics of bureaucracy.

FIGURE 8-2

HOW IT WORKS

Virginia's Bureaucracy—for This, You Get an A–

The Commonwealth of Virginia receives gold stars for its bureaucracy—it was one of the three top-ranked states (Utah and Washington were the others) in the most recent ratings conducted by the Government Performance Project. Part of what puts Virginia at the top of the class is the state's practice of holding the more than one hundred cabinet members and agency heads accountable to formal "executive agreements." These are reviewed by the governor and outline clear measurable goals for each agency against which its performance is appraised. Yearly public assessments of each agency are available online.

These scorecards evaluate performance in human resource management, government procurement, financial management, technology, and emergency preparedness. In effect, this is an assessment of those agencies' leaders and their subordinates. The table here shows only a portion of the scorecard for Virginia's executive agencies for 2009 and includes ratings for agencies in the Offices of Administration, Commerce and Trade, Education, Finance, Health and Human Services, and Public Safety. Overall, ten of the fifty-three rated agencies met expectations in every category. The remaining forty-three were rated as needing to make progress in at least one area, including five that were rated as below expectations in at least one area.

Virginia's Executive Branch Agencies 2009 Scorecard

Legend:

M = Meets Expectations   P = Progress toward Expectations   B = Below Expectations   U = Results Unavailable

Agency	Secretariat	Emergency Prepared-ness	Financial Management	Government Procurement	Human Resources	Informa-tion Tech-nology
Compensation Board	Administration	M	M	M	M	P
Department of General Services	Administration	M	M	M	M	P
Department of Human Resource Management	Administration	P	M	M	M	M
Department of Minority Business Enterprise	Administration	M	P	P	M	B
State Board of Elections	Administration	U	P	M	U	U
Department of Business Assistance	Commerce and Trade	B	P	M	M	M
Department of Housing & Community Development	Commerce and Trade	M	M	M	P	P
Department of Labor & Industry	Commerce and Trade	M	M	M	M	M
Department of Mines, Minerals & Energy	Commerce and Trade	M	M	M	M	M
Department of Professional & Occupational Regulation	Commerce and Trade	P	M	M	M	P

Agency	Secretariat	Emergency Preparedness	Financial Management	Government Procurement	Human Resources	Information Technology
Virginia Employment Commission	Commerce and Trade	M	M	M	M	M
Virginia Racing Commission	Commerce and Trade	M	M	M	M	M
Department of Education	Education	M	M	M	M	P
State Council of Higher Education for Virginia	Education	U	M	P	M	P
The Library of Virginia	Education	M	M	P	P	M
Virginia Commission for the Arts	Education	M	M	P	M	M
Virginia Museum of Fine Arts	Education	P	M	M	M	M
Department of Accounts	Finance	P	M	M	M	M
Department of Taxation	Finance	M	M	M	M	P
Department of the Treasury	Finance	P	P	M	M	P
Comprehensive Services for At-Risk Youth and Families	Health & Human Resources	P	M	M	M	P
Department of Behavioral Health and Developmental Services	Health & Human Resources	P	P	M	P	P
Department for the Blind & Vision Impaired	Health & Human Resources	P	M	P	M	P
Department of Health	Health & Human Resources	M	P	P	M	M
Department of Medical Assistance Services	Health & Human Resources	M	M	M	M	M
Department of Rehabilitative Services	Health & Human Resources	P	M	M	M	P
Department of Social Services	Health & Human Resources	P	M	M	M	P

Sources: Commonwealth of Virginia, "Organization of State Government," www.commonwealth.virginia.gov/StateGovernment/StateOrgChart/OrgChart2006–2007.pdf; "Virginia Performs: Administrative Measures, 2009," www.vaperforms.virginia.gov/agencylevel/src/ScoreCardResults.cfm.

between the ballot box and the bureaucracy. Distancing bureaucracy from elections, however, arguably makes it less accountable to the democratic process—a big concern if bureaucracy is policymaker as well as policy implementer.

Once distanced from the ballot box, public agencies and public employees discovered their own political interests and began to pursue them with vigor. Organized interests outside the bureaucracy also began to realize that being able to influence lawmaking and, especially, rule-making offered enormous political opportunities. All you have to do is get your favored policy written into the rules, and bureaucracy will enforce it well beyond the next election. The entities that get the most attention are the unions that represent most state and local government workers.

Public Labor Unions

Public-sector labor unions are a relatively new political force. Unions were almost exclusively a private-sector phenomenon until the 1960s. This changed in 1962 when President John F. Kennedy issued an executive order that recognized the right of federal employees to join unions and required federal agencies to recognize those unions. The 1960s and 1970s saw a considerable expansion in the number of state and local employees joining unions. Today, roughly three to four times as many public-sector as private-sector workers belong to unions.[49]

The reasons for the expansion in public-sector union membership are not hard to fathom. For much of their history, public employees received lower wages than their private-sector counterparts. Public employees also had limited input with regard to personnel decisions. Despite the merit system, many still saw favoritism and old-boy networks as having too much influence in pay and promotion decisions. Public-sector labor unions pushed for the right to engage in **collective**

bargaining, a process in which representatives of labor and management meet to negotiate pay and benefits, job responsibilities, and working conditions. The vast majority of states allow at least some public unions to bargain collectively.

What should not be missed here is that the outcomes of collective bargaining are important policy decisions. They are decisions in which the voter—and sometimes the legislator—has little say. Negotiations about pay and benefits for public employees are, in a very real sense, negotiations about taxes. A raise won by a public employee represents a claim on the taxpayer's pocketbook. And it is a claim that is worked out not in an open democratic process but often in closed-door negotiations.

Labor unions have given public employees more than just collective bargaining muscle; they also have started to do some heavy lifting in electoral politics. Unions that are able to deliver their members' votes can have a powerful say in who holds office. Understandably, people seeking public office pay attention to the policy preferences of public-sector unions. By raising money, mobilizing voters, and even running independent campaigns, unions exercise considerable political clout. Consider the Wisconsin Education Association Council (WEAC).

This teachers' union, long recognized as an important political actor in the state, has a well-thought-out set of legislative goals and supports candidates accordingly.[50] In the 2010 election cycle, WEAC spent roughly $1.5 million on state political campaigns.[51] That made the union the biggest-spending political action committee in state politics.

The boots-on-the-ground political organization combined with big bucks translates into considerable political clout for public labor unions, enough to shape how the merit system actually works. A basic principle of the merit system is that competence is supposed to be rewarded. Expertise and job performance are supposed to be the bases of promotion and pay increases. In contrast, unions tend to advocate **seniority**—the

---

Collective Bargaining

A process in which representatives of labor and management meet to negotiate pay and benefits, job responsibilities, and working conditions.

Seniority

The length of time a worker has spent in a position.

Federal government programs and policies directly affect state and local bureaucracies. Federal policymakers are well aware of this; the three most recent U.S. presidents all served time in state office as either governors or legislators.

length of time spent in a position—as the basis for promotions and pay increases.

In recent years, there have been several efforts to curtail the power of public unions, especially their rights to collective bargaining. The two most high-profile efforts to take on public unions were spearheaded by Scott Walker and John Kasich, respectively the Republican governors of Wisconsin and Ohio. In Wisconsin, Walker backed controversial legislation that sought to eliminate collective bargaining rights of most public employee unions, leading to mass protests, court challenges, and a failed recall attempt. In Ohio, Kasich backed a similar measure. Among other things, the Ohio law would have prevented public employees from striking and would have restricted their right to bargain collectively for wages and benefits. Opponents spearheaded a drive to overturn the law, which culminated in a statewide referendum in which the legislation was decisively defeated.

Despite efforts by their opponents to paint them otherwise, unions are far from all bad—they have fought successfully for reasonable compensation packages and safer work environments for people who perform some of society's toughest, dirtiest, and most thankless jobs, while the people who make up public-sector unions—police officers, firefighters, teachers, social workers, and the like—are appreciated at least as much as they are resented by voters.

If Not Merit . . . Then What?

Bureaucratic reform is a perennial issue in American politics. Many of the reform efforts are variations on a single theme that reflects a popular belief that government would be better if it were run more like a business. In practice, this means introducing competition into the delivery of public programs and services, making the organizations that deliver these goods and services less hierarchical, and making greater use of the private sector to deliver public services.[52] The idea is to introduce the benefits of the market into the public sector, which in theory could lead to more efficiency through lower costs while increasing responsiveness, because competition means paying attention to your customers or going out of business. The great difficulty facing reformers is how to get these benefits without leaving behind the advantages of the traditional merit-based bureaucracy.

The basic problem with trying to run government more like a business is that government is not a business. For the most part, we as citizens do not like rules and red tape—until there is a problem or a scandal. Then we want to know what went wrong and who is to blame. We want bureaucrats to be given the freedom to be flexible and make choices—until those choices result in favoritism or program failure. We like the idea of competition and the profit motive, until a private company contracted to provide public services puts profit above the public interest.

This is not to say that it is impossible to implement long-lasting changes in public bureaucracies. Indeed, the Great Recession brought about some of the biggest and potentially longest-lasting changes public agencies had experienced in at least a generation. One of the most obvious of these changes is that, personnel-wise, public

FIGURE 8-3

Monthly Changes in State and Local Government Employment, 2009–2012

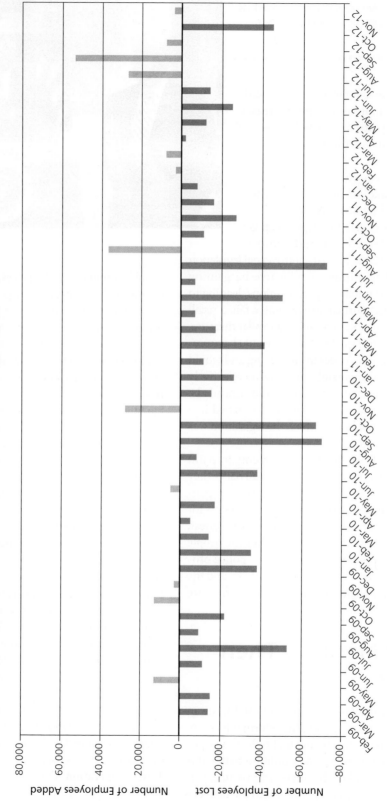

Source: "State and Local Government Employment: Monthly Data," *Governing,* www.governing.com/gov-data/monthly-government-employment-changes-totals.html.

agencies have been shrinking. Cash-strapped state and local governments started shedding jobs shortly after the financial crunch hit in 2008, and as of 2013 they were still handing out pink slips at a fairly steady clip. If citizens really want smaller government, then over the past few years they've gotten it. In 2011 alone, almost a quarter million state and local employees lost their jobs; from 2008 to 2011, the overall state and local workforce dropped from 65 employees per 1,000 population to 61 employees per 1,000 population.

The impacts of the shrinking public-sector workforce show up in different ways. In keeping with our earlier theme of governors gaining more and more power, some governors have used the financial crisis as leverage to consolidate and centralize the executive branch. For example, Kansas governor Sam Brownback folded the largely independent Kansas Health Policy Authority (which historically administered Medicaid) into the state health department, the latter being more under the direct control of his administration. Other governors have been actively seeking to merge different bureaucracies into bigger agencies that report directly to the chief executive.[53] The biggest impact, however, may be in who will show up to work in the public sector in the future. As a result of structural changes brought on by the fiscal crisis—things such as limits on collective bargaining rights and generally lower levels of public service compensation, including pension benefits—it seems clear that going forward public workers will likely be paid less and have less job security than did such workers in the past. Some scholars suggest that the end result may be a public sector that has less qualified employees and greater employee turnover.[54]

Conclusion

How did governors become the most important political figures in their states? Over the years, more and more authority has been given to them, and their offices have become the centers of state power. Once weak and unable to set policy or budgets, governors have now become unquestioned leaders. They are able to select cabinets that run most of the state agencies according to the governor's priorities. Sometimes their staff picks prove to be embarrassments, but they are also able to fire such people in the hope of seeing their agendas pushed forward by more eager replacements. Many positions are designed with staggered terms, so that governors cannot appoint their own people to every position. Strong governors, however, are able to combine their appointment powers with their ability to command attention from the mass media to set the terms of political issues and the direction these issues take in their states. That clout extends to the judicial branch, with many governors being able to appoint most of their state's judges. Governors' control of budgets and veto authority provide them with enormous sway over the legislative branch as well. Although they never get everything they want from their legislatures, they almost always get more of what they want than does any individual legislator.

A big part of governors' power comes from overseeing bureaucracies. In contrast to the popular stereotype, most public agencies tackle difficult jobs that are unlikely to be done better by any other alternative. Perhaps the most astonishing thing about bureaucracy is how much we take it for granted. Public schools, safe drinking water, working utility grids, and roads are simply there. We rarely contemplate what astounding administrative and logistical feats are required to make these aspects of everyday life appear so mundane. Some reforms, such as the rise of the merit system, can radically reshape what bureaucracy is and what it does. One theme, however, remains constant: whatever the government is, and whatever it does, it will rely on bureaucracy to get it done.

> The basic problem with trying to run government more like a business is that government is not a business.

Local Focus

Do-It-Yourself Government in Redlands, California

Officials in Redlands, California, are trying to maintain current levels of service through unusual means. One of these options is increasing the use of volunteers.

Take the police department, for example. Just a few years ago the police department in Redlands, a city of seventy-one thousand about sixty miles east of Los Angeles, employed 98 sworn officers and 208 civilians. Declining revenues brought budget cuts to the department, however, and these days the police department employs 75 sworn officers and 138 civilians, but it also draws on nearly three hundred volunteers who annually contribute a total of more than thirty-one thousand hours of their time to the city. You don't have to push too many buttons on your calculator to realize that getting that amount of human resources for free is a pretty good deal.

These volunteers are not just answering phones and making coffee. They cordon off crime scenes, direct traffic, patrol the city's fourteen parks, write parking tickets, assist with animal control, and provide crowd control at special events. They are also trained to check in parolees, assist with records processing, and take reports on property crimes. Two volunteer reserve officers even conduct investigations alongside the city's police detectives.

Such extensive use of volunteers extends beyond the police department. The city's Quality of Life Department is in charge of things such as maintenance of streets and traffic lights, the municipal airport, and city parks. As the department struggled with budget cuts of 10 percent, it turned to volunteers to help ensure that the level of services stayed the same even as its funding shrank.

Does this really work? Can volunteers really put in the hours needed and perform sensitive and highly skilled jobs? Well, sort of. Initially local agencies were using volunteers to fill gaps, but organizations such as the police department quickly realized that a better approach would be to shift a series of routine tasks to volunteers. These tasks—things like directing traffic, taking reports, and providing crime scene control—often constituted a big part of an officer's workday.

All told, the city has been able to maintain its level of public services even though city personnel have been cut by 16 percent. Still, there are limits. If a volunteer wants to stop working, she is free to do so, and there's no guarantee anyone else will be available to take her place. There may also be an ironic downside to the creative approach Redlands has taken to maintaining services. With revenues continuing to decline and the city struggling to keep up levels of service even with volunteer labor, in 2010 Redlands asked its citizens to approve a half-cent sales tax. The citizens turned it down. There was no visible sign of declining public services, so why pay more taxes for them?

Source: Adapted from John Buntin, "Does Government Work Require Government Employees?," *Governing*, April 2011.

The Latest Research

Gubernatorial powers are constantly shifting. Institutional reforms—such as increases in staff and expansion of appointment powers—may change formal power. Informal power, of course, shifts every time a new governor is elected and brings his or her own personal characteristics to the job. How do these changes shape the ability of chief executives to get their agendas enacted into law? Are these powers enough to give governors the tools they need to meet the increasingly heavy expectations voters place on them? Are those expectations—especially of the economic variety—realistic given that even the most powerful governor leads a state that is open to economic forces beyond his or her control?

Meanwhile, as discussed above, the Great Recession had an enormous and potentially long-lasting impact on public agencies. Most obviously, public-sector payrolls shrank as states and localities shed hundreds of thousands of employees in an attempt to keep the books balanced. By 2013, that exodus was tapering off, but it was clear that things were not just going to return to the way they were. The big question, of course, was what was going to happen. Would agencies stay lean and try to keep doing with less? Would they engage in more contracting out? Would the shattered traditional notion of a secure government-sector job make it more difficult for agencies to recruit the best and the brightest into careers in public service? What about representation—did the massive disruption in employment leave bureaucracies more or less representative of the constituencies they serve?

The research summarized below takes a look at some of these issues by examining the power of the chief executive and changing practices in the public agencies that make up the executive branch of government.

• •

- **Krupnikov, Yanna, and Charles Shipan.** 2012. "Measuring Gubernatorial Budgetary Power: A New Approach." *State Politics & Policy Quarterly* 12: 438–455.

The standard measure of formal gubernatorial powers used by political scientists is that developed by Thad Beyle. That index has undergone a number of changes and updates as Beyle and others have sought to provide an ever more accurate indicator of the comparative power of governors. This study takes this development a step further: the authors argue that the standard power index suffers from some important measurement errors, and they propose an alternative. The specific focus is on measuring governors' budgetary powers. The authors' central criticism of Beyle's index is that, as typically constructed, its measures of budgetary power are comparable across states but not across time. This is because, as part of its evolution and refinement, Beyle's index changed how budgetary powers were measured. This is potentially a problem for scholars using the comparative method because they often do not look at differences that make a difference in one year, but at differences that make a difference over multiple years. The authors of this study develop what they argue to be an index that is comparable from year to year as well as from state to state.

- **Bowman, Ann O'M., Neal D. Woods, and Milton R. Stark II.** 2010. "Governors Turn Pro: Separation of Powers and the Institutionalization of the American Governorship." *Political Research Quarterly* 63: 304–461.

There are two ways to think about state chief executives. The first is by looking at the person—that is, who occupies the office. The second is by looking at the office—that is, the institution of governor. The institution is where formal powers are concentrated, and the institution of governor has been expanding in many states. This research examines the growth of these institutions by using a straightforward comparative analysis; the authors look at differences in gubernatorial staffing and expenditures across states during a two-decade period and examine what other differences predict these changes. What their analysis reveals is that governors' offices get bigger and command more resources as government responsibilities increase, when the governor's party controls the legislature, and, notably, to keep pace with institutional growth in the legislature. Increases in legislative sessions and legislative staff support tend to trigger countervailing increases in the executive branch.

- **Levine, Heliss, and Eric Scorsone.** 2011. "The Great Recession's Institutional Change in the Public Employment Relationship: Implications for State and Local Governments." *State and Local Government Review* 43: 208–214.

The Great Recession made the pay and benefits of public employees a white-hot political issue. Rightly or wrongly, government employees were sometimes accused of being more insulated from economic problems than their counterparts in the private sector. This chapter has discussed the bitter fights that broke out in Wisconsin and Ohio over labor relations in the public sector, fights that were repeated on a less heated scale in many states and localities. Does all this mean that the public labor sector is undergoing a dramatic and long-term shift? If so, what does it imply? Levine and Scorsone take a crack at answering these questions. They conclude that the Great Recession has brought about one of the biggest changes in public employment in fifty years. The fallout of that change is probably lower pay and fewer benefits for government employees. As a result, public agencies of the future may struggle to attract a high-quality labor pool, which may in turn have implications for the quality if not the cost of public goods and services.

- **Joaquin, M. Ernita, and Thomas J. Greitens.** 2012. "Contract Management Capacity Breakdown? An Analysis of U.S. Local Governments." *Public Administration Review* 72: 807–816.

At least in theory, contracting out allows governments to leverage the power of the marketplace to deliver goods and services more efficiently. In practice, as the discussion of university health services in this chapter has made clear, contracting out has a mixed track record. Sometimes it works, sometimes it doesn't. This study tries to figure out what some of the underlying causes of this variation might be. Specifically, the authors look at "capacity," essentially the ability of local governments to effectively manage these contracts, which are often made with the private sector. Disturbingly, they conclude that there has been a long-term trend toward the diminishment of this capacity. This may be a result of a combination of decreasing competition and the highly complex and demanding nature of the contracts. Contracting out seems to have increased the need for public officials to undertake often very demanding evaluation responsibilities, even as their capacity to fulfill those responsibilities has shrunk. Given the huge toll the Great Recession took on the public sector, it seems that such capacity is unlikely to begin increasing in the foreseeable future.

Chapter Review

Key Concepts

- appointment powers (p. 213)
- bully pulpit (p. 220)
- bureaucracy (p. 229)
- bureaucrats (p. 229)
- collective bargaining (p. 238)
- contracting out (p. 233)
- formal powers (p. 213)
- impeachment (p. 224)
- informal powers (p. 213)
- merit system (p. 235)

- neutral competence (p. 235)
- policy implementation (p. 230)
- professionalization (p. 234)
- recall election (p. 225)
- rulemaking (p. 231)
- seniority (p. 238)
- street-level bureaucrat (p. 230)
- supermajority vote (p. 211)
- veto (p. 211)

Suggested Websites

- **www.aspanet.org.** Website of the American Society for Public Administration, the largest professional association for those who work for or study public agencies.

- **http://library.cqpress.com.** The CQ Press Electronic Library, which features an online voting and elections collection with a component for gubernatorial elections.

- **www.csg.org.** Website of the Council of State Governments, a forum for state officials to swap information on issues of common concern, such as drugs, water, and other policy matters.

- **governing.com.** Web version of *Governing* magazine, which is dedicated to covering state and local issues. Includes numerous stories and other resources on agency leaders and performance, e-government, and more.

- **www.naag.org.** Website of the National Association of Attorneys General, which has become increasingly prominent as state attorneys general have banded together on a number of high-profile cases.

- **www.nga.org.** Website of the National Governors Association, which shares information among governors and also lobbies the federal government on their behalf.

- **www.pewstates.org.** The State and Consumer Initiatives section of the website of the Pew Charitable Trusts is home to a number of analyses of government effectiveness and efficiency, including the Government Performance Project.

State Stats on the Executive Branch and Bureaucracy

Explore and compare data on the states! Go to **college.cqpress .com/sites/essentials-govstateandlocal** to do these exercises.

1. In 2003, the governor of Illinois commuted the death penalty for 167 prisoners and pardoned four more. How many death sentences have been overturned or commuted in the United States since 1973? Which

state has had the most? The least? Might there be political or cultural explanations for these numbers?

2. In 2010, Arizona citizens voted to increase the sales tax rate by a penny. How has the per capita sales tax revenue in Arizona changed between 2005 and 2011? Does this make sense? What is a possible explanation?

3. The authors refer to governors as mini-presidents. Considering the population in some of the larger states, is this the case? How do the budgets of these larger states compare to those in the smaller states? What are the implications of these differences?

4. Which state has the most law enforcement agencies? Why might it have so many, even though it may not have the highest population?

5. How does your state compare to the average in terms of per capita state and local government expenditures on welfare programs? What ramifications do you think this would have in terms of the workforce that is necessary to administer these programs?

Judges have increasingly found themselves in the crosshairs of bitter partisan battles as they rule on cases related to important legislative issues. Some judicial decisions have raised accusations that "activist judges" are legislating from the bench. Judges often rule on cases concerning issues near and dear to legislators and the public, from gun rights to education, and their rulings will never please everyone.

ch.

9

Courts

TURNING LAW INTO POLITICS

- Why are some states' judges elected and some appointed?
- Why are some states' courts more likely than those in other states to impose the death penalty?
- What effects do state campaign finance rules have on judges and on the decisions they make?

Though sometimes referred to as the non-political branch of government, courts are becoming more political all the time. Angry political rhetoric and personal attacks increasingly intrude on the once quiet hallways of courts in a big way. While campaigning for the 2012 Republican presidential nomination, former House speaker Newt Gingrich suggested sending capitol police or U.S. marshals to haul **activist judges** before Congress to explain their decisions, and GOP Representative Michele Bachmann derided judges in Iowa as "black-robed masters." From the other side of the political spectrum, *New York Times* columnist Maureen Dowd, incorrectly assuming that the U.S. Supreme Court was poised to strike down President Obama's Patient Protection and Affordable Care Act, called the Court "hacks dressed up in black robes." When Justice Roberts instead surprised conservatives by upholding the act, radio host Glenn Beck sold T-shirts with Roberts's face and the word "COWARD" boldly printed in yellow.

Railing against judges is nothing new. In 1954, when the U.S. Supreme Court, under Chief Justice Earl Warren, ordered an end to the practice of segregating schools by race, "Impeach Earl Warren" signs popped up along roadsides in many states. But, as former Supreme Court justice Sandra Day O'Connor has written, the "breadth of rage currently being leveled at the judiciary may be unmatched in American history."[1] Attacks against judges by politicians have moved beyond name-calling. According to the National Center for State Courts, judges faced more impeachment attempts in 2011 than in any previous year in history. In all but two instances, "the sole accusation was that the judges in question issued opinions that displeased members of the legislature."[2] In 2006, a handful of western states voted on ballot initiatives that were designed to rein in "out of control" judges. The most extreme was in South Dakota, where a group called JAIL 4 Judges advocated a state constitutional amendment to create special grand juries to punish judges for unpopular decisions. None of these initiatives passed, but they reflected a frustration felt by many regarding unpopular state court decisions.

Judges are often in the position of deciding cases that involve sensitive and polarizing issues, such as abortion, gun control, criminal sentencing, zoning, and school vouchers. The losing side, whether liberal or conservative, increasingly blames the outcome on "activist judges" who create new laws to fit their personal political beliefs. Judges can face criticism for "legislating from the bench"—that is, substituting their judgment for that of a democratically elected state legislature. Lee Epstein, a law and political science professor at Washington University, has suggested to her students, "Maybe the best definition of a judicial activist is a judge you don't like."[3]

Case in point: The polarizing issue of gay marriage. When Massachusetts became the first state to legalize gay marriage in 2003, it wasn't because the legislature passed a law; instead, the Massachusetts Supreme Judicial Court ruled that the state constitution required it. The years immediately following this ruling brought a period of losses for gay marriage advocates. Most other states have dealt with the issue either through legislation or ballot measures, with a majority of states voting to uphold traditional definitions of marriage but recent momentum being on the side of gay-marriage proponents.

Of the states currently recognizing same-sex marriages, only one joined Massachusetts through the action of its state supreme court. In 2009, the Iowa Supreme Court, in a unanimous decision, legalized same-sex marriage in that state. The next year, three of the seven justices were up for a retention election, usually a quiet up or down vote on a judge's qualifications. Not this time. Well-financed national organizations, including the National Organization for Marriage and the American Family Association, spent record sums opposing them, urging voters to unseat the justices with television ads accusing them of, among other things, "becom[ing] political and ignoring the will of the voters." The justices, as had been traditional in these kinds of races in the past, did not actively raise campaign money and made few public appearances in the period leading up to the election. They were all recalled. Another of Iowa's state justices, David Wiggins, faced voters in 2012. Despite Iowa's tradition of nonpartisan elections, the chairman of the Republican Party in Iowa, A. J. Spiker, issued a statement calling on voters to remove Wiggins from the

---

Activist Judges
Judges who are said to act as independent policymakers by too creatively interpreting a constitution or statute.

court as punishment for his part in the decision that legalized marriage for same-sex couples in Iowa. The *New York Times* quoted Justice Wiggins's response to the campaign against him: "Our system is built on checks and balances between independent branches of government. Two of those branches are designed to be political. It is unfortunate that Mr. Spiker apparently thinks that all three branches should be political."[4] This time the results were different; 55 percent of Iowans voted to retain Wiggins on the supreme court despite his steadfast refusal to campaign for his job.

Vast sums of money have been flooding into state judicial elections. The U.S. Supreme Court's decision in *Citizens United v. Federal Election Commission* (2010), which invalidated laws placing limits on independent corporate and union campaign spending, did not specifically involve judicial elections, but concerns voiced by Justice John P. Stevens in his dissent have proved prophetic:

> The consequences of today's holding will not be limited to the legislative or executive context. The majority of the States select their judges through popular elections. At a time when concerns about the conduct of judicial elections have reached a fever pitch . . . the Court today unleashes the floodgates of corporate and union general treasury spending in these races.[5]

Citizens United made it easier for unaffiliated groups to spend unlimited sums to elect judges. In 2012, the first judicial super PAC was created to support an incumbent state supreme court justice in a hotly contested race in North Carolina. Such money translates into more of the mud-slinging attack ads of the type we are more used to seeing from politicians. The increasing political rhetoric and money invested in judicial elections put pressure on judges to pay more attention to the potential political fallout of their decisions. And interest groups are increasingly seeing the benefit of funding high-cost judicial campaigns. After all, what is the point of getting legislation passed if a judge is going to throw it out as unconstitutional?

Ironically, at the same time that money is flooding into state court judicial elections, the state courts themselves are being starved of funds. Economic conditions across the country have led to plunging local tax revenues, and nearly all states have cut judicial branch funding. In many localities, budget cuts to local court systems have been so steep that they have placed, in the words of Georgia chief justice Carol Hunstein, "some court systems on the edge of an abyss."[6] While the judiciary is a separate and coequal branch of government, the courts depend on the political branches for funding. Dramatic budget cuts have led to closed courts, furloughed court workers, and a growing backlog of cases and delays, particularly for civil cases, which often are put on a back burner so the courts can deal with urgent criminal matters. Despite these multiple challenges, the work of the state courts continues. There is no single "right way" in which judges, justices, and courts operate. Each of the fifty states, the District of Columbia, and Puerto Rico has its own unique court system. Sometimes it seems as if every county in every state has its own way of doing things. From judicial selection to sentencing reform, states have organized their justice systems to meet the needs of the states' own unique political pressures and social dynamics.

This chapter provides an introduction to state court systems. First, we examine the types of courts and the different ways these courts are structured. Then the focus turns to the different ways state court judges are chosen and retained and the controversies that these processes create. Many issues surround the various players in state justice systems, from prosecutors and defenders to victims and jurors; we explore these before turning to a discussion of some possible areas of change.

The Role and Structure of State Courts

When people complained on old TV shows about how they felt abused or ripped off by their friends, those friends would often say, "Don't make a federal case out of it." In the real world of crime and

At the apex of most state court systems is a supreme court. State supreme court justices, such as Mississippi Supreme Court justices Jess Dickinson (left) and Michael Randolph (right), typically have the final say on appeals from lower courts.

legal conflict in the United States, there are actually relatively few federal cases, because such cases must involve violations of federal law, federal constitutional rights, or lawsuits that cross state borders.

With the exception of highly publicized trials such as the Casey Anthony murder case, state courts operate largely below the public's radar. Yet they are enormously important institutions. The federal U.S. district courts hear several hundred thousand cases a year. By comparison, close to 100 million cases are filed in the lowest state courts every year. (That number includes traffic tickets.) These courts have the responsibility of resolving the vast majority of the nation's disputes. If you crash your car or your landlord evicts you, if you get divorced and fight for child custody, if your neighbor's tree lands in your yard, or if your employer won't pay you, any legal remedy you seek will be decided in a state court. State courts are also where virtually all criminal cases are tried, from drunk driving to murder, from misdemeanors to capital offenses. If you contest a traffic ticket, you will find yourself in a state court.

There are two basic kinds of court cases: criminal and civil. **Criminal cases** involve violations of the law, with the government prosecuting the alleged perpetrators, or criminals. Those found guilty may go to jail or be put on probation. By contrast, **civil cases** involve disputes between two private parties, such as a dry cleaner and a customer with badly stained pants. In civil cases, individuals sue each other, usually for financial judgments. Both types of cases start out in **trial court**. If the parties in a case cannot reach agreement through a **settlement** or a **plea bargain**, they go to trial.

Every trial has a winner and a loser. The losing side, if unhappy with the trial's outcome, can file an **appeal**. Most states have two levels of courts that hear appeals from trial court judgments. The appeal first goes to an **intermediate appellate court**, which reviews the original trial's record to see if

Criminal Case
A legal case brought by the state intending to punish a violation of the law.

Civil Case
A legal case that involves a dispute between private parties.

Trial Court
The first level of the court system.

Settlement
A mutual agreement between parties to end a civil case before going to trial.

Plea Bargain
An agreement in which the accused in a criminal case admits guilt, usually in exchange for a promise that a particular sentence will be imposed.

Appeal
A request to have a lower court's decision in a case reviewed by a higher court.

Intermediate Appellate Court
A court that reviews court cases to find possible errors in their proceedings.

any errors were made. After the appellate court has ruled, a party who still is not satisfied can attempt to appeal to the highest state court of appeals, usually called the **state supreme court**. In most states, this court does not automatically have to take an appeal; rather, it can pick and choose among cases. Typically, a state supreme court will choose to hear only those cases whose resolutions will require novel interpretation of the state constitution or clarification of the law. Such resolutions could set **precedent** that will have consequences well beyond the specifics of the case being appealed.

The state supreme court is the highest legal body in the state court system. This gives it the ultimate power to interpret the state constitution, and its decisions are almost always final. Only the U.S. Supreme Court outranks the highest state courts. Even the nine justices in Washington, DC, however, cannot review—that is, come up with a new decision for—a state supreme court judgment unless that judgment conflicts with the U.S. Constitution or federal law.

When such federal issues are involved, there is no question that state courts must follow the rulings of the federal courts. The chief justice of the Alabama Supreme Court, Roy S. Moore, learned this lesson in 2003 after he oversaw the installation of a two-and-a-half-ton monument to the Ten Commandments in the rotunda of the state supreme court building. Federal judges ruled that such a display violated the First Amendment's separation of church and state and ordered Moore to have the monument removed. He refused and ultimately was expelled from office by a state ethics panel for having tried to place himself above the law. (He later returned, winning election to his old job in 2012.)

Trial Courts

More than 100 million cases were filed in state courts in 2009, about one case for every three citizens. These numbers have stayed relatively constant over the past ten years, although they have edged up recently. More than half the cases involved traffic offenses. The number of civil and criminal cases was roughly equal—19.5 and 20.7 million cases, respectively—and there were 7.8 million domestic and juvenile cases.[7] The vast majority of these millions of cases were resolved through plea bargains or settlements. Only a small minority ever went to trial.

The judge presides over the introduction of evidence; rules on objections, which occur when either of the parties thinks that the other party has said or done something improper, and issues of admissibility, that is, whether or not it is all right for specific evidence or facts to be included in the trial; and instructs the jury as to the relevant laws. The judge further instructs the jury members that they must apply the laws as stated to the facts as they find them. It is the jury, however, that must decide what the facts are. (In a **bench trial**, there is no jury and fact-finding is done by the judge.) The jury (or the judge in a bench trial) must decide who and what to believe and what happened. Unless the jury's final decision is based on a legal mistake, such as improper evidence, hearsay testimony (testimony based on rumor), or a misleading statement of the relevant law, the result will typically be upheld on appeal. The business of the trial court is to examine the facts to resolve the dispute. Subsequent appellate courts review the trial court's application of the law to those facts.

A key distinction among state courts is between **general jurisdiction trial courts** and **limited, or special jurisdiction, trial courts**. A general jurisdiction trial

---

Precedent
In law, the use of the past to determine current interpretation and decision making.

State Supreme Court
The highest level of appeals court in a state.

Bench Trial
A trial in which no jury is present and the judge decides the facts as well as the law.

General Jurisdiction Trial Court
A court that hears any civil or criminal cases that have not been assigned to a special court.

Limited, Or Special Jurisdiction, Trial Court
A court that hears cases that are statutorily limited by either the degree of seriousness or the types of parties involved.

A Difference
That Makes *a Difference*

The New Judicial Federalism

A century ago, state supreme courts were described as being so quiet that "you could hear the justices' arteries clog."[a] No one says this today, and the new judicial federalism is one big reason that this is so.

This no longer so "new" doctrine describes a new-found reliance on state constitutions to protect those rights not covered by the U.S. Constitution. Under the principles of federalism, each state has its own justice system—distinct from those of its neighbors and from the federal system—and its own constitution. The U.S. Constitution is the supreme law of the land, and no state court can interpret its own state's constitution in a way that limits rights secured by the federal charter. States are free, however, to interpret their own constitutions any way they like, except for that single proviso.

For most of the country's history, state constitutions were overlooked. Rarely did the courts rely on them to overturn state laws, especially on the basis of civil rights. But starting in the early 1970s, state supreme courts increasingly began to use state constitutions as independent sources of rights. By 1986, U.S. Supreme Court justice William J. Brennan was characterizing the "rediscovery by state supreme courts of the broader protections afforded their own citizens by their state constitutions [as] . . . probably the most important development in constitutional jurisprudence in our time."[b]

In many legal areas, the actual impact of judicial federalism on civil liberties has not been all that sweeping. Most state court judges continue to interpret state constitutions in lockstep with interpretations of the U.S. Constitution. One scholar found, however, that in approximately one out of every three constitutional decisions, state courts extended rights beyond federal levels.[c] In some areas, such as the interpretation of the right to exercise religion freely and in search-and-seizure rulings, state courts, relying on their own constitutions, have continued to grant rights after the U.S. Supreme Court's interpretation of the Constitution took a more conservative and restrictive turn.

In other cases, state courts rely on unique constitutional provisions. For instance, the New Jersey constitution requires a "thorough and efficient system of free public schools." Relying on explicit provisions such as these, state supreme courts have ordered legislatures to restructure the way they finance public education when inequalities are so extreme that they rise to the level of a state constitutional violation.

Today, state supreme court justices are more likely now to take a fresh look at their own constitutions than to slavishly follow the interpretations of the U.S. Supreme Court. Activists also have focused more attention on state constitutions, mounting campaigns to amend them to either extend or curtail rights.

[a]G. Alan Tarr, "The New Judicial Federalism in Perspective," *Notre Dame Law Review* 72 (1997): 1097.

[b]William J. Brennan, "State Constitutional Law," special section of *National Law Journal* 9 (September 29, 1986): S-1.

[c]James N. G. Cauthen, "Expanding Rights under State Constitutions: A Quantitative Appraisal," *Albany Law Review* 63 (2000): 1183, 1202.

court hears any case not sent to a special court, whether it is civil or criminal. The kinds of cases that can be tried in special jurisdiction courts are statutorily limited. Some are limited to cases of less seriousness, such as misdemeanors or civil cases that involve small amounts of money. Others are limited in regard to the types of parties involved, such as juvenile offenders or drug abusers.

Not all states make this distinction between types of trial courts. Illinois has no limited jurisdiction courts. In contrast, New York, the state with the largest number of judges, is also the state that relies most heavily on limited jurisdiction courts. More than three thousand of the state's 3,645 judges sit on limited jurisdiction courts.[8] (See Figure 9-1.) The majority of these limited jurisdiction courts are "town and village courts" or "justice courts." In states that do not rely on limited jurisdiction courts, appeals go directly to appellate courts. In states that make the distinction, some issues can be appealed from limited jurisdiction courts to general jurisdiction courts.

Appeals Courts: Intermediate Appeals and Courts of Last Resort

When one of the parties in a trial is dissatisfied with the outcome, that party can challenge the result by filing an appeal. An appeal must be based on a claim that there were legal errors in the original trial. It is not enough to show that an error occurred; the error had to have been **prejudicial**— that is, it had to have affected the outcome of the case. The appellant has to argue that there was a good chance the result would have been different if the error had not been made. This often is a very challenging argument to make.

To cite just one example, in 2006, the defense attorney representing the convicted murderer of an Indiana University freshman asked that the sentence be thrown out, arguing that the jurors may have been drinking during legal proceedings, given that some of the male jurors in the trial had painted their toenails and raced down a hotel hallway in a bailiff's backless high heels. "Two men with heels on, painting their toenails, it is not a normal activity unless they are intoxicated," the attorney said. The judge ruled against him, saying there was no indication of drunkenness in court or during the actual deliberations.[9]

States have made different decisions about how many levels of review to grant an appeal, how the courts must choose which cases can be appealed, and how many judges will hear an appeal. For example, not all states have both an intermediate appellate court and a supreme court. Back in 1957, only thirteen states had intermediate appellate courts. Today, only eleven states and the District of Columbia still resolve all their appeals with only one level of review. These states, which include Delaware, Montana, North Dakota, Rhode Island, South Dakota, Vermont, and Wyoming, have relatively small populations—seven have fewer than 1 million residents—and thus tend to have fewer cases to resolve than do more populous states.

In the majority of states, the sheer volume of appeals makes it impossible for one appellate court to hear and resolve every appeal. To deal with burgeoning caseloads, almost all states have created another tier of review. In these states, appeals go first to an intermediate appellate court. Only after they have been reviewed at this level can they move on to the court of last resort, usually the state supreme court. The intermediate court makes it possible for the state judicial system to hear many more appeals and creates the possibility of a second level of appeal.

Intermediate appellate courts range in size from three judges (in Alaska) to 105 judges (in California). States with many judges at the intermediate appellate level usually divide the judges' jurisdictions into specific regions. California, for example, has six appellate divisions. By contrast, New Jersey, with thirty-two appellate judges, has the largest appellate court that is not divided into judicial regions.[10]

Regional divisions help the courts to operate smoothly, but they also create a danger. All these different courts may come up with different rulings on the same or similar issues. This has the potential to set different, possibly conflicting, precedents for future litigation.

State appellate courts also vary in whether they have **discretionary jurisdiction** or **mandatory jurisdiction**. In other words, in some states the courts have a right to pick and choose which cases they hear. In other states, judges must consider every case, the principle being that everyone has the right to an appeal. It is widely accepted that a loser in a single-judge court

Discretionary Jurisdiction
The power of a court to decide whether or not to grant review of a case.

Mandatory Jurisdiction
The requirement that a court hear every case presented before it.

Prejudicial Error
An error that affects the outcome of a case.

FIGURE 9-1

HOW IT WORKS

State Court Structure in Illinois and New York

At a glance, it's easy to see why New York state's court system has been called Byzantine—just compare it to Illinois's. Although it encompasses 23 circuits with more than 850 justices, Illinois's single trial court system (its general jurisdiction courts) looks like a model of clarity and simplicity compared to New York's ten different trial courts (the courts of general and limited jurisdiction). But the differences run deeper than what a simple organizational chart can reveal. New York's three-hundred-year-old town and village justice court system, in particular, has been subject to loud and persistent criticism for cronyism, corruption, fiscal mismanagement, and plain old inefficiency. According to *New York Times* reporter William Glaberson, "the [town and village justice] courts have survived in part because the justices—most of them not even lawyers—have longstanding and deep ties to the upstate political system, and because of the substantial cost of replacing them with more professional courts."[a] With 2,300 justices involved at that level, this would indeed be a tall order.

What can be done? In 2006, New York's former chief judge Judith S. Kaye, the state's top advocate for court reform, recommended changes "across four broad areas: court operations and administration; auditing and financial control; education and training; and facility security and public protection."[b] A few of these proposed changes could be implemented right away, including requiring word-for-word records of court proceedings—a bona fide court transcript—to ensure fairness and the purchasing of recording equipment to make that possible. Other changes would require more sweeping institutional modifications. Judge Kaye called for state funds to help support the town and village justice courts, which are currently funded and operated locally. This change would require legislative approval. Her most aggressive recommendation—to simplify the trial court structure itself into a more common two-tiered organization—would require an amendment to the state's constitution. Legislators received the proposals coolly. A commission on state court reform backed some of Kaye's ideas in 2008 with its suggestion that the state eliminate as many as five hundred of the justice courts, but New York had not instituted the changes by early 2010.[c]

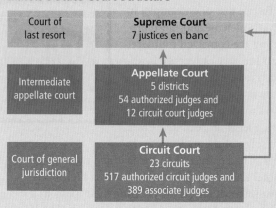

Illinois's State Court Structure

ought to have the right to at least one appeal to a court with multiple judges. This one appeal, however, is generally considered sufficient to correct any prejudicial errors made in the trial courts. Even in states in which the court of last resort has discretionary jurisdiction, appeals may be mandatory in capital punishment cases.

En Banc
Appeals court sessions in which all the judges hear a case together.

Panel
A group of (usually) three judges who sit to hear cases in a state court of appeals.

One more variable in the state court system structure involves the number of judges at each level who hear a particular appeal. At the level of either the appellate court or the court of last resort, judges may hear an appeal **en banc,** or all together, or they may sit in smaller **panels,** typically of three judges. Sitting in panels may be more convenient because appellate courts sit simultaneously in different locations. This allows more appeals to be heard and makes the courts more convenient to the parties. However, as with regional divisions, this may also lead to problems in unifying doctrine created by

New York State's Court Structure

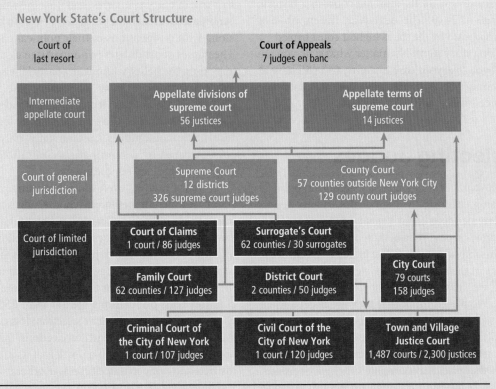

Court of last resort	**Court of Appeals** 7 judges en banc
Intermediate appellate court	**Appellate divisions of supreme court** 56 justices	**Appellate terms of supreme court** 14 justices
Court of general jurisdiction	Supreme Court 12 districts 326 supreme court judges	County Court 57 counties outside New York City 129 county court judges
Court of limited jurisdiction	**Court of Claims** 1 court / 86 judges **Surrogate's Court** 62 counties / 30 surrogates **Family Court** 62 counties / 127 judges **District Court** 2 counties / 50 judges **City Court** 79 courts 158 judges **Criminal Court of the City of New York** 1 court / 107 judges **Civil Court of the City of New York** 1 court / 120 judges **Town and Village Justice Court** 1,487 courts / 2,300 justices

[a] William Glaberson, "Justice in Small Towns to Be Upgraded," *New York Times*, November 22, 2006, A1.

[b] Judith S. Kaye and Jonathan Lippman, "Action Plan for the Justice," November 2006, available at www.state.ny.us/publications/pdfs/ActionPlan-Justice.pdf.

[c] Joel Stashenko, "Study Supports Elimination of Hundreds of Justice Courts," *New York Law Journal* 240, no. 56 (2008): 2.

various courts at the same level making different decisions.

States that use panels have a variety of techniques to limit the divergence of opinions among panels. These include conferencing drafts of opinions en banc. This means that each panel's draft opinions are circulated among all the judges, even those not on that panel. Two states, Texas and Oklahoma, have created systems in which there are two supreme courts with different subject-matter jurisdictions rather than one supreme court sitting in panels. In these states, one supreme court has largely civil

jurisdiction and one supreme court hears only criminal appeals; each of these courts sits en banc. In Texas, the intermediate appellate court has both civil and criminal jurisdiction. In Oklahoma, the intermediate appellate court has only civil jurisdiction—all criminal appeals go directly to the court of last resort for criminal cases. A few states have created systems that have intermediate appellate courts with differing subject-matter jurisdictions and then a single court of last resort.

The most common pattern, adhered to by half the states, involves an intermediate appellate court, sitting in panels, that must consider all appeals. The decisions of these panels are then subject to review by a court of last resort, such as a supreme court, sitting en banc. Usually, this highest court hears just the cases it sees fit to hear. In states without an intermediate court of appeals, often the courts of last resort must hear all the cases that are sent to them. One such state, West Virginia, eliminated discretionary review for its supreme court in a historic change in 2010. The next year, the number of appeals heard by the state's highest court tripled.

Long story short: No matter what state you are in, if you lose your case in court, you will have at least one chance—and sometimes more than one chance—to get your appeal heard.

Selecting Judges

How judges are selected is a significant political decision. Historically, such decisions have generated tremendous controversy, and the controversy continues today. Why is there no clear consensus on this important issue? The judiciary is one of the pillars of the U.S. political system, but at the same time, we want to believe that judges are above politics. We like to think that they are independent and will rule only as justice requires, based on the specific facts presented and the applicable law. But, of course, judges are only human. That's why we want them held accountable for their decisions. These competing values—independence and accountability—tug judicial selection procedures in different directions.

If independence is seen as more important than accountability, it makes sense to appoint judges for lifetime tenures. This is done in the federal system. If accountability is seen as more important than independence, it makes sense to elect judges. Elections are a key element of judicial selection at the state level. Yet they are not the only component; states have formulated a variety of selection systems in an effort to balance the competing values of independence and accountability. These specifics matter. How a state structures its courts and chooses its judiciary may affect the types of decisions made by individual judges and the

confidence citizens have in their courts to provide fair trials.

Almost no two states select judges in the exact same way, although the states can be roughly divided into two camps of about equal size. The first group includes states that choose judges through popular elections, either partisan or nonpartisan. In partisan elections, judicial candidates first run in party primaries, and then the winning candidates are listed on the general election ballot along with designations of their political parties. The names of candidates in nonpartisan elections appear on the ballot without any party labels. The second group consists of states that have appointed, rather than elected, judges. Under the appointment model, the governor or the legislature may appoint judges. In some states, only persons selected by a nominating committee are eligible for judicial appointments.

To make matters even more confusing, many states use different methods to choose judges at different levels of their judiciaries. A state might, for example, choose trial judges by popular election but appoint supreme court justices. What's more, regions within a given state often employ different methods. In Arizona, for example, trial courts in counties with populations greater than 250,000 choose judges through merit selection; less populous districts rely on nonpartisan elections. Indiana holds partisan elections in a portion of its judicial districts and nonpartisan elections in others.

Under the U.S. Constitution, the president, with the advice and consent of the Senate, appoints all federal judges. Similarly, the original thirteen states chose to appoint judges, giving the appointment power to one or both houses of the legislature or, less commonly, to the governor, either alone or with the consent of the legislature.[11]

Then, in the mid-1800s, during the presidency of Andrew Jackson—a period marked by distrust of government and a movement toward increased popular sovereignty—the appointive system came under attack. Every state that entered the Union between 1846 and 1912 provided for some form of judicial elections.[12] At the dawn of the twentieth century, concern that

The merit selection of judges, widely adopted by states across the country to fill some or all judicial vacancies, originated in Missouri from a power struggle between Governor Lloyd Stark, pictured here, and powerful political boss Tom Pendergast.

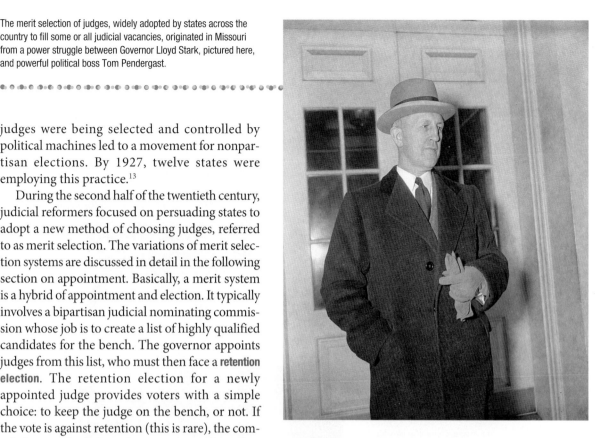

judges were being selected and controlled by political machines led to a movement for nonpartisan elections. By 1927, twelve states were employing this practice.[13]

During the second half of the twentieth century, judicial reformers focused on persuading states to adopt a new method of choosing judges, referred to as merit selection. The variations of merit selection systems are discussed in detail in the following section on appointment. Basically, a merit system is a hybrid of appointment and election. It typically involves a bipartisan judicial nominating commission whose job is to create a list of highly qualified candidates for the bench. The governor appoints judges from this list, who must then face a **retention election**. The retention election for a newly appointed judge provides voters with a simple choice: to keep the judge on the bench, or not. If the vote is against retention (this is rare), the commission goes back to work to come up with another list of candidates for the post.

Under some merit systems, all judges (not just newly appointed ones) must face periodic retention elections, although the length of term and other specifics vary from state to state. Missouri became the first state to adopt such a judicial selection method in 1940, which is why judicial merit selection is sometimes referred to as "the Missouri Plan." The movement enjoyed considerable success from the 1960s to the 1980s. The number of states that embraced merit selection for choosing supreme court justices grew from three in 1960 (Alaska, Kansas, and Missouri) to eighteen by 1980.[14]

Recently, however, this movement appears to have lost momentum. Approximately half the states still rely on merit selection to choose some or all of their judges, and no merit selection state has returned to selection through elections. However, since 1990, most states that have considered

adopting merit selection have rejected it. A poll taken in early 2007 showed that an overwhelming majority of Pennsylvanians opposed changing the method of selecting judges from election to appointment.[15] In recent years, several states have debated doing away with merit selection altogether, including Missouri, where it began. In the sections that follow, we discuss at length each method for selecting judges and the issues it raises. (Map 9-1 shows the system of selection for each state.)

Popular Elections

Why do some states elect judges? Elections allow greater popular control over the judiciary and more public accountability for judges. Proponents argue that such elections are compatible with this country's democratic traditions and that voters can be trusted to make choices for judges that are as good as those that legislators or mayors would make.

Some argue that electing judges can increase the representation of women and minorities on the bench, but studies have found negligible

---

Retention Election

An election in which a judge runs uncontested and voters are asked to vote yes or no on the question of whether they wish to retain the judge in office for another term.

MAP 9-1

Initial Judicial Selection, by Type of Court

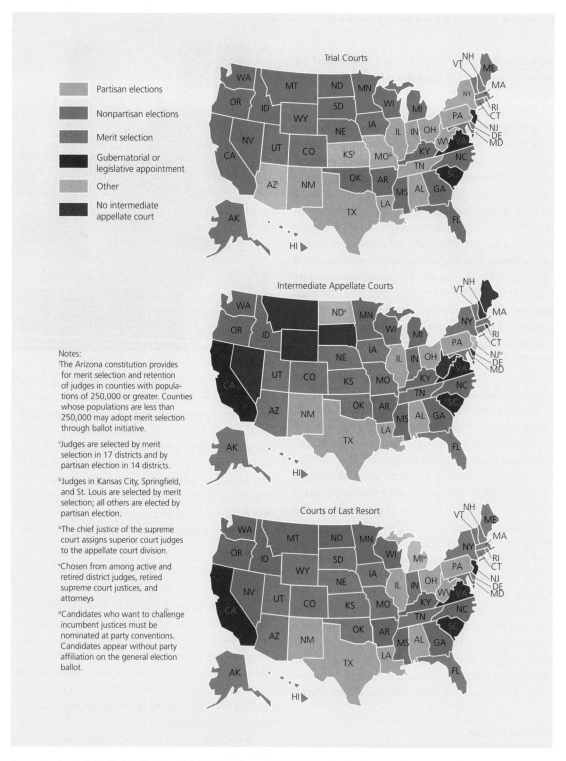

Trial Courts

Legend:
- Partisan elections
- Nonpartisan elections
- Merit selection
- Gubernatorial or legislative appointment
- Other
- No intermediate appellate court

Intermediate Appellate Courts

Courts of Last Resort

Notes:
[i]The Arizona constitution provides for merit selection and retention of judges in counties with populations of 250,000 or greater. Counties whose populations are less than 250,000 may adopt merit selection through ballot initiative.

[ii]Judges are selected by merit selection in 17 districts and by partisan election in 14 districts.

[iii]Judges in Kansas City, Springfield, and St. Louis are selected by merit selection; all others are elected by partisan election.

[iv]The chief justice of the supreme court assigns superior court judges to the appellate court division.

[v]Chosen from among active and retired district judges, retired supreme court justices, and attorneys

[vi]Candidates who want to challenge incumbent justices must be nominated at party conventions. Candidates appear without party affiliation on the general election ballot.

Source: American Judicature Society, "Methods of Judicial Selection," www.judicialselection.us/judicial_selection/methods/selection_of_judges.cfm?state=.

differences between selection methods and judicial diversity.[16] Regardless of system, state judiciaries have grown slightly more diverse over time, but the percentages of minority and women judges continue to trail their numbers in the population at large. Nationwide, as of 2010, forty-three (12 percent) state supreme court justices were members of minority groups and 111 (33 percent) were women.[17]

Those on the other side of the argument assert that judicial elections often become referendums on political issues rather than serving as forums that allow the public to evaluate the temperaments, backgrounds, and experience of the candidates. Opponents of judicial elections focus on what they see as the threat to the independence of the judiciary posed by the introduction of politics into the selection process and the danger that the need to solicit campaign contributions will make judges vulnerable to improper influence by donors.

This is a debate about more than academic ideas. How a state chooses its judges has very real political impacts, with consequences for judicial impartiality, campaign fund-raising, the role of interest groups, and the character of judicial campaigning. Some point to these problems as reasons to move away from selecting judges through judicial elections and toward a merit selection system. Others argue that there is no need to abandon elections altogether; rather, any problems can be addressed through targeted changes. Die-hard supporters of judicial election see the increased politicization of the process as a positive thing; they assert that greater competitiveness translates into more meaningful choices for voters.

Elections for state court judges, when they are held, can be either partisan or nonpartisan. Most or all of the judges in eight states (Alabama, Illinois, Louisiana, Michigan, Ohio, Pennsylvania, Texas, and West Virginia) are selected through partisan elections. Another five states (Indiana, Kansas, Missouri, New York, and Tennessee) select some of their judges this way.[18] Nonpartisan elections are held to select most or all judges in thirteen states (Arkansas, Georgia, Idaho, Kentucky, Minnesota, Mississippi, Montana, Nevada, North Carolina, North Dakota, Oregon, Washington, and Wisconsin) and some judges in another seven states (Arizona, California, Florida,

Indiana, Michigan, Oklahoma, and South Dakota).[19] In some cases, labeling a popular election partisan or nonpartisan may be a distinction without a difference. All Ohio judges and Michigan Supreme Court justices run without party labels on the ballots, but the candidates are chosen through party primaries or conventions, and the parties are heavily involved in judicial campaigns.

A lot rides on the public's belief that judges are neutral and impartial. That belief underpins the willingness to bring disputes to the courts and to abide by the results—the keys to both economic and political stability. Judges cannot, as political candidates do, make campaign promises about future decisions; to do so would be to undermine respect for the impartiality and independence of the judiciary. For the same reasons, judges cannot represent specific interest groups or constituents or even the will of the majority. There are times when all judges, when doing their jobs properly, are compelled by the law to make unpopular judgments or to protect the rights of those without political power.

In 1999, U.S. Supreme Court justice Anthony Kennedy pointed out in an interview that there are times for every judge when the law requires the release of a criminal whether the judge likes it or not. Characterizing the judge in such a case as "soft on crime" betrays a misunderstanding of the judicial process and the Constitution.[20] In the same interview, Justice Stephen Breyer also expressed concerns about the way judicial elections require judges to court public opinion. He said, "We have a different system. And our system is based upon . . . neutrality and independence."[21]

Why are some courts more likely than others to impose the death penalty? Some research indicates that state supreme court justices facing reelection in states in which capital punishment is particularly popular are reluctant to cast dissenting votes in death penalty cases.

The highly charged issue of capital punishment makes a useful test case. Why are some courts more likely than others to impose the death penalty? Some research indicates that state supreme court justices facing reelection in states in which capital punishment is particularly popular are reluctant to cast dissenting votes in death penalty cases. Researchers Paul Brace and Melinda Gann Hall found that, among politically comparable states, rulings to uphold death sentences are more likely in states with elected judges.[22] Not only that, but the closer supreme court justices are to reelection, the more likely they are to support capital punishment.[23]

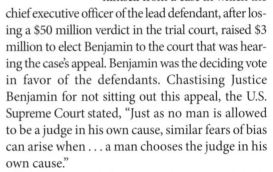

Texas and Florida have at least one thing in common—hundreds of inmates on death row with a high volume of death penalty appeals. But the similarity stops there. Texas justices are elected in partisan elections, and they almost never reverse a death sentence. In Florida, however, supreme court justices are merit selected, and the court has one of the nation's highest reversal rates.[24] It is not misguided for a judge facing reelection to fear reversing a death sentence. There are numerous examples of state supreme court justices who were voted off the bench after they were labeled as soft for opposing the imposition of capital punishment in particular cases. This occurs even when the unpopular opinions are later held to be correct by the U.S. Supreme Court.[25]

The effects of judicial selection ripple out beyond those cases that tackle politically volatile issues such as capital punishment and raise issues of improper influence on the judiciary. In 2006, the *New York Times* published the results of an examination of campaign financing over twelve years at the Ohio Supreme Court. The investigators found that justices routinely sat on cases after receiving campaign contributions from the parties involved or from groups that filed supporting briefs. Justices, on average, voted in favor of contributors 70 percent of the time, with one particular justice voting for his contributors 91 percent of the time.[26]

Okay, so this all sounds shady, but candidates running for judicial office must raise money. Frequently, this money comes from the very people who have a vested interest in the outcomes of cases that are or will be before a judge. Describing judicial fund-raising, Justice Paul E. Pfeifer, a Republican member of the Ohio Supreme Court, said, "I never felt so much like a hooker down by the bus station in any race I've ever been in as I did in a judicial race."[27] In *Caperton v. Massey* (2009), the U.S. Supreme Court ruled that Justice Brent Benjamin of the West Virginia Supreme Court of Appeals should have recused himself from a case in which the chief executive officer of the lead defendant, after losing a $50 million verdict in the trial court, raised $3 million to elect Benjamin to the court that was hearing the case's appeal. Benjamin was the deciding vote in favor of the defendants. Chastising Justice Benjamin for not sitting out this appeal, the U.S. Supreme Court stated, "Just as no man is allowed to be a judge in his own cause, similar fears of bias can arise when . . . a man chooses the judge in his own cause."

In Benjamin's case, the $3 million from the CEO of A. T. Massey Coal Co. represented about 60 percent of his electoral war chest[28]—another piece of evidence that the funds required to run a campaign have been skyrocketing, particularly in state supreme court races. From 2000 to 2009, candidates for state supreme court seats raised more than $200 million, more than double the $83 million they had raised in the previous decade.[29] Much of the money raised by judicial candidates comes from lawyers, litigants, and other groups with interests in the outcomes of litigation.

In the wake of *Citizens United* (2010), which invalidated laws placing limits on corporate campaign contributions, the spending has continued to increase, with the majority of the spending coming from corporations. As with any other political donation, there is at least some truth to the cynic's sense that campaign contributions are a good investment. The president of the Ohio state bar concluded, "The people with money to spend who are affected by court decisions have reached the conclusion that it's a lot cheaper to buy a judge than a governor or an entire legislature, and he can probably do a lot more for you."[30]

When the judicial reform organization Justice at Stake surveyed 2,428 state court judges, one-quarter said that campaign contributions influenced their decisions.[31]

Even if justices do not allow campaign contributions to affect their decisions, there's an appearance of potential conflict of interest that makes judges appear less impartial. A 2009 USA Today/Gallup poll found that 89 percent of voters believe campaign contributions to judges influence decisions.[32] Prior to 2002, judges' campaigns generally were subject to codes of judicial conduct that placed tight restrictions on campaigning to prevent judges from discussing topics that might later come before them on the bench. In *Republican Party of Minnesota v. White* (2002), however, the U.S. Supreme Court struck down such restrictions as violations of judges' free speech rights. Campaigns increasingly rely on thirty-second TV spots, which can do little more than offer simplistic sound bites about complicated issues. According to Justice at Stake, in 2002 only one in ten of these TV ads was negative; that number had risen to more than one in five by 2004.[33] In 2010, judicial candidates themselves paid for only a quarter of the negative ads, with three out of every four attack ads being purchased by noncandidate groups, including special interests and political parties.[34] In 2010, a coalition of groups seeking to oust a sitting Illinois Supreme Court justice aired a radio ad with actors purporting to be some of the state's worst criminals, recounting their crimes in grisly detail and portraying the judge as taking their side.[35] These kinds of ads can make a difference. In 2004, thirty-four judicial elections featured some form of television advertising, and in twenty-nine of them, the candidate with the most ad expenditures won.[36]

Added to this mix of expensive campaigns and thirty-second TV spots is the fact that ordinary citizens have very little information with which to make informed choices about judicial races. A 2007 poll conducted by the Colorado League of Women Voters found that 52 percent of those who did vote in judicial elections admitted to being uninformed about the candidates. When these uninformed voters were asked to describe their voting strategies,

the results were roughly evenly split between those who said they always voted to keep judges, always voted to remove them, or made random choices.[37] Both lack of voter participation and uninformed voting undermine the public's ability to keep the judiciary accountable and make judges more vulnerable to targeting by single-issue groups.

Thomas Phillips, onetime chief justice of the Texas Supreme Court, has asked,

> When judges are labeled as Democrats or Republicans, how can you convince the public that the law is a judge's only constituency? And when a winning litigant has contributed thousands of dollars to the judge's campaign, how do you ever persuade the losing party that only the facts of the case were considered?[38]

Appointment

The systems used by states in which judges are appointed rather than elected can be divided into two general categories: **pure appointive systems** and merit selection systems that rely on nominating committees. Federal judges have always been selected through a pure appointive system. The president appoints judges who, if they are confirmed by the Senate, "shall hold their Offices during good Behavior." No state, however, employs precisely this method of judicial selection.

Merit selection, initially endorsed by the American Bar Association in 1937, was conceived as a way to limit the intrusion of politics into judge selection and strike a balance between partisan election and lifetime appointment.[39] Most states that currently appoint judges rely on a method of merit selection through nominating committees. Twenty-four states and the District of Columbia rely on a merit selection plan for the initial selection of some or all judges. Another ten states use such plans to fill midterm vacancies at some or all levels of the courts.[40]

Pure Appointive System
A judicial selection system in which the governor appoints judges alone, without preselection of candidates by a nominating commission.

What puts the *merit* into merit selection? At its core, it requires that the state assemble a nonpartisan nominating committee. This committee forwards a list of names from which either the governor or the legislature chooses. How a partisan, distrustful legislature solves the problem of creating a nonpartisan committee differs in almost every state. Some states require parity of political party affiliation for the commission members. Others have adopted extremely complex methods to ensure the impartiality of nominating commissions. While the details of how a nominating committee is chosen may seem innocuous and dry, they have significant impact on just how successful a merit selection plan can be in minimizing the politicization of the judiciary. The ways in which judges are retained after they are appointed also vary by state. In most states, judges appointed through merit selection serve relatively short initial terms, usually one or two years. After that, they participate in retention elections. These special elections were conceived as a means of providing some public participation in the selection of judges while avoiding the intrusion of politics. This worked relatively well for some time, as retention elections appeared immune to the kind of big-money politics seen in partisan elections. But this all changed in the elections of 2009–2010, when incumbent justices in some states, notably Illinois, Iowa, Alaska, and Colorado, faced heavily financed opposition in races as fiercely partisan as popular elections.

Some merit selection states have dispensed with elections altogether. For instance, in Connecticut, Delaware, and Hawaii, judges are reevaluated and reappointed by the judicial selection commission. In Vermont, after an initial appointment through merit selection, a judge receives an additional term as long as the General Assembly does not vote against it.[41]

Terms of Office

The length of a judge's tenure is another element in the balance between judicial independence and judicial accountability.

With only a few exceptions, state court judges serve fixed terms of office and must therefore seek reappointment or reelection. The rare exceptions are judges in Rhode Island, who serve life terms, and judges in Massachusetts and New Hampshire, who hold their positions until the age of seventy. Judges in states with fixed terms typically serve for less than ten years. New York trial court judges serve the longest terms in the states—fourteen years—and are required to retire at age seventy.[42]

TABLE 9-1

Associate Justices' Salaries, by Rank, 2010 (dollars)

Courts of Last Resort		Intermediate Appellate Courts		Trial Courts	
Top Five		Top Five		Top Five	
California	218,237	California	204,599	California	178,789
Illinois	209,344	Illinois	197,032	Illinois	180,802
Pennsylvania	195,309	Pennsylvania	182,282	Delaware	178,449
Alaska	192,372	Alaska	181,752	Alaska	177,888
Delaware	188,751	Alabama	178,878	District of Columbia	174,000
Bottom Five		Bottom Five		Bottom Five	
Mississippi	112,530	Mississippi	105,050	Mississippi	104,170
South Dakota	118,173	New Mexico	117,506	South Dakota	110,377
Maine	119,476	Idaho	118,506	New Mexico	111,631
Idaho	119,506	Oregon	122,820	Maine	111,969
Montana	121,434	Missouri	128,207	Idaho	112,043

Source: Data compiled from the National Center for State Courts, "Survey of Judicial Salaries," January, 1, 2012, http://www.ncsc.org/~/media/Files/PDF/Information%20and%20Resources/Judicial%20Salary/judicialsalaries.ashx.

Shorter tenures bring with them the increased danger that political interests and pressures will intrude on judicial decision making. Longer terms allow for judges to be evaluated on more complete records; any particular controversial decisions may be seen as part of a larger package when there are long periods between elections.

Prosecution and Defense of Cases in State Courts

Criminal cases at the state court level most often involve a face-off between two state or county employees. The **prosecutor** pursues the case on behalf of the people and usually seeks the incarceration of the accused. Little difference exists among the states in the selection of the chief prosecutor; an elected county official almost always fills the position. The individual often is politically ambitious and views the job of chief prosecutor as a stepping-stone to higher elected office. For this reason, the policies of prosecutors tend to reflect the specific wishes of the county voters.

Private attorneys defend individuals who can afford their services. In many cases, however, a **public defender**, an attorney also on the public payroll, represents the accused. Public defenders fulfill the state's constitutional requirement to provide indigent defense services—that is, defense services for those who are poor. There is much more variety in how states organize their systems of indigent defense than there is in their systems of prosecution. Some are organized into statewide systems of public defenders. Other states have established statewide commissions that set guidelines for local jurisdictions, sometimes distributing limited state funds to local programs that follow specific standards. Still others delegate the responsibility of deciding how to provide and fund indigent defense entirely to the counties.

Prosecutor
A government official and lawyer who conducts criminal cases on behalf of the people.

Public Defender
A government lawyer who provides free legal services to persons accused of crimes who cannot afford to hire lawyers.

The Prosecutor

Commentators have gone so far as to say that the prosecutor has become the "most powerful office in the criminal justice system."[43] The prosecutor's office is run by an attorney referred to (depending on the state) as the chief prosecutor, district attorney, county attorney, commonwealth attorney, or state's attorney. Whatever the title, this lawyer represents the public in criminal and other cases. Most prosecutors are elected and typically serve four-year terms. It is a daunting job, particularly in major metropolitan districts, where the top prosecutor manages hundreds of lawyers and support staffers, deals with horrific crimes, and balances the need to serve justice with the "unavoidable scrutiny of won-lost statistics that become a factor in re-election campaigns."[44]

The authority to prosecute comes from the state, but prosecutors' offices are essentially local. A prosecutor's authority is over a specific jurisdiction, usually a county. County governments fund these offices, although close to half of them also receive some portion of their budgets from state funds.[45] Nationwide, there are more than two thousand state court prosecutors' offices, employing approximately seventy-eight thousand attorneys, investigators, and support staffers.[46] They handle more than 2 million felonies and 7 million misdemeanors a year.

Most chief prosecutors serve jurisdictions with fewer than a hundred thousand people. About one-third of chief prosecutors' offices have a total staff of four or fewer.[47] The top 5 percent of prosecutors' offices, however, serve districts with populations of five hundred thousand or more. They represent almost half the entire U.S. population.[48] In 2001, these large offices handled approximately 66 percent of the nation's serious crimes and had a median budget of more than $14 million.[49] The Los Angeles County district attorney's office has the largest staff, consisting of more than 2,200 people, including more than a thousand attorneys.[50] The types of cases handled by these offices have grown increasingly complex as prosecutors' offices have encountered high-tech crimes, including identity theft and credit card fraud, and as they have taken on homeland security responsibilities.

The prosecutor makes all decisions as to whether or not to prosecute, whom to prosecute, and with what cause of action to prosecute. Discretion in charging is, in the words of one scholar, "virtually unchecked by formal constraints or regulatory mechanisms, making it one of the broadest discretionary powers in criminal administration."[51] Charging decisions are enormously important, particularly in states where statutory guidelines set minimum sentences or where the same act can be subject to a number of different charges.

Several reasons exist for giving prosecutors such broad powers. One is the trend toward **legislative overcriminalization**, the tendency of legislatures to make crimes out of everything that people find objectionable.[52] By creating a large number of broadly defined crimes, legislatures have made it impossible for states to enforce all of their criminal statutes, even as they have made it possible for prosecutors to charge a single act under multiple, overlapping provisions.[53] This ability to charge the same act in multiple ways gives a prosecutor tremendous leverage over a defendant. It is a powerful tool for coercing a guilty plea to a lesser charge through the process of plea bargaining.

To determine how best to spend limited resources, a prosecutor must balance the severity of the crime against the probability of sustaining a conviction. Prosecutors have been reluctant to publish general guidelines regarding their charging decisions. A Florida prosecutor stated that his office declines to prosecute cases of cocaine possession when the amount of cocaine involved is deemed too small. But he refused to say just how much is too small. Understandably, he worried that drug smugglers would package their shipments in smaller batches than this arbitrary limit and thus escape prosecution.[54]

There are some limits to prosecutorial authority, for instance, in regard to the trial process itself. In many jurisdictions, before proceeding to trial the government first must obtain an **indictment**, a formal criminal charge, from a **grand jury**. The U.S. Supreme Court has noted that the grand jury historically has been regarded as the primary protection for the innocent. However, only prosecutors and their witnesses appear before a grand jury; no members of the defense are present. Prosecutors are able to offer their interpretation of the evidence and the law and have no obligation to inform the grand jury of evidence of a defendant's innocence. Grand juries hear only one side of any given case and thus almost always indict. For this reason, no discussion of grand juries is complete without mention of the immortal quip by former New York state judge Sol Wachtler that a grand jury could "indict a ham sandwich." This is also partly why many states have abolished the grand jury and now rely instead on a preliminary hearing in which a judge decides if enough evidence exists to warrant a trial.

At trial, a criminal jury must determine guilt beyond a reasonable doubt. The possibility of **jury** 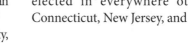 **nullification** exists if the jury does not believe a case should have been brought to court. Trials, however, rarely come into play as a check on the discretion of prosecutors—few cases actually end up going to trial. Most are resolved through plea bargaining. Plea bargaining is another area in which prosecutors have broad discretion. Judges rarely question or second-guess plea bargains reached between prosecutors and defendants. Prosecutors ultimately have to answer to the voters, because chief prosecutors are elected in everywhere other than Alaska, Connecticut, New Jersey, and Washington, DC.[55]

Defense Attorneys

Anyone with even a casual acquaintance with TV crime dramas knows that after the police make an arrest, they must inform the suspect of

---

Legislative Overcriminalization
The tendency of government to make a crime out of anything the public does not like.

Indictment
A formal criminal charge.

Grand Jury
A group of between sixteen and twenty-three citizens who decide if a case should go to trial; if the grand jury decides that it should, an indictment is issued.

Jury Nullification
A jury's returning a verdict of "not guilty" even though jurists believe the defendant is guilty. By doing so, the jury cancels out the effect of a law that the jurors believe is immoral or was wrongly applied to the defendant.

certain rights. One is that "you have the right to an attorney. If you cannot afford one, one will be appointed for you." This right derives from the Sixth Amendment of the U.S. Constitution: "In all criminal prosecutions, the accused shall enjoy the right . . . to have the assistance of counsel for his defense." In 1963, the U.S. Supreme Court found in *Gideon v. Wainwright* that this right to counsel is so fundamental and essential to a fair trial that the Constitution requires the state to provide a poor defendant with a lawyer at state expense. Nine years after *Gideon*, the Court extended this right to counsel to all criminal prosecutions, state or federal, **felony** or **misdemeanor**, that carry a possible sentence of imprisonment. The Court has also made it clear that the Sixth Amendment guarantees the right to the *effective* assistance of counsel.[56] If an attorney is unprepared, drunk, or sleeping during a trial, that can be grounds for appeal.

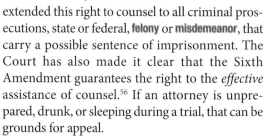

No money came along with the constitutional mandate for counsel, and its scope is tremendous because most criminal defendants in the United States cannot afford to pay for legal services. In 1991, about three-quarters of state prison inmates reported that they had been represented by a court-appointed lawyer.[57] In thirty states, a public defender system is the primary method used to provide indigent criminal defendants with lawyers.[58] In 2007, 957 public defenders' offices across the country received almost 6 million cases, at a cost of $2.3 billion. Twenty-two states' public defenders' offices are funded almost exclusively by state sources, eleven use a combination of state and

county funds, and sixteen use only county funds.[59]

Three primary models have emerged throughout the nation, with most states employing public defender programs, **assigned counsel**, **contract attorneys**, or some combination of these. The method chosen may vary from county to county within a state, or a state may rely primarily on one type and use either of the other types for casework overload or the inevitable cases involving conflict of interest. Among the nation's one hundred most populous counties in 1999 (the latest figures available), public defender programs were operating in ninety counties, assigned counsel programs in eighty-nine counties, and contract programs in forty-two counties.[60] Public defenders usually serve metropolitan areas, and assigned counsel programs and contract programs serve less populous regions.

The challenge is to fund and staff these offices adequately. In 2009, the Michigan Court of Appeals ruled in favor of criminal defendants who charged that three counties' public defense systems were so underfunded that they failed to provide adequate representation. Put simply, the defendants contended that the system was unconstitutional due to lack of funding—and the court agreed, sparking debate statewide about potential reforms.[61] In Washington, the state supreme court recently entered this debate by setting explicit limits on acceptable public defender workloads. The court set these limits after overturning convictions in a number of cases because of inadequate defenses provided by overburdened public defenders. In one such case, for instance, a twelve-year-old boy convicted of sexually molesting a neighbor child was represented by a public defender who handled about five hundred cases a year. The defender failed to investigate the case and only spoke with the boy to urge him to plead guilty. After the high court granted the boy a new trial, he was completely exonerated.[62]

Another type of system uses assigned counsel; here private attorneys are chosen and appointed to handle particular cases, either on a systematic or an ad hoc basis, and are paid from public funds. Depending on the state, individual judges, assigned counsel program offices, or the court clerk's office

---

Felony
A serious crime, such as murder or arson.

Misdemeanor
A less serious crime, such as shoplifting.

Assigned Counsel
Private lawyers selected by the courts to handle particular cases and paid from public funds.

Contract Attorney
A private attorney who enters into an agreement with a state, county, or judicial district to work on a fixed-fee basis per case or for a specific length of time.

may make the appointments. In the oldest type of assigned counsel program, judges make ad hoc assignments of counsel. Sometimes the only basis for these decisions is whoever is in the courtroom at the time. These arrangements frequently are criticized for fostering patronage (the granting of jobs to political allies), particularly in counties with small populations.

Most states using assigned counsel appoint lawyers from a roster of attorneys available for assigned cases. Generally, defense attorneys need do no more than put their names on a list to be appointed to cases. No review of their experience, qualifications, or competence is conducted. Some states, particularly those with organized plans administered by independent managers, may require that attorneys receive specific training before they can be included on the roster. Assigned counsel are generally paid either a flat fee or an hourly rate, in some cases subject to an overall fee cap. Many are paid at very low rates, such that only recent law school graduates or those who have been unsuccessful in the business of law will agree to take assignments.[63]

Contract attorney programs are another way in which states provide defense services. A state, county, or judicial district will enter into a contract for the provision of indigent representation. Such a contract may be awarded to a solo attorney, to a law firm that handles both indigent and private cases, to a nonprofit organization, or to a group of lawyers who have joined together to provide services under the contract. The contractor may agree to accept cases on a fixed-fee per case basis or to provide representation for a particular period of time for a fixed fee.

The contractor must accept all cases that come up during the duration of the contract. For this reason, some view the use of fixed-fee contracts as a quick fix that allows the funding body to limit costs and accurately project expenses for the coming year. However, such contracts have been criticized severely by the courts and by national organizations

such as the American Bar Association, because to make a profit, the contracting attorney has to spend as little time as possible on each case. Few states rely on contract attorneys to provide representation for all or even a majority of their indigent defense cases. Many indigent defense systems are plagued by lack of funding and resources, high attorney workloads, and little or no oversight of the quality of services—problems that can and do result in the conviction of innocent people. "Providing genuinely adequate counsel for poor defendants would require a substantial infusion of money and indigent defense is the last thing the populace will voluntarily direct its tax dollars to fund," writes attorney David Cole. "Achieving solutions to this problem through the political process is a pipe dream."[64]

How secure would you feel if you were facing more than twenty years in jail for a felony you didn't commit in Virginia, where your appointed lawyer could be paid a maximum of $1,235 to defend you?[65] If you don't plead guilty quickly, your lawyer will lose money on your case. Recently, a wave of successful lawsuits against underfunded and overburdened public defenders, assigned counsel programs, and contract attorneys by groups such as the American Civil Liberties Union have led legislators to enact reforms that "even the most skeptical observers admit have the potential to bring important changes to the process of criminal justice."[66] Some of these have led to successful injunctions or settlements, increased funding for indigent defense, and improved administration of such programs. Furthermore, the defense community and organizations such as the American Bar Association have been focusing on the need for standards for indigent criminal representation. The goal is to educate the policymakers who design the systems through which these legal services are delivered.

Juries

If you vote, pay a utility bill, or have a driver's license, you may be called to jury duty at some point in your life. You may be asked to decide whether a defendant in a capital case lives or dies; whether someone spends the rest of his or her life in prison; whether a civil plaintiff, injured and unable to work, should be able to collect damages; or whether a civil defendant must be bankrupted by the large amount of damages he or she is ordered to pay. Service on a jury may require spending days or weeks listening to intricate scientific evidence and expert testimony, some of it conflicting, and deciding who is credible and who is not to be believed. Or you may spend one day in a large room with other potential jurors, break for lunch, and go home at the end of that day without ever hearing a single case.

The right to a jury trial in state criminal proceedings is granted by the Sixth Amendment. Not all criminal prosecutions trigger the right to a jury trial—minor offenses involving potential sentences of less than six months do not require juries. Neither do juvenile proceedings, probation revocation proceedings, or military trials.

The jury's role in a trial is that of fact-finder. The judge has to ensure a fair and orderly trial, but it is the jurors who must determine the facts of the case. In some instances, parties may agree to forgo a jury trial and, instead, choose a bench trial, in which the judge serves as both judge and jury. In a criminal bench trial, the judge alone decides guilt or innocence.

Differences and similarities in how judges and juries rule have been the subject of much research and review. Stereotypes might lead you to think that juries are less capable than judges of separating emotion from reason or that juries decide cases more generously for injured plaintiffs or that grisly evidence in criminal cases may motivate juries to base their decisions on passion or prejudice. Not so. For instance, research shows that civil plaintiffs in product **liability** and medical malpractice cases have more success before judges in bench trials.[67]

Historically, juries in the United States have been composed of twelve people who must come to a unanimous verdict. Since 1970, however, a series of U.S. Supreme Court decisions has allowed states to move away from this standard.[68] A conviction by a twelve-member jury may be less than unanimous, whereas a six-member jury must have unanimity. A majority of states continue to require twelve-member juries to make unanimous rulings in felony criminal cases, but seven states use six-member or eight-member juries for noncapital felonies. Two states, Louisiana and Oregon, do not require unanimous

> Stereotypes might lead you to think that juries are less capable than judges of separating emotion from reason or that juries decide cases more generously for injured plaintiffs or that grisly evidence in criminal cases may motivate juries to base their decisions on passion or prejudice. Not so.

verdicts in such cases.[69] Most states provide for civil juries of six or eight members. Those that still require twelve members typically allow the parties to civil cases to agree to smaller juries. Unanimity is not required in most civil trials; instead, most states provide for verdicts based on a supermajority of either five-sixths or two-thirds.

States develop and maintain master lists from which they identify potential jurors. Their sources include driver's licenses, motor vehicle registrations, telephone directories, tax rolls, utility customer lists, voter registration rolls, and lists of actual voters. It is very hard to avoid ever being called in for jury duty. Jurors must be residents of the county in which the court sits and must generally be eighteen years old, although in Alabama and Nebraska the minimum age is nineteen and in Mississippi and Missouri it is twenty-one. States also usually have some sort of requirement regarding literacy and the ability to understand or communicate in English, or both. South Carolina requires that jurors have at least a sixth-grade education, and Tennessee explicitly excludes those of "unsound mind" and "habitual drunkards." Most states also require that jurors not be convicted felons.

Defendants' Rights Versus Victims' Rights

Numerous provisions in the Bill of Rights balance the rights of criminal defendants against the powers of the state. These defendants' rights include the following:

Liability
A legal obligation or responsibility.

- The right to be presumed innocent until proven guilty

- The right to be safe from arrest or searches and seizures unless the government has made a showing of probable cause

- The right to a lawyer

- The right to a jury trial

- The right to confront witnesses

- The rights to due process and the equal protection of laws

- If proven guilty, the right to punishment that is not cruel and unusual

In spelling out these rights, the framers sought to prevent the overreach of government power. They worried that innocent people might otherwise be railroaded into jail on charges they never had a chance to defend themselves against adequately. The Bill of Rights makes no mention of the rights of crime victims.

In the past three decades, the balance between defendants' rights and those of victims has undergone a radical transformation. Defendants still have all of the rights listed, but now state courts are increasingly balancing them against a new class of victims' rights. The movement advocating an increasing role in the courts for the victims of crime has become a formidable force and has achieved tremendous success in enacting legislation in all the states. The momentum started in 1982, when a president's task force on victims of crime described the U.S. justice system as "appallingly out of balance." That is not to say that victims were helpless—the number of state laws addressing victims' rights was already in the hundreds. By 1998, however, the number of crime victim–related statutes had soared to more than twenty-seven thousand. Twenty-nine states had passed constitutional amendments addressing victims' rights.[70]

Today, every state has either a constitutional amendment or a statutory scheme that protects victims' rights. Supporters of victims' rights frequently argue that the justice system favors defendants over victims and that, without modification, the system itself constitutes a second victimization. On the other hand, civil rights organizations fear that some victims' rights laws upset the system of checks and balances in the nation's criminal justice system and

undercut the basic due process protections designed to keep innocent people out of prison.

The specifics of victims' rights laws vary among the states. A variety of statutes and amendments guarantee that crime victims receive monetary compensation, notice of procedural developments in their cases, protection from offender harm, and more attentive treatment from the justice system. The more controversial of such laws are directed toward providing victims with significantly greater involvement in actual prosecutions. This includes providing victims the right to confer with the prosecutor at all stages, including plea bargains; the right to attend all stages of the case, even if the victim will be called as a witness; and the right to introduce victim-impact statements at the sentencing phase of the trial.

Perhaps the most controversial and interesting of the victims' rights laws concern victim-impact evidence. This may be particularly true in capital cases, in which impact statements have been described as

> highly emotional, frequently tearful testimony coming directly from the hearts and mouths of the survivors left behind by killings. And it arrives at the precise time when the balance is at its most delicate and the stakes are highest— when jurors are poised to make the visceral decision of whether the offender lives or dies.[71]

In 1991, the U.S. Supreme Court reversed itself and ruled that impact statements that detailed the particular qualities of the victim and the harm caused to the victim's family could be admissible in capital sentencing hearings.[72] Today, all states allow victim-impact evidence at the sentencing phase of a trial. Most states that allow the death penalty permit it in capital trials.

Sentencing

The total U.S. prison population has ballooned in the past thirty years, rising from less than 320,000 in 1980 to a high of 2.3 million in 2008.[73] The trend might be reversing, as 2009 and 2010 marked the first declines in total prison population in four decades.[74] Corrections has been one of the fastest-growing items in state budgets, and, although it slowed considerably owing to widespread revenue shortfalls and limited state resources after 2008, it still averaged 31 percent of total state spending and 7.3 percent of state general fund budgets in 2010.[75]

In most states, after a jury finds a defendant guilty, the judge holds a separate sentencing hearing. In capital cases, the U.S. Supreme Court has held that only a unanimous jury, and not the judge, can sentence a defendant to death.[76] In many states, capital juries are instructed that a sentence of life in prison without the possibility of parole is an option. In noncapital cases, by contrast, it is almost always the judge who sets the sentence. Only in Arkansas, Kentucky, Missouri, Oklahoma, Texas, and Virginia do juries choose the sentences of those they find guilty. In most of these states, the judge is free to reduce but not to increase the jury's sentence, except to comply with mandatory sentencing laws. Most of these states choose their judges through popular election, so having juries decide on sentences allows trial judges to evade political heat for sentencing.

Surveys indicate that attitudes toward sentencing follow regional patterns, "with residents of New England demonstrating the greatest tendency to be lenient and residents of central southern states displaying the least leniency."[77] It is not surprising, then, that state sentencing laws vary and that the punishment a convict faces depends not just on what that person did but also on where the crime was committed. Voters in California and Oklahoma, for instance, view drug offenses differently. In California state courts, a cocaine dealer is subject to a two- to four-year prison term. The same offense in Oklahoma brings a minimum of five years and a maximum of life imprisonment.[78]

A few decades ago, it was possible to talk of a predominant American approach to criminal sentencing. At all levels of the nation's criminal justice system, a concern for rehabilitation and deterrence led states to embrace **indeterminate sentencing**. Legislatures set very wide statutory sentencing margins within which judges had the discretion to

impose sentences for imprisonment with little fear of appellate review. The sentencing was indeterminate because the parole board, not the judge, had ultimate control over the actual release date. Under this system, judges and parole boards had to apply their discretion to tailor punishments to the specific rehabilitative needs of individual defendants. This practice led to wide discrepancies in the sentences imposed on different persons convicted of the same crimes.

Indeterminate sentencing came under attack from several angles during the 1970s. The lack of guidance for judges led to the potential for discrimination in sentencing based on such factors as race, ethnic group, social status, and gender. There was also criticism of the ability of parole boards to determine successfully whether inmates had or had not been rehabilitated. Finally, rehabilitation lost favor as the country entered an era of tough-on-crime rhetoric and a "just deserts" theory of criminal sentencing.[79] Reformers sought to replace indeterminate sentencing with **determinate sentencing**. This led to the adoption of federal sentencing guidelines, a structured system of binding sentencing rules that greatly limited judicial discretion in sentencing in the federal courts.

In contrast to the federal court system, there has been no single sweeping sentencing reform across all fifty states. Most states still rely on indeterminate sentencing, but all states have adopted at least some features of determinate sentencing, although in greatly differing degrees. When it comes to sentencing reform, "the states have served as hothouses of experimentation during the last thirty years, with so much activity that the diversity of provisions among the states has become exceedingly complex."[80] Some of the major reforms adopted include sentencing guidelines (either presumptive, meaning the judge can deviate with a good reason, or purely voluntary), **mandatory minimum sentences** that are

---

Indeterminate Sentencing
The sentencing of an offender, by a judge, to a minimum and a maximum amount of time in prison, with a parole board deciding how long the offender actually remains in prison.

Determinate Sentencing
The sentencing of an offender, by a judge, to a specific amount of time in prison depending on the crime.

Mandatory Minimum Sentence
The shortest sentence that an offender may receive upon conviction for a certain offense. The court has no authority to impose a shorter sentence.

imposed for conviction of specified crimes, **habitual offender laws**, and **truth-in-sentencing laws**. With the implementation of these reforms, the time served in prison by those convicted has been increasing as a percentage of the sentence imposed. In 1993, the percentage of a sentence that an offender spent in prison was 31.8 percent; that figure had increased to 46.7 percent by 2009.[81] The average length of an incarceration increased as well; offenders who were released from state prisons in 2009 had served an average of almost three years behind bars, nine months longer than those released in 1990.[82]

All fifty states and the District of Columbia have enacted some form of mandatory minimum prison sentencing laws.[83] These laws limit judicial discretion by requiring that individuals found guilty of specific crimes be incarcerated for no less than specified lengths of time. Such crimes may include drug possession or trafficking, drunk driving, and sexual offenses. The mandatory sentencing laws also may include "bump ups" that take effect if certain acts enhanced the severity of the underlying crime, for instance, if weapons were involved or if the crime occurred near a school. If a crime involved the use of a deadly weapon, New Mexico requires an additional year for the first offense and three additional years for a second offense. The use of a firearm in the commission of a crime in Nevada requires a doubling of the sentence for the underlying crime. In Ohio, the use of a deadly weapon requires an additional term of three to six years.[84]

Habitual offender laws are also common among the states. These statutes impose more severe sentences for offenders who have previously been sentenced for crimes. California's "three-strikes" law was a prototype of this kind

of legislation. The law states that if a defendant convicted of a felony has one prior conviction for a "serious" or "violent" felony, the sentence is doubled. Defendants convicted of a felony with two prior convictions for "serious" or "violent" felonies receive a life sentence without possibility of parole. The law has been severely criticized for its "unbending harshness," but it has withstood constitutional challenges.[85] According to Michael Romano, director of the Three Strikes Project, the law has sentenced people to life in prison for relatively small crimes such as drug possession or petty theft. In 2004, a ballot proposition to revise the law to impose a life term only if the third felony conviction is for a "serious or violent offense" failed. Supporters reintroduced the proposal for the 2012 elections, and this time it passed by a wide margin. Twenty-four states have enacted some form of two- or three-strikes legislation. One such state is Michigan, where the sentence is one and a half times the maximum sentence for the second conviction and twice the maximum sentence for a third conviction.[86]

Another sentencing reform movement began in the 1990s as a reaction to the sometimes jarring disparity between the sentence handed down by a judge and the actual amount of time served in prison. These "truth-in-sentencing" laws reduce the amount of discretion parole boards have to shorten sentences for good behavior. They do this by specifying the proportions of sentences that offenders must serve before they may be considered for parole. The federal government encourages truth-in-sentencing laws by conditioning the states' receipt of federal prison construction funds on the requirement that certain violent offenders serve at least 85 percent of their sentences. With this carrot, almost all states and the District of Columbia have adopted some form of truth-in-sentencing laws. Most, however, still have parole boards with some discretionary release authority and systems in which incarcerated felons can accumulate "good time" under specified formulas. Arkansas, Louisiana, Vermont, and Wyoming are among the many states that provide for a day of "good time" for each day—or less—served.

Habitual Offender Laws
Statutes imposing harsher sentences on offenders who previously have been sentenced for crimes.

Truth-In-Sentencing Laws
Laws that give parole boards less authority to shorten sentences for good behavior by specifying the proportion of a sentence an offender must serve before becoming eligible for parole.

North Dakota grants five days of good time for every month served.

These formulas can also be complicated by the accumulation of work or education credits. Some states, such as Illinois, have cut through the confusion by eliminating good time credits for certain serious offenses. Others have eliminated such credits altogether. Michigan eliminated good time for all felony offenses committed after December 2000, and the District of Columbia has not offered it since 1994.[87]

As states reduce judges' discretion and increase the amount of time that offenders spend in prison, a considerable burden has been placed on the facilities and personnel of the state prison systems. In California, atrocious conditions caused by prison overcrowding have become such a problem that the U.S. Supreme Court held in *Brown v. Plata* (2011) that California prisons violate the Eighth Amendment ban on cruel and unusual punishment. The Court ordered the release over the next several years of tens of thousands of prisoners to reduce overcrowding to 137.5 percent of capacity. For this reason, many nonviolent offenders find their prison terms greatly reduced. In November 2011, actress Lindsay Lohan served only four hours of a three-day sentence for probation violations before being released to reduce overcrowding.

While few question that putting more people in prison for longer terms has played a role in the drop in crime rates since the 1990s, longer sentences have also been the primary drivers of increasing prison costs. In a 2012 report, the Pew Center on the States put the financial impact of longer prison stays at $10 billion for offenders released in 2009 alone; the report further suggested that a significant portion of nonviolent offenders could have served shorter stays with no adverse impact on public safety.[88] In response to such research findings and increasingly tight state budgets, some states are starting to take a step back on mandatory minimum sentencing. New York, for instance, has eliminated mandatory minimums for first- and second-time nonviolent drug offenses.

In addition, most states are exploring sentencing options for their less serious offenders that are less severe than imprisonment but more serious than ordinary probation. One such option is house arrest. Offenders under house arrest are required to remain in their residences for the duration of their sentences. They often must wear electronic wrist or ankle bracelets that send continuous radio signals to verify their locations.

Many states rely on "intensive probation." This form of probation involves much closer supervision by parole officers with smaller caseloads than the norm. In such a program a parolee is typically required to hold a job, submit to urinalysis, pay restitution to victims, and perform community service. To alleviate prison overcrowding, some states release prisoners to "halfway houses" that assist with their reintegration into the community. Young first-time offenders may be sentenced for short periods to "boot camps," where they are subjected to strict military-style discipline. Nonviolent offenders may be offered work release; weekend sentencing; alcohol, drug, or mental health treatment; or release subject to appearance at daily reporting centers.

How Courts Are Changing

How state courts are organized is not static or carved in stone. States constantly evaluate the practices and procedures of their criminal justice systems as they attempt to adapt to changing demographic, economic, and political conditions. This section discusses some reforms being adopted or at least being discussed in most states. Specialized courts to handle drug offenses or family matters are currently in vogue as ways to accommodate increasing caseloads and lower costs, as are attempts to streamline and speed up court dockets. Given the controversy surrounding judicial elections, particularly following *Citizens United* (the Supreme Court decision that opened the door for unlimited campaign spending by super PACs), many states have not waited for major reforms to merit selection; instead, they have focused on modifying judicial elections to minimize the problems posed by the need for campaign contributions. Finally, this section addresses some of the pressures for court reform that stem from the lack of uniformity across the country and within individual states.

The Problem of Increasing Caseloads

Nationwide, violent crime rates are down. State courts, nonetheless, have found themselves on the front lines dealing with the results of societal problems such as substance abuse and family violence since the 1980s. From 1984 to 1999, the U.S. population grew by only 12 percent, but the number of juvenile criminal cases grew by 68 percent, and the number of domestic relations cases grew by 74 percent. Criminal cases, mostly misdemeanors, grew by 47 percent.[89]

In reaction to such growth, many states have created "problem-solving courts." These include community courts, domestic violence courts, mental health courts, and drug treatment courts. Their purpose is to deal decisively with low-level nonviolent crimes while reducing congestion in the general jurisdiction courts. The solutions often involve closely monitored treatment plans meant to stop the revolving door of **recidivism**, or relapse into criminal behavior. Drug courts, with their focus on judicially supervised treatment for nonviolent drug-addicted offenders, have been shown to contribute to the decline in violent crime and to save local and state governments millions of dollars annually from reduced incarceration rates. While it is difficult to determine the cost-effectiveness of drug courts, a definitive evaluation of a Portland, Oregon, court estimated that total savings from drug court participation were more than $5,000 per participant. With an annual caseload of three hundred participants, the program saved the state more than $1.5 million per year.[90]

States also have been experimenting with integrated family courts. These courts, referred to as "one family/one judge" courts, adopt a holistic approach to all the issues that affect a single family in a single court system. Such integrated courts can address these issues more efficiently than can multiple courts, especially in cases in which delays can leave children in foster care limbo. Many individuals who appear in such family courts traditionally would have been forced, instead, to face multiple proceedings in different courts: assault charges in county court, custody disputes in family court, and divorce issues in yet another court. The current trend is to put all of a family's problems before a single, informed judge to eliminate conflicting orders and multiple appearances. New York has estimated that its integrated domestic violence courts slashed the number of family court cases from more than three thousand to fewer than nine hundred in its first two years while reducing delay and duplication and increasing cost-effective case management.[91]

This increased focus on court administration and case management has not been confined to the criminal side of the court calendar. Until just a few years ago, crowded civil dockets and multiyear waiting periods were relatively common in many states. "Back in the 1980s, there was no incentive for an insurance company to settle a case for the first year," said Bill Sieben, who was then president of the Minnesota Trial Lawyers Association. "They knew the case wasn't even going to be nearing a trial for several years."[92] This is becoming less true as states focus on clearing their overcrowded and overly cumbersome civil dockets. Most trial judges today may insist on strong case management systems, but a generation ago, when caseloads were smaller and more manageable, not many of them did.

In recent years, not content with merely handing down verdicts, forceful judges have seized control of their courts and made it clear that things will run according to their schedules, not at the convenience of lawyers who never seem quite ready to go to trial. "A very strong component of civil cases is, just set a trial date and the case will go away," said Kevin Burke, formerly the chief judge of the Hennepin County Court in Minnesota. "Left to their own devices, lawyers aren't necessarily going to manage it to a speedy resolution."[93]

State initiatives to speed up dockets, or court case schedules, have included an increased reliance on **alternative dispute resolution**. In certain types of cases, such resolution is now mandated, and lawyers are required to inform their clients about alternatives to standard court fights. These alternatives usually

---

Recidivism
A return to, or relapse into, criminal behavior.

involve hashing things out in front of an expert mediator. Some courts have been creative in finding appropriately authoritative experts. Hennepin County courts, for instance, refer disputes involving dry cleaning—complaints about stained pants, torn dresses, and busted buttons—to a retired owner of a dry cleaning business for speedy resolution. An accountant may serve as mediator in the resolution of a financial dispute. These innovations increase the efficiency of the court system and free up trial judges for more complex cases.

Several states are experimenting with the **rocket docket**, patterned after an innovation in a Virginia federal court. In essence, this fast-tracked docket imposes tight, unbending deadlines on lawyers for the handling of pretrial motions and briefs. In the Vermont Supreme Court, the rocket docket applies to cases that present no novel issue likely to add to the body of case law. Rather than all five justices sitting en banc to hear these cases, each month they split and rotate through a smaller and less cumbersome panel of three that is able to reach consensus more quickly. The panel releases its decisions on 99 percent of rocket docket cases within twenty-four hours.

Rocket dockets are not always a panacea, however. Florida implemented the approach as thousands of home foreclosures began clogging the courts in late 2006. The foreclosure courts could clear 250 cases a day, each in a matter of minutes. But, although it represented a success for the state, attorneys found fault with the system. The few homeowners who attended the hearings had little time to be heard, and one review of 180 cases in Sarasota found that only one in four had complete paperwork. By late 2009, one judge found a way to slow the rapid-fire process, at least a

bit—he gave any homeowners who showed up at the courthouse an additional three months to work to save their homes or to move.[94]

In Colorado, rapid population growth has led to mounting lawsuits, and courts increasingly have turned to **magistrates** to resolve less important cases. Often local officials or attorneys hired on contract, these magistrates have helped the state to stay on top of an 85 percent increase in case filings despite only a 12 percent increase in the number of judges. A magistrate issues a preliminary decision that must then be upheld by a judge, but this is a formality in most cases. This modification is credited with enabling the state court system to handle routine cases efficiently and allowing more time for more complex cases, but some have complained to the Colorado Bar Association that this reliance on contract attorneys to serve as magistrates decreases the accountability of judges and does not yield sufficiently clear precedents to provide guidance to the attorneys who must practice before them.[95] Given these concerns, a task force on civil justice reform convened by then governor Bill Ritter recommended that the state create additional district and county court judgeships to alleviate the caseload strain on the system.[96] A 2007 act created forty-three new positions for judges across Colorado; however, in light of state revenue shortfalls, funding was provided for only twenty-eight.

Overhauling Judicial Selection

Nationally, 87 percent of all state judges face partisan, nonpartisan, or retention elections or some mix of these.[97] As discussed earlier, the trend in recent years has been for these elections to become more like the elections for legislative and gubernatorial offices: loud, nasty, and expensive. Some fear that this will lead to a blurring of the distinction between the judicial and political branches of government and throw into question the independent decision making of the judiciary.

Indeed, two recent decisions from the U.S. Supreme Court may have brought politics closer than

---

Alternative Dispute Resolution
A way to end a disagreement by means other than litigation. It usually involves the appointment of a mediator to preside over a meeting between the parties.

Rocket Docket
Fast-tracked cases that often have limited, specific deadlines for specific court procedures.

Magistrate
A local official or attorney granted limited judicial powers.

States Under Stress

This Court Will Not Come to Order

In Birmingham, Alabama, domestic relations judge Suzanne Childers keeps a .38-caliber Smith & Wesson revolver under her bench. That, and a can of pepper spray, have served as protection for her courtroom since budget cuts eliminated two deputies' positions. Childers's story is extreme, but hers is not the only courtroom that has been left less safe as a result of the state and local fiscal crisis. In Massachusetts, open court officer positions were not filled between the end of 2008 and early 2010, and in Maine, metal detectors in courthouses go unstaffed. "It's a question of do you want to close courthouses and run [fewer] courthouses with full security? Or do you want to keep all your courthouses open and compromise on security?" said Mary Ann Lynch, a spokeswoman for Maine's court system.[a]

When budget cuts eliminated courtroom security guards, Jefferson County, Alabama, domestic court judge Suzanne Childers resorted to keeping a .38-caliber pistol under her desk during session for protection.

In many states, courts are opening later in the day, closing earlier, and shutting their doors entirely for several days per month. Kansas and Oregon have begun closing courts on Fridays, and one court in Georgia has stopped hearing civil matters altogether to focus time on critical criminal matters. In some parts of North Carolina and Ohio, cases have ground to a halt because the courts could not afford to buy more paper. With states facing severe budget shortfalls, almost every state court system is trying to get by with less. A survey conducted by the National Center for State Courts (NCSC) in 2011 estimated that at least forty-two state court systems were facing cutbacks in their 2012 budgets, leading most courts to shrink staff and reduce hours.[b] Iowa, for instance, now has fewer employees in the judicial branch than it had twenty-four years ago, even though case filings in the state increased by 54 percent in the same period.[c]

NCSC reported that the cuts would lead to increased backlogs in civil, criminal, and family court cases. Such backlogs lead inevitably to delays; in San Francisco, it can now "take up to a year from the time you first get a [traffic] ticket until you get a trial date," says Ann Donian, communications director for San Francisco Superior Court.[d]

Making matters worse, states expected that the very programs they had implemented to help alleviate backlogs—alternative dispute resolution and problem-solving courts—would themselves end up on the chopping block.

[a]Quoted in Denise Lavoie, "Budget Cuts Force Tough Choices on Court Security," *Seattle Times*, January 10, 2010, http://seattletimes.nwsource.com/html/businesstechnology/2010758141_apuscourthousesecuritycuts.html.

[b]National Center for State Courts, "State Budget Cuts Threaten Public's Access to Courts," November 29, 2011, www.ncsc.org/Newsroom/Backgrounder/2011/Court-Budget-Cuts.aspx.

[c]Alan Greenblatt, "Sue Me? Not a Chance This Year," NPR.org, April 12, 2012, www.npr.org/2012/04/12/1504294441/sue-me-not-a-chance-this-year.

[d]Quoted in ibid.

ever to the judicial election process. First, in *Republican Party v. White* (2002), a 5–4 majority ruled that the First Amendment does not allow the government "to prohibit candidates from communicating relevant information to voters during an election." This includes judicial candidates who wish to speak publicly about disputed legal matters. At the same time, the Court acknowledged the core responsibility of judges to "be willing to consider views that oppose [their] preconceptions, and remain open to persuasion when the issues arise in a pending case." Today, states that hold elections for judicial offices, such as Ohio, Pennsylvania, and Wisconsin, feature public debates among judicial candidates similar to those held for candidates for legislative office.

Then, in 2010, the Supreme Court ruled in the controversial *Citizens United v. Federal Election Commission* that laws placing limits on campaign spending by outside groups such as corporations and unions are unconstitutional. At the time, twenty-four states had laws banning independent expenditures in judicial elections; all were rendered moot by the holding in *Citizens United*. This ruling magnified the already growing debate about the impact of increased spending in judicial elections and the best method of judicial selection.

In the wake of *Citizens United*, a dozen state legislatures proposed changing away from selecting judges through popular elections, but none was successful. States seeking to adopt merit selection are confronted with both cultural and political obstacles. They face a widely shared belief that elections are an integral part of our democracy. And, in most states, a change to merit selection would require the legislative supermajority and public approval necessary for a constitutional change.

Recognizing these barriers to the adoption of merit selection, advocates are focusing on improving popular judicial elections to minimize the threat they pose to judicial independence and impartiality. A fifty-state survey commissioned by the California legislature reviewed state trends in the wake of *Citizens United* and the unprecedented level of interest group activity in judicial elections.[98] It showed that more than half the states have proposed more stringent reporting and disclosure of campaign

contributions to increase the information available to voters. Iowa, for instance, passed a law requiring all political ads to run "paid for by" disclosures. Other states have focused on **recusal** and disqualification rules, which until recently have been very lenient, allowing judges to decide on their own whether they should recuse themselves from particular cases.

Some states have focused their reform efforts on the dangers inherent in campaign financing and have experimented with public financing of judicial campaigns. They hope that this will reduce the potential for campaign contributions to influence or appear to influence outcomes. In 2002, North Carolina became the first state to provide full public financing of elections for appeals court and supreme court candidates who accept spending limits. All North Carolina's judicial candidates participated in the plan in 2010, and Judge Wanda Bryant stated, "I've run in two elections, one with the campaign finance reform and one without. I'll take 'with' any day, anytime, anywhere."[99] In 2009, Wisconsin passed the Impartial Justice Act, which enabled the public funding of the campaigns of state supreme court candidates through a one-dollar state tax return checkoff. However, the Wisconsin reform demonstrates one of the weaknesses of public financing of judicial elections: it leaves the judiciary dependent on continuing support from lawmakers.

Conclusion

State and local courts play a profound role in state governments. They resolve civil disputes and hand out justice in criminal cases. They also protect the citizens of their states from unconstitutional behavior by the political branches of government. Despite the importance of this role, or perhaps because of it, judicial systems differ tremendously from state to state. There are organizational differences from initial trial to final appeal. Judges in some states are elected by voters and in others are appointed by the governor. Such differences reflect each state's unique orientation toward the values of politics, law, judicial independence, and accountability.

The focus in this chapter has been on the players involved as a case works its way through the judicial system. In a criminal case, the elected prosecutor has tremendous freedom to decide which charges to bring against an accused criminal. Anyone charged

---

Recusal
The disqualification of a judge because of an actual or perceived bias or conflict of interest calling the judge's impartiality into question.

with a crime has the right to an attorney, and the state must provide attorneys to those unable to afford their own. Usually the accused is represented by a public defender. If a plea bargain is not reached, the case goes to trial, and the fate of the accused rests in the hands of a panel of ordinary citizens who have been called to jury duty. Potential jurors are selected from a pool of individuals who may have done something as simple as paying a utility bill. This does not mean, however, that there is anything simple about a jury's task. Often, this group holds the future of another individual in its hands.

If an accused person is found guilty and sentenced to incarceration, the length of time the offender actually spends in jail depends a lot on how the values of rehabilitation, deterrence, and retribution have played out in a particular state's political system. Differences here can have an enormous impact. One state may try a nonviolent drug offender in a special drug court that focuses on treatment; another may try the same offense in a general trial court in which the judge has no choice under rigid minimum sentencing guidelines but to apply a sentence of lengthy incarceration.

None of the choices that states make in structuring their courts is fixed and unchanging. States are always responding to altered societal or political realities, experimenting with what works, and adapting to political movements. Some of the areas of reform and change examined in this chapter were triggered by the political rise of victims' rights movements, by the realities of changing caseloads, or by a perception that the selection of judges has become increasingly political.

The Latest Research

State courts, like state constitutions, are one of the aspects of government that remain relatively understudied by political scientists. Although there is a long record of court studies, especially by law scholars, truly systematic research using the comparative method dates back only a few decades and is considerably less common than research examining state legislatures and executives. This is unfortunate because, as this chapter has explained in detail, state courts shoulder enormous responsibility for the administration of criminal and civil justice, and their decisions have far-reaching policy implications.

As this chapter makes clear, one of the perennial controversies in this branch revolves around how states can best select judges. Above we have given a flavor of the increasing politicization of the bench. Some champion this development as increasing democratic accountability, whereas others lament it as the courts losing their independence. Ultimately, which of these values is best to emphasize in selecting judges? Below we summarize some of the latest research on state courts. All of these studies focus on the running theme of the impact of judicial elections, which are at the center of controversies regarding judicial selection.

. . . .

- **Bonneau, Chris, and Melinda Gann Hall.** 2009. *In Defense of Judicial Elections*. New York: Routledge.

An extended comparative examination of state supreme court elections, this book makes an empirical case that judicial elections have a number of benefits. The authors argue that judicial reforms aimed at depoliticizing the courts have had a number of potentially negative impacts. When states started moving toward Missouri Plan–type systems, judges' names were still showing up on ballots, but without opponents or partisan labels. The net result was that voters knew virtually nothing about judicial candidates; the courts became so low profile, accountability was lost. This, however, did not make the judicial branch any less political. The authors point to the justices of the U.S. Supreme Court as examples of judges who are appointed for life but clearly take on big political issues and decide them along roughly partisan lines. But at least the U.S. Supreme Court is high profile, and candidates for the Court are scrutinized closely in a relatively open process. There is little of this in a typical Missouri Plan setup. The authors find that competitive, partisan state supreme court elections do not just serve as accountability mechanisms, but they also confer more democratic legitimacy on the courts—voters trust the judges more because they know them and are more directly linked to them through the normal process of representative democracy.

- **Streb, Matthew, and Brian Frederick.** 2011. "When Money Cannot Encourage Participation: Campaign Spending and Rolloff in Low Visibility Judicial Elections." *Political Behavior* 33: 665–684.

One known way to increase voter turnout in legislative elections is to make those races partisan. Party labels give voters important information and a stake in the outcome of elections. Another known way to increase turnout in legislative races is to have competitive elections; competing candidates tend to spend more money and mobilize more voters. Do these same factors also increase turnout in judicial elections? This study takes a look at 172 appellate court elections between 2000 and 2008 and arrives at two key findings. First is a confirmation of the impact of partisan labels—if candidates for judicial office run on a party label, people are more likely to vote in that election. Second, and somewhat surprisingly, the authors find that campaign spending does nothing to boost turnout significantly. In these low-visibility elections, even well-resourced candidates seem to struggle to get enough information to voters to make them confident in casting their ballots. The simplest and most basic piece of political information, partisanship, seems to be the important factor for increasing participation in judicial elections.

- **Gibson, James, Jeffrey Gottfried, Michael DelliCarpini, and Kathleen Hall Jamieson.** 2010. "The Effects of Judicial Campaign Activity on the Legitimacy of the Courts: A Survey-Based Experiment." *Political Research Quarterly* 64: 545–558.

This study examines how citizens feel about the legitimacy of the Pennsylvania courts. Its key contribution is a creative experiment in which different sets of people were randomly assigned to watch different kinds of campaign ads for judicial candidates, ranging from a straightforward candidate endorsement by an interest group to negative attack ads. Overall, the authors find that elections have a positive impact—voters confer more legitimacy on the courts when judges periodically have to be approved by the voters. In contrast, some of the usual components of elections—that is, campaign ads—tend to decrease support for the courts. The positive overall impact of elections is larger than the negative impact of campaign ads, but one of the inferences that can be taken from this study is that while voters like the idea of judges being elected, they are less enthusiastic about judges actually acting like candidates for electoral office.

- **Gibson, James.** 2008. "Challenges to the Impartiality of State Supreme Courts: Legitimacy Theory and 'New-Style' Judicial Campaigns." *American Political Science Review* 102: 59–75.

Opponents of judicial elections argue that at least three components of electoral contests serve to undercut trust in and support of the courts: campaign contributions (which undermine trust by creating the perception that groups may "buy" judges), attack ads (which undermine trust in judges as individuals), and policy pronouncements (which make judges look less impartial and more partisan). This study, using a creative experiment embedded in a survey, found that the first two, contributions and attack ads, affect attitudes toward courts in pretty much the same way that they affect attitudes toward legislatures. In short, they lead to less support for and trust in the institution. The third component, taking particular policy positions, does not have the same impact. When judges promise to make certain decisions or to make decisions in certain ways, this does not chip away at the legitimacy of courts in the same fashion as judges' accepting contributions or launching attack ads.

9

Chapter Review

Key Concepts

- activist judge (p. 248)
- alternative dispute resolution (p. 272)
- appeal (p. 250)
- assigned counsel (p. 265)
- bench trial (p. 251)
- civil case (p. 250)
- contract attorney (p. 265)
- criminal case (p. 250)
- determinate sentencing (p. 269)
- discretionary jurisdiction (p. 253)
- en banc (p. 254)
- felony (p. 265)
- general jurisdiction trial court (p. 251)
- grand jury (p. 264)
- habitual offender laws (p. 270)
- indeterminate sentencing (p. 269)
- indictment (p. 264)
- intermediate appellate court (p. 250)
- jury nullification (p. 264)
- legislative overcriminalization (p. 264)
- liability (p. 267)
- limited, or special jurisdiction, trial court (p. 251)
- magistrate (p. 273)
- mandatory jurisdiction (p. 253)
- mandatory minimum sentence (p. 269)
- misdemeanor (p. 265)
- panel (p. 254)
- plea bargain (p. 250)
- precedent (p. 251)
- prejudicial error (p. 253)
- prosecutor (p. 263)
- public defender (p. 263)
- pure appointive system (p. 261)

- recidivism (p. 272)
- recusal (p. 275)
- retention election (p. 257)
- rocket docket (p. 273)
- settlement (p. 250)
- state supreme court (p. 251)
- trial court (p. 250)
- truth-in-sentencing laws (p. 270)

Suggested Websites

- **www.abanet.org.** Website of the American Bar Association, the largest voluntary professional association in the world, with a membership of more than four hundred thousand.

- **www.ajs.org.** Website of the American Judicature Society, a nonpartisan organization with a national membership that works to maintain the independence and integrity of the courts and increase public understanding of the justice system.

- **www.brennancenter.org.** Website of the Brennan Center for Justice, a nonpartisan center at New York University that conducts research and advocates on a range of judicial topics, including state court reform and campaign financing.

- **www.justiceatstake.org.** Website of the Justice at Stake Campaign, a nonpartisan effort working to keep courts fair and impartial.

- **www.ncsconline.org.** Website of the National Center for State Courts, an independent nonprofit organization that assists court officials in better serving the public.

- **www.ojp.usdoj.gov/bjs.** Website for the Bureau of Justice Statistics, which provides statistics and other information on a variety of justice system–related areas, including courts, sentencing, crimes, and victims.

State Stats on Courts

Explore and compare data on the states! Go to **college.cqpress .com/sites/essentials-govstateandlocal** to do these exercises.

1. What is the per capita state and local government expenditure on corrections in your state? How does this compare to the national average? Do you think that this amount is too little, too much, or just about right? Why?

2. Which state had the most authorized wiretaps in 2010? Which had the least? What factors may have contributed to this?

3. How many prisoners have been sentenced to death since 1973 in your state versus how many have been executed in Texas? What about in Massachusetts? Why is there such a discrepancy?

4. Which state spends the most per capita on state-supported alcohol and drug prevention programs? Which state spends the least? What are the implications of these numbers for drug and alcohol-related arrests?

5. How much do supreme court justices make in your state? Do you think that it is a fair salary considering the scope of the job? Would you raise or lower this amount? Are there some states where you think it is reasonable that justices would make more money? Why?

The ancient Greeks pledged allegiance to their cities, not to any nation-state. There are plenty of people who still make formal commitments to serve local government, including police officers and firefighters. Pictured here is the graduation ceremony of the 36th Alaska Law Enforcement Training class; these individuals will go on to work as municipal police officers and fire marshals and in other law enforcement posts in towns and cities across Alaska.

ch.

10

Local Government
FUNCTION FOLLOWS FORM

- What are the main types of local government and what do they do?
- What are the positive and negative aspects of Dillon's Rule?
- Why do the decisions of one local government affect the decisions of other local governments?
- Should there be fewer local governments or more of them?

The ancient Greeks devoted their patriotic loyalty and civic duty not to Greece but to city-states, such as Athens and Sparta. And, boy, did the Greeks take their civic duty seriously. Citizens who took the Athenian Oath pledged that, "We will never bring disgrace on this our City by an act of dishonesty or cowardice. . . . We will revere and obey the City's laws, and will do our best to incite a like reverence and respect in those above us who are prone to annul them or set them at naught."[1] Americans aren't quite that committed to their cities, but twenty-first century attitudes are not as far from the ancient Greek ideal as you might imagine. There is a long tradition of strong local government in the United States, which is unsurprising given the political system's founding principles of division and decentralization of power. Americans like to keep government close so they can keep an eye on it.

Government does not get any closer than local government—the cities, counties, and other political jurisdictions at the substate level. Americans tend to trust these governments the most, and generally want them to have more rather than less power. In 2012, only about one-third of Americans had a favorable opinion of the federal government. Nearly twice as many had a favorable opinion of local government (about half had a favorable opinion of state government).[2] So it is somewhat paradoxical that local government is, technically speaking, the weakest level of government. Federal and state governments are sovereign powers, equal partners in the federal system that draw their powers from their citizens. Pull a state out of the federal system and view it independently, however, and you have a unitary rather than a federal system. (See Figure 10-1.) This is because local governments are not sovereign; they can exercise only the powers granted to them from the central authority of the states.

An individual state, though, is a strange sort of unitary system. The state government is clearly the seat of power, but within the state are an astonishing number and variety of political jurisdictions, many piled on top of one another and related in no clear organizational fashion. For example, a city and a school district may overlap each other entirely but have different governance structures, different leaders, and different purposes. One of these governments is not the boss of the other; the city cannot tell the school district what its tax rate should be any more than the school district can tell the city to build another library.

The crazy quilt of local governments is where the grunt work of the political system takes place. Local governments provide law enforcement, roads, health services, parks, libraries, and schools; they are mostly responsible for regulating (or even providing) utilities, such as sewer and water; they run airports, public transportation systems, mosquito control programs, and community recreation centers. The list goes on. And on. Collectively, these are the public services we encounter most in our daily lives, generally take for granted, and almost certainly could not get along without. Local governments generally do a good job of handling their numerous policy responsibilities; at a minimum, citizens tend to think of their local governments as giving them good value (well, at least compared to what they get from state and federal governments). Their lack of coordination with each other is potentially a big problem. A lot of the issues they are critically involved with—transportation, poverty, crime—are more regional than purely local in nature. Local governments cannot independently address regional problems, and neither can regional governments—for the most part regional

FIGURE 10-1

Substate "Unitary" System

State-Level Unitary System

At the state level, state government grants power to local governments.

governments do not exist. This lack of regional governance makes it hard to coherently address important policy questions that are not really state-level, but go way beyond the borders of any single local government.

Given their importance and their increasing role in addressing a series of increasingly important policy issues, local governments are clearly worth getting to know. This chapter examines the powers, responsibilities, and specific forms of local government as well as the importance and difficulty of coordinating local government activity to respond to the increasing need for regional governance.

The Many Faces of Local Government

The importance of local governments to the American political system is evident, on one level, from their sheer numbers. In 2012, more than eighty-nine thousand local governments were operating in the United States; that's roughly one local government for every 3,450 people (see Table 10-1).[3]

The number, size, structure, responsibilities and powers of local governments vary wildly from state to state, differences driven by state history, culture, and administrative approach to service

TABLE 10-1

Number of Government Units, Ranked by State and Type

State	All Government	County	Municipal	Township	School Districts	All Special Districts
Illinois	6,968	102	1,298	1,431	905	3,232
Pennsylvania	4,905	66	1,015	1,546	514	1,764
Texas	4,856	254	1,214	—	1,079	2,309
California	4,350	57	482	—	1,025	2,786
Kansas	3,806	103	626	1,268	306	1,503
Missouri	3,752	114	955	312	534	1,837
Ohio	3,702	88	938	1,308	668	700
Minnesota	3,633	87	854	1,785	338	569
New York	3,454	57	617	929	679	1,172
Wisconsin	3,123	72	595	1,255	440	761
Michigan	2,877	83	533	1,240	576	445
Colorado	2,818	62	271	—	180	2,305
Indiana	2,694	91	569	1,006	291	737
North Dakota	2,666	53	357	1,314	183	759
Nebraska	2,581	93	530	419	272	1,267
South Dakota	1,979	66	311	907	152	543
Iowa	1,939	99	947	—	366	527
Oklahoma	1,854	77	590	—	550	637
Washington	1,831	39	281	—	295	1,216
Florida	1,554	66	410	—	95	1,983
Arkansas	1,543	75	502	—	239	727
Oregon	1,509	36	241	—	230	1,002

(Continued)

TABLE 10-1 (Continued)

State	All Government	County	Municipal	Township	School Districts	All Special Districts
Georgia	1,365	153	535	—	180	497
Kentucky	1,314	118	418	—	174	604
New Jersey	1,344	21	324	242	523	234
Montana	1,240	54	129	—	321	736
Alabama	1,208	67	461	—	132	548
Idaho	1,161	44	200	—	118	799
Mississippi	991	82	297	—	164	448
North Carolina	964	100	553	—	—	311
Tennessee	920	92	345	—	14	469
New Mexico	854	33	103	—	96	622
Massachusetts	852	5	53	298	84	412
Maine	841	16	22	466	99	238
Wyoming	795	23	99	—	55	618
Vermont	728	14	43	237	291	143
South Carolina	681	46	269	—	83	283
Arizona	659	15	91	—	244	309
West Virginia	658	55	232	—	55	316
Utah	613	29	245	—	41	298
Connecticut	644	—	30	149	17	448
New Hampshire	542	10	13	221	166	132
Louisiana	530	60	304	—	69	97
Virginia	497	95	229	—	1	172
Maryland	347	23	157	—	167	—
Delaware	338	3	57	—	19	259
Nevada	190	16	19	—	17	138
Alaska	177	14	148	—	—	15
Rhode Island	134	—	8	31	4	91
Hawaii	21	3	1	—	17	—

Source: U.S. Census Bureau, "2012 Census of Governments," www.census.gov/govs/cog2012/#tml.

delivery. Indeed, in terms of differences, local governments make state governments look like clones. Hawaii has few local governments, no incorporated municipalities, four counties, and the consolidated city-county government of Honolulu. Georgia has 153 counties, all of them vested with municipal-like powers. The city of New York has a resident population of more than 8 million. The city of Hove Mobile Park, North Dakota, has a population of one. That's not a typo. Hove Mobile Park is an incorporated municipality whose entire population consists of an elderly woman living in a trailer park.[4]

All these differences provide multiple opportunities to put the comparative method into practice, but they can also be confusing. Local authority, for example, overlaps—school districts sprawl across municipalities, which in turn are covered by counties. A couple may marry in the city of Chapel Hill, North Carolina, but their marriage certificate will carry the insignia of Orange County, North Carolina. This is because in most states the power to grant marriage licenses is vested in counties, not in cities. The duties and obligations of particular units of government vary from state to state, adding to the confusion. Depending on where you live, you may rely on a different set of authorities to get a pothole filled on your street, arrange for a stop sign to be installed at a dangerous intersection, or register your opinion on a bond issue for a new high school.

Despite all these differences, there are only three general forms of local government: **counties**, **municipalities**, and **special districts**. Traditionally, counties are geographical and administrative subdivisions of states. The exact definition of a municipality varies from state to state, but generally they are political units more geographically compact than counties and distinguished legally by being independent corporations. Unlike counties and cities, special districts usually are created to provide a specific public service rather than a range of services. School districts are a good example. These are geographically defined local units of government created to provide educational services. Other special districts include water management and sewage treatment districts.

The Organization and Responsibilities of Local Governments

Within each of the three basic categories of local government is considerable variation in

Counties
Geographical subdivisions of state government.

Municipalities
Political jurisdictions, such as cities, villages, or towns, incorporated under state law to provide governance to defined geographical areas; they are more compact and more densely populated than counties.

Special District
A local governmental unit created for a single purpose, such as water distribution.

organizational structure, autonomy, and responsibilities. These categories are distinct enough, however, to wrangle those more than eighty-nine thousand local governments in the United States into a general understanding of what local governments are and why they take on the forms they do.

Between the County Lines

According to U.S. Supreme Court chief justice Roger B. Taney, counties "are nothing more than certain portions of the territory into which the state is divided for the more convenient exercise of the powers of government."[5] In other words, in the name of more efficient and practical governance, states divide themselves into smaller geographical units—counties—to provide a local "branch office" of the state government.

These divisions are called parishes in Louisiana and boroughs in Alaska, and more than three thousand counties are drawn on the maps of the remaining forty-eight states, although the number in any given state varies a lot. Rhode Island and Connecticut have no county governments at all (as geographically compact states, they have no need for such administrative subunits of state government). Delaware has only three. Texas has 254, the most in the nation.

Geographically, counties are generally the largest local governments, meaning that they bear the burden of providing services widely, if not lavishly. The majority of the million citizens in California's Sacramento County, for example, live in unincorporated territory. This means that their property is not part of any city, town, or township that can provide municipal services. Hence the burden falls on the county to provide these residents with law enforcement, parks and recreation, storm water management, and other basic services.

The autonomy and authority of county governments also varies from state to state. In the Northeast, local government is traditionally centered in towns and villages, which attract the most participation, make the most high-profile

Illinois has 6,968 local governments—the mos of any state.

decisions, and are the focus of the most attention. County governments are historically viewed as just the local offices of state government. In contrast, in the South, county governments are more likely to be a central focus of local government and wield political power and policy influence. The reason for these differences primarily has to do with the more urban nature of the Northeast compared to the historically more rural South. Rural areas by definition lack substantial urban centers, meaning they lack large and powerful city or village governments. County governments thus become the locus of local politics.

As rural governments that help conduct state government business, county governments are keepers of public records (such as property deeds, birth and death certificates, and mortgages) and administrators of property taxes, local road maintenance, election results certification, criminal courts, and jails run by county sheriffs. As a general rule, counties tend to have less independence from state government than municipalities (especially large urban cities). In New Hampshire, for example, state legislators still approve county budgets. In Texas, each county is required by the state to appoint a county judge-at-large and four commissioners, regardless of whether the county's population numbers in the hundreds or the millions. Counties, in other words, are in theory and often in practice still the administrative subunits of state government.

The Structure of County Government

There are three basic forms of county government: commission, council-executive, and commission-administrator. What differentiates the three is the degree of separation between legislative and executive powers and who is responsible for the day-to-day administration of the executive side of government.

The most common form is the **county commission system**, which concentrates legislative and executive functions and powers into an elected board of commissioners. For example,

the commission exercises legislative powers by passing county ordinances and approving the budget. Further, it wields executive powers, as it is responsible for a broad range of hiring and firing decisions and exercises considerable control over many administrative offices.

An alternate form of county government is the **council-executive system**, which separates legislative and executive powers into different offices. A county government using a council-executive system typically has an independently elected officer who serves as the county-level equivalent of a governor. County executives frequently have the power to veto ordinances passed by the board of commissioners and the authority to appoint key department heads. Thus the main difference between the commission and council-executive forms of county government is the approach to separation of powers. (See Figure 10-2.)

The **commission-administrator system** stands somewhere between the commission and council-executive systems. In this form of government, an elected commission retains most legislative and executive powers but appoints a professional administrator to government operations. Commissioners typically delegate considerable powers to administrators, including the powers to hire and fire department heads and to prepare a budget for the commission's approval.

Regardless of organizational specifics, most counties have representative forms of government that include elected heads of a broad range of administrative and executive offices. These typically include a district attorney, a sheriff, a treasurer, and a clerk of records.

Municipalities

A municipality is a political jurisdiction formed by an association of citizens to provide self-governance within a clearly defined geographical

County Commission System
A form of county governance in which executive, legislative, and administrative powers are vested in elected commissioners.

Council-Executive System
A form of county governance in which legislative powers are vested in a county commission and executive powers are vested in an independently elected executive.

Commission-Administrator System
A form of county governance in which executive and legislative powers reside with an elected commission, which hires a professional executive to manage the day-to-day operations of government.

FIGURE 10-2

HOW IT WORKS

The Structure of County Government

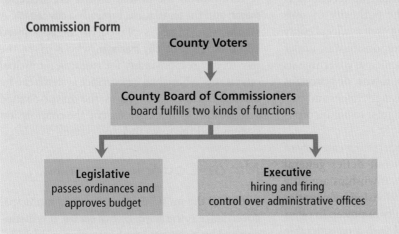

Commission Form

County Voters

County Board of Commissioners
board fulfills two kinds of functions

Legislative
passes ordinances and
approves budget

Executive
hiring and firing
control over administrative offices

The three basic forms of county government differ in the division of powers and in who is responsible for day-to-day administration of the county government. In the commission form, voters elect county commissioners who exercise legislative and executive powers and have considerable authority over day-to-day administration. In the council-executive form, voters elect commissioners who exercise legislative powers and independently elect a county executive who wields executive powers and serves as the chief administrator. In the commission-administrator form, voters elect commissioners who retain most legislative and executive powers. However, they hire a professional manager to handle the day-to-day administration of the county government.

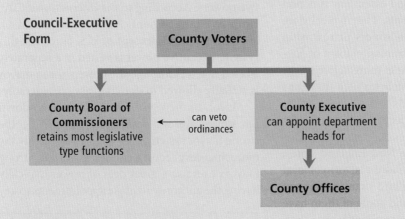

Council-Executive Form

County Voters

County Board of Commissioners
retains most legislative type functions

← can veto ordinances

County Executive
can appoint department heads for

County Offices

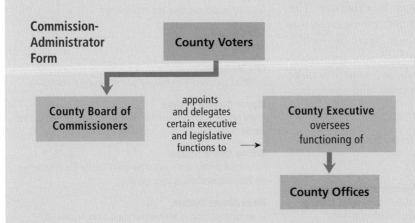

Commission-Administrator Form

County Voters

County Board of Commissioners

appoints and delegates certain executive and legislative functions to →

County Executive
oversees functioning of

County Offices

area. Municipalities encompass two basic forms of government: townships and cities. **Cities** are corporations, legal entities incorporated under state law for the purpose of self-government at the local level. This is a central difference between counties and cities. Counties were created by the state from the top down; cities are bottom-up creations. A local community seeks the authority of self-governance by incorporating itself as a legal entity with certain powers and responsibilities under state law. Such corporate municipal governments also may be called villages, towns, or boroughs (although, somewhat confusingly, *towns* and *boroughs* in some states can also refer to nonincorporated governments).

Townships constitute an interesting category of local government that all but defies general description. In some states, townships are little more than geographical subdivisions of counties vested with little responsibility or power. In other states, townships are vested with a considerable range of responsibilities and essentially function as mini-county governments. They typically are run by boards of commissioners or township supervisors—a county commission form of government in miniature. These more active townships typically are responsible for such functions as snowplowing rural roads.

In still other states, townships (or towns) exercise as much power as cities do, if not more. This is particularly true in the New England states, where the township is the traditional form of local governance. In New England many towns are incorporated, like cities, and some of them have been working units of government longer than the United States has been in existence. The Maine town of Dover-Foxcroft, for example, was incorporated in 1769, seven years before the Declaration of Independence was approved.[6] Townships, in other words, are sometimes like counties, sometimes like cities, and sometimes

little more than large geographical spaces with little in the way of governance structure at all. Which description is accurate depends on state law and the traditions of local governance.

Governance arrangements vary even more at the municipal level than at the county level. There is variation in the powers of the executive, or **mayor**, and the legislature, typically a **city council**. A strong role often is played by an appointed administrator, or **city manager**, who is given the day-to-day responsibility for running municipal operations. Municipal governance systems can be divided into four basic types: the mayor-council system, the city manager system, the commission system, and the town meeting system.

Mayor-Council Systems

One of the most common forms of municipal governance is the **mayor-council system**. It is distinguished by a separation of executive and legislative powers. According to the International City/County Management Association (ICMA), approximately 43 percent of U.S. cities use this system. Executive power is vested in a separately elected mayor, although the powers that a mayor is actually allowed to exercise vary considerably.

Mayor-council systems can be broken down into **strong mayor** and **weak mayor systems**. Under the strong mayor system, the executive is roughly the municipal-level equivalent of a governor. Strong mayors exercise a great deal of power, typically having the authority to make appointments to key

---

Cities
Incorporated political jurisdictions formed to provide self-governance to particular localities.

Townships
Local governments whose powers, governance structure, and legal status vary considerably from state to state. In some states, townships function as general-purpose municipalities; in others, they are geographical subdivisions of counties with few responsibilities and little power.

Mayor
The elected chief executive of a municipality.

City Council
A municipality's legislature.

City Manager
An official appointed to be the chief administrator of a municipality.

Mayor-Council System
A form of municipal governance in which there is an elected executive and an elected legislature.

Strong Mayor System
A municipal government in which the mayor has the power to perform the executive functions of government.

Weak Mayor System
A municipal government in which the mayor lacks true executive powers, such as the ability to veto council decisions or appoint department heads.

city offices, to veto council decisions, to prepare budgets, and to run the day-to-day operations of municipal government in general.

A weak mayor system retains the elected executive, but the mayor is more of a ceremonial than a real policymaking office. In a weak mayor system, the executive, as well as legislative, power is wielded by the council. In many cities where mayors have limited powers, individuals with strong personalities are nevertheless able to exert huge influence. They do this by fostering cooperative relationships with their powerful city managers. Examples are Pete Wilson, the mayor of San Diego in the 1970s, and Henry Cisneros, the mayor of San Antonio in the 1980s.

In both strong and weak mayor systems, the council serves as the municipal-level legislature and wields extensive policymaking power. No major policy or program can get far in a city without massaging from the city council. Councils average six members, but in many large jurisdictions twelve to fourteen or even more are elected. Chicago has a whopping fifty council members, and New York City has fifty-one. These individuals exert a major influence over a city's livability. They steer policies on such vital issues as zoning and urban renewal, as well as the provision of a wide range of public services—everything from law enforcement and fire protection to libraries and parks.

Council-Manager Systems

Rather than separating executive and legislative functions, the **council-manager system** seeks to separate the political and administrative functions of government. In such a system, a council makes policy decisions but places the implementation of

Council-Manager System
A form of municipal governance in which the day-to-day administration of government is carried out by a professional administrator.

FIGURE 10-3

Strong Mayor-Council Form of Government

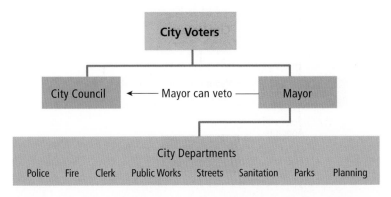

Source: John P. Pelissero, "The Political Environment of Cities in the Twenty-First Century," in *Cities, Politics, and Policy: A Comparative Analysis*, ed. John P. Pelissero (Washington, DC: CQ Press, 2003), 15.

FIGURE 10-4

Weak Mayor-Council Form of Government

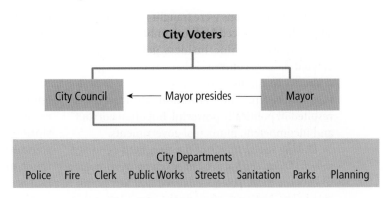

Source: John P. Pelissero, "The Political Environment of Cities in the Twenty-First Century," in *Cities, Politics, and Policy: A Comparative Analysis*, ed. John P. Pelissero (Washington, DC: CQ Press, 2003), 15.

those decisions in the hands of a professional administrator, usually called a city manager, hired by the council. (See Figure 10-5.)

This system originated in the Progressive reform movement that swept through government at all levels, beginning at the end of the nineteenth century. At the time, powerful political machines ran the typical large city in the United States. Places like Boston, Chicago, and New York were governed by charismatic politicians who took advantage of their ties to ethnic minorities, such as the Irish or the Italians. Patronage jobs were given out to their personal friends, whose chief qualification was that they were campaign

FIGURE 10-5

Council-Manager Form of Government

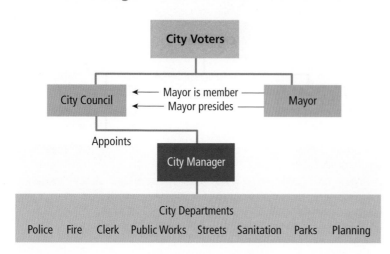

Source: John P. Pelissero, "The Political Environment of Cities in the Twenty-First Century," in *Cities, Politics, and Policy: A Comparative Analysis*, ed. John P. Pelissero (Washington, DC: CQ Press, 2003), 16.

supporters. Elections were fraught with partisanship, which produced high incumbent reelection rates. Many machine insiders got themselves elected as city commissioners and were given authority to run individual departments, including police, fire, and sanitation services. This resulted in politically powerful, but often corrupt and incompetent, municipal governments.

During the first half of the twentieth century, reform groups began pressuring city governments to become more professionalized and less politicized. The National Municipal League (now the National League of Cities), which focused on small to medium-size cities, was one such group. The U.S. Conference of Mayors, whose members head larger cities, and the ICMA were two others. In the belief that the top vote-getters in a given city may not be the best managers, the National Municipal League drafted a model charter that laid out the powers of mayors, city councils, and administrators.

In 1913, Dayton, Ohio, became the first major U.S. city to create a position for a strong manager, largely in response to suburbanization (the establishment of residential communities on the outskirts of the city) and the rise of an educated middle class. The idea was that a government run by a professional city manager would be less prone to corruption and partisan favoritism than

one led by the classic big-city mayor. Such managers are generally more interested in implementing organizational systems than they are in glad-handing voters and trolling for campaign cash. Today, the council-manager system of city government is seen in more than three thousand cities, or 49 percent of communities with populations of more than 2,500. It is most popular in medium-size cities, primarily in the South and the West. Large cities that use a manager-council system include Dallas, Texas, and San Diego and San Jose, California.[7]

Commission Systems

Similar to their county-level counterparts, municipal **commission systems** concentrate executive and legislative powers into a single elected body. These bodies make key policy decisions in the same way a legislature does. Yet each commissioner is also the head of an executive department. Commissioners run for office not as representatives in a legislative body but as the heads of particular city departments: commissioner for public safety, commissioner for public works, and so on. Most commission systems also have a mayor, but this is not an independent executive office. The position is usually held by a commissioner chosen to preside over commission meetings; it is not an independent executive office but more of a ceremonial position.

As a form of municipal (as opposed to county) governance, the commission system originated in Galveston, Texas, in the early 1900s. Galveston suffered a devastating hurricane that killed thousands and left the city in ruins. The existing city government proved ineffective in dealing with the aftermath of this disaster. In response, the Texas legislature approved a completely new form of municipal government—the commission system—to try to deal with the huge task of

City Commission System
A form of municipal governance in which executive, legislative, and administrative powers are vested in elected city commissioners.

rebuilding the city. It proved successful; Galveston was rebuilt and put back on the civic track.

This success led other municipalities to follow Galveston's lead and adopt the commission form of governance. The commission system's success, however, has been limited, and only a relative handful of cities currently operate under it. Its main drawbacks are two. First, the merging of elected and administrative positions leads to commissioners' becoming the entrenched advocates of their departments. Second, winning an election and administering a large bureaucracy are very different skills. Good politicians, in other words, do not always make good department heads. Only about 2 percent of municipalities with populations greater than 2,500 use the commission form of government.[8] The drawbacks of commission governments are much the same as the drawbacks of commission systems at the county level—executive authority is so diffuse it tends to produce a government with no real direction.

Town Meetings

The **town meeting form of government** is largely unique to the United States and is mostly found in towns in New England states (New England towns, remember, are basically municipalities, although they may also have some of the functions traditionally associated with county government in other states). Its origins are rooted in the religious communities that made up early colonial settlements in New England. A high premium was put on consensus in these communities, and the town meeting evolved as a means to reach such widespread agreement. Town meetings allowed citizens to have a direct role in deciding which laws they would pass and who would be responsible for implementing and enforcing these laws. In many cases, the politics were worked out before the actual meetings took place, with neighbors talking to neighbors across their fences and in taverns. The grassroots agreements hashed out in these informal

discussions were then expressed as community consensus in the town meeting.[9]

What all this boils down to is that the legislative functions are concentrated in the citizens themselves. A town meeting is convened through a warrant, or an announcement of the date, time, and place of the meeting and the items to be discussed. It is open to all community citizens, and all have an equal vote in matters of town policy. Such legislative power often is exercised directly; for example, budgets are approved by town meetings. Some authority, however, may be delegated to a representative board, whose members are called selectmen. The board of selectmen exercises whatever authority is granted to it and is responsible for seeing that policies enacted in the town meeting are carried out.

Towns also have incorporated some elements of the council-manager system by voting to hire professional managers to handle the administrative side of government. The manager system seems to work well with this type of government; for example, roughly 30 percent of the towns in Maine—most of them small communities with fewer than 2,500 residents—have managers but hold town meetings as well.[10]

The town meeting is probably the most idealized form of government that has ever existed in the United States. Thomas Jefferson, for example, saw this grassroots democratic approach to self-governance as "the wisest invention ever devised by man."[11] Alexis de Tocqueville, the nineteenth-century French aristocrat who wrote one of the most celebrated analyses of the American political system, referred to towns as the "fertile germ" of democracy.[12] For even modestly large communities, however, this approach simply isn't practical. A gathering of citizens that runs into the thousands would be too unwieldy, and the likelihood of getting broad agreement from such a large group on any number of policy issues is pretty low.

Special Districts

Special districts are fundamentally different from other forms of local government. Counties

---

Town Meeting Form of Government
A form of governance in which legislative powers are held by the local citizens.

The town meeting form of government is largely unique to the United States, and even in the United States is mostly confined to the Northeast. In this form of local governance, legislative powers are vested in citizens, who exercise those powers during town meetings of local residents. Here, residents in Strafford, Vermont, are meeting to discuss local issues and elect town clerks.

and municipalities are general-purpose governments providing a broad range of public services within their given jurisdictions. Special districts are mostly single-purpose governments created to provide specific services that are not being provided by a general-purpose government.

More than fifty thousand special districts have been created across the country—and often across borders of other units of government—to administer single programs or services. Most people know very little about these governments. The single biggest exception to the general rule of special district anonymity is the school district; there are more than twelve thousand independent school districts in the United States. Few might know a lot about a school district's politics, but a lot of people will know teachers, students, and administrators; how the school sports teams are doing; and which schools have a good or a poor reputation for academic performance. That level of knowledge and intimacy drops off quickly for

other types of special districts. Among the most numerous forms of special districts are sewer and water system districts, which account for about one-third of special districts nationwide. Few people know much at all about these sorts of districts, and many may be completely unaware of their existence.

Why use special districts to provide single programs or services? Why not just have the county or municipality add those services to its governing portfolio? Well, in certain situations, single-purpose governments can seem attractive solutions to political and practical problems. For example, special districts sometimes are implemented as a way of heading off threats of political annexation of one local government by another. They also are used as a tool for community and business improvement. Freed of local tax authority, administrators of special districts often can get infrastructure items built and services provided without dipping into any one locality's funds. For example, farmers in special water districts, particularly in the West, are eligible for discounted federal loans to help them with irrigation.

Working Within Limits: The Powers and Constraints of Local Government

Local governments may not be sovereign, but they are far from powerless. They have primary responsibility for delivering a broad range of public services (such as education, law enforcement, roads, and utilities), and they have broad authority to levy taxes and pass regulations and ordinances (an ordinance is a law passed by a nonsovereign government). Local governments can also exercise the power of eminent domain. Despite this, local governments are, at least technically, not equal partners in government. They are subordinate to the state governments from which they are granted their power.

Why is this the case? The short answer is the Tenth Amendment to the U.S. Constitution. The U.S. Constitution never mentions local governments, the upshot being that legally these governments fall under the purview of the Tenth Amendment's guarantee of state sovereignty. This means the power to determine the scope of authority of local governments is among the powers "reserved to the States respectively, or to the people." In other words, states get to say what localities can and cannot do.

Dillon's Rule

The legal doctrine that defines the division of power between state and local governments is known as **Dillon's Rule**, named for Iowa Supreme Court justice John F. Dillon. In 1868, Dillon formulated an argument that has served ever since as the basis for understanding and justifying the

Dillon's Rule
The legal principle that says local governments can exercise only the powers granted to them by the state government.

power—or, more accurately, the lack of power—of local government. Dillon's Rule is built on the legal principle of *ultra vires*, which means "outside one's powers." In a nutshell, it states that local governments are limited to the powers expressly granted to them by their state and to those powers indispensable to the stated objectives and purposes of each local government.

Dillon essentially built a legal argument that the Tenth Amendment secures power for state but not local governments. In a famous 1868 ruling in *City of Clinton v. Cedar Rapids and Missouri Railroad*, Dillon said that local governments are "mere tenants at the will of their respective state legislatures." The rule has structured legal thinking on the power of local governments ever since, although it has always had its critics and opponents. It was challenged as early as the 1870s, when Missouri legislators rewrote the state constitution specifically to allow municipalities a degree of independence from the constraints of state government.[13] For the most part, though, Dillon's Rule holds—state power trumps local

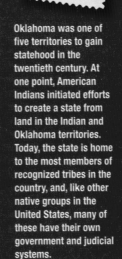

Oklahoma was one of five territories to gain statehood in the twentieth century. At one point, American Indians initiated efforts to create a state from land in the Indian and Oklahoma territories. Today, the state is home to the most members of recognized tribes in the country, and, like other native groups in the United States, many of these have their own government and judicial systems.

> Dillon's Rule is built on the legal principle of *ultra vires*, which means "outside one's powers." In a nutshell, it states that local governments are limited to the powers expressly granted to them by their state and to those powers indispensable to the stated objectives and purposes of each local government.

Policy in Practice

Eminent Domain and Local Power

Local governments are not sovereign, but this does not mean they are powerless. Many local governments, for example, have the power of eminent domain, or the right to take private property without the owner's consent.

The Fifth Amendment to the U.S. Constitution compels any government exercising such powers to offer the owner just compensation for the property taken. That, however, often does little to mollify people who have their lives or communities uprooted to make way for a new road or a new development.

In 2005, the U.S. Supreme Court significantly expanded the scope of local governments' powers of eminent domain. In *Kelo v. New London* (2005), the Court ruled that homeowners could be forced to sell not just to a city but to private developers who would add to the city's tax base. The Court reasoned that local governments have a central role in planning and that economic development cannot be halted simply because some property owner objects. In short, a city could force a property owner to sell to a developer even when the property owner wanted to do no such thing.

This significant boost to the power and reach of local governments was quickly limited, however. Indeed, the years since the *Kelo* ruling have provided an instructive lesson in Dillon's Rule. Prior to *Kelo*, only seven states had laws specifically limiting local government powers of eminent domain. As of 2012, forty-four states had passed such laws, with almost all of this legislation being driven by a reaction to the Supreme Court decision. The bottom line is that eminent domain is a power exercised by local governments, which, according to Dillon's Rule, means it is also a power that can be regulated by the states. And regulate it they have. The expanded powers the Supreme Court gave local governments in *Kelo* have been limited or taken back entirely by state governments. Even though the ruling specifically expanded local government powers, *Kelo* actually ended up underlining the limits of local government authority. Unlike state governments, local governments are not fully sovereign, and when they are given power—even if that power is given by the Supreme Court—the states can take it back.

Source: Adapted from Alan Greenblatt, "Land Law," *Governing*, August 2005.

---

government power, which means state legislatures invariably win power struggles with local governments. States have the authority to limit even traditionally exercised local government powers, such as eminent domain (see the box "Policy in Practice: Eminent Domain and Local Power").

Although Dillon's Rule says state governments control the powers of local governments, even Dillon himself thought it was a bad idea for state governments to take full advantage of this legal authority. The division of labor between local and state governments, broadly speaking, works. So it is practical and just common sense for states to respect local government autonomy. Accordingly, the independence and powers that state governments grant to localities vary considerably. Some state governments are more willing than others to

let local governments make their own decisions. Many of these differences can be explained by state culture and the degree of citizen participation. Idaho and West Virginia reserve the most local powers to the state; Oregon and Maine give localities the most freedom.[14]

In recent years, local government financial challenges created by economic recession, unfunded mandates, poor decisions, and collapsing property values have provided blunt examples of the difference in sovereignty between state and local governments. More than half of the states have laws allowing them to exercise some degree of direct supervision over financially stressed localities. Harrisburg, Pennsylvania; Central Falls, Rhode Island; and Nassau County, New York, all went bankrupt in the past few years and ended up with state-appointed rather than locally elected leaders calling the shots on a range of important decisions. In Michigan a number of struggling cities (including Detroit) have been effectively taken over by the state, with state-appointed administrators assuming virtually all local government powers.

Home Rule

While local governments are unquestionably subordinate, states are free to grant them considerable autonomy if they so choose. Many states make such grants of autonomy formal by giving local governments home rule, or the freedom to make local decisions without interference from state government. Home rule typically is enshrined in a **charter**, which spells out the powers and purposes of the local government. In effect, a charter is the municipal equivalent of a constitution.

Home rule can be granted in two basic forms. Legislatures may approve home rule in **general act charters**, which apply to all cities, or in **special act charters**, each of which affects only one community. Either type can be initiated by state legislators, local councils, or citizens' groups. In cases of citizen initiatives, advocates gather the requisite number of signatures on petitions, which are then converted into legislation or language for a ballot referendum that is put before voters.

Although voters generally support the notion of local government autonomy and generally oppose state or federal governments' making decisions on behalf of local communities, there are benefits to state or federal oversight. What is lost in local control can be offset by the deeper pockets of the larger, sovereign governments. Much of what local leaders wish to accomplish requires infusions of funds from Washington and state capitals. Those intergovernmental sources of revenue are especially critical during hard economic times, when the traditional local government sources of funding, such as property and sales taxes, tend to take a hit. With oversight, at least local governments also get some cold, hard cash. The superior capacity of state governments and the federal government to raise revenues is another limit on the powers of localities.

Participation in Local Government

Comparatively speaking, state and federal politics are dominated by political parties, which contest elections, mobilize voters, and organize government. Things are different down at the local level, where more than two-thirds of governments are nonpartisan. Since the decline of the big-city political machines of the early twentieth century, candidates for county boards and city councils run more on personal competence than on ideology or party affiliation. Only 17 percent of city councils hold partisan elections, according to the ICMA. Yet in some cities, party labels that have been abolished officially continue to play a role unofficially. This has occurred in Chicago, where city government has been officially nonpartisan since the 1930s, but Democrats continue to dominate the heavily African American city.

Council members usually run in **ward**, or **district, elections**. The advantage of organizing such elections on the basis of defined geographical areas is the assurance that each neighborhood has a local on the city council who knows the streets and residents by name. This is especially important for minorities, who may be grouped together by housing patterns. Very large cities, however, have to balance the desire to have districts small enough for council members to really know the neighborhood concerns with the practical matter of having a municipal legislature of a manageable size. In some places, the populations of council districts are themselves the equivalent of midsize cities. Los Angeles, for examples, is split into fifteen city council districts. Given the city's population of roughly 3.8 million, that means each district has something like a quarter million constituents.

Charter
A document that outlines the powers, organization, and responsibilities of a local government.

General Act Charter
A charter that grants powers, such as home rule, to all municipal governments within a state.

Special Act Charter
A charter that grants powers, such as home rule, to a single municipal government.

Ward, Or District, Election
An election in which voters in a municipal ward vote for a candidate to represent them on a council or commission.

Other local governments permit candidates to run in **at-large elections**. This means that they can hail from any part of the jurisdiction. The advantage of at-large elections is that they make room for the largest possible pool of highly qualified and talented people who, presumably, look at the interests of the city as a whole. A potential disadvantage of at-large elections is that minority candidates can have a hard time winning. In 1991, Dallas was required to switch from an at-large system to one in which fourteen city council members were chosen by districts. The result was more victories by Hispanic and African American candidates.

One of the paradoxes of local government is that, although it is the level of government that citizens support the most, it is also the level of government in which they participate the least. Voter turnout in local elections is often half the national turnout average of 55 percent in a presidential election. This reflects a general indifference among many citizens toward the prosaic affairs of local government. Neighborhood volunteer and community development organizations, although generally run by articulate and dedicated activists, often involve as little as 3 to 12 percent of the local population.[15]

The absence of popular fervor over local issues does not mean that local offices are not important. Indeed, politics at this level can have implications for state and even national politics. For example, local government offices often serve as proving grounds for up-and-coming politicians who go on to higher office at the state or national level. New immigrants, particularly Asians and Latinos, are increasingly working their way into public office on this level. By the end of the twentieth century, one-third of all cities with more than two hundred thousand residents had elected either a Hispanic or an African American mayor.[16] Many state and federal minority lawmakers come from this sort of local government background. Representative Nydia Velázquez, D-N.Y., for example, was the first Puerto Rican American woman elected to Congress and

served as the chair of the influential Congressional Hispanic Caucus. She began her career as a member of the New York city council.

The Missing Level of Government

While there are a lot of local governments, the United States has almost no real regional governments apart from the states themselves. In some ways this is understandable. There is no history or constitutional basis for a governance structure between states or localities. Regional government is thus the poor relation of the U.S. political system: little thought of and, outside the community of urban scholars and a handful of officials, not much loved.

Yet the majority of local governments in the United States are embedded in larger metropolitan regions. Allegheny County, Pennsylvania, for example, contains 273 governments—from the city of Pittsburgh to the West Mifflin Sanitary Sewer Municipal District—and that single county is itself embedded in a broader urban concentration that includes other counties. These sorts of sprawling metropolitan areas frequently have regional-level policy problems that are difficult to address because there is no regional-level government, or even any formal cooperative arrangements among the hundreds of local governments operating in that area. This absence of a regional umbrella government has been called a "fundamental flaw in America's governance structure." Why? Because "metropolitan regions have become the most important functional units of economic and social life in almost all modern societies."[17] Metropolitan regions may be intertwined economically and socially, but they are governed as if such matters can be isolated within the preexisting geographical boundaries of political jurisdictions.

The basic problem, then, is that political geography no longer lines up with economic and social geography. The center of economic and social life in the United States is increasingly less a city or a county than it is a larger metropolitan area. The U.S.

At-Large Election
An election in which city or county voters vote for council or commission members from any part of the jurisdiction.

Office of Management and Budget defines a **metropolitan area** as a region with "a large population nucleus, together with adjacent communities having a high degree of social and economic integration with that core." It is important to note that this definition goes on to specify that a metropolitan area comprises "one or more entire counties."[18]

The federal government formally defines metropolitan areas using the concept of the **metropolitan statistical area (MSA)**, an area made up of a city of fifty thousand or more people together with adjacent urban communities that have strong ties to the central city. As of 2010, there were 374 MSAs in the United States (and 8 more in Puerto Rico). More than 80 percent of U.S. residents live in MSAs, with 30 percent living in central cities.[19] These metros are where some of the most important policy challenges of the twenty-first century are not just concentrated but irretrievably interconnected. Consider traffic congestion. According to metro scholar Bruce Katz, roughly 60 percent of all the vehicular miles logged in the United States occur in the top one hundred metropolitan areas. This reflects not just the population concentration of those areas or just the challenges of traffic congestion and maintaining transportation infrastructure, but the effects of such concentration on global warming (that much traffic produces a lot of greenhouse gases) as well as on global trade, shipping, and freight.[20]

The vast majority of Americans live, work, and play in metros, routinely crossing local government jurisdictions as they go from one of these activities to another. These dense metropolitan areas often bump into each other, forming even larger urban geographical areas referred to as **megaregions**. A megaregion is an urban area made up of several large cities and their surrounding urban areas—in effect, a string of MSAs. Megaregions represent a new type of urban geography, a merging of metropolitan areas into a massive interlocking economic and social system. Megaregions may spill across multiple counties or even multiple states, yet typically there is no overarching institution at this level with anything like the powers of a municipal, let alone a state, government. Instead, within megaregions are dozens and dozens, even hundreds, of local governments. All of these share a set of common interests because a decision by any one jurisdiction in a megaregion has implications for other jurisdictions. This interdependence fuels an increasing recognition of the need for local governments to coordinate with one another in policy and decision making on everything from transportation infrastructure to economic development to public housing.

Take, for example, the rise of so-called **edgeless cities**. These are sprawling office and retail complexes that are not pedestrian friendly and often become ghost towns at night. They do have obvious economic attractions for local governments—they mean jobs, sales taxes (people who work in them buy stuff, even if it is just gas and incidentals at a convenience store), and also property taxes (office complexes are valuable properties). Yet, whatever benefits they produce for one locality, they also export a set of costs to the larger region. Most of the people who work in edgeless cities commute home to greener residential areas. This means such developments segregate and put considerable geographical distance between where people live and where they work. The end results—traffic congestion and smog—affect all communities in the region, but individually there is not much any local government can do about such problems.

Sprawl: How Metropolitan Regions Grow

The fragmented nature of local governance in metropolitan areas creates an interconnected set

---

Metropolitan Area
A populous region typically comprising a city and surrounding communities that have a high degree of social and economic integration.

Metropolitan Statistical Area (MSA)
An area with a city of fifty thousand or more people together with adjacent urban communities that have strong ties to the central city.

Megaregion
An urban area made up of several large cities and their surrounding urban areas that creates an interlocking economic and social system.

Edgeless Cities
Office and retail complexes without clear boundaries.

Critics of urban governance argue that there is a hole in local government. Not a hole quite as literal as this one, but rather the general absence of meaningful regional development. While many issues—such as transportation and highway maintenance—are essentially regional in nature, there is a notable lack of regional political jurisdictions.

of problems that are difficult to address systematically. To understand the causes and consequences of these problems, it helps to have a little historical background on the roots of metropolitan growth.

Metropolitan governance challenges are rooted in the post–World War II population boom. This created enormous pressure for new construction that typically took place on the peripheries of large cities or urban areas in the form of low-density suburban housing and commercial developments. This in turn created an interrelated set of problems that can be traced to the catchall phenomenon of **sprawl**. Although the term *sprawl* is often used generically to refer to the rapid growth of any metropolitan area, most urban scholars consider sprawl to be a particular type of growth. There is no universal definition of sprawl, but this type of growth does have a set of specific characteristics: single-use zoning, low-density development, leapfrog development, car-dependent living, and fragmentation of land use powers.

Single-use zoning. One of the central political powers of local government is control over land use. This power is typically exercised through **zoning laws**. These laws can allow land to be used for a mix of commercial, recreational, and residential development or for single-purpose developments. Local governments in metropolitan areas have tended to favor the latter approach. The end result has been the geographical separation of the places where people work, live, and play.

Low-density development. Metropolitan growth has been defined not only by single-use development but also by **low-density development**.

Sprawl
The rapid growth of a metropolitan area, typically as a result of specific types of zoning and development.

Zoning Laws
Regulations that control how land can be used.

Low-Density Development
Development practices that spread (rather than concentrate) populations across the land.

In effect, local governments have exercised their land use powers to dictate that urban areas grow out rather than up. Rather than multifamily developments such as high-rise condominiums and apartments, suburbs and other urban municipalities have favored single-family developments. These developments make for lower population densities, but obviously they also require more land. For example, the population of the Milwaukee, Wisconsin, metropolitan area increased roughly 3 percent between 1970 and 1990, but geographically the metro area increased by 38 percent.[2121]

Leapfrog development. Leapfrog developments jump—or leapfrog—over established developments, leaving undeveloped or underdeveloped land between developed areas. This puts a particular strain on infrastructure—not just on roads but also on water and sewer facilities. When new developments bypass undeveloped land, utilities have to be stretched out further to serve the newly developed areas.

Leapfrog development is partially driven by the economic incentives of developers. Most established municipalities like to create uniform requirements for developments, for example, by enforcing specific building codes. They may even impose what are sometimes called **impact fees**, which are levied on builders of new housing or commercial developments to help offset the costs of extending services such as parks, schools, law enforcement, and fire protection services. A new housing development, for instance, may require the building of a new fire station, and impact fees help offset that cost. To avoid fees and regulation, developers often favor building in unincorporated areas, typically on land with geographical (and thus regulatory) separation from municipal borders, but still close enough to make for an easy commute to the urban center.

Leapfrog Development
Development practices in which new developments jump—or leapfrog—over established developments, leaving undeveloped or underdeveloped land between developed areas.

Impact Fees
Fees that municipalities charge builders of new housing or commercial developments to help offset the costs of extending services.

Car-dependent living. Single-use, low-density development means that citizens have to be highly mobile. Getting from a suburban home to a job in a commercial office and from home to the kids' soccer game on the weekend pretty much requires an automobile. In low-density housing developments, it is often impossible—or at least impractical—to do something like "run to the corner store." Getting a six-pack to watch the game or a bag of sugar to bake cookies, or even arranging a play date for the kids, requires transportation. Because public transportation systems for the most part are not set up for convenient and efficient transportation across large, multijurisdictional geographical areas, **car dependence** becomes a necessity for anyone residing in a metropolitan area. This promotes congested commutes, increased tailpipe emissions, and constant pressure to maintain and expand road infrastructure.

The Cons of Metropolitan Growth

By now it should be fairly obvious that the characteristic sprawl-like growth of metropolitan areas over the past fifty or sixty years has contributed to, and in some cases is a primary cause of, problems such as traffic congestion and smog. According to many academics who study urban politics and growth, these same development patterns produce a wide range of other problems, including the concentration of poverty and crime in certain neighborhoods, segregation by race and class, and inequality in public services, fiscal resources, and political power.

As new low-density housing developments began popping up around core cities after World War II, the middle and upper classes began moving from the cities to the suburbs. There were "push" and "pull" reasons for the migration of the better-off classes. The lure of the lifestyle—the home with the white picket fence on a leafy suburban lane—"pulled" people out of the city. Racial desegregation of public schools in the 1960s and 1970s also meant less well-off nonwhites began to

---

Car-Dependent Living
A situation in which owning a car for transportation is a necessity; an outcome of low-density development.

make up an ever greater proportion of urban schools, which created an incentive for whites to move, "pushing" them out to the suburbs.

The racial—and perhaps racist—undertones of this demographic shift have been repeatedly noted by academics.[22] Because the middle and upper classes were largely white, this demographic phenomenon became known as **white flight**. As whites left the dense, multiuse neighborhoods of cities for the lure of single-family homes on large lots in suburbia, minorities became concentrated in the core urban areas. Because racial minorities also were much more likely to be less socioeconomically well off than whites, this meant that inner-city neighborhoods became poorer.

As the city neighborhoods became poorer, the remaining middle-class residents felt more pressure to decamp to the suburbs, and a self-reinforcing trend set in; the poor and ethnic minorities became increasingly concentrated in core city neighborhoods. In the past couple of decades, this trend has started to occur in the suburbs themselves. Minorities who managed to get far enough up the socioeconomic ladder to move to an inner-ring suburb have triggered another round of white flight; as these less white, less well-off people move into the inner-ring suburbs, the better-off move farther out. The end result of this is the increasingly racial and socioeconomic homogeneity of particular political jurisdictions.

This also results in varying levels of public services. Well-off jurisdictions have the property values necessary to support high-quality public services; notably, middle- and upper-class suburbs tend to have high-quality public schools. So do **exurbs**, or municipalities in more rural settings that serve as bedroom communities, with residents commuting to jobs in the cities or suburbs during the day and returning to their homes after work. In stark contrast, inner-city neighborhoods and inner-ring suburbs where poverty is concentrated tend to have lower property values, meaning that they cannot support high-quality public services.

It is important to note that the end result is economic *and* racial segregation based on housing patterns, a trend made apparent by school districts. In some urban areas, African Americans make up less than 3 percent of the total population but constitute 70 percent of the school population.[23] These are invariably schools that serve poor communities, where crime and other social problems place enormous strain not just on public education but also on social and economic opportunities in general. While people can, and do, experience challenge and struggle out in the suburbs, suburban communities are much more likely to have the fiscal capacity to support public services such as good school systems. And because good schools play an important role in determining where the middle class wants to live, again this becomes a self-reinforcing trend.

> Place matters because wealth is segregated by communities across metropolitan regions, communities that are themselves concentrated in different political jurisdictions. As one well-known study of metropolitan politics and policy concludes, where you live in a given metropolitan area both affects your quality of life and shapes your social and economic opportunities.

Here is a difference that makes a big difference to the quality of life of millions of people. Place matters because wealth is segregated by communities across metropolitan regions, communities that are themselves concentrated in different political jurisdictions. As one well-known study of metropolitan politics and policy concludes,

---

White Flight
A demographic trend in which the middle and upper classes leave central cities for predominantly white suburbs.

Exurbs
Municipalities in rural areas that ring suburbs. They typically serve as bedroom communities for the prosperous, providing rural homes with easy access to urban areas.

where you live affects your quality of life and shapes your social and economic opportunities. This includes access to jobs, public services, level of personal security (crime tends to be higher in some socioeconomically stressed neighborhoods), availability of medical services, and even the quality of the air we breathe (the people commuting in from the exurbs contribute to urban smog but escape to the cleaner rural air after the workday is done).[24]

Critics of sprawl argue that it leads to metropolitan areas that promote and reinforce economic and racial segregation and creates disparities in tax bases that lead to huge differences in the quality of public services among local political jurisdictions. On top of that, from a regional perspective, the patterns of metropolitan growth are economically inefficient (jobs and the labor market are disconnected) and environmentally dangerous (all those cars pump out a lot of toxic emissions).[25]

Government Reform in Metropolitan Areas

Racial and economic segregation, inequities in tax bases and public services, and, above all, the political fragmentation that makes it difficult to coordinate effective responses to regional challenges—the problems of governance in metropolitan areas are well known. But what can be done about them?

One approach is the **reform perspective**, which traces many of these problems to political fragmentation: lots of small governments making decisions that produce local benefits but export the costs to other jurisdictions. If the root cause is political fragmentation, the argument goes, then government consolidation is the obvious solution. New regional governing structures should be created to respond more effectively to the interconnected problems of large metropolitan areas.[26]

There is no general agreement on what those regional governing structures should look like.

Some argue for the creation of new pan-regional governments, while others favor merging or consolidating existing jurisdictions.

Regional Governments

Reform perspective proponents are strong advocates of creating regional authorities to address regional problems. This can be done in a couple of ways. First, new government structures can be created to sit above existing political jurisdictions and be given the authority to oversee regional land use planning. This sort of approach has been popular with a number of civic activists from the reform tradition. Former Albuquerque mayor David Rusk, former Minnesota state representative Myron Orfield, and syndicated columnist Neal Pierce have all been popular champions of pan-regional planning authorities.

A couple of well-known examples of such regional planning authorities are frequently cited as examples of the benefits of taking a top-down approach to land use regulation. The best known of these is the Metropolitan Service District in Portland, Oregon, known simply as Metro. Metro is a true regional government that covers Clackamas, Multnomah, and Washington Counties and the twenty-five municipalities in the Portland metropolitan area; all told, its jurisdiction extends over approximately 1.5 million people, or about 40 percent of Oregon residents. It is governed by an elected legislature (a six-member council) and an elected executive (the council president).[27] Metro exercises real regulatory authority in areas such as land use planning, regional transportation, recycling and garbage disposal, and a host of other policy areas that are regional rather than local in nature.

One of the notable characteristics of the Portland Metro is the presence of an **urban growth boundary (UGB)**. A UGB controls the density and type of development by establishing a boundary around a given urban area. Land inside the UGB is slated for high-density development; land outside the UGB is slated for lower-density, rural sorts of development. In

---

Reform Perspective
An approach to filling gaps in service and reducing redundancies in local governments that calls for regional-level solutions.

Urban Growth Boundary (UGB)
A border established around urban areas that is intended to control the density and type of development.

effect, this type of planning regulation forces cities to grow vertically rather than horizontally and, thus, sets limits on sprawl and the problems it generates.

Critics argue the UGBs have a significant downside. By limiting the land available for development, UGBs drive up prices for land in particular and real estate in general. The end results are high property values and limited supplies of affordable housing. This does not seem to have happened in Portland, where property values are considered reasonable compared with the rest of the West Coast. Reformers have pointed to the success of the UGB in Portland to promote the adoption of similar policies in other urban areas. Three states—Oregon, Tennessee, and Washington—now mandate cities to establish UGBs.

Regional Councils

Although a true regional government, Metro is the exception rather than the rule—the vast majority of metropolitan areas in the United States lack any form of regional government with comparable authority and policymaking power. There are, however, a large number of regional planning authorities that provide at least a rudimentary form of coordination among the local governments packed into their metropolitan areas.

Regional councils are the most common attempt to rationalize local policymaking across multijurisdictional metropolitan areas. A **regional council** is "a multi-service entity with state and locally-defined boundaries that delivers a variety of federal, state and local programs while continuing its function as a planning organization, technical assistance provider and 'visionary' to its member local governments."[28]

Regional councils are made up of member governments, such as municipalities and school districts, although other nonprofit, civic, private, or academic organizations may also be included. They originated in the 1960s and 1970s as vehicles for delivering state and federal programs to regional areas. They have grown to become an important means of coordinating region-wide policy and planning in such areas as land use, transportation, economic development, housing, and social services. There are 516 such bodies in the United States, and of the roughly thirty-nine thousand general-purpose local governments in the country (which include counties, cities, municipalities, villages, boroughs, towns, and townships), about thirty-five thousand are served by regional councils.[29]

A related form of regional authority is the **metropolitan planning organization (MPO)**. MPOs decide how federal transportation funds are allocated within their regional areas. MPOs are interesting because they represent a specific recognition by federal law that regions—as opposed to localities—are central functional policy units. The Intermodal Surface Transportation Efficiency Act of 1991 (ISTEA) mandated that every metropolitan region had to identify an MPO to serve as the central coordinating authority for federal transportation funds in that area. Some MPOs administer billions of dollars in federal transportation grants, and control over such large amounts of money, coupled with the MPOs' authority over critical transportation programs, translates into major political clout.[30] There is even a nascent effort to coordinate the decision making of MPOs within megaregions, which would extend their influence on transportation infrastructure policy across even wider geographic areas.

Regional councils and MPOs, however, should not be confused or equated with Portland's Metro. They are more a vehicle for intergovernmental cooperation than an actual form of government with executive and legislative authority independent of local government interests. Intergovernmental institutions such as regional councils are, at best, confederal sorts of regional governments that are creatures of the often conflicting interests of their members.

Regional Council

A planning and advisory organization whose members include multiple local governments. Regional councils often are used to administer state and federal programs that target regions.

Metropolitan Planning Organization (MPO)

A regional organization that decides how federal transportation funds are allocated within that regional area.

Still, in most parts of the country, they come the closest to filling the hole in the organizational structure of the federal system. A move in this direction has been growing support for regional planning efforts that emphasize **smart growth**, development practices that emphasize more efficient infrastructure and less dependence on automobiles. Smart growth is reflected in regional, or even single-jurisdiction, policies that promote mixed-use developments that are pedestrian- and bicycle-friendly, emphasize building community rather than just buildings of bricks and mortar, and consciously account for development's impact on the environment.

The bottom line on regional councils and MPOs is that, for the most part, there is a considerable mismatch between their governance capacities and the need for effective and coordinated responses to regional issues. As one study of regional councils concludes, "despite the efforts of progressive reformers to push strategies encouraging . . . strong, centralized regional government institutions, most regional institutions find it difficult to address issues affecting the quality of life in a metropolitan area."[31]

> One of the lessons to emerge from the massive economic stimulus effort initiated by the federal government in response to the Great Recession was that the existing mechanisms of disbursement—state and local governments—do not effectively connect federal dollars with their intended policy targets. Part of this disconnect is clearly due to the lack of effective regional governance.

Despite their obvious limitations, these councils are currently the only politically viable regional governance mechanisms that "most local jurisdictions can use to address multiple and cross-cutting issues."[32] And the power and role of regional councils and MPOs may be increasing because of a shift in philosophy at the federal level. One of the lessons to emerge from the massive economic stimulus effort initiated by the federal government in response to the Great Recession was that the existing mechanisms of disbursement—state and local governments—sometimes do not effectively connect federal dollars with their intended policy targets. Part of this disconnect is clearly due to the lack of effective regional governance. The overarching intent of the federal government in providing the stimulus money was to stimulate the economy, and that meant targeting metro areas, where much of the nation's economic activity takes place. Accordingly, in recent years, the federal government has begun an effort to tie federal grants to increased regional cooperation, which puts regional councils and MPOs in a good position to increase their governance capacities in the future. (See the box "States under Stress: "Tying Federal Funding to Regional Cooperation").

Many local governments also engage in looser, informal cooperative arrangements rather than creating formal institutions such as regional councils or MPOs. This sort of cooperation is known as an **interjurisdictional agreement (IJA)**, an increasingly common form of intergovernmental cooperation. An IJA may take the form of a binding agreement. For example, a town may contract with the county for law enforcement services or for dispatch services. Other IJAs may be much more informal and rest on nothing more than good-faith agreements between two or more local governments to provide a service jointly or to work together on planning or management issues. No one really knows how many IJAs there are or how effective they are in promoting effective integrated responses to regional problems. Given the shortcomings of more formal institutions such as

Smart Growth
Environmentally friendly development practices, particularly those that emphasize more efficient infrastructure and less dependence on automobiles.

Interjurisdictional Agreement (IJA)
A formal or informal agreement between two or more local governments to cooperate on a program or policy.

States Under Stress

Tying Federal Funding to Regional Cooperation

How the federal government interacts with states and localities across a wide range of policy areas is evolving, and part of that change will reshape the entire structure and process of dispensing federal funds and steering federal policy.

During the early years of the Obama administration, the White House embraced a concept, advanced largely by the Brookings Institution's Metropolitan Policy Program, that stresses the primacy of the nation's metro regions—cities or clusters of cities, plus their inner and outer suburbs and some rural areas that are linked to them economically. The Brookings mantra is that these regions are the economic drivers of the country; they do, after all, contain three-quarters of the American population and generate most of the nation's economic activity. So, the idea is for Washington to start approaching the governments below its own level not as separate states, cities, and counties but as metros.

Soon after it took office, the administration started pushing its domestic agencies to find a more regional approach to dealing with all subgovernments. Federal departments in charge of housing, transportation, energy, the environment, labor, and small businesses are trying to coordinate hundreds of programs addressing a wide range of activities. And the expectation is that the efforts they will be funding—clusters of governments acting collaboratively—must be similarly integrated. If they are, great. If not, no dough.

The federal stimulus money disbursed in an effort to blunt the effects of the Great Recession was mostly subject to the old rules because Washington wanted to pump it out as fast as possible and didn't have time to write new rules. A New York Times analysis of more than five thousand transportation projects in the first few months under Obama showed that "the 100 largest metropolitan areas are getting less than half the money from the biggest pot of transportation stimulus money. In many cases, they have lost a tug of war with state lawmakers that urban advocates say could hurt the nation's economic engines."

That prompted a rethinking of how and to whom the federal government should send its dollars. Top managers in all the relevant agencies seem serious about forcing metropolitan collaboration, particularly when it involves more than one area of domestic policy. Bruce Katz of the Brookings Institution predicts optimistically that the growing recognition of the importance of metro areas "will stimulate a new generation of political and policy organizing at the metro scale." He believes this will include reinvigorating and funding long-dormant MPOs that were resuscitated sixteen years ago when Congress passed a landmark transportation bill, only to be largely ignored in more recent years.

Of course, there are problems with this strategy, both practical and political. As columnist Mary Newsom of the Charlotte Observer points out, far too many MPOs still seem to believe that "'transportation' means only highways" and that regional organizations are little more than instruments for the protection of local turf. The Charlotte metropolitan region, Newsom notes, "is home to four separate MPOs, or five, depending on how you count. So transportation planning here is completely fragmented—and Charlotte gets shorted when dollars are divvied."

That's true in a lot of places because governors and legislatures like to spread the funds around their states rather than concentrating them in metros. And they may not be too interested in changing the process or the rules. But that is exactly what the Obama administration is pressuring them to do.

Federalism scholar Paul Posner of George Mason University has some doubts about how successful the initiative to invigorate MPOs will be, not only because states and locals have the political clout to avoid ceding too much authority but also because "the feds have a track record of good intentions over the past 50 years" that have ultimately amounted to very little.

But Posner concedes that some incremental progress is taking place. "The lesson learned," he says, "might be that the only way the federal government will succeed in institutionalizing regionalism is if it follows and supports demand from the bottom of our system, rather than seeking to create and impose demand from the top. Where the demand exists and the regional institutions are strong, there is promise. But where they are not, then progress will be much slower."

Source: Adapted from Peter Harkness, "Tying Federal Funding to Regional Cooperation," Governing, September 2009.

regional councils and MPOs, however, IJAs often represent one of the few viable alternatives for multijurisdictional governance.[33]

Government Consolidation

As discussed above, one approach to rationalizing governance in metropolitan regions is to create new types of government. An alternative is to reduce the number of existing local governments through consolidation, and a number of city and county governments have done exactly this.

On the face of it, this makes a good deal of sense. Cities and urban counties share the same geographical space and provide similar services. A classic example is law enforcement. An urban county sitting on top of a large city will have a sheriff's office and a municipal police department, each with its own jails, dispatch centers, training facilities, and purchasing departments. There is clearly a lot of redundancy and inefficiency in duplicating these services in such close quarters. Why not consolidate at least some of these functions? That is exactly what Des Moines, Iowa, and Polk County did with their city and county jails. The county and city jails sat on opposite sides of the Des Moines River—directly across from each other—and consolidating facilities and operations just seemed to make sense.

If consolidating operations can reduce redundancy and improve efficiency, why not go whole hog and merge municipal and county governments into a single government? Cities and counties often duplicate bureaucracies and paperwork, so there is an obvious logic to **city-county consolidation**. With as many as 75 percent of all major urban areas in the United States contained within single counties, you might think such mergers would be common. But, for a variety of reasons, they aren't.

According to the National Association of Counties, of the nation's more than three thousand counties, only about forty (roughly 1 percent) have

consolidated with cities. Since 1990, there have been only about forty-five formal proposals to consolidate city and county governments, and of those only about a dozen have actually passed.[34] Why do consolidation attempts have such a poor track record? Well, while consolidation is generally favored by business groups and others who favor a reorganization of government to reduce bureaucratic redundancy and to allow communities to speak "with one voice," the politics of consolidations are tricky. Middle-class suburbanites worry that mergers will benefit downtown residents while raising taxes in the suburbs; inner-city minorities fear their voting power will be diluted. Elected officials reflect these concerns and perhaps add some of their own. Consolidated governments mean fewer elected politicians and, most likely, fewer public employees. This creates internal pressure to resist merger movements. There is also plain, old-fashioned community loyalty. People identify with their local governments, tend to trust them (at least compared to state and federal governments), and are reluctant to replace them with something unknown and untested.

Despite the inherent difficulties, in the past few years there has been a renewed interest in consolidation, especially by state governments. A good deal of this interest has been driven by economic pressures stemming from the Great Recession. In Michigan, for example, there are nearly two thousand municipalities, more than a thousand fire departments, more than six hundred police departments, and a similar number of school districts. Michigan was particularly hard hit by the recession; as already mentioned, a number of its local governments fell into such precarious financial positions that they were effectively taken over by the state. The massive bureaucratic duplication at the local level did not make a whole lot of sense to Governor Rick Snyder when he took office in 2011. Snyder, whose background is primarily as a business executive, saw all that government as inefficient and made attempts to trim it down. While the governor cannot force local governments to merge, he can create incentives to do exactly that. He made hundreds of millions of dollars in state aid for cities

---

City-County Consolidation
The merging of separate local governments in an effort to reduce bureaucratic redundancy and service inefficiencies.

contingent on the elimination of duplication in areas such as fire departments and trash collection.[35]

Annexation

Rather than forming new governments like Portland's Metro or merging old ones, another option for dealing with the problems of sprawl, traffic congestion, and uneven economic development is to make the existing political jurisdictions bigger. **Annexation** is the legal incorporation of one jurisdiction or territory into another. Usually, the jurisdiction that does the annexing is more politically powerful, whereas the "annexee" is weaker and may not be enthusiastic about becoming the latest addition to a larger municipal neighbor. This approach is relatively common in the South and West,

regions where there are large tracts of unincorporated land adjacent to major cities. Cities such as El Paso, Houston, and Phoenix have annexed hundreds of square miles, turning themselves into regional governments by sheer geographical size. Oklahoma City, for example, has more than 600 square miles within its city limits, much of it having been added over the years through annexations.[36]

Annexation is principally a tool used by municipalities that want to control development along their peripheries and engage in planned expansions of their tax bases. Remember that cities like to place uniform requirements on area developers, leading developers to favor unincorporated areas where land is cheaper and there are fewer regulations. One way cities can stop developers from avoiding regulation and impose a more coherent and orderly plan on metropolitan growth is simply to annex that unincorporated land.

A city government that wishes to annex a tract of land must organize the citizens of the unincorporated area to sign a petition. Some communities seek to expand by annexing prospectively, working to incorporate still-undeveloped parcels of land farther out from suburban parcels already

being transformed from woods or farmland into subdivisions. This, in turn, may alienate rural landowners, including farmers, who value their traditional identity as separate from that of the city.[37] Annexation, in short, can create a lot of conflict, with some residents of unincorporated areas seeing it as a land grab that threatens to develop their rural communities out of existence.

Annexation can make sense from a big-picture perspective in that it can help impose the orderly expansion of urban municipalities, but there is no getting around the fact that it creates losers as well as winners. And the losers often are not interested in losing at all. For example, in Ohio, townships and counties are pushing for more say over annexations, deliberately trying to limit the ability of municipalities to gobble up unincorporated land in the name of development.[38]

Annexation also has natural limits—there has to be land available to annex. Although municipalities tend to have the upper hand over sparsely populated, unincorporated territories, if they bump up against another city, it's a different story. Unlike cities in the South and West, cities in the North and East are more likely to be ringed by incorporated suburbs; in effect, core cities are fenced in by other cities, with no real option to expand. Pittsburgh, for example, covers about 58 square miles—a fraction of Oklahoma City's 600-plus square miles. Barring a merger with county government, it is unlikely that Pittsburgh is ever going to grow to anywhere near the geographical size of Oklahoma City.

The Case Against Reform: Public Choice and the Tiebout Model

Not everyone agrees that the problems of metropolitan areas require stronger regional governments. Indeed, some argue that these problems have been exaggerated, or at least not balanced against the benefits of metropolitan growth.

Urban areas are, for the most part, pretty decent places to live. Core cities are not swirling down into

---

Annexation
The legal incorporation of one jurisdiction or territory into another.

a uniform death spiral of relentless flight to the suburbs, leaving poverty, racial segregation, and crime. In many MSAs, they remain the economic and social hubs of their regions. Scholars and musicians, business leaders and actors—people in a wide range of fields are still more likely to be attracted to the city to pursue their opportunities and dreams than to an exurb or single-use housing tract. Core cities remain exciting places, centers of innovation and culture, shopping and business activity.

Some decaying urban areas have undergone a renaissance, with old warehouses being turned into upscale condos and downtown neighborhoods becoming the focus of thriving cultural scenes. This process of physical rehabilitation of urban areas, which attracts investment from developers and drives up property values, is known as **gentrification**. Gentrified neighborhoods present something of a double-edged sword; they reinvigorate decaying urban areas, but the resulting property value increases can price poorer people out of their own neighborhoods. Regardless, it is clear that the middle and upper classes no longer find the suburbs quite as attractive as they used to. Long commutes and the falling values of suburban properties brought on by the Great Recession have made city living more attractive to younger, middle-class people. This is the demographic that started heading to the suburbs fifty or sixty years ago. We may be seeing the beginning of that demographic's return to a more urban lifestyle.

> In short, there is a glass-half-full perspective that sees in the cities innovation and vitality, high standards of living, and social and economic opportunity; this contrasts with a glass-half-empty perspective that focuses on segregation, smog, and economic inequality.

In short, there is a glass-half-full perspective that sees in the cities innovation and vitality, high standards of living, and social and economic opportunity; this contrasts with a glass-half-empty perspective that focuses on segregation, smog, and economic inequality. There are also strong theoretical arguments against any large-scale movement to replace multiple local jurisdictions with larger regional governance structures.

Public choice theory views governments and public services in market terms; governments are seen as producers of public services and citizens are seen as consumers. As in most markets, competition among producers is seen as a good thing. With lots of local jurisdictions, citizens can choose their favored "producers" by moving to the cities or towns that have the mixes of taxes and public services that suit them best. If local governments fail to satisfy individual citizen consumers—in other words, if their taxes go too high or their public services drop too low—citizens can vote with their feet and move to other jurisdictions with more attractive tax–public service packages. To work, this market model needs lots of competing local jurisdictions just as a private market needs lots of competing companies; having one big central provider of goods and services means a monopoly, and in market theory monopolies tend to be inefficient. Public choice argues that monopolies of public goods and services are likely to be just as inefficient and unresponsive to their customers as monopolies of public goods and services.

This perspective on local government was most famously articulated by Charles Tiebout in the 1950s. The **Tiebout model** of local government calls for

In June 2006, Anaheim, California, became the first major U.S. city to go wireless. Residents can subscribe to the service on a monthly basis, and visitors can purchase temporary usage capabilities.

Public Choice Model
A model of politics that views governments and public services in market terms; governments are seen as producers of public services and citizens are seen as consumers.

Tiebout Model
A model of local government based on market principles wherein a metro area is made up of a series of micropolitical jurisdictions that, on the basis of their services and costs, attract or repel certain citizens.

Gentrification
The physical rehabilitation of urban areas, which attracts investment from developers and drives up property values.

a metro area made up of a series of micropolitical jurisdictions. If each jurisdiction can control its tax-service package, fully mobile citizens will respond to the available packages by gravitating to the one that suits them best. Or, as Tiebout put it, the mobility of citizens will provide "the local public goods counterpart to the private market's shopping trip."[39]

In addition to highly mobile citizens, the Tiebout model requires informed citizens. If people do not know what different governments are offering in the way of alternative tax-service packages, they are not going to be very good local government "shoppers," and local governments may be able to take advantage of that ignorance by becoming lazy and inefficient producers of public goods and services. If the mobility and information requirements are met, the Tiebout model makes a strong theoretical case for the benefits of political fragmentation in metropolitan areas, thus arguing against the reform perspective's push for pan-regional and consolidated governments.

The "if" on the mobility and information requirements, however, is a big one. A number of studies strongly suggest that citizens are neither fully mobile nor fully informed. The constraints on mobility are fairly obvious: where you can live is determined by how much money you can earn. This means the well-off, if they so choose, can be fairly mobile. The less well-off or homeowners stuck trying to sell their homes in a tough real estate market, on the other hand, are more likely to find their mobility limited by their pocketbooks. They simply cannot afford to move to better neighborhoods, even if they want to, because property prices are too high. This has important implications. The Tiebout model is predicated on the assumption that local governments will be responsive to people who have a real exit option, that is, people who can pack up and move if they don't like what the local government is doing. If those people are defined by wealth, it means governments in metropolitan areas are likely to be more responsive to the concerns of the well-off than to those of the poor.

Rural Metropolitics

Rural governments experience different challenges than the urban areas we've been discussing. Populations in rural areas are shrinking and aging as people move from rural agricultural areas to metropolitan areas in search of educational, social, and economic opportunities. Roughly three hundred counties with populations under twenty-five thousand lost at least 10 percent of their population between 2000 and 2010.[40] This reflects a population exodus that tracks a massive consolidation in agriculture as family farms give way to corporate operations. Fewer farms means fewer agricultural jobs, which means that younger people are moving to the cities, where the jobs are, leaving smaller rural communities with fewer shoppers, fewer schools, and fewer businesses. That is a recipe for decline that can be hard to reverse.

Rather than white flight, rural states with agriculture-based economies such as Iowa, Kansas, and Nebraska face **rural flight**, the movement of the young and the middle class to more urban areas. This can create pressure for a reform that sounds familiar to any veteran of the political battles over urban growth: regional government. Iowa, for example, is a mostly rural state. It has a population of roughly 3 million and more than a thousand general-purpose governments. If special districts (schools and the like) are included, Iowa has something like one government per 1,600 residents. Most counties in Iowa do not have a lot of people; what they have is a lot of government. (See Map 10-1 for county-by-county population changes in Iowa.)

Redundant layers of government sitting on stagnant tax bases puts upward pressure on property taxes and creates incentives to make government more efficient. Consolidating governments is one way to do this, and this option is increasingly being considered in rural states. Schools are typically among the first sets of merger candidates. As student populations decrease in a rural community,

Rural Flight
The movement of youth and the middle class from rural areas to more urban areas.

MAP 10-1

Population Changes by County, Iowa, 2000–2010

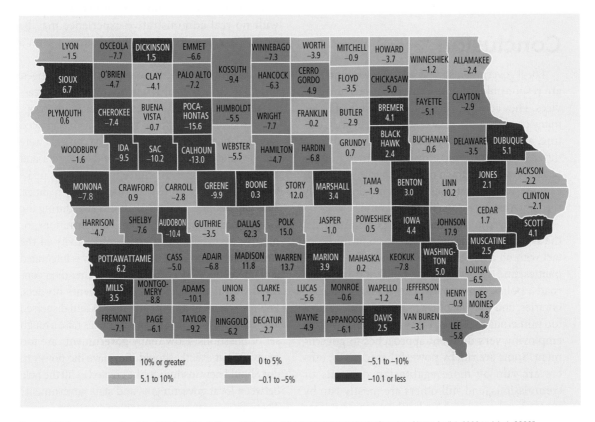

Source: U.S. Census Bureau, Population Division, Table 1, "Annual Estimates of the Resident Population for Counties of Iowa: April 1, 2000 to July 1, 2008" (CO-EST2008-01-19), release date March 19, 2009.

it is harder to fund a comprehensive K–12 school system. If there is another community within busing distance, it can make a good deal of financial sense for the two communities to split educational services—for example, to have elementary schools in both communities, the junior high in one town, and the high school in the other.

These sorts of pressures have made for a steady stream of school district consolidations in rural states. As recently as the mid-1980s, for example, Nebraska had more than a thousand public school districts. As of 2012, it had 249; in a thirty-year span, three-quarters of school districts in Nebraska consolidated or went out of business.[41] School consolidations make financial sense from the standpoint of the statewide taxpayer; larger districts can take advantage of economies of scale, rationalize class sizes, and lower per-pupil spending. From a community perspective, school

consolidations are less about dollars and cents than they are about identity, or even survival. A rural community that loses its school loses a central social and cultural institution; the loss of teachers also means losing a significant chunk of a town's middle class. The loss of a high school can be a devastating blow to a rural community.

When economics come up against strong loyalties to local governments, local loyalties often win, but these victories mean higher property taxes and fewer public services. Back in 2005, Iowa governor Tom Vilsack argued that his state simply could not support its many governments and proposed a truly radical solution—replacing the grab bag of hundreds of local governments with about fifteen regional governments. Vilsack reasoned that these would not only be cheaper but also be better positioned to drive economic development in rural areas. His plan landed with a thud; it got little support at the local level and a chilly reception in the legislature.[42] Iowans seemed to prefer higher taxes and/or lower levels of service to losing their traditional local governments.

Conclusion

Local governments wield actual power, and they are responsible for important programs and services. They come in a bewildering variety of types, many of which reflect state or regional history, culture, and preferences. Taken as a whole, all these differences can seem confusing. Yet in any single place—your hometown or local county—the government and what it does or does not do probably seems perfectly reasonable and natural.

Local government is the form of government that the average citizen is most likely to come into contact with on a day-to-day basis. Counties, municipalities, and special districts build and maintain roads, police those roads, run schools, manage libraries, and provide other programs and services too numerous to list. And they do all of this while employing very different approaches to government. Some are run by powerful executives, others are run by more egalitarian councils or commissions, and still others are mostly run by professional managers. Yet local government is far from ideal. These mini-republics are constrained by Dillon's Rule. They tend to have relatively low voter turnout for elections. The idiosyncrasies of local government structure can mean that someone with no real administrative experience may be elected to run a complicated bureaucracy with a multimillion-dollar budget.

Local governments face significant challenges, including a tough financial environment and increasing recognition that they must coordinate and cooperate to deal with regional issues. This has created renewed interest in reform. Local governments were founded and organized in a horse-and-buggy era, and those organizational structures do not always make for a rational fit with twenty-first-century realities. This gap became particularly noticeable during the Great Recession. Dense urban concentrations, or metros, are where most economic activity in the United States is located, and this activity is integrated and interconnected across a region rather than confined within a single local government's borders. Political fragmentation in urban areas and dispersed and shrinking populations in rural areas raise a tough set of questions: How many governments are too many? What exactly should they have the power to do? Should new institutions be created to fill the hole between local governments and state government? There are no easy answers to these questions.

The Latest Research

Despite their numbers and their importance to the day-to-day lives of citizens, local governments are surprisingly understudied by political scientists. Systematic comparative studies on local governance are few and far between in the discipline's major journals. Part of the reason for this may be the astonishing variety of local governments and their sometimes bewildering numbers of responsibilities. It is hard to say something generalizable about local governments because, unlike state governments, they are not necessarily comparable units. Still, how local governments should (or should not) change and how they should be held accountable are critical and pressing questions. The studies described below seek to provide at least partial answers.

• •

- **Arnold, R. Douglas, and Nicholas Carnes.** 2012. "Holding Mayors Accountable: New York's Executives from Koch to Bloomberg."

American Journal of Political Science 56: 949–963.

This study seeks to answer a simple question: How do citizens evaluate the performance of municipal executives? This question is important—one of the things we have learned from our study of state executives is that popular support is a key component of informal power, which is arguably the most important tool governors have for making policy and influencing the public agenda. Although such questions seem basic and have been the subject of intense study at the level of state executives, we have no comparable basis of knowledge at the local level. We are not even sure if citizens hold mayors accountable for the quality of municipal services or city life in general. Arnold and Carnes seek to fill that gap by doing the first-ever study to track mayoral approval across time, analyzing how approval ratings change in response to local conditions and whether that level of public opinion has electoral implications. They do this by examining responses on 150 public opinion surveys, taken over a twenty-five-year period, that included questions on mayoral approval in New York City. They find that New Yorkers hold the mayor accountable for levels of crime and economic conditions—when crime rates go up and economic conditions worsen, mayoral approval dips. Those approval ratings translate into votes. What this study suggests is that citizens treat local executives the same way they treat state executives. Even if the relevant conditions are clearly beyond a mayor's control—a weakening national economy, for example—citizens hold the mayor accountable and punish him or her at the polls if conditions do not improve.

- **Hendrick, Rebecca, Benedict Jimenez, and Kamna Lal.** 2011. "Does Local Government Fragmentation Reduce Local Spending?" *Urban Affairs Review* 47: 467–510.

This research team looks at local government spending in 126 metropolitan regions covering 538 counties. The key research question is whether greater fragmentation in these regions leads to higher spending. The answer is yes . . . and no. One of the key findings is that geographical areas with more single-purpose governments have higher levels of local government spending. This seems to support the argument for consolidation; the obvious implication is that merging the responsibilities of those single governments into fewer general-purpose governments will reduce spending. Yet another key finding of this study is that areas with more centralized governments also have higher spending. The takeaway story here is that the costs and benefits of fragmentation versus centralization are not clear-cut. Neither the many governments along the lines of the Tiebout model nor the fewer governments recommended by metro advocates are a one-size-fits-all solution. The pros and cons of more versus fewer governments depend on what sorts of governments (e.g., single purpose versus general purpose) are involved, as well as on the political, economic, and social context.

- **Bowman, Ann O'M., and Richard Kearney.** 2012. "Are U.S. Cities Losing Power and Authority? Perceptions of Local Government Actors." *Urban Affairs Review* 48: 528–546.

As the discussion of Dillon's Rule in this chapter makes clear, local governments are not sovereign—they wield only those powers that states allow them to have. This raises questions about the distribution of power, something that's becoming increasingly important given the need to address regional rather than local issues. If there really is no functioning level of regional government between states and localities, will states take on the job themselves? Will states leave local governments to keep going their own way, or will they start to exercise their sovereign authority and start to lessen the power of local authorities? Bowman and Kearney get at this question by surveying state and local government officials to get their perspectives on the evolution of state-local relationships. Their findings show that state officials generally see a reasonable distribution of power, perceiving that local officials have been given a more or less appropriate balance of authority and discretion. The authors report that the view from local officials is decidedly different: "From the perspective of city managers . . . the past decade has been one of loss of power and discretionary authority accompanied by encumbering (state) mandates in numerous policy areas." Lacking meaningful regional government structures, perhaps states are taking on the job themselves.

Chapter Review

Key Concepts

- annexation (p. 306)
- at-large election (p. 296)
- car-dependent living (p. 299)
- charter (p. 295)
- cities (p. 288)
- city commission system (p. 290)
- city council (p. 288)
- city-county consolidation (p. 305)
- city manager (p. 288)
- commission-administrator system (p. 286)
- council-executive system (p. 286)
- council-manager system (p. 289)
- counties (p. 285)
- county commission system (p. 286)
- Dillon's Rule (p. 293)
- edgeless cities (p. 297)
- exurbs (p. 300)
- general act charter (p. 295)
- gentrification (p. 307)
- impact fees (p. 299)
- interjurisdictional agreement (IJA) (p. 303)
- leapfrog development (p. 299)
- low-density development (p. 296)
- mayor (p. 288)
- mayor-council system (p. 288)
- megaregion (p. 297)
- metropolitan area (p. 296)
- metropolitan planning organization (MPO) (p. 302)
- metropolitan statistical area (MSA) (p. 297)
- municipalities (p. 285)
- public choice model (p. 307)
- reform perspective (p. 301)

- regional council (p. 302)

- rural flight (p. 308)

- smart growth (p. 303)

- special act charter (p. 295)

- special district (p. 285)

- sprawl (p. 298)

- strong mayor system (p. 288)

- Tiebout model (p. 307)

- town meeting form of government (p. 291)

- townships (p. 288)

- urban growth boundary (UGB) (p. 301)

- ward, or district, election (p. 295)

- weak mayor system (p. 288)

- white flight (p. 300)

- zoning laws (p. 298)

Suggested Websites

- **www.ampo.org.** Website of the Association of Metropolitan Planning Organizations, the national organization for MPOs. AMPO is mainly oriented toward transportation issues, but the site includes downloadable studies and publications on a range of issues facing metropolitan areas.

- **www2.icma.org/main/sc.asp.** Website of the International City/County Management Association, whose mission is to create excellence in local government by developing and fostering professional local government management worldwide.

- **www.metro-region.org.** Website of Portland, Oregon's Metro, a rare example of a true regional government in the United States; includes the history of Metro's formation and information on a range of its activities.

- **www.naco.org.** Website of the National Association of Counties, the only national organization that represents county governments in the United States.

- **www.narc.org.** Website of the National Association of Regional Councils, an organization of metropolitan planning organizations that seeks to promote cooperation between governments; covers urban, suburban, and rural governments.

- **www.nlc.org.** Website of the National League of Cities, the oldest and largest national organization representing municipal governments in the United States.

- **www.usmayors.org.** Website of the U.S. Conference of Mayors, which is the official nonpartisan organization of the 1,183 U.S. cities with populations of thirty thousand or more.

STATE STATS State Stats on Local Government

Explore and compare data on the states! Go to **college.cqpress .com/sites/essentials-govstateandlocal** to do these exercises.

1. How has local government spending across the states changed between 2000 and 2010? Where has it changed the most and the least? What might account for some of the changes?

2. In which state does the local government have the highest level of direct general expenditures? Which has the least? How does state population affect these expenditures? Why?

3. How has the number of public high schools in Nebraska changed between 2001 and 2011? Why has this change occurred?

4. New York, northern New Jersey, and portions of Pennsylvania make up the largest metropolitan statistical area in the United States. What is the average household income in these states? What might this tell us about the relationship between these states? Do we have enough information here to make this analysis?

5. One of the drawbacks of metropolitan growth is the dependence on cars that it creates. Which states have the most cars per driver? Which have the least? Why is there such a large difference?

Notes

Chapter 1

1. Peter Harkness, "Public Universities Reach a Tipping Point," *Governing*, June 2012, www.governing.com/topics/education/gov-public-universities-reach-tipping-point.html.

2. Alan Greenblatt, "Tuition? UC Riverside Students Say Bill Me Later," *Governing*, April 2012, www.governing.com/topics/education/gov-tuition-uc-riverside-students-say-bill-me-later.html.

3. National Center for Education Statistics, "Total Fall Enrollment in Degree-Granting Institutions, by Control and Type of Institution: 1963 through 2009," *Digest of Education Statistics*, April 2011, http://nces.ed.gov/pubs2011/2011015.pdf.

4. National Center for Education Statistics, "Percentage Distribution of Total Revenue of Public Degree-Granting Institutions, by Source of Funds: 2008–2009," *Digest of Education Statistics*, April 2011, http://nces.ed.gov/pubs2011/2011015.pdf.

5. National Center for Education Statistics, "Fast Facts: Financial Aid," http://nces.ed.gov/fastfacts/display.asp?id=31.

6. National Center for Education Statistics, "Fast Facts: Back to School Statistics," http://nces.ed.gov/fastfacts/display.asp?id=372.

7. Kenneth J. Meier, *Politics and the Bureaucracy* (Pacific Grove, CA: Brooks/Cole, 1993), 2.

8. Christopher Z. Mooney, "Why Do They Tax Dogs in West Virginia? Teaching Political Science through Comparative State Politics," *PS: Political Science & Politics* 31 (June 1998): 199–203.

9. Bridging the Gap, Robert Wood Johnson Foundation, "State Sales Tax on Regular, Sugar-Sweetened Soda (as of July 1, 2011)," www.bridgingthegapresearch.org/_asset/zvh93o/BTG_State_Soda_Sales_Tax_Jul012011_publuse_29Nov11.pdf.

10. Based on a standard ordinary least squares (OLS) regression analysis in which average tuition bills at public four-year universities are the dependent variable and state appropriations as thousands of dollars per enrolled student are the independent variable. Data taken from National Center for Education Statistics, *Digest of Education Statistics*, http://nces.ed.gov/pubs2011/2011015.pdf.

11. U.S. Bureau of the Census, "State and County QuickFacts," http://quickfacts.census.gov/qfd/index.html.

12. Richard Morrill, "The Urban US: Growth and Decline," *NewGeography*, April 11, 2012, www.newgeography.com/content/002769-the-urban-us-growth-and-decline.

13. Associated Press, "Not So Sunny: Florida's Growth Rate Continues to Slide, Census Reports," www.naplesnews.com/news/2010/jun/10/not-so-sunny-floridas-growth-rate-continues-slide-.

14. Daniel J. Elazar, *American Federalism: A View from the States* (New York: Crowell, 1966). This book has gone through three editions, the most recent of which was published in 1984.

15. Ibid., 88.

16. Maureen Moakley, "New Jersey," in *The Political Life of the American States*, ed. Alan Rosenthal and Maureen Moakley (New York: Praeger, 1984), 222.

17. Quoted in Robert D. Putnam, *Bowling Alone: The Collapse and Revival of American Community* (New York: Simon & Schuster, 2000), 293.

18. Russell Hanson, "Political Culture Variations in State Economic Development Policy," *Publius: The Journal of Federalism* 21, no. 2 (Spring 1991): 63–81; Kevin B. Smith, *The Ideology of Education: The Commonwealth, the Market, and America's Schools* (Albany: State University of New York Press, 2003).

19. Bureau of Economic Analysis, "Per Capita Real GDP by State," http://bea.gov/iTable/iTable.cfm?reqid=99&step=1.

20. Phillip W. Roeder, *Public Opinion and Policy Leadership in the American States* (Tuscaloosa: University of Alabama Press, 1994); J. Wolak and C. K. Palus, "The Dynamics of Public Confidence in U.S. State and Local Government," *State Politics & Policy Quarterly* 10 (2010): 421–445.

21. Bruce Wallin, "State and Local Governments Are American Too," *Political Science Teacher* 1 (1988): 1–3.

22. U.S. Bureau of the Census, "Government Employment and Payroll," www.census.gov/govs/apes.

23. U.S. Bureau of the Census, "State and Local Government Finances Summary: 2009," October 11, 2011, www2.census.gov/govs/estimate/09_summary_report.pdf.

24. Evan J. Ringquist and James C. Garand, "Policy Change in the American States," in *State and Local Politics*, ed. Ronald E. Weber and Paul Brace (New York: Chatham House, 1999).

25. David Osborne and Ted Gaebler, *Reinventing Government: How the Entrepreneurial Spirit Is Transforming the Public Sector* (New York: Plume, 1993).

Chapter 2

1. Cass Sunstein, "The Return of States' Rights," *American Prospect*, November 30, 2002, www.prospect.org/cs/articles?article=the_return_of_states_rights.

2. James Collier and Christopher Collier, *Decision in Philadelphia* (New York: Random House, 1986).

3. Quoted in ibid., 3.

4. Ellen Perlman, "The Preemption Beast: The Gorilla That Swallows State Laws," *Governing*, August 1994, 46–51.

5. Quoted in Harry N. Scheiber, "The Condition of American Federalism: An Historian's View," in *American Intergovernmental Relations*, ed. Laurence J. O'Toole Jr. (Washington, DC: CQ Press, 2000), 71.

6. Ibid.

7. Kala Ladenheim, "History of U.S. Federalism," March 16, 1999, www.cas.sc.edu/poli/courses/scgov/History_of_Federalism.htm.

8. Scheiber, "Condition of American Federalism."

9. Ellis Katz, "American Federalism, Past, Present and Future," *Issues of Democracy* 2, no. 2 (1997), www.doge.us/govecon/AmericanFederalismPast.pdf.

10. Paul L. Posner, *The Politics of Unfunded Mandates: Whither Federalism?* (Washington, DC: Georgetown University Press, 1998), 13.

11. National Conference of State Legislatures, "Mandate Monitor," www.ncsl.org/state-federal-committees/scbudg/mandate-monitor-overview.aspx.

12. Timothy Conlon, "Federalism and Competing Values in the Reagan Administration," *Publius: The Journal of Federalism* 16, no. 4 (1986): 29–47.

13. Thomas J. Anton, "New Federalism and Intergovernmental Fiscal Relationships: The Implications for Health Policy," *Journal of Health Politics, Policy and Law* 22, no. 3 (1997): 691–720.

14. Richard L. Cole and John Kincaid, "Public Opinion and American Federalism: Perspectives on Taxes, Spending, and Trust," *Spectrum: The Journal of State Government* 74, no. 3 (2000): 14–18.

15. "Same-Sex Marriage: Federal and State Authority," *Congressional Digest* 75 (November 1996): 263.

16. Peter Harkness, "Potomac Chronicle: Obama and the States," *Governing*, January 1, 2009, 18.

17. Bardon Aronson, "The Rising Tide of Federalism," CNN.com, February 1, 2001, www.cnn.com/2001/LAW/02/columns/fl.aronson.federalism.02.01.

18. Alan Ehrenhalt, "Devolution in Reverse," *Governing*, December 1, 2008, 8.

19. Michael S. Greve, *Real Federalism: Why It Matters, How It Could Happen* (Washington, DC: AEI Press, 1999), 17.

20. Jeffrey G. Homrig, "*Alden v. Maine*: A New Genre of Federalism Shifts the Balance of Power," *California Law Review* 89, no. 1 (2001): 183–205.

21. David G. Savage, "Justices Rule U.S. Can Ban Medical Pot," *Los Angeles Times*, June 7, 2005, http://articles.latimes.com/2005/jun/07/nation/na-scotus7.

22. John Dinan, "The State of American Federalism 2007–2008: Resurgent State Influence in the National Policy Process and Continued State Policy Innovation," *Publius: The Journal of Federalism* 38, no. 3 (2008): 381–415.

23. Brady Baybeck and William Lowry, "Federalism Outcomes and Ideological Preferences: The U.S. Supreme Court and Preemption Cases," *Publius: The Journal of Federalism* 30, no. 1 (2000): 73–96.

Chapter 3

1. Referendum A, Colorado, 2004.

2. Shauna Reilly and Sean Richey, "Ballot Question Readability and Roll-Off: The Impact of Language Complexity," *Political Research Quarterly* 64 (2011): 59–67.

3. See chapter 1 for a discussion of Elazar's typology of political cultures.

4. Donald Kettl, "Governor Rehnquist," *Governing*, July 1999.

5. Alan Tarr, *Understanding State Constitutions* (Princeton, NJ: Princeton University Press, 1998), 6–8.

6. Christopher Hammons, "Was James Madison Wrong? Rethinking the American Preference for Short, Framework-Oriented Constitutions," *American Political Science Review* 93, no. 4 (1999): 837.

7. Ibid., 840.

8. Ibid., 840. See also John G. Kester, "Amendment Time," *Washingtonian*, March 1995.

9. Janice C. May, "Trends in State Constitutional Amendment and Revision," in *The Book of the States 2003* (Lexington, KY: Council of State Governments, 2003), 8.

10. Robert J. Taylor, ed., *Massachusetts, Colony to Commonwealth* (New York: Norton, 1961).

11. Quoted in Willi Paul Adams, *The First American Constitutions: Republican Ideology and the Making of the State Constitutions in the Revolutionary Era* (Chapel Hill: University of North Carolina Press, 1980), 53.

12. Quoted in ibid., 61.

13. Quoted in ibid., 207

14. Tarr, *Understanding State Constitutions*, 121.

15. W. B. Stouffer, Cynthia Opheim, and Susan Bland Day, eds., *State and Local Politics: The Individual and the Governments* (New York: HarperCollins, 1996).

16. Bruce Sundlun, "R.I.'s Martyr for Democracy," *Providence Journal-Bulletin*, August 11, 2002.

17. Delaware is the only state that does not refer constitutional amendments to the electorate as a whole. The legislature may enact constitutional amendments on its own if a measure receives support in two consecutive legislative sessions.

18. *The Book of the States 2001* (Lexington, KY: Council of State Governments, 2001), 5. In South Carolina, a majority of both houses of the legislature must vote to approve a constitutional amendment a second time, after it has passed a popular referendum, before it can go into effect.

19. Initiative and Referendum Institute, www.iandrinstitute.org. The institute's website includes detailed time lines of initiative and referendum activity in each state.

20. Juan B. Elizondo Jr., "Ratliff: Time to Rewrite Constitution; Lawmaker Joined by Watchdog," *Austin American-Statesman*, October 28, 1999.

21. *The Book of the States 2003* (Lexington, KY: Council of State Governments, 2003), 3–4.

22. Warren Richey, "Unique Law Lets Florida Voters Make Changes to Constitution," *Christian Science Monitor*, May 8, 1998.

23. Quoted in Alan Ehrenhalt, "Vermont's Judicial Distillery," *Governing*, February 2000, www.governing.com/archive/archive/2000/feb/assess.txt.

24. Hammons, "Was James Madison Wrong?," 839.

25. Joni James, "Voters Hold Key to Big Shake-Up in State Cabinet: The Revision Would Eliminate Three Posts, Give the Governor More Power, and Shift Control of Education Policy," *Orlando Sentinel*, October 20, 1998, D1.

26. Stuart MacCorkle and Dick Smith, *Texas Government* (New York: McGraw-Hill, 1960).

27. Daniel Elazar, *American Federalism: A View from the States*, 3rd ed. (New York: Harper & Row, 1984), 115.

28. Hammons, "Was James Madison Wrong?," 846.

29. See ibid. for a more complete argument along these lines.

30. Melinda Gann Hall, "State Judicial Politics: Rules, Structures, and the Political Game," in *American State and Local Politics*, ed. Ronald Weber and Paul Brace (New York: Chatham House, 1999), 136.

31. National Conference of State Legislatures, "Gubernatorial Veto Authority with Respect to Major Budget Bill(s)," December 2008, www.ncsl.org/IssuesResearch/BudgetTax/GubernatorialVetoAuthoritywithRespecttoMajor/tabid/12640/Default.aspx.

32. Andrew Taylor, "Line Item Budget Barely Trims Spending at State Level," *Denver Rocky Mountain News*, January 15, 1995.

33. Scott Milfred, "Some Want to Clip Gubernatorial Wings: A Resolution in the Legislature Would Curtail Wisconsin Governor's Exceptionally Broad Veto Power," *Wisconsin State Journal*, September 23, 2001, A1.

34. Virginia Gray, Herbert Jacob, and Kenneth N. Vines, eds. *Politics in the American States: A Comparative Analysis* (Boston: Little, Brown, 1983).

35. In 2003, the U.S. Supreme Court invalidated laws prohibiting sodomy. Until that time, Alabama, Florida, Idaho, Louisiana, Massachusetts, Mississippi, North Carolina, South Carolina, Utah, and Virginia had laws that explicitly prohibited sodomy. Kansas, Oklahoma, and Texas prohibited same-sex sodomy only. LAMBDA Legal Defense and Education Fund website, www.lambda.org.

36. James Madison, *Federalist* No. 10, in Alexander Hamilton, James Madison, and John Jay, *The Federalist Papers*, ed. Charles Kesler and Clinton Rossiter (New York: Penguin Putnam, 1961), 76.

37. Ibid. Hamilton, Madison, and Jay envisioned other safeguards as well. One was the well-known principle of the separation of powers among the three branches of government. The other was the large size of the republic itself. Previous theorists of democracy had worried about republics that became too large to govern. In *Federalist* No. 10, Madison made the novel claim that a more extensive republic would be less likely to succumb to factionalism than the smaller republics of old.

38. Quoted in David Broder, *Democracy Derailed: Initiative Campaigns and the Power of Money* (New York: Harcourt, 2000), 27.

39. Ibid.

40. Initiative and Referendum Institute, "The History of Initiative and Referendum in the United States," www.iandrinstitute.org.

41. Richard Ellis, *Democratic Delusions: The Initiative Process in America* (Lawrence: University Press of Kansas, 2002).

42. Broder, *Democracy Derailed*.

43. Keon S. Chi, "Emerging Trends Shaping State Governments: 2005 and Beyond," in *The Book of the States 2005* (Lexington, KY: Council of State Governments, 2005).

44. "California Ballot Initiative Petition Signature Costs," Ballotpedia, http://ballotpedia.org/wiki/index.php/California_ballot_initiative_petition_signature_costs.

45. Broder, *Democracy Derailed*, 1.

46. Lawrence F. Keller, "Municipal Charters," *National Civic Review* 91, no. 1 (2002): 155–161.

Chapter 4

1. Phil Oliff, Chris Mai, and Vincent Palacios, "States Continue to Feel Recession's Impact," Center on Budget and Policy Priorities, www.cbpp.org/cms/index.cfm?fa=view&id=711.

2. Lucy Dadayan and Donald J. Boyd, "Recession or No Recession, State Tax Revenues Remain Negative," Rockefeller Institute of Government, Albany, NY, January 2010, 3.

3. Council of State Governments, "Federal Assistance," 2010, www.staterecovery.org/federal-assistance.

4. Tax Foundation, "State-Local Tax Burdens, All States, 1977–2009," 2011, http://taxfoundation.org/article/state-and-local-tax-burdens-all-states-one-year-1977-2009.

5. These figures and many that follow come from U.S. Department of Commerce, *Statistical Abstract of the United States, 2012* (Washington, DC: U.S. Census Bureau, 2012), www.census.gov/compendia/statab, and refer to the fiscal year that concluded in 2008, one of the most recent years for which such data are available.

6. Ibid.

7. *The Fiscal Survey of States* (Washington, DC: National Governors Association and National Association of State Budget Officers, fall 2009), vii, www.nasbo.org/sites/default/files/fsfall2009.pdf.

8. U.S. Department of Commerce, *Statistical Abstract*, Table 424.

9. Federation of Tax Administrators, "State Cigarette Excise Tax Rates and Rankings," January 1, 2012, www.taxadmin.org/fta/rate/cigarette.pdf.

10. U.S. Department of Commerce, *Statistical Abstract*, Table 435.

11. Estimated sales tax calculated at Minnesota online sales tax calculator for Bloomington, Minnesota, www.taxes.state.mn.us/taxcalc/index.shtml.

12. Tax Foundation, "A Sales Tax Word of Warning in Hawaii, New Mexico, South Dakota, and Wyoming," September 30, 2011, http://taxfoundation.org/blog/sales-tax-word-warning-hawaii-new-mexico-south-dakota-and-wyoming.

13. Katherine Barrett, Richard Greene, Michele Mariani, and Anya Sostek, "The Way We Tax: A 50-State Report," *Governing*, February 2003, www.governing.com/gpp/2003/gp3intro.htm.

14. Donald Bruce, William F. Fox, and LeAnn Luna, "State and Local Sales Tax Revenue Losses from E-Commerce," Center for Business and Economic Research, University of Tennessee, Knoxville, April 13, 2009, http://cber.bus.utk.edu/ecomm/ecom0409.pdf.

15. Cited in Penelope Lemov, "The Untaxables," *Governing*, July 2002.

16. Alan Greenblatt, "The Sales Tax Goes Online," *Governing*, December 2005.

17. "Frequently Asked Questions," Streamlined Sales Tax Governing Board, www.streamlinedsalestax.org/index.php?page=faqs.

18. Saul Hansell, "Court to Amazon: Keep Paying Sales Tax," Bits blog, January 13, 2009, http://bits.blogs.nytimes.com/2009/01/13/court-to-amazon-keep-collecting-sales-tax-to-new-yorkers.

19. "Amazon Is Now Collecting California Sales Tax," CBS News, September 15, 2012, www.cbsnews.com/8301–18563_162–57513681/amazon-is-now-collecting-california-sales-tax.

20. U.S. Department of Commerce, "State and Local Government Finances Summary: 2009," October 2011, www2.census.gov/govs/estimate/09_summary_report.pdf.

21. U.S. Department of Commerce, *Statistical Abstract*, Table 424.

22. Effective tax rate information for the nation and New Hampshire can be found in ibid., Table 436.

23. Ibid., Table 443.

24. U.S. Department of Commerce, "State and Local Government Finances Summary: 2009."

25. Alan Greenblatt, "The Loathsome Local Levy," *Governing*, October 2001.

26. U.S. Department of Commerce, "State and Local Government Finances Summary: 2009."

27. Fifteen states allow certain localities to impose income taxes as well, but for the most part, income tax receipts are a minor source of funds for cities and counties.

28. U.S. Department of Commerce, *Statistical Abstract*, Table 453.

29. Tax Foundation, "State Individual Income Tax Collections, 2010," February 15, 2012, http://taxfoundation.org/article/facts-figures-handbook-how-does-your-state-compare-0.

30. U.S. Department of Commerce, *Statistical Abstract*, Table 451.

31. Ibid., Table 436.

32. *Fiscal Survey of States*, 18.

33. U.S. Department of Commerce, *Statistical Abstract*, Table 436.

34. National Association of State Budget Officers, "Summary: NASBO State Expenditure Report," December 13, 2011, www.nasbo.org/sites/default/files/Summary%20-%20State%20Expenditure%20Report.pdf.

35. Ibid.

36. U.S. Department of Commerce, *Statistical Abstract*, Table 455.

37. Alan Greenblatt, "Enemies of the State," *Governing*, June 2002.

38. Tax Foundation, "State and Local Tax Burden per Fiscal Year 2009," http://taxfoundation.org/article/

facts-figures-handbook-how-does-your-state-compare-0.

39. U.S. Department of Commerce, *Statistical Abstract*, Table 441.

40. "Personal Income per Capita, 2007," *State and Local Sourcebook*, online supplement to *Governing*, 2010, http://sourcebook.governing.com/subtopicresults.jsp?ind=677.

41. Tax Foundation, "State-Local Tax Burdens, All States, 2008," http://taxfoundation.org/article/state-and-local-tax-burdens-all-years-one-state-1977-2010.

42. See the Mayflower Compact for further insights into the mindset of the founders of the Massachusetts Bay Colony, www.pilgrimhall.org/compact.htm.

43. John E. Petersen, "Guide to Municipal Finance: Credit Raters Make Their Mark," *Governing*, June 2005.

44. Penelope Lemov, "The Muni Market in 2012," *Governing*, January 12, 2012, www.governing.com/columns/public-finance/col-municipal-bond-market-2012.html.

45. For a detailed discussion of the state budget process, see National Association of State Budget Officers, "Budget Processes in the States," Washington, DC, January 2002.

46. These states are Connecticut, Hawaii, Indiana, Kentucky, Maine, Minnesota, Montana, Nebraska, Nevada, New Hampshire, North Carolina, North Dakota, Ohio, Oregon, Texas, Virginia, Washington, Wisconsin, and Wyoming. National Conference of State Legislatures, "State Experiences with Annual and Biennial Budgeting," April 2011, www.ncsl.org/issues-research/budget/state-experiences-with-annual-and-biennial-budget.aspx.

47. For a detailed discussion of state balanced budget requirements, see National Conference of State Legislatures, "Legislative Budget Procedures: A Guide to Appropriations and Budget Processes in the States, Commonwealths and Territories," November 2008, www.ncsl.org/?TabID=12669, www.ncsl.org/programs/fiscal/balbud2.htm.

48. Robert Zahradnik, "Rainy Day Funds: Opportunities for Reform," Center on Budget and Policy Priorities, March 9, 2005, www.cbpp.org/3-9-05sfp.htm.

49. "United States Federal State and Local Government Spending Fiscal Year 2012 per Capita," www.usgovernmentspending.com/US_per_capita_spending.html.

50. U.S. Department of Commerce, *Statistical Abstract*, Table 436; "State and Local Government Employment: Monthly Data," *Governing*, 2012, www.governing.com/gov-data/public-workforce-salaries/monthly-government-employment-changes-totals.html.

51. U.S. Department of Commerce, "State Government Finances," www.census.gov/govs/state/1000usst.html.

52. U.S. Department of Commerce, *Statistical Abstract*, Table 444.

53. "State Fiscal Support for Higher Education, by State, Fiscal Years 2006–07, 2009–10, 2010–11, and 2011–12," Grapevine: An Annual Compilation of Data on State Fiscal Support for Higher Education, http://grapevine.illinoisstate.edu/tables/FY12/Revised_March13/Table%201%20Revised.pdf.

54. National Association of State Budget Officers, "2008 State Expenditure Report," Washington, DC, December 2009, 47.

55. Ibid., 44.

56. Henry J. Kaiser Family Foundation, "Federal and State Share of Medicaid Spending, FY 2010," www.statehealthfacts.org/comparemaptable.jsp?ind=636&cat=4.

57. Georgetown University Health Policy Institute, "Medicaid and CHIP Programs," http://ccf.georgetown.edu/facts-statistics/medicaid-chip-programs.

58. Cynthia Miller, "Leavers, Stayers, and Cyclers: An Analysis of the Welfare Caseload," Manpower Demonstration Research Corporation, New York, November 2002. For a full discussion of the effects of welfare reform, see also Alan Weil, "Ten Things Everyone Should Know about Welfare Reform," no. A-52, Urban Institute, Washington, DC, May 9, 2002.

59. U.S. Department of Health and Human Services. "Federal TANF and State MOE Expenditures Summary by ACF-196 Spending Category, FY 2011," www.acf.hhs.gov/programs/ofa/data/2011fin/table_a1.pdf.

60. U.S. Department of Commerce, *Statistical Abstract*, Table 436.

61. National Association of State Budget Officers, "2008 State Expenditure Report," 66, http://www.nasbo.org/publications-data/state-expenditure-report/archives.

62. "Total State & Local Highway Spending (in millions), 2006," *State and Local Sourcebook*, online supplement to *Governing*, http://sourcebook.governing.com/subtopicresults.jsp?ind=627.

63. National Association of State Budget Officers, "2009 State Expenditure Report," Washington, DC, 2010, 64.

64. National Association of State Budget Officers, "2008 State Expenditure Report," 67.

65. "The Widening Gap Update," Pew Center on the States, Washington, DC, June 2012, www.pewstates.org/uploadedFiles/PCS_Assets/2012/Pew_Pensions_Update.pdf.

66. Greenblatt, "Enemies of the State."

67. Bill Piper, *A Brief Analysis of Voter Behavior Regarding Tax Initiatives: From 1978 to March 2000* (Washington, DC: Citizen Lawmaker Press, n.d.).

68. This section is adapted from the February 2003 *Governing* special issue on state tax systems; see Barrett et al., "The Way We Tax."

Chapter 5

1. John J. Pitney Jr., August 11, 2012, twitter.com/jpitney/status/234476224032956416.

2. Quoted in Alan Greenblatt, "Changing U.S. Electorate," *CQ Researcher*, May 30, 2008, 461.

3. Earl Black and Merle Black, *Divided America: The Ferocious Power Struggle in American Politics* (New York: Simon & Schuster, 2007), 10.

4. Chris Evans, "It's the Autonomy, Stupid: Political Data-Mining and Voter Privacy in the Information Age," *Minnesota Journal of Law, Science & Technology* 13 (2012): 868.

5. Steven Hill, *Fixing Elections: The Failure of America's Winner Take All Politics* (New York: Routledge, 2002), 119.

6. Ruy Teixeira, *America's New Swing Region: Changing Politics and Demographics in the Mountain West* (Washington, DC: Brookings Institution Press, 2012), 1.

7. Quoted in Alan Greenblatt, "Blueburbs," *Governing*, October 2008, 22.

8. Ibid.

9. Caroline J. Tolbert, John A. Grummel, and Daniel A. Smith, "The Effects of Ballot Initiatives on Voter Turnout in the American States," *American Politics Research* 29, no. 6 (2001): 625–648.

10. Interview with Rhodes Cook, December 11, 2006.

11. Kevin J. Coleman, Thomas H. Neale, and Joseph E. Cantor, "The Election Process in the United States," Congressional Research Service, Washington, DC, July 6, 1995, 69.

12. National Conference of State Legislatures, "Straight-Ticket Voting," www.ncsl.org/legislatures-elections/elections/straight-ticket-voting-states.aspx.

13. Election Data Services, *The Election Data Book: A Statistical Portrait of Voting in America* (Lanham, MD: Bernan Press, 1992), appendix.

14. Vauhini Vara, "'Instant Runoff' Faces Test," *Wall Street Journal*, October 21, 2011, http://online.wsj.com/article/SB10001424052970204774604574663121 2229446284.html.

15. Kay Lawson, "How State Laws Undermine Parties," in *Elections American Style,* ed. A. James Reichley (Washington, DC: Brookings Institution, 1987), 241.

16. Cited in William C. Binning, Larry E. Esterly, and Paul A. Sracic, *Encyclopedia of American Parties, Campaigns, and Elections* (Westport, CT: Greenwood Press, 1999), 95.

17. E-mail correspondence with Richard Winger, July 24, 2012.

18. Quoted in Greg Giroux, "Third-Party Push: Hope vs. History," *CQ Weekly*, May 4, 2007.

19. Lawson, "How State Laws Undermine Parties," 246.

20. Quoted in Jesse McKinley, "California Puts Vote Overhaul on the Ballot," *New York Times*, May 27, 2010, A1.

21. Larry Sabato, December 24, 2011, twitter.com/BuzzFeedBen/statuses/150620246800220162.

22. Binning et al., *Encyclopedia of American Parties*, 95.

23. Quoted in Dan Eggen and Amy Goldstein, "Voter-Fraud Complaints by GOP Drove Dismissals," *Washington Post*, May 14, 2007, A4.

24. Andrew Hacker, "Obama: The Price of Being Black," *New York Review of Books*, September 25, 2008, www.nybooks.com/articles/21771.

25. National Conference of State Legislatures, "Electric (or Online) Voter Registration," July 29, 2013, http://www.ncsl.org/legislatures-elections/elections/electronic-or-online-voter-registration.aspx.

26. Megan Reisz, "Register to Vote through Facebook?," *Christian Science Monitor*, July 18, 2012, www.csmonitor.com/Innovation/2012/0718/Register-to-vote-through-Facebook-Washington-reveals-new-app.

27. Phone interview with Curtis Gans, September 4, 2003.

28. Phone interview with Steven Hill, September 11, 2003.

29. Mark Hugo Lopez, "The Latino Electorate in 2010: More Voters, More Non-voters," Pew Hispanic Center, April 26, 2011, www.pewhispanic.org/2011/04/26/the-latino-electorate-in-2010-more-voters-more-non-voters.

30. Robert D. Putnam, *Bowling Alone: The Collapse and Revival of American Community* (New York: Simon & Schuster, 2000).

31. Barbara G. Salmore and Stephen A. Salmore, *New Jersey Politics and Government*, 2nd ed. (Lincoln: University of Nebraska Press, 1998), 128.

32. See "Texas Politics," Liberal Arts Instructional Technology Services, University of Texas at Austin, http://texaspolitics.lamc.utexas.edu/html/exec/index.html.

33. Associated Press, "The Decatur Daily on Windom Candidacy," October 4, 2001.

34. Quoted in Danielle Todesco, "New Mexico Governor, Attorney General, Battle over Emails," KOB Eyewitness News, July 6, 2012, www.kob.com/article/stories/S2680886.shtml.

35. Quoted in Alan Greenblatt, "Where Campaign Money Flows," *Governing*, November 2002, 44.

36. Alan Greenblatt, "The Avengers General," *Governing*, May 2003, 54.

37. Zach Patton, "Robe Warriors," *Governing*, March 2006, 34.

38. Initiative and Referendum Institute website, www.iandrinstitute.org.

39. John F. Camobreco, "Preferences, Fiscal Policy, and the Initiative Process," *Journal of Politics* 60, no. 3 (August 1998): 822.

40. Presentation at the annual meeting of the National Conference of State Legislatures, Chicago, August 9, 2012.

41. Quoted in James Dao, "Same-Sex Marriage Key to Some G.O.P. Races," *New York Times*, November 4, 2004, P4.

42. Simon Jackman, "Same-Sex Marriage Ballot Initiatives and Conservative Mobilization in the 2004 Election," http://jackman.stanford.edu/papers/ris-spresentation.pdf.

43. Ryan Holeywell, "The Rise of the Recall Election," *Governing*, April 2011, www.governing.com/topics/politics/rise-recall-election.html.

44. Alan Greenblatt, "Total Recall," *Governing*, September 2003, 27.

45. Phone interview with Randall Gnant, August 7, 2003.

46. V. O. Key, *Public Opinion and American Democracy* (New York: Knopf, 1964), 7.

47. Interview with Doug Duncan, November 15, 2006.

48. Interview with Mike Haridopolos, August 8, 2012.

49. See especially Robert S. Erikson, Gerald C. Wright, and John D. McIver, *Statehouse Democracy: Public Opinion and Policy in the American States* (New York: Cambridge University Press, 1993).

50. Paul Brace, Kellie Sims-Butler, Kevin Arceneaux, and Martin Johnson, "Public Opinion in the American States: New Perspectives Using National Survey Data," *American Journal of Political Science* 46, no. 1 (January 2002): 173–189.

51. Susan Herbst, "How State-Level Policy Managers 'Read' Public Opinion," in *Navigating Public Opinion: Polls, Policy, and the Future of American Democracy,* ed. Jeff Manza, Fay Lomax Cook, and Benjamin I. Page (New York: Oxford University Press, 2002), 176.

52. Logan Dancey and Paul Goren, "Party Identification, Issue Attitudes, and the Dynamics of Political Debate," *American Journal of Political Science* 54 (July 2010): 686–699.

53. Phone interview with Greg Shaw, September 3, 2003.

54. Phone interview with Paul Brace, September 10, 2003.

Chapter 6

1. Alan Greenblatt, "How a College Kid May Have Helped Pick a Congressman," NPR.org, May 23, 2012, www.npr.org/blogs/itsallpolitics/2012/05/22/153342541/how-a-college-kid-may-have-helped-pick-a-congressman.

2. Quoted in Alan Greenblatt, "Citizens United's Corporate Candidate," *Governing*, May 2012, www.governing.com/topics/politics/gov-citizen-uniteds-corporate-candidate.html.

3. Ed Kilgore, "Diagnosing Dems," *Blueprint*, May 17, 2006, www.ndol.org/ndol_ci.cfm?kaid=127&subid=171&contentid=253867.

4. Quoted in Alan Greenblatt, "Politics and Marketing Merge in Parties' Bid for Relevance," *Congressional Quarterly Weekly Report*, August 16, 1997, 1967.

5. Quoted in Jeff Greenfield, "Hayes's Ride," *Washington Monthly*, March 2003.

6. Alvin Kess, *Politics in New York State* (Syracuse, NY: Syracuse University Press, 1965), 29.

7. David R. Mayhew, *Placing Parties in American Politics: Organization, Electoral Settings, and Government Activity in the Twentieth Century* (Princeton, NJ: Princeton University Press, 1986), esp. 24.

8. Quoted in Bertil L. Hanson, "County Commissioners of Oklahoma," *Midwest Journal of Political Science* 9 (1965): 396.

9. Joel H. Sibley, "The Rise and Fall of American Political Parties, 1790–1990," in *The Parties Respond: Changes in the American Party System,* ed. L. Sandy Maisel (Boulder, CO: Westview Press, 1990), 9.

10. Ibid., 185.

11. John F. Bibby and Thomas M. Holbrook, "Parties and Elections," in *Politics in the American States: A Comparative Analysis*, 7th ed., ed. Virginia Gray, Russell L. Hanson, and Herbert Jacobs (Washington, DC: CQ Press, 1999), 71.

12. John F. Bibby, "State and Local Parties in a Candidate-Centered Age," in *American State and Local Politics: Directions for the 21st Century,* ed. Ronald E. Weber and Paul Brace (New York: Chatham House, 1999), 198.

13. John R. Schmidt and Wayne W. Whalen, "Credentials Contests at the 1968—and 1972—Democratic National Conventions," *Harvard Law Review* 82 (May 1969): 1456.

14. Alan Greenblatt, "History: Winds of War Blew through Chicago," *Congressional Quarterly Weekly Report*, August 17, 1996, 23.

15. Bibby, "State and Local Parties," 199.

16. Peter W. Wielhower and Brad Lockerbie, "Party Contacting and Political Participation, 1952–90," *American Journal of Political Science* 38 (February 1994): 213.

17. See John H. Kessel, "Ray Bliss and the Development of the Ohio Republican Party during the 1950s," in *Politics, Professionalism, and Power: Modern Party Organization and the Legacy of Ray C. Bliss*, ed. John C. Green (Lanham, MD: University Press of America, 1994), 49–50.

18. Leon D. Epstein, *Political Parties in the American Mold* (Madison: University of Wisconsin Press, 1986), 155.

19. Michael McDonald, "Partisan Voter Registration Totals," *Huffington Post*, October 13, 2010, www.huffingtonpost.com/michael-p-mcdonald/partisan-voter-registrati_b_761713.html.

20. Malcolm E. Jewell and Sarah M. Morehouse, *Political Parties and Elections in American States*, 4th ed. (Washington, DC: CQ Press, 2001), 76.

21. Bibby, "State and Local Parties," 198.

22. Bibby and Holbrook, "Parties and Elections," 70.

23. Ibid., 71.

24. Quoted in Ruth Marcus, "Party Spending Unleashed; Justices Say Independence from Candidate Is Key," *Washington Post*, June 27, 1996, A1.

25. Alan Greenblatt, "Soft Money: The Root of All Evil or a Party-Building Necessity?," *Congressional Quarterly Weekly Report*, September 26, 1997, 2064.

26. Agustín Armendariz and Aron Pilhofer, "McCain-Feingold Changes State Party Spending," Center for Public Integrity, May 26, 2005, www.publicintegrity .org/partylines/report.aspx?aid=690.

27. Interview with Larry J. Sabato, May 2002.

28. Alan Greenblatt, "Undoing the Split," *Governing*, February 2009.

29. Jewell and Morehouse, *Political Parties and Elections*, 22–23.

30. "Changing Hands," *Governing*, January 2003, 24.

31. Jason Szep, "Youth Turnout in Election Biggest in 20 Years," Reuters, November 8, 2006.

32. Emily Hoban Kirby and Kei Kawashima-Ginsberg, "The Youth Vote in 2008," Center for Information and Research on Civic Learning and Engagement, August 17, 2009, www.civicyouth.org/PopUps/ FactSheets/FS_youth_Voting_2008_updated_6.22 .pdf.

33. Jim Reagen, "Scozzafava: Race Became 'Referendum on Issues Far from Here,'" *Watertown Daily Times*, November 1, 2009, www.watertowndailytimes.com/ article/20091101/NEWS05/311019896.

34. Alan Ehrenhalt, "Political Pawns," *Governing*, July 2000, 20.

35. Greenblatt, "Citizens United's Corporate Candidate."

36. Quoted in Alan Greenblatt, "'Big Tent' Advocates Look Likely to Defeat Abortion Measure," *Congressional Quarterly Weekly Report*, January 10, 1998, 89.

37. David B. Magleby, Candice J. Nelson, and Mark C. Westlye, "The Myth of the Independent Voter Revisited," Working Paper 10-01, Center for the Study of Elections and Democracy, Brigham Young University, January 2010, http://csed.byu.edu/Assets/ Magleby%20Nelson%20Westlye%202010.pdf.

38. Dana Milbank, "Where Have All the Candidates Gone?," *Washington Post*, May 15, 2012, www.wash ingtonpost.com/opinions/where-have-all-the-candi dates-gone/2012/05/15/gIQA6ZRISU_story.html.

39. Quoted in Cathy Newman and Ben White, "States Left to Pick Reform Ticket," *Washington Post*, August 27, 2000, A5.

40. Greenblatt, "Politics and Marketing," 1967.

41. Pew Research Center for the People & the Press, "Independents Take Center Stage in Obama Era: Trends in Political and Core Attitudes: 1987–2009," May 21, 2009, www.people-press.org/2009/05/21/ independents-take-center-stage-in-obama-era.

42. Larry M. Bartels, "Partisanship and Voting Behavior, 1952–1996," *American Journal of Political Science* 44 (January 2000): 35.

43. Ibid., 36–37.

44. Bruce E. Keith, David B. Magleby, Candice J. Nelson, Elizabeth Orr, Mark C. Westlye, and Raymond E. Wolfinger, *The Myth of the Independent Voter* (Berkeley: University of California Press, 1992).

45. Interview with Jane Jech, August 17, 2012.

46. Quoted in Greenblatt, "Politics and Marketing," 1967.

47. Alan Greenblatt, "The Social Media Shuffle: From Kony to Spooning," NPR.org, April 19, 2012, www .npr.org/2012/04/19/150964208/young-people-turn-from-kony-to-spooning-record.

48. Ibid.

49. Frank J. Sorauf, *Political Parties in the American System* (Boston: Little, Brown, 1964), 13.

50. Clive S. Thomas and Ronald J. Hrebenar, "Interest Groups in the States," in *Politics in the American States: A Comparative Analysis*, 8th ed., ed. Virginia Gray and Russell L. Hanson (Washington, DC: CQ Press, 2004), 114–115.

51. Leah Rush, "Hired Guns," Center for Public Integrity, December 20, 2007, updated August 19, 2011, www .publicintegrity.org/2007/12/20/5895/influence-booming-business.

52. Virginia Gray and David Lowery, "Interest Representation in the States," in Weber and Brace, *American State and Local Politics*, 267.

53. Quoted in Alan Rosenthal, *The Third House: Lobbyists and Lobbying in the States*, 2nd ed. (Washington, DC: CQ Press, 2001), 17.

54. Lee Drutman, "The Complexities of Lobbying: Toward a Deeper Understanding of the Profession," *PS: Political Science & Politics* 43, no. 4 (October 2010): 835.

55. Richard L. Hall and Molly E. Reynolds, "Targeted Issue Advertising and Legislative Strategy: The Inside Ends of Outside Lobbying," *Journal of Politics* 74, no. 3 (July 2012): 888–902.

56. Christopher Swope, "Winning without Steaks and Cigars," *Governing*, November 2000. See also Rob Gurwitt, "Cookie-Jar Clampdown," *Governing*, April 2007.

57. Phone interview with John Weingart, August 18, 2010.

58. Rosenthal, *Third House*, 78.

59. Quoted in Jacob Goldstein, "So You Think You Can Be a Hair Braider?," *New York Times*, June 12, 2012, www.nytimes.com/2012/06/17/magazine/so-you-think-you-can-be-a-hair-braider.html.

60. Rosenthal, *Third House*, 45.

61. Quoted in Alan Greenblatt, "Secondhand Spokesmen," *Governing*, April 2002, www.governing. com/archive/archive/2002/apr/tobacco.txt.

62. Quoted in Rosenthal, *Third House*, 61.

63. Clive S. Thomas and Ronald J. Hrebenar, "Lobby Clout," *State Legislatures*, April 1999.

64. Thomas and Hrebenar, "Interest Groups in the States," 121–122.

65. Alan Greenblatt, "Real Power," *Governing*, June 2006, 46.

66. Phone interview with Alan Rosenthal, February 6, 2007.

Chapter 7

1. Quoted in Philip D. Duncan and Christine C. Lawrence, *Congressional Quarterly's Politics in America 1998* (Washington, DC: CQ Press, 1997), 755.

2. William M. Bulger, *While the Music Lasts: My Life in Politics* (Boston: Houghton Mifflin, 1996), 71.

3. Alexander Hamilton, *Federalist* No. 73, http://thomas.loc.gov/home/fedpapers/fed_73.html.

4. Bob Bergren, presentation at the Council of State Governments western regional meeting, October 7, 2009.

5. Quoted in Nicholas Confessore and Michael Barboro, "New York Allows Same-Sex Marriage, Becoming Largest State to Pass Law," *New York Times*, June 24, 2011, www.nytimes.com/2011/06/25/nyregion/gay-marriage-approved-by-new-york-senate.html?pagewanted=all.

6. Quoted in ibid.

7. "2011 Texas Session Statistics," State Net, September 14, 2011, www.statenet.com/resources/session_statistics.php?state=TX; "2011 Montana Session Statistics," State Net, July 29, 2011, www.statenet.com/resources/session_statistics.php?state=MT&session_id=2011000.

8. Quoted in Alan Greenblatt, "The Date-Checking Game," *Governing*, October 2006, 17.

9. Tom Loftus, "Optometrists' Kentucky Political Donations Exceed $400,000," *Louisville Courier-Journal*, February 15, 2011, www.courier-journal.com/article/20110215/NEWS01/302150097/Optometrists-Kentucky-political-donations-exceed-400–000?gcheck=1&nclick_check=1.

10. Judith C. Meredith, *Lobbying on a Shoestring*, 2nd ed. (Dover, MA: Auburn House, 1989), 4.

11. Alan Greenblatt, "Fit to Be Tied," *Governing*, August 2001, 20.

12. Quoted in Andy Sher, "GOP Claims Strides on Issues," *Chattanooga Times Free Press*, June 21, 2009, A1.

13. Alan Rosenthal, *Engines of Democracy: Politics and Policymaking in State Legislatures* (Washington, DC: CQ Press, 2009), 310.

14. Maggie Clark, "States Find Laws against Sports Head Injuries Tricky to Enact," Stateline, July 19, 2012, www.pewstates.org/projects/stateline/headlines/states-find-laws-against-sports-head-injuries-tricky-to-enact-85899405995.

15. Virginia Gray and David Lowery, "Where Do Policy Ideas Come From? A Study of Minnesota Legislators and Staffers," *Journal of Public Administration Research and Theory* 10 (January 2000): 573–597.

16. See Gary F. Moncrief, Joel A. Thompson, and Karl T. Kurtz, "Old Statehouse Ain't What It Used to Be," *Legislative Studies Quarterly* 21, no. 1 (February 1996): 57–72.

17. MSNBC interview with Amy Klobuchar, July 1, 2009.

18. Rosenthal, *Engines of Democracy*, 84.

19. Alan Rosenthal, *Governors and Legislatures: Contending Powers* (Washington, DC: CQ Press, 1990), 187.

20. Diane D. Blair, *Arkansas Politics and Government* (Lincoln: University of Nebraska Press, 1988), 182, cited in Rosenthal, *Governors and Legislatures*.

21. John Turcotte, presentation at the annual meeting of the National Conference of State Legislatures, July 21, 2009.

22. Wes Clarke, "The Divided Government and Budget Conflict in the U.S. States," *Legislative Studies Quarterly* 23, no. 1 (February 1998): 5.

23. Quoted in Alan Greenblatt, "Reformer in Power," *Governing*, January 2009, 20.

24. Meredith, *Lobbying on a Shoestring*, 34.

25. Edmund Burke, "The English Constitutional System," in *Representation*, ed. Hannah Pitkin (New York: Atherton Press, 1969).

26. Quoted in Christopher Swope, "Winning without Steak and Cigars," *Governing*, November 2000, 40.

27. Quoted in Rosenthal, *Engines of Democracy*, 237.

28. Virginia Public Access Project, "Saslaw for Senate—Richard: List of All Expenditures," www.vpap.org/committees/profile/money_out_vendors/1696?start_year=2011&end_year=2011&lookup_type=year&filing_period=all&filter_expend=all&order=amount.

29. Virginia Public Access Project, "Opportunity Virginia PAC," www.vpap.org/committees/profile/money_out_recipients/2936?end_year=2011&start_year=2011&lookup_type=year&filing_period=all.

30. Richard A. Clucas, "Principal-Agent Theory and the Power of State House Speakers," *Legislative Studies Quarterly* 26, no. 2 (May 2001): 319–338.

31. Quoted in Alan Greenblatt, "The Mapmaking Mess," *Governing*, January 2001, 23.

32. Aaron Blake, "Name That District Winner: 'Upside-Down Elephant,'" *Washington Post*, The Fix blog, August 12, 2011, www.washingtonpost.com/blogs/the-fix/post/name-that-district-winner-upside-down-elephant/2011/08/11/gIQABOTABJ_blog.html#pagebreak.

33. Nolan Hicks, "New Congressional Redistricting Maps Very Close to Greg Abbott's Plan," *Houston Chronicle*, Texas on the Potomac blog, February 28, 2012, http://blog.chron.com/txpotomac/2012/02/new-congressional-redistricting-maps-very-close-to-greg-abbotts-plan.

34. Josh Goodman, "Farming for Votes," *Governing*, November 2010, 46, www.governing.com/topics/politics/future-redistricting-rural-america.html.

35. Josh Goodman, "Introducing America's Largest State Legislative District," *Governing*, Politics blog, February 11, 2010, www.governing.com/blogs/politics/Introducing-Americas-Largest-State.html.

36. Quoted in Sean Cockerham, "Lawmakers Spar over Adding Seats to Legislature," *Anchorage Daily News*, February 2, 2010, www.adn.com/2010/02/02/1121936/lawmakers-spar-over-adding-districts.html.

37. Alan Rosenthal, Burdett Loomis, John Hibbing, and Karl Kurtz, *Republic on Trial: The Case for Representative Democracy* (Washington, DC: CQ Press, 2003), 69.

38. Quoted in Alan Greenblatt, "Real Power," *Governing*, June 2006, 46.

39. Otis White, "Making Laws Is No Job for Lawyers These Days," *Governing*, June 1994, 27.

40. Kathleen Dolan and Lynne E. Ford, "Change and Continuity among Women Legislators: Evidence from Three Decades," *Political Research Quarterly* 50 (March 1997): 137–152.

41. Center for American Women and Politics, "Women in State Legislatures 2007," January 2007, www.cawp.rutgers.edu/Facts/Officeholders/stleg.pdf.

42. Renee Loth, "The Matriarchy Up North," *Boston Globe*, April 30, 2009, 15.

43. National Conference of State Legislatures, "Percentages of Women in State Legislatures," November 21, 2011, www.ncsl.org/legislatures-elections/wln/women-in-state-legislatures-2011.aspx.

44. Interview with Barbara Lee, October 8, 2002.

45. Donald E. Whistler and Mark C. Ellickson, "The Incorporation of Women in State Legislatures: A Description," *Women and Politics* 20, no. 2 (1999): 84.

46. Ibid.

47. Kerry L. Haynie, *African American Legislators in the American States* (New York: Columbia University Press, 2001), 19.

48. Ibid., 2.

49. Ibid., 25.

50. Malcolm E. Jewell and Samuel C. Patterson, *The Legislative Process in the States* (New York: Random House, 1966), 138.

51. William Pound, "State Legislative Careers: Twenty-Five Years of Reform," in *Changing Patterns in State Legislative Careers*, ed. Gary F. Moncrief and Joel A. Thompson (Ann Arbor: University of Michigan Press, 1992).

52. James D. King, "Changes in Professionalism in U.S. State Legislatures," *Legislative Studies Quarterly* 25, no. 3 (May 2000): 327–343.

53. National Conference of State Legislatures, "Size of State Legislative Staff: 1979, 1988 1996, 2003, 2009," www.ncsl.org/legislatures-elections/legisdata/staff-change-chart-1979-1988-1996-2003-2009.aspx.

54. Josh Goodman, "Pennsylvania Takes Step toward Smaller Legislature," Stateline, April 11, 2012, www.pewstates.org/projects/stateline/headlines/pennsylvania-takes-step-toward-smaller-legislature-85899381094.

55. Ellen Perlman, "The 'Gold-Plated' Legislature," *Governing*, February 1998, 37.

56. Alan Ehrenhalt, "An Embattled Institution," *Governing*, January 1992, 30.

57. Marist Poll, "6/30: NY State Senate Unrest Irks Voters," June 30, 2009, http://maristpoll.marist.edu/630-ny-state-senate-unrest-does-not-sit-well-with-voters.

58. Field Poll, "Brown's Job Rating Remains Favorable. Very Poor Appraisal of the Legislature. Yet, Voters Oppose Having Lawmakers Work Part-Time," February 25, 2012, 6.

59. National Conference of State Legislatures, "Broadcasts and Webcasts of Legislative Floor Proceedings and Committee Hearings," March 2, 2012, www.ncsl.org/issues-research/telecom/legislative-webcasts-and-broadcasts.aspx.

60. Rosenthal, *Engines of Democracy*, 19.

61. Interview with John Hibbing, October 15, 2002.

62. Quoted in Nicholas Confessore, "Perception of Being Slighted Stoked Revolt by Lawmakers," *New York Times*, February 9, 2007, B7.

63. William Powers, "The Saturation Fallacy," *National Journal*, September 7, 2002, 2565.

64. Jonathan Walters, "How to Tame the Press," *Governing*, January 1994, 30.

65. Steve Parker, "Fewer Reporters Are Covering This Year's Super Bowl," *St. Louis Post-Dispatch*, January 27, 2009, www.stltoday.com/news/local/columns/editors-desk/fewer-reporters-are-covering-this-years-s-super-bowl/article_ff4a0baa-1fa5-53e1-9884-77485fdc7294.html.

66. Jennifer Dorroh, "Statehouse Exodus," *American Journalism Review*, April/May 2009, 20.

67. Peverill Squire, "Professionalization and Public Opinion of State Legislatures," *Journal of Politics* 55, no. 2 (1993): 479–491.

68. Interview with Gary Moncrief, October 2, 2002.

69. Quoted in Rob Gurwitt, "Can Nonprofit News Survive?," Stateline, June 9, 2011, www.pewstates.org/projects/stateline/headlines/can-nonprofit-news-survive-85899375041.

70. New Jersey Senate Democrats, "Media Advisory—Senator Whelan to Hold 'Twitter Town Hall' Live on

Monday," July 6, 2012, www.njsendems.com/release
.asp?rid=4556.

71. Glenn Blain, "Alec Baldwin Engages in Twitter War with State GOP Leader Dean Skelos," *New York Daily News*, October 27, 2011, www.nydailynews.com/news/politics/alec-baldwin-engages-twitter-war-state-gop-leader-dean-skelos-article-1.968221.

72. Jason Linkins, "Jeff Frederick's Twitter Use Foils GOP Virginia Senate Coup," *Huffington Post*, February 10, 2009, www.huffingtonpost.com/2009/02/10/jeff-fredericks-twitter-u_n_165769.html.

73. Anita Chadha and Robert A. Bernstein, "Why Incumbents Are Treated So Harshly: Term Limits for State Legislators," *American Politics Quarterly* 24 (1996): 363–376.

74. Patricia Lopez, "Coleman's Journey Crosses Typical Divide," *Minneapolis Star Tribune*, October 16, 2002, www.startribune.com/stories/462/3367928.html.

75. Quoted in Rob Gurwitt, "Southern Discomfort," *Governing*, October 2002, 32.

76. Tim Carpenter, "House Member Secretly Tapes Schmidt," *Topeka Capital-Journal*, January 17, 2012, http://cjonline.com/news/2012-01-17/house-member-secretly-tapes-schmidt.

Chapter 8

1. Interview with Dee Richard, September 5, 2012.

2. Quoted in Alan Greenblatt, "When Governors Don't Play Nice," *Governing*, November 2012, 9.

3. Remarks at the annual meeting of the National Conference of State Legislatures, August 7, 2012.

4. Quoted in Larry J. Sabato, *Goodbye to Good-Time Charlie: The American Governorship Transformed*, 2nd ed. (Washington, DC: CQ Press, 1983), 4.

5. Terry Sanford, *Storm over the States* (New York: McGraw-Hill, 1967), 185–188, quoted in Eric B. Herzik and Brent W. Brown, "Symposium on Governors and Public Policy," *Policy Studies Journal* 17 (1989): 761.

6. E. Lee Bernick, "Gubernatorial Tools: Formal vs. Informal," *Journal of Politics* 42 (1979): 661.

7. Quoted in Alan Rosenthal, *Governors and Legislatures: Contending Powers* (Washington, DC: CQ Press, 1990), 14.

8. Lynn R. Muchmore, "The Governor as Manager," in *Being Governor: The View from the Office*, ed. Thad Beyle and Lynn R. Muchmore (Durham, NC: Duke University Press, 1983), 13.

9. Quoted in Alan Greenblatt, "Governing in the Fast Lane," *Governing*, January 2004, 28.

10. Sabato, *Goodbye to Good-Time Charlie*, 4.

11. Thad Kousser and Justin H. Phillips, *The Power of American Governors* (New York: Cambridge University Press, 2012), 26.

12. Daniel C. Vock, "Govs Enjoy Quirky Veto Power," *Stateline*, April 24, 2007, www.stateline.org/live/details/story?contentId=201710.

13. Maggie Clark, "Governors Balance Pardons with Politics," *Stateline*, February 8, 2013, www.pewstates.org/projects/stateline/headlines/governors-balance-pardons-with-politics-85899449577.

14. Ibid.

15. Quoted in Alan Rosenthal, *The Best Job in Politics: Exploring How Governors Succeed as Policy Leaders* (Washington, DC: CQ Press, 2013), 28.

16. Quoted in Kousser and Phillips, *Power of American Governors*, 40.

17. Rosenthal, *Best Job in Politics*, 29.

18. Ralph Wright, *Inside the Statehouse: Lessons from the Speaker* (Washington, DC: CQ Press, 2005), 88.

19. Quoted in Laura A. Van Assendelft, *Governors, Agenda Setting, and Divided Government* (Lanham, MD: University Press of America, 1997), 71.

20. Jan Reid, "The Case of Ann Richards: Women in Gubernatorial Office," in *A Legacy of Leadership: Governors and American History*, ed. Clayton McClure Brooks (Philadelphia: University of Pennsylvania Press, 2008), 185.

21. Raphael J. Sonenshein, "Can Black Candidates Win Statewide Elections?," *Political Science Quarterly* 105 (1990): 219.

22. Rosenthal, *Best Job in Politics*, 58.

23. Quoted in Alan Greenblatt, "All Politics Is National," *Governing*, October 2012, 28.

24. Wisconsin Democracy Campaign, "Recall Race for Governor Cost $81 Million," July 25, 2012, www.wisdc.org/pr072512.php.

25. Quoted in Brian Friel, "For Governors in Congress, No More King of the Hill," *National Journal*, June 27, 2009.

26. Quoted in Clayton McClure Brooks, "Afterword: Governing the Twenty-First Century," in Brooks, *Legacy of Leadership*, 219.

27. Interview with Julia Hurst, January 5, 2004.

28. Quoted in Josh Goodman, "The Second Best Job in the State," *Governing*, April 2009, 34.

29. Quoted in Alan Greenblatt, "Where Campaign Money Flows," *Governing*, November 2002, 44.

30. Megan Verlee, "Secretaries of State at Center of Election Battles," NPR.org, January 18, 2012, www.npr.org/2012/01/18/145351397/secretaries-of-state-at-center-of-election-battles.

31. Quoted in Alan Greenblatt, "Kris Kobach Tackles Illegal Immigration," *Governing*, March 2012, 37.

32. H. H. Gerth and C. Wright Mills, *Max Weber: Essays in Sociology* (New York: Oxford University Press, 1943).

33. Ronald C. Moe and Robert S. Gilmour, "Rediscovering Principles of Public Administration: The Neglected Foundation of Public Law," *Public Administration Review* 55, no. 2 (March–April 1995): 135–146.

34. John J. Gargan, "Introduction and Overview of State Government Administration," in *Handbook of State Government Administration*, ed. John J. Gargan (New York: Marcel-Dekker, 2000).

35. National Center for Education Statistics, "Total Expenditures for Public Elementary and Secondary Education, by Function and Subfunction: Selected Years, 1990–91 through 2008–2009," *Digest of Education Statistics*, http://nces.ed.gov/programs/digest/d11/tables/dt11_188.asp.

36. Charles Barrilleaux, "Statehouse Bureaucracy: Institutional Consistency in a Changing Environment," in *American State and Local Politics*, ed. Ronald E. Weber and Paul Brace (New York: Chatham House, 1999).

37. Michael Lipsky, *Street-Level Bureaucracy* (New York: Russell Sage Foundation, 1980).

38. Cornelius Kerwin, *Rulemaking: How Government Agencies Write Law and Make Policy*, 3rd ed. (Washington, DC: CQ Press, 2003).

39. Charles T. Goodsell, *The Case for Bureaucracy: A Public Administration Polemic*, 4th ed. (Washington, DC: CQ Press, 2003).

40. U.S. Department of Commerce, *Statistical Abstract of the United States, 2012* (Washington, DC: U.S. Census Bureau, 2012), Table 461, "Governmental Employment and Payrolls (1982–2009)," www.census.gov/compendia/statab/2012/tables/12s0461.pdf.

41. Goodsell, *Case for Bureaucracy.*

42. George W. Downs and Patrick D. Larkey, *The Search for Government Efficiency* (Philadelphia: Temple University Press, 1986).

43. Kevin Abourezk, "University Health Privatization a Mixed Bag," *Lincoln Journal-Star*, September 28, 2012, http://journalstar.com/news/local/education/university-health-privatization-a-mixed-bag/article_bd064c84–4524–5581–8f07–37512ebf7ee1.html.

44. Scott Lamothe and Meeyoung Lamothe, "The Dynamics of Local Service Delivery Arrangements and the Role of Nonprofits," *International Journal of Public Administration* 29 (2006): 769–797.

45. J. Norman Baldwin, "Public versus Private Employees: Debunking Stereotypes," *Review of Public Personnel Administration* 12 (Winter 1991): 1–27.

46. Barrilleaux, "Statehouse Bureaucracy," 106–107.

47. Kenneth J. Meier, "Bureaucracy and Democracy: The Case for More Bureaucracy and Less Democracy," *Public Administration Review* 57, no. 3 (May–June 1997): 193–199.

48. Dwight Waldo, *The Administrative State* (New York: Holmes and Meier, 1948).

49. "Union Membership Edges Up, but Share Continues to Fall," *Monthly Labor Review*, January 1999, 1–2.

50. WEAC's legislative goals are described on its website, at www.weac.org/capitol/2005-06/legagenda/main.htm.

51. Wisconsin Democracy Campaign, "PAC and Corporate Spending: WEAC PAC Fall 2010," www.wisdc.org/index.php?module=wisdc.websiteforms&cmd=pacspending&year=2010&pac=500189.

52. Donald F. Kettl, *The Global Public Management Revolution: A Report on the Transformation of Governance* (Washington, DC: Brookings Institution Press, 2000).

53. Melissa Maynard, "New Governors Drive to Reorganize Agencies," Stateline, June 6, 2011, www.pewstates.org/projects/stateline/headlines/new-governors-drive-to-reorganize-agencies-85899375045.

54. Helisse Levine and Eric Scorsone, "The Great Recession's Institutional Change in the Public Employment Relationship: Implications for State and Local Governments," *State and Local Government Review* 42 (2011): 208–214.

Chapter 9

1. Sandra Day O'Connor, "The Threat to Judicial Independence," *Wall Street Journal*, September 27, 2006, A18.

2. Bill Raftery, "2011 Year in Review: Record Number of Impeachment Attempts against Judges for Their Decisions," Gavel to Gavel, December 27, 2011, http://gaveltogavel.us/site/2011/12/27/2011-year-in-review-record-number-of-impeachment-attempts-against-judges-for-their-decisions.

3. Quoted in Scott Shane, "Ideology Serves as a Wild Card on Court Pick," *New York Times*, November 4, 2005, A1.

4. Quoted in "Politics, Intolerance, Fair Courts" (editorial), *New York Times*, August 10, 2012.

5. *Citizens United v. Federal Election Commission*, 558 U.S. 310 (2010) (Stevens, dissenting).

6. Quoted in Steven M. Puiszis, ed., *Without Fear or Favor in 2011: A New Decade of Challenges to Judicial Independence and Accountability* (Chicago: DRI—The Voice of the Defense Bar, 2011), 5.

7. Robert C. LaFountain, Richard Y. Schauffler, Shauna M. Strickland, Sarah A. Gibson, and Ashley N. Mason, *Examining the Work of State Courts: An Analysis of 2009 State Court Caseloads* (Williamsburg, VA: National Center for State Courts, 2011), www.courtstatistics.org/Flashmicrosites/CSP/images/CSP2009.pdf.

8. David Rottman and Shauna M. Strickland, *State Court Organization, 2004* (Washington, DC: Bureau of Justice Statistics, 2004), www.bjs.ojp.usdoj.gov/content/pub/pdf/sco04.pdf.

9. Diana Penner, "Judge: Jurors Antics Harmless," *Indianapolis Star*, November 30, 2006, 1.

10. Court Statistics Project, "Court Structure Charts," National Center for State Courts, www.courtstatistics

.org/Other-Pages/State_Court_Structure_Charts
.aspx.

11. Sari S. Escovitz, *Judicial Selection and Tenure 4* (Chicago: American Judicature Society, 1975).

12. Caleb Nelson, "A Re-evaluation of Scholarly Explanations for the Rise of the Elected Judiciary in Antebellum America," *American Journal of Legal History* 37 (April 1993): 190–224.

13. Larry C. Berkson, "Judicial Selection in the United States: A Special Report," *Judicature* 64, no. 4 (1980): 176–193, updated 1999 by Seth Andersen, www.ajs .org/selection/berkson.pdf.

14. G. Alan Tarr, "Rethinking the Selection of State Supreme Court Justices," *Willamette Law Review* 39, no. 4 (2003): 1445.

15. Pennsylvania Keystone Poll, February 2007, produced by Franklin & Marshall College in Lancaster, Pennsylvania. Polls and other analysis available at http://politics.fandm.edu.

16. Ciara Torres-Spelliscy, Monique Chase, and Emma Greenman, "Improving Judicial Diversity," Brennan Center for Justice, New York University School of Law, 2008, http://brennan.3cdn.net/96d16b62f3 31bb13ac_kfm6bplue.pdf.

17. American Judicature Society, "Judicial Selection in the States: Diversity of the Bench," www.judicialselec tion.us/judicial_selection/bench_diversity/index .cfm?state.

18. American Judicature Society, "Judicial Selection in the States" (2012), www.judicialselection.us.

19. Ibid.

20. Frontline, "Justice for Sale: Interview with Justices Stephen Breyer and Anthony Kennedy," www.pbs .org/wgbh/pages/frontline/shows/justice/interviews/ supremo.html.

21. Ibid.

22. Paul Brace and Melinda Gann Hall, "Studying Courts Comparatively: The View from the American States," *Political Research Quarterly* 48 (1995): 5–29. See also Paul Brace and Brent D. Boyea, "State Public Opinion, the Death Penalty, and the Practice of Electing Judges," *American Journal of Political Science* 52, no. 2 (2008): 360–372.

23. Ibid.

24. Gerald F. Uelmen, "Crocodiles in the Bathtub: Maintaining the Independence of State Supreme Courts in an Era of Judicial Politicization," *Notre Dame Law Review* 72 (1997): 1135–1142.

25. Ibid., 1133, 1137.

26. Adam Liptak and Janet Roberts, "Campaign Cash Mirrors a High Court's Rulings," *New York Times*, October 1, 2006.

27. Quoted in ibid., sec. 1, 1.

28. Brennan Center for Justice, New York University School of Law, "*Caperton v. Massey*," June 8, 2009, www.bren nancenter.org/content/resource/caperton_v_massey.

29. Justice at Stake, "Money and Elections," www.jus ticeatstake.org/issues/state_court_issues/money__ elections.cfm.

30. Quoted in Sheila Kaplan, "Justice for Sale," *Common Cause Magazine*, May–June 1987, 29–30.

31. Greenberg Quinlan Rosner Research, Inc., "Justice at Stake—State Judges Frequency Questionnaire," November 5, 2001–January 2, 2002, http://www.jus ticeatstake.org/media/cms/JASJudgesSurveyResults_ EA8838C0504A5.pdf.

32. Joan Biskupic, "*Caperton v. AT Massey Coal Co*: Supreme Court Case with the Feel of a Best Seller," *USA Today*, February 16, 2009.

33. Brennan Center for Justice at New York University School of Law, "Buying Time 2004: Total Amount Spent on Judicial Advertising Peaks at $21 Million," November 18, 2004," http://www.brennancenter.org/ press-release/buying-time-2004-total-amount-spent-judicial-advertising-peaks-21-million.

34. Adam Skaggs, Maria da Silva, Linda Casey, and Charles Hall, *The New Politics of Judicial Elections 2009–10: How Special Interest "Super Spenders" Threatened Impartial Justice and Emboldened Unprecedented Legislative Attacks on America's Courts* (Washington, DC: Justice at Stake Campaign, Brennan Center for Justice, and National Institute on Money and State Politics, October 2011), 16.

35. David Kidwell, "Attack Ads Target Illinois Supreme Court Justice," *Chicago Tribune*, October 21, 2010.

36. Zach Patton, "Robe Warriors," *Governing*, March 2006.

37. Colorado League of Women Voters, "Colorado Voter Opinions on Judiciary, 2007," Institute for the Advancement of the American Legal System, University of Denver, 4, http://iaals.du.edu/images/ wygwam/documents/publications/Nov252008 .JudicialWars.pdf.

38. Quoted in Mark A. Behrens and Cary Silverman, "The Case for Adopting Appointive Judicial Selection Systems for State Court Judges," *Cornell Journal of Law and Public Policy* 11, no. 2 (Spring 2002): 282.

39. Berkson, "Judicial Selection in the United States."

40. Ibid.

41. Behrens and Silverman, "Case for Adopting," 303.

42. American Judicature Society, "Methods of Judicial Selection," www.judicialselection.us/judicial_selec tion/methods/selection_of_judges.cfm?state=.

43. Robert L. Misner, "Recasting Prosecutorial Discretion," *Journal of Criminal Law and Criminology* 86 (1996): 741.

44. Steve Weinberg, "Inside an Office: An Elected Prosecutor Explains," Center for Public Integrity, June 26, 2003, www.publicintegrity.org/2003/06/26/ 5521/inside-office.

45. Steven W. Perry, *Prosecutors in State Courts 2005*, Bureau of Justice Statistics Bulletin NCJ-213799

(Washington, DC: U.S. Department of Justice, July 2006).

46. Ibid.

47. Misner, "Recasting Prosecutorial Discretion."

48. Carol J. DeFrances, *State Court Prosecutors in Large Districts 2001*, Bureau of Justice Statistics Special Report NCJ-191206 (Washington, DC: U.S. Department of Justice, December 2001).

49. Ibid. "About two-thirds of Part I Uniform Crime Report (UCR) offenses reported to the police in 1998 occurred in the prosecutorial district served by these offices" (2).

50. Los Angeles County District Attorney's Office website, http://da.co.la.ca.us.

51. Shelby A. Dickerson Moore, "Questioning the Autonomy of Prosecutorial Charging Decisions: Recognizing the Need to Exercise Discretion—Knowing There Will Be Consequences for Crossing the Line," *Louisiana Law Review* 60 (Winter 2000): 374.

52. Wayne R. LaFave, "The Prosecutor's Discretion in the United States," *American Journal of Comparative Law* 18 (1970): 532, 533.

53. Misner, "Recasting Prosecutorial Discretion."

54. Telephone interview with Kenneth Noto, deputy chief of the narcotics section at the U.S. Attorney's Office for the Southern District of Florida, in William T. Pizzi, "Understanding Prosecutorial Discretion in the United States: The Limits of Comparative Criminal Procedure as an Instrument of Reform," *Ohio State Law Journal* 54 (1993): 1325n88.

55. Perry, *Prosecutors in State Courts 2005*.

56. *McMann v. Richardson*, 397 U.S. 759, 771 n.14 (1970), http://www.harvardlawreview.org/media/pdf/vol_12401padilla_v_kentucky.pdf.

57. Steven K. Smith and Carol J. DeFrances, "Indigent Defense," Bureau of Justice Statistics Selected Findings, NCJ-158909, U.S. Department of Justice, Washington, DC, February 1996, http://bjs.ojp.usdoj.gov/content/pub/pdf/id.pdf.

58. Ibid.

59. Lynn Langton and Donald J. Farole Jr., "Public Defender Offices, 2007—Statistical Tables," Bureau of Justice Statistics Selected Findings, NCJ-228538, U.S. Department of Justice, Washington, DC, November 2009 (revised June 17, 2010), http://bjs.ojp.usdoj.gov/content/pub/pdf/pd007st.pdf.

60. Carol J. DeFrances and Marika F. X. Litras, *Indigent Defense Services in Large Counties 1999*, Bureau of Justice Statistics Bulletin NCJ-184932 (Washington, DC: U.S. Department of Justice, November 2000).

61. Carol Lundberg, "Justice for All," *Michigan Lawyers Weekly*, June 22, 2009.

62. Gene Johnson, "State High Court Limits Public Defender Caseloads," *Seattle Times*, June 15, 2012.

63. Adele Bernhard, "Take Courage: What the Courts Can Do to Improve the Delivery of Criminal Defense

64. David Cole, *No Equal Justice: Race and Class in the American Justice System* (New York: New Press, 1999), 92.

65. Spangenberg Group, " Rates of Compensation Paid to Court-Appointed Counsel in Non-capital Felony Cases at Trial: A State-by-State Overview," June 2007, http://legis.wisconsin.gov/lc/committees/study/2010/CJFUND/files/oct22spangenberg.pdf. Virginia recently created a fund from which attorneys could petition to exceed the cap, but the fund rarely lasts for the whole year.

66. Andrew Rachlin, "Rights of Defense," *Governing*, January 2007, www.governing.com/archive/archive/2007/jan/defense.txt.

67. Kevin Clermont and Theodore Eisenberg, "Trial by Jury or Judge: Transcending Empiricism," *Cornell Law Review* 77 (1992): 1124.

68. See *Williams v. Florida*, 399 U.S. 78 (1970), approving six-member juries; and *Apodaca v. Oregon*, 406 U.S. 404 (1972), allowing nonunanimous verdicts.

69. Rottman and Strickland, *State Court Organization, 2004*.

70. U.S. Department of Justice, Office of Justice Programs, Office for Victims of Crime, "Executive Summary," in *New Directions from the Field: Victims' Rights and Services for the 21st Century* (Washington, DC: Government Printing Office, 1998).

71. Wayne A. Logan, "Through the Past Darkly: A Survey of the Uses and Abuses of Victim Impact Evidence in Capital Trials," *Arizona Law Review* 41 (1999): 177–178.

72. See *Payne v. Tennessee*, 501 U.S. 808 (1991), which reversed *Booth v. Maryland*, 482 U.S. 496 (1987).

73. "1 in 31: The Long Reach of American Corrections," Pew Center on the States, March 2009.

74. Bureau of Justice Statistics, "U.S. Correctional Population Declined for Second Consecutive Year," December 2011, http://bjs.ojp.usdoj.gov/content/pub/press/p10cpus10pr.cfm.

75. National Association of State Budget Officers, "2010 State Expenditure Report," http://www.nasbo.org/sites/default/files/2010%20State%20Expenditure%20Report.pdf, 52.

76. In *Ring v. Arizona*, 536 U.S. 584 (2002), the Supreme Court invalidated Arizona's capital sentencing procedures, holding that the jury, not the judge, must find the aggravating factors necessary to impose the death penalty. Similar procedures in Colorado, Idaho, Montana, and Nebraska were also ruled unconstitutional.

77. Michael M. O'Hear, "National Uniformity/Local Uniformity: Reconsidering the Use of Departures to Reduce Federal-State Sentencing Disparities," *Iowa Law Review* 87 (2002): 756.

78. Ibid., 749.

79. Robert Mosteller, "New Dimensions in Sentencing Reform in the Twenty-First Century," *Oregon Law Review* 92 (2003): 16–17.

80. Marguerite A. Driessen and W. Cole Durham Jr., "Sentencing Dissonances in the United States: The Shrinking Distance between Punishment Proposed and Sanction Served," *American Journal of Comparative Law* 50 (2002): 635.

81. Bureau of Justice Statistics, National Corrections Reporting Program 2009, Table 9, "First Releases from State Prison," http://bjs.ojp.usdoj.gov/index.cfm?ty=pbdetail&iid=2056.

82. "Sensible Sentences for Nonviolent Offenders" (editorial), *New York Times*, June 14, 2012.

83. Bureau of Justice Assistance, "1996 National Survey of State Sentencing Structures," NCJ-169270, 1998, Exhibit 1–1.

84. Rottman and Strickland, *State Court Organization, 2004.*

85. Driessen and Durham, "Sentencing Dissonances in the United States."

86. Rottman and Strickland, *State Court Organization, 2004.*

87. Ibid.

88. Pew Center on the States, "Time Served: The High Cost, Low Return of Longer Prison Terms," June 2012, www.pewstates.org/uploadedFiles/PCS_Assets/2012/Prison_Time_Served.pdf.

89. Brian Ostrom, Neal Kauder, and Robert LaFountain, *Examining the Work of the State Courts, 1999–2000: A National Perspective from the Court Statistics Project* (Williamsburg, VA: National Center for State Courts, 2000).

90. National Institute of Justice, *Drug Courts: The Second Decade* (Washington, DC: National Institute of Justice, 2006), 32–36, www.ncjrs.gov/pdffiles1/nij/211081.pdf.

91. Judith S. Kaye, "The State of the Judiciary, 2003: Confronting Today's Challenge," annual address, Albany, NY, January 13, 2003, 4.

92. Quoted in Alan Greenblatt, "Docket Science," *Governing,* June 2001, 40, www.governing.com/archive/archive/2001/jun/civil.txt.

93. Quoted in ibid. For more on his reforms to the Hennepin County courts, see also the profile of Kevin Burke in "Court Reform," *Governing*, November 2004.

94. Todd Ruger, "Two Minutes, and Home Goes Away," *Sarasota Herald-Tribune*, May 14, 2009, A1; Todd Ruger, "'Rocket Docket' Can Be Slowed," *Sarasota Herald-Tribune*, September 27, 2009, BN1.

95. Greenblatt, "Docket Science."

96. Rebecca A. Koppes Conway, Timothy M. Tymkovich, Troy A. Eid, Britt Weygandt, and Anthony van Westrum, "Report of the Committee on Magistrates in the Civil Justice System," Governor's Task Force on Civil Justice Reform, October 1, 2000, www.state.co.us/cjrtf/report/report2.htm.

97. David B. Rottman, Anthony Champagne, and Roy A Schotland, *Call to Action: Statement of the National Summit on Improving Judicial Selection* (Williamsburg, VA: National Center for State Courts, 2002).

98. Carmen Lo, Katie Londenberg, and David Nims, "Spending in Judicial Elections: State Trends in the Wake of *Citizens United,*" report prepared for the California Assembly Judiciary Committee, Spring 2011, http://gov.uchastings.edu/public-law/docs/judicial-elections-report-and-appendices-corrected.pdf.

99. Quoted in Bert Brandenburg, "Protecting Wisconsin's Court from Special Interest Pressure," *Milwaukee Journal Sentinel*, March 27, 2007, www.jsonline.com/news/opinion/29460844.html.

Chapter 10

1. This translation of the oath is available on the National League of Cities website, www.nlc.org/about_cities/cities_101/146.cfm.

2. Pew Research Center for the People & the Press, "Growing Gap in Favorable Views of Federal, State Governments: Republicans Like State Government, Especially in GOP-Led States," April 26, 2012, www.people-press.org/2012/04/26/growing-gap-in-favorable-views-of-federal-state-governments/?src=prc-twitter.

3. This figure is based on an estimated total population of 300 million.

4. City-Data.com website, www.city-data.com/city/Hove-Mobile-Park-North-Dakota.html.

5. Quoted in Jonathan Walters, "Cry, the Beleaguered County," *Governing*, August 1996, www.governing.com/archive/archive/1996/aug/counties.txt.

6. David Y. Miller, *The Regional Governing of Metropolitan America* (Boulder, CO: Westview Press, 2002), 26.

7. Roger L. Kemp, ed., *Model Government Charters: A City, County, Regional, State, and Federal Handbook* (Jefferson, NC: McFarland, 2003), 10.

8. William Hansell, "Evolution and Change Characterize Council-Manager Government," *Public Management* 82 (August 2000): 17–21.

9. Michael Zuckerman, *Peaceable Kingdoms: The New England Towns of the 18th Century* (New York: Knopf, 1970).

10. Miller, *Regional Governing of Metropolitan America*, 41.

11. Quoted in Anwar Syed, *The Political Theory of the American Local Government* (New York: Random House, 1966), 40.

12. Alexis de Tocqueville, *Democracy in America: A New Translation*, trans. George Lawrence, ed. J. P. Mayer (New York: HarperCollins, 2000), 33.

13. Penelope Lemov, "Infrastructure Conference Report: Building It Smarter, Managing It Better," *Governing*, October 1996," 40.

14. Ann O. Bowman, "Urban Government," in *Handbook of Research on Urban Politics and Policy in the United States*, ed. Ronald K. Vogel (Westport, CT: Greenwood Press, 1997), 133.

15. Elaine B. Sharpe, "Political Participation in Cities," in *Cities, Politics, and Policy: A Comparative Analysis*, ed. John P. Pelissero (Washington, DC: CQ Press, 2003), 81.

16. Lana Stein, "Mayoral Politics," in *Cities, Politics, and Policy: A Comparative Analysis*, ed. John P. Pelissero (Washington, DC: CQ Press, 2003), 162.

17. Anthony Downs, "The Devolution Revolution: Why Congress Is Shifting a Lot of Power to the Wrong Levels," Policy Brief no. 3, Brookings Institution, July 1996, www.brookings.edu/research/papers/1996/07/governance-downs.

18. Office of Management and Budget, "2010 Standards for Delineating Metropolitan and Micropolitan Statistical Areas," www.whitehouse.gov/sites/default/files/omb/assets/fedreg_2010/06282010_metro_standards-Complete.pdf.

19. Office of Management and Budget, OMB Bulletin No. 10–02, www.whitehouse.gov/sites/default/files/omb/assets/bulletins/b10-02.pdf.

20. Bruce Katz, "A Nation in Transition: What the Urban Age Means for the United States," speech presented at the Urban Age Conference, New York, May 3, 2007, www.brookings.edu/speeches/2007/0504community development_katz.aspx.

21. David Cieslewits, "The Environmental Impacts of Sprawl," in *Urban Sprawl: Causes, Consequences, and Policy Responses*, ed. Gregory D. Squires (Washington, DC: Urban Institute Press, 2002).

22. See, for example, Myron Orfield, *American Metropolitics: The New Suburban Reality* (Washington, DC: Brookings Institution Press, 2002).

23. Ibid., 41.

24. Peter Dreier, John Mollenkopf, and Todd Swanstrom, *Place Matters: Metropolitics for the Twenty-First Century* (Lawrence: University Press of Kansas, 2001).

25. Orfield, *American Metropolitics*, 10.

26. G. Ross Stephens and Nelson Wikstrom, *Metropolitan Government and Governance: Theoretical Perspectives, Empirical Analysis, and the Future* (New York: Oxford University Press, 1999).

27. About Metro," www.oregonmetro.gov/index.cfm/go/by.web/id=24201.

28. National Association of Regional Councils, "What Is a Regional Council?," http://narc.org/resource-center/cogs-mpos/what-is-a-council-of-government.

29. National Association of Regional Councils, "History," http://narc.org/about-narc/about-the-association/history.

30. Miller, *Regional Governing of Metropolitan America*, 103.

31. James F. Wolf and Tara Kolar Bryan, "Identifying the Capacities of Regional Councils of Government," *State and Local Government Review* 41 (2010): 61.

32. Ibid., 67.

33. Simon Andrew, "Recent Development in the Study of Interjurisdictional Agreements: An Overview and Assessment," *State and Local Government Review* 41 (2010): 133–142.

34. National Association of Counties, "City-County Consolidation Proposals, 1921–Present," www.naco.org/Counties/Documents/City%20County%20Consolidations.01.01.2011.pdf.

35. Kate Linebaugh, "Threats to Town Halls Stir Voter Backlash," *Wall Street Journal*, June 8, 2011.

36. David Rusk, *Cities without Suburbs*, 2nd ed. (Washington, DC: Woodrow Wilson Center Press, 1995).

37. Ann O. Bowman, "Urban Government," in *Handbook of Research on Urban Politics and Policy in the United States*, ed. Ronald K. Vogel (Westport, CT: Greenwood Press, 1997), 139.

38. Rob Gurwitt, "Annexation: Not So Smart Growth," *Governing*, October 2000.

39. Charles Tiebout, "A Pure Theory of Local Expenditures," *Journal of Political Economy* 64, no. 5 (October 1956): 422.

40. Dante Chinni, "Rural Counties Are Losing Population and Aging, but Are They Really Dying?," PBS NewsHour, March 4, 2011, www.pbs.org/newshour/rundown/2011/03/-as-the-2010-census.html.

41. Nebraska Department of Education, "2011–2012 Number of Districts/Systems," updated November 4, 2011, www.education.ne.gov/dataservices/PDF/11-12_Districts_Nov2011.pdf.

42. Alan Greenblatt, "Little Mergers on the Prairie," *Governing*, July 2006, 49–50.

Glossary

activist judges: Judges who are said to act as independent policymakers by too creatively interpreting a constitution or statute. (Chapter 9)

ad hoc federalism: The process of choosing a state-centered or nation-centered view of federalism on the basis of political or partisan convenience. (Chapter 2)

alternative dispute resolution: A way to end a disagreement by means other than litigation. It usually involves the appointment of a mediator to preside over a meeting between the parties. (Chapter 9)

American Recovery and Reinvestment Act (ARRA): A $787 billion federal government package intended to stimulate economic growth during the recession of 2008–2009. (Chapter 4)

annexation: The legal incorporation of one jurisdiction or territory into another. (Chapter 10)

appeal: A request to have a lower court's decision in a case reviewed by a higher court. (Chapter 9)

appointment powers: A governor's ability to pick individuals to run the state government, such as cabinet secretaries. (Chapter 8)

apportionment: The allotting of districts according to population shifts. The number of congressional districts that a state has may be reapportioned every ten years, following the national census. (Chapter 7)

appropriations bills: Laws passed by legislatures authorizing the transfer of money to the executive branch. (Chapter 3)

assigned counsel: Private lawyers selected by the courts to handle particular cases and paid from public funds. (Chapter 9)

at-large election: An election in which city or county voters vote for council or commission members from any part of the jurisdiction. (Chapter 10)

balanced budget: A budget in which current expenditures are equal to or less than income. (Chapter 4)

ballot initiative: A process through which voters directly convey instructions to the legislature, approve a law, or amend the constitution. (Chapter 3)

bench trial: A trial in which no jury is present and a judge decides the facts as well as the law. (Chapter 9)

bicameral legislature: A legislature made up of two chambers, typically a house of representatives, or assembly, and a senate. (Chapter 3)

Bill of Rights: The first ten amendments to the Constitution, which set limits on the power of the federal government and set out the rights of individuals and the states. (Chapter 2)

blanket primary: An initial round of voting in which candidates from all parties appear on the same ballot, with the top two vote-getters proceeding on to the general election. (Chapter 5)

block grants: Federal grants-in-aid given for general policy areas that leave states and localities with wide discretion over how to spend the money within the designated policy area. (Chapter 2)

bonds: Certificates that are evidence of debts on which the issuer promises to pay the holders a specified amount of interest for a specified length of time and to repay the loans on their maturity. (Chapter 4)

budget deficit, or shortfall: Cash shortage that results when the amount of money coming in to the government falls below the amount being spent. (Chapter 4)

budget process: The procedure by which state and local governments assess revenues and set budgets. (Chapter 4)

bully pulpit: The platform from which a high-profile public official, such as a governor or president, commands considerable public and media attention by virtue of holding office. (Chapter 8)

bureaucracy: Public agencies and the programs and services they implement and manage. (Chapter 8)

bureaucrats: Employees of public agencies. (Chapter 8)

candidate-centered politics: Politics in which candidates promote themselves and their own campaigns rather than relying on party organizations. (Chapter 6)

capital investments: Investments in infrastructure, such as roads. (Chapter 4)

car-dependent living: A situation in which owning a car for transportation is a necessity; an outcome of low-density development. (Chapter 10)

casework: The work undertaken by legislators and their staffs in response to requests for help from constituents. (Chapter 7)

categorical grants: Federal grants-in-aid given for specific programs that leave states and localities with little discretion over how to spend the money. (Chapter 2)

caucus: All the members of a party—Republican or Democrat—within a legislative chamber. Also refers to meetings of members of a political party in a chamber. (Chapter 7)

cause lobbyist: A person who works for an organization that tracks and promotes an issue, for example, environmental issues for the Sierra Club or gun ownership rights for the National Rifle Association. (Chapter 6)

centralized federalism: The notion that the federal government should take the leading role in setting national policy, with state and local governments helping to implement the policies. (Chapter 2)

charter: A document that outlines the powers, organization, and responsibilities of a local government. (Chapter 10)

cities: Incorporated political jurisdictions formed to provide self-governance to particular localities. (Chapter 10)

city commission system: A form of municipal governance in which executive, legislative, and administrative powers are vested in elected city commissioners. (Chapter 10)

city council: A municipality's legislature. (Chapter 10)

city-county consolidation: The merging of separate local governments in an effort to reduce bureaucratic redundancy and service inefficiencies. (Chapter 10)

city manager: An official appointed to be the chief administrator of a municipality. (Chapter 10)

civil case: A legal case that involves a dispute between private parties. (Chapter 9)

closed primary: A nominating election in which only voters belonging to that party may participate. Only registered Democrats can vote in a closed Democratic primary, for example. (Chapter 6)

coalition building: The assembling of an alliance of groups to pursue a common goal or interest. (Chapter 7)

collective bargaining: A process in which representatives of labor and management meet to negotiate pay and benefits, job responsibilities, and working conditions. (Chapter 8)

colonial charters: Legal documents drawn up by the British Crown that spelled out how the colonies were to be governed. (Chapter 3)

commission-administrator system: A form of county governance in which executive and legislative powers reside with an elected commission, which hires a professional executive to manage the day-to-day operations of government. (Chapter 10)

committee: A group of legislators who have the formal task of considering and writing bills in a particular issue area. (Chapter 7)

compact theory: The idea that the Constitution represents an agreement among sovereign states to form a common government. (Chapter 2)

comparative method: A learning approach based on studying the differences and similarities among similar units of analysis (such as states). (Chapter 1)

compromise: The result when there is no consensus on a policy change or spending amount but legislators find a central point on which a majority can agree. (Chapter 7)

concurrent powers: Powers that both federal and state governments can exercise. These include the powers to tax, borrow, and spend. (Chapter 2)

confederacy: Political system in which power is concentrated in regional governments. (Chapter 2)

constituent service: The work done by legislators to help residents in their voting districts. (Chapter 7)

constituents: Residents of a district. (Chapter 7)

constitutional amendments: Proposals to change a constitution, typically enacted by a supermajority of the legislature or through a statewide referendum. (Chapter 3)

constitutional convention: An assembly convened for the express purpose of amending or replacing a constitution. (Chapter 3)

constitutional revision commission: An expert committee formed to assess a constitution and suggest changes. (Chapter 3)

contract attorney: A private attorney who enters into an agreement with a state, county, or judicial district to work on a fixed-fee basis per case or for a specific length of time. (Chapter 9)

contract lobbyist: A lobbyist who works for different causes for different clients in the same way that a lawyer represents more than one client. (Chapter 6)

contracting out: Government hiring of private or non-profit organizations to deliver public goods or services. (Chapter 8)

cooperative federalism: The notion that it is impossible for state and national governments to have separate and distinct jurisdictions and that both levels of government must work together. (Chapter 2)

council-executive system: A form of county governance in which legislative powers are vested in a county commission and executive powers are vested in an independently elected executive. (Chapter 10)

council-manager system: A form of municipal governance in which the day-to-day administration of government is carried out by a professional administrator. (Chapter 10)

counties: Geographical subdivisions of state government. (Chapter 10)

county commission system: A form of county governance in which executive, legislative, and administrative powers are vested in elected commissioners. (Chapter 10)

criminal case: A legal case brought by the state intending to punish a violation of the law. (Chapter 9)

crosscutting requirements: Constraints that apply to all federal grants. (Chapter 2)

crossover sanctions: Federal requirements mandating that grant recipients pass and enforce certain laws or regulations as a condition of receiving funds. (Chapter 2)

crossover voting: Members of one party voting in another party's primary. This practice is not allowed in all states. (Chapter 6)

dealignment: The lack of nationwide dominance by any one political party. (Chapter 6)

delegates: Legislators who primarily see their role as voting according to their constituents' beliefs as they understand them. (Chapter 7)

determinate sentencing: The sentencing of an offender, by a judge, to a specific amount of time in prison depending on the crime. (Chapter 9)

devolution: The process of taking power and responsibility away from the federal government and giving it to state and local governments. (Chapter 1)

Dillon's Rule: The legal principle that says local governments can exercise only the powers granted to them by the state government. (Chapter 10)

direct democracy: A system in which citizens make laws themselves rather than relying on elected representatives. (Chapter 3)

direct lobbying: A form of lobbying in which lobbyists deal directly with legislators to gain their support. (Chapter 6)

discretionary jurisdiction: The power of a court to decide whether or not to grant review of a case. (Chapter 9)

discretionary spending: Spending controlled in annual appropriations acts. (Chapter 4)

district: The geographical area represented by a member of a legislature. (Chapter 7)

dividend: A payment made to stockholders (or, in Alaska's case, residents) from the interest generated by an investment. (Chapter 4)

dual constitutionalism: A system of government in which people live under two sovereign powers. In the United States, these are the government of their state of residence and the federal government. (Chapter 3)

dual federalism: The idea that state and federal governments have separate and distinct jurisdictions and responsibilities. (Chapter 2)

edgeless cities: Office and retail complexes without clear boundaries. (Chapter 10)

electorate: The population of individuals who can vote. (Chapter 3)

en banc: Appeals court sessions in which all the judges hear a case together. (Chapter 9)

entitlement: A service that government must provide, regardless of the cost. (Chapter 4)

enumerated powers: Grants of authority explicitly given by the Constitution. (Chapter 2)

establishment: The nexus of people holding power over an extended period of time, including top elected officials, lobbyists, and party strategists. (Chapter 6)

estate taxes: Taxes levied on a person's estate or total holdings after that person's death. (Chapter 4)

excise, or sin, taxes: Taxes on alcohol, tobacco, and similar products that are designed to raise revenues and reduce use. (Chapter 4)

exclusive powers: Powers given by the Constitution solely to the federal government. (Chapter 2)

expenditures: Money spent by government. (Chapter 4)

exurbs: Municipalities in rural areas that ring suburbs. They typically serve as bedroom communities for the prosperous, providing rural homes with easy access to urban areas. (Chapter 10)

factional splits, or factions: Groups that struggle to control the message within a party; for example, a party may be split into competing regional factions. (Chapter 6)

federalism: Political system in which national and regional governments share powers and are considered independent equals. (Chapter 2)

felony: A serious crime, such as murder or arson. (Chapter 9)

filibuster: A debate that under U.S. Senate rules can drag on, blocking final action on the bill under consideration and preventing other bills from being debated. (Chapter 7)

fiscal federalism: The system by which federal grants are used to fund programs and services provided by state and local governments. (Chapter 4)

fiscal year: The annual accounting period used by a government. (Chapter 4)

focused consumption taxes: Taxes that do not alter spending habits or behavior patterns and therefore do not distort the distribution of resources. (Chapter 4)

formal powers: The powers explicitly granted to a governor according to state law, such as being able to veto legislation and to appoint heads of state agencies. (Chapter 8)

Fourteenth Amendment: Constitutional amendment that prohibits states from depriving individuals of the rights and privileges of citizenship and requires states to provide due process and equal protection guarantees. (Chapter 2)

franchise: The right to vote. (Chapter 3)

full faith and credit clause: Constitutional clause that requires states to recognize each other's public records and acts as valid. (Chapter 2)

general act charter: A charter that grants powers, such as home rule, to all municipal governments within a state. (Chapter 10)

general election: A decisive election in which all registered voters cast ballots for their preferred candidates for a political office. (Chapter 6)

general jurisdiction trial court: A court that hears any civil or criminal cases that have not been assigned to a special court. (Chapter 9)

general obligation bonds: Investments secured by the taxing power of the jurisdiction that issues them. (Chapter 4)

general revenue sharing grants: Federal grants-in-aid given with few constraints, leaving states and localities with almost complete discretion over how to spend the money. (Chapter 2)

general welfare clause: Constitutional clause that gives Congress an implied power through the authority to provide for the "general welfare." (Chapter 2)

gentrification: The physical rehabilitation of urban areas, which attracts investment from developers and drives up property values. (Chapter 10)

gerrymanders: Districts clearly drawn with the intent of pressing partisan advantage at the expense of other considerations. (Chapter 7)

gift taxes: Taxes imposed on money transfers made during an individual's lifetime. (Chapter 4)

grand jury: A group of between sixteen and twenty-three citizens who decide if a case should go to trial; if the grand jury decides that it should, an indictment is issued. (Chapter 9)

grants-in-aid: Cash appropriations given by the federal government to the states. (Chapter 2)

habitual offender laws: Statutes imposing harsher sentences on offenders who previously have been sentenced for crimes. (Chapter 9)

home rule: A form of self-governance granted to towns and cities by the state. (Chapter 3)

impact fees: Fees that municipalities charge builders of new housing or commercial developments to help offset the costs of extending services. (Chapter 10)

impeachment: A process by which the legislature can remove executive branch officials, such as the governor, or judges from offices for corruption or other reasons. (Chapter 8)

implied powers: Broad but undefined powers given to the federal government by the Constitution. (Chapter 2)

income taxes: Taxes on wages and interest earned. (Chapter 4)

incumbent: A person holding office. (Chapter 7)

independent expenditures: Funds spent on ad campaigns or other political activities that are run by a party or an outside group without the direct knowledge or approval of a particular candidate for office. (Chapter 6)

indeterminate sentencing: The sentencing of an offender, by a judge, to a minimum and a maximum amount of time in prison, with a parole board deciding how long the offender actually remains in prison. (Chapter 9)

indictment: A formal criminal charge. (Chapter 9)

indirect lobbying: A form of lobbying in which lobbyists build support for their cause through the media, rallies, and other ways of influencing public opinion, with the ultimate goal of swaying legislators to support their cause. (Chapter 6)

individualistic culture: A political culture that views politics and government as just another way to achieve individual goals. (Chapter 1)

informal powers: The things a governor is able to do, such as command media attention and persuade party members, based on personality or position, not on formal authority. (Chapter 8)

insurance trust funds: Money collected from contributions, assessments, insurance premiums, and payroll taxes. (Chapter 4)

interest groups: Individuals, corporations, or associations that seek to influence the actions of elected and appointed public officials on behalf of specific companies or causes. (Chapter 6)

intergovernmental transfers: Funds provided by the federal government to state governments and by state governments to local governments. (Chapter 4)

interjurisdictional agreement (IJA): A formal or informal agreement between two or more local governments to cooperate on a program or policy. (Chapter 10)

intermediate appellate court: A court that reviews court cases to find possible errors in their proceedings. (Chapter 9)

interstate commerce clause: Constitutional clause that gives Congress the right to regulate interstate commerce. This clause has been broadly interpreted to give Congress a number of implied powers. (Chapter 2)

Jim Crow laws: Legislative measures passed in the last decade of the nineteenth century that sought to systematically separate blacks and whites. (Chapter 3)

judicial federalism: The idea that the courts determine the boundaries of state-federal relations. (Chapter 3)

judicial review: The power of courts to assess whether a law is in compliance with the constitution. (Chapter 3)

jury nullification: A jury's returning a verdict of "not guilty" even though jurists believe the defendant is guilty. By doing so, the jury cancels out the effect of a law that the jurors believe is immoral or was wrongly applied to the defendant. (Chapter 9)

laboratories of democracy: A metaphor that emphasizes the states' ability to engage in different policy experiments without interference from the federal government. (Chapter 1)

leapfrog development: Development practices in which new developments jump—or leapfrog—over established developments, leaving undeveloped or underdeveloped land between developed areas. (Chapter 10)

legislative overcriminalization: The tendency of government to make a crime out of anything the public does not like. (Chapter 9)

liability: A legal obligation or responsibility. (Chapter 9)

limited, or special jurisdiction, trial court: A court that hears cases that are statutorily limited by either the degree of seriousness or the types of parties involved. (Chapter 9)

line-item veto: The power to reject a portion of a bill while leaving the rest intact. (Chapter 3)

logrolling: The practice in which a legislator gives a colleague a vote on a particular bill in return for that colleague's vote on another bill to be considered later. (Chapter 7)

low-density development: Development practices that spread (rather than concentrate) populations across the land. (Chapter 10)

magistrate: A local official or attorney granted limited judicial powers. (Chapter 9)

majority-minority district: A district in which members of a minority group, such as African Americans or Hispanics, make up a majority of the population or electorate. (Chapter 7)

majority rule: The process in which the decision of a numerical majority is made binding on a group. (Chapter 7)

malapportionment: A situation in which the principle of equal representation is violated. (Chapter 7)

mandatory jurisdiction: The requirement that a court hear every case presented before it. (Chapter 9)

mandatory minimum sentence: The shortest sentence that an offender may receive upon conviction for a certain offense. The court has no authority to impose a shorter sentence. (Chapter 9)

mayor: The elected chief executive of a municipality. (Chapter 10)

mayor-council system: A form of municipal governance in which there is an elected executive and an elected legislature. (Chapter 10)

megaregion: An urban area made up of several large cities and their surrounding urban areas that creates an interlocking economic and social system. (Chapter 10)

merit system: A system used in public agencies in which employment and promotion are based on qualifications and demonstrated ability; such a system blends very well with the organizational characteristics of bureaucracy. (Chapter 8)

metropolitan area: A populous region typically comprising a city and surrounding communities that have a high degree of social and economic integration. (Chapter 10)

metropolitan planning organization (MPO): A regional organization that decides how federal transportation funds are allocated within that regional area. (Chapter 10)

metropolitan statistical area (MSA): An area with a city of fifty thousand or more people together with adjacent urban communities that have strong ties to the central city. (Chapter 10)

misdemeanor: A less serious crime, such as shoplifting. (Chapter 9)

model constitution: An expert-approved generic or "ideal" constitution that states sometimes use as a yardstick against which they can measure their existing constitutions. (Chapter 3)

moralistic culture: A political culture that views politics and government as the means of achieving the collective good. (Chapter 1)

municipal bonds: Bonds issued by states, counties, cities, and towns to fund large projects as well as operating budgets. Income from such bonds is exempt from federal taxes and from state and local taxes for the investors who live in the state where they are issued. (Chapter 4)

municipal charter: A document that establishes operating procedures for a local government. (Chapter 3)

municipalities: Political jurisdictions, such as cities, villages, or towns, incorporated under state law to provide governance to defined geographical areas; they are more compact and more densely populated than counties. (Chapter 10)

national supremacy clause: Constitutional clause that states that federal law takes precedence over all other laws. (Chapter 2)

nation-centered federalism: The belief that the nation is the basis of the federal system and that the federal government should take precedence over the states. (Chapter 2)

natural law, or higher law: A set of moral and political rules based on divine law and binding on all people. (Chapter 3)

necessary and proper clause: Constitutional clause that gives Congress an implied power through the right to pass all laws considered "necessary and proper" to carry out the federal government's responsibilities as defined by the Constitution. (Chapter 2)

neutral competence: The idea that public agencies should be the impartial implementers of democratic decisions. (Chapter 8)

New Federalism: The belief that states should receive more power and authority and less money from the federal government. (Chapter 2)

nonpartisan ballot: A ballot that does not list candidates by political party; this type of ballot is still often used in local elections. (Chapter 6)

nonpartisan election: An election in which the candidates do not have to declare party affiliation or receive a party's nomination; local offices and elections are often nonpartisan. (Chapter 5)

nullification: The process of a state's rejecting a federal law and making it invalid within state borders. (Chapter 2)

office group (Massachusetts) ballot: A ballot in which candidates are listed by name under the title of the office they are seeking. (Chapter 5)

open primary: A nominating election that is open to all registered voters regardless of their party affiliations. (Chapter 6)

oversight: The legislature's role in making sure that the governor and executive branch agencies are properly implementing the laws. (Chapter 7)

panel: A group of (usually) three judges who sit to hear cases in a state court of appeals. (Chapter 9)

party column (Indiana) ballot: A ballot in which the names of candidates are divided into columns arranged according to political party. (Chapter 5)

party convention: A meeting of party delegates called to nominate candidates for office and establish party agendas. (Chapter 6)

patronage: The practice of elected officials or party leaders handing out jobs to their friends and supporters rather than hiring people based on merit. (Chapter 6)

plea bargain: An agreement in which the accused in a criminal case admits guilt, usually in exchange for a promise that a particular sentence will be imposed. (Chapter 9)

plenary power: Power that is not limited or constrained. (Chapter 3)

plural executive system: A state government system in which the governor is not the dominant figure in the executive branch but, instead, is more of a first among equals, serving alongside numerous other officials who were elected to their offices rather than being appointed by the governor. (Chapter 5)

plurality: The highest number of votes garnered by any of the candidates for a particular office but short of an outright majority. (Chapter 5)

polarization: A split among elected officials or an electorate along strictly partisan lines. (Chapter 6)

policy implementation: The process of translating the express wishes of government into action. (Chapter 8)

political action committee: A group formed for the purpose of raising money to elect or defeat political candidates. PACs traditionally represent business, union, or ideological interests. (Chapter 6)

political culture: The attitudes and beliefs broadly shared by a polity about the role and responsibilities of government. (Chapter 1)

political machines: Political organizations controlled by small numbers of people and run for partisan ends. In the nineteenth and twentieth centuries these organizations controlled party nominations for public office and rewarded supporters with government jobs and contracts. (Chapter 6)

political parties: Organizations that nominate and support candidates for elected offices. (Chapter 6)

precedent: In law, the use of the past to determine current interpretation and decision making. (Chapter 9)

preemption: The process by which the federal government overrides areas regulated by state law. (Chapter 2)

prejudicial error: An error that affects the outcome of a case. (Chapter 9)

primary election: An election that determines a party's nominees for offices in a general election against other parties' nominees. (Chapter 6)

privileges and immunities clause: Constitutional clause that prohibits states from discriminating against citizens of other states. (Chapter 2)

professionalization: The process of providing legislators with the resources they need to make politics their main career, such as making their positions full-time or providing them with full-time staff. (Chapter 7) The rewarding of jobs in a bureaucratic agency based on applicants' specific qualifications and merit. (Chapter 8)

progressive tax system: A system of taxation in which the rate paid reflects ability to pay. (Chapter 4)

prosecutor: A government official and lawyer who conducts criminal cases on behalf of the people. (Chapter 9)

public choice model: A model of politics that views governments and public services in market terms; governments are seen as producers of public services and citizens are seen as consumers. (Chapter 10)

public defender: A government lawyer who provides free legal services to persons accused of crimes who cannot afford to hire lawyers. (Chapter 9)

pure appointive system: A judicial selection system in which the governor appoints judges alone, without preselection of candidates by a nominating commission. (Chapter 9)

rank-and-file members: Legislators who do not hold leadership positions or senior committee posts. (Chapter 7)

ratification: A vote of the entire electorate to approve a constitutional change, referendum, or ballot initiative. (Chapter 3)

realignment: The switching of popular support from one party to another. (Chapter 6)

recall: A way for voters to oust an incumbent politician prior to the next regularly scheduled election; they collect signatures to qualify the recall proposal for the ballot and then vote on the ouster of the politician. (Chapter 5)

recall election: A special election allowing voters to remove an elected official from office before the end of his or her term. (Chapter 8)

recidivism: A return to, or relapse into, criminal behavior. (Chapter 9)

Reconstruction: The period following the Civil War when the southern states were governed under the direction of the Union army. (Chapter 3)

recusal: The disqualification of a judge because of an actual or perceived bias or conflict of interest calling the judge's impartiality into question. (Chapter 9)

redistricting: The drawing of new boundaries for congressional and state legislative districts, usually following a decennial census. (Chapters 5 and 7)

referendum: A procedure that allows the electorate to either accept or reject a law passed by the legislature. (Chapter 3)

reform perspective: An approach to filling gaps in service and reducing redundancies in local governments that calls for regional-level solutions. (Chapter 10)

regional council: A planning and advisory organization whose members include multiple local governments. Regional councils often are used to administer state and federal programs that target regions. (Chapter 10)

regressive taxes: Taxes levied on all taxpayers, regardless of income or ability to pay; they tend to place proportionately more of a burden on those with lower incomes. (Chapter 4)

representation: Individual legislators acting as the voices of their constituencies within the house of representatives or senate. (Chapter 7)

representative government: A form of government in which citizens exercise power indirectly by choosing representatives to legislate on their behalf. (Chapter 2)

responsible party model: The theory that political parties offer clear policy choices to voters, try to deliver on those policies when they take office, and are held accountable by voters for the success or failure of those policies. (Chapter 6)

retention election: An election in which a judge runs uncontested and voters are asked to vote yes or no on the question of whether they wish to retain the judge in office for another term. (Chapter 9)

revenue bonds: Investments secured by the revenue generated by a state or municipal project. (Chapter 4)

revenues: The money governments bring in, mainly from taxes. (Chapter 4)

rider: An amendment to a bill that is not central to the bill's intent. (Chapter 7)

rocket docket: Fast-tracked cases that often have limited, specific deadlines for specific court procedures. (Chapter 9)

rulemaking: The process of translating laws into written instructions on what public agencies will or will not do. (Chapter 8)

runoff primary: An election held if no candidate receives a majority of the vote during the regular primary. The two top finishers face off again in a runoff to determine the nominee for the general election. Such elections are held only in some states, primarily in the South. (Chapter 6)

rural flight: The movement of youth and the middle class from rural areas to more urban areas. (Chapter 10)

sales taxes: Taxes levied by state and local governments on purchases. (Chapter 4)

secession: A government's or political jurisdiction's withdrawal from a political system or alliance. (Chapter 2)

secret (Australian) ballot: A ballot printed by a state that allows voters to pick and choose among different candidates and party preferences in private. (Chapter 5)

seniority: The length of time a worker has spent in a position. (Chapter 8)

separation of powers: The principle that government should be divided into separate legislative, executive, and judicial branches, each with its own powers and responsibilities. (Chapter 3)

settlement: A mutual agreement between parties to end a civil case before going to trial. (Chapter 9)

severance taxes: Taxes on natural resources removed from a state. (Chapter 4)

smart growth: Environmentally friendly development practices, particularly those that emphasize more efficient infrastructure and less dependence on automobiles. (Chapter 10)

sociodemographics: The characteristics of a population, including size, age, and ethnicity. (Chapter 1)

soft money: Money not subject to federal regulation that can be raised and spent by state political parties. A 2002 law banned the use of soft money in federal elections. (Chapter 6)

sovereign immunity: The right of a government to not be sued without its consent. (Chapter 2)

special act charter: A charter that grants powers, such as home rule, to a single municipal government. (Chapter 10)

special district: A local governmental unit created for a single purpose, such as water distribution. (Chapter 10)

sprawl: The rapid growth of a metropolitan area, typically as a result of specific types of zoning and development. (Chapter 10)

state-centered federalism: The belief that states are the basis of the federal system and that state governments should take precedence over the federal government. (Chapter 2)

states' rights: The belief that states should be free to make their own decisions with little interference from the federal government. (Chapter 2)

state supreme court: The highest level of appeals court in a state. (Chapter 9)

straight ticket: Originally, a type of ballot that allowed voters to pick all of one party's candidates at once; today, voting a straight ticket refers to voting for all of one party's candidates for various offices—for instance, voting for all Democrats or all Republicans. (Chapter 5)

street-level bureaucrat: A lower-level public agency employee who actually carries out the actions that represent law or policy. (Chapter 8)

strong mayor system: A municipal government in which the mayor has the power to perform the executive functions of government. (Chapter 10)

supermajority vote: A legislative vote of much more than a simple majority, for instance, a vote by two-thirds of a legislative chamber to override a governor's veto. (Chapter 8)

super PAC: A political action committee that can spend unlimited funds on behalf of a political candidate but cannot directly coordinate its plans with that candidate. (Chapter 6)

swing voters: Individuals who are not consistently loyal to candidates of any one party. They are true independents whose allegiance is fought for in every election. (Chapter 6)

tax burden: A measurement of taxes paid as a proportion of income. (Chapter 4)

tax capacity: A measure of the ability to pay taxes. (Chapter 4)

tax effort: A measure of taxes paid relative to the ability to pay taxes. (Chapter 4)

Tenth Amendment: Constitutional amendment guaranteeing that a broad but undefined set of powers is reserved for the states and the people. (Chapter 2)

ticket splitting: Voters' or districts' voting for different parties' nominees for different offices—for instance, supporting a Republican for president while supporting a Democrat for Congress. (Chapter 6)

Tiebout model: A model of local government based on market principles wherein a metro area is made up of a series of micropolitical jurisdictions that, on the basis of their services and costs, attract or repel certain citizens. (Chapter 10)

town meeting form of government: A form of governance in which legislative powers are held by the local citizens. (Chapter 10)

townships: Local governments whose powers, governance structure, and legal status vary considerably from state to state. In some states, townships function as general-purpose municipalities; in others, they are geographical subdivisions of counties with few responsibilities and little power. (Chapter 10)

traditionalistic culture: A political culture that views politics and government as the means of maintaining the existing social order. (Chapter 1)

trial court: The first level of the court system. (Chapter 9)

trustees: Legislators who believe they were elected to exercise their own judgment and to approach issues accordingly. (Chapter 7)

truth-in-sentencing laws: Laws that give parole boards less authority to shorten sentences for good behavior by specifying the proportion of a sentence an offender must serve before becoming eligible for parole. (Chapter 9)

unfunded mandates: Federal laws that direct state action but provide no financial support for that action. (Chapter 2)

unicameral legislature: A legislature having only one chamber. Nebraska is currently the only state with a unicameral legislature. (Chapter 3)

unitary systems: Political systems in which power is concentrated in a central government. (Chapter 2)

urban growth boundary (UGB): A border established around urban areas that is intended to control the density and type of development. (Chapter 10)

user fees: Charges levied by governments in exchange for services. Such fees constitute a type of hidden tax. (Chapter 4)

variance: The difference between units of analysis on a particular measure. (Chapter 1)

veto: The power to reject a proposed law. (Chapter 8)

voter identification: When a voter identifies strongly with one of the major parties, he or she is considered a Democrat or a Republican; many voters, however, are considered weakly aligned with either major party. (Chapter 6)

voter turnout: The percentage of voting-eligible citizens who register to vote and do vote. (Chapter 5)

ward, or district, election: An election in which voters in a municipal ward vote for a candidate to represent them on a council or commission. (Chapter 10)

wards: Divisions of municipalities, usually representing electoral districts of the city council. (Chapter 10)

weak mayor system: A municipal government in which the mayor lacks true executive powers, such as the ability to veto council decisions or appoint department heads. (Chapter 10)

white flight: A demographic trend in which the middle and upper classes leave central cities for predominantly white suburbs. (Chapter 10)

zoning laws: Regulations that control how land can be used. (Chapter 10)

Photo Credits

Index

Galveston, Texas, 290–291
Gambling, 93–94, 97 (photo)
Gamkhar, Shama, 50
Gans, Curtis, 117
GASB. *See* Governmental Accounting Standards Board
Gates, Bill, 84
Gay marriage:
   ballot initiatives, 129–130
   constitutions, state, 69
   courts and, 67, 248–249
   federalism and, 43
   legislatures and, 178
   research, latest, 78
General act charters, 295, 334
General elections, 148, 334
General jurisdiction trial courts, 251–252, 334
General obligation bonds, 94, 334
General revenue sharing grants, 40, 334
General welfare clause, 31, 334
Gentrification, 307, 334
Geography, 12–14, 70, 92–93
Geology, 93
Georgia:
   constitution, 64
   courts, 274
   elections, 115
   local government, 284
   political culture, 11
Gerrymanders, 192, 334
Gessler, Scott, 228
Gibbons, Mike, 110
Gibson, James, 277
Gideon v. Wainwright (1963), 265
Gift taxes, 84, 334
Glaberson, William, 254
Gnant, Randall, 131
Goess, Ed, 154
Gonzalez, Alberto, 117
González, Lucas, 20
Gonzalez v. Oregon (2006), 47 (table), 48
Gonzalez v. Raich (2005), 48
Good time, 270–271
Gottfried, Jeffrey, 277
Governmental Accounting Standards
   Board (GASB), 101
Government consolidation, 305–306
Government Performance Project, 236–237 (figure)
Governors:
   age requirements, 71
   appointment powers, 213–214
   budget-making power, 214, 216–217 (table)
   communication abilities, 220
   elections, 221, 224
   in legislative process, 211–212
   as National Guard commander-in-chief, 213
   office, leaving, 224–225

pardon powers, 215
as party chiefs, 212–213
party support in the legislature, 220
political parties and, 212–213, 220
popular support, 220
powers, formal, 213–215, 216–217 (table)
powers, informal, 215, 220
presidential aspirations of, 226, 239 (photo)
research, latest, 243
roles, 211–213
special sessions, power to call, 215
as spokesperson for the state, 212
by state, 222–224 (table)
term limits, 225
third parties and independents, 160–161
veto powers, 71, 72, 214–215, 216–217 (table)
weak, 67–68
See also Executive branch
"Governors Turn Pro" (Bowman, Woods & Stark), 243
Grand juries, 264, 334
Grants-in-aid, 38, 40, 41, 42 (figure), 334
Grayson, Trey, 140, 154
Great Recession:
   bureaucracy, effect on, 239, 240 (figure), 241
   federalism and, 44, 45
   finance, 82
   impact of, 14–15
"Great Recession's Institutional Change in the Public
   Employment Relationship, The" (Levine &
   Scorsone), 243–244
Greece, ancient, 282
Green, Paul, 191
Greitens, Thomas J., 244
Grisanti, Mark, 178
Groscost, Jeff, 151
Growth:
   metropolitan, 297–301
   smart, 303, 338

Habitual offender laws, 270, 334
Hacker, Andrew, 117
Hackney, Joe, 187
Hall, Melinda Gann, 260, 276–277
Hamilton, Alexander, 34, 35, 141, 177
Hamlin, Shane, 117
Hanmer, Michael, 135
Hanson, Russell L., 19–20
Harden, Jeffrey J., 20
Haridopolos, Mike, 131
Harkness, Peter, 43
Hawaii, 93, 153, 284
Haynie, Kerry L., 195
Head injuries of athletes, 184
Healthcare expenditures, 97–99
Healthcare services, contracting out, 233–234
Health insurance exchanges, 29–30

CQ Press, an imprint of SAGE, is the leading publisher of books, periodicals, and electronic products on American government and international affairs. CQ Press consistently ranks among the top commercial publishers in terms of quality, as evidenced by the numerous awards its products have won over the years. CQ Press owes its existence to Nelson Poynter, former publisher of the *St. Petersburg Times*, and his wife Henrietta, with whom he founded Congressional Quarterly in 1945. Poynter established CQ with the mission of promoting democracy through education and in 1975 founded the Modern Media Institute, renamed The Poynter Institute for Media Studies after his death. The Poynter Institute (*www.poynter. org*) is a nonprofit organization dedicated to training journalists and media leaders.

In 2008, CQ Press was acquired by SAGE, a leading international publisher of journals, books, and electronic media for academic, educational, and professional markets. Since 1965, SAGE has helped inform and educate a global community of scholars, practitioners, researchers, and students spanning a wide range of subject areas, including business, humanities, social sciences, and science, technology, and medicine. A privately owned corporation, SAGE has offices in Los Angeles, London, New Delhi, and Singapore, in addition to the Washington DC office of CQ Press.

⑤SAGE researchmethods

The essential online tool for researchers from the world's leading methods publisher

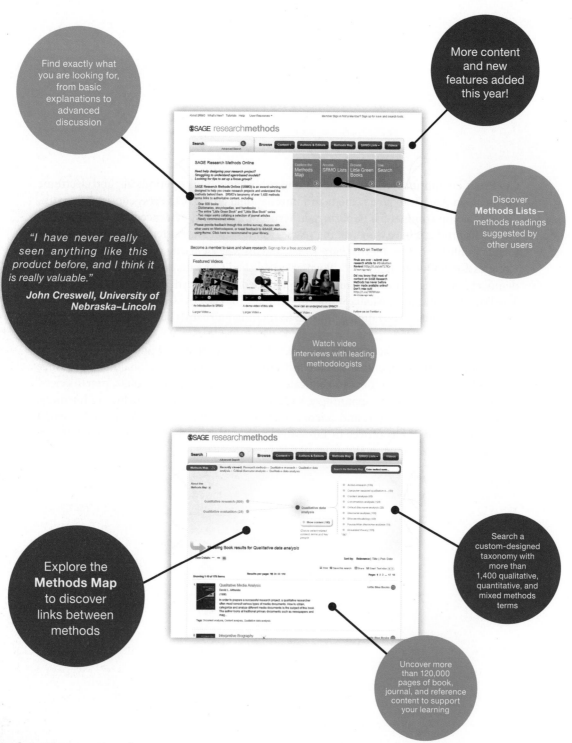

Find exactly what you are looking for, from basic explanations to advanced discussion

More content and new features added this year!

"I have never really seen anything like this product before, and I think it is really valuable."

John Creswell, University of Nebraska–Lincoln

Discover **Methods Lists**— methods readings suggested by other users

Watch video interviews with leading methodologists

Explore the **Methods Map** to discover links between methods

Search a custom-designed taxonomy with more than 1,400 qualitative, quantitative, and mixed methods terms

Uncover more than 120,000 pages of book, journal, and reference content to support your learning

Find out more at
www.sageresearchmethods.com